IB HISTORY CURRICULUM

Dr. Juan R. Céspedes, Ph.D.

Dr. Henry Charles Monteshire, Ph.D., EMER

Editor

Dr. Juan R. Céspedes, Ph.D.

ISBN: 9781081216788

VI • I • MMXIX

Mundus Novus Publishing

IB History Syllabus Outline

Prescribed subjects

(one required to be to be studied)

1. Military leaders
2. Conquest and its impact
3. The move to global war <<<<< *COVERED BY THIS BOOK*
4. Rights and protest
5. Conflict and intervention

SL and HL

World history topics (two required to be studied) *THIS BOOK HAS 3*

1. Society and economy (750-1400)
2. Causes and effects of medieval wars (750-1500)
3. Dynasties and rulers (750-1500)
4. Societies in transition (1400-1700)
5. Early Modern states (1450-1789)
6. Causes and effects of Early Modern wars (1500-1750)
7. Origins, development and impact of industrialization (1750-2005)
8. Independence movements (1800-2000)
9. Evolution and development of democratic states (1848-2000)
10. Authoritarian states (20th century) <<<<<
11. Causes and effects of 20th-century wars <<<<<
12. The Cold War: superpower tensions and rivalries (20th century) <<<<<

SL and HL

HL options: Depth studies (one required to be studied)

1. History of Africa and the Middle East

2. History of the Americas <<<<< *COVERED BY THIS BOOK*

3. History of Asia and Oceania

4. History of Europe

HL only

Internal assessment

Historical investigation

SL and HL

TABLE OF CONTENTS

AUTHORITARIAN STATES

Benito Mussolini (left), dictator of Italy from 1922 to 1943 and, Adolf Hitler (right), dictator of Germany from 1933 to 1945.

NAZI GERMANY

Type of Government

The government of Nazi Germany, the Third Reich, was an absolute dictatorship, with supreme authority in the hands of the Führer (leader), Adolf Hitler (1889–1945). The laws passed by Hitler's government superseded Germany's constitution, largely nullifying it. Though a legislature, or Reichstag, remained, it simply rubber-stamped the decrees of Hitler and the National Socialist German Workers' (Nazi) Party. Nazi Party members bowed to Hitler's will in all things. Hitler's government also rewrote judicial law to carry out its racial, political, and military agenda unconditionally.

Background

Post–World War I Germany established the Weimar Republic in 1918, with a bicameral legislative parliament: The Reichstag was the upper house of parliament and the Reichstag the lower. Though the Republic ratified the Treaty of Versailles, which ended World War I, in June 1919, many Germans considered the treaty terms to be humiliating and punitive. The terms of the treaty included German disarmament, the elimination of most of Germany's overseas territories, an official admission of responsibility for starting the war, and monetary reparations to be paid by Germany to Allied countries.

Germany's economy was severely compromised by the war, and the treaty's reparations requirement strained it even further, playing a significant role in the high unemployment, inflation, and bankruptcy rates that marked the 1920s. As the economy worsened and morale decreased, anger and unrest spread through Germany and opened the people to extremist messages that promised prosperity and the resurrection of national pride.

The Nazi Party began in 1919 as the German Workers' Party in Munich. The energetic and persuasive Adolf Hitler joined the party in 1919 and became its leader by 1921. In August 1923 Hitler led a failed coup attempt—known as the Beer Hall Putsch—in the German state of Bavaria, for which he served a year in prison. During his prison term, Hitler wrote his book *Mein Kampf* (My Struggle), an outline of his beliefs and plans. After his release in 1925, Hitler devoted himself to reshaping and controlling the Nazi Party.

At this point Germany was deeply fragmented politically, with no fewer than eight different political parties splitting power in the Reichstag during the years of the Weimar Republic. Beginning with the Spartacus Revolt of 1919—led by the Marxist revolutionaries Rosa Luxemburg (1870–1919) and Karl Liebknecht (1871–1919), both of whom were killed in the violence—communism developed a strong footing in

German politics. Like the Nazis, the German Communist Party (KPD), which was closely allied with the Communist Party in the new Soviet Russia, was violently opposed to the fledgling Weimar Republic and worked actively to destroy it. Although the two parties were bitter enemies and philosophically differed in nearly every respect, the Nazis and the Communists occasionally formed coalitions in the Reichstag to block the votes of the major parties.

Despite the chaotic nature of Weimar politics, the republic did thrive from 1923 to 1929. During that period Germany settled the issue of war reparations, attaining loans from the United States that greatly improved its economic condition, and agreed to the peaceful resolution of any outstanding border questions under the Locarno Pact of 1925. In September 1926 Germany was offered entrance to the League of Nations in recognition of the steps it had taken to overcome its image as the aggressor in World War I. The country even achieved greatness in the arts and sciences during the later Weimar period, with a thriving film industry, world-renowned avant-garde architecture, a lively cabaret scene, and numerous Nobel Prize winners.

In 1929, however, a stock market crash in the United States sparked a worldwide economic depression that left millions of Germans—33 percent of the labor force by 1932—unemployed and impoverished. American banks began calling in the loans they had issued to Germany in the early 1920s. The election of 1930 marked a turning point for the Nazis, as voters abandoned the existing democratic parties and looked to the Nazis and Communists to effect change. As the bankruptcy, suicide, and crime rates rose dramatically, both the Nazi Party and the Communist Party seized on the chaos, positioning themselves to take over when the Weimar Republic finally collapsed in early 1933.

With the two antidemocratic parties battling violently in the streets, the president, Paul von Hindenburg (1847–1934) unable to control his government, and Germans rapidly losing confidence in the concept of democracy and hoping for a strong leader to restore order, Hitler saw his chance to gain power, joining with Chancellor Franz von Papen (1879–1969) and right-wing members of the Reichstag to pressure Hindenburg to support him. Hindenburg was persuaded, against his better judgment, and on January 30, 1933, he appointed Hitler chancellor of Germany.

One of the first acts toward establishing the single-party Nazi government was Hindenburg's issuance of the Reichstag Fire Decree in February 1933, which abolished the civil rights that had been granted to German citizens by the constitution of the Weimar Republic. Having been declared chancellor in late January, Hitler convinced Hindenburg to hold elections in early March, which he hoped would allow him to dissolve the parliament. On February 27 a suspicious fire broke out at the Reichstag building. It is not known if the Nazis had anything to do with the fire, but Hitler convinced the German people that Communists were responsible and that they intended to go on a campaign of terror throughout the country. In the resulting atmosphere of hysteria and paranoia, the Nazis were able to consolidate their power and persuade Hindenburg to declare martial law for the sake of public safety. The Communist Party was disbanded and its members imprisoned, eliminating the Nazis' strongest political competition.

The election was held on March 15, 1933. While the Nazi Party did receive more votes than any other party, it won by a slim margin, leaving Hitler with a weak hold on his leadership. On March 23, Hindenburg signed the Enabling Act, which allowed the acting government—specifically Hitler—to rule by decree, passing legislation and changing the constitution without parliamentary support. The Enabling Act opened the door for Hitler and the Nazis to hold absolute power. When Hindenburg died in August 1934, Hitler took over as leader and established the Third Reich.

Government Structure

German government under the Nazis was a highly centralized and bureaucratized organization. To maintain his position as the supreme authority, Hitler depended upon a high degree of competition among the heads of his government ministries; intra- and interagency squabbling was commonplace, and establishing a personal relationship with the F"uhrer often was the best way to maintain one's position. Disappointing him could result in execution.

Passage of the Gesetz über den Neuaufbau des Reichs (Act to Rebuild the Reich) on January 30, 1934, centralized the Nazis' government by eliminating the sovereign rights of the German states and placing them under the direct control of Hitler. While the legislative body (the Reichstag) remained in existence under the Nazis, its practical influence was virtually nonexistent because of Hitler's rule by decree.

Nazi government agencies typically had overlapping duties, resulting in a confusing administrative web. Even the party's paramilitary organizations, which were essential to keeping the Nazis in power, were numerous and redundant. The Sturmabteilung (SA; also known as Brownshirts or stormtroopers) competed with the Schutzstaffel (SS), which had under its administration the secret police called the Gestapo, which in turn fell under three different agencies: the

Reichssicherheitshauptamt (RHSA), the Sicherheitsdienst (SD), and the Sicherheitspolizei (SIPO). An additional paramilitary group, the Hitler Youth, was composed of young Germans who were charged with recruiting others into party positions.

In 1933 and 1934 the Nazis eliminated the Weimar court system with its independent judges and replaced it with two courts: Sondergerichte (special court) and Volksgerichteshof (people's court). In the beginning the Special Court handled political crimes and the People's Court handled acts of treason. Each court had three judges, who were party members, and no jury. Eventually virtually any crime, major or minor (including the frequent charge of being an "antisocial parasite"), could be tried in either court, and punishment was almost always harsh, ranging from time in a concentration camp to execution. The Nazis also introduced a legal concept called *Schutzhaft* (protective custody) that allowed them to arrest and detain people without charges.

Political Parties and Factions

By the middle of 1933 the Nazi Party was the only legal political party operating in Germany. But even though other parties had been banned and the Nazis micromanaged nearly every aspect of German life, resistance and opposition groups did exist. The Communists and Social Democrats were the only organized opposition parties in the early years of the Nazis' ascent. But throughout the Nazi years a loose collection of groups and individual dissidents actively resisted Hitler's policies— occasionally plotting and even attempting to assassinate him. Leaders of the Social Democratic Party who had fled Germany and settled in Prague when the Nazis purged the Reichstag of its opposition maintained a covert membership within the German working classes, although they were never able to move beyond organizing an occasional labor strike. After Germany invaded the Soviet Union in 1941, German communists who had settled in the USSR began a campaign of espionage and sabotage against the Nazis, working with communists still living in Germany.

A fairly significant resistance came from within the government itself, mostly among members of the Army and foreign intelligence office, which Hitler had never completed persuaded to support him. Because they had access to the international community, these individuals were able to create a network for gathering and disseminating information about the internal goings-on of the Nazi government. Members of the army, for example, were able to contact Britain and France to alert them of Hitler's plans to invade Czechoslovakia in 1938. Although the Allied powers failed to act and a planned coup against Hitler never materialized, such pockets of resistance were significant considering the virulent nature of the Nazi dictatorship.

Another form of anti-Nazism took hold among the civilian population when Hitler's "final solution" was revealed and Jews and other "undesirables" were rounded up for systematic extermination in concentration camps. The Catholic Church, which had not interfered with Hitler up to that point, loudly voiced its opposition to the plan to euthanize all mentally and physically impaired people, raising a storm of protest among Germans and leading Hitler to cancel the plan. A number of wealthy or otherwise influential Germans risked their lives—and some were captured and executed for treason—hiding Jews and either employing them or helping them reach safety in other countries.

Major Events

The Nazis considered the cultural renaissance of the late Weimar years to be a period of hedonism and degeneracy, largely due to the presence of Jews in the arts and sciences. In response, they began an immediate crackdown. Artists judged to be degenerate were dismissed from teaching positions and forbidden from displaying their work. Music and films were censored. Scientific exploration was curtailed. Many creative thinkers fled the country, and what little artistic expression and scientific advancement was encouraged had to uphold the values of the Aryan race. This was the beginning of the Nazis' official policy of anti-Semitism that ultimately led to the mass extermination of Jews.

In the meantime, Hitler had begun to secretly rearm Germany. In 1935 he formally announced rejection of the military restrictions in the Versailles Treaty and passed the Nuremberg Laws that deprived Jews of the rights of citizenship and civil rights. In defiance of the Versailles Treaty, German troops occupied the country's Rhineland demilitarized zone in 1936. When European nations failed to retaliate against the treaty violation, Hitler was convinced that he could initiate more aggressive military action without consequences. At the same time, Hitler inaugurated a four-year plan for economic self-sufficiency. Although the resulting economic prosperity was due largely to militarization and not a genuine economic stimulation—low wages were legally mandated—it did inspire widespread German loyalty to the Nazi régime.

In 1937 Hitler announced to his closest associates his timetable for German domination. First, he would create a greater German Reich in the heart of Europe. Second, he would invade and occupy the rich agricultural lands of Poland and the Soviet Union and enslave their inferior populations. Third, allied with Japan and Italy, he would make Germany the strongest world power.

Hitler began to implement his plan in 1938. Without firing a shot, Nazi Germany annexed Austria and the German-speaking regions of Czechoslovakia. Instead of protesting, England and France tried to appease Hitler, hoping he would attack the Soviet Union rather than Western Europe. Instead, Hitler signed a nonaggression pact with the Soviets in August 1939, relieving him of worries about fighting a two-front war. Germany marched into Poland in September 1939. In response, Britain and France declared war, and World War II began. Germany invaded and occupied France with relative ease in May 1940. Hitler broke Germany's pact with the Soviet Union and attacked that country in June 1941. The Russians staunchly resisted the well-armed and organized German forces.

Near the end of 1938, the Nazis' virulent anti-Semitic agenda gave rise to the Kristallnacht (Crystal Night), the most violent open assault on Jews in German history. The Nazis sent almost 30,000 Jews to concentration camps and destroyed their synagogues, homes, and shops. The original plan for the Jews was to take their property, revoke their citizenship, and rid Germany of them by sending them elsewhere. But with the success of the German invasion of the Soviet Union, the plan evolved from removing Jews from Germany to exterminating all the Jews in Europe and the Soviet Union. Concentration camps began to use gas chambers for mass executions in September 1941. By the end of World War II, nearly six million Jews had died in the concentration camps, along with millions more Gypsies, homosexuals, political and religious opponents, and those Germans who did not measure up to the standards of the Aryan master race.

The United States entered the war in December 1941. At the same time, Russian troops stopped the Germans at the edge of Moscow and Leningrad. Hitler was undeterred. He dismissed any generals who disagreed with his war plans and began to direct military strategy personally. The defeat of German forces at Stalingrad in the winter of 1942–43 marked the turning point of the war. Hitler withdrew from contact with the German people and his health deteriorated.

On June 6, 1944, the Allies (primarily U.S., British, and Canadian forces) invaded Europe from the French beaches of Normandy and moved inland. At about the same time, the Soviets began a major push from the East. Convinced that the war was lost, on July 20, 1944, German military officers mounted a failed assassination attempt on Hitler. Hitler took revenge and had 5,000 Nazis killed, including many vital military leaders. Germany continued to lose territory to the Allies throughout 1944 and 1945 and saw its cities devastated by Allied bombing. In the spring of 1945 Germany collapsed, and Hitler, hiding in his mountain bunker, committed suicide on April 30. On May 8 the German high command surrendered unconditionally to the Allies, ending the Nazi régime.

Aftermath

The Third Reich lasted twelve years and three months. It was responsible for some fifty million deaths and additional millions of injuries, as well as immeasurable personal and collective suffering and economic, social, and moral devastation. The end of the war revealed the extent and nature of the Holocaust. The Reich's vast and systematic genocide shocked the world and cast a large shadow over the Allied victory.

Two meetings among the major Allies (the U.S., Great Britain, France, and the USSR)—TheYalta Conference (February 1945) and the Potsdam Conference (August 1945)—decided the fate of postwar Germany. The conference agreements reversed all of Germany's territorial annexations in Europe and shifted its eastern border westward. Germany lost about 25 percent of its 1937 territory, most of its agricultural land, and one large industrial center. France took control of its remaining coal deposits. Germany was required to make extensive war reparations but also later received aid for reconstruction under the U.S. Marshall Plan.

In November 1945 the Allies conducted the Nuremberg War Trials. Surviving Nazi leaders who had not escaped from Germany were tried for war atrocities and crimes against humanity. Some received death sentences, while others went to prison. Many of the latter group were released in the 1950s due to old age or poor health. Still others were put on trial in Israel after the establishment of that country as a Jewish state.

France, Great Britain, the United States, and the Soviet Union occupied Germany until 1955. The Soviet zone, with the exception of parts of Berlin, became the German Democratic Republic (East Germany), while the other three occupation zones became the Federal Republic of Germany (West Germany). The Allies outlawed the Nazi Party and its symbols throughout Germany and Austria. Allied dismantling of German industry ended in 1950. The severity of the occupation in West Germany also diminished when Germany came to be seen as any ally against communism. Despite the Nazi period, Germany experienced great economic and social success through the later twentieth and the early twenty-first centuries. In 1989 the East and West portions of Berlin were reunited when communism fell and the wall separating them was torn down.

Largely as a response to the Nazi persecution of the Jews, the United Nations decided in 1947 to partition Palestine into two independent states, one Arab and one Jewish. In 1948 Israel was declared an independent nation and a homeland for Jews.

Authoritarian Dictators

No inquiry of authoritarian states would be complete without an in depth analysis of the dictators Adolf Hitler of Germany and Benito Mussolini of Italy. These formed the Pact of Steel, an Alliance between Nazi Germany and Fascist Italy. Signed by Hitler and Mussolini on May 22, 1939, it formalized the 1936 Rome-Berlin Axis agreement, linking the two countries politically and militarily.

The Rise of Adolf Hitler

Hitler led the extreme nationalist and racist Nazi party and served as chancellor-president of Germany from 1933 to 1945. Probably the most effective and powerful demagogue of the 20th century, his leadership led to the extermination of approximately 6 million Jews.

Adolf Hitler and his National Socialist movement belong among the many irrationally nationalistic, racist, and fundamentally nihilist political mass movements that sprang from the ground of political, economic, and social desperation following World War I and the deeply upsetting economic dislocations of the interwar period. Taking their name from the first such movement to gain power—Mussolini's fascism in Italy (1922)—fascist-type movements reached the peak of their popular appeal and political power in the widespread panic and mass psychosis that spread to all levels of the traditional industrial and semi-industrial societies of Europe with the world depression of the 1930s. Always deeply chauvinistic, antiliberal and antirational, and violently anti-Semitic, these movements varied in form from the outright atheistic and industrialist German national socialism to the lesser-known mystical-religious and peasant-oriented movements of eastern Europe.

Early Life

Adolf Hitler was born on April 20, 1889, in the small Austrian town of Braunau on the Inn River along the Bavarian-German border, son of an Austrian customs official of moderate means. His early youth in Linz on the Danube seems to have been under the repressive influence of an authoritarian and, after retirement in 1895, increasingly short-tempered and domineering father until the latter's death in 1903. After an initially fine performance in elementary school, Adolf soon became rebellious and began failing in the *Realschule* (college preparatory school). Following transfer to another school, he finally left formal education altogether in 1905 and, refusing to bow to the discipline of a regular job, began his long years of dilettante, aimless existence, reading, painting, wandering in the woods, and dreaming of becoming a famous artist. In 1907, when his mother died, he moved to Vienna in an attempt to enroll in the famed Academy of Fine Arts. His failure to gain admission that year and the next led him into a period of deep depression and seclusion from his friends. Wandering through the streets of Vienna, he lived on a modest orphan's pension and the money he could earn by painting and selling picture postcards. It was during this time of his vagabond existence among the rootless, displaced elements of the old Hapsburg capital, that he first became fascinated by the immense potential of mass political manipulation. He was particularly impressed by the successes of the anti-Semitic, nationalist Christian-Socialist party of Vienna Mayor Karl Lueger and his efficient machine of propaganda and mass organization. Under Lueger's influence and that of former Catholic monk and race theorist Lanz von Liebenfels, Hitler first developed the fanatical anti-Semitism and racial mythology that were to remain central to his own "ideology" and that of the Nazi party.

In May 1913, apparently in an attempt to avoid induction into the Austrian military service after he had failed to register for conscription, Hitler slipped across the German border to Munich, only to be arrested and turned over to the Austrian police. He was able to persuade the authorities not to detain him for draft evasion and duly presented himself for the draft physical examination, which he failed to pass. He returned to Munich, and after the outbreak of World War I a year later, he volunteered for action in the German army. During the war he fought on Germany's Western front with distinction but gained no promotion beyond the rank of corporal. Injured twice, he won several awards for bravery, among them the highly respected Iron Cross First Class. Although isolated in his troop, he seems to have thoroughly enjoyed his success on the front and continued to look back fondly upon his war experience.

Early Nazi Years

The end of the war suddenly left Hitler without a place or goal and drove him to join the many disillusioned veterans who continued to fight in the streets of Germany. In the spring of 1919 he found employment as a political officer in the army in Munich with the help of an adventurer-soldier by the name of Ernst Roehm—later head of Hitler's storm troopers (SA). In this capacity Hitler attended a meeting of the so-called German Workers' party, a nationalist, anti-Semitic, and socialist group, in September 1919. He quickly distinguished himself as this party's most popular and impressive speaker and propagandist, helped to increase its membership dramatically to some 6, 000 by 1921, and in April that year became Führer (leader) of the now-renamed National Socialist German Workers' party (NSDAP), the official name of the Nazi party.

The worsening economic conditions of the two following years, which included a runaway inflation that wiped out the savings of great numbers of middle-income citizens, massive unemployment, and finally foreign occupation of the economically crucial Ruhr Valley, contributed to the continued rapid growth of the party. By the end of 1923 Hitler could count on a following of some 56, 000 members and many more sympathizers and regarded himself as a significant force in Bavarian and German politics. Inspired by Mussolini's "March on Rome, " he hoped to use the crisis conditions accompanying the end of the Ruhr occupation in the fall of 1923 to stage his own coup against the Berlin government. For this purpose he staged the well-known Nazi Beer Hall Putsch of Nov. 8/9, 1923, by which he hoped—in coalition with right-wingers around World War I general Erich Ludendorff—to force the conservative-nationalist Bavarian government of Gustav von Kahr to cooperate with him in a rightist "March on Berlin." The attempt failed, however. Hitler was tried for treason and given the rather mild sentence of a year's imprisonment in the old fort of Landsberg.

It was during this prison term that many of Hitler's basic ideas of political strategy and tactics matured. Here he outlined his major plans and beliefs in *Mein Kampf,* which he dictated to his loyal confidant Rudolf Hess. He planned the reorganization of his party, which had been outlawed and which, with the return of prosperity, had lost much of its appeal. After his release Hitler reconstituted the party around a group of loyal followers who were to remain the cadre of the Nazi movement and state. Progress was slow in the prosperous 1920s, however, and on the eve of the Depression, the NSDAP still was able to attract only some 2.5 percent of the electoral vote.

Rise to Power

With the outbreak of world depression, the fortunes of Hitler's movement rose rapidly. In the elections of September 1930 the Nazis polled almost 6.5 million votes and increased their parliamentary representation from 12 to 107. In the presidential elections of the spring of 1932, Hitler ran an impressive second to the popular World War I hero Field Marshal Paul von Hindenburg, and in July he outpolled all other parties with some 14 million votes and 230 seats in the Reichstag (parliament). Although the party lost 2 million of its voters in another election, in November 1932, President Hindenburg on Jan. 30, 1933, reluctantly called Hitler to the chancellorship to head a coalition government of Nazis, conservative German nationalists, and several prominent independents.

Consolidation of Power

The first 2 years in office were almost wholly dedicated to the consolidation of power. With several prominent Nazis in key positions (Hermann Göring, as minister of interior in Prussia, and Wilhelm Frick, as minister of interior of the central government, controlled the police forces) and his military ally Werner von Blomberg in the Defense Ministry, he quickly gained practical control. He persuaded the aging president and the Reichstag to invest him with emergency powers suspending the constitution in the so-called Enabling Act of Feb. 28, 1933. Under this act and with the help of a mysterious fire in the Reichstag building, he rapidly eliminated his political rivals and brought all levels of government and major political institutions under his control. By means of the Roehm purge of the summer of 1934 he assured himself of the loyalty of the army by the subordination of the Nazi storm troopers and the murder of its chief together with the liquidation of major rivals within the army. The death of President Hindenburg in August 1934 cleared the way for the abolition of the presidential title by plebiscite. Hitler became officially Führer of Germany and thereby head of state as well as commander in chief of the armed forces. Joseph Goebbels's extensive propaganda machine and Heinrich Himmler's police system simultaneously perfected totalitarian control of Germany, as demonstrated most impressively in the great Nazi mass rally of 1934 in Nuremberg, where millions marched in unison and saluted Hitler's theatrical appeals.

Preparation for War

Once internal control was assured, Hitler began mobilizing Germany's resources for military conquest and racial domination of the land masses of central and eastern Europe. He put Germany's 6 million unemployed to work on a vast rearmament and building program, coupled with a propaganda campaign to prepare the nation for war. Germany's mythical enemy, world Jewry—which was associated with all internal and external obstacles in the way of total power—was systematically and ruthlessly attacked in anti-Semitic mass propaganda, with economic sanctions, and in the end by the "final solution" of physical destruction of Jewish men, women, and children in Himmler's concentration camps.

Foreign relations were similarly directed toward preparation for war: the improvement of Germany's military position, the acquisition of strong allies or the establishment of convenient neutrals, and the division of Germany's enemies. Playing on the weaknesses of the Versailles Peace Treaty and the general fear of war, this policy was initially most successful in the face of appeasement-minded governments in England and France. After an unsuccessful coup attempt in Austria in 1934, Hitler gained Mussolini's alliance and dependence as a result of Italy's Ethiopian war in 1935, illegally marched into the Rhineland in 1936 (demilitarized at Versailles), and successfully intervened—in cooperation with Mussolini—in the Spanish Civil War. Under the popular banner of national self-determination, he annexed Austria and the German-speaking Sudetenland of Czechoslovakia with the concurrence of the West in 1938 (Munich Agreement), only to occupy all of Czechoslovakia early in 1939. Finally, through threats and promises of territory, he was able to gain the benevolent neutrality of the Soviet Union for the coming war (Molotov-Ribbentrop Pact, August 1939). Alliances with Italy (Pact of Steel) and Japan followed.

The War

On Sept. 1, 1939, Hitler began World War II—which he hoped would lead to his control of most of the Eurasian heartland—with the lightning invasion of Poland, which he immediately followed with the liquidation of Jews and the Polish intelligentsia, the enslavement of the local "subhuman" population, and the beginnings of a German colonization. Following the declaration of war by France and England, he temporarily turned his military machine west, where the lightning, mobile attacks of the German forces quickly triumphed. In April 1940 Denmark surrendered, and Norway was taken by an amphibious operation. In May-June the rapidly advancing tank forces defeated France and the Low Countries.

The major goal of Hitler's conquest lay in the East, however, and already in the middle of 1940 German war production was preparing for an eastern campaign. The Air Battle of Britain, which Hitler had hoped would permit either German invasion or (this continued to be his dream) an alliance with "Germanic" England, was broken off, and Germany's naval operations collapsed for lack of reinforcements and matériel.

On June 22, 1941, the German army advanced on Russia in the so-called Operation Barbarossa, which Hitler regarded as Germany's final struggle for existence and "living space" (*Lebensraum*) and for the creation of the "new order" of German racial domination. After initial rapid advances, the German troops were stopped by the severe Russian winter, however, and failed to reach any of their three major goals: Leningrad, Moscow, and Stalingrad. The following year's advances were again slower than expected, and with the first major setback at Stalingrad (1943) the long retreat from Russia began. A year later, the Western Allies, too, started advancing on Germany.

German Defeat

With the waning fortunes of the German war effort, Hitler withdrew almost entirely from the public; his orders became increasingly erratic and pedantic; and recalling his earlier triumphs over the generals, he refused to listen to advice from his military counselors. He dreamed of miracle bombs and suspected treason everywhere. Under the slogan of "total victory or total ruin, " the entire German nation from young boys to old men, often barely equipped or trained, was mobilized and sent to the front. After an unsuccessful assassination attempt by a group of former leading politicians and military men on July 20, 1944, the régime of terror further tightened.

In the last days of the Third Reich, with the Russian troops in the suburbs of Berlin, Hitler entered into a last stage of desperation in his underground bunker in Berlin. He ordered Germany destroyed since it was not worthy of him; he expelled his trusted lieutenants Himmler and Göring from the party; and made a last, theatrical appeal to the German nation. Adolf Hitler committed suicide on April 30, 1945, leaving the last bits of unconquered German territory to the administration of non-Nazi Adm. Karl Doenitz.

FASCIST ITALY

The political crisis of the postwar years provided an opportunity for militant, patriotic movements, including those of ex-servicemen and former assault troops, students, ex-syndicalists, and former pro-war agitators. Such was the case with the Italy in which Mussolini would rise to power. D'Annunzio in Fiume led one such movement, but the ex-Socialist journalist Benito Mussolini soon became even more prominent, founding his *fasci di combattimento* ("fighting leagues"), better known as Fascists, in Milan, in March 1919. The group's first program was a mishmash of radical nationalist ideas, with strong doses of anticlericalism and republicanism. Proposals included the confiscation of war profits, the eight-hour day, and the vote for women.

Mussolini's movement was initially unsuccessful, but Fascists soon began to agitate in the streets and against the left. In April 1919 Fascists and nationalists burned down the offices of the national Socialist daily, *L'Avanti!*, in Milan. Four people were killed, and the paper shut down for several days. This was the first demonstration of the ability of the Fascists to attack Socialist institutions. The offices of *L'Avanti!* were attacked twice more between 1920 and 1922. Organized militias began to attract support across Italy in an anti-Bolshevik crusade that united various social and political sectors and organizations. Local Fascist groups were soon founded in Emilia, Tuscany, and Puglia and by autumn 1920 were busy not only breaking up strikes but also dismantling Socialist and Catholic labour unions and peasants' cooperatives and—often with police collusion—overthrowing newly elected local councils. Fascist squads, dressed in black-shirted uniforms and often financed by landowners or industrialists, used systematic violence to destroy these organizations. Thousands of people were beaten, killed, or forced to drink castor oil and run out of town. Hundreds of union offices, employment centres, and party newspapers were looted or burnt down. In October 1920, after the election of a left administration in Bologna, Fascists invaded the council chamber, causing mayhem and nine deaths. The council was suspended by the government. Later, Socialist and Catholic deputies were run out of parliament or had their houses destroyed. The *biennio nero* ("two black years"; 1921–22) destroyed opposition to the Fascists. Union organizations were crushed. The Federterra shrank from some one million members to fewer than 6,000 in less than five years. Unable to defend basic democratic rights or to prevent the criminal activities of a private militia that operated openly and nationwide, the state had lost all credibility.

Within a few months, paramilitary Fascist squad leaders controlled many rural areas of central Italy. Local bosses built power bases in various areas—e.g., Italo Balbo in Ferrara, Roberto Farinacci in Cremona, and Leandro Arpinati in Bologna. These men became known as *ras* (meaning "provincial viceroy" in Ethiopia's Amharic language) and exercised considerable local power throughout the Fascist period. The Fascists had become a major political force, backed not only by landowners but also by many members of the urban middle class, including students, shopkeepers, and clerical workers. In May 1921, when Prime Minister Giolitti called new elections, 35 Fascists were elected to parliament as part of a government bloc of 275 deputies. In October Mussolini abandoned republicanism, and in November he formed his movement into a proper political party, the National Fascist Party (Partito Nazionale

Fascista; PNF), which by this time was well-financed if ill-disciplined and extremely disparate. Local bosses remained paramount in their areas. The Fascists also organized their own trade unions, the Fascist "syndicates," among strategic groups such as postal administrative workers and taxi drivers, to replace Socialist or Catholic organizations, to provide mass membership, and to control labour. These unions never managed to penetrate the organized working class but did have some support among the lower middle class and small landowners.

Mussolini manipulated this volatile situation in the next few months to his advantage, and the Liberal political establishment sought to conciliate him and the Fascist thugs. The police, the army, and much of the middle class sympathized with Fascist destruction of Socialist unions. Mussolini, as *duce* (leader) of fascism, gradually made himself indispensable in Rome, and the squads took over more cities in the provinces. Only a very few areas were able to resist the "Blackshirts" in street fighting, including Parma and Bari in 1922. Attempts by the left to organize defense squads against the Fascists were, in general, a failure. A major anti-Fascist protest strike, called by the Socialist-led Confederation of Labour in August 1922, quickly collapsed, strengthening Mussolini's bargaining position even further. Fascists used the opportunity to inflict further damage on the left and union institutions, and the offices of *L'Avanti!* were again attacked and razed. In October 1922 Mussolini organized a "March on Rome" by Fascist supporters. Fascist squads, numbering about 25,000 men altogether, began to converge on the capital from all over Italy on October 26, occupying railway stations and government offices. Prime Minister Facta asked the king to declare martial law, but Victor Emmanuel III eventually refused in order to avoid possible army disloyalty or even a possible civil war. Instead, he asked Mussolini to form a government on October 29, hoping to tame him by constitutional means.

Mussolini became prime minister, therefore, in a more or less constitutional manner, but only after three years of near civil war in the country and an armed invasion of Rome. He was appointed by the king, and he headed a coalition government that included nationalists, two Fascist ministers, Liberals, and even (until April 1923) two Catholic ministers from the Popular Party. For 18 months he ruled through the usual government machinery, pursued a policy of "normalization," and gradually concentrated power in his own hands. The Fascist squads were incorporated into an official Voluntary Militia for National Security. Ordinary middle-class job seekers flooded into the Fascist Party, making it more respectable and amenable; the nationalists also merged their organization into it, bringing with them much respectable backing in the south. In 1923 the electoral law was changed once more, so that a group of parties with the largest vote—even if only 25 percent of the total—would receive an absolute majority of the seats. This enabled the Fascists to attract most of the old Liberal deputies into a "national alliance." In April 1924 elections were held under this system. In a climate of violence and threats, the Fascist-dominated bloc won 64 percent of the votes and 374 seats, doing particularly well in the south. The opposition parties—by now including the Popular Party—remained divided but won a majority of the votes in northern Italy. The Socialists, indeed, had by this time split again, and the left now consisted of three rival parties, which spent much time criticizing one another: the Communists, the Socialists, and the reformist Socialists. The Popular Party was disowned by the Vatican, and its leader, Luigi Sturzo, resigned at the Vatican's request.

The End of Constitutional Rule

Mussolini's relative success as leader of a "normalizing" constitutional government did not last long. When the new parliament met, Giacomo Matteotti, leader of the reformist Socialists, denounced the recent elections as a sham and claimed there had been widespread intimidation of opposition voters. On June 10, 1924, Matteotti disappeared. His body was recovered on July 16, and he was later found to have been murdered by Fascist thugs led by the assistant to Mussolini's press office, Amerigo Dumini. The "Matteotti crisis" aroused public distrust in Mussolini and the Fascists. Mussolini was suspected of personal complicity in ordering the murder to eliminate a troublesome opponent. The press denounced the government, and the opposition parties walked out of parliament. However, Mussolini still had a majority in parliament, and the king backed him. For some time Mussolini hung on, but by autumn his Liberal supporters were drifting away, and in any case the "normalization" policy infuriated Fascist extremists in the country—especially the local bosses who were threatened with dismissal by the new militia commander, an army general. They demanded a showdown, and Mussolini—who was too weak by this time to rule by constitutional means—had to agree. On Jan. 3, 1925, he made a famous speech in the Chamber of Deputies accepting "political, moral, and historical responsibility" for Fascist rule and Matteotti's death and promising a tough crackdown on dissenters. The king made no move. On January 4, orders were given to prefects throughout Italy to control all "suspect" political organizations. Searches, arrests, and the elimination of several offices and organizations followed.

During the next two years, which included several failed assassination attempts, Mussolini disbanded most of Italy's constitutional and conventional safeguards against government autocracy. Elections were abolished. Free speech and free association disappeared, and the Fascist government dissolved opposition parties and unions. At the local level, appointed podestas replaced elected mayors and councils. Freemasonry was outlawed—a real blow to most non-Catholic anti-Fascists. A Special Tribunal for the Defense of the State, run by militia and army officers, was set up to try anti-Fascist "subversives"; it imprisoned or sent to exile on remote islands thousands of political opponents, including the Communist leader Antonio Gramsci, and it imposed 31 death penalties. Other opposition leaders, such as the Liberals Piero Gobetti and Giovanni Amendola, died at the hands of Fascist thugs. Severe controls were imposed on movement into and out of Italy. Although the repression was carried out essentially by old state institutions such as the police and the army and not by Fascist bodies, in 1927 Mussolini established the main information network of spies, the Organizzazione di Vigilanza Repressione dell'Antifascismo (Organization for the Vigilant Repression of Anti-Fascism; OVRA). This network extended abroad, where the OVRA organized assassinations of those hostile to the régime—such as the brothers Nello and Carlo Rosselli, anti-Fascist intellectuals, in France in 1937.

The prefects—mostly still career civil servants—retained their traditional dominance over local government, and the new podestas were nearly always landowners or retired army officers rather than Fascist enthusiasts. The Fascist party itself was soon swamped by more than a million job seekers and clerical workers, and thousands of the original Fascists were purged. The party, and the militia, soon had little to do except engage in propaganda and parades. The Fascist régime was mostly run by the traditional elites in the military and civilian bureaucracy, which were linked, as previously, to landowners and the court. That said, it was much more authoritarian and also much more nationalistic and interventionist than the Liberal governments had been. By the 1930s the Fascist Party dominated all aspects of daily life, from the workplace to the schools to leisure activities. However, many of the régime's opponents merely went along with its formal elements to procure space for protest and underground activity.

Fascist indoctrination was never totally successful, but the press was tightly censored, motion picture newsreels were largely government propaganda, and the régime controlled the new radio broadcasting. It also ran semi-compulsory Fascist youth movements, and new textbooks were imposed on the schools. Moreover, the government provided mass leisure activities, such as sports, concerts, and seaside holidays, which were genuinely popular. These attempts to create consent went hand in hand with the coercion imposed by the régime through the OVRA and its enormous network of spies. The fear of arrest, imprisonment, or economic marginalization hung over thousands of anti-Fascists and former oppositionists, and silence replaced the propaganda of the *biennio rosso*. Fascist control of daily life reached right down to the most basic levels. In 1938 the government imposed the use of *Voi* as the formal pronoun instead of *Lei* and banned handshakes in all places of public work. Foreign words and names were replaced. *Bordeaux* became *Barolo, film* became *pellicola*, and German place-names were Italianized. The walls of offices, schools, and public buildings were covered with slogans and murals paying homage to Mussolini and fascism, such as "Mussolini is always right" or "Better to live one day as a lion than 100 years as a sheep."

Anti-Fascist Movements

For a long time, organized anti-Fascist movements remained weak, divided, and illegal and had no access to press or radio. The Communists were soon the most significant of these movements, as they had an underground organization and some Russian support and finance, but even they had only 7,000 members at most and had great difficulty in spreading their propaganda in Italy. Spies within the movement exposed many of the underground networks before they even had a chance to put down roots. New anti-Fascist groups were founded occasionally, but the secret police soon cracked down on them. Apart from the Communists, only Justice and Liberty, an alliance of republicans, democrats, and reformist Socialists founded by Carlo Rosselli and others in 1929, managed to build up a clandestine organization in Italy and a strong organization abroad, above all in France and Switzerland. Most prominent anti-Fascists were in prison, in "confinement" on remote islands, or in exile and had little contact with Italian reality. Mussolini had disbanded unions and replaced them with new syndicates with little bargaining power. Strikes were illegal and more or less ceased to occur. Employer power was reimposed in both the countryside and the city after the union victories of the postwar years, although the welfare corporatism of the Fascist régime allowed workers important economic benefits.

The only strong non-Fascist organization in the country was the Roman Catholic Church. The Vatican implicitly supported Mussolini in the early years and was rewarded in February 1929 by the Lateran Treaty, which settled the "Roman Question" at last. Vatican City became an independent state, Italy paid a large financial indemnity to the pope for taking over his pre-1870 lands, and a concordat granted the church many privileges in Italy, including recognition of church weddings as valid in civil law, religious education in secondary as well as primary schools, and freedom for the lay Catholic organizations in Catholic Action. However, the government soon began curbing Catholic Action, seeing it as a front for anti-Fascist activity by former members of the Popular Party. The Catholic youth organizations were closed for a time in 1931. When they reopened, they had to avoid sports, but, even so, they grew considerably in the 1930s. They were a serious rival to the Fascist youth bodies and trained a new generation that often managed to avoid Fascist indoctrination. The 1929 concordat remained in force until the 1980s and was the legal basis for continued church dominance of Italian society after World War II. The Fascist régime could easily enough repress forms of local opposition such as demonstrations and strikes, but anti-Fascist feeling became more widespread after the mid-1930s.

Nonetheless, Italy sent some 60,000 "volunteer" militiamen, as well as about 800 warplanes, 90 ships, and 8,000 jeeps, to fight on the side of Mussolini's ideological cohort, Francisco Franco, in the Spanish Civil War (1936–39). This Italian force was defeated in 1937 at the Battle of Guadalajara. By the end of the war, some 4,000 Italian troops were killed and 11,000 injured. Italian anti-Fascists also fought Mussolini's troops in Spain, a rehearsal for the civil war in Italy after 1943. Many of these Italian anti-Fascists joined the Spanish Republican armies (notably, four Italian companies in 1936), inspired by Carlo Rosselli's cry "Today in Spain, tomorrow in Italy." In all, at least 3,000 Italians fought on the anti-Fascist side, about 200 of whom had traveled directly from Italy. Some 500 Italian anti-Fascists were killed and 2,000 injured in the war. Leading Italian Communists and Socialists were Togliatti and Pietro Nenni.

Italy's increasingly close alliance with Adolf Hitler's Nazi Germany was resented and feared, even by many Fascists. So too was the shocking decision to impose sweeping Nazi-like anti-Semitic laws in 1938. These laws followed a long racist campaign organized by the Fascist press and media. Under these laws and decrees, signed by the king, Jews were condemned as unpatriotic, excluded from government jobs and the army, banned from entering Italy, and banned from attending or teaching school. In addition, all Jews had to register with the authorities, limits were placed on their economic activities, and they were forbidden to marry "Aryans." In 1939 all books by Jewish authors were removed from the shops. Many Jews left Italy, while others were marginalized within Italian society. It had become clear that the Fascist government was likely to involve Italy in a disastrous European war, as indeed it did in 1940.

Economic Policy

Fascist intervention in the economy was designed to boost prestige and military strength. In the early years the Fascists compromised with the business establishment and rescued failing banks. However, in 1926 the lira was suddenly revalued for political reasons, and Italy suffered all the usual consequences of an overvalued currency. Exports fell sharply, unemployment rose, wages were frozen or even cut, and prices fell. The steel, electricity, and chemical industries expanded, for their markets were domestic, and they were helped by cheaper raw material imports; industries producing textiles, food, and vehicles, which depended on foreign markets, declined.

When the Great Depression came after 1929, these deflationary processes were accentuated, although the government increased spending on building roads and on welfare in order to provide employment. The leading banks, which had lent heavily to industry, had to be rescued in the early 1930s, as did many large industrial companies. Two new state-run holding companies, the Italian Industrial Finance Institute (Istituto Mobiliare Italiano; IMI) and the Institute for Industrial Reconstruction (Istituto per la Ricostruzione Industriale; IRI), were set up to bail out failing firms and to provide capital for new industrial investment; they also provided trained managers and effective financial supervision. Italy thus acquired a huge, state-led industrial sector, which was especially important in banking, steel, shipping, armaments, and the supply of hydroelectricity. However, these firms were not nationalized. Instead, they operated in the market as private companies and still had many private shareholders. In the long term they gave Italy a modern infrastructure—including roads and cheap energy—a sounder financial sector, and some efficient modern industries in expanding sectors such as chemicals and synthetic fibres. Most industrial development, and most workers, remained in northern Italy, although by this time large steelmaking and shipbuilding plants had been started at Naples and Taranto. After 1931 vast tracts of land were reclaimed through the draining of marshes in the Lazio region, where gleaming new towns were created with Fascist architecture and names—Littoria (now Latina) in 1932, Sabaudia in 1934, Pontinia in 1935, Aprilia in 1937, and Pomezia in 1938. Peasants were brought from the regions of Emilia and the Veneto to populate these towns. New towns, such as Carbonia, were also built in Sardinia to house miners for the revamped coal industry.

After October 1925 the Fascist syndicates, or trade unions, were the sole recognized negotiators for workers' interests. Strikes and lockouts became illegal, and wages fell between 1927 and 1934, but the syndicates had considerable political influence. They secured a shorter workweek (40 hours in November 1934), higher welfare benefits (such as family allowances, also introduced in 1934), and public works schemes, and they also helped run leisure and social activities. In 1934 the Fascists also set up "corporations"—mixed bodies of workers and employers—to resolve labour disputes and supervise wage settlements. Despite much rhetoric and propaganda about them, they had little impact in practice and virtually none on industrial management or economic policy making.

In agricultural policy, the government aimed at self-sufficiency by encouraging grain production after 1925 ("the battle for wheat"). Mussolini was filmed and photographed as he cut grain, bare-chested, in fields throughout Italy. Grain was grown for symbolic reasons in city centres such as Milan's Piazza del Duomo (Cathedral Square). A high tariff was reimposed on imported wheat, and grain prices were kept artificially high. Production rose sharply as northern farmers used more chemical fertilizers. In much of the south the climate was less favourable for growing wheat, but vineyards and olive groves were nonetheless plowed up, especially after 1929 when the world price of olive oil halved. The real beneficiaries of this policy were the large farmers of the Po valley and of the southern latifundia. These men also benefited most from the government's land-reclamation schemes, forming their own consortia and receiving government money to drain or irrigate their own land. Moreover, during the Depression they could buy land cheaply from the smaller landowners because many of the peasants who had acquired land during and after World War I were forced to sell after 1926.

After Italy's invasion of Ethiopia in 1935–36, the League of Nations subjected the Italian economy to sanctions. This led to a more extensive drive for national self-sufficiency, or autarky; imports were replaced where possible by native products, and most exports were diverted to Germany and Switzerland or to Africa. Ethiopia, once conquered, became a vast drain on resources. The government expanded its intervention and licensing role, encouraged official cartels and quasi monopolies, and shifted resources from above to heavy industry and armaments. All this led to budget deficits, big tax increases, and capital levies, which were hugely resented because they mainly went to pay for wars in Africa and Spain. Resented too was the obvious corruption of the Fascist governing clique, without whose permits—available at a price—nothing could be done. Among the members of the various conservative groups, including those in the army, the civil service, the law, and the church, which in the mid-1920s had looked to fascism to protect their interests, some had realized by the late 1930s that fascism was unreliable and began to withdraw their support.

American restrictions, European recession, and Fascist economic nationalism combined to curtail emigration drastically in the 1930s, from more than 600,000 people per annum before 1914 to fewer than 50,000 per annum. The closing of emigration outlets hit the south particularly badly. Because they could not go abroad, rural Italians moved to the cities. Rome doubled in size between 1921 and 1940, and northern cities attracted many rural emigrants, especially from the south. Fascism attempted to halt these movements through an anti-migration law in 1938. This measure banned migrants from moving within Italy without a job at their intended destination, and made many Italians "clandestine" in their own country. However, the law had little practical effect in preventing migration. Meanwhile, government policy encouraged population growth by providing tax incentives to have children and excluding the childless from public jobs. Admittedly, all this had little effect before 1937. Italians married later than ever and had fewer children than previously, so much so that in several northern and central regions the birth rate dropped below replacement level in the 1930s.

Foreign Policy

As time passed, Fascist foreign policy became more expansionist. In particular, Mussolini aimed at acquiring territory in Africa and in the Mediterranean, for which he adopted the ancient Roman term *mare nostrum* ("our sea"). Even in 1923, in his first year in office, he briefly invaded the Greek island of Corfu to avenge the murder of four Italian nationals forming part of an international boundary delegation. During the next decade he played the European statesman, and in 1924 he reached an agreement with Yugoslavia that gave Fiume to Italy. He also continued to strengthen the Italian hold on Libya, to build up the armed forces, and to plan further expansion in Africa—particularly in Ethiopia, where the defeat at Adwa in 1896 still needed to be avenged. In October 1935 Italy finally invaded Ethiopia—one of the first conquests was Adwa —and by May 1936 had conquered the country and proclaimed the Italian king, Victor Emmanuel III, emperor of Ethiopia. Ethiopia had been the only remaining country in Africa to escape colonization. Nearly 400,000 Italian troops took part in the conflict. The army employed brutal methods, including massacres and poison gas bombs. After an attempt in February 1937 on the life of the "viceroy" of Ethiopia, General Rodolfo Graziani, Italian forces arrested and shot hundreds of Ethiopians. However, the war was popular at home and among Italians abroad, especially in the Italian American community. Racist propaganda depicted the Ethiopians as backward barbarians "civilized" by the Italian army. The colonial wars coincided, not by chance, with the period when the régime enjoyed its maximum popularity.

Italy made further colonial gains in April 1939 with the invasion of Albania. Italian control over Albania already had been growing throughout the 1920s through agreements with the Albanian régime.

Moreover, in 1933 Italian had been made obligatory in Albanian schools. When Albania's King Zog refused to accept a trade agreement, however, the Italian army took control of the main strategic centres of the country and installed Italian loyalists in the civil service. Victor Emmanuel was made king of Albania. King Zog escaped to Greece.

The Italo-Ethiopian War antagonized the British and French governments, led to sanctions by the League of Nations, and isolated Italy diplomatically. Mussolini moved into Hitler's orbit, hoping that German backing would frighten the British and French into granting further concessions to Italy. However, the policy failed to bring further territorial gains in Africa. Furthermore, Italy became the junior partner in the "Rome-Berlin Axis," and in 1938 Mussolini had to accept Hitler's annexation of Austria, bringing the German Reich right up to the Italian border. In May 1939 Mussolini entered a formal military alliance with Hitler, the "Pact of Steel," which further reduced his scope for maneuver. Not only was each country committed to take part in any conflict involving the other, defensive or otherwise, but each leader was to consult the other before taking any military action. Even so, when the Germans unexpectedly invaded Poland in September 1939, Mussolini insisted on remaining neutral.

World War II

Military Disaster

Only in June 1940, when France was about to fall and World War II seemed virtually over, did Italy join the war on Germany's side, still hoping for territorial spoils. Mussolini announced his decision—one bitterly opposed by his foreign minister, Galeazzo Ciano—to huge crowds across Italy on June 10. Italy's initial attack on the French Alps in June 1940 was quickly cut short by the Franco-German armistice. The real war for Italy began only in October, when Mussolini attacked Greece from Albania in a disastrous campaign that obliged the Germans, in 1941, to rescue the Italian forces and take over Greece themselves. The Germans also had to lend support in the hard-fought campaigns of North Africa, where eventually the decisive second battle of El-Alamein (October 1942) destroyed the Italian position and led to the surrender of all of Italy's North African forces in May 1943. Meanwhile, the Italians had lost their extensive empire in eastern Africa, including Ethiopia, early in 1941; and 250,000 Italian troops in Russia, sent to help the German invaders, suffered untold hardships. The epic winter retreat of the Alpine division left thousands dead. In all, nearly 85,000 Italian troops failed to make it home from Russia.

In short, the war was an almost unrelieved succession of military disasters. Poor generals and low morale contributed much to this outcome—the Italian conscripts were fighting far from home for causes in which few of them believed. In addition, Italy had few tanks or antitank guns; clothing, food, vehicles, and fuel were all scarce; and supplies could not safely be transported to North Africa or Russia. Italian factories could not produce weapons without steel, coal, or oil, and, even when raw materials were available, production was limited because the northern Italian factories were subject to heavy Allied bombing, especially in 1942–43. Heavy attacks destroyed the iron ore production capacities on Elba, off the Tuscan coast, and damaged several industrial zones, particularly in northern Italian cities such as Genoa, La Spezia, Turin, and Milan. Naples and other southern cities also were bombed, as was the San Lorenzo district of Rome. (The San Lorenzo air raid, carried out by U.S. forces in July 1943, killed more than 3,000 people.)

Bombing indeed was one of the causes of the first major strikes since 1925. In March 1943 the leading factories in Milan and Turin stopped work in order to secure evacuation allowances for workers' families. By this time civilian morale was clearly very low, food shortages were endemic, and hundreds of thousands of people had fled to the countryside. Government propaganda was ineffective, and Italians could easily hear more-accurate news on Radio Vatican or even Radio London. In Friuli–Venezia Giulia, as in Italian-occupied Slovenia and Croatia, the local Slavic population supported armed Resistance movements, and anti-Italian terrorism was widespread. In Sicily landowners formed armed bands for possible use against mainland interference. On the mainland itself the anti-Fascist movements cautiously revived in 1942 and 1943. The Communists helped to organize strikes, the leading Roman Catholics formed the Christian Democratic Party (now the Italian Popular Party) in 1943, and the new Party of Action was founded in January 1943, mainly by republicans and Radicals. Leading Communists began to reenter Italy, and their party began to put down deep roots across the country. By this time most of the leading clandestine parties were more willing to work together to overthrow fascism. In March 1943 they signed an agreement to do so.

A further consequence of the war was the internment of hundreds of thousands of Italian emigrants across the world, especially in Britain and the United States. Italians, even with strong anti-Fascist credentials, were rounded up and sometimes stripped of their citizenship. This draconian policy left a legacy of bitterness and recrimination which lasted for years on both sides.

The Rise of Benito Mussolini

The Italian dictator Benito Mussolini (1883-1945) was head of the Italian government from 1922 to 1943. As a fascist dictator, he led Italy into three successive wars, the last of which overturned his régime.

Benito Mussolini was born at Dovia di Predappio in Forlì province on July 29, 1883. His father was a blacksmith and an ardent Socialist; his mother taught elementary school. His family belonged to the impoverished middle classes. Benito, with a sharp and lively intelligence, early demonstrated a powerful ego. Violent and undisciplined, he learned little at school. In 1901, at the age of 18, he took his *diploma di maestro* and then taught secondary school briefly. Voluntarily exiling himself to Switzerland (1902-1904), he formed a dilettante's culture notable only for its philistinism. Not surprisingly, Mussolini based it on Friedrich Nietzsche, Georges Sorel, and Max Stirner, on the advocates of force, will, and the superego. Culturally armed, Mussolini returned to Italy in 1904, rendered military service, and engaged in politics full time thereafter.

Early Career and Politics

Mussolini became a member of the Socialist party in 1900, and his politics, like his culture, were exquisitely bohemian. He crossed anarchism with syndicalism, matched Peter Kropotkin and Louis Blanqui with Karl Marx and Friedrich Engels. More Nietzschean than Marxist, Mussolini's socialism was *sui generis,* a concoction created entirely by himself. In Socialist circles, nonetheless, he first attracted attention, then applause, and soon widespread admiration. He "specialized" in attacking clericalism, militarism, and reformism. Mussolini urged revolution at any cost. In each attack he was extremist and violent. But he was also eloquent and forceful.

Mussolini occupied several provincial posts as editor and labor leader until he suddenly emerged in the 1912 Socialist Party Congress. Shattering all precedent, he became editor of the party's daily paper, *Avanti,* at a youthful 29. His editorial tenure during 1913-1914 abundantly confirmed his promise. He wrote a new journalism, pungent and polemical, hammered his readership, and injected a new excitement into Socialist ranks. On the Socialist platform, he spoke sharply and well, deft in phrase and savage in irony.

The young Mussolini proved a formidable opponent. In a party long inert, bureaucratic, and burdened with mediocrity, he capitalized on his youth, offered modernity with dynamism, and decried the need for revolution in a moment when revolutionary ferment was sweeping the country. An opportunist to his bones, Mussolini early mastered the direction of the winds and learned quickly to turn full sail into them.

From Socialist to Fascist

This much-envied talent led Mussolini to desert the Socialist party in 1914 and to cross over to the enemy camp, the Italian bourgeoisie. He rightly understood that World War I would bury the old Europe. Upheaval would follow its wake. He determined to prepare for "the unknown." In late 1914 he founded an independent newspaper, *Popolo d'Italia,* and backed it up with his own independent movement (Autonomous Fascists). He drew close to the new forces in Italian politics, the radicalized middle-class youth, and made himself their national spokesman.

Mussolini developed a new program, substituting nationalism for internationalism, militarism for antimilitarism, and the aggressive restoration of the bourgeois state instead of its revolutionary destruction. He had thus completely reversed himself. The Italian working classes called him "Judas" and "traitor." Drafted into the trenches in 1915, Mussolini was wounded during training exercises in 1917, but he managed to return to active politics that same year. His newspaper, which he now reinforced with a second political movement (Revolutionary Fascists), was his main card; his talents and his reputation guaranteed him a hand in the game.

After the end of the war, Mussolini's career, so promising at the outset, slumped badly. He organized his third movement (Constituent Fascists) in 1918, but it was stillborn. Mussolini ran for office in the 1919 parliamentary elections but was defeated. Nonetheless, he persisted.

Head of the Government

In March 1919 Mussolini founded another movement (Fighting Fascists), courted the militant Italian youth, and waited for events to favor him. The tide turned in 1921. The elections that year sent him victoriously to Parliament at the head of 35 Fascist deputies; the third assembly of his fledgling movement gave birth to a national party, the National Fascist party (PNF), with more than 250,000 followers and Mussolini as its uncontested leader, its duce.

The following year, in October 1922, Mussolini successfully "marched" on Rome. But, in fact, the back door to power had been opened by key ruling groups (industry try and agriculture, military, monarchy, and

Church), whose support Mussolini now enjoyed. These groups, economically desperate and politically threatened, accepted Mussolini's solution to their crisis: mobilize middle-class youth, repress the workers violently, and set up a tough central government to restore "law and order." Accordingly, with the youth as his "flying wedge," Mussolini attacked the workers, spilled their blood liberally over the Italian peninsula, and completed triumphantly the betrayal of his early socialism. Without scruple or remorse, Mussolini now showed the extent to which ambition, opportunism, and utter amorality constituted his very core. He was in fact eminently a product of a particular crisis, World War I, and a special social class, the petty bourgeoisie. Mussolini's capture of power was classic: he was the right national leader at the right historical moment.

Fascist State

Once in power, Mussolini attacked the problem of survival. With accomplished tact, he set general elections, violated their constitutional norms freely, and concluded them in 1924 with an absolute majority in Parliament. But the assassination immediately thereafter of the Socialist leader Giacomo Matteotti, a noted opponent, by Fascist hirelings suddenly reversed his fortunes, threw his régime into crisis, and nearly toppled him. Mussolini, however, recouped and with his pivotal speech of Jan. 3, 1925, took the offensive. He suppressed civil liberties, annihilated the opposition, and imposed open dictatorship. Between 1926 and 1929 Mussolini moved to consolidate his régime through the enactment of "the most Fascist laws" (*le leggi fascistissime*). He concluded the decade on a high note: his Concordat with the Vatican in 1929 settled the historic differences between the Italian state and the Roman Catholic Church. Awed by a generosity that multiplied his annual income fourfold, Pope Pius XI confirmed to the world that Mussolini had been sent "by Divine Providence."

As the 1930s opened, Mussolini, seated safely in power and enjoying wide support from the middle classes, undertook to shape his régime and fix its image. Italy, he announced, had commenced the epoch of the "Third Rome." The "Fascist Revolution," after the French original, would itself date civilized progress anew: 1922 became "Year I of the New Era"; 1932, Year X. The régime called itself the "Corporate State" and offered Italy a bewildering brood of institutions, all splendidly titled but sparsely endowed. For if the rhetoric impressed, the reality denied.

The strongest economic groups remained entrenched. They had put Mussolini into power, and they now reaped their fruits. While they accumulated unprecedented economic control and vast personal fortunes, while a class of nouveau riche attached itself to the régime and parasitically sucked the nation's blood, the living standard of the working majority fell to subsistence. The daily consumption of calories per capita placed Italy near the bottom among European nations; the average Italian worker's income amounted to onehalf his French counterpart's, one-third his English, and one-fourth his American. As national leader, Mussolini offered neither solutions nor analyses for Italy's fundamental problems, preferring slogans to facts and propaganda to hard results. The face of the state he indeed refashioned; its substance he left intact. The "new order" was coating only.

Il Duce ruled from the top of this hollow pyramid. A consummate poseur, he approached government as a drama to be enacted, every scene an opportunity to display ample but superficial talents. Cynical and arrogant, he despised men in the same measure that he manipulated them. Without inspired or noble sentiments himself, he instinctively sought the defects in others, their weaknesses, and mastered the craft of corrupting them. He surrounded himself with ambitious opportunists and allowed full rein to their greed and to their other, unnameable vices while his secret agents compiled incriminating dossiers. Count Galeatto Ciano, his son-in-law and successor-designate, defined Mussolini's entourage as "that coterie of old prostitutes." Such was Mussolini's "new governing class."

Mussolini's Three Wars

In 1930 the worldwide economic depression arrived in Italy. The middle classes succumbed to discontent; the working people suffered aggravated misery. Mussolini initially reacted with a public works program but soon shifted to foreign adventure. The 1935 Ethiopian War, a classic diversionary exercise, was planned to direct attention away from internal discontent and to the myth of imperial grandeur. The "Italian Empire," Mussolini's creation, was announced in 1936. It pushed his star to new heights. But it also exacted its price. The man of destiny lost his balance, and with it that elementary talent that measures real against acclaimed success. No ruler confuses the two and remains in power long. Mussolini thus began his precipitous slide.

The 1936 Spanish intervention, in which Mussolini aided Francisco Franco in the Civil War, followed hard on Ethiopia but returned none of its anticipated gains. Mussolini compounded this error with a headlong rush into Adolf Hitler's embrace. The Rome-Berlin Axis in 1936 and the Tripartite Pact in 1937 were succeeded by the ill-fated Steel Pact in 1939. Meanwhile, Mussolini's pro-Hitlerism struck internally. Having declared earlier that the racial problem did not exist for Italy, Mussolini in 1938 unleashed his own anti-Semitic blows against Italian Jewry. As the 1930s closed, Mussolini had nearly exhausted all toleration for himself and his régime within Italy.

World War II's surprise outbreak in 1939 left Mussolini standing on the margins of world politics, and he saw Hitler redrawing the map of Europe without him. Impelled by the prospect of easy victory, Mussolini determined "to make war at any cost." The cost was clear: modern industry, modern armies, and popular support. Mussolini unfortunately lacked all of these. Nonetheless, in 1940 he pushed a reluctant Italy into war on Hitler's side. He thus ignored the only meaningful lesson of World War I: the United States alone had decided that conflict, and consequently America, not Germany, was the key hegemonic power.

Disaster and Death

In 1940-1941 Mussolini's armies, badly supplied and impossibly led, strung their defeats from Europe across the Mediterranean to the African continent. These defeats constituted the full measure of Mussolini's bankruptcy. Italy lost its war in 1942; Mussolini collapsed 6 months later. Restored as Hitler's puppet in northern Italy in 1943, he drove Italy deeper into the tragedy of invasion, occupation, and civil war during 1944-1945. The end approached, but Mussolini struggled vainly to survive, unwilling to pay the price for folly. The debt was discharged by a partisan firing squad on April 28, 1945, at Dongo in Como province.

In the end Mussolini failed where he had believed himself most successful: he was not a modern statesman. His politics and culture had been formed before World War I, and they had remained rooted there. After that war, though land empire had become ossified and increasingly superfluous, Mussolini had embarked on territorial expansion in the grand manner. In a moment when the European nation-state had passed its apogee and entered decline (the economic depression had underscored it), Mussolini had pursued ultranationalism abroad and an iron state within. He had never grasped the lines of the new world already emerging. He had gone to war for more territory and greater influence when he needed new markets and more capital. Tied to a decaying world about to disappear forever, Mussolini was anachronistic, a man of the past, not the future. His Fascist slogan served as his own epitaph: *Non si torna indietro* (There is no turning back). A 19th-century statesman could not survive long in the 20th-century world, and history swept him brutally but rightly aside.

Analisi del Regime Fascista

Il Duce established a one-party state, brooked no political opposition, and created a secret police, although he controlled the country through the established police forces. Many Jews supported his régime, and there was no official anti-Semitism until 1938, when, to the surprise of many people, racial laws were enacted (and more strictly enforced in 1943, with the invasion of Italy by Germany). In the economic sphere Mussolini followed traditional policies until the Great Depression. Later he worked through nonfascist economists to establish an innovative state holding company (IRI) that rescued failing companies to save the economy. The fascists also established a corporate state, which divided the national economy into sectors run by institutions in which employers and employees were represented; in practice, however, employers had control. Both strikes and lockouts were prohibited.

In foreign policy Mussolini talked tough but was too weak to act unilaterally. The failure of the Allies to provide what he considered a proper reward led him gradually to support Hitler because he believed that he could exploit the balance of power that was emerging in the interwar period. His invasion of Ethiopia and intervention in the Spanish Civil War enmeshed him with Hitler, and he later proved unable to resist Hitler's embrace. Under Mussolini's leadership and against the advice of his foreign minister, Italy entered into the "pact of steel" with Germany on May 22, 1939. This agreement assumed that war would break out in three years and obliged both countries to coordinate their military action and economic production.

The Downward Spiral

When World War II broke out before three years had passed, Mussolini declared Italian neutrality but then, convinced that Germany would win, entered the war on its side despite Italian military unpreparedness. *Eventually he became the junior partner in this alliance. The poor performance of his nation in the conflict and the invasion of Sicily in 1943 led to the overthrow of the Duce.* Mussolini was imprisoned but freed in a daring German rescue. At this point he became a total German puppet, and the shadow of his previous self. The Germans brought him to northern Italy to head the Italian Social Republic as the Allies fought their way up the Italian peninsula. He tried to flee with the retreating Germans at the end of the war but was recognized by Italian resistance fighters, handed over by the Germans, and shot. His body, along with that of his mistress, was hung by its heels at a gas station in Milan and exposed to mob violence. The fascist state was no more, and fascism largely discredited.

A small Italian neofascist party survived the war. That movement later became more moderate, shed its extremist elements, and participated in the parliamentary structure of the Italian republic that replaced Mussolini's régime.

IMPERIAL JAPAN

First Sino-Japanese War

The First Sino-Japanese War (25 July 1894 – 17 April 1895), also known as the Chino-Japanese War, was fought between China and Japan primarily over influence in Korea. After more than six months of unbroken successes by Japanese land and naval forces and the loss of the port of Weihaiwei, the Qing government sued for peace in February 1895.

The war demonstrated the failure of the Qing dynasty's attempts to modernize its military and fend off threats to its sovereignty, especially when compared with Japan's successful Meiji Restoration. For the first time, regional dominance in East Asia shifted from China to Japan; the prestige of the Qing Dynasty, along with the classical tradition in China, suffered a major blow. The humiliating loss of Korea as a tributary state sparked an unprecedented public outcry. Within China, the defeat was a catalyst for a series of political upheavals led by Sun Yat-sen and Kang Youwei, culminating in the 1911 Xinhai Revolution (also known as the Chinese Revolution or the Revolution of 1911, establishing the Republic of China).

Second Sino-Japanese War

The Second Sino-Japanese War was a military conflict fought primarily between the Republic of China and the Empire of Japan from July 7, 1937, to September 2, 1945. It began with the Marco Polo Bridge Incident in 1937 in which a dispute between Japanese and Chinese troops escalated into a battle. Some sources in the modern People's Republic of China date the beginning of the war to the Japanese invasion of Manchuria in 1931.

China fought Japan with aid from the Soviet Union and principally the United States. After the Japanese attack on Pearl Harbor in 1941, the war merged with other conflicts of World War II as a major sector known as the China Burma India Theater. Some scholars consider the start of the full-scale Second Sino-Japanese War in 1937 to have been the beginning of World War II. The Second Sino-Japanese War was the largest Asian war in the 20th century. It accounted for the majority of civilian and military casualties in the Pacific War, with between 10 and 25 million Chinese civilians and over 4 million Chinese and Japanese military personnel dying from war-related violence, famine, and other causes.

The war was the result of a decades-long Japanese imperialist policy to expand its influence politically and militarily in order to secure access to raw material reserves, food, and labor. The period after World War I brought about increasing stress on the Japanese polity. Leftists sought universal suffrage and greater rights for workers. Increasing textile production from Chinese mills was adversely affecting Japanese production. The Great Depression brought about a large slowdown in exports. All of this contributed to militant nationalism, culminating in the rise to power of a militarist fascist faction. This faction was led at its height by the Hideki Tojo cabinet of the Imperial Rule Assistance Association under edict from Emperor Hirohito. In 1931, the Mukden Incident helped spark the Japanese invasion of Manchuria. The Chinese were defeated and Japan created a new puppet state, Manchukuo; many historians cite 1931 as the beginning of the war. This view has been adopted by the PRC government. From 1931 to 1937, China and Japan continued to skirmish in small, localized engagements, so-called "incidents".

Initially the Japanese scored major victories, capturing both Shanghai and the Chinese capital of Nanjing in 1937. After failing to stop the Japanese in the Battle of Wuhan, the Chinese central government was relocated to Chongqing (Chungking) in the Chinese interior. By 1939, after Chinese victories in Changsha and Guangxi, and with Japan's lines of communications stretched deep into the Chinese interior, the war reached a stalemate. The Japanese were also unable to defeat the Chinese communist forces in Shaanxi, which waged a campaign of sabotage and guerrilla warfare against the invaders. While Japan ruled the large cities, they lacked sufficient manpower to control China's vast countryside. During this time, Chinese communist forces launched a counter offensive in Central China while Chinese nationalist forces launched a large scale winter offensive.

On December 7, 1941, the Japanese attacked Pearl Harbor, ing day the United States declared war on Japan. The United States began to aid China by airlifting material over the Himalayas after the Allied defeat in Burma that closed the Burma Road. In 1944 Japan launched the invasion, Operation Ichi-Go, that conquered Henan and Changsha. However, this failed to bring about the surrender of Chinese forces. In 1945, the Chinese Expeditionary Force resumed its advance in Burma and completed the Ledo Road linking India to China. At the same time, China launched large counteroffensives in South China and retook West Hunan and Guangxi.

Despite continuing to occupy part of China's territory, Japan eventually surrendered on September 2, 1945, to Allied forces following the atomic bombings of Hiroshima and Nagasaki and the Soviet invasion of Japanese-held Manchuria. The remaining Japanese occupation forces (excluding Manchuria) formally surrendered on September 9, 1945, with the following International Military Tribunal for the Far East convened on April 29, 1946. At the outcome of the Cairo Conference of November 22–26, 1943, the Allies of World War II decided to restrain and punish the aggression of Japan by restoring all the territories that Japan annexed from China, including Manchuria, Taiwan/Formosa, and the Pescadores, to China, and to expel Japan from the Korean Peninsula. China was recognized as one of the Big Four of the Allies during the war and became one of the five permanent members of the United Nations Security Council.

The War from the Chinese Strategic POV

Generalissimo Chiang Kai-shek announced the Kuomintang policy of resistance against Japan at Lushan on July 10, 1937, three days after the Marco Polo Bridge Incident.

On the night of July 7, 1937, Chinese and Japanese troops exchanged fire in the vicinity of the Marco Polo (or Lugou) Bridge, a crucial access-route to Beijing. What began as confused, sporadic skirmishing soon escalated into a full-scale battle in which Beijing and its port city of Tianjin fell to Japanese forces (July–August 1937).

After 1940, the Japanese encountered tremendous difficulties in administering and garrisoning the seized territories, and tried to solve its occupation problems by implementing a strategy of creating friendly puppet governments favourable to Japanese interests in the territories conquered, most prominently the Nanjing Nationalist Government headed by former KMT premier Wang Jingwei. However, atrocities committed by the Imperial Japanese Army, as well as Japanese refusal to delegate any real power, left the puppets very unpopular and largely ineffective. The only success the Japanese had was to recruit a large Collaborationist Chinese Army to maintain public security in the occupied areas.

Japanese Expansion

By 1941, Japan held most of the eastern coastal areas of China and Vietnam, but guerrilla fighting continued in these occupied areas. Japan had suffered high casualties from unexpectedly stubborn Chinese resistance, and neither side could make any swift progress in the manner of Nazi Germany in Western Europe.

Chinese Resistance Strategy

The basis of Chinese strategy before the entrance of the Western Allies can be divided into two periods as follows:

First Period (July 1937 – October 1938)

Unlike Japan, China was unprepared for total war and had little military-industrial strength, no mechanized divisions, and few armoured forces. Up until the mid-1930s, China had hoped that the League of Nations would provide countermeasures to Japan's aggression. In addition, the Kuomintang (KMT) government was mired in a civil war against the Communist Party of China (CPC), as Chiang Kai-shek was quoted: "the Japanese are a disease of the skin, the Communists are a disease of the heart". The Second United Front between the KMT and CPC was never truly unified, as each side was preparing for a showdown with the other once the Japanese were driven out.

Even under these extremely unfavorable circumstances, Chiang realized that to win support from the United States and other foreign nations, China had to prove it was capable of fighting. Knowing a hasty retreat would discourage foreign aid, Chiang resolved to make a stand at Shanghai, using the best of his German-trained divisions to defend China's largest and most industrialized city from the Japanese. The battle lasted over three months, saw heavy casualties on both sides, and ended with a Chinese retreat towards Nanjing, but proved that China would not be easily defeated and showed its determination to the world. The battle became an enormous morale booster for the Chinese people, as it decisively refuted the Japanese boast that Japan could conquer Shanghai in three days and China in three months.

Afterwards, China began to adopt the Fabian strategy of "trading space for time" (simplified Chinese: 以空间换取时间; traditional Chinese: 以空間換取時間). The Chinese army would put up fights to delay the Japanese advance to northern and eastern cities, allowing the home front, with its professionals and key industries, to retreat west into Chongqing.

As a result of Chinese troops' scorched earth strategies, in which dams and levees were intentionally sabotaged to create massive flooding, Japanese advances began to stall in late 1938.

Second Period (October 1938 – December 1941)

During this period, the main Chinese objective was to drag out the war for as long as possible in a war of attrition, thereby exhausting Japanese resources while building up Chinese military capacity. American general Joseph Stilwell called this strategy "winning by outlasting". The NRA adopted the concept of "magnetic warfare" to attract advancing Japanese troops to definite points where they were subjected to ambush, flanking attacks, and encirclements in major engagements. The most prominent example of this tactic was the successful defense of Changsha in 1939 (and again in 1941), in which heavy casualties were inflicted on the IJA.

Local Chinese resistance forces, organized separately by both the communists and KMT, continued their resistance in occupied areas to pester the enemy and make their administration over the vast land area of China difficult. In 1940, the Chinese Red Army launched a major offensive in north China, destroying railways and a major coal mine. These constant harassment and sabotage operations deeply frustrated the Imperial Japanese Army and led them to employ the "Three Alls Policy" (kill all, loot all, burn all) (三光政策, Hanyu Pinyin: *Sānguāng Zhèngcè*, Japanese On: *Sankō Seisaku*). It was during this period that the bulk of Japanese war crimes were committed.

By 1941, Japan had occupied much of north and coastal China, but the KMT central government and military had retreated to the western interior to continue their resistance, while the Chinese communists remained in control of base areas in Shaanxi. In the occupied areas, Japanese control was mainly limited to railroads and major cities ("points and lines"). They did not have a major military or administrative presence in the vast Chinese countryside, where Chinese guerrillas roamed freely.

Relationship Between the Nationalists and Communists

After the Mukden Incident in 1931, Chinese public opinion was strongly critical of Manchuria's leader, the "young marshal" Zhang Xueliang, for his nonresistance to the Japanese invasion, even though the Kuomintang central government was also responsible for this policy, giving Zhang an order to "improvise" while not offering support. After losing Manchuria to the Japanese, Zhang and his Northeast Army were given the duty of suppressing the Red Army of the Chinese Communist Party (CPC) in Shaanxi after their Long March. This resulted in great casualties for his Northeast Army, which received no support in manpower or weaponry from Chiang Kai-shek.

Following the attack on Pearl Harbor, the United States declared war against Japan, and within days China joined the Allies in formal declaration of war against Japan, Germany and Italy. As the Western Allies entered the war against Japan, the Sino-Japanese War would become part of a greater conflict, the Pacific theatre of World War II. Almost immediately, Chinese troops achieved another decisive victory in the Battle of Changsha, which earned the Chinese government much prestige from the Western Allies. President Franklin D. Roosevelt referred to the United States, United Kingdom, Soviet Union and China as the world's "Four Policemen", elevating the international status of China to an unprecedented height after the century of humiliation at the hands of various imperialist powers.

Knowledge of Japanese naval movements in the Pacific was provided to the American Navy by the Sino-American Cooperative Organization (SACO) which was run by the Chinese intelligence head Dai Li. Philippine and Japanese ocean weather was affected by weather originating near northern China. The base of SACO located in Yangjiashan.

Chiang Kai-shek continued to receive supplies from the United States. However, in contrast to the Arctic supply route to the Soviet Union which stayed open through most of the war, sea routes to China and the Yunnan–Vietnam Railway had been closed since 1940. Therefore, between the closing of the Burma Road in 1942 and its re-opening as the Ledo Road in 1945, foreign aid was largely limited to what could be flown in over "The Hump". In Burma, on April 16, 1942, 7,000 British soldiers were encircled by the Japanese 33rd Division during the Battle of Yenangyaung and rescued by the Chinese 38th Division. After the Doolittle Raid, the Imperial Japanese Army conducted a massive sweep through Zhejiang and Jiangxi of China, now known as the Zhejiang-Jiangxi Campaign, with the goal of finding the surviving American airmen, applying retribution on the Chinese who aided them and destroying air bases. The operation started May 15, 1942, with 40 infantry battalions and 15–16 artillery battalions but was repelled by Chinese forces in September. During this campaign, the Imperial Japanese Army left behind a trail of devastation and had also spread cholera, typhoid, plague and dysentery pathogens. Chinese estimates put the death toll at 250,000 civilians.

Most of China's industry had already been captured or destroyed by Japan, and the Soviet Union refused to allow the United States to supply China through Kazakhstan into Xinjiang as the Xinjiang warlord Sheng Shicai had turned anti-Soviet in 1942 with Chiang's approval. For these reasons, the Chinese government never had the supplies and equipment needed to mount major counter-offensives. Despite the severe shortage of matériel, in 1943, the Chinese were successful in repelling major Japanese offensives in Hubei and Changde.

Chiang was named Allied commander-in-chief in the China theater in 1942. American general Joseph Stilwell served for a time as Chiang's chief of staff, while simultaneously commanding American forces in the China-Burma-India Theater. For many reasons, relations between Stilwell and Chiang soon broke down. Many historians (such as Barbara W. Tuchman) have suggested it was largely due to the corruption and inefficiency of the Kuomintang (KMT) government. Stilwell had a strong desire to assume total control of Chinese troops and pursue an aggressive strategy, while Chiang preferred a patient and less expensive strategy of outwaiting the Japanese. Chiang continued to maintain a defensive posture despite Allied pleas to actively break the Japanese blockade, because China had already suffered tens of millions of war casualties and believed that Japan would eventually capitulate in the face of America's overwhelming industrial output. For these reasons the other Allies gradually began to lose confidence in the Chinese ability to conduct offensive operations from the Asian mainland, and instead concentrated their efforts against the Japanese in the Pacific Ocean Areas and South West Pacific Area, employing an island hopping strategy.

Longstanding differences in national interest and political stance among China, the United States, and the United Kingdom remained in place. British Prime Minister Winston Churchill was reluctant to devote British troops, many of whom had been routed by the Japanese in earlier campaigns, to the reopening of the Burma Road; Stilwell, on the other hand, believed that reopening the road was vital, as all China's mainland ports were under Japanese control. The Allies' "Europe First" policy did not sit well with Chiang, while the later British insistence that China send more and more troops to Indochina for use in the Burma Campaign was seen by Chiang as an attempt to use Chinese manpower to defend British colonial holdings. Chiang also believed that China should divert its crack army divisions from Burma to eastern China to defend the airbases of the American bombers that he hoped would defeat Japan through bombing, a strategy that American general Claire Lee Chennault supported but which Stilwell strongly opposed. In addition, Chiang voiced his support of Indian independence in a 1942 meeting with Mahatma Gandhi, which further soured the relationship between China and the United Kingdom.

American and Canadian-born Chinese were recruited to act as covert operatives in Japanese-occupied China (Canadian-born Chinese who had not been granted citizenship were trained by the British army). Employing their racial background as a disguise, their mandate was to blend in with local citizens and wage a campaign of sabotage. Activities focused on destruction of Japanese transportation of supplies (signaling bomber destruction of railroads, bridges). Chinese forces invaded northern Burma in late 1943 besieged Japanese troops in Myitkyina and captured Mount Song. The British and Commonwealth forces had their operation in Mission 204 which attempted to provide assistance to the Chinese Nationalist Army. The first phase in 1942 under command of SOE achieved very little, but lessons were learned and a second more successful phase, commenced in February 1943 under British Military command, was conducted before the Japanese Operation Ichi-Go offensive in 1944 compelled evacuation.

The United States saw the Chinese theater as a means to tie up a large number of Japanese troops, as well as being a location for American airbases from which to strike the Japanese home islands. In 1944, with the Japanese position in the Pacific deteriorating rapidly, the IJA mobilized over 500,000 men and launched Operation Ichi-Go, their largest offensive of World War II, to attack the American airbases in China and link up the railway between Manchuria and Vietnam. This brought major cities in Hunan, Henan and Guangxi under Japanese occupation. The failure of Chinese forces to defend these areas encouraged Stilwell to attempt to gain overall command of the Chinese army, and his subsequent showdown with Chiang led to his replacement by Major General Albert Coady Wedemeyer.

By the end of 1944 Chinese troops under the command of Sun Li-jen attacking from India, and those under Wei Lihuang attacking from Yunnan, joined forces in Mong-Yu, successfully driving the Japanese out of North Burma and securing the Ledo Road, China's vital supply artery. In Spring 1945 the Chinese launched offensives that retook Hunan and Guangxi. With the Chinese army progressing well in training and equipment, Wedemeyer planned to launch Operation Carbonado in summer 1945 to retake Guangdong, thus obtaining a coastal port, and from there drive northwards toward Shanghai. However, the atomic bombings of Hiroshima and Nagasaki and Soviet invasion of Manchuria hastened Japanese surrender and these plans were not put into action.

Aftermath

The question as to which political group directed the Chinese war effort and exerted most of the effort to resist the Japanese remains a controversial issue.

In the Chinese People's War of Resistance Against Japan Memorial near the Marco Polo Bridge and in mainland Chinese textbooks, the People's Republic of China (PRC) claims that the Nationalists mostly avoided fighting the Japanese to preserve their strength for a final showdown with the Communist Party of China (CPC or CCP), while the Communists were the main military force in the Chinese resistance efforts. Recently, however, with a change in the political climate, the CPC has admitted that certain Nationalist generals made important contributions in resisting the Japanese. The official history in mainland China now states that the KMT fought a bloody, yet indecisive, frontal war against Japan, while the CPC engaged the Japanese forces in far greater numbers behind enemy lines. For the sake of Chinese reunification and appeasing the Republic of China (ROC) on Taiwan, the PRC has begun to "acknowledge" the Nationalists and the Communists as "equal" contributors, because the victory over Japan belonged to the Chinese people, rather than to any political party.

The Nationalists suffered higher casualties because they were the main combatants opposing the Japanese in each of the 22 major battles (involving more than 100,000 troops on both sides) between China and Japan. The Communist forces, by contrast, usually avoided pitched battles with the Japanese and generally limited their combat to guerilla actions (the Hundred Regiments Offensive and the Battle of Pingxingguan are notable exceptions). The Nationalists committed their strongest divisions in early battle against the Japanese (including the 36th, 87th, 88th divisions, the crack divisions of Chiang's Central Army) to defend Shanghai and continued to deploy most of their forces to fight the Japanese even as the Communists changed their strategy to engage mainly in a political offensive against the Japanese while declaring that the CPC should "save and preserve our strength and wait for favorable timing" by the end of 1941.

Legacy: China-Japan Relations

Today, the war is a major point of contention and resentment between China and Japan. The war remains a major roadblock for Sino-Japanese relations.

Issues regarding the current historical outlook on the war exist. For example, the Japanese government has been accused of historical revisionism by allowing the approval of a few school textbooks omitting or glossing over Japan's militant past, although the most recent controversial book, the *New History Textbook* was used by only 0.039% of junior high schools in Japan and despite the efforts of the Japanese nationalist textbook reformers, by the late 1990s the most common Japanese schoolbooks contained references to, for instance, the Nanjing Massacre, Unit 731, and the comfort women of World War II, all historical issues which have faced challenges from ultranationalists in the past.

Use of Chemical and Bacteriological Weapons

Despite Article 23 of the Hague Conventions of 1899 and 1907, article V of the Treaty in Relation to the Use of Submarines and Noxious Gases in Warfare, article 171 of the Treaty of Versailles and a resolution adopted by the League of Nations on May 14, 1938, condemning the use of poison gas by the Empire of Japan, the Imperial Japanese Army frequently used chemical weapons during the war.

According to historians Yoshiaki Yoshimi and Seiya Matsuno, the chemical weapons were authorized by specific orders given by Japanese Emperor Hirohito himself, transmitted by the Imperial General Headquarters. For example, the Emperor authorized the use of toxic gas on 375 separate occasions during the Battle of Wuhan from August to October 1938. They were also used during the invasion of Changde. Those orders were transmitted either by Prince Kan'in Kotohito or General Hajime Sugiyama. Gases manufactured in Okunoshima were used more than 2,000 times against Chinese soldiers and civilians in the war in China in the 1930's and 1940's.

Bacteriological weapons provided by Shirō Ishii's units were also profusely used. For example, in 1940, the Imperial Japanese Army Air Force bombed Ningbo with fleas carrying the bubonic plague. During the Khabarovsk War Crime Trials the accused, such as Major General Kiyashi Kawashima, testified that, in 1941, some 40 members of Unit 731 air-dropped plague-contaminated fleas on Changde. These attacks caused epidemic plague outbreaks. In the Zhejiang-Jiangxi Campaign, of the 10,000 Japanese soldiers who fell ill with the disease, about 1,700 Japanese troops died when the biological weapons rebounded on their own forces.

Analysis: Japan During World War II

Preparations for War

The decision by Japan to attack the United States remains controversial. Study groups in Japan had predicted ultimate disaster in a war between Japan and the U.S., and the Japanese economy was already straining to keep up with the demands of the war with China. However, the U.S. had placed an oil embargo on Japan and Japan felt that the United States' demands of unconditional withdrawal from China and non aggression pacts with other Pacific powers were unacceptable. Facing an oil embargo by the United States as well as dwindling domestic reserves, the Japanese government decided to execute a plan developed by the military branch largely led by Osami Nagano and Isoroku Yamamoto to bomb the United States naval base in Hawaii, thereby bringing the United States to World War II on the side of the Allies. On September 4, 1941, the Japanese Cabinet met to consider the war plans prepared by Imperial General Headquarters, and decided:

Our Empire, for the purpose of self-defense and self-preservation, will complete preparations for war ... [and is] ... resolved to go to war with the United States, Great Britain, and the Netherlands if necessary. Our Empire will concurrently take all possible diplomatic measures vis-a-vis the United States and Great Britain, and thereby endeavor to obtain our objectives ... In the event that there is no prospect of our demands being met by the first ten days of October through the diplomatic negotiations mentioned above, we will immediately decide to commence hostilities against the United States, Britain and the Netherlands.

The Vice Admiral Isoroku Yamamoto, the chief architect of the attack on Pearl Harbor, had strong misgivings about war with the United States. Yamamoto had spent time in the United States during his youth when he studied as a language student at Harvard University (1919–1921) and later served as assistant naval attaché in Washington, D.C... Understanding the inherent dangers of war with the United States, Yamamoto warned his fellow countrymen: "We can run wild for six months or maybe a year, but after that, I have utterly no confidence."

Japanese Offensives (1941–42)

The Imperial Japanese Navy made its surprise attack on Pearl Harbor, Oahu, Hawaii Territory, on Sunday morning, December 7, 1941. The Pacific Fleet of the United States Navy and its defending Army Air Forces and Marine air forces sustained significant losses. The primary objective of the attack was to incapacitate the United States long enough

51

for Japan to establish its long-planned Southeast Asian empire and defensible buffer zones. However, as Admiral Yamamoto feared, the attack produced little lasting damage to the US Navy with priority targets like the Pacific Fleet's aircraft carriers out at sea and vital shore facilities, whose destruction could have crippled the fleet on their own, were ignored. Of more serious consequences, the U.S. public saw the attack as a barbaric and treacherous act and rallied against the Empire of Japan. The United States entered the European Theatre and Pacific Theater in full force. Four days later, Adolf Hitler of Germany, and Benito Mussolini of Italy declared war on the United States, merging the separate conflicts. Following the attack on Pearl Harbor, the Japanese launched offensives against Allied forces in East and Southeast Asia, with simultaneous attacks on British Hong Kong, British Malaya and the Philippines.

By the time World War II was in full swing Japan had the most interest in using biological warfare. Japan's Air Force dropped massive amounts of ceramic bombs filled with bubonic plague infested fleas in Ningbo, China. These attacks would eventually lead to thousands of deaths years after the war would end. In Japan's relentless and indiscriminate research methods on biological warfare, they poisoned more than 1,000 Chinese village wells to study cholera and typhus outbreaks. These diseases are caused by bacteria that with today's technology could potentially be weaponised.

South-East Asia

The South-East Asian campaign was preceded by years of propaganda and espionage activities carried out in the region by the Japanese Empire. The Japanese espoused their vision of a Greater Asian Co-Prosperity Sphere, and an Asia for Asians to the people of Southeast Asia, who had lived under European rule for generations. As a result, many inhabitants in some of the colonies (particularly Indonesia) actually sided with the Japanese invaders for anti-colonial reasons. However, the ethnic Chinese, who had witnessed the effects of a Japanese occupation in their homeland, did not side with the Japanese. The brutality of the Japanese in the newly conquered colonies would soon turn most people against them.

Hong Kong surrendered to the Japanese on December 25. In Malaya the Japanese overwhelmed an Allied army composed of British, Indian, Australian and Malay forces. The Japanese were quickly able to advance down the Malayan Peninsula, forcing the Allied forces to retreat towards Singapore. The Allies lacked aircover and tanks; the Japanese had total air superiority. The sinking of HMS *Prince of Wales* and HMS *Repulse* on December 10, 1941, led to the east coast of Malaya being exposed to

Japanese landings and the elimination of British naval power in the area. By the end of January 1942, the last Allied forces crossed the strait of Johore and into Singapore. In the Philippines, the Japanese pushed the combined Filipino-American force towards the Bataan Peninsula and later the island of Corregidor. By January 1942, General Douglas MacArthur and President Manuel L. Quezon were forced to flee in the face of Japanese advance. This marked among one of the worst defeats suffered by the Americans, leaving over 70,000 American and Filipino prisoners of war in the custody of the Japanese.

On February 15, 1942, Singapore, due to the overwhelming superiority of Japanese forces and encirclement tactics, fell to the Japanese, causing the largest surrender of British-led military personnel in history. An estimated 80,000 Indian, Australian and British troops were taken as prisoners of war, joining 50,000 taken in the Japanese invasion of Malaya (modern day Malaysia). Many were later used as forced labour constructing the Burma Railway, the site of the infamous Bridge on the River Kwai. Immediately following their invasion of British Malaya, the Japanese military carried out a purge of the Chinese population in Malaya and Singapore. Over the course of a month following their victory at Singapore, the Japanese are believed to have killed tens of thousands of ethnic Chinese perceived to be hostile to the new régime.

The Japanese then seized the key oil production zones of Borneo, Central Java, Malang, Cepu, Sumatra, and Dutch New Guinea of the late Dutch East Indies, defeating the Dutch forces. However, Allied sabotage had made it difficult for the Japanese to restore oil production to its pre-war peak. The Japanese then consolidated their lines of supply through capturing key islands of the Pacific, including Guadalcanal.

Tide Turns (1942–45)

Japanese military strategists were keenly aware of the unfavorable discrepancy between the industrial potential of the Japanese Empire and that of the United States. Because of this they reasoned that Japanese success hinged on their ability to extend the strategic advantage gained at Pearl Harbor with additional rapid strategic victories. The Japanese Command reasoned that only decisive destruction of the United States' Pacific Fleet and conquest of its remote outposts would ensure that the Japanese Empire would not be overwhelmed by America's industrial might. In April 1942, Japan was bombed for the first time in the Doolittle Raid. In May 1942, failure to decisively defeat the Allies at the Battle of the Coral Sea, in spite of Japanese numerical superiority, equated to a strategic defeat for Imperial Japan. This setback was followed in June 1942 by the catastrophic loss of four fleet carriers at the Battle of

Midway, the first decisive defeat for the Imperial Japanese Navy. It proved to be the turning point of the war as the Navy lost its offensive strategic capability and never managed to reconstruct the "'critical mass' of both large numbers of carriers and well-trained air groups".

Air Raids on Japan

After securing airfields in Saipan and Guam in the summer of 1944, the United States Army Air Forces undertook an intense strategic bombing campaign, using incendiary bombs, burning Japanese cities in an effort to pulverize Japan's industry and shatter its morale. The Operation Meetinghouse raid on Tokyo on the night of March 9–10, 1945, led to the deaths of approximately 100,000 civilians. Approximately 350,000–500,000 civilians died in 66 other Japanese cities as a result of the incendiary bombing campaign on Japan. Concurrent to these attacks, Japan's vital coastal shipping operations were severely hampered with extensive aerial mining by the U.S.'s Operation Starvation. Regardless, these efforts did not succeed in persuading the Japanese military to surrender. In mid-August 1945, the United States dropped nuclear weapons on the Japanese cities of Hiroshima and Nagasaki. These atomic bombings were the first and only used against another nation in warfare. These two bombs killed approximately 120,000 to 140,000 people in a matter of minutes, and as many as a result of nuclear radiation in the following weeks, months and years. The bombs killed as many as 140,000 people in Hiroshima and 80,000 in Nagasaki by the end of 1945.

Re-entry of the Soviet Union

At the Yalta agreement in February 1945, the US, the UK, and the USSR had agreed that the USSR would enter the war on Japan within three months of the defeat of Germany in Europe. This Soviet–Japanese War led to the fall of Japan's Manchurian occupation, Soviet occupation of South Sakhalin island, and a real, imminent threat of Soviet invasion of the home islands of Japan. This was a significant factor for some internal parties in the Japanese decision to surrender to the US and gain some protection, rather than face simultaneous Soviet invasion as well as defeat by the US. Likewise, the superior numbers of the armies of the Soviet Union in Europe was a factor in the US decision to demonstrate the use of atomic weapons to the USSR, just as the Allied victory in Europe was evolving into division of Germany and Berlin, the division of Europe with the Iron Curtain and the subsequent Cold War.

Surrender and Occupation of Japan

Having ignored (Jp: *mokusatu,* meaning "treat with silent contempt") the Potsdam Declaration, the Empire of Japan surrendered and ended World War II, after the atomic bombings of Hiroshima and Nagasaki and the declaration of war by the Soviet Union. In a national radio address on August 15, Emperor Hirohito announced the surrender to the Japanese people by *Gyokuon-hōsō.* A period known as Occupied Japan followed after the war, largely spearheaded by United States General of the Army Douglas MacArthur to revise the Japanese constitution and de-militarize Japan. The Allied occupation, with economic and political assistance, continued well into the 1950s. Allied forces ordered Japan to abolish the Meiji Constitution and enforce the Constitution of Japan, then rename the Empire of Japan as Japan on May 3, 1947. Japan adopted a parliamentary-based political system, while the Emperor changed to symbolic status.

American General of the Army Douglas MacArthur later commended the new Japanese government that he helped establish and the new Japanese period when he was about to send the American forces to the Korean War:

The Japanese people, since the war, have undergone the greatest reformation recorded in modern history. With a commendable will, eagerness to learn, and marked capacity to understand, they have, from the ashes left in war's wake, erected in Japan an edifice dedicated to the supremacy of individual liberty and personal dignity; and in the ensuing process there has been created a truly representative government committed to the advance of political morality, freedom of economic enterprise, and social justice. Politically, economically, and socially Japan is now abreast of many free nations of the earth and will not again fail the universal trust. ... I sent all four of our occupation divisions to the Korean battlefront without the slightest qualms as to the effect of the resulting power vacuum upon Japan. The results fully justified my faith. I know of no nation more serene, orderly, and industrious, nor in which higher hopes can be entertained for future constructive service in the advance of the human race.

For historian John W. Dower:

In retrospect, apart from the military officer corps, the purge of alleged militarists and ultranationalists that was conducted under the Occupation had relatively small impact on the long-term composition of men of influence in the public and private sectors. The purge initially brought new blood into the political parties, but this was offset by the return of huge numbers of formerly purged conservative politicians to national as well as local politics in the early 1950s. In the bureaucracy, the purge was negligible from the outset. ... In the economic sector, the purge similarly was only mildly disruptive, affecting less than sixteen hundred individuals spread among some four hundred companies. Everywhere one looks, the corridors of power in postwar Japan are crowded with men whose talents had already been recognized during the war years, and who found the same talents highly prized in the 'new' Japan.

Post War

Repatriation of Japanese from Overseas

After World War II, most of these overseas Japanese repatriated to Japan. The Allied powers repatriated over 6 million Japanese nationals from colonies and battlefields throughout Asia. Only a few remained overseas, often involuntarily, as in the case of orphans in China or prisoners of war captured by the Red Army and forced to work in Siberia.

War Crimes

Many political and military Japanese leaders were convicted for war crimes before the Tokyo tribunal and other Allied tribunals in Asia. However, all members of the imperial family implicated in the war, such as Emperor Shōwa and his brothers, cousins and uncles such as Prince Chichibu, Prince Fushimi Hiroyasu and Prince Asaka Yasuhiko, were exonerated from criminal prosecutions by Douglas MacArthur. The Japanese military before and during World War II committed numerous atrocities against civilian and military personnel. Its surprise attack on Pearl Harbor on December 7, 1941, prior to a declaration of war and without warning killed 2,403 neutral military personnel and civilians and wounded 1,247 others. Large scale massacres, rapes, and looting against civilians were committed, most notably the Sook Ching and the Nanjing Massacre, and the use of around 200,000 "comfort women", who were forced to serve as prostitutes for the Japanese military.

The Imperial Japanese Army also engaged in the execution and harsh treatment of Allied military personnel and POWs. Biological experiments were conducted by Unit 731 on prisoners of war as well as civilians; this included the use of biological and chemical weapons authorized by Emperor Shōwa himself. According to the 2002 *International Symposium on the Crimes of Bacteriological Warfare*, the number of people killed in Far East Asia by Japanese germ warfare and human experiments was estimated to be around 580,000. The members of Unit 731, including

Lieutenant General Shirō Ishii, received immunity from General MacArthur in exchange for germ warfare data based on human experimentation. The deal was concluded in 1948. The Imperial Japanese Army frequently used chemical weapons. Because of fear of retaliation, however, those weapons were never used against Westerners, but against other Asians judged "inferior" by imperial propaganda. For example, the Emperor authorized the use of toxic gas on 375 separate occasions during the Battle of Wuhan from August to October 1938.

Hideki Tojo

No inquiry of Japan's move into political totalitarianism, ultranationalist fascism, culminating in its invasion of China in 1937 and ultimate participation in the Axis Alliance of World War II, would be complete without an in depth analysis of Hideki Tojo.

a Japanese general and premier during World War II, Hideki Tojo (1884-1948), was hanged as a war criminal. He symbolized, in his rise to leadership of the Japanese government, the emergence of Japanese Asiatic expansionism and its parochial view of the world.

Hideki Tojo was born in Tokyo on Dec. 30, 1884, the eldest son in a family of samurai descent. Tojo entered military school in 1899, following in the footsteps of his father, a professional military man who served as a lieutenant colonel in the Sino-Japanese War and as a major general in the Russo-Japanese War. Tojo likewise saw service, though briefly, in the latter war. In 1915 he graduated with honors from the army war college and was subsequently sent abroad for 3 years (1919-1922) of study in Europe. After his return he served as an instructor in military science at the war college.

Brusque, scrupulous, and hardworking, Tojo came to be known as *kamisori* (the razor) for the sharp, decisive, impatient qualities that he manifested as he rose rapidly through the military hierarchy. He was assigned first to the War Ministry and subsequently to the general staff and various command posts. Promoted to lieutenant general in 1936, Tojo became chief of staff of the Kwantung Army in Manchuria, where he worked effectively to mobilize Manchuria's economy and strengthen Japan's military readiness in the event that war broke out with the Soviet Union. When full-scale hostilities broke out instead between China and Japan following the Marco Polo Bridge incident, Tojo in his first real taste of combat experience led two brigades in a blitzkrieg that quickly brought the whole of Inner Mongolia under Japanese control. In 1938 he was recalled from field service to become vice-minister of war, a position in which he pressed resolutely for preparations that would allow Japan to wage a two-front war against both China and the Soviet Union.

In mid-1940 Tojo was appointed war minister in the second Fumimaro Konoe government, which proceeded at once to sign the Tripartite Pact with Germany and Italy. Relations with the United States gradually worsened during succeeding months as Japanese troops moved south into Indochina; but Tojo hewed to a hard line. Convinced of the righteousness of the imperial cause and of the implacable hostility of the Americans, the British, the Chinese, and the Dutch, he stoutly opposed the negotiations and concessions that Konoe contemplated. Speaking for the army command, Tojo demanded a decision for war unless the United States backed away from its embargo on all exports to Japan. When Konoe hesitated, Tojo is reported to have told him that "sometimes it is necessary to shut one's eyes and take the plunge." Konoe, however, was reluctant to take the plunge and instead tendered his resignation.

Leadership in War

An imperial mandate was then given to Tojo in October 1941 to become premier and form a new Cabinet. It was thought that only Tojo had full knowledge of recent developments and an ability to control the army. Tojo was given an imperial command to "wipe the slate clean, " review all past decisions, and work for peace. But a reconsideration of Japanese policy failed to reveal alternatives acceptable to the army, and the decision for war was taken. Within hours after the surprise attack on Pearl Harbor, Tojo broadcast a brief message to his countrymen, warning them that "to annihilate this enemy and to establish a stable new order in East Asia, the nation must necessarily anticipate a long war."

Tojo had great power at the beginning of the war and in the West was often likened to Hitler and Mussolini. Besides serving as premier, he was a general in the army, war minister, and, for a short time, home minister. Later in the war he also served as chief of the general staff. In 1942 a tightly restricted national election resulted in a pro-Tojo Diet. Nonetheless, while wielding great power, Tojo was still not a dictator like Hitler or Mussolini. The senior statesmen, the army and navy general staffs, and, of course, ultimately the Emperor still exercised considerable power independent of Tojo.

Defeat and Dishonor

By early 1944 even though the tide of battle had turned decisively against Japan, and Tojo admitted to the Diet that the nation faced "the most critical situation in the history of the Empire, " he stood firmly opposed to increasing sentiment in favor of negotiation. The fall of Saipan in July 1944, however, put American bombers within range of the home-land, and the senior statesmen together with ministers in Tojo's Cabinet forced him into retirement.

With the end of the war Tojo awaited at his Tokyo residence his arrest by the occupation forces. On Sept. 11, 1945, when Gen. MacArthur ordered his arrest, Tojo attempted to shoot himself. After his recovery he was held in Sugamo prison until his trial as a suspected war criminal by the International Military Tribunal for the Far East began in May 1946. After proceedings which stretched out over 2 years, during which Tojo willingly accepted his responsibility for much of Japan's wartime policy while declaring it legitimate self-defense, he was found guilty of having "major responsibility for Japan's criminal attacks on her neighbors" and was sentenced to death by hanging. The sentence was carried out on Dec. 23, 1948.

CULT OF PERSONALITY

A *"cult of personality"* is a pejorative term implying the concentration of all power in a single charismatic leader within a totalitarian state and the near deification of that leader in state propaganda. Totalitarian régimes use the state-controlled mass media to cultivate a larger-than-life public image of the leader through unquestioning flattery and praise. Leaders are lauded for their extraordinary courage, knowledge, wisdom, or any other superhuman quality *necessary for legitimatizing* the totalitarian régime. The cult of personality serves to sustain such a régime in power, discourage open criticism, and justify whatever political twists and turns it may decide to take. Among the more infamous and pervasive cults of personality in the twentieth century were those surrounding Hitler, Mussolini, Stalin, Mao Zedong, Francisco Franco, Vladimir Lenin, Chiang Kaishek, Ho Chi Minh, Kim Il Sung, Juan and Evita Peron, Pol Pot, Kim Jong Il, and Saddam Hussein. The term is occasionally—if idiosyncratically—applied to national leaders *who did not seek* similar godlike adulation during their lifetime or term in office, *nor have headed totalitarian régimes,* but have been later glorified by the government or in the national mass media. Examples might include George Washington, Napoléon Bonaparte, Abraham Lincoln, Mustafa Kemal Atatürk, Charles de Gaulle, Ronald Reagan, Margaret Thatcher, and others.

A cult of personality differs from Thomas Carlyle's "hero worship" in the sense that it is *intentionally* built around the national leader and is often used to justify authoritarian rule. In one of the more idiosyncratic usages, it is sometimes applied by analogy to refer to the public veneration of famous leaders of social movements such as Karl Marx, Mahatma

Gandhi, Martin Luther King Jr., Che Guevara, Malcolm X, Nelson Mandela, and others. In fact, the term itself derives from Karl Marx's critique of the "superstitious worship of authority" that had developed around his own personality, acclaimed merits, and contribution to the work of the First Socialist International in the latter half of the nineteenth century.

Historically, numerous rulers have promoted their own cults of personality. Absolute monarchies were the prevalent form of government for much of recorded history, and most traditional monarchs were held in public awe and adoration. For example, pharaonic Egypt, Imperial China, and the Roman Empire accorded their crowned sovereigns the status of revered god-kings. The doctrine of the divine right of kings claimed that absolutist monarchs such as Henry VIII, Louis XIV, or Catherine the Great sat on their thrones by the will of God. The democratic revolutions of the 18th and 19th centuries made it increasingly difficult for traditional autocrats to retain their divine aura. However, the development of the modern mass media, state-run public education, and government propaganda has enabled some more recent national leaders to manipulate popular opinion and project an almost equally extolled public image. Cults of personality developed around some of the most notorious totalitarian dictators of the twentieth century such as Hitler, Stalin, and Mao, who at the peak of their personalistic power were lionized as infallible, godlike creatures. Their portraits were hung in every private home or public building, while the country's artists and poets were expected to produce works of art idolizing the hero-leader.

The term *cult of personality* became a buzzword after Soviet leader Nikita Khrushchev bitterly denounced Stalin's near deification before a closed session of the Twentieth Party Congress on February 25, 1956:

The cult of personality acquired such monstrous dimensions mainly because Stalin himself, using all conceivable methods, supported the glorification of his own person.... One of the most characteristic examples of Stalin's self-glorification and of his lack of even elementary modesty is the edition of his Short Biography, which was published in 1948. This book is an expression of the most unrestrained flattery, an example of making a man into a god, of transforming him into an infallible sage, "the greatest leader," "sublime strategist of all times and nations." Ultimately, no more words could be found with which to praise Stalin up to the heavens. We need not give here examples of the loathsome adulation filling this book. All we need to add is that they all were approved and edited by Stalin personally and some of them were added in his own handwriting to the draft text of the book. (Khrushchev 1989)

In a country long known for its traditional worship of religious saints and czars, the public exaltation of Soviet leaders was deliberately pursued as necessary for building national unity and consensus. The result was Stalin's cult of personality—the total loyalty and dedication of all Soviet citizens to the all-powerful leader, whose demigod personality exemplified the heroism and glory of "building socialism in one country." Khrushchev's "Secret Speech" was a major break by the post-Stalin leadership with the oppressive dominance of Stalinism. "Big Brother," a fictional character in George Orwell's famous novel *Nineteen Eighty-Four*, is widely believed to be a satire of Stalin's cult of personality (even though it is equally likely to have been based on Britain's ubiquitous Lord Kitchener).

The Soviet/Communist Phenomena

At the Twentieth Congress of the Communist Party in 1956, Nikita Khrushchev denounced Josef Stalin's "Cult of Personality" in the so-called "Secret Speech." He declared, "It is impermissible and foreign to the spirit of Marxism-Leninism to elevate one person, to transform him into a superman possessing supernatural characteristics akin to those of a god." In addition to enumerating Stalin's repression of the Communist Party during the purges, Khrushchev recounted how in films, literature, his *Short Biography,* and the *Short Course of the History of the Communist Party,* Stalin displaced Vladimir Lenin, the Party, and the people and claimed responsibility for all of the successes of the Revolution, the civil war, and World War II. Khrushchev's speech praised Lenin as a modest "genius," and demanded that "history, literature and the fine arts properly reflect Lenin's role and the great deeds of our Communist Party and of the Soviet people." Khrushchev's formulation reveals the paradox of the "cult of personality." While denigrating the cult of Stalin, Khrushchev reinvigorated the cult of Lenin.

Analysts have traced the leader cult back to the earliest days of the Soviet Union, when a personality cult spontaneously grew up around Lenin. The cult grew among Bolsheviks because of Lenin's stature as Party leader and among the population due to Russian traditions of the personification of political power in the tsar (Tucker, 1973, pp. 59–60). Lenin himself was appalled by the tendency to turn him into a mythic hero and fought against it. After the leader's death in 1924, however, veneration of Lenin became an integral part of the Communist Party's quest for legitimacy. Party leaders drew on both political and religious traditions in their decision to place a mausoleum containing the embalmed body of Lenin at the geographic and political center of Soviet power in Moscow's Red Square. Once Lenin was enshrined as a sacred figure, his potential successors scrambled to position themselves as his true heirs.

After Stalin consolidated his power and embarked on the drive for socialist construction, he began to build his own cult of personality. Stalin's efforts were facilitated by the previously existing leader cult, and he trumpeted his special relationship with Lenin. Early evidence of the Stalin cult can be found in the press coverage of his fiftieth birthday in 1929, which extolled "the beloved leader, the truest pupil and comrade-in-arms of Vladimir Ilich Lenin" (Brooks, 2000, p. 61). In the early 1930s, Stalin shaped his image as leader by establishing himself as the ultimate expert in fields other than politics. He became "the premier living Marxist philosopher" and an authoritative historian of the Party (Tucker, 1992, pp. 150–151). Stalin shamelessly rewrote Party history to make himself Lenin's chief assistant and adviser in 1917. Soviet public culture of the 1930s and 1940s attributed all of the achievements of the Soviet state to Stalin directly and lauded his military genius in crafting victory in World War II. Stalin's brutal repressions went hand in hand with a near-deification of his person. The outpouring of grief at his death in 1953 revealed the power of Stalin's image as wise father and leader of the people.

Once he had consolidated power, Nikita Khrushchev focused on destroying Stalin's cult. Many consider Khrushchev's 1956 attack on the Stalin cult to be his finest political moment. Although Khrushchev criticized Stalin, he reaffirmed the institution of the leader cult by invoking Lenin and promoting his own achievements. Khrushchev's condemnation of the Stalin cult was also limited by his desire to preserve the legitimacy of the socialist construction that Stalin had under-taken. After Khrushchev's fall, Leonid Brezhnev criticized Khrushchev's personal style of leadership but ceased the assault on Stalin's cult of personality. He then employed the institution of the leader cult to enhance his own legitimacy.

Like Stalin's cult, Brezhnev's cult emphasized "the link with Lenin, [his] … role in the achievement of successes … and his relationship with the people" (Gill). The Brezhnev-era party also perpetuated the Lenin cult and emphasized its own links to Lenin by organizing a lavish commemoration of the centennial of Lenin's birth in 1970. The association of Soviet achievements with Brezhnev paled in comparison to the Stalin cult and praise of Brezhnev's accomplishments often linked them to the Communist Party as well. Both Khrushchev and Brezhnev sought to raise the status of the Communist Party in relation to its leader. Yet Stalin, Khrushchev, and Brezhnev all conceived of the role of the people as consistently subordinate to leader and Party.

It was not until Gorbachev instituted the policy of glasnost, or openness, in the mid-1980s that the institution of the cult of personality came under sustained attack. The Soviet press revealed Stalin's crimes and then began to scrutinize the actions of all of the Soviet leaders, eventually including Lenin. The press under Gorbachev effectively demolished the institution of the Soviet leader cult by revealing the grotesque falsifications required to perpetuate it and the violent repression of the population hidden behind its facade. These attacks on the cult of personality undermined the legitimacy of the Soviet Union and contributed to its downfall.

In the post-Soviet period, analysts have begun to see signs of a cult of personality growing around Vladimir Putin. Other observers, however, are skeptical of how successful such a leader cult could be in the absence of a Party structure to promote it and given the broad access to information that contemporary Russians enjoy. The cult of personality played a critical role in the development of the Soviet state and in its dissolution. The discrediting of the cult of the leader as an institution in the late Soviet period makes its post-Soviet future uncertain at best.

THE MOVE TO
GLOBAL WAR

German King Tiger tanks

The 20th century crystallized the concept of "total war", a form of warfare, characteristic of modern industrial society, involving the total and maximum mobilization of all military, social, and economic resources of a country for armed conflict, usually entailing the exposure of the civilian population and economy to enemy attack. Distinct therefore from regional or local war, and from nuclear as distinct from conventional conflict.

THE IMPACT OF TOTAL WAR

World War II was larger than previous wars and was fought in more parts of the world. But it was different in another way, too. It came closer than any prior conflict to being a total war. It was not fought just by soldiers and sailors. Instead, each country tried to use all its resources to support the war. Victory in World War II depended, more than anything else, on supplying armies with huge quantities of industrial products. A country needed modern weapons, including planes, bombs, tanks, submarines, aircraft carriers, and machine guns. It needed the ships, railroads, and trucks to transport them; the fuel to run them; and the grease to lubricate them. It needed enough boots, uniforms, and helmets for its soldiers. The people who built these products, as well as the scientists and engineers who developed new weapons (see Chapter 15) and the writers and filmmakers who waged psychological warfare (see Chapter 16), were as important to the war effort as the soldiers in the armies.

If all the people of a country were involved in the war, then the country could ask the civilian population to make major sacrifices to win the war. And if the civilian population were necessary for victory, then they were also targets for the enemy. Rationing of consumer goods was common as production shifted to the needs of the military. If World War II were a war of the people, then the people were its victims as well as its fighters.

Total war has been practiced for centuries, but *outright total warfare* was first demonstrated in the nineteenth century, *and flourished* with conflicts in the twentieth century. When one side of a conflict participates in total war, they dedicate not only their military to victory, but the civilian population still at home to working for victory as well. It becomes an ideological state of mind for those involved, and therefore, represents a very dangerous methodology, for the losses are great whether they win or lose.

The threat of total devastation to the earth and humankind through nuclear warfare in the mid-twentieth century caused a change in thinking. Such a war does not require the mobilization of the whole population, although it would result in their destruction. Since that time, therefore, the arena of war has retreated to smaller powers, and major powers have not been involved in a total war scenario. However, this has not necessarily reduced the casualties or the suffering of those involved in wars and the threat of widespread violence remains. Ultimately, humankind must move beyond the age of resolving differences through acts of violence, and establish a world in which war, total or otherwise, no longer exists.

Origin and Overview

The concept of total war is often traced back to Carl von Clausewitz and his writings *Vom Kriege (On War)*, but Clausewitz was actually concerned with the related philosophical concept of absolute war, a war free from any political constraints, which Clausewitz held was impossible. The two terms, absolute war and total war, are often confused:

Clausewitz's concept of absolute war is quite distinct from the later concept of "total war." Total war was a prescription for the actual waging of war typified by the ideas of General Erich von Ludendorff, who actually assumed control of the German war effort during World War One. Total war in this sense involved the total subordination of politics to the war effort—an idea Clausewitz emphatically rejected, and the assumption that total victory or total defeat were the only options.

Indeed, it is General Erich von Ludendorff during World War I (and in his 1935 book, *Der Totale Krieg—The Total War*) who first reversed the formula of Clausewitz, calling for total war—the complete mobilization of all resources, including policy and social systems, to the winning of war.

There are several reasons for the changing concept and recognition of total war in the nineteenth century. The main reason is industrialization. As countries' natural and capital resources grew, it became clear that some forms of conflict demanded more resources than others. For example, if the United States was to subdue a Native American tribe in an extended campaign lasting years, it still took much less resources than waging a month of war during the American Civil War. Consequently, the greater cost of warfare became evident. An industrialized nation could distinguish and then choose the intensity of warfare that it wished to engage in.

Additionally, this was the time when warfare was becoming more mechanized. A factory and its workers in a city would have greater connection with warfare than before. The factory itself would become a target, because it contributed to the war effort. It follows that the factory's workers would also be targets. Total war also resulted in the mobilization of the home front. Propaganda became a required component of total war in order to boost production and maintain morale. Rationing took place to provide more material for waging war.

There is no single definition of total war, but there is general agreement among historians that the First World War and Second World War were both examples. Thus, definitions do vary, but most hold to the spirit offered by Roger Chickering:

Total war is distinguished by its unprecedented intensity and extent. Theaters of operations span the globe; the scale of battle is practically limitless. Total war is fought heedless of the restraints of morality, custom, or international law, for the combatants are inspired by hatreds born of modern ideologies. Total war requires the mobilization not only of armed forces but also of whole populations. The most crucial determinant of total war is the widespread, indiscriminate, and deliberate inclusion of civilians as legitimate military targets.

Examples

Peloponnesian War

The first documented total war was the Peloponnesian War, as described by the historian, Thucydides. This war was fought between Athens and Sparta between 431 and 404 B.C. During the Peloponnesian War, the fighting lasted for years and consumed the economic resources of the participating city-states. Atrocities were committed on a scale never before seen, with entire populations being executed or sold into slavery, as in the case of the city of Melos. The aftermath of the war reshaped the Greek world, left much of the region in poverty, and reduced once influential Athens to a weakened state, from which it never completely recovered.

The Thirty Years War

The Thirty Years War may also be considered a total war. This conflict was fought between 1618 and 1648, primarily on the territory of modern Germany. Virtually all of the major European powers were involved, and the economy of each was based around fighting the war. Civilian populations were devastated. Estimates of civilian casualties are approximately 15-20 percent, with deaths due to a combination of armed conflict, famine, and disease. The size and training of armies also grew dramatically during this period, as did the cost of keeping armies in the field. Plunder was commonly used to pay and feed armies.

French Revolution

The French Revolution introduced some of the concepts of total war. The fledgling republic found itself threatened by a powerful coalition of European nations. The only solution, in the eyes of the Jacobin government, was to pour the nation's entire resources into an unprecedented war effort—this was the advent of the *levée en masse*. The following decree of the National Convention on August 23, 1793, clearly demonstrates the enormity of the French war effort:

From this moment until such time as its enemies shall have been driven from the soil of the Republic all Frenchmen are in permanent requisition for the services of the armies. The young men shall fight; the married men shall forge arms and transport provisions; the women shall make tents and clothes and shall serve in the hospitals; the children shall turn linen into lint; the old men shall betake themselves to the public squares in order to arouse the courage of the warriors and preach hatred of kings and the unity of the Republic.

Taiping Rebellion

During the Taiping Rebellion (1850-1864) that followed the secession of the Tàipíng Tiānguó (太平天國, Wade-Giles T'ai-p'ing t'ien-kuo) (Heavenly Kingdom of Perfect Peace) from the Qing empire, the first instance of total war in modern China can be seen. Almost every citizen of the Tàipíng Tiānguó was given military training and conscripted into the army to fight against the imperial forces.

During this conflict, both sides tried to deprive each other of the resources to continue the war and it became standard practice to destroy agricultural areas, butcher the population of cities, and, in general, exact a brutal price from captured enemy lands in order to drastically weaken the opposition's war effort. This war truly was total in that civilians on both sides participated to a significant extent in the war effort and in that armies on both sides waged war on the civilian population as well as military forces. In total, between 20 and 50 million died in the conflict, making it bloodier than the First World War and possibly bloodier than the Second World War as well, if the upper end figures are accurate.

American Civil War

U.S. Army General William Tecumseh Sherman's "March to the Sea" in 1864 during the American Civil War destroyed the resources required for the South to make war. He is considered one of the first military commanders to deliberately and consciously use total war as a military tactic. Also, General Phillip Sheridan's stripping of the Shenandoah Valley was considered "total war." Ulysses S. Grant was the general to initiate the practice in the Civil War.

World War I

Almost the whole of Europe mobilized to wage World War I. Young men were removed from production jobs and were replaced by women. Rationing occurred on the home fronts.

One of the features of total war in Britain was the use of propaganda posters to divert all attention to the war on the home front. Posters were used to influence people's decisions about what to eat and what occupations to take (women were used as nurses and in munitions factories), and to change the attitude of support towards the war effort.

After the failure of the Battle of Neuve Chapelle, the large British offensive in March 1915, the British Commander-in-Chief Field Marshal Sir John French claimed that it failed because of a lack of shells. This led to the Shell Crisis of 1915, which brought down the Liberal British government under the Premiership of H.H. Asquith. He formed a new coalition government dominated by Liberals and appointed Lloyd George as Minister of Munitions. It was a recognition that the whole economy would have to be geared for war if the Allies were to prevail on the Western Front.

As young men left the farms for the front, domestic food production in Britain and Germany fell. In Britain, the response was to import more food, which was done despite the German introduction of unrestricted submarine warfare, and to introduce rationing. The Royal Navy's blockade of German ports prevented Germany from importing food, and the Germans failed to introduce food rationing. German capitulation was hastened in 1918, by the worsening food crisis in Germany.

World War II

United Kingdom

Before the onset of the Second World War, the United Kingdom drew on its First World War experience to prepare legislation that would allow immediate mobilization of the economy for war, should future hostilities break out.

Rationing of most goods and services was introduced, not only for consumers but also for manufacturers. This meant that factories manufacturing products that were irrelevant to the war effort had more appropriate tasks imposed. All artificial light was subject to legal blackouts.

Not only were men and women conscripted into the armed forces from the beginning of the war (something which had not happened until the middle of World War I), but women were also conscripted as Land Girls to aid farmers and the Bevin Boys were conscripted to work down in the coal mines.

The Dunkirk evacuation by the British, was the large evacuation of Allied soldiers from May 26 to June 4, 1940, during the Battle of Dunkirk. In nine days, more than three hundred thousand (338,226) soldiers—218,226 British and 120,000 French—were rescued from Dunkirk, France, and the surrounding beaches by a hastily assembled fleet of about seven hundred boats. These craft included the famous "Little Ships of Dunkirk," a mixture of merchant marine boats, fishing boats, pleasure craft, and RNLI lifeboats, whose civilian crews were called into service for the emergency. These small craft ferried troops from the beaches to larger ships waiting offshore.

Huge casualties were expected in bombing raids, and so children were evacuated from London and other cities en masse to the countryside for compulsory billeting in households. In the long term, this was one of the most profound and longer lasting social consequences of the whole war for Britain. This is because it mixed up children with the adults of other classes. Not only did the middle and upper classes become familiar with the urban squalor suffered by working class children from the slums, but the children got a chance to see animals and the countryside, often for the first time, and experience rural life.

Germany

In contrast, Germany started the war under the concept of blitzkrieg. It did not accept that it was in a total war until Joseph Goebbels' Sportpalast speech of February 18, 1943. Goebbels *demanded from his audience a commitment to total war*, the complete mobilization of the German economy and German society for the war effort. For example, women were not conscripted into the armed forces or allowed to work in factories. The Nazi party adhered to the policy that a woman's place was in the home, and did not change this even as its opponents began moving women into important roles in production.

The commitment to the doctrine of the short war was a continuing handicap for the Germans; neither plans nor state of mind were adjusted to the idea of a long war until it was too late. Germany's armament minister, Albert Speer, who assumed office in early 1942, nationalized German war production and eliminated the worst inefficiencies. Under his direction, a threefold increase in armament production occurred and did not reach its peak until late 1944. To do this during the damage caused by the growing strategic Allied bomber offensive is an indication of the degree of industrial under-mobilization in the earlier years. It was because the German economy through most of the war was substantially under-mobilized that it was resilient under air attack. Civilian consumption was high during the early years of the war and inventories both in industry and in consumers' possession were high. These helped cushion the economy from the effects of bombing. Plant and machinery were plentiful and incompletely used, thus it was comparatively easy to substitute unused or partly used machinery for that which was destroyed. Foreign labor, both slave labor and labor from neighboring countries who joined the Anti-Comintern Pact with Germany, was used to augment German industrial labor which was under pressure by conscription into the *Wehrmacht* (Armed Forces).

Soviet Union

The Soviet Union (USSR) was a command economy which already had an economic and legal system allowing the economy and society to be redirected into fighting a total war. The transportation of factories and whole labor forces east of the Urals as the Germans advanced across the USSR in 1941, was an impressive feat of planning. Only those factories which were useful for war production were moved because of the total war commitment of the Soviet government.

During the battle of Leningrad, newly-built tanks were driven— unpainted because of a paint shortage—from the factory floor straight to the front. This came to symbolize the USSR's commitment to the Great Patriotic War and demonstrated the government's total war policy.

To encourage the Russian people to work harder, the communist government encouraged the people's love of the Motherland, and in a Machiavellian move, even allowed the reopening of Russian Orthodox Churches as it was thought this would help the war effort.

The ruthless movement of national groupings like the Volga German and later the Crimean Tatars (who Stalin thought might be sympathetic to the Germans) was a development of the conventional scorched earth policy. This was a more extreme form of internment, implemented by both the UK government (for Axis aliens and British Nazi sympathizers), as well as the U.S. and Canadian governments (for Japanese-Americans).

The Policy of Unconditional Surrender

After the United States entered World War II, Franklin D. Roosevelt declared at Casablanca conference to the other Allies and the press that unconditional surrender was the objective of the war against the Axis Powers of Germany, Italy, and Japan. Prior to this declaration, the individual régimes of the Axis Powers could have negotiated an armistice similar to that at the end of World War I and then a conditional surrender when they perceived that the war was lost.

The unconditional surrender of the major Axis powers caused a legal problem at the post-war Nuremberg Trials, because the trials appeared to be in conflict with Articles 63 and 64 of the Geneva Convention of 1929. Usually if such trials are held, they would be held under the auspices of the defeated power's own legal system as happened with some of the minor Axis powers, for example in the post World War II Romanian People's Tribunals. To circumvent this, the Allies argued that the major war criminals were captured after the end of the war, so they were not prisoners of war and the Geneva Conventions did not cover them. Further, the collapse of the Axis régimes created a legal condition of total defeat *(debellatio)* so the provisions of the 1907 Hague Conventions over military occupation were not applicable.

Present Day

Since the end of World War II, no industrial nations have fought such a large, decisive war, due to the availability of weapons that are so destructive that their use would offset the advantages of victory. With nuclear weapons, the fighting of a war became something that instead of taking years and the full mobilization of a country's resources, such as in

World War II, would instead take hours, and the weaponry could be developed and maintained with relatively modest peace time defense budgets. By the end of the 1950s, the super-power rivalry resulted in the development of Mutually Assured Destruction (MAD), the idea that an attack by one superpower would result in a war of retaliation which could destroy civilization and would result in hundreds of millions of deaths in a world where, in words widely attributed to Nikita Khrushchev, "The living will envy the dead."

As the tensions between industrialized nations have diminished, European continental powers for the first time in 200 years started to question if conscription was still necessary. Many are moving back to the pre-Napoleonic ideas of having small professional armies. This is something which despite the experiences of the first and second world wars is a model which the English speaking nations had never abandoned during peace time, probably because they have never had a common border with a potential enemy with a large standing army. In Admiral Jervis's famous phrase, "I do not say, my Lords, that the French will not come. I say only they will not come by sea."

The restrictions of nuclear and biological weaponry have not led to the end of war involving industrial nations, but a shift back to the limited wars of the type fought between the competing European powers for much of the nineteenth century. During the Cold War, wars between industrialized nations were fought by proxy over national prestige, tactical strategic advantage, or colonial and neocolonial resources. Examples include the Korean War, the Vietnam War, and the Soviet invasion of Afghanistan. Since the end of the Cold War, some industrialized countries have been involved in a number of small wars with strictly limited strategic objectives which have motives closer to those of the colonial wars of the nineteenth century than those of total war; examples include the Australian-led United Nations intervention in East Timor, the North Atlantic Treaty Organization intervention in Kosovo, the internal Russian conflict with Chechnya, and the American-led coalitions which invaded Afghanistan and twice fought the Iraqi régime of Saddam Hussein.

Total war, however, is still very much a part of the political landscape. Even with the disarmament of nuclear weapons and biological weapons, total war is still possible. Some consider the genocides in Rwanda and Darfur as acts of total war. The break up of Yugoslavia in the early 1990s and the resulting "ethnic cleansing" also has familiar elements of total war. Civil wars between a nation's own populations can be regarded as total war, especially if both sides are committed wholly to defeating the other side. Total war between industrialized nations is theorized to be non-existent, simply because of the interconnectivity between economies. Two industrialized nations committed in total war would affect much of the world. However, countries in the process of industrializing and countries that have not yet industrialized are still at risk for total war.

Death from the Air

One of the ways in which the war was brought home to civilian populations during World War II was by attacks from the air. In the first days of the war, the German air force (the Luftwaffe) heavily bombed Warsaw, the Polish capital. Then the Luftwaffe destroyed the center of the Dutch port of Rotterdam in May 1940. In both places, many civilians were killed and injured, and there was heavy damage to nonmilitary structures such as homes, schools, and hospitals. Shortly after, when large numbers of civilians clogged the roads of Belgium and France trying to escape the advancing Germans, Luftwaffe planes sometimes swooped down and fired machine guns at them to increase their panic and to block the movement of the Allied armies.

The Impact of Total War on Children

British children were also impacted by World War II in a dramatic way. When the war began, British experts were sure that German air raids on London and other English cities would kill hundreds of thousands of people a week. They also expected the Germans to drop bombs containing poison gas. Because of these fears, in September 1939, at the very beginning of the war, more than 800,000 children were evacuated—without their parents—from London and other large cities and sent to small towns or villages in the countryside. Half a million mothers of preschoolers, with their children, were also evacuated.

Most returned within a few months, during the period known as the phony war, when there were no German attacks on Britain. (This period is described in Chapter 2.) When German air attacks began again, many again left London. The same thing happened in 1944, when the V-weapon attacks began. (See Chapter 15.) Apart from physical dangers and shortages, one of the most dramatic effects of the war on children in countries such as Britain and the United States was the way it disrupted normal ways of growing up. An English child who was eight when the war began was fourteen when it finally ended—and probably could no longer remember a time before the war. Soldiers might be separated from their families for years, and no one could be sure if they would ever come back. Every child knew a friend whose father or older brother or uncle was killed in the war.

Victims and Orphans

Children in countries conquered by the Nazis suffered much more. The clearest example was the Holocaust, the Nazis' attempt from 1941 to 1945 to kill all the Jews of Europe. (Chapter 7 describes the Holocaust.) Even before the war, Jewish children in Germany suffered constant discrimination. They were expelled from schools and attacked by Nazi thugs. Many Jewish families left Germany, but fleeing became increasingly difficult. In the last ten months before the war, German Jewish parents, who were unable to leave themselves, sent about 9,000 of their children to Britain. They traveled through Europe on special trains called *kindertransporte* ("children's transports"). Although separated from their parents, friends, and homeland, these children were the lucky ones.

The overwhelming majority of Jewish children in German-controlled Europe, perhaps 85 percent, were murdered during the war—a much higher rate than adults. In extermination camps such as Auschwitz, designed to kill thousands of people a day, healthy adults might be spared and used as slave labor, but children were killed immediately. In addition, in the ghettos, the walled-in Jewish sections of towns that the Germans established in eastern Europe, there was starvation and constant epidemics of diseases caused by malnutrition, exhaustion, and inadequate sanitation. Children, especially very young children, were more likely to die from these causes than adults. Children were also less likely to survive by hiding in forests or escaping over mountains. Something like 1.5 million Jewish children died in the Holocaust.

Even so, many thousands of Jewish children survived the war, usually by being hidden by non-Jewish families or by Christian churches, even though their parents had died. But they were not the only children left alone. There were 1 million orphans in Poland at the end of the war and tens of thousands in France. One of every eight children in Greece was without parents. In 1945, when Germany surrendered, more than 10 million children in Europe had—at least temporarily—been abandoned or lost by their parents.

Germany: Fanatics and Rebels

For years, the Nazis had heavily pressured young people in Germany to join official Nazi organizations like the Hitler Youth and the League of German Girls. By 1939, membership was legally required. These groups sponsored sporting events and similar social activities. But they also taught young Germans Nazi ideas, gave the youths uniforms, and marched them in Nazi parades. Older boys received military training, and many entered the army. In 1944, an entire armored division, called the Hitler Youth Division, was formed entirely from young men who had just "graduated" from the Hitler Youth. It fought with great courage and determination, but it was also the unit that murdered captured Canadian soldiers during the Battle of Normandy. (See Chapter 11.) In other words, the Hitler Youth had trained these young men to be fanatical Nazis.

Not all German young people participated in official Nazi groups, despite the law. In fact, some wanted to stay out so much that they became rebels against the Nazi government. In some of the big cities, especially in the Rhineland region of western Germany, loose groups of unskilled workers —usually between fourteen and eighteen years old—formed. They had various names, but the best-known groups were called Edelweiss Pirates. The edelweiss is a white flower that grows high in the Alps, the great mountain range of western Europe, and the Pirates wore one, or sometimes a white pin, hidden under the left lapel of their coats.

Originally, many of the Edelweiss Pirates just wanted to hike or go camping without Nazi interference. Soon, however, they began mocking Hitler and the Nazis in songs and in the graffiti they scrawled on walls. They attacked members of the Hitler Youth on the streets and tried to assassinate local Nazi officials. Sometimes they engaged in industrial sabotage, intentionally destroying machines or products.

The government considered the Pirates criminal street gangs, and, in some ways, some of them were. But their targets, and the things they wrote and said, made it clear that they hated everything the Nazis stood for. Because of this, the Gestapo (the Nazi secret police), whose job was to crush enemies of the government, hunted them. Although twelve Pirates were publicly hanged, without trial, in Cologne in 1944, the Gestapo never succeeded in destroying them entirely.

Of the 600,000 German civilians killed in bombing raids during the war, about 120,000 were children.

Arthur "Bomber" Harris

A week after the RAF adopted the strategic air offensive directive, Air Marshal Arthur Harris, soon known as "Bomber" Harris, became head of Bomber Command. He was a firm believer in the new policy. Harris argued that long-term bombing attacks that would destroy the enemy's industrial resources and demoralize its population was the only correct use of bombers. He opposed the use of bombers in any other operations. Indeed, he even tried to prevent the temporary interruption of the strategic air offensive in spring 1944, when the British transferred the bombers to France, where they were needed to attack railroads and bridges before the Allies could invade Normandy. WIth bombed-out roads, the Germans would be prevented from bringing reinforcements to the invasion beaches. Harris claimed that bombers were not suited for this job, and General Dwight D. Eisenhower, the supreme Allied commander, had to threaten to resign before Harris would give in.

Military experts and historians agree that the campaign Harris opposed so strongly was probably the most successful air campaign of the war and perhaps the bombers' most important contribution to the Allied victory in Europe.

The Nazis used area bombing to help convince average Germans that the British—not the Nazis—were barbarians who made war against defenseless children.

American Bombing of Germany

The American strategic bombing campaign against Germany generally avoided area bombing. (The United States did use area bombing against Japan, described in Chapter 14.) Instead, the American air force, concentrated on hitting specific industrial targets. The targets were chosen after economic experts analyzed which factories were most needed and would be the most difficult to replace. For example, the Americans attacked a plant that was one of Germany's few sources of ball bearings, which are needed in all motor vehicles. But sites like these were strongly defended, and the American daylight raids suffered heavy losses, just as Air Marshal Arthur Harris and the Royal Air Force predicted.

The most important target for the Americans became Germany's production of gasoline and aviation fuel. Germany had few sources of petroleum and increasingly relied on synthetic (chemically produced) fuel made from coal and other sources. The plants that produced fuel could not be broken up into smaller units and were difficult to hide. The campaign against the synthetic oil plants eventually became tremendously successful, but only after the introduction of a new American plane, the P-51 Mustang. This was the first fighter that had the fuel capacity to accompany the bombers all the way to their targets and protect them against German attack. The shortage of fuel, especially aviation fuel, was a key factor in the final collapse of the German armies.

Another major American target was the transportation system, which was more important than ever because the big factories were scattered around Germany. In fact, the collapse of German industry in 1945 was probably caused by the destruction of the transportation system, rather than because the industries themselves had been bombed. But by the time this collapse occurred, Allied ground troops were pouring through Germany, so it is impossible to know what part the bombing itself played.

The greatest danger was that planes would drop poison gas bombs onto cities in air raids.

Rationing, Recycling, and Fellowship

Rationing and recycling were facts of life in Britain during World War II. Nothing was wasted, and anything that could be recycled was recycled: even potato peels were saved to feed to pigs. The government limited the clothing styles that could be manufactured. To save material, men's pants could not have cuffs, and women's skirts were made shorter. Clothing was severely rationed, and buying new wearing apparel was extremely rare. Children wore hand-me-downs. New shoes for civilians, including children, were unavailable: leather was reserved for soldiers' boots. People were allowed to buy new furniture only if their house had been bombed. Only one pattern of dishware was produced.

Tea and fresh eggs were difficult to get. Oranges and other imported fresh fruit almost disappeared. So did chocolate. Even ordinary food like butter and meat were rationed. People did not eat as much and had less variety in their diets.

There were other inconveniences, too. The blackout, in which all lights had to be off at night, made it hard to go anywhere after dark. In many places, street signs and road names were removed to delay the Germans if they invaded, but this only confused residents.

Although the shortages and rationing were inconvenient, many British people viewed the wartime atmosphere in a positive way. They liked the feeling that the whole country was working together for a common goal. Everyone seemed to belong to one of the numerous volunteer organizations. Many were air raid wardens, who made sure people got into shelters, which many families built in their backyard. In London, thousands of people went into the subway stations during air raids. Everywhere posters urged people not to repeat any information they learned because German spies were supposedly everywhere ("Loose Lips Sink Ships" was the most famous slogan). Other posters showed Prime Minister Winston Churchill with a defiant look on his face. Many people remember that England seemed much friendlier in those years. There were fewer trains, so they were more crowded—but strangers traveling together now spoke to each other instead of reading their newspapers. In the cities, the crowded air raid shelters became neighborhood meeting places.

A Child's View of the War

In 1940, when she was five years old, Ann Stalcup watched the German bombers overhead, on their way to attack the city of Bristol in western England, less than 20 miles from her home in the small town of Lydney. She heard the explosions and saw the flames' reflection on the river that passed her town.

In 1943, German prisoners of war were put to work on some farms near Lydney. Stalcup remembers that when they first arrived, they had only bloody rags to wear until the local people found old clothes for them. "No one blamed the soldiers for the war. The war was Hitler's fault. I was only eight but I was sure of that."

WORLD WAR II

The Second World War was history's largest and most significant armed conflict. It served as the breeding ground for the modern structure of security and intelligence, and for the postwar balance of power that formed the framework for the Cold War. Weapons, materiel, and actual combat, though vital to the Allies' victory over the Axis, did not alone win the war. To a great extent, victory was forged in the work of British and American intelligence services, who ultimately overcame their foes' efforts. Underlying the war of guns and planes was a war of ideas, images, words, and impressions—intangible artifacts of civilization that yielded enormous tangible impact for the peoples of Europe, east Asia, and other regions of the world.

Scope and Consequences of the War

The war pitted some 50 Allied nations, most notable among which were the United States, United Kingdom, Soviet Union, and China, against the Axis nations. The name "Axis," a reference to the straight geographic line between the capital cities of Rome and Berlin, came from a pact signed by Germany and Italy in 1936, to which Japan became a signatory in 1940. Ultimately a number of other nations would, either willingly or unwillingly, throw in their lot with the Axis, but Germany and Japan remained the principal powers in this alliance.

Although the roots of the conflict lay before the 1930s, hostilities officially began with the German invasion of Poland on September 1, 1939, and ended with the Japanese surrender to the United States six years and one day later. The war can be divided into three phases: 1939–41, when Axis victory seemed imminent; 1941–43, when Axis conquests reached their high point even as the tide turned with the U.S. and Soviet entry into the war; and 1943–45, as the Allies beat back and ultimately defeated the Axis.

Over those six years, armies, navies, air units, guerrilla forces, and clandestine units would fight across millions of square miles of sea and land, from Norway's North Cape to the Solomon Islands, and from Iran to Alaska. The war would include more than a dozen significant theatres in western Europe, the north Atlantic, Italy, eastern and southern Europe, Russia, North Africa, China, southern Asia, Southeast Asia, and the Pacific islands. Less major, but still significant, engagements took place in East Africa, the Middle East, and West Africa. There were even extremely limited engagements—mostly at the level of diplomacy, espionage, or propaganda—in South America and southern Africa.

Death Toll

World War II and its attendant atrocities would exact an unparalleled human toll, estimated at 50 million military and civilian lives lost. Combat deaths alone add up to about 19 million, with the largest share of this accounted for by 10 million Soviet, 3.5 million German, 2 million Chinese, and 1.5 million Japanese deaths. (The United States lost about 400,000, and the United Kingdom some 280,000.)

Adolf Hitler and the Nazis killed another 15.5 million in a massive campaign of genocide that included the "Final Solution," whereby some 6 million Jews were killed. Another 3 million Soviet prisoners of war, along with smaller numbers of Gypsies, homosexuals, handicapped persons, political prisoners, and other civilians rounded out the total. Principal among the Nazi executioners was the SS, led by Heinrich Himmler, which operated a network of slave-labor and extermination camps throughout central and eastern Europe.

About 14 million civilian deaths have been attributed to the Japanese. They imposed a system of forced labor on the peoples of the region they dubbed the "Greater East Asia Co-Prosperity Sphere," and literally worked millions of civilians and prisoners of war (POWs) to death in their camps. The Japanese also conducted massacres of civilians that rivaled those undertaken by the Nazis in Russia.

Soviet non-combat atrocities accounted for another 7 million deaths. Victims included members of deported nationalities, sent eastward to prevent collaboration with the Nazis; murdered German POWs; returning

Soviet POWs killed because of their exposure to the West; and other campaigns of genocide conducted by Soviet dictator Josef Stalin.

World War II served as a watershed between the multi-polar world of the nineteenth and early twentieth centuries, and the bipolar world of the Cold War. It ended the military dominance of European powers, but also ushered in an era in which Europe, heavily aided in its recovery by the United States so as to avoid another European war, became a major economic power.

The war transformed the United States from an isolationist giant, with little interest in affairs outside the Western Hemisphere, to a modern superpower. Symbolic of this transformation was the construction of the Pentagon building, commenced just before the United States entered the war. The war also marked the birth of the modern U.S. intelligence apparatus, of which the Office of Strategic Services (OSS), led by Major General William Donovan, was the progenitor. OSS would cease to function soon after the war's conclusion, but two years later, it would be replaced by a far more lasting organization, the Central Intelligence Agency (CIA).

Despite the wartime alliance with the Soviet Union, and the creation of the United Nations in an effort to settle international differences peacefully, the Cold War was an all but inevitable result of the war, which left only two superpowers in its wake. Thenceforth, the world would be divided between the United States and its allies—among which would be its two wartime enemies, West Germany and Japan—and the Soviet Union and its affiliates. These would include East Germany and eastern Europe; Communist China from 1949 to the Sino-Soviet rift of the late 1950s; and a number of states in the gradually emerging developing world of the Middle East, Africa, and Asia.

The conflict spelled an end to the European colonial empires, and brought independence to dozens of countries in the Middle East, Africa, and south and east Asia. Among the many states that owed their existence to the war was Israel. The effects of the Holocaust moved Western leaders to action, and Western sympathy helped ensure support for the establishment of a Jewish state.

The Axis and the Causes of the War

The victory of Benito Mussolini's Black Shirts in Italy in October 1922, introduced the world to Fascism, which reinterpreted nationalism in totalitarian terms, i.e., as an all-encompassing political movement intended to supplant all other centers of influence, such as religion, in the life of the individual. Hitler regarded Mussolini as a mentor, yet the Nazis would eclipse the Fascists in terms of strength, influence, and impact on world history.

Not only was Germany's militarily more powerful than Italy's, but the agenda of the Nazis, who took power in January 1933, had a much greater sense of urgency.

Central to Hitler's plans, outlined in his manifesto *Mein Kampf* (1924), was the elimination of central and eastern European Jews, who Hitler regarded as the principal barrier to German European dominance. Intimately tied with this plan was his vision of conquest and colonization in Russia and eastern Europe, which would—after the Jews and Slavs had been exterminated—constitute a German empire or *reich* that Hitler predicted would last a thousand years.

This consciously millenarian vision drew on German history and national mythology, citing as the first and second reichs the Holy Roman Empire of the Middle Ages and the German Empire of 1870–1918 respectively. It appealed not only to longstanding strains of anti-Semitism in Europe, which dated back at least to the time of Crusades, but also to disaffection with what the Germans regarded as their betrayal and humiliation in World War I and with the Versailles Treaty of 1919. In a country that had recently been devastated by inflation—Germany's economic crisis preceded the worldwide Great Depression by several years, and was even more severe—Nazism seemed to offer a solution for strengthening a once-great nation that had fallen on difficult times.

Communism and the Spanish Civil War

At a rhetorical and symbolic level, Hitler opposed Communism, and used the threat of Soviet Russia as justification for his moves to arm Germany in the 1930s. In reality, the Nazis and Soviets provided one another with mutual assistance, continuing a pattern begun in World War I, when imperial Germany had aided V. I. Lenin. After the war, German aristocrats, nationalists, and Communists all opposed, and helped bring down, the liberal democratic Weimar Republic. Though Hitler killed thousands of Communists after he gained power in January 1933, German military forces trained in Russia, and Germany provided Russia with equipment.

This secret relationship would become public when the two sides signed the Non-Aggression Pact on August 23, 1939, but until that time, Hitler and Stalin made much of their putative opposition to one another. The Spanish Civil War (1936–39) provided them with a proxy battleground, as Germany and Italy tried out new armaments in support of the Nationalists, led by Francisco Franco. The Republican side turned to Stalin for help, but he gave them little assistance while siphoning resources and leaders, some of whom went to Moscow and never returned.

On the other hand, the romance and mythology of the Republican cause provided the Soviets with a propaganda victory that comported well with their current "Popular Front" strategy. In accordance with the latter, Communists worldwide ceased calls for world revolution, and instead formed alliances with liberal, socialist, and anarchist movements. Later, Stalin would form a "popular front" on a grand scale, as he aligned himself with the United States and Great Britain.

Munich and Mussolini

Hitler's rhetorical opposition to Communism won him tacit support from Britain and France, which in the 1930s regarded Nazism as the lesser of two evils. At Munich in September 1938, British and French complicity yielded Germany title to a portion of Czechoslovakia known as the Sudetenland. In the view of many historians, the Munich conference and the appeasement efforts of British Prime Minister Neville Chamberlain rendered war all but inevitable.

Munich also sealed the relationship between Mussolini and Hitler. Despite their later alliance, Mussolini, a former Communist, rightly perceived significant differences between his nationalism and Hitler's racism. If Britain and France perceived Hitler as a buffer against Stalin, then Mussolini in the early 1930s seemed like a buffer against Hitler. What brought Italy and Germany together was the same complex of factors that eventually forged a three-way alliance with Japan: a shared desire for greater power, territorial ambitions that had supposedly been frustrated by the democratic powers, and a string of diplomatic and military successes that encouraged ever bolder moves.

Japan, Militarism, and Expansionism

When its troops marched into Manchuria in 1931, Japan launched the first in the series of conquests and invasions during the 1930s that set the stage for the war. Though nominally led by an emperor, Hirohito, by that time the nation had come under the control of military officers, who had imposed a dictatorship. The Japanese lacked a single powerful leader until Hideki Tojo emerged at the top in 1941.

Although certainly authoritarian and strictly controlled, the Japanese system was technically not totalitarian, in the sense that it did not have a specific, animating modern ideology. Instead, it relied on ancient national myths, combined with an abiding sense that Japan had been wronged in its struggle to make a place for itself as a world power. The Japanese belief system combined nationalistic and racial themes: like the Nazis, they regarded all other peoples as inferior. This would have seemingly made the Japanese and Nazi systems mutually exclusive, but because they were at opposite sides of the world, it provided a convenient formula for dividing the planet between them.

Each of the three future participants in the Axis Pact set out to test the resolve of the other powers to oppose them, and found such opposition all but nonexistent. The League of Nations, formed to put an end to wars after World War I, failed to act decisively when Italy conquered Ethiopia in 1935–36, when Germany occupied the Rhineland in 1936, when Japan conquered most of eastern China in 1937–38, or when Germany annexed Austria in 1938.

1939–41: The Axis Triumphant

Over the course of the first nine months of 1939, Germany added the rest of Czechoslovakia, while Italy occupied Albania. Having signed the Non-Aggression Pact with Stalin in August, Hitler invaded Poland on September 1. Britain and France, which on March 29 had pledged to support Poland, declared war, but did not attack Germany. During the next few weeks, Germany and Russia divided Poland between themselves, and in November, the Soviet Union launched a separate war with Finland.

Although the Soviets eventually emerged victorious in March 1940, the Russo-Finnish War convinced Hitler of Stalin's vulnerability. Stalin had decimated his officer corps with his purges in the 1930s, and his collectivization efforts had been accompanied by the imprisonment, starvation, and deaths of millions. The Soviet Union was to prove much stronger, however, than Hitler imagined. And if Hitler believed that Japan would join him in making war on the Soviets, he was mistaken; the Soviet performance against the Japanese during the little-known tank battle at Nomonhan in Manchuria in August, 1939, effectively convinced the Japanese of Russia's true strength.

From 1939 to 1941, the Axis unquestionably had the upper hand in the conflict. During the first part of this period, nicknamed "the Phony War," hardly a shot was fired in western Europe. Only in the spring of 1940 did Hitler's forces resume action, conquering Denmark, Norway, the Low

Countries, and France. The French, who relied on the defenses of the Maginot Line (designed to fight a World War I–style conflict of limited movement), surrendered after a nominal resistance effort. Most of the country fell under direct Nazi control, which a small portion to the southeast, with the town of Vichy as its capital, formed a pro-Axis government.

The speedy capitulation of the French left the British alone in opposition to the Nazis. In May 1940, Chamberlain resigned, and was replaced by Winston Churchill. In this change, the British people gained an unexpected advantage; over the next five years, Churchill, widely regarded as one of history's great orators, would stir his people to action with a series of memorable speeches. Yet, the position of the British was perilous, and as the Nazi Luftwaffe launched an aerial campaign against them in August, it seemed that German victory was only a matter of time.

Axis Victories and Blunders

At about the same time that the Battle of Britain began, Mussolini attacked the British in North and East Africa. He thus unexpectedly offered England a venue for fighting the Axis outside of Europe, and eventually German forces would be diverted into the Africa campaign.

In southern Europe, Hitler managed to compel Bulgaria, Hungary, and Romania into joining the Axis, but this advantage was overshadowed by another diversion of forces caused by Mussolini. Mussolini invaded Greece in October 1940, and Greek resistance proved so fierce that in April 1941, German forces rolled into southern Europe. Churchill attempted to oppose them in Greece, but the Germans pushed back British forces, and in history's first airborne invasion, took the isle of Crete—an important Mediterranean base—in May.

By mid-1941, virtually all of Western Europe, except Britain and neutral Switzerland, Spain, and Sweden, belonged to the Axis. But the Balkan campaign had pushed back Hitler's timetable for the most important campaign of the war, the invasion of Russia. The purpose of all other fighting up to that point had been to eliminate opposition as Germany invaded the Soviet Union, and rather than conquer Britain, Hitler preferred to enlist it as an ally against Stalin. He called off attacks on British air bases in May 1941, but by then the Nazi bombardment had inflamed British sentiment against Germany.

1941–43: The Tide Turns

On June 22, 1941, the Nazis invaded Russia. Operation Barbarossa, as it was called—its name a reference to the twelfth century Holy Roman Emperor Frederick I Barbarossa—was the largest land invasion in history. Fought according to the blitzkrieg ("lightning war") tactics already demonstrated elsewhere in Europe, the invasion relied on mechanized infantry divisions and Panzer (tank) columns with heavy aerial support.

The invasion would initially yield enormous victories for the Nazis, who quickly doubled the size of their territory by annexing most of western Russia. However, the Germans had started the invasion relatively late in the year and were eventually delayed in their advances, given the challenges posed by the Russian winter. This delay was partly due to the incursion into southern Europe, but also resulted from arguments between Hitler and his general staff, which put off the invasion for several weeks.

Not content to be Germany's *Führer* or supreme leader, Hitler also wished to be generalissimo, and eventually he would push aside all military planners and take personal control of the war effort. Not only did Hitler, a corporal in World War I, lack the generals' understanding of strategy, but he tended to be bold where prudence counseled caution, and vice versa. When he had a good chance of taking Britain, he demurred, but a year later, he swept into Russia without taking adequate stock of the consequences.

German troops were not equipped with clothing for the winter. This was in part a consequence of the fact that Hitler resisted apprising his armies or his people of the sacrifices necessary for war. Whereas the Allies immediately undertook rationing efforts, Hitler was slow to enact rationing for fear of unleashing discontent. Likewise, he was ill-inclined to equip his men for a long campaign, and thus admit that such a campaign likely awaited them.

America Enters the War

Japan launched its first major offensive of the war in early December 1941, when, in addition to attacking the United States at Pearl Harbor, it swept into the Philippines, Malaya, Thailand, and Burma. The result of these decisive attacks, combined with German victories in Russia, was to bring the Axis to the height of its powers in 1942. At that point, it seemed possible that the two major Axis powers, taking advantage of anti-British unrest in Iran and India, might even link up, thus controlling a swath of land and sea from Normandy to the Solomon Islands.

In actuality, events of 1941 would serve to bring an end to Axis hopes of world conquest. While the invasion of Russia would ultimately cripple the German Wehrmacht, or army, the introduction of the United States to the war would give the Allied force a seemingly bottomless supply of equipment with which to wage the war. It also brought in a vast military force that, alongside the British, would drive back the Germans in North Africa (despite impressive resistance by the tank commander German Erwin Rommel) and make two key landings on the European continent, in Italy and France.

Thus, the attack on Pearl Harbor, intended as a first strike to eliminate American opposition, would prove a miscalculation on a par with Hitler's invasion of Russia. Hitler welcomed the Japanese surprise attack on Pearl Harbor at the time, and quickly declared war on the United States, thus, giving him justification for sinking U.S. ships crossing the north Atlantic in order to deliver supplies to Britain. This proved a benefit to President Franklin D. Roosevelt, who, up to then, had been confronted by strong isolationist opposition to war with Germany.

1943–45: The Allies Victorious

Unlike the Axis, the Allies were not bound by one single formal alliance. Instead, there were agreements such as Lend-Lease, whereby the United States provided equipment to Great Britain even before it entered the war. Later, America would extend Lend-Lease to the Soviet Union, providing considerable assistance to its future Cold War enemy.

There were also a number of conferences whereby the leaders of the Allied nations planned the postwar world. These included Newfoundland in August 1941, and Casablanca in January 1943, (United States and Britain only), Teheran in November 1943, Yalta in February 1945, and Potsdam in July 1945. (By the latter point, Roosevelt had died and was replaced by Vice-President Harry S. Truman, while Churchill had been voted out in favor of Clement Atlee and the Labour Party.)

As with the Axis alliance of Germany and Italy, there was an alliance within this alliance—that of the United States and Britain. Between Roosevelt and Churchill was a strong personal bond that reflected the ultimate commonality of aims between their two nations. More strained was the relation of these leaders with Stalin. The alliance with Soviet Russia was a marriage of convenience, as all three powers faced a common enemy in Nazi Germany, but Churchill in particular never let down his guard where Stalin was concerned. (And he was right to do so, as Stalin's intelligence services were busy gathering secrets in England.)

To a much smaller extent, the United States and United Kingdom made common cause with the Chinese Nationalists, led by Chiang Kai-shek, and the Free French under General Charles de Gaulle. In neither case did these leaders speak for their entire nations. Chiang's Nationalists expended greater resources on fighting the Communists, led by Mao Tse-tung, than they did against the Japanese invaders. The Communists, who enjoyed widespread peasant support, proved able defenders, and though they would become enemies of the United States, at the time America regarded them as a useful ally against the Japanese. As for de Gaulle, who operated from London, he represented only a tiny portion of France, most of which made little effort to resist Nazi and Vichy rule.

Driving Back the Axis in Europe

In Russia, the Germans got as far as the suburbs of Moscow before the winter—along with the resurgent Red Army and a defiant populace—caught up with them. Lengthy sieges at Stalingrad and Leningrad (the latter lasting more than 800 days) would spell an end to German hopes of conquest. Led by Georgi Zhukov, the Red Army gradually drove back the Germans and began the long, steady push into central Europe.

After defeating the Germans in North Africa in late 1942, the Allies invaded Sicily in July 1943, and Italy itself on September 9. This forced Mussolini to retreat to northern Italy, where he would serve as puppet ruler of a Nazi-controlled state for the remaining two years of his life. On June 6, 1944, an Allied force of some 2,700 ships and 176,000 U.S., British, Canadian, and other troops landed at Normandy, in the largest amphibious invasion in history.

By the end of 1944, Allied victory in Europe began to seem all but imminent, but a number of obstacles still stood in the way. Hitler's scientists had developed the V2 rocket, precursor of modern missiles, and Germany fired several of them against England. The Allies, meanwhile, relentlessly bombed German cities, bringing the Reich to its knees. The Battle of the Bulge in the Ardennes forest in December 1944 was the later major Axis offensive in Europe.

With the Soviets surrounding Berlin, Hitler on April 30, 1945, committed suicide in his bunker with his mistress, Eva Braun, along with propaganda minister Josef Goebbels and Goebbels's family. Two days earlier, Mussolini and his mistress, captured by Italian resistance fighters, had been shot. The Germans surrendered to the Allies on May 7. Only after the surrender did the full magnitude of the Holocaust become apparent, and for this and other crimes, those German military and political leaders who did not commit suicide would be tried before the World Court.

The Defeat of Japan

In the carrier-dominated Battle of the Coral Sea in May 1942, the first naval battle in which opposing ships never caught sight of one another, neither side gained a clear victory, but the Allies won the upper hand at the Battle of Midway the following month. Later that summer, the U.S. Marines fought the Japanese at Guadalcanal in the Solomon Islands, one of the bloodiest battles of the war. Late in 1943, the Marines began a series of assaults on Pacific islands, including the Gilbert, Marshall, Caroline, and Mariana chains. Allied forces under General Douglas MacArthur liberated the Philippines in the fall of 1944.

Early in 1945, Allied forces under Major General Curtis LeMay began dropping incendiary bombs on Japanese cities, while the Marines took the nearby islands of Iwo Jima and Okinawa. Still, the Japanese resisted, and Allied leaders contemplated a land invasion, to begin in November. The invasion, they calculated, would cost as many as 1 million American lives, with untold casualties on the among the Japanese.

Instead of invading Japan, the United States unleashed the results of the Manhattan Project, which it had begun secretly 1942. Before dropping the atomic bomb, the Allies issued one more plea for the Japanese to surrender, and when they did not, the American B-29 bomber *Enola Gay* dropped a bomb on the city of Hiroshima. Despite the devastation wrought by this, the first use of a nuclear weapon in warfare, the Japanese still refused to surrender. On August 9, the United States dropped a second bomb, this one on Nagasaki. At this point, Hirohito urged the nation's leaders to surrender. Tojo and several others committed suicide, and on September 2, 1945, Japanese representatives formally surrendered.

A War of Information, Images, and Ideas

The Manhattan Project was the most dramatic expression of a theme that ran through the entire conflict, that ideas and information often contribute as much to a successful military effort as do troops and weapons. Though the First World War brought airplanes into widespread use, along with tanks, and resulted in the popularization of radio soon afterward, the Second World War saw the first true marriage of science and defense to yield the military-industrial complex familiar today. Its legacy is evident in the many technological innovations that were either introduced during its course, or very soon after the fighting ended. In addition to nuclear power and the missile, these include radar, computers, jet engines, and television.

The war also introduced modern concepts of covert and special operations, on the part of the OSS, the British Special Operations Executive (SOE), military intelligence units, and special warfare units that included the Rangers and the precursors to the Navy SEALS of today. The Germans had their spies as well, some of whom even managed to infiltrate the United States, but their efforts in this regard were never as successful as those of the Allies.

Cryptology

In the cryptologic war, the Allies were the unquestioned victors. Perhaps the single greatest intelligence success of the war was the British deciphering of the Germans' secret system of communications. Early in the war, British and Polish intelligence officers obtained a German Enigma cipher machine, to which a team of mathematicians at Bletchley Park applied their expertise. The result was Ultra, the British system for reading the German ciphers.

Thanks to Ultra, the British knew many of the targets in advance during the Battle of Britain. In north Africa in 1942, Ultra helped Field Marshal Bernard Montgomery predict Rommel's actions. So vital was the Ultra secret that the British used it with the utmost of caution, careful not to act to often or too quickly on information it revealed for fear that this might tip off the Germans. Only in the 1970s did the world learn of the Ultra secret.

American successes included the breaking of the Japanese RED cipher by the U.S. Navy, and the PURPLE cipher by the U.S. Army Signal Intelligence Service prior to the war. During the war, the navy proved more successful at breaking the ciphers of its counterpart than did the army. Also notable was the American use of codetalkers transmitting enciphered messages in the Navajo Indian language, which made their transmissions indecipherable to the Japanese. Neither the Japanese nor the Germans scored any major cryptologic victory against the Allies.

Deception, Secrets, and Covert Operations

The Allied invasion of Italy was accompanied by a number of behind-the-scenes moves. Just before the invasion of Sicily, British naval intelligence obtained the body of a man who had recently died, and arranged for his body—clad in the uniform of a major in the Royal Marines—to wash up on a shore in Spain. On his person were documents laying out a British plan for an imminent invasion of the Balkans, information the British knew the Germans (who had numerous agents in Spain) would acquire. The ruse, known as Operation Mincemeat (subject of the 1953 film *The Man Who Never Was*) left the Germans unprepared for the subsequent invasion.

The surrender of most of Italy by Marshal Pietro Badoglio appears to have been the result of behind-the-scenes talks with the Allies. During the moments of turmoil in the capital as Mussolini's government was over-thrown, a British intelligence officer provided Badoglio with a safe haven. In 1945, Allen Dulles—future director of the CIA—secretly negotiated with SS General Karl Wolff for the surrender of all German forces in Italy.

Another deception campaign, known as Bodyguard, preceded the Normandy invasion of June 1944. Using German agents in England who had been turned by British intelligence, the Allies conducted an elaborate campaign designed to convince the Germans that they were attacking anywhere but Normandy. Radio transmission from Scotland seemed to indicate a thrust toward Norway, while the appearance of Montgomery near Gibraltar suggested an invasion through Spain. (In fact "Montgomery" was actually a British actor who resembled the general.)

The Normandy deception included the creation an entire unit, the First U.S. Army Group (FUSAG), from thin air. FUSAG, which was supposed to be landing at Calais rather than Normandy, had a putative commander in General George S. Patton, fresh from victories in North Africa and Italy. Large tent encampments created the illusion of massive troop strength, while fake tanks, landing craft, and other equipment gave indications that the Allies were gearing up for a major operation. So, too, did radio communications from Patton's headquarters, as well as a heavy Allied bombing campaign over Calais in the days leading up to June 6. The ploy succeed in diverting 19 German divisions from Normandy.

The race to develop an atomic bomb involved several covert operations, including British sabotage directed against Nazi weapons materials in Norway, as well as an intelligence-gathering operation known as Alsos. The name was chosen by Major General Leslie Groves, who oversaw the Manhattan Project, because *alsos* is Greek for "grove." Members of the Alsos team, which included both U.S. Army and Navy personnel, scoured research laboratories in Germany, Italy, France, and Belgium for information on Axis bomb-making efforts.

Propaganda

At the simplest level of ideas, propaganda—though a feature of wars since the beginning of history—played a particularly significant role in the Second World War. Its importance to the Nazis is symbolized by the fact that in his final hours, Hitler had Goebbels beside him. Goebbels, who like Mussolini was a former Communist, had powerful instincts for making appeals to the populace, using all available media, including print, radio, and film. (The Nazis even conducted early experiments with television.)

Films by Leni Riefenstahl in the 1930s romanticized the myth of Aryan superiority, while cruder propaganda from Goebbels' office excited hatred toward Jews. During the war, Axis powers on both sides of the world made considerable use of radio through broadcasters such as Lord Haw Haw (a.k.a. William Joyce), Axis Sally (Mildred Gillars, an American), and a number of Asian females collectively dubbed "Tokyo Rose" by U.S. forces. The Allies conducted a propaganda war of their own, through radio broadcasts and the efforts of the U.S. Office of War Information and the Voice of America.

CONSEQUENCES OF WORLD WAR II

The war had a greater effect on the external position of the Soviet Union than on its internal organization and structure. The Soviet Union became a dominant regional power and quickly thereafter an atomic superpower. The wartime alliance soon fell apart, but the Soviet Union soon replaced it with a network of compliant neighboring states in central and eastern Europe and remodeled them in its own image. This set the stage for the Cold War. In the process the popular sympathy in the west for the Soviet Union's wartime struggle quickly dissipated.

Within the country, the victory of the wartime alliance gave rise to widespread hopes for political relaxation and an opening outward but these hopes were soon dashed. Living conditions remained extremely tough. Millions were homeless; it was just as hard to restore peacetime production as it had been to convert to a war footing; and the pressure to restore food supplies on top of a bad harvest led to one million or more famine deaths in Ukraine and Moldavia in 1946. In addition, Stalin used the victory not to concede reforms but to strengthen his personal dictatorship, promote nationalism, and mount new purges although with less publicity than before the war. After an initial phase of demobilization, the nuclear arms race and the outbreak of a new conventional war in Korea resulted in resumed growth of military expenditures and revived emphasis on the readiness for war. Not until the death of Stalin did the first signs of real relaxation appear.

After the famine of 1946 the Soviet economy restored prewar levels of production of most commodities with surprising speed. It took much longer, possibly several decades, to return to the path that the economy might have followed without a war. It also took decades for the Soviet population to return to demographic balance; in 1959 women born between 1904 and 1924 outnumbered men of the same generation by three to two, despite the fact that women also fought and starved.

One of the most persistent legacies of the war resulted from the wartime evacuation of industry. After the war, despite some reverse evacuation, the war economy of the interior was kept in existence. Weapons factories in the remote interior, adapted to the new technologies of nuclear weapons and aerospace, were developed into closed, self-sufficient company towns forming giant, vertically integrated systems; they were literally taken off the map so that their very existence became a well kept secret. Thus, secretiveness and militarization were taken hand in hand to new levels.

It is easier to describe the Soviet Union after the war than to say what would have happened if the war had gone the other way. World War II was a defining event in world history that engulfed the lives of nearly two billion people, but the eastern front affected the outcome of the war to a much greater extent than is commonly remembered in western culture and historical writing.

THE COLD WAR

For America and the Soviet Union, Cold War was the natural condition of the twentieth century. Throughout the existence of the Soviet Union, both superpowers defined themselves, and incidentally justified their military budgets, by invoking the threat of the other, not merely as a geographic enemy or competitor but as an embodiment of an utterly antithetical way of life. American persecution of its homegrown (or immigrant) Communists got into high gear with the Palmer Raids of 1919 and became a long-lasting national pastime in the 1920s as J. Edgar Hoover (1895–1972) solidified his power base in what would become the Federal Bureau of Investigation (FBI). Throughout the New Deal and World War II, Hoover and others maintained a policy of demonizing American dissent by suggesting that all Communists were agents of an unfriendly foreign power. Until Hitler's invasion of Russia, America saw Nazi Germany as less of a threat than its fellow "dictator nation," the Soviet Union. World War II put the US-Soviet conflict on hold, as President

Franklin D. Roosevelt (1882–1945) and Joseph Stalin (1879–1953) led their countries in an alliance against fascism.

The Cold War properly began in the late 1940s, with a freeze in relations between East and West fueled by paranoia, to an extent justified, on both sides. The lesson of Hiroshima and Nagasaki, not lost on Moscow, was that the United States not only had the atom bomb but was also prepared to drop it, while half of Europe turned out to have been saved not for democracy but as a buffer of "satellite states" almost as oppressed as they had been under Hitler. Though it lasted at least until the dismantling of the Berlin Wall in 1989, the peak of the Cold War is usually reckoned from Winston Churchill's (1874–1965) "Iron Curtain" speech in 1948 to the Cuban missile crisis of 1962. This was an eventful period: nuclear buildup in both camps, with a procession of A- and H-bomb tests by both superpowers; an actual skirmish between the sides in Korea, later replayed on a larger scale in Vietnam; Communist insurgencies against old colonial powers Britain and France in Malaya and Indonesia; the "loss" of China to Communism, which created an equally fractious relationship between Red China and the Soviet Union; the extensive persecution of comparatively few American Communists and far more merely left-leaning or liberal Americans, many of whom had been associated with the New Deal or had spoken for the Russian ally during the war; and the beginnings of the space race, sparked by Russia's initial triumphs in launching Sputnik and putting a cosmonaut in orbit—all this, and a wave of juvenile delinquency fanned by rock and roll, horror comics, and hot rods.

The Cold War Warriors

Architects of the conflict that gripped the world for nearly fifty years, the cold warriors were the men, and women, who gave shape to the ongoing conflict between the United States and the Soviet Union from 1945 to 1989. They built the Cold War's institutions, forged its diplomacy, oversaw its military flare-ups and its diplomatic stand-downs, and supplied its fierce rhetoric and its silent espionage. In the West, the so-called free world, cold warriors were usually well-born and well educated. In revolutionary societies and communist countries, high class standing was no asset for a leader, so cold warriors either came from humble stock or claimed that they did. The most prominent cold warriors were men of power—commanders of great armies, of the masses, of economic might, of words and ideas. Cold warriors were frequently messianic in their convictions, believing they represented the one best political, economic, and social system. They were serious men, disinclined to joke about their work and for the most part innocent even of a sense of irony about it; with the exception perhaps of their hubris, they masked their emotions, though they could never fully erase them. Cold warriors were often pragmatic men, able to calculate their nations' interests and if necessary to negotiate with their adversaries in order to protect those interests. Still, despite their pragmatism cold warriors contained within their bodies the cells of history and ideology that compelled them to the contest, in the belief that they were defending their nations' values or in the hope of spreading their values to others beyond their borders.

Cold warriors lived most obviously in the United States and the Soviet Union, but because the Cold War enveloped the world its warriors were everywhere. They included the presidents of the United States, from Harry S. Truman to George H. W. Bush, and their secretaries of state, among them John Foster Dulles, Dean Rusk, and Henry Kissinger. Many other U.S. government officials were cold warriors: appointees such as George F. Kennan, Paul Nitze, and Jeane Kirkpatrick, and elected representatives including senators William Knowland, Joseph McCarthy, and Hubert H. Humphrey. There were members of the intelligence community (J. Edgar Hoover, Edward G. Lansdale, William Colby), prominent journalists who interpreted the Cold War to the American people (Walter Lippmann, James Reston), and theologians, among them Reinhold Niebuhr and Billy Graham, who saw the Cold War as a moral challenge to Americans. In the Soviet Union a commitment to the Cold War was necessary for the leaders who followed Joseph Stalin after 1953, from Nikita Khrushchev to Konstantin Chernenko. The ideologue Andrei Zhdanov was a cold warrior of the first magnitude. Soviet diplomats carried out their superiors' orders but contributed as well their own mite to the conflict; among them were the longtime foreign minister Vyacheslav Molotov and the ambassador to the United States Andrei Gromyko. Lavrenti Beria, head of Stalin's secret police, maintained a bloodstained vigil against all forms of Cold War heterodoxy.

Outside the United States and the Soviet Union, cold warriors fought their own battles in the shadows cast by their powerful allies. Their Cold Wars were similar to the principal super-power conflict in their ideological and geopolitical purposes, but different to the extent that they were influenced by histories that preceded the Cold War and in some ways transcended it, and also different because local concerns pressed down upon a broad Cold War foundation, reshaping it as wood construction forms mold wet concrete. There were British cold warriors, among them Winston Churchill, prime minister and influential statesman, foreign ministers Ernest Bevin and Anthony Eden, and in the last decade of the Cold War, Prime Minister Margaret Thatcher. In Canada there was Lester Pearson (prime minister, 1963–1968). France had Charles de Gaulle (whose Cold War had an overwhelmingly Gallic flavor), South

Africa Hendrik Verwoerd (prime minister 1958–1966, who invoked the Soviet threat in order to defend white supremacy in his country), and the Philippines Ferdinand Marcos (president 1965–1986), who traded his support for U.S. military bases on his islands for U.S. help against his domestic enemies, communist or not. On the other side were Kim Il Sung of North Korea, Vietnam's revolutionary nationalist Ho Chi Minh, Walter Ulbricht of East Germany, and Cuban leader Fidel Castro.

There were thousands of cold warriors; the four profiled here were selected because they represented different sides of the conflict and because, taken together, their influence spanned nearly the length of the Cold War. Joseph Stalin was dictator of the Soviet Union from the late 1920s until his death in 1953. Dean Acheson was U.S. undersecretary of state from 1945 to 1947, secretary of state from 1949 to 1953, and foreign policy adviser without portfolio thereafter. Mao Zedong led the communists to victory in China in 1949 and became the nation's supreme ruler for nearly thirty years. And Ronald Reagan, U.S. president from 1981 to 1989, stoked the flickering fire beneath the Cold War cauldron. All of these men made decisions that had enormous consequences for the world in which they lived and for the world inherited by the next generation of leaders. Strenuous as it was to fight the Cold War, it proved even harder to unmake it.

JOSEPH STALIN

That Stalin came to lead the Soviet Union following Vladimir Ilych Lenin's death in 1924 was a surprise to nearly everyone. Stalin was a man people underestimated. He was short (five feet, four inches tall) and stocky, with a face pitted by smallpox and a left arm bent permanently by a childhood accident. He mumbled or talked so quietly that he was hard to hear; possibly he was embarrassed at his poor grasp of Russian, which he spoke with an accent. On the eve of the October 1917 revolution, one of Stalin's colleagues on the Executive Committee of the Petrograd Soviet wrote that he gave "the impression ... of a grey blur which flickered obscurely and left no trace. There really is nothing more to be said about him." But some by then could see in his eyes a fixity of purpose that promised a good deal more. "He's not an intellectual," noted the American journalist John Reed in 1920. "He's not even particularly well informed, but he knows what he wants. He's got will-power, and he's going to be on top of the pile some day."

He was born in 1879, in the Russian state of Georgia. His family name was Dzhugashvili. (Joseph would take the name Stalin, meaning "man of steel," in the early 1900s.) Possibly he was illegitimate. His father, or the man who raised him, was a cobbler, while his mother was a domestic servant. Joseph attended local schools and was a good student, though inclined to challenge the authority of his teachers. His boyhood hero was Koba, a character in a novel called *The Patricide,* who battled against the forces of injustice and rewarded the downtrodden with the spoils of his victories. Joseph identified so fully with this Russian Robin Hood that he later took "Koba" as one of his code names.

Stalin had no philosophy in the usual sense of the word. Unlike Marx or Lenin he was not much good at theorizing. He understood Russian history as a narrative of triumph and tragedy and took from it the lesson that an unguarded Russia would be ripe for exploitation or worse. Russia had saved Europe from the Mongols in the thirteenth century, had stopped Napoleon in the nineteenth, and would destroy Adolf Hitler's Reich in the 1940s. Each of these hard-won triumphs had saved civilization. Yet it seemed to Stalin that Russia's reward for its sacrifice was to be attacked yet again; the nation was surrounded by enemies who wished for its demise. Superimposed on this view of Russia's haunted history was a particular version of revolutionary communism. Stalin believed that the revolution required a long period of incubation at home, that it would not be ready for export to other nations until it had totally transformed Russia. Agriculture must be collectivized. The state must control industry, goading factory workers to new heights of production. Art, literature, and even science ought to reflect the noble purposes of the communist state, valorizing the proletariat and refusing to indulge in bourgeois fripperies. Suspicious of Russia's neighbors, suspicious of ideological deviation, suspicious, really, of almost everyone, Stalin built by the 1930s an industrial power and a state ruled by intimidation and terror.

No one knows how many Soviet citizens died as a result of Stalin's agricultural policy or by his direct order. Judging the rich peasants, or kulaks, inherently selfish and therefore incompatible with the goal of collectivization, Stalin eradicated them as a class. When grain production fell short of expectations in 1932, Stalin demanded more. The result was the starvation of perhaps five million Russians. Between 1936 and 1938 Stalin instituted the Terror, in which millions more of his political opponents real or imagined were deported to Siberia or executed following a show trial. On one December day in 1937 Stalin and Molotov signed 3,167 death warrants, then went to a movie. A cult of Stalin developed throughout the country. Poems and songs celebrated the dictator. One of his speeches was pressed onto seven sides of a gramophone record; the eighth side contained nothing but applause.

Once disclosed, the horrors of the Stalinist gulag convinced many observers that Stalin's foreign policy would proceed, by comparably brutal steps, to threaten the world with a bloodbath in the guise of revolution. There was a germ of logic to this fear. If Stalin did not hesitate to murder Russian citizens, why should he have scruples about killing foreigners? Revolutionary ideology would not respect national boundaries. The metaphors used to describe it by those who dreaded it— a conflagration, a disease, or even, in George Kennan's more measured analysis, "a fluid stream"—suggested that Stalinist communism was relentlessly expansionistic.

The reality was a good deal more complicated. Certainly Stalin was opportunistic, looking for trouble spots or turmoil to exploit. He had not abandoned hope of inspiring revolution in other countries, only shelved it temporarily in favor of consolidating control at home. Yet Stalin's first concern was always the preservation of the Soviet state from invasion or erosion from without. There was much to lose—including, of course, his own power. A shrewd foreign policy must, therefore, state the Soviet Union's claim to survival while nevertheless avoiding antagonizing neighboring countries that were capable of destroying the motherland. This meant, for example, that when Germany was restored to its military power under Hitler during the 1930s, Stalin would seek to offset German strength by finding friends among the bourgeois states that were ideologically anathema to him. When it became clear, after the Munich Pact of 1938, that the British and French had no stomach for opposing Hitler's absorption of other countries, Stalin decided to make his own arrangement with the Germans. The result was the Nazi-Soviet Pact of August 1939, in which the two nations agreed not to fight each other, and (secretly) to divide Poland and the Baltic states between them. Stalin even promised that if Germany seemed in danger of losing a war, he would send a hundred divisions to the West to defend his new ally. It turned out badly for the Soviet Union, which in June was invaded by the Germans.

Stalin was at first shocked into near paralysis. "Lenin founded our state, and we've fucked it up!" he said. He fled Moscow and failed to communicate with his generals, who were desperate for instructions. But he recovered and began issuing orders. Russia would not surrender. There would be bloody battles, and many lives would be lost—indeed, well over twenty million by the war's end. Germany would be beaten, and the Soviet Union would have a peace that would at last guarantee the protection of the nation against all outside forces.

The Soviet victory over Germany was bought with help from the United States, which provided equipment through President Franklin D. Roosevelt's Lend-Lease program. Stalin was grudgingly appreciative of this aid. Still, he believed that the Americans, along with the British, could have done much more, and he suspected that his new allies wanted Russians and Germans to kill each other in droves, leaving Roosevelt and British prime minister Winston Churchill free to dictate the peace. Stalin was especially angry at the allies' failure to open a meaningful second front against Germans in Europe before mid-1944.

It seemed to Stalin that the Russians bore the brunt of the German attack. Over time, however, Stalin found the policy could work to his advantage. Once the Nazis had been defeated at Stalingrad, in February 1943, they fell into retreat, pursued by the Red Army. By the spring of 1944, as the Americans and British were preparing at last to invade Normandy, the Russians had begun arriving at the eastern frontiers of the European nations that had made common cause with the Nazis.

Ultimately, by dint of having the largest army in the region, the Soviets gained predominant influence after the war in Romania, Bulgaria, Hungary, Czechoslovakia, Poland, and the eastern quarter of Germany. Yugoslavia was controlled by communists. To gain these prizes seemed to Stalin nothing more than a reasonable division of the postwar spoils. He did not picture the eastern European satellites as an entering wedge toward world domination but rather as recompense for Russian suffering at Nazi hands and the logical result of occupation policies established by his allies. And he sought a buffer zone of politically compliant states along the western face of the Soviet Union.

It was not so much ideological conformity as simple cooperation that Stalin sought, in eastern Europe and elsewhere. He hoped that the Americans and British would allow him the buffer zone and a good deal of reconstruction aid as well. Churchill, after all, had in 1944 conceded major Soviet influence in several eastern European countries. Franklin Roosevelt endorsed a spheres of influence arrangement in the postwar world, to include a Soviet sphere roughly east of the Elbe River. Meeting with Stalin at Yalta in February 1945, Churchill and Roosevelt had seemed to accept a face-saving formula on the composition of the emerging Polish government. Stalin felt sure that the others would permit him to do essentially what he wanted there. "The logic of his position was simple," as one of Stalin's biographers has written. "He had won the war in order to have good next-door neighbors." He thought his allies accepted this.

Elsewhere Stalin probed in places where his predecessors had long had interests. He pressured the Turks to revise the Montreux Convention, up for renewal, and grant him joint management of the strategically vital Dardanelles strait. He dragged his feet on the matter of withdrawing Soviet troops from northern Iran in 1946, though he had previously agreed to pull out. And he demanded a share of the occupation authority in Japan, having sent his armies against Japanese forces in China in the last days of the war. When the allies remonstrated or acted firmly against him, however, Stalin backed down. The Dardanelles remained Turkish, Soviet troops left Iran without having guaranteed Moscow's access to Iranian oil, and Stalin pretty much conceded his exclusion from Japanese affairs after 1945. He did not want a confrontation with the United States. He emphatically did not want war.

But between April 1945 and March 1946 Stalin came to believe that the British and Americans sought a confrontation with him. Roosevelt's death in April 1945 deprived Stalin of a rival who had nevertheless shown flexibility in negotiations and apparent sympathy for Soviet predicaments. Roosevelt's successor, Harry S. Truman, seemed less inclined to give Stalin the benefit of the doubt. The American use of atomic bombs against Japan in August was a shock. The Russians had known and had been receiving information that scientists in the United States were working on the bomb, but until he read reports of what had happened at Hiroshima and Nagasaki Stalin had not appreciated the power of the new weapon. He immediately authorized a major effort to build the bomb; unless the Soviets tested their own weapon, he believed, they remained subject to intimidation by the United States. The Soviet bomb was tested successfully in August 1949. Finally, as the disagreements mounted between Russia and the West—quarrels over the disposition of postwar Germany, reparations or loans or aid due the Soviet Union, and the future of atomic weapons— the United States and Great Britain seemed to conspire against the Russians. The rhetoric on both sides intensified; the Cold War had begun.

To statesmen in the West, Stalin's culpability seemed obvious. He had clamped down ruthlessly in eastern Europe, suppressing freedom throughout the region, most outrageously in Czechoslovakia in early 1948. He stripped Soviet occupation zones of their factories, refused to bargain reasonably over German reunification, and in 1948 blockaded Berlin. He reestablished the Cominform to coordinate the menacing activities of communist parties everywhere. It looked different to Stalin. He wished only for security, prosperity, and noninterference by other nations in Russia's affairs. Just five years after defeating Germany, the Soviet Union was threatened with encirclement once more.

The emergent Cold War was not confined to Europe. In China a long-simmering civil war between the Nationalist forces of Generalissimo Chiang Kai-shek and the communist peasant army of Mao Zedong came to a full boil following Japan's surrender. Stalin did not at first embrace Mao's revolutionary quest and doubted the efficacy of Mao's movement;

however, Mao was able to establish the People's Republic of China on 1 October 1949. Stalin hoped to preserve Soviet influence in China, which the 1945 treaty provided, and could not afford to subsidize the People's Republic to the extent that Mao would have liked. Strains developed between the two men: Stalin was suspicious of Mao's plans, while Mao resented what he considered to be his second-class treatment in Moscow. While the two men agreed on a treaty of friendship in mid-February 1950, the differences between the communist leaders remained.

The most strenuous test of the new Sino-Soviet relationship, and the most dangerous flare-up of the Cold War to that point, was the Korean War. The North Korean leader, Kim Il Sung, visited Stalin at least twice, in April 1949 and March 1950, and corresponded with him at other times. Stalin at first splashed cold water on Kim's assertion that he could reunite Korea by military means. Stalin worried, as ever, that the United States would intervene, thus threatening Soviet security. By the early spring of 1950, though, Stalin had come around. Assured by Kim that his forces were far superior to those in the south, that the Americans were unlikely to act, and that there were 200,000 communists in South Korea who would rise up in support of the North Korean invaders, Stalin went along with Kim's plan to attack. Stalin offered increased military aid and some military advisers. At the same time, he urged Kim to ask Mao for help.

The Truman administration's decision to intervene in the Korean War, buttressed by the United Nations Security Council (from which the Soviet representative was conveniently absent), confirmed Stalin's worst fears. It was a measure of his reluctance to venture too deeply into conflicts with the United States, even those in places close to Russia's border, that he would not commit Soviet troops to the fray. He did nudge the Chinese forward, promising aid and support to Chinese brave enough to go to war, but the aid came stintingly, and Soviet air cover appeared over Korean airspace a full month after the first Chinese soldiers crossed the Yalu River into North Korea. Stalin, who had worried about a U.S.–China rapprochement, was not unhappy to see Americans and Chinese killing each other.

The Korean War became a bloody stalemate in 1951, and by then Stalin's health was failing. He continued to rule with an iron hand, arresting those of whom he contrived any reason to be suspicious, reducing more and more the size of the trusted circle around him. But his body had weakened, and his thinking was no longer clear. He had a brain hemorrhage on the night of 28 February–1 March 1953, though he managed to remain alive for another four days. Just as he died, according to his daughter, "he suddenly lifted his left hand as though he were pointing to something up above and bringing down a curse on us all. The gesture was incomprehensible and full of menace." It was a fitting end for a man who had brought so much suffering to Russian citizens, while nevertheless making the Soviet Union a nation to be respected, or feared, throughout the world.

DEAN ACHESON

When Dean Acheson became U.S. secretary of state in early 1949 he hung in his office two portraits: one of John Quincy Adams, the other of Henry Stimson. These were significant choices. Adams, perhaps the greatest secretary of state in U.S. history, had conceived the first American empire but had warned his overzealous compatriots against going "abroad in search of monsters to destroy." Stimson, who had served as secretary of state for Herbert Hoover and became secretary of war (for the second time) under Franklin Roosevelt in 1940, had preserved Adams's imperial vision. Both men were among the best and brightest of their generations: Adams the scion of the famous political family, Stimson a partner in Elihu Root's law firm. And both men were dedicated to the service of their country, had a keen sense of right and wrong, and believed that gentlemen should behave honorably—as Stimson said, they did not read one another's mail. Dean Acheson believed these things too.

Acheson was born and raised in Connecticut. His father, Edward, was an Episcopal rector; his mother, Eleanor (Gooderham), was a grande dame with a sense of humor. Both were British subjects. Eleanor spoke with a British accent, and the family celebrated the queen's birthday. Thus was Acheson's Anglophilia instilled at an early age. He went to Groton and Yale, finishing both (Groton barely) without academic distinction. His Yale classmate Archibald MacLeish recalled that Acheson was "socially snobby with qualities of arrogance and superciliousness." Seriousness arrived in his second year at Harvard Law School, when he took a class with Felix Frankfurter. The law captured him, especially for its possibilities as training for government service. Frankfurter arranged a clerkship with Supreme Court Justice Louis Brandeis.

Acheson's career in government began in 1933, when he was named Roosevelt's treasury undersecretary. The appointment was short-lived. Acheson opposed FDR's plan to buy gold to shore up prices, and he was asked to resign that fall. But he had made himself known to Roosevelt's men, and early in 1941 Secretary of State Cordell Hull brought Acheson to the State Department as assistant secretary for economic affairs. Acheson quickly made his presence felt. He helped negotiate the lend-lease agreement with the British, into which, and despite his Anglophilia, he inserted a clause demanding an end to preferential economic arrangements within the British empire. Acheson also insisted on tightening an embargo on oil shipments to Japan. And after the United States had entered the war, he became one of the American architects of the International Monetary Fund and the World Bank, both of which would do much to stabilize the economy of the capitalist nations following the war. When, in late 1944, Hull was replaced by Edward Stettinius, Acheson became assistant secretary of state for congressional relations and international conferences.

Acheson fortuitously had had a lengthy meeting with Truman two days before Roosevelt's death in April 1945. Truman made "a very good impression. He is straightforward, decisive, simple, entirely honest." He would "learn fast and inspire confidence." But Acheson was not at first moved to stay on in the government, and after seeing through to completion the drafting of the United Nations Charter, in midsummer he submitted to the president a letter of resignation. Truman and his new secretary of state, James Byrnes, refused to accept it. They wanted Acheson to stay in the administration and to promote him to undersecretary of state, second in command in the department. Acheson hesitated but finally agreed to return.

He was thrust immediately into the maelstrom. Byrnes was a clever politician but a poor administrator, and the volume of information flowing into the department, as well as the demands placed on its employees by the developing Cold War, threatened to overwhelm all of them. Acheson became the department's leading organizer and troubleshooter. Truman assigned him to the crucial task of finding a way to control atomic energy without sacrificing American security. His report, written with David Lilienthal and submitted in March 1946, was a sincere (if doomed) effort to accommodate Soviet concerns about the American nuclear monopoly by establishing an international agency to regulate the production of atomic energy. Yet Acheson found himself, along with his president, moving toward a tougher stance against the Soviet Union. If Stalin thought by early 1946 that his capitalist enemies were encircling him despite the reasonableness of his position, the view from Washington was different. U.S. policymakers came to believe that the Soviets would push and probe and stir up trouble anywhere they were not met with resistance, including potential military action. While the hallmark of American resolve was George Kennan's 1947 essay "The Sources of Soviet Conduct," in which he called for the employment of "counterforce" against the Soviets "at a series of constantly shifting geographical and political points," the Truman administration had in fact been pursuing an ad hoc version of this containment strategy since early 1946. Acheson was its lead author. It was he who wrote Stalin a stern note, delivered by Kennan, demanding the withdrawal of Russian troops from northern Iran. And it was Acheson who wrote the Truman administration's sharp response to the Soviet demand, in August 1946, that Turkey agree to a joint Russian-Turkish defense of the Dardanelles. Acheson's note, along with arrival in the area of a U.S. naval task force, caused the Soviets to back down.

Acheson also played a vital role in shaping the political and economic institutions of Truman's Cold War. In early 1947, with Byrnes out and George Marshall in as the secretary of state, the anticommunist governments of Turkey and Greece claimed to be under severe Soviet pressure and could not guarantee their own survival. Convinced that the United States must help the Turkish and Greek governments, the administration nevertheless faced the difficult task of persuading a fiscally careful Congress to provide the aid needed to shore up these governments. On 27 February, Truman called a meeting between administration officials and a handful of leading senators and members of congress in hopes of winning over the legislators. Acheson described this encounter as "Armageddon." Marshall spoke first, emphasizing the need for the United States to act because it was the right thing to do and because no one else would help. The legislators seemed unmoved. Was it America's fight? Was the bill likely to be enormous? Acheson asked to speak. Immediately he changed the terms of the debate. The crisis in southeastern Europe, he said, was no local dustup but one that involved the two Cold War powers. The Soviets were pressuring Turkey and Greece as they had pressured Iran. At stake was a vast portion of the free world, for if Greece went communist, "like apples in a barrel infected by one rotten one, the corruption of Greece would infect Iran and all to the east. It would also carry infection to Africa through Asia Minor and Egypt, and Europe through Italy and France," which faced communist threats of their own. Only the United States stood in the way of a communist onslaught that would, if successful, snuff out freedom and destroy all hope of economic recovery in parts of three continents. The congressional leaders were impressed, and the pronouncement of the Truman Doctrine followed on 12 March, promising that the United States would fight communism everywhere.

The world's biggest problems remained economic, and the chief area of concern for Acheson, as always, was neither Iran nor Greece but western Europe. Policymakers in Washington believed that communism fed on economic distress; European nations were vulnerable to radicals promising the redistribution of wealth as a panacea for poverty. Economic aid from the United States—and in far greater magnitude than that proffered to Turkey and Greece—was essential to Europe's economic recovery, its revival as a market for U.S. exports, and its people's continued faith in democracy. Acheson said as much in a speech he gave in Cleveland, Mississippi, in early May 1947. His call for massive economic aid to Europe found its manifestation in the Marshall Plan, announced by the secretary of state at Harvard the following month. If the Truman Doctrine had made the strategic case for containment, the Marshall Plan was designed to give economic spine to American's closest friends and trading partners in western Europe. Once more, Acheson had played a crucial role in shaping the new policy.

Acheson had previously decided to leave the administration, and when he tendered his resignation effective 1 July 1947, Truman this time reluctantly let him go. He was, however, receptive when Truman, surprisingly victorious in the 1948 election, invited him to return to public life, this time as secretary of state.

The problems to which Acheson returned in January 1949 were even knottier than they had been when he had departed eighteen months earlier. Europeans and Soviets no longer doubted American resolve. But the Nationalist government of China was in the final stages of collapse; as Acheson remarked ruefully, he arrived back in service just in time to have it fall on him. There was not yet a peace treaty with Japan, and France's effort to return to power in its colony of Indochina had met with firm resistance from Vietnamese nationalists associated with communism. The Soviet Union would explode its first atomic bomb later that year. Above all, at least as far as Acheson was concerned, Europe remained dangerously unstable. The Italian and French governments turned over with distressing frequency, threatening Europe's stability and ultimately its solvency. Great Britain still depended on U.S. aid, and a slight U.S. recession in the spring of 1949 undermined the sterling pound and forced a new round of austerity on London. Germany remained divided, with Berlin under siege in the East and with the West, its capital at Bonn, a seeming out-post of Western interests thrust provocatively into the Soviet bloc, economically infirm and utterly defenseless. Here especially, thought Acheson, something had to be done.

Acheson addressed the problems systematically, blending a staunch anticommunism, a fervent faith in liberal capitalism, and a healthy measure of pragmatism. There was not much to be done about China: Chiang Kai-shek was plainly a loser and it would be necessary to "let the dust settle" following the communists' victory. Japan would have a peace treaty in 1952. Vexed by French behavior in Indochina but unwilling to weaken France further or cede more territory to what he construed as world communism, Acheson supplied some economic and military aid to the French-backed (read "puppet") government of Bao Dai in Vietnam. What Europe and especially West Germany needed was an infusion of confidence that the United States would come to the rescue in the unlikely event that the Soviet Union attacked. Working with the Europeans, Acheson helped fashion, in the spring of 1949, the North Atlantic Treaty, which created a group of like-minded nations committed to the proposition, as article 5 of the treaty put it, that "an armed attack against one ... shall be considered an attack against them all." For Acheson the treaty was valuable as a morale boost for U.S. allies, as well as a means to permit, someday, the military restoration of (West) Germany under multilateral aegis.

Acheson had not spent much time thinking about Korea. His State Department predecessors, and the military, had already put into motion the withdrawal of U.S. forces from South Korea. In a speech in January 1950 Acheson described a U.S. "defense perimeter" in East Asia that incorporated various islands, among them the Philippines and Okinawa. It was possible to take from Acheson's words the implication that mainland Asian nations, including South Korea, fell outside the U.S. picket, though this was a strained interpretation; Acheson did say that the United States had "direct responsibility" for Korea. Certainly Acheson was naive to assume, as he told the Foreign Relations Committee, that South Korea "could take care of any trouble started by" the North. But no cold warrior of Acheson's type would have invited an attack on an ally, even one as troublesome as Syngman Rhee's South Korea. The proof of Acheson's commitment came in the last days of June, once Kim Il Sung had launched his offensive. Truman, closely advised by Acheson and the military, committed U.S. forces to the conflict, seeking UN support for this step afterward.

The Korean War would ultimately serve the ends of the containment strategy. The North Koreans, who were presumed by Acheson to be proxy soldiers for Moscow, were stopped. Still, Acheson's reputation suffered as a result of the war. Conservatives attacked him because he had not seen it coming. He would have, they argued, had he understood the implications of his do-nothing policy on China; his abandonment of Chiang had encouraged communists throughout Asia to think they could launch attacks with impunity. Republicans led by Senator Joseph McCarthy accused Acheson of appeasement or worse. He was part of a "crimson crowd," said McCarthy. Senator Hugh Butler exclaimed: "I look at that fellow. I watch his smart-aleck manner and his British clothes, and that New Dealism in everything he says and does, and I want to shout, 'Get out, Get out. You stand for everything that has been wrong with the United States for years!'"

Truman and Acheson could not achieve a truce in Korea. An armistice was signed only in July 1953, six months after Dwight Eisenhower and John Foster Dulles had succeeded them as the nation's chief cold warriors. Out of harness Acheson drifted. He wanted badly to have influence again on U.S. diplomacy. This was not possible in the Eisenhower administration: Acheson was tainted by his association with the humiliations of the United States in East Asia. In any case he disparaged the administration's reliance on nuclear weapons, a strategy dubbed "massive retaliation," and thought Dulles sanctimonious. Nor would Democrats embrace him. Adlai Stevenson, the Democrats' presidential nominee in 1952 and 1956, thought Acheson irascible and controversial, and kept his distance. In Germany in 1957 Ambassador David Bruce, who was Acheson's friend, found the former secretary "devastating, clever, bitter and not constructive.... Dean is overfull of bile and it is sad."

John F. Kennedy, the Democrat who won the presidency in 1960, did consult with Acheson. Kennedy took Acheson's advice on cabinet appointments (Secretary of State Dean Rusk was Acheson's suggestion, though Acheson later regretted having made it) and the need to build NATO forces in Europe. Elsewhere Kennedy resisted Acheson's increasingly reflexive militancy. During the Cuban Missile Crisis, Acheson, a member of Kennedy's high-level ExCom, urged the president to bomb Soviet missile sites and was disgusted when JFK decided to interdict Russian ships instead, a tactic Acheson thought timid. As the war in Vietnam expanded, particularly under Kennedy's successor, Lyndon Johnson, Acheson found himself more and more in demand as an adviser. Johnson treated Acheson with deference. And Acheson's early position on Vietnam—that the United States had no choice but to fight until South Vietnam was preserved against a communist takeover—matched Johnson's.

Averell Harriman said in 1970: "Some people's minds freeze. Acheson's hasn't changed since 1952." That was unfair. While Acheson never lost his suspicion of the Soviet Union, and thus remained convinced of the necessity of containment, and while his contempt for his intellectual inferiors, especially those in Congress, remained undiminished, he came to see the Vietnam War as a waste of American power. Harriman himself, along with Undersecretary of State George Ball, made Acheson see by early 1968 that Vietnam was a peripheral Cold War theater. At a meeting of Johnson's Vietnam "wise men" on 25 March 1968, Acheson spoke bluntly and eloquently of the need for the administration to disengage from the conflict. Johnson, shaken, announced less than a week later that he would seek to negotiate with Hanoi. He added, almost as an afterthought, that he would not seek reelection in 1968 but would instead devote all his energy to finding a way out of the morass in Southeast Asia.

Acheson had come full circle. He had started his public career as a man of principle, demanding to see evidence that one policy choice was better than another, just as Felix Frankfurter and Louis Brandeis had taught him. His Cold War—like Stalin's, ironically—sprang from ideology tempered by pragmatism. There was assertiveness but no adventurism in the man who helped shape the United Nations, the Bretton Woods economic system, the Truman Doctrine, the Marshall Plan, and NATO. But the harsh criticism of conservatives inclined Acheson toward greater militancy and left him unable to resist the temptations of victory in Korea. Thereafter he grew increasingly sharp with those with whom he disagreed. That never changed. But the Vietnam War restored Acheson to his former view that the United States could not solve every world problem, especially not by military means. When Acheson died on 12 October 1971 he left a legacy worthy, in ambition and execution, of the two secretaries of state he admired most.

MAO ZEDONG

The Chinese Communist leader Mao Zedong and Dean Acheson were exact contemporaries, born in 1893. But while Acheson enjoyed a comfortable boyhood and moved rather casually through Groton and Yale, Mao left school at thirteen to help with the family farm, married at age fourteen (and was widowed at seventeen), and in 1911 joined the Republican army in its quest to unite and strengthen China. When he was twenty years old Mao, who came from the rural province of Hunan, returned to school and came under the influence of a teacher named Yang, who inspired in him a passion for reform, a strong ethical sense, and an enthusiasm for exercise, generally taken in the nude. When Yang got a job at Beijing University, Mao went north with him. It was the young farmer's first time out of Hunan.

He took a job as a clerk at the university library and came to know a corps of intellectuals who published an influential magazine called *New Youth,* which became the literary centerpiece of an inchoate but determined reformist movement that emerged following the formal end of the Qing dynasty and the establishment of a republic in 1912. Sun Yat-sen, a Japanese-educated radical from Canton, was the movement's leading political light, but his faith in republicanism was not shared by some young Chinese who sought the end of class oppression. Li Dazhao proclaimed an interest in Marxism and endorsed the Bolshevik revolution. Hu Shih, who had a degree from Cornell, was a literary critic who wrote on women's liberation. Mao was not in their intellectual circle, but the yeastiness of the Beijing scene plainly affected him.

Mao returned to Hunan and the city of Changsha in the early spring of 1919. He thus missed the great urban demonstrations of 4 May, out of which would flow reformist currents that would dominate China for the next thirty years. But Mao contributed a small tributary of his own. He taught history at local schools. And he edited a journal called the *Xiang River Review,* for which he wrote nearly all the articles. His writing heralded the forthcoming "liberation of mankind," which would arrive when people lost their fear of those who ruled them and the superstitions that held them in thrall. When the local warlord stopped publication of the *Review,* Mao shifted to another journal; when it, too, was suppressed, he wrote for Changsha's biggest newspaper.

On 23 July 1921 thirteen Chinese and two members of the Soviet-sponsored Comintern (one Dutch, one Russian), met in Shanghai for the First Congress of the Chinese Communist Party. Mao Zedong was among them. After days of discussion the Congress decided that it should devote its efforts to organizing the working class, putting off plans to mobilize the peasants and the army. The capitalists would be overthrown and "social ownership" of land and machinery would ensue. Buoyed by these resolutions, and presumably in agreement with them, Mao returned to Hunan to begin building a mass movement.

He organized workers and orchestrated strikes. Mao did not attend the Second Party Congress meeting in July 1922, but he soon after learned that the party, nudged by the Comintern agents, had decided to enter into coalition with the Nationalist, or Kuomintang, Party, then headed by Sun Yat-sen. Communists were instructed to form "a bloc within" the party. In this way, they would work alongside the bourgeois elements in China to overthrow the feudal oppressors, all the while securing their bonds to the working class and awaiting the revolutionary situation that would someday emerge in the country. Mao dutifully joined the Kuomintang. Certainly the Communist decision to create a United Front with the Kuomintang seemed reasonable at the time and was consistent with Marxist doctrine. The Kuomintang under Sun was a militant organization, sympathetic to workers and willing to help them strike for their rights. Nor were there many Communist Party members in China, and the party was broke. The Communists could decide their ultimate course as events unfolded.

Sun Yat-sen died in 1925, and leadership of the Kuomintang, and thus the United Front, was grasped by Chiang Kai-shek, a general who was commandant of the United Front's military academy. In the spring of 1926 Chiang led his forces north out of Canton, determined to destroy the power of local warlords and unite the nation under United Front rule. Communists marched alongside Kuomintang troops, but even more important were the Chinese Communist Party (CCP) organizers, among them Mao, who were assigned to prepare the way for Chiang's soldiers. The men and women of the CCP served as agitators, turning peasants and workers against their local régimes in order to soften them up for the expedition forces. Alarmed at the success of CCP organizers in mobilizing workers, Chiang decided to purge the United Front of its Communists, thus purifying the Kuomintang ideologically and eliminating any awkwardness about power sharing in the future. Chiang's purge was bloody everywhere, but particularly so in Shanghai, where Kuomintang troops killed thousands of their recent allies in April 1927. As the ideological cleansing spread westward, Mao found himself the de facto leader of a demoralized peasant army whose ranks dwindled daily. Increasingly isolated, he moved his remaining supporters to a mountainous area on the border between Hunan and Jiangxi provinces.

His force, as he noted at the time, consisted of "ten thousand messy people." The description was not altogether disparaging. In 1927 Mao had written a report on the peasants in two Hunan counties. Contrary to the Comintern view that peasants were benighted and thus unlikely revolutionary tinder, Mao discovered that the country people were doing a remarkable job of radicalizing and organizing themselves. The Communist Party was at a crossroads: it could continue to deny the revolutionary potential of the rural masses, or it could break with Moscow-inspired orthodoxy, take its place at the revolutionary vanguard, and guide the peasants to victory. For Mao the second road seemed best; however, this decision put Mao at odds with the Comintern and Stalin.

Under pressure from Kuomintang forces, in 1930 Mao and his peasants moved to a new border base and created a government in what they called the Jiangxi Soviet. Mao's grasp of power now slipped. He fell seriously ill several times. In 1932 the national CCP leadership removed to Jiangxi, and the bosses pushed Mao to the side. It was they who decided that the Soviet had become indefensible, and that the Communists would have to leave, though exactly where they would end up was unsettled. Thus began the Long March, an event that would assume legendary status among the Communists, especially as the passage of time dimmed memories of its horrors. Some eighty-six thousand people left Jiangxi in the fall of 1934, Mao among them, though without a leading role. Harried by Kuomintang troops, exploited by the locals, frozen, hungry, and sick, the Communists lost marchers at an alarming rate. As the former Soviet leaders were blamed for the debacle, Mao's star rose. By the time the remnants of the column—only eight thousand people—reached far off Shaanxi province a full year after its departure from the Soviet, Mao was back in charge.

The Communists made their new headquarters in the town of Yan'an. Living in caves carved into the sere hillsides, they worked to create their version of a just society, to include some land redistribution and respect for the local peasantry. Mao was the acknowledged leader in these efforts. He insisted that intellectuals learn from rather than teach the masses. But he abandoned sociology in favor of political theory that he represented as unassailable.

In July 1937 the Japanese forced a clash with Chinese troops at the Marco Polo Bridge near Beijing, then used the incident as a pretext to launch a full-scale assault against China. The Japanese attacked the major eastern cities, took Shanghai, then drove Chiang's Nationalist Kuomintang out of its capital at Nanjing, committing appalling atrocities as they did so. The spreading war forced Chiang to reinstitute the United Front with the CCP. Mao welcomed this step, though he understood that it was born purely of expediency; once the Japanese were defeated, he knew, war between the parties would resume.

Nationalist and Communist troops frequently fought hard against the Japanese, but they cooperated minimally and kept a wary eye on each other. When the war ended in August 1945 Japanese troops remained on Chinese soil. The Americans, who had sent representatives to Yan'an during the war and had encouraged the maintenance of the United Front, were nevertheless determined to help Chiang regain political and military superiority. They gave weapons to the Kuomintang, ferried its troops north to accept the Japanese surrender and thus their weapons as well, and kept Japanese soldiers armed in order to prevent Communist advances. The Russians, for their part, ushered Communist troops into Manchuria in the wake of their own departure. Thus did the Cold War come implicitly to China.

Hoping to prevent the resumption of civil war, President Truman sent George Marshall to China in late 1945. Marshall wanted a coalition between the Communists and the Nationalists, a desire that was as sincere as it was unrealistic. Mao, whose postwar position seemed weaker than Chiang's, proved cooperative, agreeing to remove Communist fighters from southern China and accepting in principle Marshall's proposal for a unified Chinese army. Chiang balked at nearly every American suggestion, preferring to pursue his war against the Communists. When a discouraged Marshall left China in January 1947 he labeled Chiang "the leading obstacle to peace and reform" on the scene. Yet the Americans would not abandon Chiang. He was, the Truman administration judged, the only hope for a united, noncommunist China.

Mao may have hoped for a more genuinely balanced U.S. policy but he could not have been shocked when the Americans sided with Chiang. Never, despite his pretensions, a sophisticated political theorist, Mao soon proved his abilities as a battlefield strategist. He maintained high morale and fought relentlessly and without quarter. Within each new area seized from the Kuomintang, Mao instituted land reform, with the understanding that the beneficiaries in their gratitude would become eager recruits for the Communist army. Beginning in the fall of 1947 CCP forces won battle after battle against the Kuomintang. On 1 October 1949 Mao declared in Beijing the founding of the People's Republic of China. Chiang Kai-shek fled to Taiwan, taking with him the remnants of the Kuomintang government and vowing to reconquer the mainland.

China desperately needed help. There had been a flicker of hope of establishing a diplomatic relationship with the United States. Even after the failure of Marshall's mission, Mao had signaled that he would welcome American assistance, and Mao's compatriot Zhou Enlai, who would become premier of the People's Republic, had seemed even more willing to make overtures to Washington. But in June 1949 Mao had given a speech in which he declared the need for China to "lean to one side" in the Cold War, specifically toward the Soviet Union. Mao's pronouncement did not ensure that the Soviets would embrace the Chinese Communists. Stalin had all along treated the Chinese revolution as an odd and ominous strain of the species, and he remained ambivalent about its prospects even after the CCP had won. Mao came to resent the widely held perception that he was Stalin's junior partner in revolution, and he was not reassured by the treatment he received when he arrived in Moscow in December, seeking a new relationship with the Kremlin and a good deal of economic aid. He got far less than he had hoped for with the Sino-Soviet Treaty of Friendship signed in February 1950.

Mao's most important goal was to consolidate the revolution at home, which required the establishment of Communist political legitimacy and economic policies that would eradicate poverty. He was also intent on liberating Taiwan from Chiang; without this step, the revolution would remain unfinished. Stalin promised no help, but when the Americans indicated their disinterest in defending the island, Mao began to concentrate his forces along China's southwest coast in preparation for an attack across the Formosa Strait. But Kim Il Sung moved faster. Having received Stalin's permission to go to war, Kim came to Beijing in May 1950, seeking Mao's blessing as well.

Mao was unenthusiastic about Kim's plans and asked him to reconsider. Kim refused. In the end Mao offered Kim a green light but promised nothing in the way of help, and Kim did not then pursue the matter, figuring he was likely to win quickly or that the Soviets would give him any assistance he needed. Mao was also surprised when the Americans intervened to halt the North Korean attack and placed their fleet in the Formosa Strait. The United States, Mao decided, was determined to destroy the People's Republic, and had taken its first step toward doing so in Korea. In response Mao began redeploying troops to northeast China near the Korean border. In September, following Douglas MacArthur's successful landing at Inchon and the subsequent rout of the North Korean army, Mao wrote to a Manchurian comrade: "Apparently, it won't do for us not to intervene in the war. You must accelerate preparations."

On 16 October Chinese units crossed the Yalu River in force. Mao professed confidence in their ultimate victory. Once the Chinese had bloodied U.S. forces in battle the American people would demand an end to the conflict. Privately Mao looked for additional help from the Soviet Union. Stalin was not at first forthcoming; he evidently wanted to test Chinese determination, and he remained wary of antagonizing the Americans. But as the Chinese routed UN forces and gave every indication that they intended to stay the course, Stalin relented, putting Soviet warplanes into action over Korea in mid-November.

Military stalemate came in Korea by the spring of 1951. The negotiations toward ending the war then dragged on for two frustrating years. During this time Mao used the war to rally people to the CCP. He mounted campaigns aimed at rooting out "counterrevolutionaries," crypto-capitalists, and Kuomintang sympathizers. His own power grew. By 1953 he was not only chairman of the Communist Party but also chairman of the People's Republic of China itself and in charge of its armed forces. Stalin's death in March left Mao unrivaled as a source of revolutionary wisdom and experience. He became the leading symbol of the communist Cold War, dispensing advice to would-be revolutionaries throughout the world, rattling sabers at the capitalist powers and their "running dog" allies, and threatening, as always, to absorb Taiwan.

The relationship between the People's Republic of China and the Soviet Union, tense during the best of times, deteriorated rapidly following Stalin's death. Nikita Khrushchev, who ultimately succeeded Stalin and who exposed some of Stalin's crimes to the world, found Mao cruel and megalomaniacal. At a time when Khrushchev was seeking to coexist with the United States, Mao seemed always to be courting war. In Moscow in 1957 Mao, according to Khrushchev, told Communist Party delegates that they should not fear "atomic bombs and missiles." If the imperialists started a war China might "lose more than three hundred million people. So what? War is war. The years will pass, and we'll get to work producing more babies than ever before." The Russians present were appalled. The following year Mao confronted the United States (for a second time) over the status of Quemoy and Matsu, two Nationalist-held islands in the Formosa Strait. Having precipitated a crisis Mao then backed down, which suggested to Khrushchev that the Chinese leader was better at creating confrontations than he was at resolving them. (Mao would say the same thing about Khrushchev following the Cuban missile crisis in 1962.)

By then the breach between the People's Republic of China and the Soviet Union was total. The Russians found intolerable Chinese abuse of Soviet advisers sent to help China develop its oil and build an atomic bomb, and in 1960 the Soviets removed their people. Mao, meanwhile, was incredulous that the Soviets would sell advanced MIG jets to India in 1962, given the friction that existed on the border between China and India. For his sixty-ninth birthday that year, Mao wrote a poem that contained the defiant lines "Only the hero dares pursue the tiger,/Still less does any brave fellow fear the bear." It may be presumed that Mao himself was the "hero," even more contemptuous of the Russian bear than of the paper tiger of imperialism.

As ever Mao's Cold War abroad directly affected his domestic policies. In 1958 Mao inaugurated a program of economic acceleration called the Great Leap Forward, in which all farm cooperatives would be joined into twenty thousand enormous communes and in which the nation's steel production would be increased through the efforts of workers who would erect blast furnaces in their backyards. Mao also announced a campaign to "let a hundred flowers bloom, and a hundred schools of thoughts contend." This seemed encouragement to Chinese to write or say anything, even if it was critical of their government. Both policies proved catastrophic. The Great Leap Forward resulted in a famine that killed twenty million in 1960–1961. Intellectuals and journalists who took seriously Mao's invitation to let flowers bloom quickly found themselves branded as "poisonous weeds" by an orchestrated "anti-rightist" campaign. Mao grew increasingly dictatorial and unpredictable.

He also seemed to withdraw from the battlements of the Cold War. He continued to support revolution around the world, and he was helpful in particular to the North Vietnamese in their war with the United States after 1965. China, not the contemptibly revisionist Soviet Union, would summon what Mao called "the mighty revolutionary storm" in the Third World. But Mao had never been greatly interested in affairs beyond China's borders, or he was circumspect about China's ability to control them. He did not leave China for the last twenty years of his life. It is too much to say that he mellowed, but he nevertheless came to understand that the world was changing. Seeking to offset the emerging détente between the United States and the Soviet Union, Mao invited President Richard Nixon to China. The two men met on 17 February 1972, shaking hands in front of a thicket of cameras in Mao's study. Mao apologized for his slurred speech and waved away Nixon's compliments. The policy implications of the visit were left to men other than Mao to sort out. Still, Mao enabled the meeting to take place, and he, along with Nixon, could take credit for initiating the first improvement in Sino-American relations since the establishment of the People's Republic of China.

Like other cold warriors, Mao Zedong, who died on 9 September 1976, left a mixed legacy. He was one of those responsible for introducing ideology into the realm of foreign policy, for defining opponents as enemies, for menacing others with his rhetoric, for maintaining large military forces and authorizing construction of an atomic bomb. Yet like the others, in the end Mao granted pragmatism primacy over ideology in foreign affairs. That he regarded the Americans as imperialists would not stand in the way of cultivating them if that proved necessary to preserve China's security and well-being in an increasingly complicated world.

RONALD REAGAN

By the time Mao Zedong died in the year of the U.S. bicentennial, it was clear that the Cold War had changed significantly. The Soviet Union, under Khrushchev and his successors, had thrown aside the cult of Joseph Stalin and had proved willing to consider limiting its nuclear arsenal if the United States would reciprocate.

The man who won the American presidency in 1980 and again in 1984 was instinctively suspicious of this effort for conciliation. Ronald Reagan was born (6 February 1911) and raised in small towns in Illinois. His memoir begins: "If I'd gotten the job I wanted at Montgomery Ward, I suppose I would never have left Illinois." Later in life Reagan recalled not small-town parochialism and racism, nor his father's alcoholic rages, but a life of summer days, lifeguarding at Lowell Park in Dixon, having fun at Eureka College, and after college taking a job in Des Moines in which he broadcast Chicago Cubs baseball games as if he were watching them, while in fact reconstructing them from a running telegraphic account sent from the field. He went to Hollywood in 1937 with a six-month contract from Warner Brothers studio. He became a star in B movies and took leadership of the Screen Actors Guild. He did not leave the United States during World War II, though he later claimed to have done so, even asserting that he had filmed Nazi concentration camps for the army. In fact, Reagan made war movies at home.

By the early 1950s Reagan was convinced that communists had infiltrated Hollywood and the Actors Guild, and he so told the FBI. His career in film was waning. But in 1954 the General Electric Company asked Reagan to host a weekly dramatic show on television. To promote the show Reagan went around the country talking with workers at GE plants about life in Hollywood and about the virtues of private enterprise. In 1960 Reagan switched his party affiliation from Democrat to Republican, and in 1966 he surprised nearly everyone by beating the two-term Democratic incumbent for the California governorship.

Reagan served two terms as governor, a tenure marked by incendiary rhetoric. He insisted that people who accepted government welfare were chiselers or cheats, and he threatened a "bloodbath" if students in Berkeley kept taking to the streets to protest against Vietnam War. Reagan's stature grew. In 1976 he challenged the Republican president, Gerald Ford, and nearly gained the nomination by attacking Secretary of State Kissinger's policy of détente. When Ford lost the election to Jimmy Carter, Reagan was established as the Republican frontrunner in 1980. He thrashed Carter in that election, returning to themes that had made him famous: the venality of big government, the horrors of communism, and the unique ability of Americans to overcome all their problems and secure a luminous future.

Reagan's Cold War was a product of his experience in Middle America, in Hollywood, and on the circuit for GE; his chief source of information about the Soviet Union was *Reader's Digest*. He was not much interested in foreign countries. Like Mao he traveled abroad only reluctantly. Still Reagan knew what he did not like. The Soviet Union was an "evil empire," and its agents, he said at his first presidential press conference, "reserve unto themselves the right to commit any crime, to lie, to cheat," in order to foment "world revolution." The Berlin Wall should be ripped down, free elections should be held throughout eastern Europe, and the Soviet government should stop violating the human rights of its citizens. The Vietnam War had been "a noble cause." ("We should declare war on Vietnam," Reagan had said in October 1965. "We could pave the whole country and put parking stripes on it and still be home by Christmas.") Revolutions, or even experiments in socialism, were the result of Soviet imperialism.

Reagan brought to office a set of convictions rather than a foreign policy. He delegated to his advisers the task of turning his dreams and fears into directives. This might have worked if everyone agreed on how to do a thing, but as Reagan's men and women often disagreed among themselves, the result was frequently chaos.

Again and again Reagan displayed an alarming ignorance of his own nation's foreign policy. He misstated the name given by the CIA to the Soviets' largest long-range missile, and when his error was pointed out to him he accused the Soviets of changing the name in order to fool the West. He mistook defensive weapons for offensive ones, failed to understand the strategic difference between placing missiles in silos or putting them on mobile carriers, and claimed that neither bombers nor submarines carried nuclear weapons. He prepared for his 1986 summit meeting with Soviet leader Mikhail Gorbachev, to be held in Reykjavik, Iceland, by reading the Tom Clancy thriller *Red Storm Rising* —because, he said, much of it was set in Iceland. Briefings of the president had to be short and snappy, reducible to a few small note cards or film clips. These were by definition devoid of detail or ambiguity, which tended to reinforce Reagan's black-or-white view of the world.

Yet the president was not altogether without assets as a foreign policymaker. He commanded the world's strongest economy. He put it into recession early in his first term, and ran up an enormous national debt thereafter, but the Gross Domestic Product nevertheless increased through the 1980s. Possessed of a sense of humor and an actor's charm, Reagan was liked even by those who disagreed with him. And despite his caustic characterizations of the Soviets and his resolve to build American military power until his enemies cried uncle, Reagan feared a nuclear holocaust and was determined to find a way to prevent it. Back in 1979 Reagan had visited the headquarters of the North American Aerospace Defense Command (NORAD), at Cheyenne Mountain, Colorado. At the end of his tour Reagan asked the base commander what the United States could do if the Russians launched a missile at an American city. NORAD could track the missile, the commander replied, but could do nothing to stop it.

Reagan was astonished. "We have spent all that money and have all that equipment, and there is nothing we can do to prevent a nuclear missile from hitting us," he said. To Reagan it seemed that, armed to the teeth with weapons of mass destruction, the United States and the Soviet Union had come to the brink of Armageddon.

There might be a way out. The loophole was a system of lasers or rockets, deployed in space, that could destroy or knock off course any missile launched by Russia at the United States. Proposed by Reagan at the end of a defense budget speech to the nation on 23 March 1983, the Strategic Defense Initiative (SDI), popularly known as "Star Wars," soon after became the centerpiece of the administration's strategic planning. To Reagan it was a matter of logic and simple humanity: if you can prevent something as awful as a nuclear warhead from striking your nation, it would be irresponsible not to do so. But the Soviets reacted strongly against SDI. What Reagan had not said, they pointed out—and they assumed he realized it—was that a U.S. monopoly on missile defense would tempt the Americans to launch a first strike against them, secure in the knowledge that the Russians could not effectively retaliate. They were also concerned about a new arms race. The Americans would have to spend billions to develop SDI technology, while the Russians would be forced to increase their offensive capabilities in the hope of defeating the American shield. (The possibility of bankrupting the feeble Soviet economy had occurred to Reagan, though the strategic hazards of missile defense perhaps had not.) In any case, the Soviets said, meaningful arms negotiations could not take place between the powers so long as SDI remained on the table.

Reagan was disinclined to grant the Soviets any sympathy; moreover, he had found arms control distasteful. The Soviets continued, in his judgment, to stir up trouble around the globe: in the Middle East, Africa, and in Latin America, of special concern because of its proximity to the United States. When Reagan took office in 1981 the hot spot in Latin America was Nicaragua. Convinced that the Sandinista government was not only Marxist but a hemispheric agent of world communism, Reagan sought ways to unseat it. At the urging of William Casey, the director of the CIA, Reagan authorized the creation of an anti-Sandinista army, dubbed the contras, that would train in Honduras and harass the Sandinistas across the border. The contras were constituted mostly of members of Somoza's National Guard; at their peak they numbered about 7,500.

U.S. aid to the contras, and its related efforts to overthrow the Sandinistas, proved impossible to hide. In April 1984 the *Wall Street Journal* revealed that the CIA had mined Sandino harbor, hoping to discourage Nicaragua's trade. Congress now put its foot down, refusing to allow further funding of the anti-Sandinista war. Reagan branded the Sandinista government "a Communist reign of terror," and insisted that the United States had a moral right to overthrow it. The contras were "freedom fighters" similar to the American Founders. The administration would find alternative sources of funding for its sunshine patriots.

The Israel is refused to help, but the Saudis and the sultan of Brunei agreed to back the contras financially. Then National Security Council aide Oliver North, in the company of Casey and national security adviser Robert C. "Bud" McFarlane, had what North called "a neat idea." The fundamentalist Islamic government of Iran desperately wanted weapons to continue its war against Iraq. Despite its antipathy for the United States it was willing to buy U.S. arms and might out of gratitude intervene to secure the release of several American hostages then being held in Lebanon. North saw another benefit from selling arms to Iran: the money paid by the Iranians for the weapons might then be diverted to the contras. It would work as long as it was kept secret.

Word of the arms for hostages deal leaked out of the Middle East in November 1986. The contra connection was then uncovered as well. Congressional investigators wanted to know what role the president had played in the arms for hostages scheme and the diversion of monies to the contras, but either because he was stonewalling or because he genuinely could not remember what he had authorized and when, Reagan was unhelpful. He denied that he had known about the attempted swap, but documents indicated otherwise, and Reagan confessed, almost: "A few months ago I told the American people I did not trade arms for hostages. My heart and my best intentions still tell me that's true, but the facts and the evidence tell me it's not." He continued to deny that he had known about the diversion of funds to the contras. Senator William Cohen, a member of the congressional group that investigated Iran-Contra, participated in two interviews with Reagan and concluded, "with Ronald Reagan, no one is there."

The Iran-Contra affair and the nuclear freeze movement undoubtedly made him more tractable in negotiations with the Soviet Union. Mikhail Gorbachev, who emerged as the leader of the Soviet Union, declared his intention to reform the Soviet economy and pursue greater flexibility in foreign affairs, especially to move forward with arms control. At first suspicious that Gorbachev's offer to negotiate a meaningful arms agreement was a ploy to weaken U.S. vigilance, Reagan came ultimately to accept Gorbachev's sincerity, but he would not fully grasp the opportunity provided by Gorbachev's policy.

The obstacle to a full-scale nuclear rollback was SDI. At summits with Gorbachev in 1985, 1986, and 1988, Reagan continued to insist that defense against a nuclear attack could not be wrong, especially if Armageddon loomed. When Gorbachev pointed out that a missile shield would enable the United States to launch a first strike with impunity, Reagan, who was amazed that anyone would think the United States capable of such a thing, offered to share SDI technology with the Soviets. Gorbachev thought this unlikely. He urged Reagan to agree to confine SDI to the laboratory for ten years; Reagan refused. Still, Gorbachev wanted arms reduction enough that he was willing to make cuts in the Soviet arsenal even in the absence of an agreement on SDI. The result was the Intermediate Nuclear Force (INF) treaty of 8 December 1987, by which the Americans and Russians agreed to eliminate all intermediate-range nuclear missiles from Europe. But Reagan's commitment to SDI slowed the progress of further arms negotiations.

Gorbachev then unmade the Cold War. He ended the bloody Soviet intervention in Afghanistan, released Soviet control of the eastern European satellites and the Baltic states, allowed the destruction of the Berlin Wall, wrenched the Soviet economy off its rusty statist moorings, began opening Soviet archives to scholars, and traveled the world, creating about himself an international cult far more Reaganesque than Stalinist. He brought change so quickly and with such verve that Reagan and his successors mistrusted it. George H. W. Bush, who followed Reagan to the presidency in 1989, reacted so slowly to Gorbachev's revolution that critics charged him with being "nostalgic for the Cold War." Bush finally got it and embraced what he called "the new world order," which meant that the United States would now call the shots. Meanwhile Ronald Reagan returned to California, firm in the belief that his policies had brought about the end of the Cold War but not fully understanding how. He was the last cold warrior. The Alzheimer's disease that dissolved his memory made for a sad yet fitting metaphor: a dark era had passed, and there was a world to be remade.

A Military & Ideological Struggle (1945–91)

In essence the Cold War (1945–91) was a military and ideological struggle between capitalist/democratic economies and those of Marxist/totalitarian single party states. The Causes of the Grand Alliance of the United States, Great Britain, and the Soviet Union was the indirect creation of Adolf Hitler. Only such a challenge as Nazi Germany could bring together the world's leading capitalist democracy, the world's greatest colonial empire, and the world's major Communist state. Relations between the Anglo–Americans and the Russians, moreover, had been marked by ideological clash and distrust since the Bolshevik Revolution. The Western powers had intervened in the Russian civil war against the Bolsheviks, and the United States had refused to recognize the Soviet Union from 1917 to 1933. Prewar diplomacy, particularly Western appeasement of Hitler and rejection of collective security with the Soviet Union, followed by the Nazi–Soviet Pact in August 1939, led each side to be wary of the other's intentions and motives.

During World War II, President Franklin D. Roosevelt set forth two parallel strategies for postwar peace. The first was the continuation of the Grand Alliance. Best symbolized by the United Nations, this path sought continued cooperation with the Soviet Union, great power control over different spheres of influence, and incorporation of socialist economies into a world trade system. The other strategy was based on American power, the "open door," policy, and unilateral planning. It was best represented by the development of the atomic bomb, which Roosevelt refused to share with the Russians. Though Roosevelt wished for continued cooperation with the Soviets, he was also willing to hedge his bets and keep his options open. Underlying both approaches was Roosevelt's tactic of delaying the major decisions on boundaries, governments, occupation policies, and reparations and reconstruction aid until the end of the war, when American power would be at its height. With his characteristic optimism, Roosevelt believed that time would allow the conflicts in these approaches to be worked out.

The Yalta Conference in February 1945 appeared to expose the problems and contradictions of Roosevelt's two-track approach. The Allies clashed over the composition of Poland's government, and could not reach firm agreements on the crucial questions of the occupation of Germany and postwar reparations and loans. Roosevelt, believing any truly representative government in Warsaw would be anti-Soviet, accepted a vague compromise that allowed the Soviet-imposed government to maintain control without technically violating the agreement. Four zones of occupation were established for Germany, and $10 billion was adopted as a working figure for German reparations to the Soviet Union, with the details to be settled later. Still, Roosevelt saw the common desire to prevent a resurgence of German power, along with Soviet needs for postwar reconstruction, to be firm roads to continued cooperation among the Big Three (the United States, the United Kingdom, and the USSR). He believed that concessions to Soviet security concerns in Eastern Europe were necessary in the short run until the West could demonstrate its good faith through American economic aid and guarantees against German remilitarization. Once Soviet dictator Josef Stalin was persuaded that the West did not intend to allow Germany again to threaten Europe's peace, and that it would assist the Soviet Union in its recovery, Moscow would no longer need to dominate its neighbors. The Soviet Union would find its security protected within the collective arrangements of the United Nations Security Council.

Roosevelt's hopes of resolving the contradictions of his policy died with him on 12 April 1945. The new president, Harry S. Truman, was by all accounts unaware of Roosevelt's plans, generally uninformed about foreign policy and military matters, and therefore initially reliant upon a set of advisers that included Ambassador to the Soviet Union Averell Harriman, Secretary of War Henry L. Stimson, and Truman's choice for secretary of state, James Brynes. This group tended to take a harder line toward the Soviet Union than had Roosevelt. Truman believed in cooperation, but he thought it should be on American terms. He stated that he did not expect to get his way every time, but he did believe "we should be able to get eighty-five percent." In his first meeting with the Soviet foreign minister, V. M. Molotov, in late April 1945, Truman used blunt language in accusing the Soviets of failing to carry out their promise of establishing a democratic government in Poland. In July, when Truman learned of the successful testing of the atomic bomb, he wrote privately that he now had an "ace in the hole," which he could use to end the war in the Pacific and in negotiations with the Soviets. The unilateral approach was winning out over cooperation and negotiation.

The bombings of Hiroshima and Nagasaki did indeed add to Soviet distrust of the United States, but Soviet leaders in the Kremlin continued in 1945 to seek cooperation with the West. The reasons for this were compelling. The devastation of the Soviet Union by the Germans was unprecedented. Over 20 million Soviet citizens died during the war, and over 1,700 cities, 70,000 villages, and 31,000 factories were destroyed. To ensure more secure borders, rebuild, and prevent a future resurgence of German strength seemed to demand continued good relations with the United States. Only Washington could ensure Soviet security through its occupation policies and provide funds for reconstruction. Cooperation, for Stalin, was a means to ensure the Soviet sphere of influence, control Germany, and secure vital economic aid.

Yet, from Washington's perspective Soviet actions in Eastern Europe more and more came to be seen not as necessary steps for security but as aggressive actions that threatened American plans for postwar peace and prosperity. From the outset of World War II, officials in the Roosevelt administration were determined that the United States would seize its "second chance" (the first chance had been lost after World War I) to shape the postwar world in such a way as to promote American interests and peace. It was an article of faith for advocates of American internationalism that the United States had an obligation to accept responsibility for postwar leadership and to see to it that the world adopted American ideas of self-determination, free trade, arms limitations, and collective security. These were not only good for the United States but beneficial to all nations. With isolationism discredited, the objective was to maintain the principles of the Grand Alliance as set out in the Atlantic Charter. The United States had fought the war in part to protect self-determination and open trade.

It was therefore necessary to combat spheres of influence and closed trading systems. No one nation or group of powers could be allowed to establish a competing system to the one the U.S. government envisioned for the world. Truman and his advisers believed that political and economic freedoms were interrelated and necessary for American prosperity and international peace. Any restrictions of trade or exclusive economic spheres would lead to a repetition of the 1930s. As Truman declared in 1947, "peace, freedom, and world trade" were inseparable; "the grave lessons of the past have proved it." Limiting a Soviet sphere of influence was perceived as necessary to postwar peace. This understanding led to great fears among American officials that if they did not respond to Soviet actions, the United States would find itself once again in a world of trade blocs and international competition. To compel the Soviets to accept American interpretations of agreements, the Truman administration denounced Soviet behavior in Poland, Romania, and elsewhere, threatened action over Soviet involvement in Iran, and held up economic assistance until the Soviets demonstrated their willingness to cooperate on American terms. Truman, believing he had either the power to force Soviet compliance or the ability to achieve American goals without the Kremlin's cooperation, was convinced by the end of 1945 that it was time to "stop babying the Soviets." "Unless Russia is faced with an iron fist and strong language," he said, "another war is in the making."

The arrival of George F. Kennan's Long Telegram from Moscow in February 1946 served to provide coherence to the developing hard line against the Soviets. Kennan argued that the Soviet Union was motivated by a combination of traditional Russian desires to expand and by Marxist ideology that taught there could be no cooperation with capitalist states. There was therefore no room for compromise and negotiation. The Soviets would take advantage of all sincere efforts at peace and only honor agreements when it was expedient to their goals. He portrayed Stalin as acting on a coherent design, rather than as a man responding to events in the interests of his nation. The obvious conclusion for Kennan —and the one drawn by the Truman administration—was that the Soviets had no legitimate grievances. There was thus no need to try to understand and meet Soviet concerns. Rather, a policy of opposition and the containment of Soviet power was necessary.

A few weeks later in Fulton, Missouri, former British prime minister Winston S. Churchill delivered his "Iron Curtain" speech sounding the call for an Anglo–American alliance against the Soviets, whom he said had established a dictatorial régime behind an "iron curtain" from "Stettin in the Baltic to Trieste in the Adriatic." Problems seemed to be multiplying around the world, and from the White House it appeared that more often than not the source of the difficulties was the Soviet Union. In Asia, revolutionary nationalist movements, often headed by Communists, were fighting against the restoration of Europe's colonial empires, while civil war between the Nationalists and Communists resumed in China. In Europe, economic recovery was slow, food and other essential goods short, and Communist parties, particularly in France and Italy, were gaining ground. Truman's advisers warned him that time was running short. The Soviet strategy, they argued, was to weaken the position of the United States in Europe and Asia to create confusion and collapse. The threat was not necessarily a military one, but a political and economic challenge.

Other apparent challenges appeared in Turkey and Iran. In 1946, the Soviets pushed for access to the strategic Dardanelles Straits while simultaneously delaying the removal of troops from Iran's northern provinces.

The event that spurred Truman to action was the British government's announcement in February 1947 that it was pulling out of Greece. It could no longer afford to finance the Greek royalist forces in their civil war against a Communist-led rebellion. Rather than viewing the war as a civil conflict revolving around Greek issues, American policymakers incorrectly interpreted it as a Soviet effort. Secretary of State Dean Acheson told congressional leaders that the "Soviet Union was playing one of the greatest gambles in history at minimal cost" in an effort to expand into the Middle East, Asia, and Africa. The United States alone could stop this. In March 1947, the president announced the Truman Doctrine. It "must be the policy of the United States," Truman declared, "to support free peoples who are resisting attempted subjugation by armed minorities or outside pressures." This was followed in June by the Marshall Plan (1948–52), a pledge of economic assistance to Europe to stimulate recovery and trade.

By 1947, U.S. policy was predicated on the containment of the Soviet Union. In its efforts to establish a postwar order based upon American institutions and ideals, the Truman administration came to see the Soviet Union as a threat to U.S. interests. In the late 1940s, containment and anticommunism were globalized to include Asia, Africa, and Latin America. Competing security and economic demand in Europe shattered the Grand Alliance and brought about the Cold War.

The Role of Nuclear Weapons

By 1949, both countries possessed nuclear weapons. There has been much debate over the exact role of these weapons in the Cold War. Many historians argue that the only reason the Cold War never became "hot" was that the fear of nuclear annihilation effectively deterred each side from directly attacking the other. Others disagree, pointing to the fact that the Cold War had already reached a fever pitch before the Soviets had nuclear weapons, and that until the widespread development of hydrogen bombs in the 1950s, atomic weapons were only slightly more deadly than the most concentrated conventional attacks.

Without question, nuclear weapons were an integral aspect of the Cold War, and it is impossible to understand the history of the conflict without an appreciation for how large the threat of these weapons loomed, not just over Washington and Moscow but throughout the world. The rapid growth of nuclear arsenals altered the nature of international relations and made both nuclear superpowers far more wary of military confrontation with one another than they might otherwise have been.

After the Cuban Missile Crisis in October 1962, both sides made strenuous efforts to establish a modus vivendi. A period of detente continued until 1979, when the Soviet invasion of Afghanistan contributed to renewed American military spending and to the election of President Ronald Reagan, who pursued what is sometimes known as the "second Cold War." This lasted from 1979 to 1986, when Reagan and the reform–minded Soviet premier, Mikhail Gorbachev, came to an agreement in Iceland. The final years, between 1986 and 1991, saw the rapid dissolution of the Soviet Union. Its collapse in December 1991 marked the end of a Cold War that had all but sputtered out in the previous five years.

Phase One: 1945–1946

After Potsdam, the United States and the Soviet Union approached each other warily. Throughout the fall of 1945, the two countries shifted attention from the European and Asian wars that had consumed them for the past five years. As they did so, they found that their visions for a post–Cold War world differed, most noticeably in Poland and occupied Germany. The United States envisioned a world dominated by democracy and free market economics, while the USSR saw that vision as a thinly veiled strategy to dominate the Soviet Union. By the end of 1946, the level of antagonism between the two nations had risen precipitously. Each viewed the other as the primary foreign policy threat, and both governments mobilized resources and planned strategy with one goal in mind: maximizing their own influence and minimizing that of the other.

Phase Two: 1947–1962

The second phase was the most intensive of the Cold War, and the most dangerous. During this period, the United States and the Soviet Union constructed formidable nuclear arsenals and enormous conventional forces, and at several points the two countries nearly came to blows.

In 1947, the U.S. government reorganized. The National Security Act created a unified Department of Defense, a Central Intelligence Agency (CIA), and a National Security Council. These would be the primary bureaucracies for American policy in the Cold War. Responding to a Communist insurgency in Greece and to Stalin's pressure on Turkey to allow Soviet military access to the straits connecting the Black Sea to the Mediterranean, Truman requested Congress to authorize a $400 million aid program. In order to mobilize isolationists in the Republican Congress, the Democratic president heightened the rhetorical stakes, painting the Cold War as a contest between "free institutions and representative government" and those who were forcibly ruled by "the will of the minority." The struggle between the two sides in the Cold War was more than military, strategic, or economic; it was also profoundly ideological, with each side presenting the other as the embodiment of evil.

The Truman Doctrine was followed by an announcement of European aid by Secretary of State George C. Marshall, in June 1947. The twin policies of the Truman Doctrine and the Marshall Plan led to billions in economic and military aid to Western Europe and the eastern Mediterranean. With American assistance, the Greek military defeated the insurgents, and the Christian Democrats in Italy defeated the powerful Communist–Socialist alliance in the elections of 1948.

At the same time, tension over Germany grew. Unable to agree on a partition of Germany, both Soviet and U.S. troops remained in Berlin, and in an attempt to force the Americans out, the Soviets blockaded Berlin in the summer of 1948. Rather than backing down, the United States orchestrated the Berlin airlift of supplies to Berlin, which lasted nearly a year until Stalin realized that his blockade had failed in its aims.

The year 1949 saw three developments that deepened the conflict. In April, a Western military alliance, the North Atlantic Treaty Organization (NATO), was created, and it bound the United States to the defense of Western Europe. In September, the Soviet Union successfully tested a nuclear weapon; and in October, the Communist forces of Mao Zedong defeated the last remnant of the Nationalist Army and took power in China. In response to these events, the National Security Council in Washington drew up a plan in early 1950 known as NSC 68, which called for a massive buildup of American conventional and nuclear forces and an aggressive military response to Communist expansionism throughout the world.

When war erupted between North and South Korea in June 1950, Truman and his advisers barely hesitated before acting on NSC 68 and sending U.S. troops to bolster South Korea. By late fall, more than 1 million Chinese troops crossed the Yalu River in North Korea and entered the Korean War against American, South Korean, and other United Nations troops. The war turned into a stalemate that lasted until an armistice in 1953 that returned Korea essentially to its pre-1950 dividing line.

The inauguration of Dwight D. Eisenhower as president in January 1953 and the death of Josef Stalin that March shifted the dynamic of the Cold War somewhat. Eisenhower and his secretary of state, John Foster Dulles, initiated the "New Look" strategy, which called for a greater reliance on nuclear weapons to deter China and the Soviet Union. Dulles enunciated a doctrine of massive retaliation that called for a severe American response to any Soviet aggression and violence, and the "New Look" also drew the United States more closely into Third World politics. The Soviets, now led by Nikita Khrushchev, moved away from the depredations of Stalinism, but in foreign policy they remained dedicated to global competition with the United States.

The Cold War in Europe settled into an uneasy armed truce, with NATO troops stationed in West Germany and Warsaw Pact and Soviet forces stationed throughout Eastern Europe. In 1956, the Soviets invaded Hungary rather than allow the Hungarians to move out of the Soviet orbit. Berlin remained divided and contested, and in 1961, the East Germans erected a wall to prevent their citizens from fleeing to West Berlin.

The other arena for the Cold War during the 1950s was the Third World, where nationalist movements in countries such as Guatemala, Iran, and the Philippines were often allied with or led by Communist groups. The United States and the Soviet Union began to compete by proxy in the Third World, and the U.S. government utilized the CIA as well as various forms of covert operations in order to remove certain Third World governments and support others. Third World countries reacted by rejecting the impetus to choose sides in the Cold War. At Bandung, Indonesia, in 1955, dozens of Third World governments gathered and resolved on staying out of the Cold War. This resolve culminated with the creation of the Non-Aligned movement in 1961.

During the 1950s, the Soviets and the Americans created a new generation of nuclear weapons—hydrogen bombs—which magnified exponentially the potential damage of nuclear war. In the late 1950s, the Soviets launched the first of the reconnaissance satellites, Sputnik, while the United States developed U–2 spy planes. Both innovations soon led to aerial reconnaissance, allowing Cold War adversaries to gain a clearer picture of the military strength of the other.

But in 1960, U.S. reconnaissance did not prevent the CIA and the American military from overestimating the strength of the Soviet military. During the presidential election of 1960, John F. Kennedy criticized the Eisenhower administration for allowing an alleged "missile gap" to develop with the Soviet Union, even though in reality the United States was ahead of the Soviets in missiles, in particular, intercontinental missile development. On his inauguration as president, Kennedy promised that the United States would not fall behind the Soviet Union in military strength.

Kennedy and Khrushchev held a summit in Vienna in June 1961, but it did not go well. Kennedy felt bullied, and Khrushchev felt that Kennedy was a weak man surrounded by hawkish advisers. At the same time, Khrushchev knew that the only missile gap was on the Soviet side, and he intended to redress that imbalance. In the summer of 1962, Khrushchev decided to station nuclear missiles in Cuba, where the anti-American Fidel Castro had recently come to power and thwarted a CIA-sponsored invasion by Cuban exiles. An American U–2 overflight of Cuba detected these missiles, and that discovery set off what has since become known as the Cuban Missile Crisis.

For thirteen days in October 1962, Kennedy and Khrushchev played a deadly game of "chicken," each threatening to escalate the crisis to the brink of nuclear war. After a tense standoff, Khrushchev decided to withdraw the weapons from Cuba in return for a pledge from Kennedy that the United States would not invade the island. Though the crisis was a victory for Kennedy, it signaled to both the United States and the Soviet Union that the cost of direct confrontation in an era of nuclear weapons was greater than any potential gain. In 1963, the two countries agreed on a Limited Test Ban Treaty, which marked the first step toward normalization of relations.

Phase Three: 1963–1979

After 1963, the United States and the Soviet Union entered the period that came to be known as *detente*. Ideological passions gradually dissipated in favor of a more pragmatic approach to international politics. The United States turned its attention to the Vietnam War, and until 1973, it remained mired there. The civil war in Vietnam was part of the Cold War insofar as it was the logical outgrowth of American policies of containment and rollback, but with its military attention locked on Vietnam and beset by severe domestic unrest, the administration of Lyndon B. Johnson focused less on Moscow. President Richard M. Nixon, while disengaging from Vietnam, worked assiduously to establish a diplomatic rapport with the Soviets, aided in that task by his chief foreign policy official, Henry Kissinger.

The Soviets until the very end of this period focused on their bitter rivalry with Mao's China; after Khrushchev's ouster in 1964, the Soviet leadership turned inward to attend to the many domestic problems that plagued the Soviet Union. Soviet rulers such as Alexei Kosygin and Leonid Brezhnev warily embraced the notion of detente, although like the Americans they continued to expend considerable energies trying to win various Third World states to their side.

The year 1972 was the apogee of detente. Nixon and Kissinger orchestrated a stunning and secretive rapprochement with Communist China. For their part, the Chinese had sought improved relations with the Americans in order to gain advantage over the Soviets. In February, Nixon traveled to the Forbidden City in Beijing and met with Mao and Chou En-Lai. Then, in June, Nixon and Kissinger met with Brezhnev and Soviet military officials in Moscow. The result was the first of the SALT Treaties (an acronym for Strategic Arms Limitation Talks), which pledged the United States and the USSR to limit the deployment of antiballistic missiles and set restrictions on offensive nuclear missiles as well. SALT I was followed in 1974 by SALT II, which went even further in specifying numbers of warheads each side could possess.

President Jimmy Carter came into office in 1977 with SALT II unratified, and he announced that his administration would make human rights a central concern. Carter had great success brokering a Middle East peace agreement between Israel and Egypt, the Camp David Accords (1979). However, though relations with the Soviets and the Chinese were civil, the spirit of detente began to dissipate. In December 1979, Brezhnev ordered Soviet troops to invade Afghanistan to support a tottering pro-Moscow régime. The U.S. Embassy in Teheran, Iran, had been seized a month earlier by Islamic militant students allied with the Ayatollah Khomeini, and the American hostages were held until the day Ronald Reagan was inaugurated in January 1980. The dual effects of the Iranian hostage crisis and the Soviet invasion of Afghanistan led to a significant increase in U.S. military spending in Carter's last year, to the election of Reagan, and to the end of detente.

Phase Four: 1980–1986

Reagan arrived in office determined to restore American pride and power. He and his advisers believed that both the realpolitik of Kissinger and the weakness of Carter had sacrificed America's ideological and strategic advantage in the Cold War. Calling the Soviet Union an "evil empire," Reagan embarked on a huge military buildup that ranged from new aircraft carrier groups to research for a space missile defense system known as the Strategic Defense Initiative (or "Star Wars"). The most visible manifestation of Reagan's renewed Cold War fervor was the support given to the Contra rebels in Nicaragua, who were fighting a guerrilla war against the Communist Sandinista government.

The Soviets attempted to match Reagan's military spending. But the war in Afghanistan deteriorated, and Moscow discovered that the ailing industry and economy of the Soviet Union simply could not keep pace with the Americans. In 1985, a young, dynamic Mikhail Gorbachev became premier, and he instituted a series of domestic reforms known as *glasnost* (openness) and *perestroika* (restructuring the economy).

At first, the Reagan administration saw these initiatives as a ruse. They were not. Meeting with Gorbachev in Reykjavik, Iceland, in October 1986, Reagan made what was for him a leap of faith, agreeing to both the INF Treaty (Intermediate Nuclear Forces) and the START Treaty (Strategic Arms Reduction, the stepchild of SALT II). At Reykjavik, the Cold War began to thaw.

Phase Five: 1987–1991

Few could have predicted how quickly the ice would melt. Although glasnost was designed to save and strengthen the Soviet Union, it helped cause the Soviet system to collapse. The economy was in shambles, and the pressures of war in Afghanistan and deep structural reform were simply more than the system could bear. In 1989, taking their cue from Moscow, people throughout the Eastern bloc demanded change. In Poland, Hungary, East Germany, and Czechoslovakia, Communist régimes fell and were replaced by interim governments dedicated to democracy and the free market. At the same time, in the Soviet Union itself, the Baltic states declared their independence, and Gorbachev significantly refused to authorize the use of the military to force either Eastern European or the Baltics back into the Soviet fold.

The end came in 1991. In August, Gorbachev survived a coup attempt by hard-liners opposed to any further reforms, but he survived largely because the newly elected Russian president, Boris Yeltsin, rallied army units and crowds to oppose the coup in Moscow. Gorbachev returned, but only for a brief time, before the Ukraine, Belarus, and the Russian Federation declared their independence. In December 1991, Gorbachev resigned as president of the defunct Soviet Union.

Assessment

The end of the Cold War came as a surprise to Moscow, Washington, and to the world. Almost no one had thought that the conflict would end so suddenly with one side collapsing internally. Both the Americans and the Western Europeans were unprepared for the rapid demise of Soviet military and economic power, and in the years after 1991, the major players in the Cold War tried to find a new strategic template that would organize their foreign policy. With the possible exception of China, that template proved elusive in the 1990s.

Like the Westphalian system in 1648 after the Thirty Year's War, and that of the Congress of Vienna in 1815 after the Napoleonic Wars, the Cold War was as much an international system following a major war as it was a struggle between two nuclear superpowers. It was a system that dominated all aspects of world politics between 1945 and 1991, and one that both exacerbated conflict in the Third World and prevented armed nuclear confrontation between the United States and the Soviet Union.

The Endgame

The collapse of the U.S.-Soviet détente in the late 1970s left no doubt about the staying power of the Cold War. One of the reasons that Ronald Reagan won the U.S. presidency in 1980 is that he was perceived as a stronger leader at a time of heightened U.S.-Soviet antagonism. Although the renewed tensions of the early 1980s did not spark a crisis as intense as those in the early 1950s and early 1960s, the hostility between the two sides was acute, and the rhetoric became inflammatory enough to spark a brief war scare in 1983.

Even before Reagan was elected, the outbreak of a political and economic crisis in Poland in the summer of 1980, giving rise to the independent trade union known as "Solidarity," created a potential flashpoint in U.S.-Soviet relations. The relentless demand of Soviet leaders that the Polish authorities crush Solidarity and all other "anti-socialist" elements, demonstrated once again the limits of what could be changed in Eastern Europe. Under continued pressure, the Polish leader, General Wojciech Jaruzelski, successfully imposed martial law in Poland in December 1981, arresting thousands of Solidarity activists and banning the organization. Jaruzelski's "internal solution" precluded any test of Moscow's restraint and helped prevent any further disruption in Soviet-East European relations over the next several years.

Even if the Polish crisis had never arisen, East-West tensions over numerous other matters would have increased sharply in the early 1980s. Recriminations about the deployment of intermediate-range nuclear forces (INF) in Europe, and the rise of antinuclear movements in Western Europe and the United States, dominated East-West relations in the early 1980s. The deployment of NATO's missiles on schedule in late 1983 and 1984 helped defuse popular opposition in the West to the INF, but the episode highlighted the growing role of public opinion and mass movements in Cold War politics.

Much the same was true about the effect of antinuclear sentiment on the Reagan administration's programs to modernize U.S. strategic nuclear forces and its subsequent plans to pursue the Strategic Defense Initiative (SDI). These efforts, and the rhetoric that surrounded them, sparked dismay not only among Western antinuclear activists, but also in Moscow. For a brief while, Soviet leaders even worried that the Reagan administration might be considering a surprise nuclear strike. In the United States, however, public pressure and the rise of a nuclear freeze movement induced the Reagan administration to reconsider its earlier aversion to nuclear arms control. Although political uncertainty in Moscow in the first half of the 1980s made it difficult to resume arms control talks or to diminish bilateral tensions, the Reagan administration was far more intent on pursuing arms control by the mid-1980s than it had been earlier.

This change of heart in Washington, while important, was almost inconsequential compared to the extraordinary developments in Moscow in the latter half of the 1980s. The rise to power of Mikhail Gorbachev in March 1985 was soon followed by broad political reforms and a gradual reassessment of the basic premises of Soviet foreign policy. Over time, the new thinking in Soviet foreign policy became more radical. The test of Gorbachev's approach came in 1989, when peaceful transformations in Poland and Hungary brought noncommunist rulers to power. Gorbachev not only tolerated, but actively encouraged this development. The orthodox communist régimes in East Germany, Bulgaria, Czechoslovakia, and Romania did their best to stave off the tide of reform, but a series of upheavals in October–December 1989 brought the downfall of the four orthodox régimes.

The remarkable series of events following Gorbachev's ascendance, culminating in the largely peaceful revolutions of 1989, marked the true end of the Cold War. Soviet military power was still enormous in 1989, and in that sense the Soviet Union was still a superpower alongside the United States. However, Gorbachev and his aides did away with the other condition that was needed to sustain the Cold War: the ideological divide. By reassessing, recasting, and ultimately abandoning the core precepts of Marxism-Leninism, Gorbachev and his aides enabled changes to occur in Europe that eviscerated the Cold War structure. The Soviet leader's decision to accept and even facilitate the peaceful transformation of Eastern Europe undid Stalin's pernicious legacy.

The Unforeseen Collapse of the Soviet Empire

By the early 1970s, the Union of Soviet Socialist Republics (i.e.; the U.S.S.R., or Soviet Union) was at the peak of its power. The Communist Party remained the sole political force in the Soviet Union, but decades of post-Stalinist economic reforms left the Soviet empire with a seemingly robust economy and an increased standard of living for Soviet citizens. Wages in the Soviet Union increased sharply. The Soviet Union was the world's leading producer of steel and oil. Urban dwellers enjoyed modern appliances, such as televisions and dishwashers, and lived mostly in numbers of newly-constructed single-family apartments never seen before in the Soviet Union.

In addition to these economic advantages at home, the Soviet Union attempted to assert itself as the world's dominant superpower. For nearly every Soviet success in the early 1970s, the United States suffered a setback. While the oil-rich Soviet economy continued to grow, the economy of the United States strained under the pressure of the OPEC imposed oil embargo of 1972 and 1973.

The Soviet Union also prevailed on the international stage. Soviet-backed North Vietnamese forces expelled American troops after a prolonged conflict. The communist victory in Vietnam, coupled with U.S. public opposition to the conflict, signaled an end to the American policy of communist containment in Southeast Asia. With further containment of communism in doubt, the United States had to reposition itself on the international scene. The administration of President Richard M. Nixon embarked on a policy of détente with China, culminating with Nixon's trip to China, and, to some degree, with the Soviet Union. The pace of Soviet nuclear weapon production greatly alarmed Washington. Fearing a Soviet advantage in the arms race, Nixon signed the Strategic Arms Limitations Talks (SALT I).

In addition to Southeast Asia, Soviet ideology was gaining support in other parts of the world, including Latin America. Soviet-supported troops in Central and South America alarmed American officials, who feared communist expansion in the Western Hemisphere. Still deeply

wounded by opposition to the Vietnam War, however, America resorted to conducting covert operations in Latin America. During the administration of President James E. Carter, communist backed Sandinistas overthrew Nicaragua's government. President Ronald Reagan later provided financial and material support to anti-Sandinista rebels. Reagan also backed anti-communist forces in El Salvador, even though Congress did not always agree with the White House on the issue of Nicaragua and El Salvador.

With proxy victories in Southeast Asia and Latin America and with a booming national economy, the power of the Soviet Union appeared formidable under Soviet Premier Leonid Brezhnev. To many outside observers, the Soviet Union appeared to be on the verge of winning the Cold War. The post-Brezhnev years, however, would see the internal collapse of the Soviet Union. Even while the Soviet Union was soaring to new heights, cracks were beginning to form in the monolithic empire. Economic troubles, military failures, and emerging nationalism would soon result in the end of the Soviet Union and communist régimes in Eastern Europe.

Economic Stagnation and the Arms Race

The vigorous Soviet economy of the late-1960s and early 1970s quickly fell victim to the very factors that had contributed to its success, central planning and raw materials allocation. Brezhnev recognized that the Soviet economy was slowing, and attempted to patch problems rather than completely overhaul the system. His efforts failed. Even if Brezhnev had attempted to overhaul the Soviet economy, the highly entrenched special interests that made their living by manipulating the Soviet Union's centrally planned economy could have defeated Brezhnev's efforts.

Throughout the 1970s and into the mid-1980s, the Soviet Union's GNP and industrial output continued to increase, but at a lessening pace, eventually leading to economic stagnation. The Ninth Five Year Plan (1970–1975) saw a growth rate of approximately 3%. The period of 1975–1980 experienced a growth rate of between 1% and 1.9%, depending on whether revised Soviet numbers or the West's estimate is examined. Likewise, 1980–1985 saw a further decline in economic growth, between 0.6% and 1.8%. Declining economic growth rates were not confined to the Soviet Union. Eastern Europe, with its economies intertwined with the Soviet Union's, suffered a similar fate.

This declining growth rate in the 1970s and 1980s resulted in the Soviet Union receiving a diminishing rate of return on capital investment. This proved disastrous for the Soviet economy, because by 1980, the Soviet Union was spending nearly one-third of its GNP on capital investment, with most of the sum dedicated to the military. The military was consuming such a large portion of the Soviet economy for two reasons: the Soviet involvement in Afghanistan and the arms race with the United States. These two events would weigh heavily in the Soviet economic demise and lead to its inevitable fall. A weak economy prevented the Soviet Union from reacting appropriately to each experience.

The stagnant Soviet economy of the 1970s would have faired far worse had it not been for vast oil and natural gas production propping up the economy. By the late 1970s, technological backwardness and poor management under the centrally planned Soviet economy resulted in depleted oil and gas reserves. This led Brezhnev to turn his eye towards the oil and gas reserves of Central Asia. Afghanistan had long been a relatively undeveloped country comprised of numerous semi-autonomous ethnic groups. Brezhnev assumed that the Soviet Union could achieve a quick and decisive victory over the country and expand its influence of Communism into Central Asia.

The United States and the rest of the world quickly condemned the Soviet invasion of Afghanistan in 1979. The United States also provided covert support to the mujahideen, or Afghani resistance fighters. Rapid turnover in Soviet leadership following the death of Brezhnev in 1982 also hampered the war effort. The short-lived régimes of Yuri Andropov and Konstantin Chernenko provided for an inconsistent Afghan policy. The Soviet military operation quickly bogged down and faced stiff resistance in the harsh terrain of Afghanistan.

The Soviets erroneously assumed that since the Afghans were economically disadvantaged, they would be quickly defeated and embrace communism. The opposite result happened. As the Afghans had little to lose by continuing to fight, instead of driving Afghanistan to communism, the Soviet invasion forged the Afgani Islamic resistance. A decade after the invasion, Soviet troops withdrew.

The war in Afghanistan had an even more adverse effect on the Soviet Union than the Vietnam War had on the United States. Thousands of Soviet troops died in a conflict that resulted in the defeat of a superpower by a developing country. Moreover, the conflict strained an already weak economy. The conflict angered Soviet citizens, and they began demanding accountability from the state. Brezhnev and his successors intended the war in Afghanistan to reassert the supremacy of the Soviet Union. Instead, the conflict proved that the superpower's might was waning.

The war in Afghanistan also distracted the Soviet Union from its arms race with the United States, thus allowing America to gain a technological advantage. The United States ratcheted up pressure on the U.S.S.R. through several means. The Reagan administration began placing missiles in Western Europe, primarily in Western Germany, strategically located to intimidate Eastern Europe and the Soviet Union. Reagan also began building up the U.S. military. Reagan commissioned new aircraft carriers and expanded America's stealth aircraft program. To the Soviets, these actions signaled a widening weapons gap, particularly in terms of technologically advanced weapons.

Perhaps the greatest threat to the Soviet Union was the United States' Strategic Defense Initiative (SDI), also known conventionally as Star Wars. The SDI was a planned satellite based weapons system that would detect and destroy missiles fired at the United States. Such a technological advancement would have rendered Soviet ICBMs useless. The Soviet Union tried to dissuade the United States from implementing the SDI, but the Reagan administration refused to back away from the proposal. In reality, the SDI was only in the technological planning stages; the Soviets, however, bought America's bluff, prompting a quick and expensive advance in their lagging military technology. This increased spending further accelerated the Soviet economic decline.

Realizing a weapons gap, the Soviet Union began pushing the Reagan administration for nuclear arms talks following the death of Brezhnev in 1982. The U.S. soon entered negotiations over the Strategic Arms Reduction Treaty (START). However, numerous changes in post-Brezhnev Soviet leadership, Solidarity strikes in Poland, and other issues prevented the completion of the START during the Reagan administration.

Gorbachev and the End of the Cold War

After a decade of over-inflated military expenditures, dwindling oil revenue, and a centrally-planned economy that was too rigid to adapt to consumer demands, Mikhail Gorbachev, upon assuming office, declared the Soviet economy to be in a "pre-crisis." Gorbachev immediately transformed the face of Soviet politics. Gorbachev quickly appointed new members to the Politboro and Secretariat, ridding each of many hardline, longtime bureaucrats. Gorbachev also attempted to reform the KGB, replacing many agents and bureaucrats. Despite the shake-up, the KGB's operational power emerged from Gorbachev's early reforms relatively unscathed.

After reforming the government, Gorbachev set out to reform the economy and ultimately, Soviet society. Gorbachev's economic reforms (*perestroika,* or restructuring), were perceived as noble, but poorly executed. The Twelfth Five Year Plan tried ambitiously and quickly to reform the Soviet economy. Gorbachev sought to update industrial equipment and computer systems, while simultaneously expecting workers to produce higher quality products in greater quantities. Gorbachev also tried to decentralize the economy by giving different regions greater control over industry. All of these goals proved to be unrealistic given Gorbachev's timetable to dismantle the gargantuan Soviet bureaucracy in favor of a more streamlined and efficient system.

By 1986, Gorbachev also began experimenting with the notion that greater democracy, if presented in the proper format, would lead to increased socialism. Gorbachev wanted to strip away Stalinism and its accompanying bureaucracy and return to the communism of Lenin. Initially, Gorbachev underestimated the effect that allowing Soviet citizens to question the past, in particular the brutality of Stalin, would have upon the citizenry, leading them to follow their lines of questioning up to the present day. Soon, however, Gorbachev came to accept and embrace the concept that he termed *glasnost,* or "openness."

Glasnost initially allowed only the divulgence of information by the state. Gorbachev held that if the Soviet Union was more open and honest about its past, then Soviet and Eastern European citizens would be more likely to follow Gorbachev's economic lead. Even a large number of bureaucrats in the KGB supported glasnost. The KGB's information network had become burdened and as ineffective as the bureaucracy that it supported. Therefore, many KGB officials assumed that fostering an atmosphere of openness would result in new and better informants.

Although Gorbachev intended glasnost to strengthen the communist régime, he did not initiate a crack-down when Soviet citizens went beyond the original intent of glasnost. Soviet intellectuals began questioning the very tenets of Soviet Communism and attacked the Communist Party in newspapers, journals, film, and books. Eastern European thinkers followed the lead of their Soviet counterparts.

Consequently, glasnost had the unintended effect of spurring nationalist and anti-communist movements in Eastern Europe and the Soviet republics. Dissidents in Poland, East Germany, Czechoslovakia, and other Soviet-satellite states staged labor demonstrations. Citizens took to the streets, demanding that the Communist Party step aside and allow democratic elections. In fall 1989, the Berlin Wall, long a symbol of the division between Eastern Europe and the world, fell, allowing East and West Berliners to cross freely. The Communist Party and its East Germany secret police organization, the Stasi, had lost power. Within months of the fall of the Berlin Wall, other Eastern European countries broke away from Moscow's influence and expelled their communist leaders. With the exception of Romania, most of the revolutions of 1989 and early 1990 were relatively peaceful.

In the wake of the Eastern European revolts and the euphoria that followed, the Soviet Union had little choice but to allow greater freedoms. In February, 1990, the Communist Party agreed to relinquish its political monopoly. Many of the civic groups that had been voicing displeasure with the Soviet system formed political parties. Most of these new parties, especially those outside of Russia had a nationalist agenda. Within a month, the Baltic republic of Lithuania declared itself an independent state. Other Soviet republics quickly followed.

In June 1991, Gorbachev allowed free elections to choose a president of the Russian Republic. Boris Yeltsin, a former Gorbachev-supporter, won a landslide victory over Gorbachev's chosen candidate. In August, 1991, a group of communists hardliners attempted a poorly organized coup while Gorbachev was on vacation at the Black Sea. The coup failed, and strengthened Boris Yeltsin, the primary target of the coup. The coup also undermined the leadership of Gorbachev, who continued to govern ineffectively until his resignation on December 25, 1991. The following day, the Supreme Soviet officially declared an end to the Soviet Union.

Civil Rights and the Cold War

During the cold war, civil rights violations within the United States captured the interest of the world, causing many to wonder whether race discrimination undermined the nation's global leadership. How could American democracy be a model for the world to follow, peoples of other nations asked, when within the United States citizens were disenfranchised, segregated, and sometimes lynched because of their race? Discrimination was widely seen as the nation's Achilles' heel.

In 1947, after violent attacks on African American World War II veterans in the South raised concern at home and abroad, President Harry S. Truman's Committee on Civil Rights issued a report which argued that the United States needed to improve its civil rights record, in part because race discrimination harmed U.S. foreign relations. By the late 1940s, the Soviet Union used racial discrimination in America as a principal anti-U.S. propaganda theme. Soviet propaganda was often exaggerated, but propaganda on race was particularly effective, simply because there was so much truth to it.

Global interest gave the civil rights movement international allies. In 1947 W. E. B. Du Bois wrote a petition for the National Association for the Advancement of Colored People (NAACP) to the new United Nations, "An Appeal to the World," to enlist U.N. support for the rights of African Americans. Du Bois, Paul Robeson, and others who criticized American race discrimination in an international context, lost their passports during the 1950s. Meanwhile, through the Voice of America and overseas information programs, the U.S. government tried to rehabilitate the image of American race relations, casting it as a story of enlightened progress under democracy. Some civil rights leaders, such as NAACP Executive Secretary Walter White, were staunchly anti-Communist and tried to aid the effort to convince peoples of other nations that African Americans could flourish in the United States, and that democracy was a better system of government than communism. Ultimately, however, American leaders believed that only civil rights progress would dampen the negative effect of racial problems on U.S. foreign relations.

In 1952 the Justice Department filed an Amicus Curiae brief in support of school desegregation in *Brown v. Board of Education* (1954), citing Secretary of State Dean Acheson as authority, and arguing that a crucial national interest was at stake in the case: foreign relations. When the Supreme Court ruled that segregation was unconstitutional, the decision was celebrated around the world. A challenge soon arose when Arkansas governor Orval Faubus blocked nine African American students from attending Little Rock's Central High School (1957). The Little Rock Crisis generated global criticism, and led jazz artist Louis Armstrong to cancel a State Department–sponsored trip to the Soviet Union; if "people over there ask me what's wrong with my country," Armstrong asked, "what am I supposed to say?" (Giddins 2001, p. 127). President Dwight D. Eisenhower, concerned with damage to U.S. foreign relations and other factors, sent in federal troops to escort the students into school. The world press lauded the president for putting the force of the U.S. government behind civil rights.

International interest gave the civil rights movement important leverage in the 1960s. The Nobel Peace Prize awarded to Martin Luther King Jr. in 1964 was one sign of global support. When Police Commissioner Eugene "Bull" Connor ordered fire fighters and police to use high-powered fire-hoses and police dogs on civil rights demonstrators marching in Birmingham, Alabama, in 1963, images of these violent tactics filled the world press. Domestic and international pressure led President John F. Kennedy to call for a strong civil rights bill. Passage of the Civil Rights Act of 1964 was celebrated around the world as a sign that the U.S. government was firmly behind civil rights reform. Formal legal change helped restore the image of America, even though inequities in American communities remained.

THE BLACKLIST

In Hollywood, the wave of anti-Communist investigation that was later termed "McCarthyism" actually began in 1947, three years before Senator Joseph McCarthy (1908–1957) embarked on his personal crusade (eventually becoming chair of the Subcommittee on Investigations in the US Senate). The House Un-American Activities Committee (HUAC) had convened before the war to investigate allegations of Communist influence in the movie industry but suspended its activities for the duration of the war. In 1947 Chairman J. Parnell Thomas (1895–1970), replacing the late Martin Dies, interrogated the "unfriendly" witnesses who became known as the Hollywood Ten. For refusing to answer questions that would have involved implicating others, the Ten were convicted of "contempt of Congress" and mostly served short prison sentences before emerging to face unemployability. The Ten would have been Eleven, but Bertolt Brecht (1898–1956)—whose latest work, significantly, was a play about Galileo—pretended not to understand English well enough to answer questions in his first session, then fled the country. After years of appeals, two of the Hollywood Ten, Lester Cole and Ring Lardner Jr. (1915–2000), arrived in Danbury Prison to serve their terms, only to find Congressman Thomas, convicted in the interim of embezzling from the federal purse, among their fellow inmates.

The Hollywood Communists suffered for slipping "subversive" dialogue into scripts: the line "hare and share alike, that's democracy" in Edward Dmytryk's (1908–1999) *Tender Comrade* (1943) tipped off Ginger Rogers's (1911–1995) mother that the writer Dalton Trumbo (1905–1976) was a Red. Yet it is hard to detect traces of anything that might count as Communist or even socialist propaganda in any of the films, good or bad, made by the Ten. The Ten were mostly talented journeymen: Cole, writer of *The Invisible Man Returns* (1939), which has a miners' strike subplot; Lardner, who later wrote *M*A*S*H* (1970); Trumbo, who wrote *A Guy Named Joe* (1943) and *Spartacus* (1960); Dmytryk, director of *Captive Wild Woman* (1943) and *Murder, My Sweet* (1944); John Howard Lawson (1895–1977), writer of *Terror in a Texas Town* (1958); Herbert Biberman (1900–1971), director of *Meet Nero Wolfe* (1936), writer of *King of*

Chinatown (1939); Adrian Scott (1912–1973), producer of *Murder, My Sweet* and *Crossfire* (1947); Alvah Bessie, writer of *Northern Pursuit* (1943) and *Hotel Berlin* (1945); Albert Maltz, writer of *This Gun for Hire* (1942) and *The Man in Half Moon Street* (1944); and Samuel Ornitz (1890–1957), writer of *Hit Parade of 1937* (1937) and *Little Orphan Annie* (1939).

Other "unfriendlies," former or current radicals eventually blacklisted, included actors Gale Sondergaard (1899–1985), John Garfield (1913–1952), Kim Hunter (1922–2002), Zero Mostel (1915–1977), and Lionel Stander (1909–1994), writers Dashiell Hammett (1894–1961) (who went stubbornly to jail), Carl Foreman (1914–1984), and Walter Bernstein (b. 1919) (who dealt with the period in his autobiographical script *The Front*, 1976), and directors Joseph Losey (1909–1984), Jules Dassin (b. 1911), and Cy Endfield (1914–1995). Most of these had, at one time or another, been "card-carrying" Communists, that is, members of the American Communist Party (CPUSA). Some directors (Losey, Endfield) went to Europe and eventually became successful there; some writers used pseudonyms or fronts until it was safe to be credited again. Many endured long periods of forced inactivity. Abraham Polonsky (1910–1999) did not direct between *Force of Evil* (1948) and *Tell Them Willie Boy Is Here* (1969), managing only one further feature in the remaining thirty years of his life. On the strength of his debut feature, it seems obvious that without the blacklist he would have had a career at least on a level with Edward Dmytryk (who eventually named names) and possibly on a level with Elia Kazan (1909–2003) (who famously became a "friendly"). Actors, of course, were hardest hit of all: some (Sam Wanamaker [1919–1993]) became refugees, but others cracked and informed (Lee J. Cobb [1911–1976], Sterling Hayden [1916–1986], Lloyd Bridges [1913–1998]) to resume their careers.

Under Thomas, HUAC obsessively alleged that "Red writers" insidiously worked the Party Line into Metro-Goldwyn-Mayer musicals or Fox thrillers, polluting the minds of American audiences. Investigations failed to turn up *any* concrete incidences of subversion beyond Lionel Stander whistling "Internationale" while waiting for an elevator in *No Time to Marry* (1938). Subtly, the thrust of the crusade changed: as in later investigations into the civil services, universities, and other spheres, including dentistry and the US mail, the purpose of the Hollywood hearings was to render unemployed and unemployable anyone who was or had been a Communist or "fellow traveler." Liberals like John Huston (1906–1987) or Kirk Douglas (b. 1916) survived only through canniness —a combination of undoubted box office track record, token anti-Red statements (or films), and an independent streak that would lead to work outside the troubled studio system (other federal committees were breaking up monopolies on exhibition and production), eventually becoming free of the powers who could actually draw up and enforce blacklists.

There was, of course, no formal blacklist. It operated on threat and innuendo, with a complex system of extortion, blackmail, and intimidation, even including approved methods for getting off the list through strategic self-abasement (cooperation with the FBI) or actual bribery. Initially, the blacklisted were names compiled by HUAC for their hearings, but the work was taken up enthusiastically by the American Legion and a private firm called American Business Consultants, who "exposed" subversives in their publications (*Firing Line, Counterattack, Red Channels*). If studios continued to hire those named, the studios would become the victims of organized boycott campaigns. In television, pressure was brought not on the broadcast companies but on the sponsors who underwrote their programs. Mistakes were made—actress Martha Scott (1914–2003) was confused with singer Hazel Scott (1920–1981) and was blacklisted.

Studio heads, their power eroded by other factors (television, antitrust legislation, impatient heirs), embraced the blacklist as a "bolting the stable door after the horse has gone" measure. Few of the men who had founded the studio system in the 1920s were in office by the end of the decade, but they tended to be eased into extraordinarily monied retirement, whereas a great many of their former employees were ostracized, persecuted, denied their professions, and forced into poverty.

THE COLD WAR COMES TO HOLLYWOOD

Anthony Mann's (1907–1967) *Strategic Air Command* (1955) opens with Dutch Holland (James Stewart), a professional baseball player, being approached by his former commanding officer and asked to reenlist in the peacetime air force. "Where's the fire?" asks Dutch, who has done "his share" in two wars, seconded by a 1950s wife (June Allyson) who wants him at their home in the suburbs, not off on some far-flung base. But the thrust of the film is that it is Dutch's duty to get back in harness and maintain the peace against the ever-present (if rarely specified) Russian threat. The fetishist treatment of weapons of mass destruction, central to Stanley Kubrick's (1928–1999) *Dr. Strangelove, or: How I Learned to Stop Worrying and Love the Bomb* (1964), begins here. Mann's camera ogles the lines and curves of the B-47 that Stewart (a real-life bomber pilot) gets to fly (with the new family of nuclear weapons, a B-47 with a crew of three carries the destructive power of the entire B-29 forces used in World War II). Dutch's eventual commitment to the Strategic Air Command seems to suggest that his plane is sexier than the starched, maternal Allyson.

At first, Hollywood reacted to the Cold War much like Dutch, when he was asked to stop playing ball and start practicing bomb runs. After years of turning out war propaganda, a policy the movies embraced before the government (e.g., *Confessions of a Nazi Spy*, Anatole Litvak, 1939), the studios felt they had done their "share" and believed that audiences wanted Technicolor musical escapism or *film noir* romantic agonies rather than more gray, grim, depressing privation-leads-to-victory stories. If anything, Hollywood needed to mop up after World War II, tracking down Nazi war criminals who might be infiltrating America (*The Stranger*, Orson Welles, 1946) or reflecting on the situations of returning veterans who found their homeland not quite the paradise they thought they were fighting for. A wave of films, many made by people who would soon be facing HUAC, dealt with heroic black, Jewish, or even Nisei soldiers suffering from bigotry or racial assault, including murder: *Crossfire* (Edward Dmytryk, 1947), *Gentleman's Agreement* (Elia Kazan, 1947), *Home of the Brave* (Mark Robson, 1949), and *Bad Day at Black Rock* (1955) by John Sturges (1911–1993). A decade before *Strategic Air Command*, Dana Andrews found his war record suited him for no peacetime employment and rendered him as obsolete as the fields of junked bombers in *The Best Years of Our Lives* (1946) by William Wyler (1902–1981). Within a few years, films like this (another Oscar® winner) would be seen as either suspect or anti-American.

THE "HIP" COLD WAR

Ian Fleming's (1908–1964) early James Bond novels, published in the 1950s, often pit the British superspy against SMERSH, a division ("Death to Spies") of Soviet intelligence. When Bond (Sean Connery) emerged in film, from *Dr. No* (1962) on, SMERSH was downplayed in favor of SPECTRE, a fantastical, apolitical criminal organization along the lines of those once run by Dr. Mabuse or Fu Manchu. In the novel *From Russia with Love*, plans are laid against Bond by SMERSH, but in the 1964 film, the Soviets subcontract the job to SPECTRE. Though theoretically a Cold Warrior, Bond has in later films as often allied with Russians as clashed with them. Even the title *From Russia with Love* suggests a thaw in relations.

In the Kennedy-Krushchev period, when the Cold War chess game (a recurrent image in the media) seemed to become more deadly over missiles in Cuba (and Turkey), popular culture was inclined to take a more cynical, callous attitude to the superpower face-off. The key film is *The Manchurian Candidate* (1962) by John Frankenheimer (1930–2002), scripted by George Axelrod (1922–2003) from Richard Condon's (1915–1996) novel, which caricatures McCarthy as the know-nothing Senator John Yerkes Iselin (James Gregory), who picks the easy-to-remember number (57) of Communists he claims to have identified in the State Department off a ketchup bottle, and partners him with a monstrous wife (Angela Lansbury) who wants him swept into the White House with "powers which will make martial law look like anarchy." This indictment of the blacklist mind-set coexists with plot developments that suggest McCarthy was not paranoid *enough*. The Iselins are actually Communist tools out to undermine America (the inspiration is the suggestion that McCarthy could not have hurt the United States more if he were a paid Soviet agent); Mrs. Iselin has collaborated with the transformation of her own son, Raymond (Laurence Harvey), through brainwashing by Sino-Soviet villains into a zombie assassin.

The Manchurian Candidate is a thriller meant to shock, signified by the splattering of blood and brains over a poster of Stalin during a demonstration of Raymond's killing abilities. It has a certain "plague on both your houses" tone, far more vicious in its attack than Peter Ustinov's (1921–2004) across-the-curtain romantic comedy *Romanoff and Juliet* (1961), and it is as much remembered for its prescience in the matter of presidential assassination and conspiracy theory as its acute dissection of the paranoia of both West and East. A stark, black-and-white nightmare, with stylish bursts of martial arts action and walking political cartoons, its zero-degree cool bled into the highly colored cynicism of the Bond films. These wallow in luxury and voluptuousness, brush off murders with flip remarks ("shocking!"), and routinely climax with an intricate world-threatening scheme, foiled by individual heroism and the prompt arrival of an Anglo-American assault team to overwhelm the diabolical mastermind's secret base. These tactics failed in the real world at the Bay of Pigs, an operation badly fumbled by Bond fan Kennedy, just as the Cuban missile crisis led to closer scrutiny of the mechanics of the balance of terror.

Dr. Strangelove, like Sidney Lumet's (b. 1924) more serious *Fail-Safe* (1964), is a brink-of-doom thriller, a possible prequel to all those "life-in-the-radioactive-ruins" quickies of the 1950s (*Five*, 1951; *The Day the World Ended*, 1956; *The World, the Flesh and the Devil*, 1959). Here, the world is not imperiled by aggressive ideologies but by neuroses—a US Air Force general (Sterling Hayden), driven by impotence to rail against the Communist threat to his "precious bodily fluids," and a Soviet régime that invests in a cheap Doomsday Machine because the people are clamoring for washing machines. In a way, Kubrick's film—a satire adapted from a dead-straight novel, *Red Alert* (1958) by Peter George (1924–1966)—is a sigh of relief that the world has come through Korea and Cuba without self-annihilation, but it is also an awful warning and a declaration that a third world war cannot be won. *Invasion USA* (1952) is the only American atomic war film to suggest that after nuclear attack, the Communist enemy would attempt to occupy the United States like stereotypical conquerors. Later films (including the Yugoslav *Rat*, 1960) blame both sides equally, with war as likely to result from accident or a failure of diplomacy. The ultimate message of *The War Game* (1967) by Peter Watkins (b. 1935) is that governments should not be trusted with nuclear weapons, while *Ladybug Ladybug* (Frank Perry, 1963)—echoing an outstanding *Twilight Zone* episode, "The Shelter"—goes so far as to suggest that civil preparedness contributes to a breakdown of society, as shelter-owners arm themselves not against the military enemy but their own neighbors.

The 1960s saw many fantastical Bondian superspies (the Flint and Matt Helm adventures), Strangelovian satires (*The Russians Are Coming! The Russians Are Coming!*, Norman Jewison, 1966; *The President's Analyst*, Theodore J. Flicker, 1967), and "realistic" espionage dramas (*The Spy Who Came In from the Cold*, Martin Ritt, 1965; *The Ipcress File*, Sidney J. Furie, 1965) riffing on the Cold War. Taking their cue from *The Manchurian Candidate*, all these films tend to suggest that "our side" is as bad (or, less often, good) as "their side"—the mission of the *Spy Who Came In from the Cold* is to discredit a clever and idealistic Jewish East German counterintelligence agent to save a former Nazi working as a double agent for the West—and, eventually, that the power elites of both sides are so dependent on the Cold War to retain their positions that they have become interchangeable.

As in so much later twentieth-century history, events suggest George Orwell's (1903–1950) novel *Nineteen Eighty-Four* (1949), in which a permanent state of hostilities is an excuse for the real war, waged by rulers against the populace. From the mid-1960s, popular culture shifted from worrying about the Communists to that other deadly prong of the 1950s, rock and roll (representing youth, rebellion, and even unrestrained capitalist consumerism)—but was unsure whether to worry or celebrate. With *Bonnie and Clyde* (Arthur Penn, 1967), *Easy Rider* (Dennis Hopper, 1969), and *Night of the Living Dead* (George A. Romero, 1968) offering counterarguments to increasingly uncomfortable Americanist crusades like John Wayne's *The Green Berets* (1968), battle lines were drawn for new wars, between young and old, powerful and powerless, black and white, hip and square. Old-style patriotism would resurge in the Reagan years (1980–1988), but even the red-bashing Rambo is by no means simplistic, as he grapples with masculinity, the legacy of Vietnam, and America's self-image. When the Berlin Wall came down in 1989, few victory parades were held in America. The movies were not there—

round-the-clock news footage had told the story so quickly that it was stale by the time a film (e.g., Frankenheimer's *The Fourth War*, 1990) could be made.

The Berlin Airlift

Europe's economy was in crisis after World War II. By 1947, the Soviets had taken over much of Eastern Europe using the strength of the Red (Soviet) Army. As communism spread throughout Eastern Europe, the United States began a postwar recovery program known as the Marshall Plan. The plan helped restore Western Europe's economy. The Soviet Union its communist satellite nations of Eastern Europe opposed the plan, fearing the revival of the German economy, as well as the implication that free-market capitalist measures (and not a Marxist planned economy) were viable solutions to Europe's woes.

After World War II, the victorious Allies —the United States, Great Britain, France, and the Soviet Union—had agreed to divide defeated Germany into four zones, each of which was occupied by one of the Allies. Germany's capital, Berlin, was similarly divided into four sectors. Because of the city's location in the Soviet-occupied part of Germany (what later became communist East Germany), the U.S., British, and French sectors of Berlin were completely surrounded by the Soviet occupation zone. In 1948, the Soviet Union restricted access into West Berlin in 1948 by setting up blockades into the city. As of June 24, the city was not accessible by road, train, or canal. It had enough coal to last forty-five days and enough food to last thirty-six days. President Truman had to maintain a Western presence in the city if the Marshall Plan was to be successful. On June 26, he officially approved what became known as the Berlin airlift. During the airlift, which lasted 321 days, planes delivered daily supplies of coal, food, and other necessities to the more than two million people living in Berlin behind the blockade. By May 12, 1949—the end of the airlift—1,592,787 tons of supplies had been delivered to

Berlin. It was a magnificent achievement that cost very few lives. When the Soviet Union realized that the airlift could continue indefinitely, Stalin was forced to back down and remove the blockades.

CUBA, VIETNAM, AND THE PRAGUE SPRING, 1962–1969

East Germany was a Soviet showpiece in the Cold War. Another, more recent, was Cuba. After Fidel Castro (b. 1926) and his guerrillas seized power from a corrupt but pro-American régime in 1959, they became increasingly dependent on Soviet aid as they turned the country into a socialist state. Cuba was only ninety miles from America, and Kennedy did his best to overthrow the Castro government. In the autumn of 1962 Khrushchev responded by introducing medium-range nuclear missiles into Cuba. He tried to do so secretly, but American spy planes detected the buildup and Kennedy went public on 22 October, announcing a blockade of the island. After an increasingly frenzied week of negotiation, Khrushchev, aware that the U.S. nuclear arsenal was far superior to his own, backed down and pulled out the missiles. This massive humiliation, played out on the world stage, was a major factor in his enforced resignation in 1964.

But Kennedy's advantage was short-lived. He was assassinated in November 1963, having already laid the groundwork for America's own nemesis—Vietnam. After the French pulled out of this divided country in 1954, the United States propped up the anticommunist régime in the south with massive amounts of aid, and in 1960 the North embarked on a massive guerrilla war. Kennedy, seeing Vietnam as a Cold War test case of American virility, began to introduce "military advisors." Although the Soviets were not anxious to escalate the conflict, the increasingly radical government of China, now bitterly at odds with Russia, provided aid to the North, and Moscow had to follow suit or lose face in the communist world. With South Vietnam in danger of collapse in 1965, Kennedy's successor, Lyndon B. Johnson (1908–1973), committed combat troops and started massive bombing of North Vietnam. But his escalation failed to end the conflict and also caused immense popular protest in America and across the world.

The growing anti-American feeling in Western Europe was reflected at the top of the Western alliance. Critical of what he saw as excessive American domination, the French president Charles de Gaulle (1890–1970) withdrew his country from NATO's integrated command system in 1966.

But the 1960s also brought another reminder of the nature of Soviet rule. Reformers in Czechoslovakia under Alexander Dubček (1921–1992) promoted democratic change in what became known as the "Prague Spring." Eventually Warsaw Pact troops reimposed Soviet control in August 1968—another military success that was also a propaganda disaster.

Implications of the Communist World's Collapse

Stated simply, the Cold War ended in 1989–1991 when most of the world's communist régimes collapsed, Germany was reunited, and the Soviet Union ceased to exist. In that sense, the West and especially the

United States won the Cold War. This was certainly the verdict of many American conservatives.

But other factors mattered as well. Leaders, for instance, were crucial, particularly in the Soviet Union: the Cold War grew out of Stalin's paranoid sense of insecurity; conversely, Gorbachev's belief that security was not a zero-sum game helped bring it to an end.

The Cold War was also a phase in social history. It was made possible by the development of mass media, particularly television and film, and their use by governments to shape public ideology in the Soviet Union and the United States. The explosion of new electronic media under looser official control ushered in a new historical era. Equally important in the Soviet bloc was the growth of an educated middle class, which made Stalinism increasingly difficult to maintain.

At the time, the Cold War seemed an all-encompassing phenomenon, particularly to Americans. Yet much associated with the Cold War has outlived it. The People's Republic of China—the world's most populous country and a coming power of the twenty-first century—is still a communist state, albeit in modified form. Final verdicts on Marxism-Leninism will depend heavily on how China evolves. And although the Cold War and the atomic bomb came of age together in 1945, the problem of nuclear weapons has survived the Soviet collapse. Evaluating the Cold War and its legacies will preoccupy historians for decades to come.

TOTALITARIANISM IN THE 20TH CENTURY

Left to right: Marx, Engels, Lenin, Stalin, Mao.

Totalitarianism is a concept rooted in the horror of modern war, revolution, terror, genocide, and, since 1945, the threat of nuclear annihilation. It is also among the most versatile and contested terms in the political lexicon. At its simplest, the idea suggests that despite Fascist/Nazi "particularism" (the centrality of the nation or the master race) and Bolshevist "universalism" (the aspiration toward a classless, international brotherhood of man), both régimes were basically alike— which, as Carl Friedrich noted early on, is not to claim that they were wholly alike. Extreme in its denial of liberty, totalitarianism conveys a régime type with truly radical ambitions. Its chief objectives are to rule unimpeded by legal restraint, civic pluralism, and party competition, and to refashion human nature itself.

Coined in May 1923 by Giovanni Amendola, *totalitarianism* began life as a condemnation of Fascist ambitions to monopolize power and to transform Italian society through the creation of a new political religion. The word then quickly mutated to encompass National Socialism, especially after the Nazi "seizure of power" in 1933. By the mid-1930s, invidious comparisons among the German, Italian, and Soviet systems as totalitarian were becoming common; they increased considerably once the Nazi-Soviet pact was signed in 1939. Meanwhile, recipients of the totalitarian label took different views of it. Although, in the mid 1920s, Benito Mussolini and his ideologues briefly embraced the expression as an apt characterization of their revolutionary élan, Nazi politicians and propagandists saw a disconcerting implication. Granted, Adolf Hitler and Joseph Goebbels, during the early 1930s, had a penchant for cognate expressions such as "total state"; so, too, did sympathetic writers such as Ernst Forsthoff and Carl Schmitt. At around the same time, Ernst Jünger was busy expounding his idea of "total mobilization." But "totalitarianism" was treated with greater circumspection. The *Volksgemeinschaft* (national community), Nazi spokesmen insisted, was unique: the vehicle of an inimitable German destiny based on a national, racially based, rebirth. *Totalitarianism* suggested that German aspirations were a mere variant on a theme; worse, a theme that current usage extrapolated to the Bolshevist foe.

Once Fascism and Nazism were defeated, a new global conflict soon emerged, and with it a reinvigorated role for "totalitarianism." Anxiety over Soviet ambitions in Europe prompted Churchill's use of the term twice in his "Iron Curtain" speech on March 5, 1946, at Fulton, Missouri. A year later, the Truman Doctrine entrenched the word in American foreign policy and security jargon. Then the Cold War took its course, punctuated by the Berlin Airlift, the building of the Berlin Wall, the Sino-Soviet treaties, the Korean War, the Cuban Missile Crisis, and the Hungarian, Czech, and Polish uprisings. At each turn, the language of totalitarianism received a further boost, though there were significant national variations in the credence it received. In the United States, the language of totalitarianism, despite dissenting voices, had wide appeal across the political spectrum. In France, by contrast, it had practically none until the decay of existentialism and the appearance of Solzhenitsyn's work on the Soviet Gulag triggered a major attitudinal shift. Postwar Germany represents an intermediate case: officially sanctioned by the Federal Republic, *totalitarianism* became the focus of major intellectual controversy from the late 1960s onward.

Even periods of engagement with the Soviet Union—notably détente and the Ronald Reagan–Mikhail Gorbachev dialogue—stimulated debate over totalitarianism. Some commentators optimistically announced its softening and demise, while others deplored collaborating with the totalitarian enemy. During the Soviet Union's last decade, Western academics and foreign policy experts argued over the distinction between two kinds of régime. Authoritarian régimes (sometimes also called "traditional" or "autocratic") typified the apartheid state in South Africa, Iran under the Pahlavis, and the South American military juntas. Though hierarchical, vicious, and unjust, they had limited goals, and they left large parts of society (religious practice, family, and work relations) untouched. Conceivably, they were capable of reformist evolution toward representative government. In contrast, totalitarian régimes were depicted as utopian, inherently expansionist, and indelibly tyrannical, an evil empire. Treating them as normal states was folly. Meanwhile, in central Europe, embattled oppositionists during the late 1970s and 1980s were coining terms that suggested novel permutations on the classical model. "Post-totalitarian" régimes, suggested Václav Havel in *The Power of the Powerless* (1978), retained a brutal apparatus of coercion but were no longer able to enthuse their populations with faith. Resistance required puncturing a hollow, mechanically recited ideology by everyday acts of noncompliance and by "living in truth" (that is, by speaking and acting honestly).

Following the collapse of the Soviet Union, twenty-first-century Islamism and the "war against terror" continued to keep the idea of totalitarianism salient. Yet if all these experiences are inseparable from the discourse of totalitarianism, its longevity has also been promoted by three rather different factors. One factor is the term's elasticity. It can be applied either to institutions or to ideologies, to governments or to movements, or to some combination of all of these. Additionally, it can be invoked to delineate an extant reality or a desire, myth, aim, tendency, experiment, and project. *Total* and its cognates (*totality, total war,* etc.) are commonplaces of the current age, so it is unsurprising that *totalitarianism* is also one. A second factor, more important still, is the role played by journalists, novelists, poets, playwrights, and filmmakers in publicly disseminating the images of totalitarian domination. Their role was to ensure that totalitarianism never became a recondite, academic term but one central to the vernacular of educated people. Totalitarianism was a buzzword of political journalism before it received, in the late 1940s and 1950s, searching treatment by social science and political theory. Its first literary masterpiece was Arthur Koestler's *Darkness at Noon* (1941) with its sinister portrayal of the Communist confessional. Many great works on a similar theme followed, making totalitarianism vivid and unforgettable to readers electrified by the pathos and terror such writing evoked.

Still, no novelist is more responsible for the notion that totalitarianism penetrates the entire human personality, dominating it from within, than George Orwell (Eric Arthur Blair, 1903–1950). That view appeared nothing less than prescient when stories later circulated in the 1950s about "brainwashing" of captured prisoners of war (POWs) during the Korean War. Orwell deserves a special place in any historical audit of totalitarianism for another reason. *Nineteen Eighty Four* (1949) introduced terms—"Thought Police," "Big Brother," "Doublethink"—that have since entered the English language as unobtrusively as those of Shakespeare and the King James Bible. So long as his work appears in the secondary school and university curricula, totalitarianism as an idea will survive. In a similar way, no one is more responsible for informing a general public about the Soviet Gulag than Aleksandr Solzhenitsyn (b. 1918). To his extraordinary novels, memoirs, and what he called "experiments in literary investigation," one may add the work of Osip Mandelstam, Nadezhda Mandelstam, Anna Akhmatova, Boris Souvarine, and Boris Pasternak. Each bequeathed a searing portrait of the depravity and recklessness of "totalitarian" systems.

Finally, totalitarianism's endurance as a term owes much to its capacity for provocative and counterintuitive application. It was not only heterodox Marxists such as Herbert Marcuse who indicted modern pluralist régimes for a systemically imbecilic, one-dimensional, and totalitarian mass culture. Liberals such as Friedrich Hayek also warned in 1944 of totalitarian developmental tendencies—particularly the fetish with state planning and intervention—that were paving the "road to serfdom." Many critics of the New Deal took a similar view; Herbert Hoover notoriously called Franklin Delano Roosevelt a "totalitarian liberal." Also disquieting was the sociologist Erving Goffman's contention in *Asylums* (1961) that Nazi death camps were broadly comparable to widely accepted "total institutions" such as the asylum, prison, barracks, and orphanage. The implication was that totalitarianism was not an exotic species of régime "over there" but a legitimized institution or trend deeply embedded within modernity as a whole.

Origins, Trajectory, Causation

Theorists of totalitarianism take very different views of its origins. For some, Hannah Arendt foremost among them, totalitarianism is radically new, an unprecedented development that attended Europe's economic, political, and moral ruination during and after World War I. From this perspective, attempts to locate a long-established lineage of totalitarianism are fundamentally mistaken. So, too, are analogies of totalitarianism with Caesarist, Bonapartist, and other dictatorial régimes. Totalitarianism is conjunctural or unique, not an extreme version of something previously known. The point of using the term is precisely to show the novelty of the régime type and the crisis it denotes. Other writers, conversely, believe that totalitarianism has deeper roots. Hence it might be said that totalitarianism is a perverted outgrowth of the Martin Luther–sanctioned authoritarian state, or an exaggerated legacy of tsarist intolerance. Or it might be agued that "totalitarian dictatorship" is ancient, prefigured in the Spartan state or the Roman imperial régime of Diocletian (r. 284–305). That was the judgment of Franz Neumann, who in addition claimed that National Socialism had revived the "fascist dictatorship" methods of the fourteenth-century Roman demagogue Cola di Rienzo. Nor, according to still others, should totalitarianism be understood as an exclusively occidental institution. Karl Wittfogel in *Oriental Despotism* (1957) found "total power" in the hydraulic governance of ancient China. And while sinologists have major reservations about describing Maoism as totalitarian, victims such as Harry Wu, imprisoned for nineteen years in the Chinese Laogai, exhibit no such compunction. Totalitarianism has also been located in Africa, for instance, in the rule of Shaka Zulu, while the Soviet Union itself was often depicted as a hybrid entity, more "Asian" than Western.

The search for the roots of totalitarian ideas, as distinct from institutions, has generated yet another fertile literature. Karl Popper found protototalitarianism in Plato. Max Horkheimer and Theodor Adorno spied a totalitarian dialectic evolving out of an "Enlightenment" fixation on mathematical formalization, instrumental reason, and the love of the machine. J. L. Talmon discovered a creedal, "totalitarian democracy" arising from one tendency among eighteenth-century philosophies. Enunciated by Jean-Jacques Rousseau (1712–1778), Morelly (fl. mid-eighteenth century), and Gabriel Bonnot de Mably (1709–1785); radicalized by the French Revolution, especially during its Jacobin phase; reincarnated in the Babouvist conspiracy, "totalitarian democracy" amounted to a leftist "political messianism" that preached the arrival of a new order: homogenous, egalitarian, yet supervised by a virtuous revolutionary vanguard able to divine the general will. This reminds one of Alexis de Tocqueville's observation, in *The Ancien Regime and the French Revolution* (1856), that the Revolution's "ideal" was nothing less than "a regeneration of the whole human race. It created an atmosphere of missionary fervor and, indeed, assumed all the aspects of a religious revival." That "strange religion," he continued, "has, like Islam, overrun the whole world with its apostles, militants, and martyrs" (p. 44).

Tocqueville's reference to Islam was deliberately discomfiting. It reminded his audience of what a modern "enlightened" European revolution shared with a declining Oriental civilization. Less than a century later, Bertrand Russell augmented that idea when he suggested that Bolshevism was like Islam, while John Maynard Keynes, in lapidary mood, remarked that "Lenin [was] a Mahomet, and not a Bismarck." Yet since Al Qaeda's suicide attack on the World Trade Center and the Pentagon on September 11, 2001, a growing number of commentators have contended that it is *modern* Islam, or at least the current of Islamism associated with the legacy of the Egyptian Muslim Brotherhood and the Saudi Wahhabite movement, with which previous European revolutions are best compared. On this account, twenty-first century Islamist (and perhaps Ba athi) ideology, practice, and organization bear many disquieting parallels with National Socialism and Bolshevism.

Modern Islamism is a radical movement in which pluralism is anathema, and in which politics itself is derided as a sphere of venality. To that extent it mirrors Islamic doctrine more generally since the suras of the Koran make no categorical or principled distinction between public and private spheres: every duty emanates from God alone. The state has no independent authority. Among Islamist militants, the substitute for political institutions is, above all, the fellow-feeling and camaraderie bestowed by membership of a secret society and the existential tests that confront the believer. "Muslim totalitarianism" reconfigures the capillary, decentralized organization of its Western precursors. Islamist militants combine the conspiratorial anti-Semitism of the Nazis (for whom they entertain a nostalgic admiration) with the pan-territorial ambitions of Bolshevik universalism. Islamist language is also replete with millenarian images of struggle, merciless destruction, and "sacred terror." Bent on purifying the world of Zionism, liberalism, feminism, and Crusader (U.S.) hegemony, Islamist ideology articulates a mausoleum culture of submission, nihilism, suicidal martyrdom for the cause, and mythological appeal to a world about to be reborn. That archaic demands for the reestablishment of the hallowed caliphate are pursued with all the means modern technology affords is consistent with the "reactionary modernism" of earlier totalitarian movements.

Such totalitarian parallels or intellectual lineages do not satisfy those who insist that family resemblance is no substitute for attributable historical causation. And since the early 1950s it has frequently been acknowledged that theorists of totalitarianism are much more adept at constructing morphologies than they are at establishing the precise relationship of totalitarian régimes to one another. François Furet argued this point eloquently, claiming too that Arendt's hodgepodge reconstruction of totalitarianism's career had failed to explain the "very different origins" of fascism and communism. Like Ernst Nolte, Furet was convinced that a "historico-genetic" approach to these movements was required to supplement the standard typological one. Like Nolte, as well, he believed that Bolshevism and National Socialism were historically linked, still a taboo contention among many leftists. Yet Furet disagreed with Nolte's contention that, essentially, National Socialism was a reaction to Bolshevism, a defensive if evil posture that gained credibility owing to the disproportionate influence of Jews in Marxist and socialist parties. According to Furet, the genealogical relationship between Bolshevism and National Socialism was not principally cause and effect. Each had its own endogenous history. The two movements' affinity derived instead from the fact that both of them (and Italian Fascism too—Mussolini was once a revolutionary socialist) emerged from the same "cultural" atmosphere: a late-nineteenth-, early-twentieth-century milieu suffused with "hatred of the bourgeois world." Deep and bitter loathing of that world was well established before World War I and thus also before the October Revolution. Equally, German anti-Semitism did not require Jews to be major spokesmen and leaders of the left to be an object of detestation. Anti-Semitism was already firmly established before Bolshevism erupted, because Jews were seen as a vanguard of democracy itself. Bourgeois democracy was the common enemy of totalitarian movements: the "communist sees it as the breeding ground of fascism, while the fascist sees it as the antechamber of Bolshevism (Furet and Nolte, p. 33)."

Totalitarian Characteristics

A conventional way of describing totalitarianism is to present a list of characteristics common to Italian Fascism, German National Socialism, and Soviet Bolshevism. (Other régimes may also be included—notably, Chinese Communism under the rule of Mao, the Democratic People's Republic of Korea (North Korea), and Pol Pot's "Democratic Cambodia.") But how capacious should that portmanteau be? In *Totalitarianism,* published in 1954, Carl Friedrich itemized five elements, which, in a subsequent collaboration with Zbigniew Brzezinski, he increased to six. Yet, before that, Arthur M. Hill concocted fifteen points that Norman Davies, in *Europe: A History* (1997), expanded to seventeen. Recurrently mentioned features of totalitarianism include the following:

- A revolutionary, exclusive, and apocalyptical ideology that announces the destruction of the old order—corrupt and compromised—and the birth of a radically new, purified, and muscular age. Antiliberal, anticonservative, and antipluralist, totalitarian ideology creates myths, catechisms, cults, festivities, and rituals designed to commemorate the destiny of the elect.

- A cellular, fluid, and hydralike political party structure that, particularly before the conquest of state power, devolves authority to local militants. As it gains recruits and fellow believers, the party takes on a mass character with a charismatic leader at its head claiming omniscience and infallibility, and demanding the unconditional personal devotion of the people.

- A régime in which offices are deliberately duplicated and personnel are continually shuffled, so as to ensure chronic collegial rivalry and dependence on the adjudication of the one true leader. To the extent that legal instruments function at all, they do so as a legitimizing sham rather than a real brake on the untrammeled use of executive power. Indeed, the very notion of "the executive" is redundant since it presupposes a separation of powers anathema to a totalitarian régime.

- Economic-bureaucratic collectivism (capitalist or state socialist) intended to orchestrate productive forces to the régime's predatory, autarchic, and militaristic goals.

- Monopolistic control of the mass media, "professional" organizations, and public art, and with it the formulation of a cliché-ridden language whose formulaic utterances are designed to impede ambivalence, nuance, and complexity.

- A culture of martial solidarity in which violence and danger (of the trenches, the street fight, etc.) are ritually celebrated in party uniforms, metaphors ("storm troopers," "labor brigades"), and modes of address ("comrade"). Youth are a special audience for such a culture, but are expected to admire and emulate the "old fighters" of the revolution.

- The pursuit and elimination not simply of active oppositionists but, and more distinctively, "objective enemies" or "enemies of the people"—that is, categories of people deemed guilty of wickedness in virtue of some ascribed quality such as race or descent. Crimes against the state need not have actually been committed by the person accused of them. Hence the "hereditary principle" in North Korea where punishment is extended to three generations (the original miscreants, their children, and their grandchildren). Under totalitarianism, it is what people are, more than what they do that marks them for punishment. As Stéphane Courtois observes, "the techniques of segregation and exclusion employed in a 'class-based' totalitarianism closely resemble the techniques of 'race-based' totalitarianism" (p. 16). Soviet and Chinese Marxism may have claimed to represent humanity as a whole, but only a humanity divested first of millions—classes, categories—who were beyond the pale of Marxist doctrine. Its universalism was thus always, like National Socialism, an exclusive affair.

- Continual mobilization of the whole population through war, ceaseless campaigns, "struggles," or purges. Moreover, and notwithstanding ideological obeisance to ineluctable laws of history and race, totalitarian domination insists on febrile activity. The mercurial will of the leader and the people as a whole must constantly be exercised to produce miracles, combat backsliding, and accelerate the direction of the world toward its cataclysmic culmination.

- The pervasive use of terror to isolate, intimidate, and regiment all whom the régime deems menacing. Charged with this task are the secret police rather than the army, which typically possesses significantly fewer powers and less status than it does under a non-totalitarian dictatorship or "authoritarian" régime.

- The laboratory of totalitarian domination is the concentration camp. The experiment it conducts aims to discover the conditions under which human subjects become fully docile and pliable. In addition, a slave labor system exists side by side with a racial and/or class-oriented policy of genocide. In Nazi Germany, Jews were the principal objective enemy—over six million were murdered—but there were others such as Slavs and Gypsies. In the Soviet Union, key targets of annihilation or mass deportation were Cossacks (from 1920), kulaks (especially between 1930–1932), Crimean Tartars (1943), Chechens, and Ingush (both in 1944). The Great Purge of 1937–1938 is estimated to have killed close to 690,000 people, but this is dwarfed by the systematically induced famine in Ukraine in 1932–1933, thought to have killed around six million. Pol Pot's Cambodian Communist Party had a similar penchant for mass extermination, as did the Chinese Communist Party (CCP) under Mao: the Chairman boasted that 700,000 perished in the 1950–1952 campaign against "counterrevolutionaries." The CCP targeted landlords and intellectuals, and through a policy of accelerated modernization created the famine of the Great Leap Forward that claimed around 30 million victims.

It should be noted that there is widespread disagreement among commentators about whether Italian Fascism is properly classified as a totalitarian system. Hannah Arendt and George Kennan thought otherwise. Mussolini's régime, on such accounts, is best comprehended as an extreme form of dictatorship or, according to Juan Linz, a species of "authoritarianism." Though preeminent, it shared power with other collective actors such as the monarchy, the military, and the Catholic Church in a way that was utterly alien to National Socialism and Bolshevism. Official anti-Semitism was less intense and less vigorously policed. And Mussolini was domestically ousted in a way that indicates a far more precarious grip on power than either Hitler or Stalin evinced.

The Coherence of Totalitarianism

Since the 1950s, the majority of academic commentators who favor the term have acknowledged that totalitarianism was never fully successful in its quest for complete domination. (Critics of the concept of totalitarianism are considered in the final section of this entry.) This was the key intuition of David Riesman in his correspondence with Hannah Arendt (he read in manuscript the last part of *The Origins of Totalitarianism* [1951]). It was also a theme of the Harvard Project on the Soviet Social System and its literary offspring—notably, Alex Inkeles and Raymond Bauer's *The Soviet Citizen: Daily Life in a Totalitarian Society* (1961). To that extent, as Daniel Bell remarked, totalitarianism was always a concept in search of reality. Unlike political philosophers, moreover, social scientists tend to see totalitarianism as an ideal-type, a one-sided model constructed for research purposes, which also suggests that totalitarianism in the flesh can be of greater or lesser virulence. Studies of inmate camp "culture" lend further credence to the oxymoronic concession that totalitarianism had its limits. Tsvetan Todorov and Anne Applebaum show that even under conditions expressly designed to expunge all traces of solidarity, acts of "ordinary virtue" persisted. Hence there were always people who maintained their dignity (by keeping as clean as they could), who cared for others (sharing food, tending the sick), and who exercised the life of the mind (by reciting poetry, playing music, or committing to memory camp life so as to allow the possibility of its being fully documented later). Michel Mazor's luminous, yet astonishingly objective, autobiographical account of the Warsaw Ghetto (*The Vanished City,* 1955) expresses a similar message of hope. Survivors of death camps and Gulags have typically conveyed a different message, however. Crushed by a merciless régime determined to exterminate not only an individual's life, but the concept of humanity itself, inmates endured a vertiginous "gray zone" of collaboration and compromise.

Any list of totalitarian features, such as the one itemized above, raises an obvious question: What gives the typology its coherence? Or, to put the matter differently, is there some property that furnishes the whole with its master logic or integral animation? Two frequently rehearsed, and related, answers are discernible. The first takes up the pronounced totalitarian attachment to the will, dynamism, and movement. As early as 1925, Amendola was struck by the "wild radicalism" and "possessed will" of the Italian Fascists. Mussolini himself spoke proudly of "*la nostra feroce volonta totalitaria*" (It.: "our fierce totalitarian will"). And the virtue of "fanaticism," "will," and "the movement" for the nation's well-being was tirelessly rehearsed by Hitler and Goebbels, as it was later by Mao. *Yundong* (movement, campaign) was among the most salient ideas of the Chairman, who specifically emphasized the importance of chaos. Sinologist Michael Schoenhals observes that in its original Maoist sense (since disavowed by Deng Xiaoping and his successors, who prefer to speak of an incremental *fazhan* or "development"), *yundong* entails the deliberate "shattering of all regular standards," the suspension of all stabilizing rules, norms, and standards that may apply in ordinary times. The goals of this regularized suspension—there were sixteen major national "movements" between 1950 and 1976—were to orchestrate hatred against the Party's latest enemy (often previously hallowed figures within the Party), to arouse superhuman efforts in support of economic targets, and incessantly to combat "revisionism" and the emergence of new elites. The Soviet Union during the heyday of Stalinism exhibited similar characteristics, as Boris Pasternak's Dr. Zhivago explains:

The point is, Larissa Fyodorovna, that there are limits to everything. In all this time something definite should have been achieved. But it turns out that those who inspired the revolution aren't at home in anything except change and turmoil: that's their native element; they aren't happy with anything that's less than on a world scale. For them, transitional periods, worlds in the making, are an end in themselves.

The centrality of flux and activism to the idea of totalitarianism is integral to classical academic accounts of the phenomenon. It prompted Franz Neumann, in *Behemoth: The Structure and Practice of National*

Socialism (1942), to call the Third Reich a "movement state," and Ernst Fraenkel to describe it as a "dual state" in which the "normal" functions of the legal and administrative apparatus were constantly undermined by Party "prerogative"—Fraenkel's term for the maelstrom of feverish Nazi initiatives that unleashed bedlam without respite. Similarly, Sigmund Neumann entitled his comparative study of the Nazi, Fascist, and Bolshevist hurricanes *Permanent Revolution: The Total State in a World at War* (1942).

Still, the most influential account along these lines was that proffered by Hannah Arendt. Totalitarianism, she argued, was a mode of domination characterized far less by centralized coordination than by unceasing turbulence. To confuse totalitarianism with dictatorship or to see it as a type of dictatorship (or even state) was to miss a fundamental distinction. Once consolidated, dictatorships—for instance, military juntas—typically become routinized and predictable, domesticating and detaching themselves from the movements that were their original social basis. Totalitarian régimes, in contrast, rise to power on movements that, once installed in office, employ motion as their constitutive "principle" of domination. The volcanic will of the leader whose next decision could nullify all previous ones; rule by decree rather than law; the continual manufacture of new enemies; police institutions, Gulags, and death camps whose only purposes are to transform citizens into foes and transform individuals into an identical species and then into corpses: All these features characterize a régime-type of eternal transgression. "Terror," remarks Arendt, is itself "the realization of the law of movement; its chief aim is to make it possible for the force of nature or of history to race freely through mankind, unhindered by any spontaneous human action" (p. 465). Indeed, it is the grotesque destructiveness and futility of totalitarian systems, their attack on every norm that might anchor human life in something stable, that makes them so resistant to methodical analysis.

A second thread that runs through discussions about totalitarianism is the pagan ardor that Fascism, National Socialism, and Bolshevism were capable of generating. Once more, Amendola was a pioneer in this line of interpretation, calling Fascism a "war of religion" that demands total devotion. More sympathetically, the philosopher Giovanni Gentile, ghost-writer of Mussolini's "The Doctrine of Fascism" (1932), stressed the new movement's penetrative spirit. Of special significance was the myth of rebirth: the creation of a new nation or a world without classes, and the formation of a selfless New Man or Woman, untainted by decrepit habits. Fascism, Mussolini avowed, was the author of the Third Italian Civilization (the previous two being the Roman Empire and the Renaissance). Nazi ideology was also replete with notions of national redemption, the spirit of a rejuvenated people, and even the divine mission of the SS. World War I, and the community of front-line soldiers (*Frontsgemeinschaft*) or "trenchocracy" it witnessed, was typically identified as the crucible of this steely resurrection. Coup d'état strategizing, the battles to defeat the Whites during the civil war, and the perennial trumpeting of the class struggle, promoted a similar mentality among the Bolshevik leaders.

Commentators who stress the mythological component of totalitarianism —writing of "ersatz religions," "political religions," the "myth of the state," the "sacralization of politics," and "palingenesis"—include Raymond Aron, Albert Camus, Ernst Cassirer, Norman Cohn, Waldemar Gurian, Jacob Talmon, and Eric Voegelin. Worthy successors are Michael Burleigh, Roger Griffin, and Emilio Gentile. Gentile, while desisting from the view that political religion is the most important element of totalitarianism, nonetheless affirms that it is "the most dangerous and deadly weapon" in its ideological arsenal (p. 49). Civic religions, such as those found in the United States and France, are different from political religions because they celebrate a republican concept of freedom and law. Church and state are separated, but each has its legitimate sphere of activity. In contrast, the sacralization of politics under totalitarian rule, together with its liturgies, festivals, and cults, is marked by the deification of the leader; idolatrous worship of the state, which arrogates to itself the exclusive right to determine Good and Evil; marginalization or destruction of traditional religion; orgiastic mass rallies; immortalization of the party fallen; the appeal to sacrifice; and the cult of death. Interpretations of totalitarianism that emphasize political religion have one notable implication. They suggest that totalitarianism is best understood not as a singular event, or a unique set of institutions, but as a recurrent possibility of the modern world shorn of its customary restraints.

Criticisms and Responses

At the risk of simplification, criticisms of the concept of totalitarianism may be divided into two main, though overlapping, types: moral-political and scientific. The first type of criticism takes different forms but often hinges on the argument that *totalitarianism* was employed during the Cold War as an ideological weapon of a particularly Manichaean, self-serving, and self-righteous kind. Starkly dividing the world into liberal democratic white-hats and communist black-hats, Abbott Gleason remarks, conveniently omitted the extent to which Western governments supported military and other régimes with bleak and bloody human-rights records. Describing military juntas as authoritarian rather than totalitarian made no difference to the people they murdered. A twist on this criticism, found among American disciples of the Frankfurt School, is that liberal democracy itself is not in principle the antithesis of totalitarianism, because both are disastrous permutations of "Enlightenment modernity." A rather different objection is that totalitarianism is an opportune way for former collaborators of Nazism, Bolshevism, and so forth, to dodge responsibility for their actions. Its exculpatory value turns on the claim that "resistance was impossible" or that "we were all brainwashed." Yet the charge of double standards is also made by those, such as Martin Malia, who vehemently defend the pertinence of *totalitarianism* as a label. Disavowing that term all too often means denying the evil symmetry of Nazism and Bolshevism. By recapitulating earlier leftist dogmas—that genuine antifascism required support for the Soviet Union, that comparisons with Nazi Germany are unacceptable because they play into the hands of U.S. imperialism—such denials can become an expedient means of rescuing Marxism from its real, sanguinary history. In a similar way, loose talk of the "dialectic of Enlightenment" is less a challenge to common sense than it is a meretricious affront to its very existence. In any case, the term *totalitarianism* preceded the Cold War by more than two decades.

Scientific objections to totalitarianism as an idea typically focus on a diverse set of issues. Critics argue that the notion is mistaken because:

- Totalitarianism is a fictive Orwellian dystopia instead of an empirical reality. The Soviet system, for instance, "did not exercise effective 'thought control,' let alone ensure 'thought conversion,' but in fact depoliticized the citizenry to an astonishing degree" (Hobsbawm, p. 394). Official Marxism was unspeakably dull and irrelevant to the lives of most people.

- *Totalitarianism* is a misnomer because in neither the Soviet Union nor Nazi Germany was terror total. Instead it was always focused on particular groups. In the Soviet Union, terror formed a radius in which danger was greatest the nearer one was to power and purge. In Germany, once active domestic opposition to the Nazis was defeated, and Jews were deported to the camps, most citizens existed at peace with a régime they deemed legitimate. The majority would never have considered themselves as terrorized by it. Distinguishing between seasoned adversaries and pesky grumblers, the undermanned Gestapo rarely intruded into normal life. Denunciation by citizens of one another was a more effective means of garnering information than the prying eye of the security state.

- The theory of totalitarianism fails to specify a mechanism to explain the internal transition of the Soviet Union and China to non-totalitarian phases. Indeed, the very evolution of such régimes toward humdrum routinization flies in the face of the idea that totalitarianism is above all a movement that cannot be pacified, and is the antithesis of all forms of political normality.

- Totalitarian régimes are too heterogeneous for them to be classified under a single rubric. Under Mao, for instance, the People's Liberation Army was a more powerful organ of control than the security forces, while Mao's prestige was periodically checked, and occasionally deflated, by other CCP leaders. The contrasts between Hitler and Joseph Stalin are, Ian Kershaw suggests, even more telling. While Stalin was a committee man who ascended to rule within a recently established system, Hitler was a rank outsider, strongly averse to bureaucratic work of all kinds. Similarly, while Stalin was an interventionist micromanager, Hitler had little to do with the actual functioning of government. People did not so much directly follow his detailed orders, of which there were few, as second guess what he wanted them to achieve, thereby "working toward the Führer." Then again, Hitler was a spectacular and mesmerizing orator; Stalin's words were leaden by comparison. Mass party purges characterize one system, but not the other (the liquidation of the Röhm faction in 1934 was a singular event). And finally the systems over which the men prevailed had a different impetus. Stalin's goal of rapid modernization was, some say, a humanly understandable, if cruelly executed, objective; that the end justifies the means is a standard belief of all tyrants. Conversely, the mass slaughter of the Jews and others was, for Hitler, an end in itself, unquestionably irrational if not insane.

All these objections are themselves the targets of rebuttal. Modernization at the expense of the nation it is intended to benefit seems hardly rational. Its victims rarely thought so. And did not Hitler, too, think in terms of instrumental means and ends? The goal was a purified Aryan civilization, regenerate, martial, manly, and beautiful. To achieve it, putative nonhumans had to vanish from the face of the earth. Moreover, the transitions that Soviet and Chinese Communism witnessed by no means nullify the totalitarian model. They only appear to do so, Victor Zaslavsky argues, because of failure to distinguish between "system building" and "system maintenance" phases; the latter represents a more stable development, but one still mired in the militarization of society and mass surveillance. Where previous thinkers have erred is in identifying the "system building" stage with totalitarianism *tout court.*

Finally, critics of the total-itarian model often object to it on spurious grounds. For to argue that totalitarianism was never systematic in its rule, never fully synchronized, but rather "chaotic," "wasteful," and "anarchic" is hardly a criticism of those such as Arendt who made such attributes pivotal to their theory. In good measure, her emphasis on movement is vindicated even by those who employ a different terminology. Examples include "régimes of continuous revolution" (enunciated by Michael Mann) and "cumulative radicalization" (preferred by Hans Mommsen).

Conclusion

As a vehicle for condemnation as well as analysis, *totalitarianism* is likely to remain a vibrant idea long into the twenty-first century. Its extension to radical Islam is already evident. And as a potent reminder of the terrible deeds of which humans are capable, the concept has few conceptual rivals. Principled disagreements as well as polemics about its value continue to mark its career. Present dangers, and anxious debates about how they should best be characterized, suggest that the age of totalitarianism is not yet over.

Totalitarian Systems

The most promising way to gain an understanding of totalitarianism is to compare those systems to which the term is usually applied both to one another and to their *non-totalitarian* opposites.

Nazi Germany under Hitler and the Soviet Union under Stalin are usually regarded as prototypal totalitarian systems, to which Communist China has been added more recently. Although the term itself was first applied by Mussolini to his fascist state, his rule of Italy—in retrospect, and in comparison with its National Socialist German and Communist Russian contemporaries—is not usually described as totalitarian. Nor does the term apply to other fascist or dictatorial régimes, such as those of Horthy in Hungary, Pilsudski in Poland, Franco in Spain, Salazar in Portugal, and Peron in Argentina. Disagreement prevails about the proper classification of smaller member states of the Soviet bloc. Are Poland, Hungary, North Vietnam, or Cuba genuinely totalitarian on their own or merely under the direct or indirect control of the totalitarian rulers of the Soviet Union or China? The futility of this question again points to the inherent difficulties of the definitional approach.

Communists themselves naturally reject the label of totalitarianism, which scholars, publicists, and propagandists of the West have tried to pin on them. But the communists do not return the charge by calling their opponents "totalitarians." Rather, they call them "capitalists," "imperialists," or "colonialists" and call their systems of government "minority dictatorships of the bourgeoisie." Since the Marxists conceive of the first postrevolutionary stage toward socialism and communism as the dictatorship of the proletariat, the communists evidently object not to dictatorship itself but to minority dictatorship, which they regard as reactionary or nonprogressive. They remain silent on the issue of totality of control. In this they resemble some non-Marxists who consider the trend toward totality of political control a common feature of all industrial societies, regardless of ideological persuasion.

Distinctive Features

The most distinctive features of the three major political systems of the twentieth century that have generally been considered totalitarian may be listed, in descending order of distinctiveness: (1) commitment to a single, positively formulated substantive goal— such as industrialization, racial mastery, or proletarian unity—and a concomitant lack of commitment to maintenance of procedural stability; (2) unpredictability and uncertainty, resulting from the condition of procedural flux, under which yesterday's hero is today's traitor and today's loyal behavior becomes tomorrow's subversion; (3) the large-scale use of organized violence by military and paramilitary forces and uniformed and secret police; parallel efforts (4) to bring into line or suppress organizations and associations not geared to the substantive aim of the régime and (5) to enforce universal participation in public organizations dedicated to the single goal; and (6) universalization of the goal toward the remaking of all mankind in the image of the totalitarian system itself.

Operational commitment to an ideology is omitted from the list, because this also characterizes systems not generally classified as totalitarian. Many democratic socialists, for example, seem as firmly committed to their ideology as Nazis or Stalinists to theirs. The difference lies not in the commitment to but in the content of the ideologies. All three of these ideologies changed over time, although by different processes. Similarly, adherents of many organized religions also demonstrate ideological commitment. Moreover, in the cold war repeated efforts have been made, particularly in the United States, to fashion an ideology for the "free world" with which to combat the Soviet ideology. The aim of these efforts is to marshal popular commitment to the values incorporated in the new ideology, but it is not to further the establishment of totalitarianism in the West. Ideological commitment consequently does not appear to be a distinctive feature of totalitarianism.

The six apparently distinctive features will now be examined in ascending order of distinctiveness.

Universalism. Universalization of the single substantive goal of the system toward the reshaping of all mankind in its image is listed as the least distinctive aspect of prototypal totalitarianism because clearly non-totalitarian régimes have at times displayed a similar orientation. Like their occasional tendency toward ideologism, this seems related to economic, cultural, and social conditions increasingly prevalent in all modern or modernizing societies.

Forced participation. Enforced general participation in public organizations is especially marked under totalitarianism. This would be particularly obvious if voting participation were taken as the only index, since both the Soviet Union and Nazi Germany came close to enforcing almost 100 per cent participation at the polls, whereas in constitutional democracies only between 40 and 80 per cent of the electorate normally vote.

Apart from such formal practices as voting, however, the technology of communications has not only facilitated but made inevitable inclusion of the entire population in the political, or at least the "public," process.

Suppression of associations. The suppression of organizations not dedicated to the substantive goal of the régime manifests itself as the concomitant of the enforced political coordination *(Gleich-schaltung)* of associations whose existence antedates the establishment of the régime. The effort to coordinate is, in turn, an aspect of enforced participation. In constitutional systems, coordination and suppression are used mainly in crises and emergencies. In Nazi Germany, Stalinist Russia, and Communist China, they were in constant evidence—although to varying degrees depending on the persistence and relative innocuousness, in different periods, of organizations like churches.

Violence. The widespread use of organized violence still more clearly distinguishes the systems most frequently designated as totalitarian. In the eyes of the leaders, military and police violence on a large scale is made necessary, and therefore justified, by the urgency with which they pursue the goal to whose attainment the whole system is geared. Nazi extermination camps and the liquidation of the kulaks under Stalin illustrate this point. Although the violence in the first instance is directed against classes of the internal population, like Jews or remnants of the bourgeoisie, these classes are usually identified by the régime with an external enemy.

Unpredictability. Unpredictability and uncertainty was the rule of life for ordinary men and for both high and low members of the dominant party under Hitler and Stalin. Although Hitler never bothered to abrogate or replace the Weimar constitution, under which he came into office as chancellor, an enabling act passed by the Reichstag in March 1933 made it possible for him, under color of legality, to amend the constitution by decree to the point of its utter transformation. Hitler himself became supreme lawgiver *(oberster Rechtsherr);* his will was "law," and his mind provided such constitutional provisions as Germany had under his rule. Whenever he changed his mind, he could also have changed not only the personnel but the most basic institutions of party and state. And although Stalin, in 1936, elaborately provided the Soviet Union with the constitution named after him, he never allowed it to become the framework of political processes. Stalin not only constantly changed his personnel and remade institutions but he also kept the interpretation of Marxism-Leninism-Stalinism in a condition of continuous flux, controlled only by himself. Communist China's Mao Tse-tung seems to have presided over a similar process, for example, by first promulgating and then revoking the doctrine of "letting a hundred flowers bloom and a hundred schools of thought contend."

In none of these cases was there either a regular publicly known procedure for effecting change or means by which individuals could anticipate which institutions or policies would be changed, and when. Stalin, in particular, skillfully manipulated and exploited this uncertainty. He would, for instance, appear to be moving to the ideological left, thereby enticing others to go even further in that direction through attempted imitation of the leader, and then apparently execute an extreme swing to the right, leaving his former followers ideologically exposed and ready for liquidation. The feeling of uncertainty created by such maneuvers probably contributed much more to the atmosphere of terror, which is generally associated with totalitarianism, than did the massive internal use of organized violence. Uncertainty meant, among other things, that the victims of liquidation might not know the reasons for their fate and, more important, that those who wanted to avoid liquidation in the future had no rational means for doing so. They could escape from the dilemmas of uncertainty neither by withdrawing from politics, because of enforced participation, nor by mouthing the current party line, because that would expose them to condemnation for merely mechanical commitment. Repeated executions of chiefs of the secret police can serve as a paradigm for this process. In non-totalitarian police states, by contrast, one chief of secret police often serves for several decades in that post.

Although unpredictability and uncertainty are the most distinctive features of the totalitarian characteristics discussed so far, they are also the ones most likely to be moderated, or even eliminated, in political systems that retain or develop the other totalitarian traits. And although non-totalitarian systems sometimes seem to be developing the other features discussed, even long-established totalitarian systems seem to move away from unpredictability and toward more constitutional methods. For example, the longest-lived of the prototypal régimes, the Soviet Union, has emphasized "socialist legality" in the post-Stalin period, and some students of Soviet affairs have noticed the emergence of more clearly discernible social groups— party, bureaucracy, the military, management, and others—that may be trying to stabilize relations between one another and the internal operating procedures within each.

The Single and Ultimate Goal

Ruthless pursuit of a single, positively formulated goal is the most distinctive common denominator of totalitarianism.

The single-minded pursuit of a substantive goal, such as racial hegemony, the dictatorship of the proletariat, or the rapid industrialization of a backward economy, *in utter disregard* of all other possible goals and seen as an "indispensable positive" by the régime, is characteristic of totalitarianism. All the resources of the system are ruthlessly harnessed to the attainment of the one great goal. An ideology is constructed to explain all reality with reference to this goal and to the obstacles encountered on the road toward it. Whatever is considered efficient with respect to overcoming these obstacles is done. Whatever is considered distracting from this single-mindedness of purpose is condemned and eliminated. As a result, no procedures are worked out for the resolution of disagreements. All disagreement within the system is identified as evil. Internal politics is, therefore, banned. But when unanticipated new substantive problems arise, as they inevitably do in the ever-changing modern environment, then there is a lack of adaptive procedures by means of which these problems can be tackled and disagreements about them resolved. The elite, as well as ordinary people, lack experience with or commitment to such workable procedures. For the same reason, the leadership cannot admit the achievement of its original goal, since to pursue this aim is its only *raison dêtre*.

Sigmund Neumann (1942) aptly described totalitarianism as "permanent revolution," since under totalitarianism the fundamental procedures of political adaptation are in continuous flux [*à la* Mao's China]. The most distinctive aspect of constitutional systems, by contrast, is the comparatively procedural bias of sources of authority prevailing in them and the relatively strong procedural commitment of their leaders.

Origins and Causes

Explanations of the rise of totalitarianism vary according to conceptions of the phenomenon. Those who focus on centralized, total control point to the complexities of modern societies and, more particularly, of modern economies. They often link socialism with totalitarianism and, for example, underline the inclusion of socialism in the title of Hitler's National Socialist German Workers' party. They also emphasize the totalitarian potential of the "creeping socialism" allegedly hiding behind the welfare policies of contemporary non-totalitarian states with mixed economies.

A second type of explanation relates totalitarianism to the rise of the masses to political participation and to the great military and economic catastrophes of the twentieth century. These disasters eroded whatever commitment to older values the masses may have had and, along with this, also weakened private organizations, thereby "atomizing" the masses and making them easy prey for totalitarian manipulators. Adherents of this theory usually emphasize the features of enforced participation and suppression of private organizations. The totalitarian distinctiveness of these features seems to be backed up by these explanations, but they do not account for the failure of similarly afflicted mass societies like the United States to develop the more distinctive and more vicious features of totalitarianism.

A third category of explanation traces the origin of totalitarianism in the realm of political philosophy, for example, as the logical conclusion of doctrines of majority rule or as the final development of Rousseau's concept of the general will. Because Marxism belongs to both these lines of descent and the prototypal totalitarian ideologies have related themselves, either positively or negatively, to Marxism, a heavy burden of blame is placed upon Marxism. But such explanations exaggerate the independent influence of philosophies and ignore the ideological diversity of totalitarianism and, indeed, of the modern world. Why did neither the English-speaking countries, as heirs to the modern advocates of liberal majoritarianism, nor the French-speaking countries, as heirs to Rousseau, become totalitarian? Or, if all are believed to be moving in that direction, is not the concept of totalitarianism devoid of the minimal specificity of meaning required of useful tools of comparison and analysis?

A fourth theory relates the origins of totalitarianism to anti-Semitism and to racial imperialism, especially in South Africa (Arendt 1951). It emphasizes the utter unpredictability of the Nazi and Soviet systems, stresses the role of secrecy and the secret police, and suggests that the dictators are not motivated by utilitarian pursuit of their stated goals but by a desire to eliminate the capacity to distinguish fact from fiction and to persuade mankind of the superfluousness of human beings. This interpretation, by assuming that the dictators intended to bring about the effects ascribed to their rule, overlooks the extent to which they themselves may have been victims of the uncertainty they created. This explanation of the origins of totalitarianism also fails to account for the rise of totalitarianism in some countries, say, Germany and Russia, and its absence in others, say, Great Britain, France, and Italy.

George Orwell

While many twentieth–century professors and government experts have challenged the practicality of non–democratic systems, the best known and most influential modern critic of authoritarianism and totalitarianism was neither a political scientist nor a policy maker. That person was a socialist novelist who took the pen name George Orwell. Orwell (1903–1950) did more than anyone else in the twentieth century to shape popular notions about the dehumanizing effects of overly controlling government systems. In his novels *Animal Farm* (1945) and *1984* (1949), Orwell painted a vividly grim picture of totalitarian régimes. Stalin's Soviet Union was the obvious target of both books, but Orwell was also concerned that milder forms of government, even Britain's, could become oppressive while presenting a front of benevolence.

Born in India, where his father worked for the British colonial administration, Orwell returned to England for his secondary education. He did not attend university, but instead spent time working for the colonial police in India and living with the poor in London and Paris. A socialist, his goal was to learn about the plight of the underprivileged and to develop his skills as a writer. In 1936, he went to Spain to fight on the side of the socialists against the dictator Francisco Franco. Back in England, he worked as an editor and writer until he died of TB in 1950.

1984 describes a dreary totalitarian society. The year is 1984, far in the future from when Orwell wrote. The place is England, now called Airstrip One, part of vast country named Oceania (England, North America, South Africa, and Australia). Two other huge countries, both totalitarian as well, rule the rest of the world. At all times, one of the countries, although never the same one, is Oceania's ally, the other its mortal enemy. The book's main character, Winston Smith, is a writer in the Ministry of Truth. Winston's job is to rewrite records such as old newspaper articles so that they conform to whatever the government says is the truth. In Oceania, the thought and actions of party members are molded and closely monitored by the state. In every room, a TV screen spews forth a constant barrage of propaganda while a hidden camera spies on an individual's every activity. As in the Soviet Union, where pictures of Stalin were ubiquitous, portraits of Big Brother were ever in view. The goal of government was to make every person believe that Big Brother loved and cared for them and to believe, in turn, that they loved Big Brother.

Orwell's portrayal of Oceania bore all the traits of twentieth century totalitarianism. Thought control (either through peaceful propaganda or the violence of the Thought Police), purges, forced confessions, spying, torture, mass rallies, and compulsory citizen activities were all designed to shape the hearts and minds of an unthinking population. Doublespeak, a language that called forced labor "joycamps" and labeled the War Department, the Ministry of Love, twisted falsehood into truth. If Big Brother said two plus two equaled five, people were obligated to accept that as fact. An external enemy also served to unify the people in support of Big Brother. The constant struggle against an enemy enabled government to justify the country's low standard of living and tight economic rationing imposed by the authorities. Mandatory Two Minute Hate drills and a more formal Hate Week against Oceania's foes were used by government to divert people's attention away from the dismal realities of their own life.

While Winston Smith was a low–level party member, as in the Soviet Union the great majority of Oceania's population were not party members. The "proles"—the term was an obvious reference to the proletariat or working class—lived in oppressive poverty. Although Big Brother did not attempt to monitor their thought or actions with the same degree of intensity as for party members, the proles had no time or energy to think about politics. Work, easy sex, and mindless entertainment filled their days.

George Orwell's *1984* has been read by millions of readers around the world. Even people with little knowledge of political theory or government policies came to regard totalitarianism as dismal, cruel, aggressive, and hypocritical. Although claiming to govern for the good of the people, totalitarian leaders were exposed by Orwell as self–serving predators. In Orwell's view, not only did they insist on political obedience, they extracted the very humanity of their victims. Clearly, George Orwell intended to condemn Soviet, and also German, totalitarianism. Nevertheless, the fact that Airstrip One is England indicates that he was issuing a prophetic warning to the people of his own country. Totalitarianism could be in their future. And, they could be brainwashed to love it.

Hannah Arendt

On the academic front, the German political thinker Hannah Arendt (1906–1975) did the most to define totalitarianism and to claim it as an entirely novel and evil political phenomenon. Focusing on Nazism in Germany and Communism in Russia, she claimed that Hitler and Stalin had introduced an entirely new type of political system that previously had not existed. Totalitarianism, she argued, developed out of the breakdown of social structures and ideals that had characterized Europe in the nineteenth century. With the chaos of World War I, the economic crisis following the war, the migration of millions of people, and the decline of stable political systems, the citizens of Europe were plunged into hopelessness and deep anxiety. They felt profoundly lonely, rootless, and superfluous. To them, the world seemed both meaningless and inexplicable. Furthermore, the people had no faith that their leaders would be able to do anything to remedy the tragic emptiness that so dominated their lives.

According to Arendt, totalitarianism offered a suicidal solution for the grim void of post–World War I Europe. People such as Hitler and Stalin provided people with direction and meaning. Both Hitler and Stalin embodied evil in a form so radical and absolute that they introduced political forms unlike anything the world had ever experienced before. The evil of Nazism, Arendt argued, surpassed the evil of any previous régime. This evil was more than just an exaggerated self–interest, greed, lust for power, cowardice, or resentment. The evil of Nazi totalitarianism was an unmitigated passion for destruction (nihilism). First, the Nazi's believed they needed to completely destroy the existing world in order to create the new world to which they aspired. Second, by exercising the power of destruction, the Nazis demonstrated their own unlimited power. Why, Arendt, asked did the Nazis need the death camps and why did they engineer the Holocaust? Certainly not for any rational political or military advantage. From a practical point of view, the death camps were a liability. But, as a symbol of complete power and domination, the death camps served the Nazi's aims. The death camps allowed the Nazis to treat others as sub–human and to inflict infinite revenge on other human life. By their despicable acts, the Nazis were attempting to escape their own feelings of smallness and impotence. Ordinary people responded in a supportive way because they too wanted to escape their weakness.

Because both the Nazi leaders ers lost their ability to see the humanity in those they classified as sub human, they were able to extinguish those people without any feelings of remorse or discomfort. Just as the vast power difference between humans and insects allows most people to kill such creatures with no thought, so too the Nazis were able to kill undesirables in a routine, meticulous, and unemotional manner. While the Nazis exterminated people such as Jews and Gypsies, they effectively destroyed the humanity and individuality of all the German people. For Arendt, one of the ways to prevent totalitarianism was to encourage free citizens to participate in politics. Citizens who took an active role in the political realm would not allow a totalitarian régime to control their minds, emotions, and conscience. They would not lose themselves to a state trying to obliterate the humanity of all its subjects.

CUBAN IMPACT ON HEMISPHERIC AND WORLD AFFAIRS

Cuba is a relatively small country, but engages in the foreign policy of a major league international player. It has carried out such a policy since the start of Castro's 1959 revolution. Because of its close alliance with the Soviet Union, by the early to mid 1960's it had the external resources, internal conditions, and lack of significant US opposition to begin to visibly impact conditions throughout the world; from Latin America, to Africa and Asia. At times, the close relationship to the USSR (and corresponding partnership with Communist Bloc countries) made many perceive its autonomy in foreign affairs as close to zero. Viewed from the perspective of analysts in the American Department of State, it is easy to see Castro's Cuba as an unofficial province of the Soviet Union. The Cuban foreign policy that has been both aggressive ideologically, militaristic, yet highly pragmatic.

The Castro brothers saturated the media with altruistic images of themselves in a campaign to justify and encourage, or directly spread, radical change. A totalitarian state was created where Fidel Castro could claim "unanimous support" for revolutions which could defy the United States and its allies. Participation in the state-orchestrated exportation of Marxism quickly became a requirement for existence in a Cuba that prohibited all forms of dissent. Devoted leftists who aided Castro's rise, but later resisted disastrous economic policies and challenged the one-party state, found themselves silenced, imprisoned, or executed. Cuba's communist government has engaged in political subversion throughout the world, either through direct military intervention, or disguised as development aid for health, economic, and civic programs.

Geographically, Cuba is the largest island in the Caribbean, slightly smaller than the US state of Florida (42,426 sq.m. in comparison to Florida's 65,755 sq.m.), and the second-most populous after the island of Hispaniola, with 11,270,000 inhabitants. Cuba's foreign policy is uncharacteristic for such a minor, developing country. Coupled with

Castro's leadership of the faux Non-Aligned Movement[1] and Cuba's medical-based internationalism, it has increased the country's profile on the international stage and earned its dictatorial leader great respect in the third world.

Contrary to the highly successful efforts of the Castro-communist régime to paint pre-revolutionary Cuba as a backward developing nation, Cuba had Latin America's highest per capita consumption rates of meat, vegetables, cereals, and highest ownership or usage of automobiles, telephones, TV sets, newspapers, and radios. Cuba's Gross Domestic Product per capita was roughly equal to that of Italy and richer than Japan in the 1950s, and its GDP per capita was a sixth as large as that of its neighboring economic giant, the United States; an impressive economic comparison. The country in general, and Havana specifically, had a modern transportation system rivaling any major city in the United States[2]. The *La Rambla* section of Havana, was in the same league with, and arguably exceeded in "never sleeping" with New York's Broadway or Times Square. The United States Bureau of Foreign Commerce summarized in 1956: "the worker in Cuba...has wider horizons than most Latin American workers and expects more out of life in material amenities than many European workers...".[3] However, there was growing popular resentment against President Fulgencio Batista y Zaldívar, who had been the power behind the throne, or directly in government, since the Sergeant's Revolt of 1933 that overthrew the authoritarian rule of President Gerardo Machado y Morales.[4]

After running unsuccessfully for the presidency in 1952, Batista staged a coup deposing President Carlos Prío Socarrás. Initially, the coup was widely welcomed, but Batista increasingly became more repressive. He

---

[1] Dr. Céspedes has referred to the Non-Aligned Movement as *faux*, or false, because it was obvious (except for the most politically naïve) that it was never, as it claimed, non-aligned between the "Communist World" and the ostensible "Free World"; it contained in its membership Communist countries, the largest of which was Maoist China! Its founders, in 1955, were Nehru, Nasser, Tito, Sukarno and Chou-en-lai; none of whom could be disguised as friends of the West.

[2] For example, public buses made stops in Havana pick-up locations every 5-8 minutes.

[3] Farber, 2015.

[4] Batista was elected democratically and served from 1940–1944 as a popular president. He was the first non-white Cuban, a mulatto, in that position. Batista supported business development, admired the United States, enacted a variety of pro-labor laws, supported labor unions, and carried out major social reforms.

outlawed the Cuban Communist Party in 1952. Political unrest and instability led to Batista's overthrow in January 1959 by the 26th of July Movement, led by Fidel Castro. Batista fled Cuba by air for the Dominican Republic just hours into New Year's Day on 1 January 1959.

[Image 2: Busy Havana street in front of El Malecon, 1956. The new Focsa luxury condominium, center, is surrounded by smaller modern multi-story buildings.]

International Involvement Pre-1959

World War II

Because of the island's strategic geographical location at the entrance of the Gulf of Mexico, Cuba was an important participant in the American Theatre of War and beneficiary of the Lend-Lease program (receiving 6.6 million dollars). The armed forces of the Republic of Cuba were not involved in heavy combat during World War II, although president Batista at the time suggested a combined Latin American/U.S. strike on Francisco Franco's Spain in order to overthrow its pro-Axis régime and outflank Germany.

In December, 1941, Cuba declared war on the Axis Powers, and by 1945 its military had developed a reputation as being the most cooperative and efficient of all the Caribbean nations. Without losing a single warship or aircraft to enemy action, the Cuban Navy escorted hundreds of Allied ships through hostile waters; sailing nearly 400,000 miles on convoy and patrol duty, flying over 83,000 hours on convoy and patrol duty, and rescuing more than 200 U-boat victims from the sea.

On May 15, 1943, a squadron of three Cuban submarine chasers, CS-11, CS-12 and CS-13, sailed from Isabela de Sagua (on the north coast of the province of Villa Clara in central Cuba) toward Havana, escorting the Honduran merchant ship *Wanks*, and the Cuban ship *Camagüey*. The CS-13, commanded by Second Lieutenant Mario Ramirez Delgado, made sonar contact and launched two attacks with depth charges, which annihilated U-176, a German long-range Type IXC submarine under the command of Reiner Dierksen.

The German Abwehr sent an intelligence agent named Heinz Lüning to Havana with orders to establish a secret radio station and then transmit the information he collected to agents in South America. Cuban security uncovered and captured Lüning, who was tried, found guilty of espionage and executed in November 1942. Heinz Lüning was the only German spy to be put to death in Latin America during World War II.[5]

[Image 3: United States Navy battleship USS Texas (BB-35) entering Havana Harbor in February 1940. Morro Castle is in the background.]

---

[5] Schoonover, 2008.

Post 1959 International Relations

At first, the United States government reacted favorably to the 1959
· assent of Fidel Alejandro Castro Ruz, later known simply as Fidel Castro,
seeing it as part of an overall movement toward democratic government
in Latin America. However, once it was obvious that Cuba was adopting
a totalitarian Marxist–Leninist political and economic system, opposition
increased not only by dissident Cubans and other political organizations,
but by the United States as well.

With Castro's assent to power, many non-Marxist, anti-Batista rebel
leaders were forced into exile, executed in a Bolshevik-like reign of
terror, or eliminated in failed uprisings. It was estimated by the US State
Department that a minimum of 3,200 people were executed from 1959 to
1962. This estimate is probably far too conservative. Other estimates for
the total number of political executions range from 4,000 to 33,000.

Appalled at the increasing repression of civil liberties, and seizing of all
private property and collectivization of the Cuban economy, anti-
communist Cuban insurgents fought a six year insurgency in the
Escambray Mountain range against the Castro government (1959 to
1965). The rebellion involved more soldiers and lasted longer than the
initial struggle against the Batista government. The Castro government
disparagingly dubbed the rebellion "the war against the bandits" (*La
lucha contra los bandidos*) in its propaganda. The vast majority of the so-
called bandits were poor farmers (the very *"guajiros"* the revolution was
to have enfranchised), and former guerrillas who had previously fought
as allies of Castro against Batista. The anti-Castro forces included
Commandante Raúl Menendez Tomassevich, founding member of the
Cuban Communist Party. The government's tactics were genocidal, and
employed a "no-prisoners" strategy (Law 988, enacted in 1961, decreed
that by virtue of being "outlaws", the *alzados* forfeited both their lives
and their property). It has been estimated that between 3,500 to 5,000
alzados (and *campesino* non-combatant sympathizers) were killed in the
bloody Escambray campaign. With vastly superior numbers (as many as
250,000 government troops), the Castro forces eventually crushed the
counter-insurgency.

[Image 4: Fidel Castro arrives at MATS (Military Air Transport Service) Terminal, Washington, D.C., April 15, 1959.]

SPOTLIGHT ON CASTRO

Fidel Alejandro Castro Ruz, known simply as Fidel Castro, a first-generation Cuban, was born August 13, 1926, to a wealthy farming family in the eastern region of Oriente. Their 11,000 hectares produced wood, sugarcane, and cattle. His father had migrated from Galicia, Spain, while his religious peasant mother had been born in Cuba of Spanish parents. Both parents learned to read and write although neither went to school. Fidel Castro was one of six children.

When Castro was three years old, the worldwide economic depression hit rural Cuba. From 1929 to 1933 the island experienced widespread social and political upheaval, culminating when Fulgencio Batista (1901–1973), a sergeant, led a military revolt that put a democratic/liberal government in power.

Castro initially went to a small rural school. At age six, in 1932, he left for a private Catholic elementary boarding school in Santiago de Cuba. Later he went to the leading elite Jesuit secondary school, Colegio Belén, in Cuba's capital city of Havana. From the Spanish priests he learned self-discipline. In 1943 he earned an award as the country's best secondary-school athlete. During school breaks, he visited the family farm and read newspaper reports about the Spanish Civil War (1936–1939) or World War II (1939–1945) to his parents and workers. In the Spanish conflict, his family supported Francisco Franco (1892–1975).

ENTERING POLITICS

In September 1945, at the age of nineteen, Castro entered the University of Havana. The campus was his springboard to national politics. Just the previous year, national elections had allowed the Partido Revolucionario Cubano (PRC), also known as the Auténtico Party, to set up a government. The PRC promised major social reforms and greater national independence. Castro immediately became involved in the tumultuous politics of the time. Students and professors transformed courses into discussions of Cuba's social, economic, and political problems.

In 1947 he participated in setting up a new populist political party, the Partido del Pueblo Cubano, or Ortodoxo Party, which had separated from the PRC. The Ortodoxos shared the same values as the PRC but claimed the Auténtico government had failed to deliver on its promised reforms and instead had become thoroughly corrupt.

Early in his life Castro had absorbed anticapitalist ideas based on Catholic counter-reformation conservative thought. While attending high school, he discovered the nationalist writings and biography of the Cuban patriot José Martí (1853–1895). At the University of Havana he became immersed in radical leftist ideology, including those of the German political philosopher Karl Marx (1818–1883) and the Russian Communist leader Vladimir Lenin (1870–1924). He claims that in those days he became a communist.

During his university years, from 1945 to 1950, Castro was a political activist. In September 1947 he joined an armed expeditionary force composed of Cubans and exiles from the Dominican Republic intending to oust the government of the dictator Rafael Leónidas Trujillo (1891–1961). The invasion was never launched. The next year, in April 1948 as a representative of the Law Students Association of Cuba, Castro went to a Latin American University Students Congress in Bogotá, Colombia, which coincided with the United States' initiation of the Organization of American States and the advent of civil war in Colombia. The populist leader of the opposition was assassinated. For two days Castro participated in some of the early armed skirmishes, and then he returned home. Both incidents indicate that he, like many contemporaries in Cuba, identified with political struggles in the region. He was also involved in a political organization promoting the independence of Puerto Rico. By then he had acquired lifelong contacts with Latin American leftist parties and leaders.

He graduated in 1950 with a law degree, having specialized in international law and social sciences. His main interests were politics, sociology, history, theory, and agriculture. He was a radio commentator, and investigative political journalist, and developed a following among young leftist ideologues. The Ortodoxo Party recognized his oratorical and organizational skills and nominated him for the planned June 1952 national congressional election. However, on March 10, 1952, the military, led by Batista, carried out a second coup d'état, ending hopes that electoral politics could reform the island and throwing Cuba's constitutional system into a crisis.

ARMED REVOLUTIONARY

The young Ortodoxos became committed revolutionaries, clandestinely organizing to oust the new military rulers. On July 26, 1953, civilians led by Castro attacked Santiago de Cuba's Moncada army barracks, the second largest in the country. It ended in abject failure. Some men were killed in the confrontation; others were captured and then assassinated. It is reported that Fidel was the first to run away when the shooting started. The survivors ended up in prison. From the summer of 1953 to May 1955, Castro was imprisoned at the Isle of Pines, but he continued to organize his associates inside and outside prison. Because of his youth and family connections, he was given by Batista a comfortable imprisonment and was treated kindly, a favor that he would not extend to his political opponents in the future. In mid-May 1955, the *Moncadistas* were granted a political amnesty. Batista hoped such a move would earn him legitimacy. By serving time, Castro had become one of the national opposition leaders in Cuba.

He spent May 1955 to November 1956 in exile in Mexico, where he organized and trained a guerrilla force. On December 2, 1956, eighty-two men who had embarked from the Mexican port of Tuxpan days earlier landed in Cuba in the southern portion of the Oriente. The guerrilla insurgency had begun. The guerrillas gained control of significant portions of territory in the mountains, launched an agrarian reform, and recruited peasants. Castro broadcast daily from a rebel shortwave radio station. From the Sierra Maestra Mountains, he coordinated the military and political struggle. From 1957 to 1958 the guerrillas were able to build a peasant-class front against the dictatorship.

On December 31, 1959, the Batista régime collapsed. This was a first in Latin America: an insurgency that defeated a regular military force supported by the U.S. government.

Post 1959 International Relations

At first, the United States government reacted favorably to the 1959 assent of Fidel Alejandro Castro Ruz, later known simply as Fidel Castro, seeing it as part of an overall movement toward democratic government in Latin America. However, once it was obvious that Cuba was adopting a totalitarian Marxist–Leninist political and economic system, opposition increased not only by dissident Cubans and other political organizations, but by the United States as well.

With Castro's assent to power, many non-Marxist, anti-Batista rebel leaders were forced into exile, executed in a Bolshevik-like reign of terror, or eliminated in failed uprisings. It was estimated by the US State Department that a minimum of 3,200 people were executed from 1959 to 1962. This estimate is probably far too conservative. Other estimates for the total number of political executions range from 4,000 to 33,000.

Appalled at the increasing repression of civil liberties, and seizing of all private property and collectivization of the Cuban economy, anti-communist Cuban insurgents fought a six year insurgency in the Escambray Mountain range against the Castro government (1959 to 1965). The rebellion involved more soldiers and lasted longer than the initial struggle against the Batista government. The Castro government disparagingly dubbed the rebellion "the war against the bandits" (*La lucha contra los bandidos*) in its propaganda. The vast majority of the so-called bandits were poor farmers (the very *"guajiros"* the revolution was to have enfranchised), and former guerrillas who had previously fought as allies of Castro against Batista. The anti-Castro forces included Commandante Raúl Menendez Tomassevich, founding member of the Cuban Communist Party. The government's tactics were genocidal, and employed a "no-prisoners" strategy (Law 988, enacted in 1961, decreed that by virtue of being "outlaws", the *alzados* forfeited both their lives and their property). It has been estimated that between 3,500 to 5,000 *alzados* (and *campesino* non-combatant sympathizers) were killed in the bloody Escambray campaign. With vastly superior numbers (as many as 250,000 government troops), the Castro forces eventually crushed the counter-insurgency.

A Dependable Soviet Proxy

Castro-Cuba's close relationship with the USSR's, its modeling of the collectivized Soviet economy, and totalitarian government was the *raison d'être* of its expansionist policies. A marionette of the Kremlin, Cuba sought to export Marxist ideology worldwide, establish leftist dictatorships friendly to the Soviet bloc, and sought to counter American diplomatic efforts worldwide, especially in Latin America.

Cuban foreign policy specifically backed the establishment of Marxist governments in the Dominican Republic, Chile, Nicaragua, El Salvador, and Grenada, and sent troops to aid allies in the Yom Kippur War, Ethio-Somai War, the Congo, and Angolan Civil War, among many other interventions.

In addition to Latin America, Africa was the parallel objective of Cuban foreign policy. The Cuban military employed troops or advisers in 10 nations throughout Africa, also sustaining exchanges with the preponderance of the countries in the continent, although the most significant numbers were with Ethiopia, Angola, and the "front-line"[6] countries in southern Africa. In addition to troops, Cuba provided educational and medical personnel, veterinarians, agronomists, and technicians. The renamed Isle of Youth of the southern coast of Cuba (formerly the Isle of Pines) was the destination for thousands of young Africans who studied in Cuba, mostly in special schools set up especially for foreigners.

Coupled with Castro's leadership of the faux Non-Aligned Movement and Cuba's medical internationalism, these policies increased Cuba's profile on the world stage, and earned it respect in the developing world.

---

[6] In communist parlance, referring to countries that are in the vanguard; the front-line troops of insurgents leading in the revolutionary struggle against the colonial, neo-colonial, or capitalist allies of the western powers, led by the United States. An example would be the Marxist MPLA fighting the Portuguese in Angola, but also the MPLA later fighting the pro-western/anti-communist forces of UNITA.

[Image 5: Fidel Castro and Nikita Khrushchev hug in Cuba, 1961.]

Première Expérience - Santo Domingo

Castro provided the first serious threat to the Dominican Republic's leader, Rafael Trujillo, on June 14, 1959. In a mission Castro personally approved, Cuban-trained guerrillas under the leadership of Captain Enrique Jimenez Moya attempted to infiltrate the Dominican Republic's northern coast. Departing from Nipe Bay, in Oriente Province, Moya's two fast motor launches were escorted by three Cuban Navy frigates to the coast of Samana Bay. However, the Dominican military detected the invasion and its air and naval forces destroyed the launches. Captain Moya and the guerrillas who made it to shore were shot.

At the same time, a Castroite Air Force plane in Oriente Province, Cuba, was boarded by 56 guerrillas. Disguised with false Dominican markings, the plane took off from an airfield near the city of Manzanillo. Comandante Delio Gomez Ochoa, who led the Rebel Army's Fourth Front in Oriente Province during the insurgency against Batista, led the group. The invaders landed at Costanza airport, surprising and overpowering the Dominican guards. Lacking ground transportation and overloaded with ammunition, the invaders failed in their goal of reaching the mountains. Additionally, the invaders were recognized easily due to inconsistencies in their uniforms. An estimated 10 Cubans and 200 Dominican exiles were killed or captured.

[Image 6: Dominican rebels at Mil Cumbres training camp in Cuba.]

The Congo

The Congo Crisis was a period of political upheaval in the Republic of the Congo (renamed the Republic of Zaïre since 1971) that commenced with its independence from Belgium, and ended with the seizing of power by Joseph Mobuto Sese Seko. During the Congo Crisis, a Cuban expedition led by Ernesto "El Che" Guevara trained Marxist rebels to fight against the weak central government of Joseph Kasavubu, the first president of the newly independent country, in alliance with Mobutu. This would be Cuba's first military action outside of Latin America and in Africa.

The Marxist "Simbas" ("Lions" in Kiswahili, the common language of much of the Congo), the principal rebel group as they were known, saw the violent expulsion of Europeans from their territory in the northern region around Stanleyville as their principal goal, to be performed with the greatest savagery. The rebels murdered thousands in a rampage driven by hostility toward Congolese officials of any kind, past colonial policies, as well as interethnic rivalries between the Africans themselves. However, Guevara's dream of a Marxist Congo had evaporated by November 1965 against the reality of his African allies' military incompetence *vis-à-vis* the anti-communist Western powers.

[Image 7: Che Guevara holding an unidentified Congolese baby while participating in an guerrilla insurgency in the Congo in 1965.]

Failure in the Bolivian Ñancahuazú

The next target of Cuban foreign policy was the South American country of Bolivia, where Castro hoped to foment an insurgency that would spread throughout the continent. Guevara was the man chosen to head the mission, and on November 3, 1966, he secretly entered the country using a false identity; Adolfo Mena González, an Uruguayan businessman. Three days later Guevara started his guerrilla operations in the remote Ñancahuazú region. The indigenous people proved to be indifferent or even hostile to Guevara's recruitment, and little was accomplished. His band of insurgents, operating under the name *Ejército de Liberación Nacional,* or ELN (Army of National Liberation) never numbered more than 50 men. The ELN engaged units of the Bolivian Army, which was unaccustomed to guerrilla warfare and generally undertrained, in a series of skirmishes in 1967 in which it was relatively successful.

However, two major factors stymied Cuban operations. The first was the continued inability of the guerrillas to recruit additional members from the population. The second was that, unbeknownst to Guevara, his earlier successes caused the Bolivian government to overestimate the size of the his forces and seek help from the US. Henceforth, Bolivian units were trained, advised, and supplied in anti-insurrection tactics by the CIA's Special Activities Division and the US Army Special Forces. Eventually, the Communist forces were whittled away and Guevara's main encampment was detected and encircled. Guevara was captured (he is reputed to have yelled "Don't shoot, I'm Che Guevara and worth more to you alive than dead!"[7]), and interrogated. The CIA wanted to question him further, but he was executed by a Bolivian firing squad on the orders of the Bolivian President. CIA analysts estimated that Castro sent Guevara on a mission that would likely lead to his destruction because of policy and personality issues (see Appendix A: "CIA, *The Fall of Che Guevara...*").

[Image 8: Guevara in rural Bolivia, shortly before his death in 1967, in a customary photo-op with unidentified Bolivian children and peasant.]

1961: The Revolution Imperiled

In March 1960, the Eisenhower administration gave the go ahead to a CIA plan to arm and train a force of Cuban exiles to overthrow the Castro

---

[7] This author's personal interview with Félix Rodríguez, 2011, the Cuban-born CIA operative present during Guevara's capture, whose cover at the time was that of a Bolivian major.

government. The Eisenhower plan included the destruction of the Castroite airforce *by the exiles* prior to an invasion, and a landing near the city of Trinidad, on Cuba's south coast. The final operation, known as the Bay of Pigs Invasion (or *Playa Girón,* as it is usually referred to by Cubans) took place on April 14, 1961. Fortunately for the Castro régime, the Kennedy administration cancelled air operations after the first air strike, and changed the invasion site to the remote Bay of Pigs area which is surrounded by the Zapata swamps, in an effort to maintain a degree of "plausible denial". These changes essentially guaranteed the failure of the invasion. Approximately 1,500 Cuban exiles of Brigade 2506 disembarked on the beaches of the aforementioned bay, but failed in their attempt to overthrow the régime.

During the night of April 16-17, a mock diversionary landing was organized by CIA operatives near Bahia Honda in Pinar del Rio Province, which briefly lured Fidel Castro's forces away from the main invasion area. By the late morning of 18 April, Cuban troops and militia, supported by T-54 tanks imported previously from the Soviet Union, took Playa Larga after Brigade forces had retreated towards Girón. Later during the day, Brigade forces were forced to retreat to San Blas along the two roads from Covadonga and Yaguaramas.

Without sufficient air support, short of ammunition, and no way to maneuver, Brigade 2506's ground forces retreated to the beaches in the face of a considerable onslaught from the communist artillery, tanks and infantry.

During the 1961 economic conference of the Organization of American States in Uruguay, Ernesto "Che" Guevara sent a note to Kennedy via Richard Goodwin, Secretary of the Treasury and acting representative for the White House. It read: "Thanks for Playa Girón. Before the invasion, the revolution was weak. Now it's stronger than ever." Guevara also stated in the meeting that Cuba's ties to the Soviet Union and the communist bloc came about as the result of "natural sympathies and common beliefs."[8] The failure of the US at Bay of Pigs greatly emboldened Cuba's expansionistic and antagonistic foreign policy, and was seen as a weakness of American will to contain communism, as evidenced by Castro connivance with Khrushchev in the missile crisis that was to follow.

---

[8] Lazo, 1968, 1970.

[Image 9: Czech-made anti-aircraft gun employed by Castro forces at Bay of Pigs. Nicknamed by the Cubans *"Cuatro Bocas"* (Spanish: "Four Mouths").]

Operation Mongoose

The embarrassment caused by the Bay of Pigs compelled the Kennedy administration to continue to seek ways to topple Castro and seek to save face. In November 1961 Operation Mongoose was devised for this purpose. General Edward Lansdale was given the responsibility of coordinating activities between the CIA, Defense Department, and State Department. The President's brother, Robert Kennedy, ultimately oversaw the program.

A wide range of activities encompassed Mongoose, including infiltrating insurgents into Cuba, intelligence gathering, sabotage (especially sugar production), attempts to "turn" key military against the régime, and a variety of schemes to assassinate Castro.[9]

---

[9] Among the many assassination schemes was poisoning his cigars. A lethally contaminated box was prepared and actually delivered to Havana.

The placement of Soviet missiles in Cuba in 1962, discussed in the next section, resulted in the stoppage of Mongoose undertakings by the still waffling Kennedy administration. Operation Mongoose formally ceased its activities at the end of 1962.

The half-hearted and poorly conceived policies of the Kennedy administration bred stronger resistance from *La Revolución*, much like an incomplete regimen of antibiotics. The communist "germ" was in the Americas to stay, much to the consternation of the United States. Such failures to topple Castro militarily, or foment an anti-Castro rebellion, only strengthened the impression that the United States was anemic and inept, and conversely made stronger Castro's hand.

[Image 10: Minutes of Meeting of the Special Group on Operation Mongoose, October 4, 1962, page 1.]

Cuban Missile Crisis

By 1962 it was obvious that the Castro government had modeled Cuba after the one-party marxist economic system of the Soviet Union. In October 1962, the world was confronted by the Cuban missile crisis. In the geopolitical chess game of nations, the Russians were placing nuclear missiles in Cuba in response to US nuclear missiles in Turkey and the Middle East, and the Americans were demanding they be immediately withdrawn. General Curtis LeMay, of WWII fame, wanted immediate military action. The Cubans were happy to host the missiles and argued consistently with the Soviets that these new defense arrangements should have been made public from the start. For Castro, this represented an ascension in political and military prestige, national security, as well as an opportunity for a proverbial tweaking the American nose. The Kremlin thought differently. Khrushchev wanted to confront the Americans with a surprise *fait accompli*. The Soviets had also given Cuba a large conventional arsenal, as well as creating the largest foreign military base ever seen in the history of the Caribbean.

The Soviets and Americans soon came to an agreement to end the crisis. The Soviets would remove the missiles from Cuba and the Americans would remove missiles from Turkey and the Middle East (an agreement so embarrassing that it was kept secret from the American public for nearly ten years). When the missiles were withdrawn the Castro government was angry: the Cubans were never part of the negotiations or consulted. Castro would never fully trust Khrushchev again. Yet the Cubans won a significant victory, securing a tacit agreement from the American government that another 'Bay of Pigs' would not be repeated – an assurance that has lasted to the date of this writing. The revolution would survive.

[Image 11: CIA reference photograph of Soviet medium-range ballistic missile (SS-4 in U.S. documents, R-12 in Soviet documents) in Red Square.]

Early Diplomatic Coup: Schism in the OAS

Cuba was suspended from membership in the Organization of American States (OAS) from January 21, 1962, to June 3, 2009, due to pressure exerted by the United States and initially by the Kennedy administration. The US aims, as conceptualized by President Kennedy, were to not only be bar the Castro government from the organization and avoid its inevitable political mischief, but that the OAS would also place sanctions against the island, largely as a response to Castro's many and onerous human rights violations. However, the Cuban government was successful in securing the opposition to the US plan from Argentina, Brazil, Chile, Mexico, Bolivia, and Ecuador during 1962 the OAS meeting in Punta del Este, Uruguay.

[Image 12: Castro at a meeting of the UN General Assembly, September 22, 1960.]

Chile

Cuba had been a reference point for Chilean leftist political parties since the 1960s. The rise of Salvador Allende, a Chilean physician and self-proclaimed Marxist who ruled from 1970 to 1973, gave Cuba an important geopolitical opportunity.

Allende, a leading member of the Socialist Party of Chile, came to power in 1970 after narrowly beating his two closest opponents with 36.3

percent of the vote in a three-way race. Allende was straightforward in publicly voicing his desire to dramatically "transform" his country by instituting a plan called the "Chilean way to socialism" (*La vía Chilena al socialism*).

Upon assuming power Allende increasingly expropriated private sector businesses, industry, private property and farmland. The media wrote extensively of Allende's economic failures and the flight of Chilean capital. Cuban-Chilean relations became unprecedentedly close, as well as Chilean relations with the USSR and communist bloc nations. Strikes and shutdowns caused massive inflation, shortages and political unrest.

Shortly after the election of Allende, Cuba's internal security apparatus (the DI, or *Dirección General de Inteligencia*) worked closely with their Chilean counterparts in strengthening and solidifying Allende's position. The Cuban DI station chief Luis Fernandez Oña even married Allende's daughter Beatriz (who later committed suicide in Cuba).

Allende was implicated in the assassination of several political opponents, according to US intelligence reports. Additionally, KGB files smuggled out of Russia by Major Vasily N. Mitrokhin (secretly a dissident who worked in the KGB archives) indicate that Allende received funds from the Soviet Union. The Chilean parliament formally condemned Allende for systematically destroying democracy in Chile and violating the constitution. In a resolution of August 22, 1973, the Chilean Chamber of Deputies accused Allende of torture, illegal arrests, censoring the press supporting anti-government armed groups, confiscating private property, and barring Chileans from leaving the country.

In the "Cuban Packages Scandal" that precipitated the 1973 coup led by General Augusto Pinochet, Chilean authorities uncovered large quantities of automatic weapons, ammunition, and grenades sent from Cuba to arm Marxist groups which intended to keep Allende in power. The discovery was just the tip of the iceberg of a constant smuggling of weapons from Cuba, hidden inside diplomatic pouches, that were delivered with regularity twice a week via the Cuban airline *Cubana de Aviación*.

The September 11, 1973, military coup orchestrated by Army Commander-in-Chief Pinochet (who later became President) resulted in the death of Allende; either by suicide, the ensuing battle for the Presidential Palace, or execution by the putschists.

Allende's overthrow was fiercely protested by the Cuban government (and many in the US) who criticized the CIA's alleged involvement. The

Senate Intelligence Committee under Senator Frank Church (a liberal Democrat) investigated the role of the US and exonerated the Nixon administration of any unlawful activity.

[Image 13: Fidel Castro and Salvador Allende embrace.]

Nicaragua

The Kremlin had this Central American in it sights for some time. In July, 1961, the head of the KGB, Alexander N. Shelepin, sent a memorandum to Soviet premier Nikita Khrushchev containing plans to organize an armed insurgency in Nicaragua in coordination with Cuba. Approving the memo, Khrushchev forwarded it to his deputy, Frol R. Kozlov, a member of the Politburo Central Committee, and on August 1st, it was passed as a major directive, albeit with minor revisions.

With the backing of the Castro government, the Sandinista National Liberation Front (FSLN: *Frente Sandinista de Liberación Nacional*) was formed in 1961 by Carlos Fonseca Amador (an avowed Marxist[10]) Silvio Mayorga, and Tomás Borge Martínez. The Cubans advised the Sandinistas to seek support from students, peasants and anti-Somoza

---

[10] Fonseca will not live to see the Sandinistas triumph, he was killed in the mountains of Nicaragua three years before the FSLN took power.

elements within Nicaraguan society when organizing their group. Cuba also helped to align the leftist government of General Omar Efraín Torrijos, dictator of Panama from 1968 to 1981, and the government of Carlos Andrés Pérez (often referred to as "El Gocho"[11]), President of Venezuela from 1974 to 1979 and again from 1989 to 1993, with help from the FSLN. The FSLN coalition was strong enough by the 1970s to commence a military campaign against the régime of longtime dictator Anastasio Somoza Debayle (known as "Tachito" to his close friends). The Sandinistas would eventually overthrow the pro-western Somoza, ending a dynasty that had been in power since 1936.

During the civil war that followed with the anti-communist Contras, Cuba gave substantial military aid and ideological training to the Sandinistas. Once the multi-party post Somoza government was formed in 1979, under the leadership of Daniel José Ortega Saavedra, it quickly became dominated by the Sandinistas, who quickly started on the familiar path of expropriating private land and turning to the Marxist socio-economic model. The Inter-American Commission on Human Rights (IACHR, an autonomous organ of the Organization of American States, or OAS) found in a 1981 report evidence of mass executions by the Sandinistas in the period following the revolution[12].

Ortega also travelled to Cuba to receive training and solidify his Marxist allegiances. The FSLN additionally created neighborhood captains, similar to the Cuban Committees for the Defense of the Revolution (Fidel Castro proclaimed them "a collective system of revolutionary vigilance"; in other words, neighbors spying upon neighbors) called Sandinista Defense Committees (*Comités de Defensa Sandinista,* or CDS). The Cubans and Nicaraguans quickly began aiding Marxist revolutionary movements throughout other Latin American countries, starting with El Salvador and Guatemala.

---

[11] In May 1993 he was forced out of the office by the Venezuelan Supreme Court for the embezzlement of 250 million bolívars.

[12] According to the Nicaraguan Commission of Jurists, the Sandinistas carried out over 8,000 political executions within three years of the revolution. The number of "anti-revolutionary" Nicaraguans who had "disappeared" in Sandinista hands or had died "trying to escape" were numbered in the thousands. By 1983, the number of political prisoners in the Sandinistas' ruthless tyranny were estimated at 20,000. Torture was institutionalized.

Cuban and East Germans advisors helped the Sandinistas form a secret police force modeled after the feared *Stasi* in East Germany. Cuban military and DGI advisors (*Dirección General de Inteligencia*, or Intelligence Directorate), initially brought in during the Sandinista insurgency to maintain control over the population in "liberated" areas, would swell to over 2,500 and operated within all levels of the Sandinista government.

Cuban aid went further. Cuba provided Nicaragua with volunteer teachers on a yearly basis and was instrumental in the Nicaraguan Literacy Campaign, and donated audiovisual equipment and teaching materials. Additionally, about 2,000 primary and secondary Nicaraguan students were sent to study on the Cuban Isle of Youth, with the cost covered by the host country (Cuba). The curriculum naturally included ideological training.

More than 1,500 Cuban doctors were sent to Nicaragua, and Nicaraguan workers were trained by Cubans in the use of machinery imported from the USSR and other Soviet bloc countries. Close to 3,000 Nicaraguans went to Cuba for short periods of three to six months to receive industrial and mechanical training. Cuba helped Nicaragua in large infrastructure projects such as the building of roadways, sugar mills, and power plants.

Due to its repressive policies, the Sandinista régime soon found itself fighting a guerrilla war with the Reagan-backed, pro-democracy Contras. The largest among the Contra groups was the the Nicaraguan Democratic Force (*Fuerza Democrática Nicaragüense*, or FDN).[13]

The conflict ended with the 1990 presidential election where Daniel Ortega lost to Violeta Barrios de Chamorro, widow of Pedro Joaquín Chamorro, a journalist working at his family's newspaper, *La Prensa*, which was highly critical of the Somoza régime. Chamorro led a 14 party alliance of pro-democracy groups known as the National Opposition Union (*Unión Nacional Opositora*, or UNO).

---

[13] The term "contra" is an contraction of the Spanish *el contra-revoluciónario*, in English "the counter-revolutionary". Some Contras disliked the term, feeling that it described their cause in a negative manner, implying a desire to restore the old *Somocista* order. Contras usually referred to themselves as *comandos* ("commandos"), while peasant supporters called the counter-insurgents *los primos* ("the cousins").

[Image 14: Fidel Castro and Daniel Ortega in Managua, Nicaragua, 1985.]

El Salvador

The Salvadoran Civil War was fought by the Salvadoran government against rebels headed by the Farabundo Martí National Liberation Front (FMLN), an umbrella coalition of five leftist guerrilla groups. The rebels were supplied by Cuba with advisors and Soviet weapons. The Salvadoran military, backed by the Reagan administration, waged a punishing counter-insurgency program derived and adapted from US strategy during the war in Vietnam and taught by American military advisors. The war had claimed some 70,000 lives by the time of the January 16, 1992, Chapultepec Peace Accords. In the accords, the FMLN metamorphosed from a guerrilla army to a legitimate political party.

[Image 15: Salvadoran guerrillas operating in the countryside.]

Grenada

The Marxist-Leninist New Jewel Movement (NJM), under the leadership of Maurice Bishop, overthrew the government of Eric Gairy while Gairy was on a trip abroad in 1979. The armed coup was conducted by the People's Revolutionary Army (PRA), which had been formed in secrecy within the NJM. The NJM suspended the constitution and announced draconian laws. The People's Revolutionary Government of Grenada and Cuba established diplomatic relations.

After the NJM seized power, the Grenadian army expanded rapidly, far outnumbering their combined Eastern Caribbean neighbors. The Soviet Union and Cuba supplied nearly all of the weapons, and especially selected soldiers and officers were trained in the USSR to insure ideological purity. Deputy Prime Minister Bernard Coard orchestrated an additional coup, with Cuban and Soviet sanction, in order to speed up the Grenadian conversion to a communist state. Coard had Bishop first placed under house arrest, and eventually killed.

The United States accused Grenada of constructing facilities to aid a Soviet-Cuban military build-up in the Caribbean, and assisting the Cuban infiltration of weapons to subversives operating in Central America. Thus, on October 25, 1983, at 5:00 AM, 7,600 troops, mostly from the United States, along with 350 members from the Eastern Caribbean Peace Force (ECPF), invaded Grenada encountering sporadic resistance from 1,200 to 1,500 troops of the People's Revolutionary Army. Although many of the Grenadian troops surrendered, some put up stiff resistance against the US-led invasion force. At the time of the invasion there were 722 Cuban soldiers deployed on the island to prop up the leftist government. Cuban losses during the fighting were 25 killed, 59 wounded, and 638 captured. Also present were 60 advisors from the Soviet Union, East Germany, Bulgaria, Libya, and North Korea.

[Image 16: Marxist allies (left to right) Daniel Ortega, Maurice Bishop, and Fidel Castro.]

Yom Kippur War

Cuba joined the Soviet sponsored multinational efforts against Israel, sending approximately 4,000 troops, including tank and helicopter crews to Syria, in the three week conflict against the Israeli Defense Forces. These men performed well but were unable to defeat the Israeli Army. Precise Cuban casualty numbers have remained a state secret.

[Image 17: Hundreds of Cuban tanks took part in the 1973 Arab-Israeli War.]

Ethio-Somali War

This conflict between Mohamed Siad Barre's Somali Democratic Republic, and Mengistu Haile Mariam's People's Democratic Republic of Ethiopia, between 1977 and 1978 is also known as the Ogaden War. Fighting erupted in the Ogaden region as Somalia attempted to "liberate" the area. The USSR, finding itself supplying both sides of a war, attempted to mediate a ceasefire between its Marxist propagates. When their efforts failed, the Soviets abandoned Somalia. Naturally, their Cuban surrogates followed in the abandonment. All aid to Siad Barre's régime was halted, while arms shipments to Ethiopia were increased. Somalia abrogated the Treaty of Friendship and Cooperation with the USSR, expelled all Russian advisers, and broke diplomatic relations with Cuba.

When the USSR began supporting the Ethiopian Derg[14] government instead of the Somalis, other Communist bloc nations dutifully followed (sending at least $850 million in armaments—including 400 tanks and 50

---

[14] The Derg, Common Derg or Dergue (meaning "committee" or "council") is the short name of the *Coordinating Committee of the Armed Forces, Police, and Territorial Army* that ruled Ethiopia from 1974 to 1987. It took power following the ousting of Emperor Haile Selassie I. Soon after it was established, the committee was formally renamed the *Provisional Military Administrative Council*, but continued to be known popularly as "the Derg". In 1975, it embraced communism as the official state ideology.

MiGs). The Cuban military deployed 15,000 combat troops along with artillery, tanks, helicopters and aircraft to support the Derg government and the USSR military advisors in the region.[15] The conflict ended with a Somali retreat. The Somalis lost 8,000 men (one-third of its military), three-quarters of its armored units, and half of its air force.

[Image 18: Column of Cuban-manned Ethiopian tanks seen near Jijiga, in March 1978.]

Angolan Civil War

In 1975, as many as 5,500[16] Cuban troops had been airlifted to the African country to support the leftist People's Movement for the Liberation of Angola (MPLA) (see Appendix B: "The Shipment of Comrades to Angola and Mozambique"), as it sought dominance over the war-torn region — while the United States and South Africa had been supporting the opposition National Union for the Total Independence of Angola (UNITA) and the more conservative National Liberation Front of Angola (FNLA).

By 1977 the MPLA and Cuban forces had control over the southern cities, but roadways in the south came under repeated attacks by UNITA. Insisting on Cuban withdrawal, UNITA's Savimbi stated "The real enemy is Cuban colonialism," warning, "The Cubans have taken over the country, but sooner or later they will suffer their own Vietnam in

---

[15] Due to the Sino-Soviet rift, the People's Republic of China supported Somalia, but sent only token military assistance.

[16] Eventually the Cuban contingent would reach 40,000 troops in February 1985.

Angola."[17] The MPLA and Cuban troops used flame throwers, bulldozers, and napalm airstrikes to destroy villages in a 1.6-mile (2.6 km) wide area along the Angola-Namibia border. Only women and children were able to pass through this area, called the "Castro Corridor," because MPLA troops had executed all males ten years of age or older to prevent them from joining the UNITA forces. Toxicology reports indicate that the Cuban military used nerve gas against its opponents. Cuban military intervention in Angola ended in 1991, while the civil war continued until 2002.

[Image 19: A Cuban T-62 tank crew in Angola in 1987.]

Cuba's Role in the Non-Aligned Movement

The revolutionary government in Havana prioritized building diplomatic alliances throughout the Third World since its inception, and the Non-Aligned Movement (NAM - the largest international body besides the United Nations) became a primary venue for strengthening its international profile and prestige. Non-alignment, a term created by the newly independent Indian state to define its foreign policy position in relation to the Cold War, referred generally to the rejection of military blocs and the associated international politics in favor of more politically neutral and democratic relations between countries. Cuba and other faux nonaligned members reoriented NAM global policy toward anti-western strategies couched in egalitarian and usually pro-Soviet verbiage

---

[17] Wood, 2016.

regarding economic inequality, cultural preservation, medical care, human rights, and peaceful coexistence.

Cuba is one of NAM's founding members. Deeply involved in the organization, Cuba twice hosted the NAM's triennial summit of heads of state, chairing the Movement until the subsequent summits. Considering the criteria set up in 1961 for NAM membership, which ruled that member countries could not be involved in defense or military alliances with the US or USSR, the historically pawn-like relationship between Cuba and the Soviet Union is contradictory and highly ironic.

[Image 20: Fidel Castro is met by Indira Gandhi on his arrival in India for the Non- Aligned Movement summit.]

Medical Internationalism

Cuba engages in an aggressive "Doctor Diplomacy".[18] In the 1960s, more than 28,000 Cuban health workers worked in 37 Latin American countries, more than 30,000 in 33 African countries, and nearly 8,000 in 24 Asian countries. Cuba sent 67,000 health workers to structural cooperation programs in 94 countries over a period of four decades, usually committed to work for a period of at least two years. This is an average of 3,350 health workers working abroad every year between 1960 and 2000. The medical personnel "perform[ed] a critical function in

---

[18] Sometimes lampooned as "Castro-Care", with an obvious reference to "Obama-Care".

consolidating socialist consciousness"[19]. Many doctors take the opportunity of working abroad to defect. Cuban doctors working in other countries are reported to be monitored and accompanied by "minders", and subject to strict curfews, preventing an exodus of thousands of healthcare professionals.

[Image 21: Cuban doctors and medical personnel before being shipped on "a mission".]

Drug Trafficking & the Ochoa Trial

As early as 1975, US intelligence received the first reports that the Castro government was providing the protection of Cuban ports and territorial waters to major drug smugglers. At first, these reports were greeted with healthy skepticism. However, the evidence was undeniable by the fall of 1981. Cuba's cash-starved economy was indubitably being aided by the millions of nacro-dollars smugglers pumped into it, according to intelligence reports from federal and state law-enforcement agencies. Marxist guerrilla movements in Colombia, El Salvador, Guatemala, and throughout Latin America also benefitted from the additional millions the Cubans apportioned to their cause.

The Castro régime found itself in an awkward situation. Fidel Castro boasted internationally that his government was intolerant of drug trafficking, but DEA surveillance tapes and interviews with former Cuban officials and drug-runners confirmed it was using drug smuggling as a political weapon. The growing narco-trafficking scandal was

---

[19] Ceasar, 2007.

potentially more dangerous for Castro than any previous domestic crisis. Caught in a lie, the régime faced additional problems. By mid-1989, the economic malaise and political changes then taking place on the island and abroad[20] had already resulted in a shared sense among the Cuban leadership that a crisis might be at hand.

Given Fidel Castro's resistance to instituting any political or economic reforms similar to those then being carried out in the Soviet Union under Mikhail Gorbachev, the Havana government decided that a shakeup of Cuba's security apparatus was in order. As a result of the purges that followed, the authority of the Ministry of Interior was diminished as many career intelligence officers were forced out of the institution and replaced by military personnel.

Then there was General Ochoa.

Arnaldo T. Ochoa Sánchez was a widely decorated and respected army officer who was not only popular among his men, but as the recipient of the country's highest decoration, a Hero of the Republic, Ochoa was a potential challenger to the authority to Fidel and Raúl Castro.

General Ochoa was next in line to take over as the chief of the Western Army in June 1989, a mere six months after returning home from a tour of duty as the commander of Cuba's forces in Angola. It was the most important of the FAR's three territorial commands. Instead, on June 13, the well-known general was arrested and charged with "serious acts of corruption and illegal use of economic resources."[21]

On June 30, 1989, the court martial began. The government charged three other officers, in addition to Ochoa, as the key players in a supposed conspiracy that included drug and diamond trafficking, money laundering, and other illegal activities. The televised proceedings were a "show trial" that was reminiscent of the Stalinist era in the Soviet Union. The four officers were executed by firing squad in July.

---

[20] Beginning in Poland, and continuing in East Germany, Czechoslovakia and throughout Eastern Europe and the Soviet Union, the desire to cast off the shackles of communism had achieved an unstoppable momentum in 1989. The desire for greater liberalization was sparked by the ascension of reform-minded Soviet leader Mikhail Gorbachev and felt world-wide, including the long repressed Cuban populace.

[21] Hudson, 2001.

Former Cuban Air Force Brigadier General Rafael del Pino, who defected to the United States, believes it was "virtually impossible" for Ochoa to have been involved in drug trafficking. Many ranking Cuban officers, as well as many in the general population, believe that as well. Rather, they believe that the popular General was a convenient scapegoat, and that his principal "crimes" were in fact questioning the Castro brother's authority.

If the Castro's were willing to sacrifice their closest supporters, then who was safe in Cuba? The Ochoa affair has very serious implications for sycophants of the régime.

[Image 22: Before his conviction and execution, General Arnaldo T. Ochoa Sánchez was a shining star in Castro's Cuba.]

Guinea-Bissau

The war in Guinea-Bissau had been termed "Portugal's Vietnam". The Marxist African Party for the Independence of Guinea and Cape Verde (Portuguese: *Partido Africano da Independência da Guiné e Cabo Verde)* or PAIGC, the main indigenous guerrilla movement, received substantial support from safe havens in neighboring Senegal and Guinea-Conakry. PAIGC insurgents were also well-trained, well-led, and well-equipped.

By 1963, the PAIGC, led by Amílcar Cabral, also known by his *nom de guerre* Abel Djassi, began to openly receive military support from Cuba, China, and the Soviet Union. Although he claimed to not be a Marxist, he was deeply influenced by Marxist ideology, met with Soviet bloc leaders such as Romania's Nicolae Ceaușescu, and became an inspiration to revolutionaries and independence movements throughout the world.

While PAIGC rebels fought Portuguese soldiers, Cuban instructors accompanied them, Cuban military personnel took to the field with them, and Cuban doctors staffed their medical stations. Starting in 1966, and remaining through the end of the war in 1974, this was the longest Cuban involvement in Africa before Angola. It was also a pivotal military contribution, as *No Pintcha*, a Guinean paper declared, "The Cubans' solidarity was decisive for our struggle".[22] The Cuban's knowledge in using the sophisticated weapons that the PAIGC received from the Soviets was invaluable. One PAIGC commander remarked. "They trained us on the spot. We called our first bazookas 'Cubans.' They were made in the United States, but it was the Cubans who gave them to us and taught us how to use them."[23]

---

[22] Gleijeses, 1997, p. 45

[23] Gleijeses, 2002, p. 197

[Image 23: Amílcar Cabral with Romanian Communist dictator Nicolae Ceaușescu.]

Mozambique

After a decade of intermittent guerrilla warfare and Portugal's return to democracy (the Carnation Revolution of April, 1974), FRELIMO, or the The Mozambique Liberation Front (Portuguese: *Frente de Libertação de Moçambique*) took control of the former colony by June 25, 1975. The new Marxist government, predictably anti-European and anti-capital, emptied the country of the 250,000 Portuguese in Mozambique. Former FRELIMO general and now minister of the interior, Armando Guebuza, issued a confiscatory new law ordering the Portuguese to leave the country with only 20 kilograms (44 pounds) of luggage within 24 hours. Many had already fled in fear of the increasing violence toward anyone connected to the *ancien régime*. Deprived of all their personal possessions, they returned to Portugal destitute.

The new revolutionary government, under the leadership of Samora Machel, a Marxist and admirer of Lenin, established a single party state intolerant of any opposition. The FRELIMO government quickly turned into a client state of the Soviet Union, receiving military support from the Russians and from Cuba. The usual failed policies of expropriation of private property and centralized planning were instituted, resulting in economic collapse and famine. The Marxist government executed tens of thousands of its citizens while trying to broaden its control throughout the countryside, and sent others to "re-education"[24] camps where thousands more died. However, as in many other places, opposition to the new régime did not disappear. The anti-Communist and pro-western Mozambican National Resistance (Portuguese: *Resistência Nacional Moçambicana* - RENAMO) began a protracted struggle against FRELIMO which lasted from 1977 to 1992. RENAMO also had to contend with 230 Soviet and 800 Cuban military advisors in the country to insure its pro-communist orientation.

---

[24] A euphemism used by Communists for a forced labor camp where prisoners were usually worked to death.

[Image 24: Fidel Castro and Samora Machel.]

Yemen and Oman

After unstable Marxist South Yemen (People's Democratic Republic of Yemen) attacked North Yemen (Yemen Arab Republic) in a 1979 border dispute, Cuba's military aided the attack with advisors, artillery, armored vehicles, rockets, MiG pilots, logistics, and communications (predictably, the Soviet Union and East Germany helped). Daily patrols over the Red Sea and the Gulf of Aden were flown by Cuban pilots. Jordan, Saudi Arabia, and Britain aided North Yemen. The Cuban armed forces also trained Dhofari guerrillas, whose objective was the overthrow of the Omani government, a Sultinate.

[Image 25: South Yemeni leadership (left to right); President Salim Rubai Ali, Secretary General of the National Liberation Front of Yemen Abdul Fattah Ismail, and Prime Minister Ali Nasir Muhammad.]

Trinidad and Tobago Meeting

US President Barack Obama stated on April 17, 2009, during a summit in Trinidad and Tobago that "the United States seeks a new beginning with Cuba",[25] and nullified the Bush Administration's prohibition on travel and remittances by Americans from the United States to the island. Comfortable with his re-election, on December 17, 2014, Obama continued the process of restoring relations between Cuba and the United States, generally referred to as the "Cuban Thaw". The agreement was brokered in part by the government of Canada and Pope Francis. On April 14, 2015, the Obama administration announced that the US would remove Cuba from the American government's list of nations which sponsor terrorism. On June 30, 2015, Cuba and the US finalized an agreement to reopen embassies in their respective capitals on July 20, 2015. President Obama has been heavily criticized for these diplomatic moves. Prior to the historic trip, the Castro government was arresting dissidents and reporters, maintaining an unwavering anti-American stance internationally, and supporting dictatorial régimes.

---

[25] NBC News, 2009.

[Image 26: President Obama stands in front of a mural of Che Guevara on the Ministry of the Interior, Cuba.]

Intelligence Directorate

All state organs of law enforcement come under the jurisdiction and control of the Cuban Ministry of the Interior, which is supervised by the Revolutionary Armed Forces (Spanish: *Fuerzas Armadas Revolucionarias*—FAR). Another important state organ is the Intelligence Directorate (Spanish: *Dirección de Inteligencia*, or DI, also known as G2) which is tasked with internal and external security and intelligence and maintains close ties with the Russian Federal Security Service, or FSB[26]. Almost since its inception the the DI has been active in aiding leftist movements throughout Latin America, Africa, and the Middle East. It maintained training camps for terrorists, such as the

---

[26] The FSB is the principal security agency of Russia and is the successor to the the feared Committee of State Security (the KGB) of the Soviet era. There is no difference in the tactics and methodology used by the Cuban DI and the FSB/KGB.

nefarious "Carlos"[27], on Cuban soil. Havana has avoided the usual terrorist stunts, such as airplane hijacking, that attract maximum and unfavorable international attention. The Castros shrewdly do not publicly threaten to unleash terrorists against the West in their legendary and lengthy diatribes. This is in sharp contrast to other leftist dictatorships, and also to the current alphabet soup of radical Muslim organizations. Cuban intelligence invented or refined many of the techniques of present-day urban terrorism, which they dutifully passed on in dozens of training camps worldwide to thousands of Argentinians, Brazilians, Chileans, Colombians, Ecuadorians, Hondurans, Nicaraguans, Salvadorans, and Uruguayans, Basques, Namibians, Palestinians West Germans, and Yemenis, to name a few. It is reputed that the DI helped interrogate American POWs held by the North Vietnamese during the war. Havana may be encouraged to continue its support of terrorism because of the removal of all diplomatic and economic restraints by the Obama administration.

[Image 27: Fidel Castro shaking hands with Communist soldiers in Quang Tri Province, North Vietnam.]

---

[27] "Carlos the Jackal", was the cover name of Ilich Ramírez Sánchez, a Venezuelan militant who orchestrated some of the highest-profile terrorist attacks of the 1970s and 1980s. In 1994 French agents captured Carlos and returned him to France for trial where he was sentenced to life in prison.

Cuba's Military Machine

Cuba has become the most utterly militarized nation on the planet. As of 2010, Cuba allocated $94.3 million for military expenditures annually, or more than 10 percent of its GDP. Starting in the early 1960s, Cuba built up one of the largest armed forces in Latin America. Its military spending is greater than even the South American giant, Brazil, which spent $38.13 million the same year. Military service is compulsory for 2 years for persons 17-28 years of age, and both sexes are subject to military service.

Always dependent on the USSR for its military supplies[28], from 1975 until the late 1980s, Soviet military aid empowered Cuba to greatly enhance its military capabilities. However, after the loss of Soviet subsidies in 1991, Cuba was forced to reduce the numbers of its military. Even so, Cuba remains heavily militarized. As of 2010, Cuban active frontline personnel numbered 90,000 (these are backed by at least 110,000 reservists, who are trained for forty-five or more days each year), total available personnel number 6 million, those fit for service number approximately 4,835,000, and those reaching military age each year number 142,000. In comparison, the Canadians, with a population that is two and a half times that of Cuba, have far greater wealth and sobering responsibilities with the United Nations and NATO, rely upon a regular army of only 95,000.

The Cubans have accumulated an astounding 300 T-62 and 650 T-54/55 Soviet-made main battle tanks, 60 amphibious and light tanks, 650 other assorted armored vehicles, 600 anti-tank guns, and 1,400 artillery pieces.

The Cuban Navy is relatively small, yet it maintains four older model submarines and six North Korean Yugo class midget submarines, two guided-missile frigates, and a large number of minesweepers and patrol craft. The Cuban Air Force has a strength of 250 combat aircraft in various stages of readiness, mostly MiG-21, 23, and 27 models. Although there are no exact figures available, Western analysts estimate that a few as 41 are combat operational. Although the Cuban military machine is considerably more powerful than that of any other Latin American country, it is unable to project power beyond its borders without the aid of a benefactor.

---

[28] In early 1961, Castro's army was able to fend of the Bay of Pigs invasion force with recently arrived Soviet T-34 medium tanks, IS-2 heavy tanks, and SU-100 tank destroyers, in addition to various other equipment.

The Cuban military, invariably a highly conspicuous symbol of Castro's revolution and power, heralds an antagonistic and adverse message for those desiring peace and prosperity throughout the world. The degree to which Castro has militarized Cuban society is such that, as English historian Hugh Thomas has stated, "Batista's tyranny seems, from the angle of the present, a mild and indolent undertaking."[29]

[Image 28: Cuban military in light armored vehicles on parade.]

The "Special Period"

After Fidel Castro seized power in Cuba in 1959, a joke soon started circulating throughout Cuban society: the signs at the Havana zoo that previously read "Please do not feed the animals" were soon changed to "Please do not take the animals' food". When the so-called "special period" started in the early 1990s after the collapse of the USSR and the subsequent withdrawal of its aid to Cuba, the times became even harder and the joke became edgier. The new signs, so the latest version of the joke went, begged the zoo visitors not to *eat the animals*.

The collapse of the Soviet bloc trade organization, COMECON (the Council for Mutual Economic Assistance), presented new difficulties for the Cuban government, which in the best of times delivered an austere

---

[29] 1998, p. 262.

standard of living that barely satisfied the basic needs of the Cuban people in providing food, housing, and consumer goods. This new challenge to Cuban Communism became known in Cuba as the *Special Period*.

Further food and fuel shortages, as well as a punishing economic downturn, followed the withdrawal of Soviet subsidies totaling more than $6 billion per year. Exports fell by 79 percent and imports by 75 percent, the budget deficit tripled, and the gross national product contracted by as much as 50 percent by 1993.[30] Not surprisingly, the already spartan[31] economic existence of the population declined sharply.

In the first half of the nineties, the most terrible years of the crisis, Cubans simply went hungry, leading to grave nutritional deficiencies that resulted in 1991 in an outbreak of optical neuropathy[32] that affected more than fifty thousand people.

Buses, transportation, and public services nosedived, and those without remittances of hard currency from abroad found life nearly impossible. Wages also declined steeply, and as late as 2013 they had only reached 27 percent of 1989 levels.

---

[30] In the 1980s, for example, 88 percent of Cuba's trade took place with the USSR and the Soviet bloc. The revolution had shaped agriculture under the principles that the state is the central force in production. Cuban agriculture was similar to the Soviet model in that it was large-scale, oriented towards export, and heavily subsidized. The rural economy in Cuba slowed and then practically came to a standstill. Tractors stood motionless in fields, electric pumps went dry, crops wilted, and breeding stock animals were slaughtered as food disappeared.

[31] In Cuba socialism was often sarcastically lauded by the public as the widespread sharing of scarcity: the rationing of foodstuffs and goods, the unavailability of many basic goods, the persistence of visible poverty amongst the population, and the lack of housing, child-care facilities, public health, and public transportation. *La libreta,* the Cuba ration booklet, encapsulates the fact that food is still rationed after more than 50 years of socialism, the rations in the booklet have always been inadequate, and have been shrinking over the decades.

[32] Loss of vision or blindness due to optic nerve abnormalities or damage, in this case from diminished caloric consumption, malnutrition, or toxic exposure from lack or hygiene (shortages in the water supplies or contamination thereof, soap and cleaning products, etc.).

The "Special Period" also impacted the health care system. Patients have to bring their own bedding to the hospitals, and assorted other items such as light bulbs, soap, and even containers of water. "Gratuities" to medical personnel became common. Teachers and other professionals have fled their respective fields to find higher wages in other sectors such as tourism or the ubiquitous black market.

Equally important, since the fall of the USSR, the support for the Castro régime has fallen substantially, especially among Cuban youths. This does not mean that there is open opposition to the government, which would result in a rapid and usually brutal confrontation with the one thing that *always* functions smoothly on the island: the security apparatus. Periodically, the government releases political prisoners (they can always be rounded up again with relative ease, since movement is both closely monitored and limited) and increasingly, but slowly, allows for a small degree of social liberalization (for example, in terms of permitting religious institutions[33] and travel abroad), but still maintains a one-party police state. The government continuously employs close surveillance, harassment, and frequent arrests of dissidents and suspected dissidents. The court system is a complete sham, as agreed upon by international jurists and legal experts.

On August 5, 1994, Havana experienced spontaneous protests against the government, called *El Maleconazo,* which continued throughout the day. Thousands of Cubans took to the streets, shouting *"libertad"* (Spanish: *liberty*). Protestors threw stones at shop windows. State security dispersed the protestors, shooting at unarmed civilians and beating them with truncheons.

However, the Castro régime continued to cling to tried and failed Marxist principles, and refused to democratize the political process. Eventually, Cuba found an economic lifeline and political support in the People's Republic of China. Leftist Hugo Chávez, then President of Venezuela, (signing Cuba to the Bolivarian Alliance for the Americas[34]), and equally

---

[33] Priests and other religious persons must take care to limit their speech to religious matters and not to criticize the government's policies or the Castro brothers.

[34] Founded by Cuba and Venezuela in 2004, it is associated with socialist governments in the Americas wishing to consolidate economic integration exclusive of the United States, and based on a vision of social welfare, bartering, and mutual economic assistance.

leftist Evo Morales, President of Bolivia, made common cause with Castro; both countries being major oil and gas exporters.

In 2006 an aging Fidel Castro transferred his duties to the First Vice-President, his brother Raúl Castro, who formally assumed the presidency on February 24, 2008, continuing the family dynasty. Raúl promised that some of the government restrictions on the Cuban economy would be removed during his inauguration speech. Minor adjustments were introduced, such as more relaxed foreign investment laws and the opening of private, but still highly regulated, small businesses and agricultural stands. The Cuban government's economic survival strategy now requires the cultivation of foreign investment and improved political relations with market-economy countries.

[Image 29: Plain clothed and uniformed police arrest and brutalize a demonstrator during *El Maleconazo*.]

A Look Toward the Future

In August 2015 there occurred a graphic representation of the future of Cuba, as the US flag was raised again in Havana. Eight months earlier, Barack Obama and Raúl Castro had made public their intent to normalize diplomatic relations between the two countries. The Obama administration is intent on overlooking Cuba's past transgressions, as well as its present policies, in the hopes of establishing a new legacy and changing the political dynamics... with a a high degree of naïveté, according to many critics. With this, the Obama administration aided in the renewal and revitalization an otherwise moribund economic carcass.

Still, the Castro brother's revolution finds itself forced to gradually chart a new heading, or face extinction.

The daily flights from and to Miami join others from around the world, and Cubans can now obtain licenses to operate small private businesses (ironically, foreigners have been establishing large enterprises, such as hotels closed to Cuban nationals, for some time). Still, Cubans find it hard to afford "luxury" goods taken for granted in the US and Europe. Money from family members living abroad is a necessity.

Fidel Castro admitted on December 2, 1961, "I am a Marxist-Leninist and will remain one until the last day of my life."[35] Whether or not Castro had *always* been a communist, or whether he had been "pushed" into the arms of the Soviets, as his apologists insisted, was a topic hotly debated in many political circles during that time period. The statement was no surprise to those who knew Castro's background. Prior to Castro triumphantly entering Havana on January 1, 1959, Former Assistant Secretary of State Spruille Braden (who also served as US ambassador to Cuba from 1943 to 1945) gave an interview in mid-1957 to *Human Events,* a Washington weekly, citing Castro's communist activities.

Today, the Communist Party remains the only political party permitted, and the ruling elite, all tied to the Castro family and the Armed Forces, jealously guard their privilege and power. Many have attempted to analyze the nature of the régime in Cuba. Some have done so in an attempt to excuse it for its inhumane politics and manifest flaws. The middle and working classes of Cuba did not share Fidel's well-hidden agenda when he stated in 1959 "I am not a communist and neither is the revolutionary movement..."[36] The truth is that Fidel and and Raúl Castro are above all else *Castristas*, much more so than they are *Communistas*. Marxism was the perfect ideology for Fidel, Raúl, and those wishing to implement total political control over a country. The Castro brothers would have called themselves *Fascistas* if the pages of history would have been written differently. Marxism was the historically viable ideology at the time; the ideology of convenience and political perpetuation.

---

[35] Fidel Castro. (n.d.). BrainyQuote.com. Retrieved from http://www.brainyquote.com/quotes/quotes/f/fidelcastr178573.html

[36] Cold War Quotations. Alpha History. Retrieved from http://alphahistory.com/coldwar/cold-war-quotations/

The Cuban economy, as well as the government's previous military expansionism, has experienced a myopathic crippling with the Soviet Union's demise. The government is attempting to offset this by encouraging foreign investment. In this regard, the Cuban government is following the Chinese model of adopting Gorachev's *perestroika without glasnost* (and certainly no *demokratizatsiya*).[37] However, the easing of the government's grip on the economy does not equal an increase in the respect for human rights. As of this writing, more than one million Cubans have sought exile throughout the world, escaping Castro's 'socialist paradise'. The United Nations (UN) Human Rights Commission, Amnesty International, and other international groups have denounced Cuba's communist government for its blatant and continuous human rights violations to the Cuban people.

Fidel Castro was the cement which held the 1959 Cuban revolution together for decades. His cult of personality cannot be underestimated. Even a putrescent Castro continues to draw international headlines with his defiant writings. What will follow after the last links to the Fidel legacy are severed upon his death, after he is interred in a mimicked *Mavzoléy Lénina*[38] and revered by leftists worldwide as a Marxist demigod? Will there be another, greater and perhaps unstoppable, *Maleconazo* like the one in 1994? Conceivably, but the aspirations of the Cuban populace are low, and made increasingly so by the relaxation of economic restrictions that have brought a small degree of comfort. Additionally, the population knows that the engines of repression will quickly be brought to bear upon any anti-government demonstrators with unrestrained brutality.

A coup d'état by the military? Equally unlikely. The army has been entirely co-opted and made part of the Mafiosi. Indeed, it is a lynchpin in the present liberalization of the economy. Dubbed *El Sistema de Perfeccionamiento Empresarial* (the System of Empresarial Perfectionism), high ranking officers manage business firms with a considerable degree of freedom from the government's central planning

---

[37] Russian for "restructuring", "transparency" or "openness", and "democratization" respectively.

[38] Lenin's Mausoleum (Russian: Мавзоле́й Ле́нина). Mao Zedong has his as well. It seems that the officially atheist state must have an embalmed leader-demigod in a shrine for Marxist pilgrimage, public reverence, and dutiful remembrance. This writer predicts that the construction of Fidel's shrine is a very likely scenario, although such plans have not been announced by the Cuban government as of this writing.

committee. The military has incorporated more and more firms, expanding into sectors such as manufacturing, tobacco production, and tourism.

In spite of being crippled economically, Cuban foreign policy seeks to aggravate and militarize regional and internationalize problems. Cuba is a relatively small country with the foreign policy of a major world player. In Latin America, an area where sorely is needed stable, non-corrupt, and democratic governments interested in economic development, Cuba is acerbating existing problems by encouraging and aiding leftist authoritarian régimes. Cuba aims to stimulate violence and destabilize its democratic neighbors, and wherever possible disrupt normal diplomatic relations in the hemisphere. Classically Machiavellian in their foreign policy aims, the existence of diplomatic ties with Cuba will not negate their attempts to destabilize any established *diplomatic entente*. As investigated previously in this tome, Cuban foreign policy is primarily aimed at subverting democracy, and backed by an extensive intelligence, political, propaganda, and military apparatus. One can only conclude that as the Cuban economy improves with increasing injections of capitalism *à la Chinois*, their efforts will redouble.

The escalating influence of the military and the *Raúlistas* in Cuba will constitute to be two critical variables during a post-communist transition, in the event that such a transition would occur in the future. Cuba is their personal fiefdom, and throughout history fiefdoms have seldom been relinquished without bloodshed.

[Image 30: The new leftist alliances in the Americas (left to right); Schafik Handal of the FMLN in El Salvador, Hugo Chavez of Venezuela, Fidel Castro of Cuba, and Evo Morales of Bolivia, 2004.]

SPOTLIGHT ON MAO ZEDONG

Mao Zedong (previously, under the Wades-Giles system written: "Mao Tse-tung") is undisputedly the preeminent figure in modern Chinese history, and also a commanding presence in the history of the twentieth century. The Mao-led Communist revolution in 1949 ended China's century of humiliation and laid the foundations of the rapidly developing nation of the early twenty-first century. But Mao also created much unnecessary social turmoil in the latter part of his political career; he did not know when to exit the historical stage gracefully. As a result, most Chinese today have a mixed view of Mao—a great leader who united and rejuvenated their massive country, but also one who left considerable human suffering in his wake. Mao is often compared to Qin Shihuangdi (259 bce–210 bce) by the communist government, the First Emperor of Qin, a brilliant but bloody leader who created the first unified Chinese empire in 221 bce.

Mao was a complex personality who was torn between admiration for China's past imperial glory and despair at its parlous condition in the closing decades of the nineteenth century, when he was born. As a young man, he struggled to reconcile the dichotomy in his mind (and in the minds of many others in his generation) between China's traditional civilization and the increasing demands of a modern world dominated by the advanced nations of Europe and North America. In Marxist-Leninist theory, Mao discovered a penetrating Western critique of the West, which enabled him to adopt many of its revolutionary premises (and promises) without abandoning China's own impressive cultural heritage. In direct intellectual descent from Mao, China's succeeding leaders continue to claim they are building socialism with Chinese characteristics, a somewhat ambiguous concept that has yet to be fully articulated, which (at least in the narrower area of economics) is often referred to as "market socialism".

RISE TO POWER

Mao was born on December 26 into a moderately well-off peasant family in the village of Shaoshan in Xiangtan County, Hunan province, in south-central China, not far from the provincial capital of Changsha. He developed an early interest in political and international affairs, and his years at the First Provincial Normal School in Changsha, where he studied to be a teacher, brought him into contact with young men and women from all over the province. Seeking a wider stage after graduation, Mao set out for Beijing in 1918, where he studied and worked part-time in the library at Peking University, the nation's premier institution of higher education, and, at the time, a hotbed of radical political thinking among many of the faculty and students.

Mao took an active interest in the student-inspired May Fourth movement, which sparked off a country-wide nationalist upsurge directed against unwanted European and Japanese influence in China. Soon after, Mao declared himself to be a Marxist-Leninist, without actually undertaking a thorough study of either the revolutionary doctrine or the Russian Revolution in 1917. After a short period as an elementary school principal and political activist back home in Hunan, he became a founding member of the Chinese Communist Party, which was formally established in Shanghai on July 23, 1921.

Consolidating Power

Mao's rural background gave him a special interest in the peasantry, and he was often at odds with his more urban-oriented colleagues. In early 1927, after an intensive study of rural conditions in his native province, Mao wrote his seminal "Report on an Investigation of the Peasant Movement in Hunan," in which he predicted that the peasant masses would soon rise up and sweep away the old, feudal system of land ownership that exploited and oppressed them. The Communists, he argued, should lead the peasants or get out of the way. Chiang Kai-shek's (1887–1975) bloody coup in the spring of 1927 effectively destroyed the Communist organizations in Shanghai and other major cities, forcing them to find refuge in Jiangxi province, in the mountainous hinterland in south-central China, adjacent to Hunan where Mao had been born and raised. Mao was elected chairman of the new Jiangxi Soviet (local Communist government) in this isolated base area, but soon lost power to the Returned Student group (a reference to their study in Moscow), which took over party leadership and pushed him aside.

Mao finally came into his own during the famous Long March in 1934 to 1936, when the Communists had to flee from Nationalist leader Chiang Kai-shek's fifth and finally successful military encirclement campaign to surround their base area and destroy them. At the decisive Zunyi conference in January 1935, in the early part of this arduous 6,000-mile trek, Mao was recognized as the political and military leader of the Communist movement. At the Communists' new base area in Yan'an, a small county seat in China's arid northwest region, Mao built an elaborate system of ideology, organization, guerrilla warfare, and rural recruitment that led quickly to the emergence of a powerful political movement, backed up by its own military forces (the Red Army). Both the party and the army grew rapidly during the war against Japan, which had invaded China in July 1937, and the Communists emerged as a formidable competitor for state power with the Nationalists.

By the end of the war in 1945, Mao was hailed as the Party's leading political and military strategist, and, coincidentally, its preeminent ideological thinker. What was now called Mao Zedong thought was said to represent the Sinification of Marxism, that is to say, the adaptation of Marxist theory to China's actual historical conditions. Mao's thought, reinforced through a powerful personality cult and an oppressive rectification campaign to tame his critics, was to become the ideological foundation of the Chinese Communist movement in subsequent years.

SUCCESS—AND FAILURE

Despite unfavorable odds, the Red Army (renamed the People's Liberation Army) employed superior strategic tactics to defeat the Nationalists in the civil war (1946–1949). Mao wasted no time in consolidating Communist rule; he proclaimed the founding of the People's Republic of China on October 1, 1949, and moved decisively to consolidate its borders and occupy and reintegrate Tibet. His intention was not merely to rebuild the shattered nation, but also transform it, which, with a staggering population of over 400 million, was the world's largest. In late 1949 to early 1950, Mao traveled to Moscow (his first trip abroad) and signed an alliance with the Soviets; but Mao and Soviet leader Joseph Stalin (1879–1953) neither liked nor trusted each other and their relationship was to prove unstable. The Korean War (1950–1953) could not have come at a worse time for the new régime, but at great cost Chinese troops succeeded in repulsing the U.S. advance into the north, near the Yalu River on the Chinese border.

Despite these international concerns, Mao launched a wide-ranging program of reconstruction and nationalization in major industrial and commercial cities such as Shanghai and Guangzhou (Canton). In the countryside, land was confiscated from the landlord class, many of whom were summarily executed by makeshift tribunals, and land passed (if only briefly) into the hands of the ordinary peasants. A comprehensive range of social reforms was also launched, including marriage reform favoring the female; a crackdown on crime, drugs, and prostitution; and clean-up campaigns targeted at government and business corruption. Although U.S. intervention had placed Taiwan beyond their grasp, by the mid to late-1950s the Communists had consolidated their power on the mainland, and for this much credit must go to Mao and his fellow party leaders.

But Mao had ever more ambitious plans. He wanted to speed up the pace of economic growth, based on industrial development and the collectivization of agriculture; and he wanted to emancipate China from the bonds of the Soviet alliance, which he found increasingly restrictive. Unfortunately it was at this juncture, in the late 1950s, that Mao's hitherto deft political touch began to fail him and he launched two disastrous political campaigns that convulsed the country and ultimately damaged his reputation. The Great Leap Forward in 1958, calling for the establishment of small backyard factories in the towns and giant people's communes (consolidated cooperative enterprises) in the countryside, resulted in an economic lurch backward. The consequent three bitter years (1959–1961) saw rural peasants perish in the millions due to harsh conditions for the very young, the very old, and the disadvantaged. Chastened, and under criticism from his more moderate colleagues, Mao agreed to step back from the forefront of leadership; he turned his attention to the growing ideological polemic marking the growing Sino-Soviet split and left it to others to repair the untold damage at home.

In his heart, Mao believed that the Great Leap Forward had failed largely because too many party officials (cadres) did not boldly implement his policies (not because of Marxist economic policies); disparagingly, he compared them to old women tottering about in bound feet. He decided to purge these revisionist (pro-Soviet) officials and others said to be taking the capitalist road (more open to Europe and North America generally) from positions of authority. Mao and his militant party faction (the Gang of Four) called upon the nation's youth (primarily high school and university students) to rise up and call the errant officials to account. The result was the Great Proletarian Cultural Revolution, which witnessed the unusual spectacle of the top Communist leader declaring war on his own party organization. Millions of inflamed students and others donned Red Guard armbands, and, waving the *Little Red Book* (1966) of selected Mao quotations, they proceeded to carry out their assigned mission. The campaign tore the country apart from 1966 to 1969, forcing Mao to call for military intervention to restore order, and it dragged on destructively until his death in 1976. Still, from the perspective of foreign policy, the Cultural Revolution's sharp anti-Soviet orientation succeeded in liberating China from its underlying dependency on the Soviet Union, and prepared the nation for a more independent role in international affairs in the years ahead.

A BEGINNING, AND AN END

Despite his miscalculations with the Great Leap Forward and the Cultural Revolution, Mao wisely decided to play the American card in order to counterbalance growing Soviet military power on the conflict-prone Chinese border. With the surprise invitation to a U.S. table tennis team then in Japan to visit China, Mao set in motion the ping-pong diplomacy that led to U.S. president Richard Nixon's state visit to China in February 1972, which culminated in the landmark Shanghai communiqué calling for a more constructive relationship between the countries. Mao and Nixon toasted each other cordially in the Great Hall of the People in Beijing, laying to rest a generation of bitter enmity and setting the stage for the remarkable flowering of Sino-American relations that has continued into the early twenty-first century. It was to be Mao's final hurrah; already in declining health (possibly suffering from Parkinson's disease), he gradually faded from the scene and passed away peacefully at age eighty-two on September 9, 1976.

In an official assessment of his lengthy career, the Communist Party hailed Mao as an illustrious national hero who laid the foundations of the new China, but at the same time a tragic figure with all too human frailties. Mao is buried in a grand mausoleum in Tiananmen Square in Beijing and he enjoys considerable popular approbation despite his rather clouded historical record. But while many people revere Mao, many others revile him, as they do the First Emperor of Qin, who lived some two thousand years earlier. For most Chinese though, many of whom were born well after Mao's death, he remains the human embodiment of China's national regeneration and its reemergence as a great world power.

English historian Lord Acton (1834–1902), in his controversial observation on power, concluded that "great men are almost always bad men," and, in the case of Mao, there is considerable truth to this. Mao was a dogmatic visionary who set himself seemingly impossible goals, but he had the necessary qualities of leadership, persistence, and ruthlessness to implement them. In addition to his political and military prowess, he is also considered a talented calligrapher and poet in the classical style, and he left behind a small corpus of work that is generally well regarded. But he was also something of an uncouth peasant who lacked personal polish, could be vulgar in his choice of words, and (even in his declining years) overly enjoyed the company of young women. As he aged, he became increasingly out of touch with political reality, vainly attempting to force the entire nation onto the Procrustean bed of his own ideological convictions (ideological fantasies, some would say).

Will history remember Mao Zedong? Undoubtedly, for Mao occupies a historical position comparable to individuals such as Alexander the Great, Julius Caesar, Genghis Khan, Napoleon Bonaparte, and Qin Shihuangdi—these individuals were a frustrating mix of good and bad, but they all left a distinctive imprint on their own historical ages. Like playwright William Shakespeare's Caesar, they "bestrode the narrow world like a Colossus," and to this day their achievements and failures are enshrined in countless volumes for future generations to read and ponder. The same will quite likely be true of Mao Zedong.

SPOTLIGHT ON JOSEPH STALIN

The Russian leader Joseph Stalin (1879-1953) was the supreme ruler of the Soviet Union and the leader of world communism for almost 30 years. Under Joseph Stalin the Soviet Union greatly enlarged its territory, won a war of unprecedented destructiveness, and transformed itself from a relatively backward country into the second most important industrial nation in the world. For these achievements the Soviet people and the international Communist movement paid a price that many of Stalin's critics consider inhuman and excessive. The price included the loss of millions of lives; massive material and spiritual deprivation; political repression; an untold waste of resources; and the erection of an inflexible authoritarian system of rule thought by some historians to be one of the most offensive in recent history and one that many Communists consider a hindrance to further progress in the Soviet Union itself.

Formative Years

Stalin was born Iosif Vissarionovich Dzhugashvili on Dec. 21, 1879, in Gori, Georgia. He was the only surviving son of Vissarion Dzhugashvili, a cobbler who first practiced his craft in a village shop but later in a shoe factory in the city. Stalin's father died in 1891. His mother, Ekaterina, a pious and illiterate peasant woman, sent her teen-age son to the theological seminary in Tpilisi (Tiflis), where Stalin prepared for the ministry. Shortly before his graduation, however, he was expelled in 1899 for spreading subversive views.

Stalin then joined the underground revolutionary Marxist movement in Tpilisi. In 1901 he was elected a member of the Tpilisi committee of the Russian Social Democratic Workers party. The following year he was arrested, imprisoned, and subsequently banished to Siberia. Stalin escaped from Siberia in 1904 and rejoined the Marxist underground in Tpilisi. When the Russian Marxist movement split into two factions, Stalin identified himself with the Bolsheviks.

During the time of the 1904-1905 revolution, Stalin made a name as the organizer of daring bank robberies and raids on money transports, an activity that V. I. Lenin considered important in view of the party's need for funds, although many other Marxists considered this type of highway robbery unworthy of a revolutionary socialist.

Stalin participated in congresses of the Russian Social Democratic Workers party at Tampere, London, and Stockholm in 1905 and 1906, meeting Lenin for the first time at these congresses. In 1912 Stalin spent some time with Lenin and his wife in Crakow and then went to Vienna to study the Marxist literature concerning the nationality problem. This study trip resulted in a book, *Marxism and the National Question.* In the same year Lenin co-opted Stalin into the Central Committee of the Bolshevik party.

Stalin's trips abroad during these years were short episodes in his life. He spent the major portion of the years from 1905 to 1912 in organizational work for the movement, mainly in the city of Baku. The secret police arrested him several times, and several times he escaped. Eventually, after his return from Vienna, the police caught him again, and he was exiled to the faraway village of Turukhansk beyond the Arctic Circle. He remained here until the fall of czarism. He adopted the name Stalin ("man of steel") about 1913.

First Years of Soviet Rule

After the fall of czarism, Stalin made his way at once to Petrograd, where until the arrival of Lenin from Switzerland he was the senior Bolshevik and the editor of *Pravda,* the party organ. After Lenin's return, Stalin remained in the high councils of the party, but he played a relatively inconspicuous role in the preparations for the October Revolution, which placed the Bolsheviks in power. In the first Cabinet of the Soviet government, he held the post of people's commissar for nationalities.

During the years of the civil war (1918-1921), Stalin distinguished himself primarily as military commissar during the battle of Tsaritsyn (Stalingrad), in the Polish campaign, and on several other fronts. In 1919 he received another important government assignment by being appointed commissar of the Workers and Peasants Inspectorate. Within the party, he rose to the highest ranks, becoming a member of both the Political Bureau and the Organizational Bureau. When the party Secretariat was organized, he became one of its leading members and was appointed its secretary general in 1922. Lenin obviously valued Stalin for his organizational talents, for his ability to knock heads together and to cut through bureaucratic red tape. He appreciated Stalin's capabilities as a machine politician, as a troubleshooter, and as a hatchet man.

The strength of Stalin's position in the government and in the party was anchored probably by his secretary generalship, which gave him control over party personnel administration—over admissions, training, assignments, promotions, and disciplinary matters. Thus, although he was relatively unknown to outsiders and even within the party, Stalin doubtless ranked as the most powerful man in Soviet Russia after Lenin.

During Lenin's last illness and after his death in 1924, Stalin served as a member of the three-man committee that conducted the affairs of the party and the country. The other members of this "troika" arrangement were Grigori Zinoviev and Lev Kamenev. The best-known activity of this committee during the years 1923-1925 was its successful attempt to discredit Leon Trotsky and to make it impossible for him to assume party leadership after Lenin's death. After the committee succeeded in this task, Stalin turned against his two associates, who after some hesitation made common cause with Trotsky. The conflict between these two groups can be viewed either as a power struggle or as a clash of personalities, but it also concerned political issues—a dispute between the left wing and the right wing of bolshevism. The former feared a conservative perversion of the revolution, and the latter were confident that socialism could be reached even in an isolated and relatively backward country. In this dispute Stalin represented, for the time being, the right wing of the party. He and his theoretical spokesman, Nikolai Bukharin, warned against revolutionary adventurism and argued in favor of continuing the more cautious and patient policies that Lenin had inaugurated with the NEP (New Economic Policy).

In 1927 Stalin succeeded in defeating the entire left opposition and in eliminating its leaders from the party. He then adopted much of its domestic program by initiating a 5-year plan of industrial development and by executing it with a degree of recklessness and haste that antagonized many of his former supporters, who then formed a right opposition. This opposition, too, was defeated quickly, and by the early 1930s Stalin had gained dictatorial control over the party, the state, and the entire Communist International.

Stalin's Personality

Although always depicted as a towering figure, Stalin, in fact, was of short stature. His personality was highly controversial, and it remains shrouded in mystery. Stalin was crude and cruel and, in some important ways, a primitive man. His cunning, distrust, and vindictiveness seem to have reached paranoid proportions. In political life he tended to be cautious and slow-moving. His style of speaking and writing was also ponderous and graceless. Some of his speeches and occasional writings read like a catechism. He was at times, however, a clever orator and a formidable antagonist in debate. Stalin seems to have possessed boundless energy and a phenomenal capacity for absorbing detailed knowledge.

About Stalin's private life, little is known beyond the fact that he seems always to have been a lonely man. His first wife, a Georgian girl named Ekaterina Svanidze, died of tuberculosis. His second wife, Nadezhda Alleluyeva, committed suicide in 1932, presumably in despair over Stalin's dictatorial rule of the party. The only child from his first marriage, Jacob, fell into German hands during World War II and was killed. The two children from his second marriage outlived their father, but they were not always on good terms with him. The son, Vasili, an officer in the Soviet air force, drank himself to death in 1962. The daughter, Svetlana, fled to the United States in the 1960s.

Stalin's Achievements

In successive 5-year plans, the Soviet Union under Stalin industrialized and urbanized with great speed. Although the military needs of the country drained away precious resources and World War II brought total destruction to some of the richest areas of the Soviet Union and death to many millions of citizens, the nation by the end of Stalin's life had become the second most important industrial country in the world.

The price the Soviet Union paid for this great achievement remains staggering. It included the destruction of all remnants of free enterprise in both town and country and the murder of hundreds of thousands of Russian peasants. The transformation of Soviet agriculture in the early 1930s into collectives tremendously damaged the country's food production. Living standards were drastically lowered at first, and more than a million people died of starvation. Meanwhile, Stalin jailed and executed vast numbers of party members, especially the old revolutionaries and the leading figures in all areas of endeavor.

In the process of securing his rule and of mobilizing the country for the industrialization effort, Stalin erected a new kind of political system characterized by unprecedented severity in police control, bureaucratic centralization, and personal dictatorship. Historians consider his régime one of history's most notorious examples of totalitarianism.

Stalin also changed the ideology of communism and of the Soviet Union in a subtle but drastic fashion. While retaining the rhetoric of Marxism-Leninism, and indeed transforming it into an inflexible dogma, Stalin also changed it from a revolutionary system of ideas into a conservative and authoritarian theory of state, preaching obedience and discipline as well as veneration of the Russian past. In world affairs the Stalinist system became isolationist. While paying lip service to the revolutionary goals of Karl Marx and Lenin, Stalin sought to promote good relations with the capitalist countries and urged Communist parties to ally themselves with moderate and middle-of-the-road parties in a popular front against the radical right.

From the middle of the 1930s onward, Stalin personally managed the vast political and economic system he had established. Formally, he took charge of it only in May 1941, when he assumed the office of chairman of the Council of Ministers. After Nazi Germany invaded the Soviet Union, Stalin also assumed formal command over the entire military establishment.

Stalin's conduct of Russian military strategy in the war remains as controversial as most of his activities. Some evidence indicates that he committed serious blunders, but other evidence allows him credit for brilliant achievements. The fact remains that under Stalin the Soviet Union won the war, emerged as one of the major powers in the world, and managed to bargain for a distribution of the spoils of war that enlarged its area of domination significantly, partly by annexation and partly by the transformation of all the lands east of the Oder and Neisse rivers into client states.

Judgments of Stalin

Stalin died of a cerebrovascular accident on March 5, 1953. His body was entombed next to Lenin's in the mausoleum in Red Square, Moscow. After his death Stalin became a controversial figure in the Communist world, where appreciation for his great achievements was offset to a varying degree by harsh criticism of his methods. At the Twentieth All-Union Party Congress in 1956, Premier Nikita Khrushchev and other Soviet leaders attacked the cult of Stalin, accusing him of tyranny, terror, falsification of history, and self-glorification.

SPOTLIGHT ON POL POT

Pol Pot (born 1928) was a key figure in the Cambodian Communist movement, becoming premier of the government of Democratic Kampuchéa (DK) from 1976 to 1979. He directed the mass murder of intellectuals, professional people, city dwellers—perhaps one-fifth of his own people.

Pol Pot was born Saloth Sar on May 19, 1928. He was the second son of a conservative, prosperous, and influential small landowner. Pol Pot's father had social and political connections at the royal court at the Cambodian capital of Phnom Penh, some 70 miles south from Prek Sbau, the small hamlet in Kompong Thom, the province where Pol Pot was born. Visits by court officials—and, on at least one occasion, even by King Monivong himself—to Pol Pot's father's home appear to have been common. Pol Pot consistently denied that he was Saloth Sar, probably because his family and educational background clashed with Communist proletarian perceptions and because his tactical and organizational skills seemed to have flourished best in an atmosphere of extreme secrecy. Even after he had become premier of the victorious Communist Democratic Kampuchéa (DK) régime in Phnom Penh on April 5, 1976, there was widespread uncertainty about who he was.

The Education of a Radical

Pol Pot's intellectual development showed a sharp break from traditional toward radical values. He was educated in a Buddhist monastery and a private Catholic institution in Phnom Penh and then enrolled at a technical school in the provincial quiet and security of the town of Kompong Cham to learn carpentry. Despite his later claims, there is no evidence that as early as his mid-teens he joined Ho Chi Minh's Viet Minh resistance for a while. He seemed at first destined for a trade in carpentry. However, the program of French colonial policymakers to accelerate development of a more diversified "polytechnic" elite in the overseas territories enabled Pol Pot in 1949 to obtain a government scholarship to study radio and electrical technology in Paris.

In France Pol Pot joined a small circle of leftist Cambodian students— some of whom later became prominent Marxist and/or Communist Party leaders (such as Ieng Sary, the future DK foreign minister, and Hou Yuon, an independent Marxist radical who repeatedly served in Prince Norodom Sihanouk's cabinets until his death in 1975 in the Pol Pot holocaust). Pol Pot soon became an anti-colonialist, Marxist radical. Among the European countries he visited during this period was Yugoslavia, whose determination to chart its own national Communist course of thoroughgoing reform reportedly particularly impressed him.

Upon his return to Cambodia in 1953, Pol Pot first drifted into the Viet Minh "United Khmer Issarak (Freedom) Front" of underground Cambodian Communists and radical nationalists. After 1954 the Issarak's principal above-ground organizational mainstay became the Krom Pracheachon ("Citizens Association"). The Front, along with other Cambodian political groups, opposed both the remnant of French colonial power in Cambodia and the government of Sihanouk. The latter was perceived by many Cambodians to be a French puppet. Pol Pot served for several months with Viet Minh and Issarak units, some of whom had joined in the loose leftist radical resistance groups supervised by the Krom Pracheachon. But Cambodia's 1954 achievement of independence from the French also found him increasingly involved in the organization of the Khmer People's Revolutionary Party (KPRP), the first Cambodian Communist party, founded in 1951.

In the post-independence era Pol Pot appears to have resented as much the continued heavy Communist Vietnamese influence in the KPRP and its armed units as the hothouse atmosphere of partisan political intrigues in the capital deftly manipulated by the wily Sihanouk. Pol Pot's contempt for intellectuals and politicians jockeying for favor and power was greatly increased and helped shape his own ruthless radical reforms once he assumed power. Pol Pot's mentor in these years was Tou Samouth, the onetime Unified Issarak Front's president and later the KPRP's secretary general. Like Pol Pot, Samouth was primarily interested in building the KPRP into a genuinely Cambodian, broad-based organization capable of rallying all opposition elements among peasants, urban workers, and intellectuals against the Sihanouk régime.

This effort led to tensions with the Vietnamese, who continued to try to dominate the left and anti-Sihanouk Cambodian resistance.

Building a Revolutionary Party

On September 28, 1960, Pol Pot, Tou Samouth, Ieng Sary, and a handful of followers reportedly met in secret in a room of the Phnom Penh railroad station to found the "Workers Party of Kampuchea" (WPK). Samouth was named secretary general and Pol Pot became one of three Politburo members. But on February 20, 1963, at the WPK's second congress, Pol Pot succeeded Samouth as party secretary. The latter had disappeared on July 20, 1963, under mysterious circumstances and subsequently was reported to have been assassinated. Whether Pol Pot was involved in Samouth's murder remains uncertain.

For the next 13 years, as the WPK increasingly seemed to distance itself from Hanoi, Pol Pot and other top WPK cadres virtually disappeared from public notice. They set up their main party encampments in a remote forest area of Ratanakiri province. During this period Pol Pot appears not only to have been consolidating his own leadership position in the WPK, but he also gradually and successfully contested pro-Hanoi elements in the anti-Sihanouk resistance generally. However, Pol Pot at this time carefully avoided an open breach with the Vietnamese Communists, who were consolidating their hold on the Ho Chi Minh trail and adjacent pockets of Cambodian territory. Nevertheless, a 1965 visit by Pol Pot to Hanoi designed to win acceptance as top party leader was shrouded in mutual mistrust. More successful was Pol Pot's journey and extended stay in Beijing in the same year. He remained in China for some seven months, during which time he likely received ideological and organizational schooling. Pol Pot's pro-Chinese orientation became more pronounced upon his return to Cambodia in September 1966. The WPK soon changed its name to Communist Party of Kampuchea (CPK).

CPK-instigated demonstrations against the Sihanouk régime now steadily mounted. The prince's blanket denunciation and execution of scores of what his government termed the *Khmer Rouge* ("Red Khmers") solidified the CPK-led opposition. At the same time it made that opposition appear more formidable than it actually was. In December 1969 and January 1970 Pol Pot and other CPK leaders again visited Hanoi and Beijing, evidently in preparation for a final drive against the Sihanouk régime. But the drive was preempted as on March 18, 1970, a right-wing coup in Phnom Penh overthrew Sihanouk, bringing Lon Nol to the Cambodian presidency.

Although some CPK members and other Communist Pracheachon resistance leaders—including Pol Pot's colleague the future DK President Khieu Sampan—rallied to Sihanouk's call for a united front against Lon Nol, Pol Pot himself remained aloof. After Sihanouk's fall, Hanoi had begun infiltrating some 1, 000 Vietnamese-trained Cambodian Communists into Cambodia. But on orders of Pol Pot most of these were identified and quickly killed. Despite this action and clashes with Pol Pot's followers in Kompong Chom province, Hanoi avoided rupture in the interest of winning first a decisive Communist victory throughout Indochina.

In mid-September 1971 a new CPK congress reelected Pol Pot as secretary general and as commander of its "Revolutionary Army." Tensions between Hanoi and Pol Pot increased further when the CPK refused a Vietnamese request to negotiate with the Lon Nol régime and the United States as Vietnamese-U.S. discussions took place in Paris. In keeping with the Paris Accords, the Vietnamese in the early months of 1973 left some of their Cambodian encampments. But CPK "Revolutionary Army" units quickly took their place as Pol Pot further strengthened his power base. Clashes between Lon Nol's forces and Pol Pot's guerrillas, as well as new "Revolutionary Army" raids on pro-Hanoi Cambodian resistance units and on followers of Sihanouk's coalition exile government continued, however. Yet throughout 1974, in letters to Hanoi and Vietnamese party leaders and in public messages, Pol Pot affirmed his friendship and gratitude.

A Holocaust on His Own People

On April 17, 1975, Phnom Penh fell to several Communist Cambodian and Sihanoukist factions. The CPK and Pol Pot quickly managed to establish hegemony over the capital. Fighting continued between Pol Pot's "Revolutionary Army" and Vietnamese troops in disputed border territories and on islands in the Gulf of Thailand. At a meeting with Vietnamese representatives along the border in early June 1975, Pol Pot reportedly apologized for his troops' "faulty map reading." Tensions between Pol Pot and his associates and the Vietnamese did not abate, however, despite another Pol Pot visit to Hanoi in order to suggest a friendship treaty.

For nearly a year Pol Pot and other Cambodian Communists, as well as the embattled Norodom Sihanouk (in exile), struggled for power in the newly proclaimed state of "Democratic Kampuchea." Another CPK party congress in January 1976 reaffirmed Pol Pot's position as secretary general but also revealed emergent leadership rifts between Pol Pot and some outlying zone organizations of the party. Relations with Hanoi continued to worsen. On April 14, 1976, after CPK-controlled elections for a new "People's Representative Assembly" and the resignation as head of state of Sihanouk, a new DK government was proclaimed. Pol Pot, who officially had been elected to the assembly as a delegate of a "rubber workers organization," now became premier.

However, his authority still was being contested both by Hanoi-influenced party cadres and rival party zone leaders. Beginning in November 1976 Pol Pot accelerated extensive purges of rivals, including cabinet ministers and other top party leaders. This provoked repeated explosions of unrest in Kompong Thom and Oddar Meanchey.

Meanwhile, the fury of Pol Pot's social and economic reform policies carried out by the mystery-shrouded Angka, or "inner" party organization, eventually was to make Pol Pot's name synonymous with one of the modern world's worst holocausts. Forced evacuation, through extended death marches, of the inhabitants of major cities and resettlement and harshly exploitive labor of tens of thousands in agricultural work projects; deliberate withholding of adequate food and medical care; systematic mass killings of all "old dandruff"—i.e., suspected subversives, especially those who had white collar or intellectual occupations or political experience—all these reflected Pol Pot's brand of ideology in which Rousseauist purism and Stalinist terrorism were uniquely blended. Great emphasis was placed in Pol Pot's policies on the training of the young and on the creation of a "New Man" in Cambodia. Even after Pol Pot was driven from power, young teenagers remained among his dedicated followers in the DK's "Revolutionary Army." But the killings and deliberate neglect by the Pol Pot régime cost some 1.6 million Cambodians their lives—nearly 20 percent of the country's total population.

Régime policies prompted mounting opposition among divisional commanders and party cadres. Pol Pot's visit to China and North Korea in September and October 1977 solidified his standing among other Asian Communist leaders, even as fighting with Vietnamese border forces intensified. On December 31, 1977, all diplomatic relations with Hanoi were severed, Pol Pot charging that the Vietnamese were seeking to impose their hegemony on both Laos and Cambodia through an "Indochinese Federation."

The Fall of a Dictator

On May 26, 1978, Eastern Zone party leaders and their followers rose up in revolt against Pol Pot. But the rising failed, and thousands of cadres either were killed or, like Heng Samrin (who would succeed Pol Pot as premier), made good their escape to Vietnam. Some Eastern Zone leaders charged Pol Pot with selling Cambodia to the Chinese. Vietnamese attacks on and military penetration of DK territory became more severe and extensive during the second half of 1978. Pol Pot's premiership also became more precarious and his overtures toward the Chinese to deter Vietnamese intervention found little response. In the wake of a final Vietnamese military drive, Pol Pot and other DK leaders were forces to flee Phnom Penh on January 7, 1979. They eventually regrouped their forces and established an underground government in Western Cambodia and in the Cardamom mountain range.

On July 20, 1979, Pol Pot was condemned to death in absentia, on grounds of having committed genocide. The verdict was issued by a "People's Tribunal" of the new government of the "People's Republic of Kampuchea, " installed with the aid of Vietnamese forces. As growing world attention focussed on the plight of wartorn Cambodia and on the bloody violence of the Pol Pot era, Pol Pot himself increasingly became a liability to his Chinese backers and the underground DK leaders. At a CPK congress on December 17, 1979, Pol Pot stepped down as DK prime minister, and the post was taken over by DK President Khieu Sampan. However, he remained as party secretary general and as head of the CPK's military commission, making him in effect the overall commander of the DK's 30, 000-man guerrilla force battling the Vietnamese in Cambodia. (But throughout most of the 1980s the Vietnamese army controlled Cambodia (Kampuchea) under the presidency of Heng Samrin.)

After leaving his premiership little was known of Pol Pot's whereabouts or activities. Reportedly he repeatedly sought medical attention for a cardio-vascular condition in Beijing in the course of 1981-1983. On September 1, 1985, the DK's clandestine radio announced that Pol Pot had retired as commander of the DK's "National Army" and had been appointed to be "Director of the Higher Institute for National Defense."

Pol Pot was married to Khieu Ponnary, a former fellow student activist of his Paris days and later the CPK women's movement leader in Phnom Penh.

Captured at Last

After several years of living underground, Pol Pot was finally captured on June 18, 1997, by a rival communist faction. The Khmer Rouge had suffered from internal factionalism in recent years, and finally splintered into opposing forces, the largest of which, in the northern zone, joined with the government of Cambodia under Sihanouk and hunted down their former leader. Upon capturing him, the guerrillas sentenced Pol Pot, leader of the modern day reign of terror, to life in prison.

The Cult of Personality

No true understanding of authoritarian and totalitarian systems of government can be complete without fully grasping and appreciating the significance of the phenomenon referred to as a *cult of personality* within these systems.

Cult of personality is a pejorative term implying the concentration of all power in a single charismatic leader within a totalitarian state and the near deification of that leader in state propaganda. Totalitarian régimes use the *state-controlled* mass media to cultivate a larger-than-life public image of the leader through unquestioning flattery and praise. Leaders are lauded for their extraordinary courage, knowledge, wisdom, or any other superhuman quality necessary for legitimating the totalitarian régime. The cult of personality serves to sustain such a régime in power, discourage open criticism, and justify whatever political twists and turns it may decide to take. Among the more infamous and pervasive cults of personality in the twentieth century were those surrounding Hitler, Mussolini, Stalin, Mao Zedong, Francisco Franco, Fidel Castro, Chiang Kai-shek, Ho Chi Minh, Kim Il Sung, Juan and Evita Peron, Pol Pot, Augusto Pinochet, Kim Jong Il, and Saddam Hussein. The term is occasionally—if idiosyncratically—applied to national leaders *who did not seek* similar godlike adulation during their lifetime or term in office but have been later glorified by the government or in the national mass media. Examples might include George Washington, Napoléon Bonaparte, Abraham Lincoln, Vladimir Lenin, Mustafa Kemal Atatürk, Charles de Gaulle, Ronald Reagan, Margaret Thatcher, and others.

A cult of personality differs from Thomas Carlyle's "hero worship" in the sense that it is intentionally built around the national leader and is *used to justify authoritarian rule*. In one of the more idiosyncratic usages, it is sometimes applied by analogy to refer to the public veneration of famous leaders of social movements such as Mahatma Gandhi, Martin Luther King Jr., Nelson Mandela, and others. In fact, the term itself derives from Karl Marx's critique of the "superstitious worship of authority" that had developed around his own personality, acclaimed merits, and contribution to the work of the First Socialist International in the latter half of the nineteenth century.

Historically, numerous rulers have promoted their own cults of personality. Absolute monarchies were the prevalent form of government for much of recorded history, and most traditional monarchs were held in public awe and adoration. For example, pharaonic Egypt, Imperial China, and the Roman Empire accorded their crowned sovereigns the status of revered god-kings. The doctrine of the divine right of kings claimed that absolutist monarchs such as Henry VIII, Louis XIV, or Catherine the Great sat on their thrones by the will of God. The democratic revolutions of the eighteenth and nineteenth centuries made it increasingly difficult for traditional autocrats to retain their divine aura. However, the development of the modern mass media, state-run public education, and government propaganda has enabled some more recent national leaders to manipulate popular opinion and project an almost equally extolled public image. Cults of personality developed around some of the most notorious totalitarian dictators of the twentieth century such as Hitler, Stalin, and Mao, who at the peak of their personalistic power were lionized as infallible, godlike creatures. Their portraits were hung in every private home or public building, while the country's artists and poets were expected to produce works of art idolizing the hero-leader.

Many lesser known autocrats have engaged in similar self-glorification, subordinating nearly all aspects of national life to their fickle vanity, megalomania, and conceit. In post-Soviet Turkmenistan, for instance, the late president-for-life Saparmurat Niyazov encouraged his own cult of personality, dotting the local landscapes with public monuments to himself and even renaming the months of the year to pay homage to himself and his family. After declaring Turkmenistan's independence in October 1991, the former chairman of the Sovietera Council of Ministers and first secretary of the Turkmen Communist Party quickly established himself as the center and source of all political authority in the new country. Niyazov became the first president of independent Turkmenistan and won the uncontested 1992 election, which was the only presidential election held during his rule. He assumed the title of *Turkmenbashi* ("head of all the Turkmen"), and the country's obedient legislature proclaimed him president for life. He even authored a book—the *Ruhnama*, or "Book of the Spirit"—that became a compulsory part of the curricula at all levels of the national educational system.

The term *cult of personality* became a buzzword after Soviet leader Nikita Khrushchev bitterly denounced Stalin's near deification before a closed session of the Twentieth Party Congress on February 25, 1956:

The cult of personality acquired such monstrous dimensions mainly because Stalin himself, using all conceivable methods, supported the glorification of his own person.... One of the most characteristic examples of Stalin's self-glorification and of his lack of even elementary modesty is the edition of his *Short Biography*, which was published in 1948. This book is an expression of the most unrestrained flattery, an example of making a man into a god, of transforming him into an infallible sage, "the greatest leader," "sublime strategist of all times and nations." Ultimately, no more words could be found with which to praise Stalin up to the heavens. We need not give here examples of the loathsome adulation filling this book. All we need to add is that they all were approved and edited by Stalin personally and some of them were added in his own handwriting to the draft text of the book. (Khrushchev 1989)

In a country long known for its traditional worship of religious saints and czars, the public exaltation of Soviet leaders was deliberately pursued as necessary for building national unity and consensus. The result was Stalin's cult of personality—the total loyalty and dedication of all Soviet citizens to the all-powerful leader, whose demigod personality exemplified the heroism and glory of "building socialism in one country." Khrushchev's "Secret Speech" was a major break by the post-Stalin leadership with the oppressive dominance of Stalinism. "Big Brother," a fictional character in George Orwell's famous novel *Nineteen Eighty-Four*, is widely believed to be a satire of Stalin's cult of personality (even though it is equally likely to have been based on Britain's ubiquitous Lord Kitchener).

DEATH BY COMMUNISM

Skulls of Khmer Rouge victims

Why is it, wonders Juan R. Céspedes in *The Myopic Vision: The Causes of Totalitarianism, Authoritarianism, & Statism* (2013) that the Nazi and Soviet régimes are treated so differently in the popular mind-set and the media at large? Many young people who would never purchase a t-shirt emblazoned with a swastika or a photograph of Adolf Hitler would think little (if at all) of sporting one with a hammer and sickle or a portrait of the Marxist revolutionary, and murderer of thousands of Cubans, Ernesto "Che" Guevara. Indeed, identifying oneself as a socialist, leftist, Marxist, Marxist-Leninist, or even a communist, has become a ubiquitous countercultural symbol and *appel populaire* to rebellion, even a sort of boastful global insignia in popular culture. Lenin, the founder of the Union of Soviet Socialist Republics, rejected multi-party governments and peaceful political evolution. Even a cursory reading of contemporary history reveals that Lenin's murderous despotism was to be emulated, then surpassed, by Stalin and other communists from Cuba to North Korea and throughout the world. The question remains: how did this change in thinking come about? The pivotal year was 1945; Germany and Italy had been defeated on the battlefield, their governments and economies crushed, and more importantly, they were discredited ideologically. Fascism, once a dangerous rival to communism, was no more. Thus, at the end of the war, the Soviet Union not only inherited Eastern Europe, but it also inherited a greatly enhanced level of international prestige.

Sadly, the communist killing machine surpassed that of the Nazis. Ever since Aleksandr Solzhenitsyn published his magisterial three-volume history of the Soviet concentration-camp network, "The Gulag Archipelago," in the early 1970's, the grim details of life in the Soviet totalitarian system have been well known. From arrest by the Soviet secret police for even *suspicion* of being against the régime, to torture and interrogation, to deportation and forced hard labor; the life-and-death cycle of the gulag is a familiar story. Other witnesses, like Varlam Shalamov and Evgeniya Ginzburg, have also brilliantly described prisoners' constant struggle against mistreatment, hunger, cold and disease. A great deal of information about the soul-stifling apparatus of socialist systems has been told and is plentifully available, even to the minimally acquainted with contemporary history.

When Solzhenitsyn's writings first appeared, they had an enormous impact. Yet he soon fell from favor, dismissed by the political left as an anti-communist eccentric, an obsessive and unfair critic, and by others as an extreme nationalist or anti-Semite. As documents from the Soviet archives have now shown, much of this defamation campaign was financed and promoted by the K.G.B. But the attacks had their effect: a group of revisionist historians, who dominated the study of the Stalin years in the United States and Britain during the 1980's, waged a war against the portrayal of the Soviets as ruthless oppressors of democracy.

The American political left often had a flirtatious relationship with the Soviets, their politics, and their policies. There were many times during the days of the Cold War, and continuing thereafter for decades, when leftists and liberals *wanted* the United States to adopt pro-Soviet policies. The man the Russians sought first to help was Henry A. Wallace, former vice president for F.D.R. and secretary of Commerce under Truman. Wallace became the first public figure to oppose Harry Truman's "get-tough policy" with the Soviets, which he adopted after it became clear that the Soviets were seeking to expand their empire to control Eastern Europe. Back in 1943, Wallace already had made his views clear in a speech in which he said that "fascist interests motivated largely by anti-Russian bias" were trying to "get control of our government." The American political left wanted to share the secrets of the a-bomb with the Soviets, called for recognizing Soviet spheres of influence—in effect, occupation zones—as just and necessary, opposed the creation of NATO, opposed the Marshall Plan to reconstruct Europe, and argued that the Communist coup of 1948 in Czechoslovakia was a necessary measure to prevent a "fascist" takeover of the country.

During the latter years of the Cold War, when Ronald Reagan became President, his stance towards the "Evil Empire," as he called the Soviet Union, hardened. Democrats called Reagan every name in the book, from "fascist" to a "warmonger" who could trigger a nuclear war. Reagan mirrored Truman's policy to back regimes fighting the Soviets in Europe, like the opponents of the Communists in the Greek civil war. Reagan did this by supporting the Contras in Nicaragua and opposing the attempts of local Communists to take-over Central American nations, especially El Salvador and Guatemala. The Democrats fought all of these anti-communist initiatives.

Instead of an evil empire, liberal revisionist historians stressed the Soviets's rapid economic development and urbanization which started under Stalin, which supposedly fostered widespread support for the régime among the Russian people. None questioned the existence of the gulag. Rather, they minimized its place in Soviet life and *denied that the population as a whole was ever terrorized.*

Unbiased research weighs in heavily in support of the fact that the legacy of communist régimes worldwide has been oppression and death. This is backed not only by a careful use of the vast memoir literature but also by a thorough mining of the long-closed Soviet archives. Most importantly, Solzhenitsyn's central argument is confirmed: that *the gulag was not some incidental Stalinist accretion to Lenin's visionary concept of Socialism. The cancer of police terror was embedded in the original DNA of Lenin's creation, "an integral part of the Soviet system".* Under Lenin, the first concentration camps were created; the first mass executions were carried out. Lenin bequeathed to his Russian successors, and his sycophants throughout the world a well-functioning machine of repression and death.

Extensive and repeated mass murders occurred under 20th-century Communist régimes. Death estimates vary widely, depending on the definitions of deaths included. The higher estimates of mass killings account for crimes against civilians by governments, including executions, destruction of population through government created hunger and deaths during forced deportations, imprisonment and through forced labor. Terms used to define these killings include "mass killing", "democide", "politicide", "classicide" and a broad definition of "genocide".

Terminology

Several different terms are used to describe the intentional killing of large numbers of noncombatants and according to Professor Anton Weiss-Wendt there is no consensus in the field of comparative genocide studies on a definition of "genocide". The following terminology has been used by individual authors to describe mass killings of unarmed civilians by Communist governments, individually or as a whole:

- Genocide – under the Genocide Convention, the crime of genocide generally applies to mass murder of ethnic rather than political or social groups. Protection of political groups was eliminated from the United Nations resolution after a second vote because many states, including Joseph Stalin's Soviet Union, anticipated that clause to apply unneeded limitations to their right to suppress internal disturbances. "Genocide" is also a popular term for mass political killing, which is studied academically as "democide" and "politicide". Killing by the Khmer Rouge in Cambodia has been labeled "genocide" or "auto-genocide" and the deaths under Leninism and Stalinism in the Soviet Union and Maoism in China have been controversially investigated as possible cases. In particular, the Soviet famine in the 1930s and the famine in China during the Great Leap Forward have been "depicted as instances of mass killing underpinned by genocidal intent".

- Politicide – the term "politicide" is used to describe the killing of groups that would not otherwise be covered by the Genocide Convention. Professor Barbara Harff studies "genocide and politicide", sometimes shortened as "geno-politicide", in order to include the killing of political, economic, ethnic and cultural groups. Professor Manus I. Midlarsky uses the term "politicide" to describe an arc of large-scale killing from the western parts of the Soviet Union to China and Cambodia. In his book *The Killing Trap: Genocide in the Twentieth Century*, Midlarsky raises similarities between the killings of Stalin and Pol Pot.

- The term "Red Holocaust" was coined by the *Munich Institut für Zeitgeschichte*. It has been used by some state officials and non-governmental organizations. Professor Steven Rosefielde used it as a name for his monograph about crimes of Communism. According to Jörg Hackmann, this word is not popular among scholars in Germany or internationally. The usage of this metaphor has been condemned as an attempt to usurp and undermine the history of European Jews and to introduce various "double genocide" theories, an essential component of the Holocaust obfuscation. Alexandra Laignel-Lavastine condemned usage of this metaphor that "allows the reality it describes to immediately attain, in the Western mind, a status equal to that of the extermination of the Jews by the Nazi régime".

- Democide – Professor R. J. Rummel defined "democide" as "the intentional killing of an unarmed or disarmed person by government agents acting in their authoritative capacity and pursuant to government policy or high command". His definition covers a wide range of deaths, including forced labor and concentration camp victims; killings by "unofficial" private groups; extrajudicial summary killings; and mass deaths due to the governmental acts of criminal omission and neglect, such as in deliberate famines as well as killings by *de facto* governments, i.e. civil war killings. This definition covers any murder of any number of persons by any government and it has been applied to killings perpetrated by communist régimes.

- Mass killing – Professor Ervin Staub defined "mass killing" as "killing members of a group without the intention to eliminate the whole group or killing large numbers of people without a precise definition of group membership. In a mass killing the number of people killed is usually smaller than in genocide". Referencing earlier definitions, Professors Joan Esteban, Massimo Morelli and Dominic Rohner have defined "mass killings" as "the killings of substantial numbers of human beings, when not in the course of military action against the military forces of an avowed enemy, under the conditions of the essential defenselessness and helplessness of the victims". The term has been defined by Professor Benjamin Valentino as "the intentional killing of a massive number of noncombatants", where a "massive number" is defined as at least 50,000 intentional deaths over the course of five years or less. This is the most accepted quantitative minimum threshold for the term. He applied this definition to the cases of Stalin's Soviet Union, China under Mao Zedong and Cambodia under the Khmer Rouge while admitting that "mass killings on a smaller scale" also appear to have been carried out by régimes in North Korea, Vietnam, Eastern Europe and Africa. Professors Frank Wayman and Atsushi Tago used the term "mass killing" from Valentino and concluded that even with a lower threshold (10,000 killed per year, 1,000 killed per year, or even 1 killed per year) "autocratic régimes, especially communist, are prone to mass killing generically, but not so strongly inclined (i.e. not statistically significantly inclined) toward geno-politicide".

- Repression – Professor Stephen Wheatcroft notes that in the case of the Soviet Union terms such as "the terror", "the purges" and "repression" are used to refer to the same events. He believes the most neutral terms are "repression" and "mass killings", although in Russian the broad concept of repression is commonly held to include mass killings and is sometimes assumed to be synonymous with it, which is not the case in other languages.

- Classicide – Professor Michael Mann has proposed the term classicide to mean the "intended mass killing of entire social classes". "Classicide" is considered "premeditated mass killing" narrower than "genocide" in that it targets a part of a population defined by its social status, but broader than "politicide" in that the group is targeted without regard to their political activity.

- Crime against humanity – Professor Klas-Göran Karlsson uses the term "crimes against humanity", which includes "the direct mass killings of politically undesirable elements, as well as forced deportations and forced labour". He acknowledges that the term may be misleading in the sense that the régimes targeted groups of their own citizens, but considers it useful as a broad legal term which emphasizes attacks on civilian populations and because the offenses demean humanity as a whole. Historian Jacques Sémelin and Professor Michael Mann believe that "crime against humanity" is more appropriate than "genocide" or "politicide" when speaking of violence by Communist régimes.

Estimates

According to Klas-Göran Karlsson, discussion of the number of victims of Communist régimes has been "extremely extensive and ideologically biased".

Although any attempt to estimate a total number of killings under Communist régimes depends greatly on definitions, several attempts to compile previously published data have been made:

- According to R. J. Rummel's book *Death by Government* (1994), about 110 million people, foreign and domestic, were killed by Communist democide from 1900 to 1987. In 1993, Rummel wrote: "Even were we to have total access to all communist archives we still would not be able to calculate precisely how many the communists murdered. Consider that even in spite of the archival statistics and detailed reports of survivors, the best experts still disagree by over 40 percent on the total number of Jews killed by the Nazis. We cannot expect near this accuracy for the victims of communism. We can, however, get a probable order of magnitude and a relative approximation of these deaths within a most likely range".

- In his introduction to the *Black Book of Communism* (1999), Stéphane Courtois gave a "rough approximation, based on unofficial estimates" approaching 100 million killed. In his foreword to the book, Martin Malia noted "a grand total of victims variously estimated by contributors to the volume at between 85 million and 100 million".

- According to Benjamin Valentino in 2005, the number of non-combatants killed by Communist régimes in the Soviet Union, People's Republic of China and Cambodia alone ranged from a low of 21 million to a high of 70 million. Citing Rummel and others, Valentino stated that the "highest end of the plausible range of deaths attributed to communist régimes" was up to 110 million".

- In his book *Red Holocaust* (2010), Steven Rosefielde said that Communism's internal contradictions "caused to be killed" approximately 60 million people and perhaps tens of millions more.

- In 2011, Matthew White published his rough total of 70 million "people who died under communist régimes from execution, labor camps, famine, ethnic cleansing, and desperate flight in leaky boats", not counting those killed in wars.

- In 2016, the Dissident blog of the Victims of Communism Memorial Foundation made an effort to compile updated ranges of estimates and concluded that the overall range "spans from 42,870,000 to 161,990,000" killed, with 100 million the most commonly cited figure.

- In 2017, Professor Stephen Kotkin wrote in The Wall Street Journal that Communism killed at least 65 million people between 1917 and 2017: "Though communism has killed huge numbers of people intentionally, even more of its victims have died from starvation as a result of its cruel projects of social engineering".

The criticisms of some of the estimates were mostly focused on three aspects: (i) the estimates were based on sparse and incomplete data when significant errors are inevitable; some critics said the figures were skewed to higher possible values; and (iii) some critics argued that victims of Holodomor and other man-made famines created by Communist governments should not be counted.

Proposed Causes

Ideology

Klas-Göran Karlsson writes: "Ideologies are systems of ideas, which cannot commit crimes independently. However, individuals, collectives and states that have defined themselves as communist have committed crimes in the name of communist ideology, or without naming communism as the direct source of motivation for their crimes". Scholars such as R. J. Rummel, Daniel Goldhagen, Richard Pipes and John N. Gray consider Communism as a significant causative factor in mass killings. *The Black Book of Communism* claims an association between Communism and criminality, saying: "Communist régimes [...] turned mass crime into a full-blown system of government" while adding that this criminality lies at the level of ideology rather than state practice.

Christopher J. Finlay has argued that Marxism legitimates violence without any clear limiting principle because it rejects moral and ethical norms as constructs of the dominant class and "states that it would be conceivable for revolutionaries to commit atrocious crimes in bringing about a socialist system, with the belief that their crimes will be retroactively absolved by the new system of ethics put in place by the proletariat". Rustam Singh notes that Karl Marx had alluded to the possibility of peaceful revolution, but after the failed Revolutions of 1848 emphasized the need for violent revolution and "revolutionary terror".

Literary historian George G. Watson cited an 1849 article written by Friedrich Engels called "The Hungarian Struggle" and published in Marx's journal *Neue Rheinische Zeitung*, stating that the writings of Engels and others show that "the Marxist theory of history required and demanded genocide for reasons implicit in its claim that feudalism, which in advanced nations was already giving place to capitalism, must in its turn be superseded by socialism. Entire nations would be left behind after a workers' revolution, feudal remnants in a socialist age, and since they could not advance two steps at a time, they would have to be killed. They were racial trash, as Engels called them, and fit only for the dung-heap of history". Watson's claims have been criticized by Robert Grant for "dubious evidence", arguing that "what Marx and Engels are calling for is [...] at the very least a kind of cultural genocide; but it is not obvious, at least from Watson's citations, that actual mass killing, rather than (to use their phraseology) mere 'absorption' or 'assimilation', is in question". Talking about Engels' 1849 article and citing Watson's book, historian Andrzej Walicki has said; "It is difficult to deny that this was an outright call for genocide".

According to Rummel, the killings committed by Communist régimes can best be explained as the result of the marriage between absolute power and an absolutist ideology—Marxism. "Of all religions, secular and otherwise", Rummel positions Marxism as "by far the bloodiest – bloodier than the Catholic Inquisition, the various Catholic crusades, and the Thirty Years War between Catholics and Protestants. In practice, Marxism has meant bloody terrorism, deadly purges, lethal prison camps and murderous forced labor, fatal deportations, man-made famines, extrajudicial executions and fraudulent show trials, outright mass murder and genocide". He writes that in practice the Marxists saw the construction of their utopia as "a war on poverty, exploitation, imperialism and inequality – and, as in a real war, noncombatants would unfortunately get caught in the battle. There would be necessary enemy casualties: the clergy, bourgeoisie, capitalists, 'wreckers', intellectuals, counterrevolutionaries, rightists, tyrants, the rich and landlords. As in a war, millions might die, but these deaths would be justified by the end, as in the defeat of Hitler in World War II. To the ruling Marxists, the goal of a communist utopia was enough to justify all the deaths".

Benjamin Valentino writes that mass killings strategies are chosen by Communists to economically dispossess large numbers of people:

"Social transformations of this speed and magnitude have been associated with mass killing for two primary reasons. First, the massive social dislocations produced by such changes have often led to economic collapse, epidemics, and, most important, widespread famines. [...] The second reason that communist régimes bent on the radical transformation of society have been linked to mass killing is that the revolutionary changes they have pursued have clashed inexorably with the fundamental interests of large segments of their populations. Few people have proved willing to accept such far-reaching sacrifices without intense levels of coercion".

Daniel Chirot and Clark McCauley write that especially in Stalin's Soviet Union, Mao's China and Pol Pot's Cambodia a fanatical certainty that socialism could be made to work motivated Communist leaders in "the ruthless dehumanization of their enemies, who could be suppressed because they were 'objectively' and 'historically' wrong. Furthermore, if events did not work out as they were supposed to, then that was because class enemies, foreign spies and saboteurs, or worst of all, internal traitors were wrecking the plan. Under no circumstances could it be admitted that the vision itself might be unworkable, because that meant capitulation to the forces of reaction". Michael Mann writes that communist party members were "ideologically driven, believing that in order to create a new socialist society, they must lead in socialist zeal. Killings were often popular, the rank-and-file as keen to exceed killing quotas as production quotas".

According to Jacques Sémelin, "communist systems emerging in the twentieth century ended up destroying their own populations, not because they planned to annihilate them as such, but because they aimed to restructure the 'social body' from top to bottom, even if that meant purging it and recarving it to suit their new Promethean political *imaginaire*".

Political System

Anne Applebaum asserts that "without exception, the Leninist belief in the one-party state was and is characteristic of every communist régime" and "the Bolshevik use of violence was repeated in every communist revolution". Phrases said by Vladimir Lenin and Cheka founder Felix Dzerzhinsky were deployed all over the world. She notes that as late as 1976 Mengistu Haile Mariam unleashed a Red Terror in Ethiopia. Said Lenin to his colleagues in the Bolshevik government: "If we are not ready to shoot a saboteur and White Guardist, what sort of revolution is that?".

Robert Conquest stressed that Stalin's purges were not contrary to the principles of Leninism, but rather a natural consequence of the system established by Lenin, who personally ordered the killing of local groups of class enemy hostages. Alexander Yakovlev, architect of perestroika and glasnost and later head of the Presidential Commission for the Victims of Political Repression, elaborates on this point, stating: "The truth is that in punitive operations Stalin did not think up anything that was not there under Lenin: executions, hostage taking, concentration camps, and all the rest". Historian Robert Gellately concurs, saying: "To put it another way, Stalin initiated very little that Lenin had not already introduced or previewed".

Stephen Hicks of Rockford College ascribes the violence characteristic of 20th-century socialist rule to these collectivist régimes' abandonment of protections of civil rights and rejection of the values of civil society. Hicks writes that whereas "in practice every liberal capitalist country has a solid record for being humane, for by and large respecting rights and freedoms, and for making it possible for people to put together fruitful and meaningful lives", in socialism "practice has time and again proved itself more brutal than the worst dictatorships prior to the twentieth century. Each socialist régime has collapsed into dictatorship and begun killing people on a huge scale".

Eric D. Weitz says that the mass killing in Communist states are a natural consequence of the failure of the rule of law, seen commonly during periods of social upheaval in the 20th century. For both Communist and non-Communist mass killings, "genocides occurred at moments of extreme social crisis, often generated by the very policies of the régimes". They are not inevitable, but are political decisions. Steven Rosefielde writes that Communist rulers had to choose between changing course and "terror-command" and more often than not chose the latter.mMichael Mann argues that a lack of institutionalized authority structures meant that a chaotic mix of both centralized control and party factionalism were factors in the killing.

Other Causes

Martin Malia called Russian exceptionalism and the war experience general reasons for barbarity. Russian and world history scholar John M. Thompson places personal responsibility directly on Joseph Stalin. According to him, "much of what occurred only makes sense if it stemmed in part from the disturbed mentality, pathological cruelty, and extreme paranoia of Stalin himself. Insecure, despite having established a dictatorship over the party and country, hostile and defensive when confronted with criticism of the excesses of collectivization and the sacrifices required by high-tempo industrialization, and deeply suspicious that past, present, and even yet unknown future opponents were plotting against him, Stalin began to act as a person beleaguered. He soon struck back at enemies, real or imaginary". Historian Helen Rappaport describes Nikolay Yezhov, the bureaucrat in charge of the NKVD during the Great Purge, as a physically diminutive figure of "limited intelligence" and "narrow political understanding. [...] Like other instigators of mass murder throughout history, [he] compensated for his lack of physical stature with a pathological cruelty and the use of brute terror".

States Where Mass Killings Have Occurred

Soviet Union

Sign for the Memorial about Repression in USSR at Lubyanka Square which was erected in 1990 by the human rights group Memorial in the Soviet Union in remembrance of the more than 40,000 innocent people shot in Moscow during the "years of terror"

Genocide scholar Adam Jones claims that "there is very little in the record of human experience to match the violence unleashed between 1917, when the Bolsheviks took power, and 1953, when Joseph Stalin died and the Soviet Union moved to adopt a more restrained and largely non-murderous domestic policy". He notes the exceptions being the Khmer Rouge (in relative terms) and Mao's rule in China (in absolute terms).

Estimates on the number of deaths brought about by Stalin's rule are hotly debated by scholars in the field of Soviet and Communist studies. The published results vary depending on the time when the estimate was made, on the criteria and methods used for the estimates and sources available for estimates. Some historians attempt to make separate estimates for different periods of the Soviet history. Prior to the collapse of the USSR and the archival revelations, some historians estimated that the numbers killed by Stalin's régime were 20 million or higher. In the latest 2007 revision of his book *The Great Terror,* Robert Conquest estimates that while exact numbers will never be certain, the Communist leaders of the Soviet Union were responsible for no fewer than 15 million deaths. Michael Parenti writes that estimates on the Stalinist death toll vary widely in part because such estimates are based on "anecdotes" in absence of reliable evidence and "speculations by writers who never reveal how they arrive at such figures".

According to historian Stephen G. Wheatcroft, Stalin's régime can be charged with causing the "purposive deaths" of about a million people. Wheatcroft excludes all famine deaths as "purposive deaths" and claims those that do qualify fit more closely the category of "execution" rather than "murder". Others posit that some of the actions of Stalin's régime, not only those during the Holodomor, but also dekulakization and targeted campaigns against particular ethnic groups, can be considered as genocide at least in its loose definition. Modern data for the whole of Stalin's rule was summarized by Timothy Snyder, who concluded that Stalinism caused six million direct deaths and nine millions in total, including the deaths from deportation, hunger and Gulag deaths. Michael Ellman attributes roughly 3 million deaths to the Stalinist régime, excluding excess mortality from famine, disease and war.

Wheatcroft asserts that prior to the opening of the archives for historical research, "our understanding of the scale and the nature of Soviet repression has been extremely poor" and that some scholars who wish to maintain pre-1991 high estimates are "finding it difficult to adapt to the new circumstances when the archives are open and when there are plenty of irrefutable data" and instead "hang on to their old Sovietological methods with round-about calculations based on odd statements from emigres and other informants who are supposed to have superior knowledge". After the Soviet Union dissolved, evidence from the Soviet archives became available, containing official records of the execution of approximately 800,000 prisoners under Stalin for either political or criminal offenses, around 1.7 million deaths in the Gulags and some 390,000 deaths during kulak forced resettlement—for a total of about 3 million officially recorded victims in these categories. However, official Soviet documentation of Gulag deaths is widely considered inadequate. Golfo Alexopoulos, Anne Applebaum, Oleg Khlevniuk and Michael Ellman write that the government frequently released prisoners on the edge of death in order to avoid officially counting them. A 1993 study of archival data by J. Arch Getty et al. showed that a total of 1,053,829 people died in the Gulag from 1934 to 1953. Subsequently, Steven Rosefielde asserted that this number has to be augmented by 19.4 percent in light of more complete archival evidence to 1,258,537, with the best estimate of Gulag deaths being 1.6 million from 1929 to 1953 when excess mortality is taken into account. Alexopolous estimates much higher totals, at least 6 million died in the Gulag or shortly after release. Jeffrey Hardy has criticized Alexopoulos as basing her assertions primarily on indirect and misinterpreted evidence and Dan Healey has called her work a "challenge to the emergent scholarly consensus".

Red Terror

The Red Terror was a period of political repression and executions carried out by Bolsheviks after the beginning of the Russian Civil War in 1918. During this period, the political police (the Cheka) conducted summary executions of tens of thousands of "enemies of the people". Many victims were "bourgeois hostages" rounded up and held in readiness for summary execution in reprisal for any alleged counter-revolutionary provocation. Many were put to death during and after the suppression of revolts, such as the Kronstadt rebellion of Baltic Fleet sailors and the Tambov Rebellion of Russian peasants. Professor Donald Rayfield claims that "the repression that followed the rebellions in Kronstadt and Tambov alone resulted in tens of thousands of executions". A large number of Orthodox clergymen were also killed.

According to Nicolas Werth, the policy of decossackization amounted to an attempt by Soviet leaders to "eliminate, exterminate, and deport the population of a whole territory". In the early months of 1919, perhaps 10,000 to 12,000 Cossacks were executed and many more deported after their villages were razed to the ground. According to historian Michael Kort: "During 1919 and 1920, out of a population of approximately 1.5 million Don Cossacks, the Bolshevik régime killed or deported an estimated 300,000 to 500,000".

Soviet Induced Famine of 1932–1933

Within the Soviet Union, forced changes in agricultural policies (collectivization), confiscations of grain and droughts caused the Soviet famine of 1932–1933 in Ukraine, Northern Caucasus, Volga Region and Kazakhstan. The famine was most severe in the Ukrainian SSR, where it is often referenced as the Holodomor. A significant portion of the famine victims (3.3 to 7.5 million) were Ukrainians. Another part of the famine was known as Kazakh catastrophe, when more than 1.3 million ethnic Kazakhs (38% of all indigenous population) died. Many scholars say that the Stalinist policies that caused the famine may have been designed as an attack on the rise of Ukrainian nationalism and thus may fall under the legal definition of genocide (see Holodomor genocide question).

The famine was officially recognized as a genocide by the Ukraine and other governments. In a draft resolution, the Parliamentary Assembly of the Council of Europe declared the famine was caused by the "cruel and deliberate actions and policies of the Soviet régime" and was responsible for the deaths of "millions of innocent people" in Ukraine, Belarus, Kazakhstan, Moldova and Russia. Relative to its population, Kazakhstan is believed to have been the most adversely affected. Regarding the Kazakh catastrophe, Michael Ellman states that it "seems to be an example of 'negligent genocide' which falls outside the scope of the UN Convention of genocide".

Great Purge (Yezhovshchina)

Stalin's attempts to solidify his position as leader of the Soviet Union led to an escalation of detentions and executions, climaxing in 1937–1938 (a period sometimes referred to as the Yezhovshchina, or Yezhov era) and continuing until Stalin's death in 1953. Around 700,000 of these were executed by a gunshot to the back of the head. Others perished from beatings and torture while in "investigative custody" and in the Gulag due to starvation, disease, exposure and overwork.

Modern historical studies estimate a total number of Stalinism repression deaths during the Great Purge (1937–1938) as 950,000–1,200,000. These figures take into account the incompleteness of official archival data and include both execution deaths and Gulag deaths during that period. Former "kulaks" and their families made up the majority of victims, with 669,929 people arrested and 376,202 executed.

Arrests were typically made citing counter-revolutionary laws, which included failure to report treasonous actions and in an amendment added in 1937 failing to fulfill one's appointed duties. In the cases investigated by the State Security Department of the NKVD from October 1936 to November 1938, at least 1,710,000 people were arrested and 724,000 people executed.

Citing church documents, Alexander Nikolaevich Yakovlev has estimated that over 100,000 priests, monks and nuns were executed during this time. Regarding the persecution of clergy, Michael Ellman has stated that "the 1937–38 terror against the clergy of the Russian Orthodox Church and of other religions (Binner & Junge 2004) might also qualify as genocide".

National Operations of the NKVD

In 1930s, the NKVD conducted a series of national operations which targeted some "national contingents" suspected of counter-revolutionary activity. A total of 350,000 were arrested and 247,157 were executed. Of these, the Polish operation which targeted the members of *Polska Organizacja Wojskowa* appears to have been the largest, with 140,000 arrests and 111,000 executions. Although these operation might well constitute genocide as defined by the UN convention, or "a mini-genocide" according to Simon Sebag Montefiore, there is as yet no authoritative ruling on the legal characterization of these events.

Great Purge in Mongolia

In the summer and autumn of 1937, Stalin sent NKVD agents to the Mongolian People's Republic and engineered a Mongolian Great Terror in which some 22,000 to 35,000 people were executed. Around 18,000 victims were Buddhist lamas.

Soviet Killings During World War II

Following the Soviet invasion of Poland in September 1939, NKVD task forces started removing "Soviet-hostile elements" from the conquered territories. The NKVD systematically practiced torture which often resulted in death. According to the Polish Institute of National Remembrance, 150,000 Polish citizens perished due to Soviet repression during the war. The most notorious killings occurred in the spring of 1940, when the NKVD executed some 21,857 Polish POWs and intellectual leaders in what has become known as the Katyn massacre.

Executions were also carried out after the annexation of the Baltic states.

During the initial phases of Operation Barbarossa, the NKVD and attached units of the Red Army massacred prisoners and political opponents by the tens of thousands before fleeing from the advancing Axis forces.

Mass Deportations of Ethnic Minorities

Soviet leader Joseph Stalin and Lavrenti Beria (in foreground), who was responsible for mass deportations of ethnic minorities as head of the NKVD

The Soviet government during Joseph Stalin's rule conducted a series of deportations on an enormous scale that significantly affected the ethnic map of the Soviet Union. Deportations took place under extremely harsh conditions, often in cattle carriages, with hundreds of thousands of deportees dying en route. Some experts estimate that the proportion of deaths from the deportations could be as high as one in three in certain cases. Regarding the fate of the Crimean Tatars, Amir Weiner of Stanford University writes that the policy could be classified as "ethnic cleansing". In the book *Century of Genocide*, Lyman H Legters writes: "We cannot properly speak of a completed genocide, only of a process that was genocidal in its potentiality".

People's Republic of China

Main article: History of the People's Republic of China (1949–1976)

The Chinese Communist Party came to power in China in 1949 after a long and bloody civil war between Communists and Nationalists. There is a general consensus among historians that after Mao Zedong seized power, his policies and political purges directly or indirectly caused the deaths of tens of millions of people. Based on the Soviets' experience, Mao considered violence to be necessary in order to achieve an ideal society that would be derived from Marxism and as a result he planned and executed violence on a grand scale.

The first large-scale killings under Mao took place during his land reform and the counterrevolutionary campaign. In official study materials that were published in 1948, Mao envisaged that "one-tenth of the peasants" (or about 50,000,000) "would have to be destroyed" to facilitate agrarian reform. The actual number killed during land reform is believed to have been lower, but at least one million people. The suppression of counterrevolutionaries targeted mainly former Kuomintang officials and intellectuals suspected of disloyalty. At least 712,000 people were executed while 1,290,000 were imprisoned in labor camps.

Benjamin Valentino claims that the Great Leap Forward was a cause of the Great Chinese Famine and the worst effects of the famine were steered towards the régime's enemies. Those labeled as "black elements" (religious leaders, rightists and rich peasants) in earlier campaigns died in the greatest numbers because they were given the lowest priority in the allocation of food. In *Mao's Great Famine*, historian Frank Dikötter writes that "coercion, terror, and systematic violence were the very foundation of the Great Leap Forward" and it "motivated one of the most deadly mass killings of human history". Dikötter estimates that at least 2.5 million people were summarily killed or tortured to death during this period. His research in local and provincial Chinese archives indicates the death toll was at least 45 million: "In most cases the party knew very well that it was starving its own people to death". In a secret meeting at Shanghai in 1959, Mao issued the order to procure one third of all grain from the countryside, saying: "When there is not enough to eat people starve to death. It is better to let half of the people die so that the other half can eat their fill". In light of additional evidence of Mao's culpability, Rummel added those killed by the Great Famine to his total for Mao's democide for a total of 77 million killed.

Sinologists Roderick MacFarquhar and Michael Schoenhals estimate that between 750,000 and 1.5 million people were killed in the violence of the Cultural Revolution in rural China alone. Mao's Red Guards were given *carte blanche* to abuse and kill the ones perceived to be enemies of the revolution. For example, in August 1966, over 100 teachers were murdered by their students in western Beijing.

According to Jean-Louis Margolin in *The Black Book of Communism*, the Chinese Communists carried out a cultural genocide against the Tibetans. Margolin states that the killings were proportionally larger in Tibet than they were in China proper and that "one can legitimately speak of genocidal massacres because of the numbers that were involved". According to the Dalai Lama and the Central Tibetan Administration, "Tibetans were not only shot, but they were also beaten to death, crucified, burned alive, drowned, mutilated, starved, strangled, hanged, boiled alive, buried alive, drawn and quartered, and beheaded". Adam Jones, a scholar who specializes in genocide, notes that after the 1959 Tibetan uprising the Chinese authorized struggle sessions against reactionaries, during which "communist cadres denounced, tortured, and frequently executed enemies of the people". These sessions resulted in 92,000 deaths out of a total population of about 6 million. These deaths, Jones stressed, may not only be seen as a genocide, but they may also be seen as an "eliticide", meaning "targeting the better educated and leadership oriented elements among the Tibetan population". However Patrick French, the former director of Free Tibet Campaign in London, states that there is "no evidence" to support the figure of 1.2 million Tibetans killed as a result of Chinese rule after examining archives in Dharamsala. Rather, French estimates that as many as half a million Tibetans died from repression and famine under Chinese rule.

Cambodia (Democratic Kampuchea)

The "Killing Fields" were a number of sites in Cambodia where large numbers of people were killed and buried by the Khmer Rouge régime during its rule of the country from 1975 to 1979 after the end of the Vietnam War.

The results of a demographic study of the Cambodian genocide concluded that the nationwide death toll from 1975 to 1979 amounted to 1,671,000 to 1,871,000, or 21 to 24 percent of the Cambodian population before the Khmer Rouge took power. According to Ben Kiernan, the number of deaths caused by executions is still unknown because many victims died from starvation, disease and overwork. Researcher Craig Etcheson of the Documentation Center of Cambodia suggests that the death toll was between 2 and 2.5 million, with a "most likely" figure of

2.2 million. After five years of researching some 20,000 grave sites, he concluded that "these mass graves contain the remains of 1,112,829 victims of execution". A study by French demographer Marek Sliwinski calculated slightly fewer than 2 million unnatural deaths under the Khmer Rouge out of a 1975 Cambodian population of 7.8 million, with 33.5% of Cambodian men dying under the Khmer Rouge compared to 15.7% of Cambodian women. The number of suspected victims of execution found across 23,745 mass graves is estimated at 1.3 million according to a 2009 academic source. Execution is believed to account for roughly 60% of the full death toll during the genocide, with other victims succumbing to starvation or disease.

Helen Fein, a genocide scholar, states that although Cambodian leaders declared adherence to an exotic version of agrarian communist doctrine, the xenophobic ideology of the Khmer Rouge régime resembles more a phenomenon of national socialism, or fascism. Henri Locard argues that the "fascist" label was applied to the Khmer Rouge by their enemy, the Vietnamese Communists, as a form of "revisionism", but that repression under the Khmer Rouge was "similar (if significantly more lethal) to the repression in all communist régimes". Daniel Goldhagen explains that the Khmer Rouge were xenophobic because they believed the Khmer were "the one authentic people capable of building true communism". Sociologist Martin Shaw described the Cambodian genocide as "the purest genocide of the Cold War era". Steven Rosefielde claims that Democratic Kampuchea was the deadliest of all Communist régimes on a per capita basis, primarily because it "lacked a viable productive core" and "failed to set boundaries on mass murder".

Others

Mass killings have also occurred in Vietnam and North Korea. According to Benjamin Valentino, most régimes that described themselves as Communist did not commit mass killings. He has suggested that there may also have been other mass killings (on a smaller scale than his standard of 50,000 killed within five years) in Communist states such as Bulgaria, Romania and East Germany, although lack of documentation prevents definitive judgement about the scale of these events and the motives of the perpetrators.

Bulgaria

According to Benjamin Valentino, available evidence suggests that between 50,000 and 100,000 people may have been killed in Bulgaria beginning in 1944 as part of agricultural collectivization and political repression, although there is insufficient documentation to make a definitive judgement. In his book *History of Communism in Bulgaria*, Dinyu Sharlanov accounts for about 31,000 people killed under the régime between 1944 and 1989.

Cuba

As of this writing, human rights in Cuba are under the scrutiny of human rights organizations, who accuse the Cuban government of systematic human rights abuses, including arbitrary imprisonment and one-sided trials. In Cuba there is no freedom of expression, association, assembly, movement, due process, and the press. The government maintains tight control on religious institutions, affiliated groups, and individual believers. According to the report of Human Rights Watch from 2017 the government continues to rely on arbitrary arrest and imprisonment to harass and intimidate critics, independent activists, political opponents, and others.

The *Cuba Archive* project (www.cubaarchive.org) has verified the names of 10,723 victims of the Castro regime and the circumstances of their deaths [through 2016]. Archive researchers meticulously insist on confirming stories of official murder from two independent sources.

Cuba Archive President Maria Werlau says the total number of victims could be higher by a factor of x 10. Project Vice President Armando Lago, a Harvard-trained economist, has spent years studying the cost of the revolution and he estimates that almost 78,000 innocents may have died trying to flee the dictatorship. Another 5,300 are known to have lost their lives fighting communism in the Escambray Mountains (mostly peasant farmers and their children) and at the Bay of Pigs. An estimated 14,000 Cubans were killed in Fidel's revolutionary adventures abroad, most notably his dispatch of 50,000 soldiers to Angola in the 1980s to help the Soviet-backed regime fight off the pro-western UNITA insurgency.

Cuba Archive finds that some 5,600 Cubans have died in front of firing squads and another 1,200 in "extrajudicial assassinations." Che Guevara was a gleeful executioner at the infamous La Cabana Fortress in 1959 where, under his direct orders, at least 151 Cubans were lined up and shot. Children have not been spared. Of the 94 minors whose deaths have been documented by Cuba Archive, 22 died by firing squad and 32 in extrajudicial assassinations.

East Germany

According to Valentino, between 80,000 and 100,000 people may have been killed in East Germany beginning in 1945 as part of denazification by the Soviet Union, but other scholars argue that these figures are inflated.

Immediately after World War II, denazification commenced in occupied Germany and the regions the Nazis had annexed. In the Soviet occupation zone, NKVD established prison camps, usually in abandoned concentration camps and interned alleged Nazis and Nazi German officials along with some landlords and Prussian Junkers. According to files and data released by the Soviet Ministry for the Interior in 1990, all in all 123,000 Germans and 35,000 citizens of other nations were detained. Of these prisoners, a total of 786 people were shot and 43,035 died of various causes. Most of the deaths were not direct killings, but caused by outbreaks of dysentry and tuberculosis. Death by starvation did also occur on a notable scale, in particular from late 1946 to early 1947, but these deaths do not appear to be deliberate killings as food shortages were widespread in the Soviet occupation zone. The prisoners of the "silence camps", as the NKVD special camps were called, did not have access to the black market and were unable to get food other than what they were handed by authorities. Some prisoners also died because of execution and perhaps torture. In this context, it is unclear if the prisoner deaths in the silence camps can be categorized as mass killings. It is also unclear how many of the dead were German, East German, or of other nationalities.

In 1961, East Germany erected the Berlin Wall following the Berlin crisis. Even though crossing between East Germany and West Germany was possible for motivated and approved travelers, thousands of East Germans tried to defect by crossing the wall illegally. Of these, between 136 and 227 people were killed by the Berlin Wall guards in the years 1961 to 1989.

Romania

Further information: Danube-Black Sea Canal § Construction of the canal in 1949-1953

According to Valentino, between 60,000 and 300,000 people may have been killed in Romania beginning in 1945 as part of agricultural collectivization and political repression.

Yugoslavia

Further information: Bleiburg repatriations, Macelj massacre, Tezno massacre, Kočevski Rog massacre, Barbara Pit massacre, Communist purges in Serbia in 1944–45, Foibe massacres, and Goli Otok

Josip Broz Tito made bloody repression and several massacres of POW after second world war; European Public Hearing on "Crimes Committed by Totalitarian Régimes" reports "The decision to "annihilate" opponents must had been adopted in the closest circles of Yugoslav state leadership, and the order was certainly issued by the Supreme Commander of the Yugoslav Army Josip Broz Tito, although it is not known when or in what form".

Dominic McGoldrick writes that as the head of a "highly centralised and oppressive" dictatorship, Broz Tito wielded tremendous power in Yugoslavia, with his dictatorial rule administered through an elaborate bureaucracy which routinely suppressed human rights. The main victims of this repression were known and alleged Stalinists during the first years, such as Dragoslav Mihailović and Dragoljub Mićunović, but during the following years even some of the most prominent among Tito's collaborators were arrested. On 19 November 1956 Milovan Đilas, perhaps the closest of Tito's collaborator and widely regarded as Tito's possible successor, was arrested because of his criticism against Tito's régime. The repression did not exclude intellectuals and writers, such as Venko Markovski who was arrested and sent to jail in January 1956 for writing poems considered anti-Titoist.

Tito's Yugoslavia remained a tightly controlled police state. According to David Mates, outside the Soviet Union, Yugoslavia had more political prisoners than all of the rest of Eastern Europe combined. Tito's secret police was modeled on the Soviet KGB. Its members were ever-present and often acted extrajudicially, with victims including middle-class intellectuals, liberals and democrats. Yugoslavia was a signatory to the International Covenant on Civil and Political Rights, but scant regard was paid to some of its provisions.

Democratic People's Republic of Korea

According to Rummel, forced labor, executions and concentration camps were responsible for over one million deaths in the Democratic People's Republic of Korea from 1948 to 1987. Others have estimated 400,000 deaths in concentration camps alone. A wide range of atrocities have been committed in the camps including forced abortions, infanticide and torture. Former International Criminal Court judge Thomas Buergenthal, who was one of the UN report's authors and a child survivor of Auschwitz, told *The Washington Post* "that conditions in the [North]

Korean prison camps are as terrible, or even worse, than those I saw and experienced in my youth in these Nazi camps and in my long professional career in the human rights field". Pierre Rigoulot estimates 100,000 executions, 1.5 million deaths through concentration camps and slave labor, and 500,000 deaths from famine.

Estimates based on a North Korean census suggest that 240,000 to 420,000 people died as a result of the 1990s famine and there were 600,000 to 850,000 excess deaths in North Korea from 1993 to 2008. The famine, which claimed as many as one million lives, has been described as the result of the economic policies of the North Korean government and deliberate "terror-starvation". In 2010, Steven Rosefielde stated that the "Red Holocaust" "still persists in North Korea" as Kim Jong Il "refuses to abandon mass killing".

Democratic Republic of Vietnam

Valentino attributes 80,000–200,000 deaths to "communist mass killings" in North and South Vietnam.

According to scholarship based on Vietnamese and Hungarian archival evidence, approximately 15,000 suspected landlords were executed during North Vietnam's land reform from 1953 to 1956. The North Vietnamese leadership planned in advance to execute 0.1% of North Vietnam's population (estimated at 13.5 million in 1955) as "reactionary or evil landlords", although this ratio could vary in practice. Dramatic errors were committed in the course of the land reform campaign. Vu Tuong states that the number of executions during North Vietnam's land reform was proportionally comparable to executions during Chinese land reform from 1949 to 1952.

Democratic Republic of Afghanistan

According to Frank Wayman and Atsushi Tago, although frequently considered an example of Communist genocide, the Democratic Republic of Afghanistan represents a borderline case. Prior to the Soviet invasion, the People's Democratic Party of Afghanistan executed between 10,000 and 27,000 people, mostly at Pul-e-Charkhi prison. Mass graves of executed prisoners have been exhumed dating back to the Soviet era.

After the invasion in 1979, the Soviets installed the puppet government of Babrak Karmal, but it was never clearly stabilized as a Communist régime and was in a constant state of war. By 1987, about 80% of the country's territory was permanently controlled by neither the pro-Communist government and supporting Soviet troops nor by the armed opposition. To tip the balance, the Soviet Union used a tactic that was a combination of "scorched earth" policy and "migratory genocide". By systematically burning the crops and destroying villages in rebel provinces as well as by reprisal bombing entire villages suspected of harboring or supporting the resistance, the Soviets tried to force the local population to move to Soviet controlled territory, thereby depriving the armed opposition of support. Valentino attributes between 950,000 and 1,280,000 civilian deaths to the Soviet invasion and occupation of the country between 1978 and 1989, primarily as counter-guerrilla mass killing. By the early 1990s, approximately one-third of Afghanistan's population had fled the country. M. Hassan Kakar said that "the Afghans are among the latest victims of genocide by a superpower".

People's Democratic Republic of Ethiopia

Amnesty International estimates that half a million people were killed during the Ethiopian Red Terror of 1977 and 1978. During the terror, groups of people were herded into churches that were then burned down and women were subjected to systematic rape by soldiers. The Save the Children Fund reported that victims of the Red Terror included not only adults, but 1,000 or more children, mostly aged between eleven and thirteen, whose corpses were left in the streets of Addis Ababa. Mengistu Haile Mariam himself is alleged to have killed political opponents with his bare hands.

Debate on Famines

According to Soviet historian J. Arch Getty, over half of the 100 million deaths attributed to Communism were due to famine. Stéphane Courtois argues that many Communist régimes caused famines in their efforts to forcibly collectivize agriculture and systematically used it as a weapon by controlling the food supply and distributing food on a political basis. He states that "in the period after 1918, only Communist countries experienced such famines, which led to the deaths of hundreds of thousands, and in some cases millions, of people. And again in the 1980s, two African countries that claimed to be Marxist-Leninist, Ethiopia and Mozambique, were the only such countries to suffer these deadly famines".

Scholars Stephen G. Wheatcroft, R. W. Davies and Mark Tauger reject the idea that the Ukrainian famine was an act of genocide or intentionally inflicted by the Soviet government. Getty posits that the "overwhelming weight of opinion among scholars working in the new archives is that the terrible famine of the 1930s was the result of Stalinist bungling and rigidity rather than some genocidal plan". Russian novelist and historian

Aleksandr Solzhenitsyn opined on 2 April 2008 in *Izvestia* that the 1930s famine in the Ukraine was no different from the Russian famine of 1921 as both were caused by the ruthless robbery of peasants by Bolshevik grain procurements.

Pankaj Mishra questions Mao's direct responsibility for famine, noting: "A great many premature deaths also occurred in newly independent nations not ruled by erratic tyrants". Mishra cites Nobel laureate Amartya Sen's research demonstrating that democratic India suffered more excess mortality from starvation and disease in the second half of the 20th century than China did. Sen wrote that "India seems to manage to fill its cupboard with more skeletons every eight years than China put there in its years of shame".

Benjamin Valentino writes: "Although not all the deaths due to famine in these cases were intentional, communist leaders directed the worst effects of famine against their suspected enemies and used hunger as a weapon to force millions of people to conform to the directives of the state". Daniel Goldhagen says that in some cases deaths from famine should not be distinguished from mass murder: "Whenever governments have not alleviated famine conditions, political leaders decided not to say no to mass death – in other words, they said yes". He claims that famine was either used or deliberately tolerated by the Soviets, the Germans, the Communist Chinese, the British in Kenya, the Hausa against the Ibo in Nigeria, Khmer Rouge, Communist North Koreans, Ethiopeans in Eritrea, Zimbabwe against regions of political opposition and political Islamists in southern Sudan and Darfur.

Authors including Seumas Milne and Jon Wiener have criticized the emphasis on communism and the exclusion of colonialism when assigning blame for famines. Milne argues that if the Soviets are considered responsible for deaths caused by famine in the 1920s and 1930s, then Britain would be responsible for as many as 30 million deaths in India from famine during the 19th century, lamenting: "There is a much-lauded *Black Book of Communism*, but no such comprehensive indictment of the colonial record". Weiner makes a similar assertion while comparing the Ukrainian famine and the Bengal famine of 1943, stating that Winston Churchill's role in the Bengal famine "seems similar to Stalin's role in the Ukrainian famine". Historian Mike Davis, author of *Late Victorian Holocausts*, draws comparisons between the Great Chinese Famine and the Indian famines of the late 19th century and argues that both the Maoist régime and the British Empire share the same level of criminal responsibility for these events respectively.

Michael Ellman is critical of the fixation on a "uniquely Stalinist evil" when it comes to excess deaths from famines and asserts that catastrophic famines were widespread in the 19th and 20th centuries, such as "in the British empire (India and Ireland), China, Russia and elsewhere". He argues that a possible defense of Stalin and his associates is that "their behaviour was no worse than that of many rulers in the nineteenth and twentieth centuries". He also draws comparisons to the actions of the Group of Eight (G8) in recent decades, saying "the world-wide death of millions of people in recent decades which could have been prevented by simple public health measures or cured by application of modern medicine, but was not, might be considered by some as mass manslaughter—or mass death by criminal negligence—by the leaders of the G8 (who could have prevented these deaths but did not do so)".

Legal Status and Prosecutions

According to a 1992 constitutional amendment in the Czech Republic, a person who publicly denies, puts in doubt, approves, or tries to justify Nazi or Communist genocide or other crimes of Nazis or Communists will be punished with a prison term of 6 months to 3 years.

Barbara Harff wrote in 1992 that no Communist country or governing body has ever been convicted of genocide. In his 1999 foreword to *The Black Book of Communism*, Martin Malia wrote: "Throughout the former Communist world, moreover, virtually none of its responsible officials has been put on trial or punished. Indeed, everywhere Communist parties, though usually under new names, compete in politics".

At the conclusion of a trial lasting from 1994 to 2006, Ethiopia's former ruler Mengistu Haile Mariam was convicted of genocide, war crimes and crimes against humanity and sentenced to death by an Ethiopian court for his role in Ethiopia's Red Terror. Ethiopian law is distinct from the UN and other definitions in that it defines genocide as intent to wipe out political and not just ethnic groups. In this respect, it closely resembles the definition of politicide.

In 1997, the Cambodian government asked the United Nations assistance in setting up a genocide tribunal. The prosecution presented the names of five possible suspects to the investigating judges on July 18, 2007. On July 26, 2010, Kang Kek Iew (Comrade Duch), director of the S-21 prison camp in Democratic Kampuchea where more than 14,000 people were tortured and then murdered (mostly at nearby Choeung Ek), was convicted of crimes against humanity and sentenced to 35 years. His sentence was reduced to 19 years in part because he had been behind bars for 11 years. Nuon Chea, second in command of the Khmer Rouge and its most senior surviving member, was charged with war crimes and crimes against humanity, but not charged with genocide. On August 7, 2014, he was convicted of crimes against humanity by the Khmer Rouge Tribunal and received a life sentence.

In August 2007, Arnold Meri, an Estonian Red Army veteran and cousin of former Estonian President Lennart Meri, faced charges of genocide by Estonian authorities for participating in the deportations of Estonians in Hiiumaa in 1949. The trial was halted when Meri died March 27, 2009 at the age of 89. Meri denied the accusation, characterizing them as politically motivated defamation, saying: "I do not consider myself guilty of genocide".

On November 26, 2010, the Russian State Duma issued a declaration acknowledging Stalin's responsibility for the Katyn massacre, the execution of over 21,000 Polish POW's and intellectual leaders by Stalin's NKVD. The declaration stated that archival material "not only unveils the scale of his horrific tragedy but also provides evidence that the Katyn crime was committed on direct orders from Stalin and other Soviet leaders".

Memorials and Museums

Monuments to the victims of communism exist in almost all the capitals of Eastern Europe and there are several museums documenting communist rule, such as the Museum of Occupations and Freedom Fights in Lithuania, the Museum of the Occupation of Latvia in Riga and the House of Terror in Budapest, all three of which also document Nazi rule.

In Washington D.C., a bronze statue based upon the 1989 Tiananmen Square *Goddess of Democracy* sculpture was dedicated as the Victims of Communism Memorial in 2007, having been authorized by the Congress in 1993. The Victims of Communism Memorial Foundation plans to build an International Museum on Communism in Washington.

In 2017, Canada's National Capital Commission approved the design for a memorial to the victims of Communism to be built at the Garden of the Provinces and Territories in Ottawa.

The Wall of Grief in Moscow, inaugurated in October 2017, is Russia's first monument ordered by presidential decree for victims of political persecution by Joseph Stalin during the country's Soviet era.

On August 23, 2018, Estonia's Victims of Communism 1940–1991 Memorial was inaugurated in Tallinn by President Kersti Kaljulaid. The memorial construction was financed by the state and is managed by the Estonian Institute of Historical Memory. The opening ceremony was chosen to coincide with the official EU European Day of Remembrance for Victims of Stalinism and Nazism.

WAR: ITS CAUSES AND EFFECTS

Soviet troops charging German positions near Leningrad, World War II.

War, armed conflict between states or nations (international war) or between factions within a state (civil war), prosecuted by force and having the purpose of compelling the defeated side to do the will of the victor. Among the causes of war are ideological, political, racial, economic, and religious conflicts. Imperialism, nationalism, and militarism have been called the dynamics of modern war. According to Karl von Clausewitz, war is a "continuation of political intercourse by other means." As such it often occurs after arbitration and mediation have failed. War has been a feature of history since primitive times. In ancient states warfare was usually a community enterprise, but as society divided on a functional basis a warrior class developed, and the army and navy became component parts of the state. In many instances, both recent and historic, the military has ruled the state. The use of fighting forces as instruments of war became a scientific art with the development of strategy and tactics. Modern war was been even more greatly influenced by industrial development, scientific progress, and the spread of popular education; a new era of machine warfare, prosecuted by masses of troops raised by conscription, rather than by rulers and the military class alone, developed after the wars of Napoleon I. Modern total war calls for the regimentation and coordination of peoples and resources; the state is compelled to demand a surrender of private rights in order that unity of purpose may enable it to prosecute the war to a victorious conclusion. Wars are waged not only against a nation's government and armed forces but also against a nation's economic means of existence and its civilian population in order to destroy the means and will to continue the struggle. Organized efforts to end war began with the peace congresses of the 19th cent. and culminated in the formation of the League of Nations after World War I and the United Nations after World War II. The threat of nuclear war has created a movement for nuclear disarmament (see disarmament, nuclear). During the cold war the threat of nuclear retaliation has restrained the use of nuclear weapons; instead there was an arms race, a succession of regional wars, and a proliferation of guerrilla wars and counterinsurgency campaigns. The end of the cold war has made arms control a more realistic goal.

WHY WAR?

The ubiquity and importance of war have made analyses of its causes a central concern of scholars for over two millennia. Many of the fundamental questions about the causes of war were raised by Thucydides in the fifth century b.c., but the vast amount of work on the topic since that time has produced ongoing debates instead of generally accepted answers. Studies of war can be divided into three broad categories (reviews of the literature using similar frameworks are provided by Waltz 1959; Bueno de Mesquita 1980; and Levy 1989). The first type takes the system as whole as the unit of analysis and focuses on how characteristics of the interstate system affect the frequency of war. States are the unit of analysis in the second type, which explores the relationships among the political, economic, and cultural features of particular states and the propensity of states to initiate wars. The third type analyzes war as an outcome of choices resulting from small group decision making.

Some debates focus on characteristics of the interstate system that are thought to increase or decrease the chance of war. Are wars more likely during a period of economic prosperity or one of economic contraction? Which is more likely to maintain peace, a balance of power in the international system or a situation in which one state is hegemonic? Has the increasing power of transnational organizations such as the United Nations changed the likelihood of war in the contemporary world?

There is also no consensus on which model of individual decision making is most appropriate for the study of war. Is the decision to go to war based on a rational calculation of economic costs and benefits, or is it an irrational outcome of distortion in decision making in small groups and bureaucracies? Are wars based on nationalist, ethnic, or religious conflicts generated more by emotions or values than by rational choices?

CAPITALISM, DEMOCRACY, AND WAR

One of the longest and most heated debates about the causes of war concerns the effects of capitalism. Beginning with Adam Smith, liberal economists have argued that capitalism promotes peace. Marxists, by contrast, suggest that capitalism leads to frequent imperialist wars.

Liberal economic theories point to the wealth generated by laissez-faire capitalist economies, the interdependence produced by trade, and the death and destruction of assets caused by war. Since capitalism has increased both the benefits of peace (by increasing productivity and trade) and the costs of war (by producing new and better instruments of destruction), it is no longer rational for states to wage war. The long period of relative peace that followed the triumph of capitalism in the nineteenth century and the two world wars that came after the rise of protectionist barriers to free trade often are cited in support of liberal economic theories, but those facts can be explained by hegemonic stability theorists as a consequence of the rise and decline of British hegemony.

In contrast to the sanguine views of capitalism presented by liberal economic theories, Marxists argue that economic problems inherent in advanced capitalist economies create incentives for war. First, the high productivity of industrial capitalism and a limited home market resulting from the poverty of the working class result in chronic "underconsumption" (Hobson [1902] 1954). Capitalists thus seek imperial expansion to control new markets for their goods. Second, Lenin ([1917] 1939) argued that capitalists fight imperialist wars to gain access to more raw materials and find more profitable outlets for their capital. These pressures lead first to wars between powerful capitalist states and weaker peripheral states and then to wars between great powers over which of them will get to exploit the periphery.

In contrast to the stress on the political causes (power and security) of war in most theories, the Marxist theory of imperialism has the virtue of drawing attention to economic causes. However, there are several problems with the economic causes posited in theories of imperialism. Like most Marxist arguments about politics, theories of imperialism assume that states are controlled directly or indirectly by dominant economic classes and thus that state policies reflect dominant class interests. Since states are often free of dominant class control and since many groups other than capitalists often influence state policies, it is simplistic to view war as a reflection of the interests of capitalists. Moreover, in light of the arguments made by liberal economists, it is far from clear that capitalists prefer war to other means of expanding markets and increasing profits.

With the increasing globalization of economies and the transition of more states to capitalist economies, the debates about the effects of capitalism, trade, and imperialism on war have become increasingly significant. If Adam Smith is right, the future is likely to be more peaceful than the past, but if Marxist theorists are right, there will be an unprecedented increase in economically based warfare.

The form of government in a country also may determine how often that country initiates wars. Kant ([1795] 1949) argued that democratic states (with constitutions and separation of powers) initiate wars less often than do autocratic states. This conclusion follows from an analysis of who pays the costs of war and who gets the benefits. Since citizens are required to pay for war with high taxes and their lives, they will rarely support war initiation. Rulers of states, by contrast, have much to gain from war and can pass on most of the costs to their subjects. Therefore, when decisions about war are made only by rulers (in autocracies), war will be frequent, and when citizens have more control of the decision (in democracies), peace generally will be the result.

Empirical research indicates that democratic states are less likely than are nondemocratic states to initiate wars, but the relationship is not strong (Levy 1989, p. 270). Perhaps one reason for the weakness of the relationship is that the assumption that citizens will oppose war initiation is not always correct. Many historical examples indicate that in at least some conditions citizens will support war even though it is not in their economic interest to do so. Nationalism, religion, ethnicity, and other cultural factors often are cited as important causes of particular wars in journalistic and historical accounts, but there still is no general theory of the conditions in which these factors modify or even override economic interests. Many classical sociological arguments suggested that these "premodern" and "irrational" sources of war would decline over time, but the late twentieth century has demonstrated the opposite. Nationalist and ethnic wars have become more common and intense. This raises the general issue of the factors affecting the choices individuals make about war initiation: Can these factors be modeled as rational maximization of interests, or is the process more complex?

DECISION MAKING AND WAR

Although the assumptions may be only implicit or undeveloped, all theories of war must contain some assumptions about individual decision making. However, few theories of war focus on the individual level of analysis. One notable exception is the rational-choice theory of war developed and tested by Bueno do Mesquita (1981).

Bueno de Mesquita begins by assuming that the decision to initiate war is made by a single dominant ruler who is a rational expected-utility maximizer. Utilities are defined in terms of state policies. Rulers fight wars to affect the policies of other states, essentially to make other states' policies more similar to their interests. Rulers calculate the costs and benefits of initiating war and the probability of victory. War is initiated only when rulers expect a net gain from it.

This limited set of assumptions has been used to generate several counterintuitive propositions. For example, common sense might suggest that states would fight their enemies and not their allies, but Bueno de Mesquita argues that war will be more common between allies than between enemies. Wars between allies are caused by actual or anticipated policy changes that threaten the existing relationship. The interventions of the United States in Latin America and of the Soviet Union in eastern Europe after World War II illustrate the process. Other counterintuitive propositions suggest that under some conditions a state may rationally choose to attack the stronger of two allied states instead of the weaker, and under some conditions it is rational for a state with no allies to initiate a war against a stronger state with allies (if the distance between the two is great, the weaker state will be unable to aid the stronger). Although these propositions and others derived from the theory have received strong empirical support, many have argued that the basic rational-choice assumptions of the theory are unrealistic and have rejected Bueno de Mesquita's work on those grounds.

Other analyses of the decision to initiate war focus on how the social features of the decision making process lead to deviations from rational choice. Allison (1971) notes that all political decisions are made within organizations and that this setting often influences the content of decisions. He argues that standard operating procedures and repertoires tend to limit the flexibility of decision makers and make it difficult to respond adequately to novel situations. Janis (1972) focuses on the small groups within political organizations (such as executives and their cabinet advisers) that actually make decisions about war. He suggests that the cohesiveness of these small groups often leads to a striving for unanimity that prevents a full debate about options and produces a premature consensus. Other scholars have discussed common misperceptions that distort decisions about war, such as the tendency to underestimate the capabilities of one's enemies and overestimate one's own. In spite of these promising studies, work on deviations from rational choice is just beginning, and there still is no general theoretical model of the decision to initiate war.

CONCLUSION

The failure to develop a convincing general theory of the causes of war has convinced some scholars that no such theory is possible, that all one can do is describe the causes of particular wars. This pessimistic conclusion is premature. The existing literature on the causes of war provides several fragments of a general theory, many of which have some empirical support. The goal of theory and research on war in the future will be to combine aspects of arguments at all three levels of analysis to create a general theory of the causes of war.

War: Legal Questions

For many centuries, western European attitudes toward the legality of war were dominated by the teachings of the Roman Catholic Church. War was regarded as a means of obtaining reparation for a prior illegal act, and was sometimes regarded as being commanded by God. In this way much of the debate centered on the distinction between just and unjust wars, a distinction that began to break down in the late sixteenth century. In time, leaders justified wars if they were undertaken for the defense of certain vital interests, although there were no accepted objective criteria for determining what those vital interests were. In the twenty-first century, international lawyers and states rarely use the term *war*. This is because "war" has a technical and somewhat imprecise meaning under international law, and states engaged in hostilities often deny there is a state of war. The difference between war and hostilities falling short of war may appear very fine, but it can have important consequences especially in regard to the relations between states. Since the adoption of the United Nations Charter in 1945, there is a general prohibition on the use of force by states except in accordance with the provisions of the Charter itself. In this way the question is more about the use of force than the right to declare war. This is reflected in the difficulty government representatives have had in finding an acceptable definition for the crime of aggression under the 1998 Rome Statue of the International Criminal Court.

Laws of War/International Humanitarian Law

Among the equivalent and interchangeable expressions, the "laws of war," the "law of armed conflict," and "international humanitarian law," the first is the oldest. War crimes come under the general umbrella of international humanitarian law, and may be defined as the branch of international law limiting the use of violence in armed conflicts. The expression "laws of war" dates back to when it was customary to make a formal declaration of war before initiating an armed attack on another state.

In the twenty-first century, the term *armed conflict* is used in place of *war*, and while the military tend to prefer the term *law of armed conflict,* the International Committee of the Red Cross and other commentators use the expression "international humanitarian law" to cover the broad range of international treaties and principles applicable to situations of armed conflict. The fundamental aim of international humanitarian law is to establish limits to the means and methods of armed conflict, and to protect noncombatants, whether they are the wounded, sick or captured soldiers, or civilians.

International humanitarian law is comprised of two main branches; the law of the Hague and the law of Geneva. The law of the Hague regulates the means and methods of warfare. It is codified primarily in the regulations respecting the Laws and Customs of War on Land ("the Hague Regulations") annexed to the 1907 Hague Convention IV ("the Hague Regulations"). These govern the actual conduct of hostilities and include matters such as the selection of targets and weapons permissible during armed conflict. The law of Geneva is codified primarily in four conventions adopted in 1949, and these are known collectively as the Geneva Conventions for the Protection of War Victims. Their aim is to protect certain categories of persons, including civilians, the wounded, and prisoners of war.

After the piecemeal development of international humanitarian law at the end of the nineteenth century and the beginning of the twentieth century, the experience of World War II exposed the shortcomings in the legal regulation of this field dramatically. This realization led to the adoption of the four Geneva Conventions for the Protection of War Victims in 1949. The adoption of the Conventions, coupled with the earlier well developed body of Hague law governing the conduct of hostilities by armed forces, meant that traditional interstate wars, or "armed conflicts" to use the language of the Conventions, were now well-regulated, in theory at least. The phrase "armed conflict" was employed to make it clear that the Conventions applied once a conflict between states employing the use of arms had begun, whether or not there had been a formal declaration of war.

As the majority of armed conflicts in the cold war period were not interstate wars of the kind envisaged by traditional international humanitarian law, obvious gaps in the legal regulation governing armed conflicts remained. The adoption of the Geneva Conventions marked a break with the past in that Article 3, which was common to all four Conventions, sought to establish certain minimum standards of behavior "in the case of armed conflict not of an international character." In an attempt to address deficiencies in the 1949 Geneva Conventions, Additional Protocols I and II were adopted in 1977.

Protocol I applies to international armed conflict and brought what was often referred to as "wars of national liberation" within the definition of international conflicts. Protocol II, on the other hand, did not apply to all non-international armed conflicts, but only to those that met a new and relatively high threshold test. Despite the time and effort that was involved in drafting and agreeing the Protocols, the result was less than satisfactory, especially from the point of view of classifying armed conflicts to determine which Protocol, if any, applies in a given case. The applicability of Protocol II is quite narrow, and this helps explain in part why so many states are party to it.

Codification of War Crimes

The United Nations Commission for the Investigation of War Crimes was established in the aftermath of World War II in order to prepare the groundwork for the prosecution of war criminals arising from atrocities committed during the war. One of the features of the 1945 Charter of the International Military Tribunal at Nuremberg is that the crime of genocide did not appear in its substantive provisions. Consequently, the Tribunal convicted the Nazi war criminals of "crimes against humanity" for the crimes committed against the Jewish people in Europe.

The relationship between war crimes, genocide, and crimes against humanity is somewhat complex due to the historical development of each category of international crime. The most significant practical legal issue to be considered is the necessity for some form of armed conflict before there can be a war crime. In the case of genocide, there is no requirement for such crimes to take place in the context of a war or armed conflict. However, such crimes can often be committed as part of a wider conflict to achieve some of the broader aims of participants. The chaos and breakdown in law and order characteristic of armed conflict provides potential perpetrators with an opportunity to pursue illegitimate objectives and methods.

Historically, it was also probably easier to evade responsibility for such crimes when they were committed in the course of an armed conflict. With the advent of the International Criminal Tribunals for the former Yugoslavia and Rwanda, Special Courts and the International Criminal Court, this situation no longer prevails.

The concept of a war crime is broad and encompasses many different acts committed during an armed conflict. It is synonymous in many people's minds with ethnic cleansing, mass killings, sexual violence, bombardment of cities and towns, concentration camps, and similar atrocities. War crimes may be defined as a grave or serious violation of the rules or principles of international humanitarian law—for which persons may be held individually responsible. The Geneva Conventions oblige states to provide effective penal sanctions for persons committing, or ordering to be committed grave violations of the Conventions. In fact, in such cases all states are required to assume power to prosecute and punish the perpetrators. Such provisions only apply if the violations were committed in the course of an international armed conflict. In reality, it is often difficult to determine if a particular situation amounts to an "international" or a "non-international armed conflict." However, although legally of some significance, it does not alter the serious nature of the crimes in the first instance.

Furthermore, decisions of the International Criminal Tribunals for the former Yugoslavia and Rwanda have ruled that many principles and rules previously considered applicable only in international armed conflict are now applicable in internal armed conflicts, and serious violations of humanitarian law committed within the context of such internal conflicts constitute war crimes. Such decisions, and the adoption of the Rome Statute of the International Criminal Court, have tended to blur the legal significance of the distinction between international and non-international armed conflicts.

Genocide and Crimes Against Humanity

The judgment of the International Military Tribunal at Nuremberg was controversial in some respects. One of the main reasons why it was considered necessary to draft a convention that dealt specifically with the crime of genocide was the limited scope given to "crimes against humanity" at the time.

A crime against humanity referred to a wide range of atrocities, but it also had a narrow aspect, and the prevailing view in the aftermath of World War II was that crimes against humanity could only be committed in association with an international armed conflict or war. The Allies had insisted at Nuremberg that crimes against humanity could only be committed if they were associated with one of the other crimes within the Nuremberg Tribunal's jurisdiction, that is, war crimes and crimes against peace. In effect they had imposed a requirement or nexus, as it became known, between crimes against humanity and international armed conflict. For this reason many considered that a gap existed in international law that needed to be addressed. The General Assembly of the United Nations wanted to go a step further recognizing that one atrocity, namely genocide, would constitute an international crime even if it were committed in time of peace. The distinction between genocide and crimes against humanity is less significant today, because the recognized definition of crimes against humanity has evolved and now refers to atrocities committed against civilians in peacetime and in wartime. The Rome Statute of the International Criminal Court provides that crimes against humanity must have been committed as part of a "widespread or systematic attack directed against any civilian population."

Some states were concerned that international law did not seem to govern atrocities committed in peacetime (as opposed to during a time of armed conflict or war) and called for the preparation of a draft convention on the crime of genocide. The Convention on the Prevention and Punishment of the Crime of Genocide was adopted in 1948, and entered into force on January 11, 1951.

Under the Convention, the crime of genocide has both a physical element —certain listed acts such as killing, or causing serious mental or bodily harm to members of a racial group—and a mental element, which upholds the acts must be committed with intent to destroy, in whole of in part, a national, ethnic, racial or religious group "as such." Although earlier drafts had included political groups, this was later dropped during final drafting stages. In this way, the killing of an estimated 1.5 million Cambodians by the Khmer Rouge is not generally considered to have been genocide as defined under the Genocide Convention (both the perpetrators and the majority of the victims were Khmer). However, its widespread and systematic nature qualifies it as one of the twentieth century's most notorious crimes against humanity. The definition in the Convention is essentially repeated in Article 6 of the Rome Statute of the International Criminal Court, and in the relevant statues of the International Criminal Tribunals for the former Yugoslavia and Rwanda.

THE NATURE OF WAR

The nature of war definitions of war have varied, but any attempt to understand it must include the following critical elements.

- First, war is an organized violent activity, waged not by individuals but by men (sometimes joined by women) in groups.

- Second, war is a mutual activity; whatever takes place in it relates, or should relate, primarily to the enemy's movements with the aim of defeating him and avoid being defeated oneself.

- Third, the conduct of war is conditioned on the hope for victory, or at the very least self-preservation. Where that hope does not exist there can be no war, only suicide.

The "American" Way of War

Military institutions and war reflect in part the society that creates them. Although many Americans view themselves as a peace-loving people and war as an aberration, war has been a regular part of American history, integral to the way the nation developed.

Despite divisions among Americans, the United States has justified its wars as in defense of American lives, property, or ideals. Policymakers have also taken the nation into war for various strategic, economic, and political reasons. But since the old world idea of balance-of-power wars, or wars of subjugation over other nations, has been anathema to Americans' self-image, the United States has usually mobilized for war in highly idealistic crusades—for liberty or democracy.

America views itself generally as anti-militaristic because for most of its history, the nation relied in wartime on *ad hoc* citizen armies rather than large standing forces, and because civilian control of the military is seen as a fundamental principle. This antimilitarism was reinforced by isolationism. Secure behind vast oceans, the United States did not develop large peacetime standing forces until the Cold War.

Another paradox is that although Americans generally view themselves as peace loving, they have been capable of engaging in the most devastating kind of warfare—war aimed at total victory and complete elimination of the enemy threat, sometimes of the enemy themselves. This view of warfare emerged from European Americans' wars with Native Americans.

The Civil War had led the United States to adopt the doctrine of Gen. Ulysses S. Grant, which emphasized overwhelming and continual military force applied directly against the enemy army and indirectly through deprivation of the enemy's civilian population and resources. In the twentieth century, during two world wars, and limited wars in Korea and Vietnam, the U.S. Army would pursue this strategy against the enemy forces, while the air force and navy pursued the indirect campaign, through bombing and blockade, against the enemy's material resources and political will.

As the United States industrialized, optimism about America's fighting ability focused on superior weaponry. At the turn of the century, Adm. Alfred T. Mahan's doctrine of Sea Power emphasizing the use of a modern fleet promised swift and total victory. In the 1920s and 1930s, Gen. Billy Mitchell of the Army Air Service helped develop the doctrine of Strategic Airpower as a technological means to achieve quick and total victory. In World War II, in response to the Japanese attack on Pearl Harbor and in a crusade against fascism, Americans waged war on land, sea, and air, including conventional and ultimately nuclear bombing of urban areas to achieve decisive victory and unconditional surrender of the enemy.

The Cold War posed a major challenge to American views of war and the military. Containment of the Soviet Union led to large standing military forces, but even these did not produce a sense of military security, for the USSR also developed intercontinental ballistic missiles and thermonuclear weapons. Before it ended in 1991, with the total collapse of the Soviet empire, the forty-year Cold War represented an unprecedented period of U.S. uncertainty over national security.

During the Cold War, the U.S. government refrained from the use of total military force in Korea and Vietnam. But the policy of limited war clashed with the traditional goal of total victory. The Korean War ended in a frustrating stalemate, the Vietnam War ultimately in defeat. After the United States had fought for more than seven years to prevent it, the Communist victory in Vietnam was a severe blow to Americans' optimism, sense of righteousness, and sense of military prowess, which did not return until the collapse of the USSR and the American victory in the Persian Gulf War of 1991.

The U.S.-led coalition assault in Operation Desert Storm seemed quite justified and resulted in a quick, decisive victory that drove the forces of Iraqi dictator Saddam Hussein out of Kuwait. Although the Baghdad régime continued in power, its threat to the region was dramatically curtailed. More than any other U.S. military engagement since World War II, the Gulf War to liberate Kuwait conformed to the traditional American way of war.

Peace and Anti-War Movements

Ideas on the causes of war held by various American peace and antiwar movements, often had little basis in reality. Since the early nineteenth century, these movements have, at various times, offered eight main prescriptions that embody their central ideas: (1) arbitration treaties and an international court to arbitrate disputes (popular ideas from the 1840s until 1914); (2) treaties forbidding resort to force (such as the 1920s movement for the "outlawry of war"); (3) disarmament or quantitative arms reductions; (4) collective security (popular during and after World War I); (5) some form of world government; (6) U.S. isolationism or strict neutrality (popular in the late 1930s); (7) pacifist noncooperation with national military programs; (8) dovish U.S. policies toward U.S. adversaries (e.g., Vietnamese Communists or Nica raguan Sandinistas). Some peace groups have also emphasized the need to cultivate pacific values through public moral education and by emphasizing the horrors of war.

When tried, these prescriptions usually proved infeasible or ineffective. Many arbitration treaties were signed before 1914, but they proved useless: governments freely ignored arbitration rulings that went against them. The Kellogg-Briand Treaty supposedly "outlawed" war in 1928, yet it proved to be an empty stunt that had no political effects. Quantitative disarmament rests on a proposition—that the incidence or intensity of warfare increases with the quantity of modern weapons available—that remains unproven and seems wrong. (Ancient history offers evidence against it, recording many immensely destructive wars fought wholly without modern weapons.) The collective security idea, embodied in the League of Nations, proved ineffective in the 1930s while distracting Americans from more feasible ways to prevent World War II, such as early U.S. moves to deter or contain Germany and Japan. World government is now among those ideas so discredited they are no longer seriously discussed. U.S. neutrality, codified in the U.S. Neutrality Acts of 1935–39, helped embolden Adolf Hitler to start World War II while failing to keep the United States out of that war, and thus must be reckoned as more a cause of war than peace. Pacifism also helped embolden Hitler, who saw British and American pacifism as easing his road to European hegemony. Pressure for dovish policies did end one or two wars (e.g., the Indochina and Nicaraguan Contra wars), but only after these wars had burned for years. Overall, peace movements' main prescriptions seem generally unsound in retrospect.

Another misdirected approach to the causes of war has come in the twentieth century from anti–Communist conservatives. Their analysis rested on two main hypotheses: (1) communism causes war because Communist states will seek to expand by force against capitalist states; and (2) appeasement of communism causes war by emboldening Communist states in their expansionism. Their second hypothesis was arguably valid, at least in some situations, but their first was not. Communist states proved to be only modestly aggressive. The USSR was an opportunistic but cautious aggressor, not a Hitlerian juggernaut. Soviet leaders committed vast crimes against their own people but only modest international aggressions.

Assumptions Based on Great Historical Victories

After three great victories—in the wake of World War I and World War II, and after the Cold War, which ended in 1991—the United States has sought to shape a durable peace based on its assumptions about the causes of war.

Woodrow Wilson's post–World War I policies rested on poor theories of war's causes. Wilson offered six main prescriptions, framed in his famous Fourteen Points: (1) Replace balance–of–power politics and competitive alliance making (which Wilson believed caused war) with a collective security system. But collective security was infeasible, as the League's later failure showed. (2) Reduce armaments to "the lowest level consistent with national safety." Here Wilson was misled by the myth that quantitative disarmament could reduce violence between states. (3) End secret diplomacy in favor of "open covenants … openly arrived at," a change Wilson believed would bolster popular control of foreign policy, promoting peace. This soon–forgotten notion was a false corollary to the stronger hypothesis that democracy promotes peace. (4) Grant self–determination to freedom–seeking peoples. But this was infeasible in a post–1919 Europe of much intermingled ethnicities. (5) Remove trade barriers. This was a sound economic idea but a poor peace program, because free trade can cause war as well as peace, as illustrated by the way U.S. trade with the Allies helped draw the United States into World War I. (6) End colonialism. This was a humane idea that addressed a non–cause of the world war (European colonial rivalries had largely ended by 1914).

In World War II, President Franklin D. Roosevelt's ideas about the causes of war and peace echoed Wilson's in part and differed in part. Like Wilson, Roosevelt believed that arms reductions, free trade, and national self–determination would promote peace. Unlike Wilson, Roosevelt also believed that aggressor states could best be tamed by completely defeating, disarming, and occupying them. His core belief, however, was that the best cornerstone of peace would be a concert system resembling the 1815 Concert of Europe, run through the cooperation of the "four policemen" (the United States, Britain, Nationalist China, and the Soviet Union). Roosevelt's concert scheme failed because a concert requires an underlying consensus among the great powers—something rare in history and absent after 1945.

In the 1990s, the administrations of George Bush and Bill Clinton built their post–Cold War peace on better ideas and got better results. They continued U.S. security guarantees to primary U.S. allies in Europe and Asia, backed by a continued overseas U.S. military presence. They pressed Europe's newly freed states to respect the rights of ethnic minorities. Echoing Wilson, they pressed Europe's dictatorships to democratize, believing that democracies seldom fight each other. Finally, they pushed former Communist states to "marketize" their economies, believing that marketization would promote prosperity, which would bolster democracy and peace. These post–Cold War policies, produced a softer landing than the policies of 1919 and 1945.

The Effects of War on the Economy

The most persistent and perhaps most important question relating to the effects of America's wars and their related costs on the U.S. economy is whether military expenditures have been a prop or a burden for economic growth. This question has continued relevance because the United States in the 1990s spent a larger part of its gross domestic product (GDP) on defense (3.8% in 1995) than any other G7 industrial nation, almost four times Japan's expenditure and nearly twice as much as Germany's—America's two most important economic competitors. The fact that Russia in the 1990s spent almost three times more of its GDP on defense —and was in economic chaos—only strengthened this concern.

Historians and economists have waxed and waned with regard to the effect of military expenditures on the U.S. economy. Charles and Mary Beard in The Rise of American Civilization (1927) and Louis Hacker in The Triumph of American Capitalism (1940) argued that the Civil War destroyed not only slavery but also the Southern slaveocracy, thus allowing the balance of political power to shift to Northern industrialists and hence spurring American economic growth. Prior to these accounts, the classical economists (Adam Smith, David Ricardo, and Thomas Malthus) were concerned with the effects of war on aggregate demand. The eighteenth and early nineteenth centuries saw very high levels of military expenditures in Britain, for example, which these economists believed had a negative impact on industrial growth. The national debts resulting from war, Smith believed, "enfeebled every state ... enriching in most cases the idle and profuse debtor at the expense of the industrious and frugal creditor."

Critics of the capitalist system in more recent years have argued that capitalist societies are prone to periodic stagnation, and that only wars of the magnitude of World War II are capable of curing massive unemployment. Alternatively, liberal economists argue that war, and particularly World War II, was the strongest influence establishing Keynesian economics as a guideline and a justification for U.S. government fiscal policies for the postwar era—policies that led to widespread employment, high earnings, and a modest measure of income redistribution. Even some strong opponents of the Vietnam War began to argue in the mid–1990s that full employment was only possible in the late 1960s because of that war.

Paul Kennedy, in his widely read Rise and Fall of the Great Powers (1987), is perhaps the best known historian for the view that persistent and high military expenditures have played an important role in the relative economic decline of major nations since 1500. In this and subsequent works, he argues that the United States now runs the risk of "imperial overstretch"; that America's global commitments are greater than its capacity to fund them. For him, war is not only a burden, but continuous high levels of defense spending can and generally have turned major nations into minor ones. Although his is a popular view, he had yet to persuade the experts that the United States was well down the road to relative economic decline.

The most sophisticated studies on the prop v. burden issue—whether defense spending contributes to economic growth and well-being by stimulating the economy, or whether defense spending uses up scarce resources or diverts resources into less productive channels—tend to emphasize that growth in the GDP has been rather constant, with little lasting impact from the nine major wars America has fought since independence. Wars temporarily reduce long-run productive capacity by reducing the growth of population and the inflow of immigrants; but the general burden of any given war falls largely on the current generation, according to Chester Wright in a seminal study on the more enduring economic consequences of American wars to 1940. More recently, Todd Sandler and Keith Hartley demonstrated that defense spending generally inhibits economic growth in developed countries by crowding out public and private investment, and siphoning off of R & D resources. Indeed, since the late 1980s, world military expenditures as a percentage of GDP have decreased dramatically without any evidence of harmful effects on the world economy. In truth, the overall economic burden of America's wars is less significant than the inequitable manner in which so much of that burden has been placed upon the working class and those with modest education, while others largely escape or even profit from such wars.

If the effect of military spending during the war years is the most obvious point of impact on the economy, the most lasting one has to do with veterans' benefits paid after the war to veterans and their dependents. Veterans' benefits have been paid for every war since the American Revolution. They amounted to about two-thirds of the total dollar cost of the Revolutionary War; more than half the cost of the War of 1812; and 3.7 times the cost of mobilizing the Union forces in the Civil War. Surprisingly, these benefits continued to rise for about forty to sixty years after the end of each of these wars and did not cease until well over a century later. Benefits for Civil War veterans and spouses ceased only in the 1980s; World War II benefits will be paid until sometime after 2070. To date, World War II veteran's benefits have amounted to more than $300 billion, only somewhat less than the original cost of that war in current dollars. Clearly, veterans' benefits have been a major infusion of funds into the economy, and were the major direct federal subsidy to families prior to the welfare state. Compared to other countries, American soldiers and their dependents received benefits much earlier (since 1783) and in more generous amounts than elsewhere. The average payment to a still-living World War I veteran, for example, was $6,500 in 1992. Confederate soldiers, of course, received no federal veterans benefits, although some southern states sought to add them.

The most troubling problem concerning the impact of war on the economy has to do with rapidly rising public debt. Large but temporary public debts have occurred in all of America's wars; all were paid off in time until the 1970s, when U.S. public debt rose dramatically owing to large defense increases and major tax cuts under President Ronald Reagan. In the 1990s, U.S. net public debt (most of which is war–related) was at an unprecedented peacetime level. High public debt levels—a problem in all G7 nations—boost real interest rates, retard the accumulation of private capital, and limit gains in living standards, according to the International Monetary Fund. Reducing this unsustainable public debt, the most significant legacy of recent American wars, will be one of the United States's greatest challenges in the twenty-first century.

MORAL JUSTIFICATIONS FOR WAR

Jus ad bellum

Can war be morally justified? Most war doctrines include two considerations: first, the conditions under which one may have recourse to war (*jus ad bellum*); second, the rules and codes by which war may be conducted (*jus in bello*). The act of war, a license to kill, tests our adherence to morality, our acceptance of what we assume are human and civilized codes of behavior, our notion of the distinctions between the divine and the profane, our understanding of authority and legitimacy, and our sense of self-and moral consciousness. There are two main discourses dealing with *jus ad bellum.* The first makes a distinction between just and unjust wars, and the second makes distinctions between offensive and defensive wars.

St. Augustine of Hippo (354–430 A.D.) first grappled with the Christian ideal of love that prohibited killing and wounding in one's own defense but also obliged Christians to aid others, thus justifying the use of force on the aggressors. Yet Augustine did not provide a theory that isolated causes for a just war, nor did he suggest that a Christian cause was most just. Instead, he proposed that Christian ethics gave people and their leaders a capacity to know the moral limits of armed action but did not provide them with the attributes to "compare unerringly the over-all justice of régimes and nations" (Ramsey, p. 32). For Augustine, as all parties in war are engaging in wrongdoing, the warring parties cannot be divided into good versus bad, but rather Christian ethics provide guidance and the parameters for conduct in war of all parties involved.

St. Thomas Aquinas (1225–1274) expanded the idea of a just war and also initiated a shift from "voluntarism" to "rationalism" in understanding the nature of the political community, emphasizing a natural-law notion of justice (Ramsey, p. 32). According to Aquinas, a just war had three necessary requirements: declaration by a legitimate constitutional authority, a just cause, and the right intention. Francisco de Vitoria (1486?–1546) and Francisco Suárez (1548–1617) added further conditions: the means of war should be proportional to the injustices being prevented or remedied by war, all peaceful means to remedy injustices should be exhausted, and the war should have a reasonable hope of success.

In reflecting on the morality of the Gulf War, several authors came up with different conclusions. George Weigel argues that opposing the aggression of Saddam Hussein's invasion of Kuwait was justified in both intention and execution according to the criteria set out by just-war theory. Jean Bethke Elshtain, on the other hand, argues that war cannot be justified merely by checking off the list of criteria associated with the just-war theory. Instead, she suggests that the theory begs us to pause, to think about the ramifications of war, and to show some skepticism and queasiness about war. Above all, she asks that in drawing the balance sheet for the Gulf War, we evaluate technological accuracy and military might alongside the devastation and long-term effects of war on Iraqi children and society.

The just-war mode of reasoning attempts to reconcile the requirements of national defense with the moral obligations of protecting the innocent. In the age of modern warfare, where nuclear deterrence is the most significant element in preventing wars, the ideas behind just-war theory require a lot of tweaking before it begins to make any sense at all. In evaluating the justifiability of a contemporary war, some of the rules pertaining to *jus ad bellum,* particularly the rules of proportionality and reasonable hope of success, are seriously challenged. With the capacity and probability of killing large numbers of innocent people in warfare, the tensions inherent between *jus ad bellum* and *jus in bello* become sharper.

Can war be controlled? Carl von Clausewitz says war is an act of force, and "there is no logical limit to the application" of force (Clausewitz, p. 77). However, others see war as a social activity that demands social organization and control, requiring a military that uses violence with deliberation for political objectives. As instruments of the state, the military employs violence (or uses force) in a purposeful, deliberate, and legitimate manner. Two criteria that maintain order and military discipline in war are the general value system of culture and the presupposition that the cost of war should not outweigh its benefits.

News Media, War, and the Military

From the earliest days of the republic, American leaders encountered difficulties trying to balance the need for secrecy in diplomatic and military affairs with America's tradition of a free and independent press. As early as 1792, Secretary of State Thomas Jefferson wrote to President George Washington that "No government ought to be without censors and where the press is free, no one ever will." Yet, only three years earlier, Congress passed a statute requiring each department to establish regulations for the custody, use, and preservation of official documents. That seemingly innocuous statute implicitly included rules for classification and censorship. The imposition of such rules has been especially important during periods of international crisis and war when citizens have been asked by presidents, who controlled the flow of government information, to surrender their lives and treasure to defend national security. Looking over America's military past, many observers would agree with Senator Hiram Johnson (R–Calif.) who said in 1917 that "The first casualty when war comes is truth."

Obviously, few citizens in any nation approve the publication in wartime of information about troop movements and military strategies that would help their enemies defeat their fighting men and women. Not all citizens agree about the necessity of government suppression or censorship of journalists or those opposed to war who allegedly give aid and comfort to the enemy by criticizing presidents or generals or organizing antiwar groups.

After the United States entered World War I in April 1917, the War Department, following the policies of the European nations, established its first formal accrediting procedure for war correspondents. A journalist had to agree in writing to submit dispatches to military censors and to behave "like a gentleman of the press." In addition, back in Washington, Woodrow Wilson established the controversial Committee on Public Information, which was not only in charge of censorship but also ran an elaborate propaganda campaign at home and abroad. For example, the committee employed 75,000 speakers who delivered 750,000 four-minute pep talks, often in movie theaters, in 5,000 cities and towns in support of the war.

The administration also obtained from Congress the Espionage and Sedition Acts of World War I. The former permitted the Postmaster General to refuse to mail magazines or other publications detrimental to the war effort; the latter prohibited speech that did not support that effort. Under such laws, Socialist Party presidential nominee Eugene V. Debs was sent to jail, as was a movie producer for making a film about the Revolutionary War in which the British appeared as villains.

During World War II, military authorities again imposed strict censorship at the source for correspondents who numbered as many as 1,000 in Europe alone. Among other matters deemed threatening to national security were stories and, especially, pictures that portrayed too graphically G.I. injuries and death, or reported incidents of cowardice, as was the case during the Battle of the Bulge, or revealed information embarrassing to the United States and its Allies. And as in previous wars, once they learned the rules, correspondents practiced self–censorship so that they would not have to rewrite their articles completely after censors got through with them.

Back home, the government issued a voluntary code of wartime practices for the media, to which, in most cases, the mainstream press adhered. The *Chicago Tribune* was a notable exception when it revealed mobilization plans on the eve of the attack on Pearl Harbor, and later ran a story about the breaking of Japanese codes. Although the Office of Censorship did intercept and read letters and cablegrams and tap phone calls, most Americans accepted the abridgment of their First Amendment rights during the global crisis.

The Office of War Information (OWI), headed by radio commentator Elmer Davis, coordinated propaganda activities. Somewhat more sophisticated than the Creel Committee of World War I, OWI staffers met regularly with the media, including the heads of Hollywood studios, to suggest political themes they wanted to promote.

No such elaborate activities were needed during the limited Korean War. From June through December 1950, journalists at the front adhered to a voluntary code of self–censorship. But when South Korean leaders began complaining about articles critical of their repressive actions, Washington imposed full military censorship. Few Americans ever learned the truth about the nature of their ally or of the devastating American bombing of civilians in North Korea that resulted in hundreds of thousands of deaths.

Such was not the case in the Vietnam War—the most controversial war in American history in many ways, including the relationship between the media and the military. According to critics of press performance, journalists in the combat theater, not subject to censorship, wrote stories and shot television footage that distorted and hurt the war effort—most controversially, media coverage of the Tet Offensive of early 1968. That charge dramatically influenced the way the government subsequently limited journalists' access during the 1983 U.S. intervention in Grenada, the 1989 Panama intervention, and, above all, the 1991 Persian Gulf War.

The political left believes that the charge that the media "lost the war" in Vietnam was a myth. Except for a brief period during the Kennedy administration when several young journalists who supported the war criticized military tactics and the venality of the Saigon régime, most of the coverage favored administration policies, at least until 1968. Even during that earlier period, the government in Saigon expelled American journalists, and Washington influenced publishers to alter their coverage. [Others point to] several celebrated cases—notably Morley Safer's 1965 account on CBS of Marines burning hooches, and his later coverage of the Tet Offensive—the media apparently contributed to the growth of antiwar sentiments, but no more so than the American rates of casualties. But the fact that reporters shared the national Cold War consensus and that the tenets of so-called objective journalism demanded that they report official briefings (the "Five O'clock Follies"), often uncritically, guaranteed a relatively favorable press until almost the end. The Johnson administration did not institute full censorship because it wanted to play down the importance of this undeclared war.

Another view suggests that the Vietnam War was the first televised live or "living-room war." But it was not projected live into viewers' homes. In this era before the development of satellite hookup, the news film for stories emanating either from Saigon or Japan was flown by air to New York, then edited and broadcast. As in World War II, those in charge of deciding what to air generally eliminated pictures of bloodied soldiers and the other worst horrors of war.

The situation was different during the Persian Gulf War in 1991, with strict censorship and "pool" reporting for the more than 1,000 journalists who covered the fighting in real time—primarily from hotels in Saudi Arabia. Military authorities banned several magazines from the combat theater and arrested at least eight American correspondents for violating aspects of the censorship rules. Aside from reports from the Cable News Network's (CNN) Peter Arnett in Baghdad, which were themselves censored by the Iraqis, most of what Americans saw on television was exactly what the military wanted Americans—and anyone else tuning in —to see.

Beginning in the 1980s, worldwide television news services, led by CNN, began to play an increasingly important role in crises and wars. Before the Gulf War broke out, Saddam Hussein, the Iraqi leader, was encouraged by strong congressional opposition to President George Bush's policies, broadcast by satellite to Iraq. Later, coalition commander Gen. H. Norman Schwarzkopf tailored his televised briefings for those in Baghdad who were watching. In 1991, Haitian dictator Gen. Raoul Cédras's viewing of congressional and other opposition to American policies, brought to him by the ubiquitous CNN, may have contributed to his recalcitrance.

As nations become even more completely electronically connected to one another in years to come, the problems inherent in maintaining a free press during times of international crisis may become even more severe.

DIRECT IMPACT ON HUMANS AND THE ENVIRONMENT

War is perhaps the most serious of all public health problems. Public health has been defined by the Institute of Medicine as "what we, as a society, do collectively to assure the conditions in which people can be healthy." Using this definition, war is clearly antithetical to public health. It not only causes death and disability among military personnel and civilians, but it also destroys the social, economic, and political infrastructure necessary for well-being and health. War violates basic human rights. As a violent method of settling conflicts, it promotes other forms of violence in the community and the home. War causes immediate and long-term damage to the environment. And war and preparation for war sap human and economic resources that might be used for social good.

Worldwide, there were over 45 million deaths among military personnel during the twentieth century—a mean annual military death rate of 183 deaths per 1 million population. This rate was more than sixteen times greater than the reported rate for the nineteenth century, despite enormous progress in surgical treatment of war injuries and in the prevention and treatment of infectious diseases. In addition, since an increasing percentage of wars are civil wars or are indiscriminate in the use of weapons, civilians are increasingly caught in the crossfire. Civilian deaths as a percentage of all war-related deaths rose from 14 percent during World War I to 90 percent during some wars of the 1990s. Moreover, during civil wars civilians may find it difficult to receive medical care and may be unable to obtain adequate and safe food and water, shelter, medicinal care, and public health services. The physical, mental, and social impacts of war on civilians are especially severe for vulnerable populations, including women, children, the elderly, the ill, and the disabled. Further, war is responsible for many million refugees and internally displaced persons.

INDIRECT IMPACT ON HUMANS AND THE ENVIRONMENT

War also has a severe, indirect impact on humans and the environment through the diversion of human and economic resources. The governments of many developing countries spend five to twenty-five times more on military than on health expenditures. From this culture of violence people learn at an early age that violence is the way to try to resolve conflicts. War and preparation for war use huge amounts of nonrenewable resources, such as fossil fuels, as well as toxic and radioactive substances that cause pollution of the air, water, and land.

INDISCRIMINATE HARM TO NONCOMBATANTS

Of particular concern to public health is the indiscriminate harm done to noncombatants. This includes not only the use of so-called weapons of mass destruction, such as nuclear, chemical, and biological weapons, but also some uses of conventional weapons. Examples of the latter include the carpet bombing of Warsaw, Rotterdam, Coventry, Dresden, Hamburg, Tokyo, and other cities during World War II; and collateral damage caused by bombs and missiles in recent conflicts in Iraq, Serbia, and Kosovo. Anti-personnel land mines also cause indiscriminate injury and death and, like biological and chemical weapons, have been banned by international convention.

Chemical and biological weapons have been used since antiquity. Chemical weapons, which are used to produce toxic effects rather than explosions or fire, include vesicant agents such as mustard gas; agents producing pulmonary edema such as chlorine and phosgene; agents affecting oxidizing enzymes such as cyanide; and anticholinesterase inhibitors known as nerve agents. Chemical weapons were used extensively in World War I, leading to the negotiation of the Geneva Protocol of 1925, which banned the use of chemical and bacteriologic weapons. During World War II, chemical weapons were stockpiled by several nations, but were little used. The Chemical Weapons Convention (CWC), which was opened for signature in 1993 and entered into force in 1997, bans the development, production, transfer, and use of chemical weapons. The Organization for the Prohibition of Chemical Weapons (OPCW), headquartered in The Hague, has broad enforcement powers under the CWC. The United States and Russia are proceeding with destruction of stockpiles of chemical weapons, but there remains controversy about the health consequences of the methods being used. In

1995, the Aum Shinrikyo sect in Japan released nerve agent gas in the Tokyo subway, resulting in a number of deaths and many injuries. This incident heightened the concern about future use of chemical weapons.

Biological weapons, which are used to cause disease in living organisms, were developed and stockpiled by the United States, Great Britain, and other nations during World War II, but saw only very limited use by Japan in China. In 1969 the United States unilaterally renounced the use of biological weapons and announced the destruction of its stockpiles. The Biologic Weapons Convention (BWC), which was opened for signature in 1972 and entered into force in 1975, is much weaker than the CWC. It permits "defensive" research, which has led to suspicion that offensive research and development is being done. Efforts are currently being made to strengthen the BWC. Concern has recently been raised about the possible use of biological agents by groups or individuals to attack civilian populations.

The Anti-Personnel Landmine Convention (ALC) was opened for signature in 1997 and entered into force in 1999, setting precedents both for the speed of its ratification and for the work of nongovernmental organizations in bringing it about. The International Campaign to Ban Landmines and its leader, Jody Williams, were awarded the 1997 Nobel Peace Prize. By February 2000 the ALC had been signed by 137 governments, but not by the United States, Russia and the other states of the former USSR, and most countries of the Middle East. The ALC, in addition to banning any further production or placement of mines, calls for destroying stockpiles, removing mines from the ground, and helping landmine survivors.

Nuclear weapons were used by the United States in 1945 to destroy the Japanese cities of Hiroshima and Nagasaki. In each city, a bomb of explosive power equivalent to about 15 kilotons of TNT caused approximately 100,000 deaths within the first few days. Nuclear weapons have not been used in war since, but enormous quantities of nuclear and thermonuclear weapons have been stockpiled by the United States and the Soviet Union. Explosive tests of these weapons have been conducted by these two nations and by the United Kingdom, France, China, South Africa, and, in 1998, India and Pakistan. There have been 518 tests documented in the atmosphere, under water, or in space and, after the signing of the 1963 Limited Nuclear Test Ban Treaty, approximately 1,500 tests underground. The U.S. National Cancer Institute estimated in 1997 that the release of Iodine-131 in fallout from U.S. atmospheric nuclear test explosions was responsible for 49,000 excess cases of thyroid cancer among U.S. residents. Another study estimated that radioactive fallout from nuclear test explosions would be responsible for 430,000 cancer deaths by the year 2000. A Comprehensive Test Ban Treaty was negotiated in 1997, but a number of nations, including the United States, have refused to ratify it.

There are now approximately 35,000 nuclear weapons stockpiled in the seven nations that have declared possession—the U.S., Russia, the United Kingdom, France, China, India, and Pakistan. Israel is also widely believed to possess nuclear weapons. The declared nuclear-weapons nations agreed in the 1970 Nuclear Non-Proliferation Treaty (NPT) to work toward elimination of these weapons, but progress has been slow. The International Court of Justice in a unanimous advisory opinion in 1996 ruled that the nuclear weapons states were obligated under the NPT "to pursue in good faith ... negotiations leading to nuclear disarmament." The International Physicians for the Prevention of Nuclear War was awarded the 1985 Nobel Peace Prize for its work to reduce the risk of nuclear weapons use by the United States and the Soviet Union. With the dissolution of the USSR, there has also been concern about leakage of nuclear weapons to other nations, to groups, and even to individuals.

WORLD WAR I

World War I (1914–18): Although the United States did not enter World War I until 1917, the outbreak of that war in 1914, and its underlying causes and consequences, deeply and immediately affected America's position both at home and abroad. In the debate on neutrality and later on peace aims, much was made of European secret diplomacy, which was rejected on the U.S. side of the Atlantic, of militarism and the escalating arms race before 1914, and of the impact of colonialism. Undoubtedly, all these factors contributed to the origins of the European catastrophe, but they do not explain why the war broke out when it did. This question can only be answered more precisely by looking at the political and military decision–making processes in the last months, weeks, and days of peace in 1914.

After decades of debate about whether Europe "slithered over the brink" (David Lloyd George's phrase) owing to general crisis mismanagement among all participant nations or because of the actions of a clearly identifiable group of people, the overwhelming majority consensus has emerged among historians that the primary responsibility rests in Berlin and Vienna, and secondarily perhaps on St. Petersburg. Judging from the documents, it has become clear that the German kaiser and his advisers encouraged Vienna to settle accounts with Serbia following the assassinations of the heir to the Austro–Hungarian throne, Archduke Ferdinand, and his wife at Sarajevo in Bosnia–Herzegovina on 28 June 1914.

By issuing a "blank check" to Austria–Hungary on 5 July 1914, the German government took the first step in escalating a crisis that involved the risk of a world war among the great powers. This risk was high not only because these powers had been arming over the previous years, but also because they had regrouped into two large camps: the Triple Alliance (Germany, Austria–Hungary, Italy) and the Triple Entente (Britain, France, Russia). And when, after various diplomatic maneuvers, it became clear toward the end of July that such a world war might indeed be imminent, Berlin refused to deescalate although the decision makers there were in the best position to do so.

The Czarist government, as Serbia's protector, also had a role in this development; but it was primarily a reactive one after Vienna had delivered a stiff ultimatum in Belgrade and subsequently began to invade its smaller Balkan neighbor. So, while the main responsibility for the outbreak of war is therefore to be laid at the kaiser's door, the question of why he and his advisers pushed Europe over the brink continues to be a matter of debate. The German historian Fritz Fischer has argued that the kaiser's government saw the Sarajevo crisis as the opportunity for aggressively achieving a *Griff nach der Weltmacht (Breakthrough to World Power Status)*, as the 1961 German version of Fischer's first, and highly controversial, book on the subject was entitled. The American historian Konrad Jarausch and others, by contrast, have asserted that Berlin's and Vienna's initial strategy was more limited. By supporting Austria–Hungary against the Serbs, the two powers hoped to weaken Slav nationalism and Serb expansionism in the Balkans and thus to restabilize the increasingly precarious position of the ramshackle Austro–Hungarian empire with its many restive nationalities. According to this interpretation, the assumption was that Russia and its ally, France, would not support Serbia, and that, after a quick localized victory by the central powers in the Balkans, any larger international repercussions could be contained through negotiation following the fait accompli.

It was only when this strategy failed owing to St. Petersburg's resistance that the German military got its way to launch an all–out offensive, the first target of which would be Russia's ally, France. This was the sole military operations plan, the "Schlieffen Plan," first developed by Gen. Alfred von Schlieffen, that the kaiser still had available in 1914. The alternative of an eastern attack on Russia had been dropped several years before. Worse, since the German Army was not strong enough to invade

France directly through Alsace–Lorraine, Helmut von Moltke, chief of the General Staff, had further reinforced the right flank of the invasion force with the aim of reaching Paris swiftly from the north. However, this could only be achieved by marching through Belgium, and it was this violation of Belgian neutrality that brought Britain into the conflict, definitely turning it into a world war.

In a further radicalization of his argument, Fischer asserted in his second book, War of Illusions (1973), that the German decision to start a world war had been made at a "War Council" on 8 December 1912, and that Berlin used the next eighteen months to prepare it. However, this view has not been generally accepted by the international community of scholars. Unless new documents supporting Fischer emerge, possibly from the Russian archives, the most plausible argument seems to be the one developed by Jarausch and others of a miscalculated "limited war" that grew out of control.

While diplomatic historians and political scientists have dominated the debate on the outbreak of World War I, social historians have more recently begun to examine the attitude of the "masses" in that summer of 1914. The older view has been that there was great enthusiasm all–round and that millions in all participant countries flocked to the colors expecting to achieve victory no later than Christmas 1914. No doubt there was strong popular support, reinforced by initial serious misconceptions about the nature of modern industrialized warfare. But there have been recent challenges to this view, and it appears that divisions of contemporary opinion were deeper and more widespread than previously believed. French social historians have shown that news of the mobilization was received in some parts of the country with tears and consternation rather than joy and parades. In Germany, too, feeling was more polarized than had been assumed. Thus, there were peace demonstrations in major cities to warn Austria–Hungary against starting a war with Serbia. And when the German mobilization was finally proclaimed, the reaction of large sections of the population was decidedly lukewarm. As one young trade unionist wrote after watching cheerful crowds around him near Hamburg's main railroad station on 1 August 1914: "Am I mad or is it the others?"

Considering the unprecedented slaughter that began shortly thereafter in the trenches of the western front as well as in the east, this was certainly a good question, and further research may well open up new perspectives on the mentalities of the men and women in 1914 and on the socioeconomic and political upheavals that followed, which ultimately also involved the United States as a participant.

THE SPANISH CIVIL WAR

The Spanish Civil War broke out on July 17, 1936, as a result of the revolutionary process begun under the democratic Second Republic of Spain, which had been inaugurated in 1931. Democracy had brought large-scale political and social mobilization, while the left launched a series of four revolutionary insurrections between 1932 and 1934. In 1935 an alliance of the moderate and the revolutionary left formed a Popular Front that won the election of February 1936. This produced a weak minority government of the moderate left that could not restrain the revolutionaries, whose violence, disorder, seizure of property, and corruption of electoral processes provoked a military revolt.

Though Spanish political society was strongly polarized between right and left, each polarity was badly fragmented. The military revolt brought scarcely more than half the army out in revolt, though it was assisted by rightist militia. The leftist Republican government in power abandoned constitutional rule and engaged in what was called "arming the people," which meant giving weapons and de facto power to the revolutionary organizations.

The result was the Spanish revolution of 1936–1937, the most intense and spontaneous outburst of worker revolution seen in modern Europe, not excepting the Russian Revolution of 1917. It collectivized much farmland and most of urban industry, and it was marked by an extensive Red Terror—the mass execution of political opponents, directed against all conservative organizations, and especially the Catholic Church—which destroyed countless churches. Nearly 7,000 clergy were killed, and at least 55,000 people perished in the Republican zone.

After two months, the military insurgents elected General Francisco Franco as their commander-in-chief. Franco also acted as dictator and permanent chief of state. By the second week of the Civil War, he had successfully sought military assistance from Nazi Germany and Fascist Italy, and he mounted a military drive on Madrid. The rebels quickly termed themselves Nationalists and mounted a savage repression of their own, which was more concerted and effective than that of the Republicans and eventually claimed even more victims.

General Franco organized a single-party state, partially modeled on that of Fascist Italy, in April 1937. He combined the Spanish fascist party with rightist groups to form the Falange Española Tradicionalista (Traditionalist Spanish Phalanx, or FET). Franco succeeded in establishing almost complete political unity among the rightist forces, enabling him to concentrate almost exclusively on the war effort, and in the process he developed a more effective and professionally led military force than did his opponents.

The revolutionary Republic proved ineffective militarily, relying on disorganized revolutionary militia. After the first two weeks it lost battle after battle, resulting in the organization of a new Republican government on September 4, 1936, led by the Socialist Francisco Largo Caballero. It eventually included all the leftist forces in a single government and began the creation of a new centralized Ejército Popular (People's Army).

Though France was led by a Popular Front government at this time, it was becoming dependent on Great Britain, which counseled against involvement in Spain. The French government therefore took the lead in organizing the Non-Intervention Committee, which gained the collaboration of nearly all European governments and took up deliberations in London in September 1936, though it was unsuccessful in ending the involvement in the war of the three major European dictatorships.

Germany and Italy were already intervening on behalf of Franco, and the Republicans urgently requested military assistance from the Soviet Union, the only other revolutionary state in Europe. Stalin finally decided to send assistance in September 1936, and Soviet military assistance began to arrive soon afterward. This assistance was paid for by shipping most of the Spanish gold reserve (the fifth largest in the world) to Moscow. Late-model Soviet planes and tanks, which arrived in large quantities, outclassed the weaponry provided by Hitler and Mussolini. These weapons, together with hundreds of Soviet military specialists, were accompanied by the first units of the International Brigades, a volunteer force organized by the Communist International, which eventually numbered approximately 41,000. By the end of 1936 the war was turning into a stalemate, and it promised to become a long struggle of attrition.

In this situation, the Spanish Communist Party, which had been weak prior to the war, expanded rapidly. Soviet assistance helped it become a major force on the Republican side, emphasizing the importance of restraining the revolution of the extreme left and concentrating all resources on the military effort. This provoked great tension, leading to the "May Days" of May 1937 in Barcelona, the center of the revolution. This was a mini-civil war within the civil war, with the extreme revolutionary left fighting the more disciplined forces of the Communists and the reorganized Republican state. The latter dominated, leading to the formation that same month of a new Republican government led by the

Socialist Juan Negrín, which deemphasized the socioeconomic revolution and sought to concentrate all its activity on the military effort.

The Soviet escalation of military intervention in October 1936 was quickly countered by a counter-escalation from Mussolini and Hitler, who sent an Italian army corps of nearly 50,000 men and a 90-plane German aerial unit, the Condor Legion, to Spain. This guaranteed that Franco would continue to receive the support necessary to maintain the military initiative. In 1937 he conquered the Republican northern zone, and in April 1938 his army sliced through Aragon to the Mediterranean, dividing the remaining Republican zone in two. During the conquest of the northern zone, the most famous (and infamous) incident of the war occurred. This was the bombing of the Basque town of Guernica by German and Italian planes in April 1937.

Though Mussolini desired a quick and complete Nationalist victory to strengthen Italy's position in the Mediterranean, Hitler was in no hurry. He preferred that the Spanish war continue for some time. It had become the main focus of European diplomacy during 1936–1937, and it served to distract attention from the rearmament of Germany and the beginning of its expansion in central Europe. The French government covertly supported the Republican cause in a policy of "relaxed nonintervention," which served as a conduit for military supplies from the Soviet Union and other countries. By 1937, Stalin was in turn increasingly distracted by the Japanese invasion of China. In 1938 he sought disengagement from Spain, but he could find no terms that would not involve a loss of face.

Franco's forces slowly but steadily gained the upper hand. His government in the Nationalist zone maintained a productive economy and a relatively stable currency. The revolutionary Republican zone, by contrast, was wracked with inflation and suffered increasingly severe shortages, producing widespread hunger by 1938. The Communists, in turn, developed a political and military hegemony under the Negrín government, though never complete domination. The policy of both Negrín and the Communists was to continue resistance to the bitter end, hoping that a general European war would soon break out, during which France would come to the relief of the Republicans. This was increasingly resented by the other leftist parties, however, who finally rebelled in Madrid in March 1945, overthrowing Negrín and the Communists, and then soon surrendering to Franco, who declared the end of the war on April 1, 1939.

The Spanish Civil War was a classic revolutionary-counter revolutionary civil war, somewhat similar to those that occurred in eastern and southeastern Europe after each of the world wars. It became a highly mythified event, often presented as a struggle between "fascism and democracy," "fascism and communism," or "Christian civilization and Asian barbarism." It has also been viewed as the "opening battle of World War II (1939–1945)." All such epithets are exaggerated, however. While there was fascism on the side of Franco's Nationalists, there was no democracy on the Republican side. In Spain, Hitler and Stalin were on opposite sides, but they joined forces in August-September 1939 to begin World War II in Europe. Germany and Italy did gain their goals in Spain, however, while Soviet policy failed.

Militarily, the war was notable for the introduction of late-model weaponry, especially new warplanes and tanks. The Soviet military studied the war with great thoroughness, but they sometimes drew the wrong conclusions from it, as did some other countries. Germany learned important lessons on the use of combined arms and air-to-ground support, but it failed to improve its armored forces. The victorious Franco régime remained neutral during World War II, and Franco remained in power until his death in 1975.

THE CHINESE CIVIL WAR

Beginning with the ambiguous Yalta Conference (1945), the United States and the Soviet Union failed to agree on the future political shape of Asia or to control their Asian allies and clients (as they did in postwar Europe). Manchuria, which Yalta had effectively awarded to the USSR, played the pebble that starts an avalanche.

After the Japanese surrender, the U.S. transport moved Chinese government armies from the southwest to key cities such as Peking, Tientsin, and Shanghai, and 50,000 U.S. troops landed in China proper. The Soviets who arrived in Manchuria in August 1945 excluded Nationalist forces and helped bring Chinese Communist main forces there from Northwest China.

Fearing deep involvement in China, the United States attempted to deal with this and other issues primarily by negotiations between Nationalists and Communists, sponsored first by Ambassador Patrick Hurley (1945) and then by Gen. George C. Marshall (1945–47). Unrealistic to begin with, this approach was further undermined by a clear American tilt toward the Nationalists, made worse by the abandonment of the direct U.S. contact with the Communists that had been provided, for example, by the military "Dixie Mission" of 1944.

The Chinese Communists' concentration on civil administration rather than military preparation in Man churia suggests that they expected an East European–style outcome: a stable partition and the establishment of a "Red China" in Manchuria under Soviet tutelage. Their calculations were upset by Soviet withdrawal and by the unexpected initiation, in early 1946, of a massive Nationalist offensive that saw American–equipped elite Nationalist divisions quickly throw the Communists into full retreat. The Communists in Manchuria were saved when Marshall evidently pressured Chinese Nationalist leader Chiang Kai–shek to stop the offensive, in June 1946, just short of Harbin.

Thereafter the tide of war shifted toward the Communists, and American public opinion became increasingly concerned. In October 1947, an Army Advisory Group was formed to counsel Chiang and $27.7 million in aid was supplied. The Nationalists requested far more and eventually another $400 million was paid, but only in 1948, long after the Truman administration had lost faith in Chiang's Nationalist government. In 1949, after Truman won reelection, he refused further aid and ordered the U.S. ambassador not to follow the retreating Nationalists to Taiwan but rather to remain in Nanking to establish contact with the Communists.

THE KOREAN WAR

War came to the Korean peninsula in 1950–53 as the first military clash of the Cold War between the forces of the Soviet Union and its Communist clients, and the United States and its allies. It was, therefore, potentially the most dangerous war in the post WWII era.

Even before the war against Germany and Japan drew to a close in 1945, the United States and the Soviet Union assumed competing roles in shaping the postwar world. As the two undisputed victorious powers, they influenced the course of every political problem emerging from the debris of war. Unfortunately, hostility between the two powers increased at the same time and threatened the outbreak of another war, which after 1949 risked the use of atomic weapons.

The conservative forces eventually coalesced in the Republic of Korea under the leadership of President Syngman Rhee. A North Korean state, The Democratic People's Republic created by the Soviet Union and headed by Premier Kim Il–sung, adopted a policy of opposition to Rhee's government and for unification of the Korean peninsula by armed force.

North Korean ground forces crossed the 38th Parallel into South Korea about 4:30 A.M. on 25 June 1950 (24 June Washington time). The main attack, led by two divisions and a tank brigade, aimed at Uijongbu and

Seoul. In the central mountains, two North Korean divisions drove toward Yoju and Wonju and on the east coast, a reinforced division headed for Samchok.

In an emergency session on Sunday, 25 June, the UN Security Council (with the USSR boycotting because of the refusal to admit the People's Republic of China) adopted an U.S.-sponsored resolution branding the North Korean attack a breach of the peace and calling on the North Korean government to cease hostilities and withdraw. The North Koreans did not respond to the UN resolution, so on the following Tuesday, the United States offered a follow-up proposal that "the members of the United Nations furnish such assistance to the Republic of Korea as may be necessary to repel the armed attack and to restore international peace and security in the area." Subsequently, the UN Security Council designated the president of the United States as its executive agent for the war in Korea. President Truman, in turn, appointed Gen. Douglas MacArthur as the Commander in Chief, United Nations Command (CICUNC). The military organization to wage war was in place.

Saving South Korea was certainly the most urgent UN war aim, but President Harry S. Truman also believed that the Soviet Union was the most dangerous threat to the western allies. The UN Command had to stop the North Koreans and eject them from South Korea by military means, no small task with the North Korean army rolling south and no UN troops on the ground. Moreover, while accomplishing this, the UN coalition had to avoid expanding the war into Asia and to Europe by provoking China or the Soviet Union to enter the struggle. So the Truman administration adopted additional, unilateral war aims designed to keep the violence confined to the Korean Peninsula, to keep the Soviets out of the war, to maintain a strongly committed UN (and NATO) coalition, and to buy time to rearm the United States and its allies.

At first, MacArthur had little choice in how to fight the North Koreans. Somehow he had to slow down their offensive sufficiently to give him time to mount a counter-attack against their flanks or rear. His forces consisted of four undermanned and partially trained U.S. Army divisions comprising Gen. Walton Walker's Eighth Army, the South Korean army, then falling back in front of the enemy, an ill-equipped U.S. air force, and growing naval U.S. strength. When the President ordered use of American troops, the Joint Chiefs of Staff (JCS) immediately sent additional army forces, marines, and air and naval forces to strengthen MacArthur's command. As these units began to deploy, MacArthur requested more reinforcements that included between four and five additional divisions.

In all, fifty-three UN member nations promised troops to assist South Korea. Of all, the nations of the British Commonwealth were most ready to fight when war broke out. Great Britain, Australia, New Zealand and Canada were the first to send air, sea, and ground forces. Eventually UN allies sent over 19,000 troops to Korea. All were assigned to the U.S. Eighth Army.

MacArthur's first task was to block what appeared to be the enemy's main attack leading to the port of Pusan in the south. Rushing American ground and air forces from Japan to Korea, he hoped to delay the enemy column and force it to deploy, then withdraw UN forces to new delaying positions and repeat the process. With any luck, he could gain enough time to muster an effective force on the ground. For this task he ordered General Walker to send units to confront the enemy on the road to Pusan. Walker sent a small infantry force—Task Force Smith—to lead the way. While reinforcements were moving to Korea, MacArthur pushed the rest of Walker's Eighth Army (less the 7th Infantry Division) into Korea to build up resistance on the enemy's main axis of advance. With these forces and the South Koreans, Walker hoped to delay the enemy north and west of a line following the Naktong River, to the north, then east to Yongdok on the Sea of Japan. If forced to withdraw farther, he proposed to occupy the Naktong River line as the primary position from which Eighth Army would defend the port of Pusan.

With the main enemy force applying heavy pressure along the primary axis aimed at Pusan, Walker had to fight off two North Korean divisions, advancing around the west flank deep into southwest Korea. From there they could turn east and strike directly at Pusan. To head off this threat, Walker sent the 25th Infantry Division to meet the North Koreans west of Masan and stop them. In savage battle, the 25th slowed the North Koreans, and Walker pulled the Eighth Army and Republic of Korea Army (ROKA) behind the Naktong River line to defend Pusan.

Walker's retirement into the Pusan Perimeter fit MacArthur's plans perfectly. Now he could exercise close control over both the battle on the peninsula and preparations for an amphibious counterstroke, now planned for mid-September. As reinforcements poured into Pusan and combat strength began to favor Walker, MacArthur started to shunt units, equipment, and individual replacements to Japan to rebuild a corps for use in the amphibious operation. With complete superiority of air power and growing strength in tanks, artillery, and infantry, MacArthur believed that Eighth Army and the ROKA could hold Pusan.

North Koreans launched violent, piecemeal attacks against the perimeter beginning on 5 August. By the end of August, the defenders had thrown back the first barrage of attacks, but a new onslaught began on the night of 31 August. This time the enemy hit simultaneously and even more savagely. American reinforcements had, however, greatly increased the combat power of the allies, and by 12 September the North Korean offensive had spent itself on all fronts against Walkers' skillful defense.

While the Eighth Army fought to hold Pusan, Mac Arthur readied the forces he had assembled in Japan to eject the North Koreans from Korea. He selected the port of Inchon near Seoul as the objective in spite of undesirable hydrographic characteristics. High tides, swift currents, and broad mud flats threatened the safety of an amphibious assault force. But Inchon also had some features that convinced MacArthur that the prize was worth the risk. The North Koreans, concentrated around Pusan in the south, would be vulnerable to an attack so far to the north, and the capture of Inchon would lead directly to the fall of Seoul. Because Seoul, the capital of South Korea, was the intersection of most of the major roads and railroads in South Korea, its capture would trap the North Koreans and force them to surrender or escape to the mountains, abandoning all their heavy equipment. MacArthur believed he could defeat the North Koreans in one decisive battle—the Inchon Landing.

Early in September, naval air forces struck targets up and down the west coast of Korea. As D−day for Inchon approached, surface gunfire support ships began to add their weight. On 15 September, U.S. Marines of the newly formed X Corps successfully assaulted the port, paving the way for army troops that followed. In the ensuing campaign, North Korea forces fought bitterly to hold the capital. On September 28, Seoul fell, and by October 1, Marines held a line close to the 38th Parallel, blocking all roads and passes leading to Seoul and its port at Inchon.

Weakened by the heavy fighting of July and August, the Eighth Army could not at first break out of the Pusan perimeter. Finally, a week after X Corps landed at Inchon, the North Koreans began to waver. On 23 September they began a general withdrawal, and Eighth Army units advanced to link up with X Corps. MacArthur had won his battle and the UN was poised to exploit his success.

In retrospect, the turning point in the Korean War was the decision now made to cross the 38th Parallel and pursue the retreating enemy into North Korea. At President Truman's direction, the National Security Council (NSC) staff had studied the question and recommended against crossing the 38th because ejecting the North Koreans from South Korea was a sufficient victory. To this, the JCS objected. MacArthur, they argued, must destroy the North Korean army to prevent a renewal of the aggression. On 11 September—four days before the Inchon Landing—the president adopted the arguments of the JCS. Most importantly, Truman changed the national objective from saving South Korea to unifying the peninsula. After the UN Assembly passed a resolution on 7 October 1950 calling for unification of Korea, MacArthur was free to send forces into North Korea.

MacArthur's attack on North Korea never achieved the success of his earlier operations. Beginning 7 October, he sent the weakened Eighth Army in the main attack against the North Korean capital of P'yongyang without adequate combat support. As the supporting attack, he planned another powerful amphibious assault by X Corps to strike the east coast port of Wonsan on 20 October. Although the Eighth Army advanced rapidly toward P'yongyang against light resistance, the amphibious attack by X Corps was six days late landing in its objective area because mine sweepers had to clear an elaborate minefield. On 11 October, Wonsan fell to a South Korean corps, almost two weeks before the marines could land. P'yongyang fell on the 19 October.

After the capture of P'yongyang and Wonsan, allied troops streamed north virtually unopposed. Truman worried about possible Chinese intervention, but at a conference at Wake Island on 15 October, MacArthur belittled this possibility and was optimistic about an early victory. There was, however, little time to enjoy the successes of mid-October. Beginning on the 25 October, a reinvigorated enemy struck the Eighth Army in a brief but furious counterattack. By 2 November intelligence officers had accumulated undeniable evidence from across the front that Chinese forces had intervened, and the Eighth Army had to stop its advance.

Chinese leaders had tried to ward off a direct confrontation with the Americans by warning the UN not to cross the 38th Parallel. American leaders interpreted these statements as bluff rather than policy. But they were wrong; Josef Stalin, the Soviet premier, asked Mao Zedong, the Chinese premier, to send Chinese forces to the aid of his clients, the North Koreans. After much deliberation, Mao decided to intervene. On 19 October Chinese Peoples Volunteers (CPV) crossed the Yalu River and massed some 260,000 troops in front of the UN Command.

After replenishing supplies, MacArthur's forces were ready. On 24 November the troops of the Eighth Army, unaware of the presence of massed Chinese forces, crossed their lines of departure. Within twenty—

four hours after the Eighth Army jumped off, the Chinese struck back, aiming their main attack at the South Korean ROKA II Corps on the army's right flank. Two days later the CPV hit U.S. X Corps as it advanced into the mountains of eastern Korea. Stunned and outnumbered, American and South Korean units recoiled, beginning a long retreat that ended in January 1951, only after the UN forces fell back south of the 38th Parallel and once again gave up the city of Seoul. X Corps fought its way back to the port of Hungnam on the east coast and then rejoined Eighth Army in the south.

During the first week of December 1950 when reports from the front were incomplete and most grim, President Truman met in Washington with Prime Minister Clement Attlee of the United Kingdom. Though initially far apart, Truman and Attlee, after four days of intense discussion, reached a compromise solution on Korea. They would continue to fight side–by–side, find a line and hold it, and wait for an opportunity to negotiate an end to the fighting from a position of military strength. Moreover, they reaffirmed their commitment to "Europe first" in the face of Soviet hostility toward NATO. In this way, the decision to unify Korea was abrogated and a new war aim adopted.

The most immediate military effect of the talks was to prevent MacArthur from exacting revenge for his humiliating defeat. The JCS limited his reinforcements to replacements, shifted the priority of military production to strengthening NATO forces, and wrote a new directive for MacArthur requiring him to defend in Korea as far to the north as possible. MacArthur disagreed with giving priority to Europe at the expense of the shooting war in Korea. He was outraged at the thought of going on the strategic defensive and fought against his new directive with all his might. Nevertheless, on 12 January 1951, the JCS sent him the final version of the directive, and the UN coalition had a new war aim designed to bring about a negotiated settlement.

Just two days before Christmas 1950, the command of the Eighth Army passed to Lt. Gen. Matthew B. Ridgway after Gen. Walker died in a truck accident. From his position on the Department of the Army staff in Washington, Ridgway came to the Eighth Army well informed of the strategic situation in Korea. He arrived at his new headquarters determined to attack north as soon as possible. Somehow he had to stop the retreat and turn the army around; until then the Eighth Army continued to withdraw. In early January 1951 UN forces gave up Seoul.

Finally, Ridgway's front line units began reporting light contact with the enemy. Sensing the opportunity to turn on the Chinese, Ridgway stopped the army on a line from P'yongt'aek in the west, through Wonju in the center, to Samch'ok on the east coast. When American divisions, withdrawn with X Corps, moved up to thicken the line in the lightly held center, Ridgway ordered his forces to patrol north and find the enemy. In a series of increasingly powerful offensives, he then sent the Eighth Army north: Operation Thunderbolt jumped off in January, Roundup in February (though a tactical setback), Killer in late February, Ripper in March, and Rugged in April. By this time, Ridgway's army had once again crossed the 38th Parallel where its forward units dug into strong defensive ground in anticipation of an enemy counteroffensive. Surprisingly, the shock came, not from the enemy as Ridgway expected, but from Washington, when MacArthur was dismissed by President Truman.

MacArthur's dismissal resulted from his rejection of Truman's policy. As Ridgway neared the 38th again, the position of military strength envisioned in the Truman–Attlee conference had seemed near at hand. Truman took advantage of Ridgway's success to invite the Communists to negotiate a cease fire. After reading the text of Truman's proposed message, MacArthur broadcast a bellicose ultimatum to the enemy commander that undermined the president's plan. Truman was furious. MacArthur had preempted presidential prerogative, confused friends and enemies alike about who was directing the war, and directly challenged the president's authority as Commander in Chief. As Truman pondered how to handle the problem, Congressman Joseph W. Martin, Minority (Republican) Leader of the House of Representatives, released the contents of a letter from MacArthur in which the general repeated his criticism of the administration. The next day Truman began the process that was to end with Mac Arthur's being relieved from command on 11 April 1951.

After MacArthur's dismissal, Ridgway took his place as Commander in Chief, Far East and CINCUNC. Lt. Gen. James A. Van Fleet, an experienced and successful World War II combat leader, took command of the Eighth Army. On 22 April, as Van Fleet's Eighth army edged north, the CPV opened the expected general offensive, aiming their main attack toward Seoul in the west. The Chinese, numbering almost a half million men, drove Van Fleet once again below the 38th Parallel. On 10 May, the Chinese jumped off again after shifting seven armies to their main effort against the eastern half of the UN line. Taking advantage of the Chinese concentration in the east, Van Fleet attacked suddenly in the west, north of Seoul. The effect was dramatic; surprised CPV units pulled back, suffering their heaviest casualties of the war, and by the end of May found themselves retreating into North Korea. By mid–June, UN forces had regained a line, for the most part, north of the 38th Parallel.

Regardless of UN success on the battlefield, ending the war turned out to be a maddeningly long process. U.S. planners knew that the Truman–Attlee agreement made it unlikely that the war would end in a conventional victory. The UN allies had even adopted negotiating an armistice as a war aim. The time seemed right for the Chinese and North Koreans as well since they needed a respite from the heavy casualties suffered in the UN offensive. They agreed to meet with UN representatives when in late June 1951, the Soviets proposed a conference among the belligerents.

Negotiations were initially hampered by silly haggling over matters of protocol and the selection of a truly neutral negotiating site. Even so, on 26 July 1951 the two sides finally reached an agreement on an agenda containing four major points: selection of a demarcation line and demilitarized zone, supervision of the truce, arrangements for prisoners of war (POWs), and recommendations to the governments involved in the war. With an agreed agenda in hand, and Panmunjom—a town between opposing lines, suitable to hold talks—the negotiators began the lengthy process of debating each item. Handling POWs proved to be the most difficult problem on the agenda, but fixing the demarcation line was the most damaging. By dealing with the final position of the armies *first*, the UN negotiators blundered into an agreement that permitted the Communists to stalemate the battlefield and to wage a two–year political war at the negotiating table.

At issue was a U.S. scheme seeking quick agreement on a demarcation line. On 17 November the UN delegation proposed the current line of contact as the demarcation line providing that all remaining agenda items were resolved within thirty days. The communists accepted the proposal on 27 November debated the remaining agenda items for thirty days, and then failed to reach agreement. They used the thirty days to create a tactical defense so deeply dug in that both sides had to accept a stalemate.

From that moment on, the battlefield changed to a static kind of war, more reminiscent of World War I than anything that had happened since. Beginning in the winter of 1951–1952, the war came to be defined by elevated sites named Porkchop Hill, Sniper's Ridge, Old Baldy, T–Bone, Whitehorse, Punchbowl and a hundred other hilltops between the two armies. There followed a seemingly endless succession of violent fire fights, most of them at night, to gain or maintain control of hills that were a little higher and ridges that were a bit straighter. All of them, no matter how large the forces engaged, were deadly encounters designed to provide leverage for one side or the other in the protracted political battle going on at Panmunjom. In an historical age when technology enabled greater mobility than at any other time, tactical warfare in Korea went through a regression that can only be explained in terms of its close relationship to the negotiations. Constant pressure was its purpose, not decisive victory.

In Panmunjom negotiators plodded through the remaining agenda items. Supervising the armistice agreement was an extremely complex issue, but a compromise emerged that permitted rotation of 35,000 UN troops and supplies each month through specified ports of entry. In addition, both sides accepted Swedish, Swiss, Polish, and Czech membership on an armistice commission. Political recommendations to the belligerents were agreed in the astonishingly short period of eleven days. Both sides called for a conference to convene three months after a cease fire. At that time all political issues that had not been settled during the negotiations would be discussed.

What to do about prisoners of war was the major obstacle to final agreement. The UN Command wanted prisoners to decide for themselves whether or not they would return home. The Communists insisted on forced repatriation. To restore movement to the talks, the International Red Cross polled prisoners as to where they wanted to go. The results, announced early in April 1952, surprised everyone. Of 132,000 Chinese and North Korean POWs screened, only 54,000 North Koreans and 5,100 Chinese wanted to go home. The communist delegation was incredulous and accused the United Nations of influencing the poll. From that moment on, negotiations bogged down on the POW issue.

At about this time, May 1952, General Ridgway left Tokyo to become Supreme Allied Commander, Europe. Gen. Mark Clark, who had made his reputation during World War II in Italy, replaced Ridgway as CINCUNC and inherited a difficult situation. Unable to carry the war to the enemy in a decisive way and stalemated in the armistice talks, Clark —with the approval of the administration—finally ordered the UN delegation to walk out of Panmunjom on 8 October. With no one to talk to, the Communists hammered away at UN treatment of POWs and alleged UN violations of the neutral zones surrounding the negotiating site.

Over the fall and winter of 1952–53, three events broke the impasse. In November, Dwight D. Eisenhower won the election for the presidency, ushering in a new style of toughness toward the Communists—including discussion of using atomic weapons. In December, Clark read about an International Red Cross resolution calling for the exchange of sick and wounded POWs. In February 1953 Clark sent letters to the Chinese and North Korean leaders proposing that they exchange the sick and wounded. Before the Communists could respond, the third and perhaps most important event occurred: Josef Stalin died on 5 March 1953.

So achieving a cease–fire was the result of a complex set of circumstances and interwoven pressures. Eisenhower's toughness increased the pressure on the battlefield. He believed that the Truman strategy was the only practical one, but still something ought to be done to give the Communists an incentive to reach agreement. He permitted Clark's aircraft to bomb dams in North Korea, flooding the countryside. He instructed the JCS to prepare plans for more intensive maneuver—even atomic warfare—should negotiations break down. He authorized movement of atomic delivery aircraft to the Far East and initiated training for low–level attack with atomic bombs. And he sent John Foster Dulles, his Secretary of State, to India in April to let it be known that the United States was prepared to renew the war at a higher level unless progress was made at Panmunjom.

Clearly, Chinese leaders carefully considered these news signals, but it is conjectural to connect Ike's toughness and Stalin's death directly to the Communist agreement to end the war. Still, we do know that Stalin's death resulted in a deadly power struggle in the Kremlin that probably focused Soviet leaders on settling their internal problems rather than supporting a prolonged war. Moreover, East European states needed to be kept in line after Stalin's death, and something had to be done to restore deteriorating relations with the governments of China and North Korea, both of which had lost confidence in the Soviet government for not taking a more active part in the war.

On 26 April, negotiating sessions resumed at Panmunjom where a final solution to handling the remaining POWs took shape in the months that followed. Those who chose not to go home were to be turned over to a neutral repatriation commission. If they still did not want to go home, the neutral commission would release them to whichever government they chose. As the delegations wrapped up the details, it seemed that a cease–fire was not far off.

While the UN worked diligently toward an armistice, South Korean President Syngman Rhee became obstructive. Rhee saw the rush toward an armistice as contrary to South Korea's best interest, and he did not trust the Communists should the UN Command pull out. So on the night of 18 June, Rhee ordered his guards on the POW compounds to release some 25,000 friendly North Koreans. The Communists cried "foul." Eisenhower, feeling betrayed, was outraged. But in order to save the cease-fire, he negotiated with the South Korean president, pledging a mutual security pact after the cease-fire, long term economic aid, expansion of the South Korean armed forces, and coordination of U.S. and ROK objectives at the political conference. Though costly for the United States, the agreement secured Rhee's cooperation and cleared the way for an armistice.

While negotiating the final details of a truce, the Chinese communists sought one last military advantage. They mounted a limited offensive that was designed to push UN negotiators toward a settlement more agreeable to the Communist side; managed carefully, the offensive might also create the illusion of a peaceful settlement following a Communist victory. The attacks began on 10 June 1951 and by 16 June the UN line had been pushed back some 4,000 yards. Although some ground was recovered, fighting slackened as commanders of contending armies prepared to sign the truce. At 10 A.M. 27 July 1953, the darkest moment in Mark Clark's life, he signed the armistice documents to end the Korean War.

For a war intended to be limited, the human toll was staggering. Although Chinese and North Korean casualties are unknown, estimates of total losses amounted to almost two million, plus perhaps a million civilians. The UN Command suffered a total of 88,000 killed, of which 23,300 were American. Total casualties for the UN (killed, wounded, missing) were 459,360, 300,000 of whom were South Korean.

Nevertheless, limiting the war in Korea made a significant contribution to the history of the art of war. First, the Korean War demonstrated alternative strategies designed to gain national objectives without resorting to atomic war. For this reason, the Korean War is less about tactical evolution than about political goals, the strategy to achieve those goals, and the operational art designed to make the strategy succeed. Second, the war caused the U.S. government to arm the nation and its allies on a permanent basis and to bring its military force to a high state of combat readiness, prepared to respond quickly to any threat to national or alliance security. Never again would the United States find itself as ill-prepared as it had been when the Korean War began.

THE VIETNAM WAR

The Vietnam War (1960–75): Causes Most American wars have obvious starting points or precipitating causes: the Battles of Lexington and Concord in 1775, the capture of Fort Sumter in 1861, the attack on Pearl Harbor in 1941, and the North Korean invasion of South Korea in June 1950, for example. But there was no fixed beginning for the U.S. war in Vietnam. The United States entered that war incrementally, in a series of steps between 1950 and 1965. In May 1950, President Harry S Truman authorized a modest program of economic and military aid to the French, who were fighting to retain control of their Indochina colony, including Laos and Cambodia as well as Vietnam. When the Vietnamese Nationalist (and Communist−led) Vietminh army defeated French forces at Dienbienphu in 1954, the French were compelled to accede to the creation of a Communist Vietnam north of the 17th parallel while leaving a non−Communist entity south of that line. The United States refused to accept the arrangement. The administration of President Dwight D. Eisenhower undertook instead to build a nation from the spurious political entity that was South Vietnam by fabricating a government there, taking over control from the French, dispatching military advisers to train a South Vietnamese army, and unleashing the Central Intelligence Agency (CIA) to conduct psychological warfare against the North.

President John F. Kennedy rounded another turning point in early 1961, when he secretly sent 400 Special Operations Forces–trained (Green Beret) soldiers to teach the South Vietnamese how to fight what was called *counterinsurgency* war against Communist guerrillas in South Vietnam. When Kennedy was assassinated in November 1963, there were more than 16,000 U.S. military advisers in South Vietnam, and more than 100 Americans had been killed. Kennedy's successor, Lyndon B. Johnson, committed the United States most fully to the war. In August 1964, he secured from Congress a functional (not actual) declaration of war: the Tonkin Gulf Resolution. Then, in February and March 1965, Johnson authorized the sustained bombing, by U.S. aircraft, of targets north of the 17th parallel, and on 8 March dispatched 3,500 Marines to South Vietnam. Legal declaration or no, the United States was now at war.

The multiple starting dates for the war complicate efforts to describe the causes of U.S. entry. The United States became involved in the war for a number of reasons, and these evolved and shifted over time. Primarily, every American president regarded the enemy in Vietnam—the Vietminh; its 1960s successor, the National Liberation Front (NLF); and the government of North Vietnam, led by Ho Chi Minh—as agents of global communism. U.S. policymakers, and most Americans, regarded communism as the antithesis of all they held dear. Communists scorned democracy, violated human rights, pursued military aggression, and created closed state economies that barely traded with capitalist countries. Americans compared communism to a contagious disease. If it took hold in one nation, U.S. policymakers expected contiguous nations to fall to communism, too, as if nations were dominoes lined up on end. In 1949, when the Communist Party came to power in China, Washington feared that Vietnam would become the next Asian domino. That was one reason for Truman's 1950 decision to give aid to the French who were fighting the Vietminh.

Truman also hoped that assisting the French in Vietnam would help to shore up the developed, non−Communist nations, whose fates were in surprising ways tied to the preservation of Vietnam and, given the domino theory, all of Southeast Asia. Free world dominion over the region would provide markets for Japan, rebuilding with American help after the Pacific War. U.S. involvement in Vietnam reassured the British, who linked their postwar recovery to the revival of the rubber and tin industries in their colony of Malaya, one of Vietnam's neighbors. And with U.S. aid, the French could concentrate on economic recovery at home, and could hope ultimately to recall their Indochina officer corps to oversee the rearmament of West Germany, a Cold War measure deemed essential by the Americans. These ambitions formed a second set of reasons why the United States became involved in Vietnam.

As presidents committed the United States to conflict bit by bit, many of these ambitions were forgotten. Instead, inertia developed against withdrawing from Vietnam. Washington believed that U.S. withdrawal would result in a Communist victory—Eisenhower acknowledged that, had elections been held as scheduled in Vietnam in 1956, "Ho Chi Minh would have won 80% of the vote"—and no U.S. president wanted to lose a country to communism. Democrats in particular, like Kennedy and Johnson, feared a right−wing backlash should they give up the fight; they remembered vividly the accusatory tone of the Republicans' 1950 question, "Who lost China?" The commitment to Vietnam itself, passed from administration to administration, took on validity aside from any rational basis it might once have had. Truman, Eisenhower, and Kennedy all gave their word that the United States would stand by its South Vietnamese allies. If the United States abandoned the South Vietnamese, its word would be regarded as unreliable by other governments, friendly or not. So U.S. credibility seemed at stake.

Along with the larger structural and ideological causes of the war in Vietnam, the experience, personality, and temperament of each president played a role in deepening the U.S. commitment. Dwight Eisenhower restrained U.S. involvement because, having commanded troops in battle, he doubted the United States could fight a land war in Southeast Asia. The youthful John Kennedy, on the other hand, felt he had to prove his resolve to the American people and his Communist adversaries, especially in the aftermath of several foreign policy blunders early in his administration. Lyndon Johnson saw the Vietnam War as a test of his mettle, as a southerner and as a man. He exhorted his soldiers to "nail the coonskin to the wall" in Vietnam, likening victory to a successful hunting expedition.

When Johnson began bombing North Vietnam and sent the Marines to South Vietnam in early 1965, he had every intention of fighting a limited war. He and his advisers worried that too lavish a use of U.S. firepower might prompt the Chinese to enter the conflict. It was not expected that the North Vietnamese and the NLF would hold out long against the American military. And yet U.S. policymakers never managed to fit military strategy to U.S. goals in Vietnam. Massive bombing had little effect against a decentralized economy like North Vietnam's. Kennedy had favored counterinsurgency warfare in the South Vietnamese countryside, and Johnson endorsed this strategy, but the political side of counterinsurgency—the effort to win the "hearts and minds" of the Vietnamese peasantry—was at best underdeveloped and probably doomed. Presidents proved reluctant to mobilize American society to the extent the generals thought necessary to defeat the enemy.

As the United States went to war in 1965, a few voices were raised in dissent. Within the Johnson administration, Undersecretary of State George Ball warned that the South Vietnamese government was a functional nonentity and simply could not be sustained by the United States, even with a major effort. Antiwar protest groups formed on many of the nation's campuses; in June, the leftist organization Students for a Democratic Society decided to make the war its principal target. But major dissent would not begin until 1966 or later. By and large in 1965, Americans supported the administration's claim that it was fighting to stop communism in Southeast Asia, or people simply shrugged and went about their daily lives, unaware that this gradually escalating war would tear American society apart.

During 1966 Westmoreland requested more ground troops, and by year's end the U.S. ground force level "in country" reached 385,000. These were organized into seven divisions and other specialized airborne, armored, special forces, and logistical units. With U.S. aid, the ARVN also expanded to eleven divisions, supplemented by local and irregular units. While MACV was getting men and munitions in place for large-unit search and destroy operations, army and marine units conducted smaller operations. Although the "body count"—the estimated number of enemy killed—mounted, attrition was not changing the political equation in South Vietnam. The NLF continued to exercise more effective control in many areas than did the government, and Vietcong guerrillas, who often disappeared when U.S. forces entered an area, quickly reappeared when the Americans left.

In 1967, Westmoreland made his big push to win the war. With South Vietnam's forces assigned primarily to occupation, pacification, and security duties, massive U.S. combat sweeps moved to locate and destroy the enemy. In January, Operation Cedar Falls was a 30,000-man assault on the Iron Triangle, an enemy base area forty miles north of Saigon. From February through April, Operation Junction City was an even larger attack on nearby War Zone C. There was major fighting in the Central Highlands, climaxing in the battle of Dak To in November 1967. U.S. forces killed many enemy soldiers and destroyed large amounts of supplies. MACV declared vast areas to be "free-fire zones," which meant that U.S. and ARVN artillery and tactical aircraft, as well as B-52 "carpet bombing," could target anyone or anything in the area. In Operation RANCH HAND, the USAF sprayed the defoliant Agent Orange to deprive the guerrillas of cover and food supplies. Controversy about the use of Agent Orange erupted in 1969 when reports appeared that the chemical caused serious damage to humans as well as to plants.

Late in 1967, with 485,600 U.S. troops in Vietnam, Westmoreland announced that, although much fighting remained, a cross-over point had arrived in the war of attrition; that is, the losses to the NVA and Vietcong were greater than they could replace. This assessment was debatable, and there was considerable evidence that the so-called "other war" for political support in South Vietnam was not going well. Corruption, factionalism, and continued Buddhist protests plagued the Thieu-Ky government. Despite incredible losses, the Vietcong still controlled many areas. A diplomatic resolution of the conflict remained elusive. Several third countries, such as Poland and Great Britain, offered proposals intended to facilitate negotiations. These formulas typically called upon the United States and DRV to coordinate mutual reduction of their military activities in South Vietnam, but both Washington and Hanoi firmly resisted even interim compromises with the other. The war was at a stalemate.

De-Escalation

The decisive year was 1968. In the early morning of 30 January, Vietcong forces launched the Tet Offensive, named for the Vietnamese holiday then being observed. In coordinated attacks throughout South Vietnam, the Vietcong assaulted major urban areas and military installations in an attempt to spark a popular uprising against the Saigon régime and its American backers. Heavy fighting ensued for three weeks, some of the most brutal at Hué. Westmoreland claimed victory because no cities were lost and thousands of casualties were inflicted upon the attackers. Indeed, the Vietcong lost so many soldiers that thereafter the PAVN took over much of the conduct of the war. The Tet Offensive, however, was a great strategic gain for North Vietnam and its southern adherents. U.S. and ARVN losses were high, and the fighting generated thousands of refugees that further destabilized the South. Most importantly, as a result of the massive surprise attack and the pictures from Saigon, the U.S. press and public began to challenge the Johnson administration's assurances of success and to question the value of the increasingly costly war.

At the same time as the Tet Offensive, the siege of Khe Sanh underscored the image of the war as an endless, costly, and pointless struggle. From 20 January to 14 April 1968, 30,000 to 40,000 NVA forces surrounded 6,000 U.S. Marines and ARVN at the remote hilltop outpost of Khe Sanh in the northwest corner of South Vietnam. Using artillery and air power, including B-52 strikes, the United States eventually broke the siege and forced an NVA withdrawal. At the end of June, however, the Marines abandoned the base to adopt a more mobile form of fighting in the DMZ area. Once again, a major engagement left seemingly intangible results.

In March 1968, Johnson decided that the size of the U.S. effort in Vietnam had grown as large as could be justified. Prompted by a request from Westmoreland and JCS Chairman General Earle G. Wheeler for 206,000 more men, the president asked his new secretary of defense, Clark Clifford, for a thorough policy review. Johnson's sense that a limit had been reached seemed confirmed when the "Wise Men," a group of outside advisers including such elder statesmen as former Secretary of State Dean Acheson and Gen. Omar Bradley, recommended against further increases. The president authorized only 13,500 more soldiers and bluntly informed Thieu and Ky that their forces would have to carry more of the fighting. He then announced on television on 31 March 1968 that the United States would restrict the bombing of North Vietnam and pursue a negotiated settlement with Hanoi. Johnson also revealed that he would not seek reelection.

Meanwhile, combat raged in South Vietnam. Over 14,000 Americans were killed in action in Vietnam in 1968, the highest annual U.S. death toll of the war. The worst U.S. war crime of the conflict occurred on 16 March 1968 (although not revealed in the press until 6 November 1969) when American infantrymen massacred some 500 unresisting civilians, including babies, in the village of My Lai. In April and May 1968 the largest ground operation of the war, with 110,000 U.S. and ARVN troops, targeted Vietcong and NVA forces near Saigon. Peace talks began in Paris on 13 May but immediately deadlocked. On 10 June 1968, Gen. Creighton Abrams succeeded Westmoreland as MACV commander. In the fall Abrams began to shift U.S. strategy from attrition to a greater emphasis on combined operations, pacification area security, and what was called "Vietnamization," that is, preparing the ARVN to do more of the fighting.

When Richard M. Nixon became president in 1969, the U.S. war effort remained massive, but the basic decision to de-escalate had already been reached. Nixon owed his political victory to voter expectation that somehow he would end the war. He and his principal foreign policy adviser, Henry Kissinger, rejected precipitate U.S. withdrawal. With the ground war stalemated, the new administration turned increasingly to air bombardment and secretly expanded the air war to neutral Cambodia. Publicly the White House announced in June the first withdrawal of 25,000 U.S. troops and heralded Vietnamization as effective. In fact, South Vietnam's armed forces remained problem-plagued. To bolster the South, the administration leaked to the press dire threats of a "go for broke" air and naval assault on the North—possibly including nuclear weapons. Kissinger also began secret meetings with North Vietnamese representatives in Paris hoping to arrange a diplomatic breakthrough.

The morale and discipline of U.S. troops declined in 1969 as the futility of the ground war and the beginnings of U.S. withdrawal became more obvious. After an intense ten-day battle in May, infantrymen of the 101st Airborne Division (Air Mobile) took a ridge in the A Shau Valley that they had dubbed Hamburger Hill. Having fought bravely and suffered significant losses, the soldiers were bitter when the site soon was abandoned. Such inability to see progress, and an awareness among the troops that politicians back home were giving up on the war, helped undermine military effectiveness. Simple survival of their twelve-month tour of duty became the only motivation for many soldiers. Incidents of insubordination, mutiny, fatal assaults on officers, drug use, racial tensions, and other serious problems increased.

Faced with mounting public dissatisfaction, the slow pace of Vietnamization, and diplomatic frustration, Nixon boldly sent U.S. units into Cambodia in April 1970. U.S. military leaders had long complained about the sanctuary that neutral Cambodia provided Vietcong and NVA forces. This Cambodian incursion lasted until the end of June and provided some tactical gains, but it also sparked sharp controversy and demonstrations by the Vietnam antiwar movement in the United States over what seemed an expansion of the war to another country. U.S. troop reductions continued with only 334,600 in the South as 1970 ended.

Nixon stuck with more of the same in 1971. Responding to domestic critics, he continued to order U.S. troops home, leaving only 156,000 by December. To support Vietnamization, heavy U.S. air attacks continued against Communist supply lines in Laos and Cambodia, and so-called protective-reaction strikes hit military targets north of the Demilitarized Zone and near Hanoi and its port city of Haiphong. Tactical air support continued, with the heaviest coming in March during a South Vietnamese assault into Laos. Code named Lam Son 719, this operation ended in a confused retreat by the ARVN that further sullied the notion of Vietnamization.

During 1971, Kissinger made progress in the secret negotiations by offering to separate the arrangement of a ceasefire from discussion of the future of the Saigon government. In 1972 Nixon traveled to China and the USSR in diplomatic initiatives, trying to isolate Hanoi from its suppliers. With the shrinking American forces nearing 100,000 (only a small portion being combat troops), General Giap launched a spring 1972 offensive by Communist forces against the northern provinces of South Vietnam, the Central Highlands, and provinces northwest of Saigon. In most of the battles, the ARVN was saved by massive B-52 bombing. Nixon also launched the heavy bombers against North Vietnam itself in a campaign called Linebacker, and the United States mined the harbor at Haiphong. Over the course of the war, total U.S. bombing tonnage far exceeded that dropped on Germany, Italy, and Japan in World War II.

Wearied by the latest round of fighting, the United States and North Vietnamese governments agreed in October on a ceasefire, return of U.S. prisoners of war (POWs), at least the temporary continuation of Thieu's government, and, most controversially, permission for NVA troops to remain in the South. Objections from Thieu caused Nixon to hesitate, which in turn led Hanoi to harden its position. In December, the United States hit North Vietnam again with repeated B-52 attacks, codenamed Linebacker II and labeled the Christmas Bombing by journalists. On 27 January 1973, the United States, North Vietnam, South Vietnam, and the

Provisional Revolutionary Government representing the NLF signed the Paris Peace Agreements Ending the War and Restoring Peace in Vietnam, which basically confirmed the October terms.

By 1 April 1973, U.S. forces were out of Vietnam (except for a few embassy guards and attaches) and 587 POWs had returned home (about 2,500 other Americans remained missing in action). Congress cut off funds for the air war in Cambodia, and bombing there ended in August. Over Nixon's veto, Congress passed the War Powers Resolution in November 1973. It limited presidential power to deploy U.S. forces in hostile action without congressional approval.

Nixon characterized the Paris Peace Agreements of 1973 as "peace with honor," but primarily they allowed the U.S. military to leave Vietnam without resolving the issue of the country's political future. Without U.S. air and ground support, South Vietnam's military defenses steadily deteriorated. In the spring of 1975, an NVA thrust into the Central Highlands turned into an ARVN rout. On 30 April, as NVA and Vietcong soldiers entered the city, the last remaining Americans abandoned the U.S. embassy in Saigon in a dramatic rooftop evacuation by helicopters.

The United States failure in Vietnam raised important questions. Should the United States have fought the war at all? Did the United States fight the war the wrong way? Many analysts believe that the strategic importance of Vietnam was vastly exaggerated. An alternative view is that even if the odds were poor for U.S. success, the United States had to make the effort to maintain its moral and strategic credibility in the world. On the question of how the war was fought, the debate centers on whether the United States used its military power adequately and effectively. Assuming that more is better, some critics argue that a greater use of U.S. force, either against North Vietnam or to isolate the battlefield in South Vietnam, would have produced victory. Throughout the conflict, however, the Saigon régime proved incapable of translating military success into political success. Also, massive U.S. assistance seemed to prove North Vietnam's and the Vietcong's claims that South Vietnam was not a Vietnamese but an American creation. Finally, a larger war would have risked a dangerous military conflict with China and the Soviet Union. Most scholars conclude that the Vietnam War was a tragic event whose costs far exceeded any benefits for the United States.

GUERRILLA WARS

In the modern era, guerrilla warfare (or asymmetric war) refers to armed resistance by paramilitary or irregular groups toward an occupying force. Guerrilla warfare also describes a set of tactics employed by smaller forces against larger, better equipped, and better supplied forces. Guerrilla warfare tactics often rely on isolating smaller units of the larger occupying force so as to attack parts of the larger force by ambush. Guerrilla forces often practice espionage, industrial sabotage, and wage propaganda campaigns by portraying themselves as a popular but suppressed political movement. In many areas of the world, guerrilla warfare is practiced by local groups against government forces, and is especially effective in areas with a rugged natural topography or areas of dense vegetation (e.g., forest or jungle) that provide natural hiding places from which to stage guerrilla operations.

Derived from the Spanish term for "little war," guerrilla warfare has a long history. Although the term was not used until Spanish partisans resisted the intrusions of Napoleon during the Peninsular War in the early nineteenth century, American colonist revolutionaries practiced guerrilla warfare tactics against British forces to win independence from what was arguably the finest military power in the world at the time. During the twentieth century, communist guerrilla forces fought succedfullly against French and then American forces in Vietnam.

Confederate raiders—including Quantrill's raiders (led by William C. Quantrill) and Mosby's raiders (led by John S. Mosby) practiced guerrilla warfare against Union forces during the American Civil War. Following the acquisition of the Philippines after the Spanish-American War, U.S. President Theodore Roosevelt's administration and U.S. forces struggled to suppress Filipino guerrilla forces led by Emilio Aguinaldo.

Although usually confined to mountainous or forested terrain, Arab forces inspired by T. E. Lawrence (Lawrence of Arabia) and led by King Faisal al-Husayn used the harsh environment of the desert to fight a successful guerrilla war against superior Turkish forces during World War I.

During World War II guerrilla forces (also termed "partisan" or "underground" forces) in France and other countries fiercely resisted Nazi occupation.

Well known modern guerrilla wars that resulted in permanent changes in government occurred in China, Vietnam, and Cuba. Chinese communist guerrillas led by Mao Zedong, prevailed against a number of opponents to eventually take power after WWII. Communist Viet Minh forces led by Ho Chi Minh and later Viet Cong guerrilla forces outlasted French and then American forces in Vietnam. In Cuba, Fidel Castro and Ernesto (Che) Guevara fought a three year long guerrilla war from 1956 to 1959 that eventually ousted the launched a guerrilla war in Cuba against the government of Fulgencio Batista.

Guevara's writings became politically influential for a number of guerrilla groups that organized across Central and South America. Guevara wrote that "popular forces can win a war against (an) army" and that "it (was) not necessary to wait until all conditions for making revolution exist; the insurrection can create them."

Other nationalist movements sprung from guerrilla movement roots in Algeria (against the French in 1954); Cyprus (Greek nationalists against the British in the late 1950s).

Although often portraying themselves as a popular front, guerrilla forces seizing power often engage in bloody "cleansing" and destruction of local populations once loyal to the former government. After seizing power in Cambodia, the Khmer Rouge led by Pol Pot (also known as Soloth Sar) killed an estimated two million Cambodians.

Although sometimes only a matter of semantics, there is often considerable debate concerning the overlap of guerrilla tactics with tactics employed by terrorists (e.g., hijacking, kidnapping). There are no easily agreed upon definitional lines to distinguish the two groups. In general, most historians hinge such distinctions not necessarily upon tactics employed, but rather on relations between the opposing parties and the targets selected. Although there are many historical exceptions, terrorists generally represent minority or extreme viewpoints and target civilian, military, or government targets. Guerrilla forces generally represent broader popular movements and generally attack occupying military or government forces. A key element in defining guerrilla forces as opposed to other types of forces or movements involves the general principle that guerrilla forces are generally accepted—in fact often supported and sheltered—by local populations. In accord with international law, in stark contrast to the legal treatment of terrorist groups, guerrilla forces are to be treated as combatants in accord with the rules of the Geneva Convention if the forces operate in uniform or carry as distinctive emblem (e.g., patch, red scarf, etc.).

In many cases, whether to declare a particular group a group of freedom fighters, a guerrilla force, or a terrorist organization is often a matter of political or geographical perspective.

Cyberspace opens new opportunities and perils for what may come to be considered a new form of guerrilla warfare in the twenty-first century as activists (also known as "hacktivists") use Internet technology to combat electronic monitoring and Internet censorship by governments in many parts of the world.

NUCLEAR WAR

The Nazi death camps and the mushroom cloud of nuclear explosion are the two most potent images of the mass killings of the twentieth century. As World War II ended and the cold war began, the fear of nuclear annihilation hung like a cloud over the otherwise complacent consumerism of the Eisenhower era. The new technologies of mass death exacted incalculable costs, draining the treasuries of the United States and the Soviet Union and engendering widespread apocalyptic fatalism, distrust of government, and environmental degradation.

The advent of nuclear weapons fundamentally altered both the nature of war and the relationship of the military with the rest of society. A 1995 study by John Pike, the director of the space policy project at the Federation of American Scientists, revealed that the cost of nuclear weapons has constituted about one-fourth to one-third of the entire American military budget since 1945. President Eisenhower, in his farewell speech on the threats posed by the "military-industrial complex," warned of the potential of new technology to dominate the social order in unforeseen ways. The "social system which researches, chooses it, produces it, polices it, justifies it, and maintains it in being," observed British social historian E. P. Thompson, orients its "entire economic, scientific, political, and ideological support-system to that weapons system" (Wieseltier 1983, p. 10).

Throughout the cold war, U.S. intelligence reports exaggerated the numbers and pace of development of the Soviet Union's production of bombs and long-range nuclear forces, thus spurring further escalations of the arms race and the expansion of the military-industrial complex. In the 1950s there was the bomber gap, in the 1960s it was the missile gap, in the 1970s the civilian defense gap, and in the 1980s the military spending gap. The Soviet Union and the members of the NATO alliance developed tens of thousands of increasingly sophisticated nuclear weapons and delivery systems (e.g., cannons, bombers, land- and submarine-based intercontinental ballistic missiles) and various means of protecting them (e.g., hardened underground silos, mobile launchers, antiballistic missiles). With the possible exception of the hydrogen bomb, every advance in nuclear weaponry—from the neutron bomb and X-ray warheads to the soldier-carried Davy Crockett fission bomb—was the product of American ingenuity and determination.

A Brief History of Cold War Nuclear Developments

During World War II, while German research resources were largely invested in developing the V-1 and V-2 guided missiles, similar investments were being made by the United States and selected allies in producing the ultimate bomb through the highly secret Manhattan Project. The first nuclear device was detonated before dawn on July 16, 1945, at the Alamogordo Test Range in south central New Mexico. Within two months, atomic bombs were dropped on the Japanese cities of Hiroshima and Nagasaki. The U.S. government claimed that these bombings were necessary to shorten the war and avoid the anticipated heavy casualties of a land invasion of Japan, but later revisionist historians have disputed that motivation, claiming rather that the blasts were intended as an advertisement of American power over the Soviet Union.

The United States continued to develop the new weaponry despite the fact the war had concluded. Whether this was the reason why the Soviet Union embarked on its own weapon program, or if it would have done so if the U.S. had ceased production, remains a matter of debate. The Soviets deeply feared that the United States, having demonstrated its willingness to use the weapon on civilian populations, might not hesitate to do so again during the cold war. Two weeks after Hiroshima's destruction, Stalin ordered a crash program to develop an atomic bomb using Gulag prisoners to mine uranium and construct weapons facilities, putting the needs of his people behind those of the bomb. The race for nuclear supremacy had begun.

The 1940s saw the dawn of the cold war: the Soviet blockade of Berlin, Mao's victory over the Nationalists in China, discoveries and accusations of espionage, and, in September 1949, evidence that the Russians had tested their own bomb. Major General Curtis LeMay, head of the newly formed Strategic Air Command, was ordered to prepare his Air Force unit for possible atomic attack. His first war plan, based on a concept called "killing a nation," involved attacking seventy Soviet cities with 133 atomic bombs.

Fears of imminent nuclear war swept the globe. President Truman believed that if the Russians had the bomb, they would use it. The physicist Edward Teller pushed for a thermonuclear weapon whose virtually unlimited power would dwarf the atomic bombs produced under the Manhattan Project. The "Super," as it would be called, was the hydrogen bomb. In January 1950 Truman approved its development. Five months later, North Korea, with Stalin's support, attacked South Korea. Later that year, when in retreat, the North Koreans were reinforced by another Russian ally, Communist China. The cold war was in full swing, and the climate of fear and suspicion fueled McCarthyism. In 1952 the first hydrogen bomb was detonated, releasing a force some 800 times greater than the weapon that had destroyed Hiroshima. The bomb, initially sixty-two tons, was later made smaller and lighter, allowing its placement on missiles.

It was then that President Eisenhower's Secretary of Defense, John Foster Dulles, presented the impression that the United States would instigate nuclear war if there were any communist encroachments upon the "free world." Peace was maintained through the deterrent of fear: "Mutually Assured Destruction" (MAD) became the principle nuclear strategy for the rest of the twentieth century, making it inconceivable that politicians would risk the destruction of the planet by actually deploying the weapons they were so busily and alarmingly developing and stockpiling. To ensure retribution following a first strike, stockpiles continued growing to the point where human populations could be killed many times over.

Nuclear anxieties intensified with the development of strategic intercontinental rockets capable of delivering a nuclear warhead anywhere in the world within minutes. Because atomic war would basically be a one-punch affair, the alacrity and thoroughness of the first strike became the preoccupation of strategic planners. The race between the United States and Russia to refine German rocket technology intensified during the 1950s. When Russia launched the first satellite, Sputnik, in 1957, Americans panicked at the thought of Soviet hardware overhead and its ability to drop weapons from orbit. To recoup lost face and bolster national confidence, the United States entered the space race with its own orbital missions and even considered a plan to detonate a Hiroshima-size nuclear bomb on the moon that would be visible to the naked eye. In 1961 the Soviets placed the first man, Yuri Gargarin, into orbit as the nuclear-arms race combined with the space race as the key instruments of cold war rivalry between the Soviet Union and the United States.

But the critical event of the 1960s was the 1962 discovery that Russians had deployed forty-eight offensive ballistic missiles in Cuba. In a showdown of nuclear brinkmanship, both the Soviet Union and the United States went on highest alert in their preparations for war. For thirteen days the cold war almost went hot. As the Russian nuclear missiles were nearing operational status the Kennedy administration weighed such options as mounting an air strike, staging an invasion, or conducting a naval blockade. After the latter was selected, a Russian fleet steamed west to break it; a U.S. spy plane was shot down over Cuban territory killing the pilot. Eventually, though, diplomacy and level heads prevailed. The missiles were removed in exchange for a U.S. pledge not to invade the communist country and to remove its obsolete Jupiter missiles from Turkey. The nations' closeness to the unthinkable contributed to their agreeing on the 1963 Nuclear Test Ban Treaty.

There was one final peaking of fears and expenditures before the collapse of the Soviet Union: the entry of another communist superpower on the nuclear game board. China, which had detonated its first atomic bomb in 1964, claimed thirteen years later to have successfully tested guided missiles with nuclear warheads. Reports surfaced of nuclear shelters being constructed in Manchuria. The 1970s concluded with six members in the nuclear club and with memories associated with the seventy-fifth anniversary of the beginning of World War I and how an unpredictable chain of events could set into motion unwanted global conflict.

In 1982 President Reagan unilaterally discontinued negotiations for a comprehensive test ban of nuclear weapons, echoing the military's claims of a "testing gap" with the Soviet Union. In fact, as of the beginning of 1985, the United States had over the previous four decades (since 1945) conducted some 200 more nuclear tests than had the Soviets. The President proposed the Strategic Defense Initiative, popularly known as "Star Wars," to protect the nation from missile attack by using exotic technologies that were still on the drawing board. Pure scientific research in physics, lasers, metallurgy, artificial intelligence, and dozens of other areas became largely focused on direct military uses. By the mid-1980s, 70 percent of American programs in research and development and testing and evaluation were defense-related, and nearly 40 percent of all U.S. engineers and scientists were involved in military projects.

Compounding public anxieties was a 1982 forecast by U.S. intelligence agencies that thirty-one countries would be capable of producing nuclear weapons by 2000. From the scientific community came highly publicized scenarios of a postwar "nuclear winter," possibly similar to conditions that led to the extinction of dinosaurs following the impact of an asteroid. Groups such as Physicians for Social Responsibility warned that such a conflict would lead to the return to the Dark Ages. Books like Jonathan Schell's The Fate of the Earth (1982) and media images such as ABC television's special The Day After (1983) produced a degree of public unease not seen since the 1962 Cuban Missile Crisis.

The collapse of the Soviet Union and the end of the cold war in the late 1980s did not conclude American research and development—nor fears of a nuclear holocaust. In Russia, equipment malfunctions have accidentally switched Russian nuclear missiles to a "combat ready" status, and deteriorating security systems have increased the likelihood of weapons-grade materials falling into the hands of rogue states and terrorists. In the United States, major military contractors sought long-term sources of revenue to compensate for their post–cold war losses, and Republicans continued pushing for a defensive missile shield. In the mid-1990s the Department of Energy approved expenditures of hundreds of millions of dollars for superlasers and supercomputers to simulate weapons tests. A sub-critical nuclear weapons test, called Rebound, was conducted in 1997 at the Nevada Test Site. At the beginning of President George W. Bush's term, the 2001 Defense Authorization Bill was passed requiring that the Energy and Defense Departments study a new generation of precision, low-yield earth penetrating nuclear weapons to "threaten hard and deeply buried targets."

The Proliferation of Nuclear Weapons

Through espionage, huge national investments, and a black market of willing Western suppliers of needed technologies and raw materials, the American nuclear monopoly was broken with the successful detonations by the Soviet Union (1949), the United Kingdom (1952), France (1960), China (1964), India (1974), and Pakistan (1998).

Although the Western allies made the Soviet Union the scapegoat for the proliferation of nuclear weapons, it has been the export of Western technology and fuel that has given other countries the capability of building their own bombs. Although publicly dedicated to controlling the proliferation of "the bomb," in the fifty years following the Trinity detonation the United States shipped nearly a ton of plutonium to thirty-nine countries, including Argentina, India, Iran, Iraq, Israel, Japan, New Zealand, Pakistan, South Africa, Sweden, Turkey, Uruguay, and Venezuela.

The countries suspected of having (or having had) nuclear weapons programs include Iraq, Romania, North Korea, Taiwan, Brazil, Argentina, and South Africa. There is little doubt that the sixth member of the nuclear club is Israel, which was supplied a reactor complex and bomb-making assistance by the French as payment for its participation in the 1956 Suez Crisis. Despite its concerns over nuclear proliferation, the United States looked the other way as the Israeli nuclear program progressed, owing to the country's strategic position amid the oil-producing countries of the Middle East. When a Libyan airliner strayed over the highly secretive Negev Nuclear Research Center in 1973, Israeli jets shot it down, killing all 104 passengers.

Living with the Bomb

In By the Bomb's Early Light (1985) Paul Boyer asks how a society lives with the knowledge of its capacity for self-destruction. However such thinking was in vogue with the approach of the West's second millennium, with the media saturated with doomsday forecasts of overpopulation, mass extinctions, global warming, and deadly pollutants. By the end of the 1990s, half of Americans believed that some manmade disaster would destroy civilization.

The real possibility of nuclear war threatens the very meaning of all personal and social endeavors, and all opportunities for transcendence. In 1984, to dramatize the equivalency of nuclear war with collective suicide, undergraduates at Brown University voted on urging the school's health service to stockpile "suicide pills" in case of a nuclear exchange.

Such existential doubts were not mollified by the government's nuclear propaganda, which tended to depict nuclear war as a survivable natural event. Americans were told that "A Clean Building Seldom Burns" in the 1951 Civil Defense pamphlet "Atomic Blast Creates Fire," and that those who fled the cities by car would survive in the 1955 pamphlet "Your Car and CD [civil defense]: 4 Wheels to Survival."

Not even the young were distracted from thinking about the unthinkable. Civil defense drills became standard exercises at the nation's schools during the 1950s, including the "duck and cover" exercises in which students were instructed to "duck" under their desks or tables and "cover" their heads for protection from a thermonuclear blast. In the early 1980s, a new curriculum unit on nuclear war was developed for junior high school students around the country. Psychologists wrote about the implications of youngsters expecting never to reach adulthood because of nuclear war.

The Impacts of the Nuclear Arms Race on Culture and Society

In the words of Toronto sociologist Sheldon Ungar, "Splitting the atom dramatically heightened the sense of human dominion; it practically elevated us into the empyrean. The control over nature's ultimate power was also taken as a sign of grace, an indication of America's moral superiority and redemptive capacity" (1992, p. 5). But this seeming benefaction turned into a nightmare, destroying Western faith in moral progress and providential history.

Scholars and essayists have speculated liberally on the psychological and cultural effects of growing up with the possibility of being vaporized in a nuclear war. For instance, did it contribute to permissive parenting strategies by older generations seeking to give some consolation to their children? Or the cultural hedonism and dissolution of mores evidenced when these children came of age? It certainly did contribute to the generational conflicts of the 1960s, as some baby boomers laid blame for the precarious times on older generations.

It is in the arts that collective emotions and outlooks are captured and explored, and fears of the atomic unknown surfaced quickly. As nuclear weapons tests resumed in Nevada in 1951, anxieties over radioactive fallout were expressed cinematically in a sci-fi genre of movies featuring massive mutant creatures. These were to be followed by endof-the-world books (e.g., Alas, Babylon in 1959), films (e.g., On the Beach in 1959, Fail-Safe in 1964, Dr. Strangelove in 1964), television series Planet of the Apes, and music (e.g., Bob Dylan's "Hard Rain" and Barry McGuire's "Eve of Destruction").

The bomb also opened the door to UFOs. In the same state where the first nuclear bomb exploded two years earlier, near Roswell, New Mexico, an alien space ship supposedly crashed to Earth, although later reports have debunked that story despite the stubborn beliefs in an alien visitation by various UFO aficionados. Were they contemporary manifestations of angels, messengers carrying warnings of humanity's impending doom? Or did our acquisition of the ultimate death tool make our neighbors in the cosmos nervous? The latter idea was the theme of the 1951 movie The Day the Earth Stood Still, where the alien Klaatu issued an authoritarian ultimatum to earthlings to cease their violence or their planet will be destroyed.

Harnessing the Atom for Peaceful Purposes

The logic of the death-for-life tradeoff runs deep throughout all cultural systems. It is a price we see exacted in the natural order, in the relationship between predator and prey, and in the economic order in the life-giving energies conferred by fuels derived from the fossils of long-dead animals. Over 80 percent of American energy comes from coal, oil, and gas, whose burning, in turn, produces such environment-killing by-products as acid rain.

This logic extends to attempts to harness nuclear energy for peacetime uses. In theory, such energy can be virtually limitless in supply. In the words of the science writer David Dietz, "Instead of filling the gasoline tank of your automobile two or three times a week, you will travel for a year on a pellet of atomic energy the size of a vitamin pill. . . . The day is gone when nations will fight for oil . . ." (Ford 1982, pp. 30–31). But it is a Faustian bargain because the by-products, most notably plutonium, are the most lethal substances known to man. Thousands of accidents occur annually in America's commercial nuclear plants. Collective memory remains vivid of the meltdown at the Chernobyl nuclear plant in the former Soviet Union in 1986 and the 1979 accident at Three Mile Island in Pennsylvania.

The Ecological Legacy

A comprehensive 1989 study by Greenpeace and the Institute for Policy Studies estimated that at least fifty nuclear warheads and 9 nuclear reactors lie on ocean floors because of accidents involving American and Soviet rockets, bombers, and ships. Radiation leaks south of Japan from an American hydrogen bomb accidentally dropped from an aircraft carrier in 1965. In the 1990s equipment malfunctions led to Russian missiles accidentally being switched to "combat mode," according to a 1998 CIA report.

The cold war rush to build nuclear weapons in the 1940s and 1950s led to severe contamination of the land and air. In one 1945 incident at the 560-square-mile Hanford nuclear reservation in Washington State, over a ton of radioactive material of roughly 350,000 to 400,000 curies (one curie being the amount of radiation emitted in a second by 1,400 pounds of enriched uranium) was released into the air. There, the deadly by-products of four decades of plutonium production leaked into the area's aquifer and into the West's greatest river, the Columbia. Fish near the 310-square-mile Savannah River site, where 35 percent of the weapons-grade plutonium was produced, are too radioactive to eat. Federal Energy Department officials revealed in 1990 that 28 kilograms of plutonium, enough to make seven nuclear bombs, had escaped into the air ducts at the Rocky Flats weapons plant near Denver.

Such environmental costs of the cold war in the Untied States are dwarfed by those of the former Soviet Union. In the early years of their bomb program at Chelyabinsk, radioactive wastes were dumped into the Techa River. When traces showed up 1,000 miles away in the Arctic Ocean, wastes were then pumped into Karachay Lake until the accumulation was 120 million curies—radiation so great that one standing on the lake's shore would receive a lethal dose in an hour.

The Corruption of Public Ethics

Perhaps even more devastating than the environmental damage wrought by the nuclear arms race was its undermining of public faith in government. Public ethics were warped in numerous ways. Secrecy for matters of national security was deemed paramount during the cold war, leaving Americans unaware of the doings of their government. The secrecy momentum expanded beyond matters of nuclear technologies and strategies when President Truman issued the first executive order authorizing the classification of nonmilitary information as well.

Some instances of severe radioactivity risk were kept secret from the public by federal officials. Thousands of workers—from uranium miners to employees of over 200 private companies doing weapons work—were knowingly exposed to dangerous levels of radiation. Though many of these firms were found by various federal agencies to be in violation of worker safety standards set by the Atomic Energy Commission, there were no contract cancellations or penalties assessed that might impede the pace of weapons production. After three decades of denials and fifty-seven years after the Manhattan Project began processing radioactive materials, the Federal government finally conceded in 2000 that nuclear weapons workers had been exposed to radiation and chemicals that produced cancer in 600,000 of them and early death for thousands of others.

The dangers extended well beyond atomic energy workers; ordinary citizens were exposed to water and soil contaminated toxic and radioactive waste. From 1951 to 1962, fallout from the Atomic Energy Commission's open-air nuclear blasts in the Nevada desert subjected thousands to cancer-causing radiation in farm communities in Utah and Arizona. According to a 1991 study by the International Physicians for the Prevention of Nuclear War, government officials expected this to occur but nevertheless chose this site over a safer alternative on the Outer Banks of North Carolina, where prevailing winds would have carried the fallout eastward over the ocean. The study predicted that 430,000 people will die of cancer over the remainder of the twentieth-century because of their exposures, and millions more will be at risk in the centuries to come.

According to a 1995 report of the Advisory Committee on Human Radiation Experiments, between 1944 and 1974 more than 16,000 Americans were unwitting guinea pigs in 435 documented radiation experiments. Trusting patients were injected with plutonium just to see what would happen. Oregon prisoners were subjected to testicular irradiation experiments at doses 100 times greater than the annual allowable level for nuclear workers. Boys at a Massachusetts school for the retarded were fed doses of radioactive materials in their breakfast cereal. And dying patients, many of whom were African Americans and whose consent forms were forged by scientists, were given whole-body radiation exposures.

Conclusion

Nuclear anxieties have migrated from all-out war among superpowers to fears of nuclear accidents and atomic attacks by rogue nations. According to Valentin Tikhonov, working conditions and living standards for nuclear and missile experts have declined sharply in post–Communist Russia. With two-thirds of these employees earning less than fifty dollars per month, there is an alarming temptation to sell expertise to aspiring nuclear nations. During its war with Iran, Iraq in 1987 tested several one ton radiological weapons designed to shower radioactive materials on target populations to induce radiation sickness and slow painful deaths. And during May of 1998, two bitter adversaries, India and Pakistan, detonated eleven nuclear devices over a three-week period.

Some believe that with the advent of nuclear weapons, peace will be forever safeguarded, since their massive use would likely wipe out the human race and perhaps all life on Earth. Critics of this outlook have pointed out that there has never been a weapon developed that has not been utilized, and that the planet Earth is burdened with a store of some 25,000 to 44,000 nuclear weapons.

The amount of scientific research and technological advance wrought by the Cold War is truly incredible. Both the American and Soviet space programs were the result of national pride and fear of the other's missiles. When the Soviet Union launched Sputnik, the U.S. military saw, instead of a small satellite in orbit, a potential bomb flying over the pole toward New York. The Cold War and the space program brought the world miniature electronics, home computers, wireless telephones, Velcro, fuel cells, communications and weather satellites, and more. In addition, scientists in any number of specialties benefited, even if their research was only peripherally related to war. Astronomers, for example, benefited from advances in optics spurred by the Strategic Defense Initiative (SDI) (popularly known as "Star Wars"); the Human Genome Project, initially conceived as a way to better understand the genetic effects of radiation, was initiated by the Department of Energy.

The SDI program warrants special mention. Begun under the Reagan administration in the early 1980s, this ambitious program aimed to design a space-based system that could detect and destroy a full-blown Soviet nuclear attack. It is widely thought that Soviet fear of American technological prowess and the rapid development of Star Wars induced the Soviet government to spend more than it could afford on its military efforts. This may well have hastened the collapse of the Soviet Union and the overthrow of Communist governments throughout Eastern Europe at the Cold War's close. Though SDI's initial goals may have been ambitious, subsequent efforts have turned to intercepting small-scale launches by rogue nations rather than stopping a full-scale attack.

The cultural aspects of nuclear weapons were important, too. Movies like the original Godzilla and Them postulated monsters created by exposure to radiation from nuclear-weapons testing. American school children were taught to "duck and cover" in case of a nuclear attack. People dug bomb shelters beneath or beside their homes in case of a nuclear attack, and other movies, such as On the Beach, Dr. Strangelove, and Failsafe looked at nuclear war from a number of aspects. In some parts of the world, particularly Europe, these fears may have been even greater, as they were positioned between the two nuclear-armed superpowers.

The end of the Cold War removed many of these fears. Although the United States and Russia still possess enough nuclear weapons to destroy human civilization, both nations have agreed to reduce their stockpiles. That and other political events have since made an all-out nuclear war less likely. Replacing the fear of global nuclear catastrophe, however, is the fear of local nuclear war or of nuclear terrorism. The collapse and impoverishment of the former Soviet Union raised many fears that a combination of desperation, hunger, and poverty could lead former Soviet nuclear scientists to work for rogue governments, helping them obtain the materials and expertise needed to build their own weapons. Where Cold War movies explored total nuclear war, post-Cold War movies imagine nuclear terrorism.

We now find ourselves in a world dominated not by fears of global catastrophe, but, rather, by fears of nuclear terrorism or small-scale nuclear war between minor nuclear powers. It remains to be seen how and to what extent nuclear weapons will shape the geopolitical balance and social consciousness around the world.

HISTORY OF THE AMERICAS

Mexican fighter pilot and air crew, World War II.

20th Century North America

As a part of the British Empire, Canada immediately entered World War I when it broke out in 1914. Canada bore the brunt of several major battles during the early stages of the war, including the use of poison gas attacks at Ypres. Losses became grave, and the government eventually brought in conscription, despite the fact this was against the wishes of the majority of French Canadians. In the ensuing Conscription Crisis of 1917, riots broke out on the streets of Montreal. In neighboring Newfoundland, the new dominion suffered a devastating loss on July 1, 1916, the First day on the Somme.

The United States stayed out of the conflict until 1917, when it joined the Entente powers. The United States was then able to play a crucial role at the Paris Peace Conference of 1919 that shaped interwar Europe. Mexico was not part of the war, as the country was embroiled in the Mexican Revolution at the time.

The 1920s brought an age of great prosperity in the United States, and to a lesser degree Canada. But the Wall Street Crash of 1929 combined with drought ushered in a period of economic hardship in the United States and Canada. From 1936 to 1949, there was a popular uprising against the anti-Catholic Mexican government of the time, set off specifically by the anti-clerical provisions of the Mexican Constitution of 1917.

Once again, Canada found itself at war before its neighbors, however even Canadian contributions were slight before the Japanese attack on Pearl Harbor. The entry of the United States into the war helped to tip the balance in favour of the allies. Two Mexican tankers, transporting oil to the United States, were attacked and sunk by the Germans in the Gulf of Mexico waters, in 1942. The incident happened in spite of Mexico's neutrality at that time. This led Mexico to enter the conflict with a declaration of war on the Axis nations. The destruction of Europe wrought by the war vaulted all North American countries to more important roles in world affairs, especially the United States, which emerged as a "superpower".

The early Cold War era saw the United States as the most powerful nation in a Western coalition of which Mexico and Canada were also a part. In Canada, Quebec was transformed by the Quiet Revolution and the emergence of Quebec nationalism. Mexico experienced an era of huge economic growth after World War II, a heavy industrialization process and a growth of its middle class, a period known in Mexican history as *"El Milagro Mexicano"* (the Mexican miracle). The Caribbean saw the beginnings of decolonization, while on the largest island the Cuban Revolution introduced Cold War rivalries into Latin America.

The civil rights movement in the U.S. ended Jim Crow and empowered black voters in the 1960s, which allowed black citizens to move into high government offices for the first time since Reconstruction. However, the dominant New Deal coalition collapsed in the mid 1960s in disputes over race and the Vietnam War, and the conservative movement began its rise to power, as the once dominant liberalism weakened and collapsed. Canada during this era was dominated by the leadership of Pierre Elliot Trudeau. In 1982, at the end of his tenure, Canada enshrined a new constitution.

Canada's Brian Mulroney not only ran on a similar platform but also favored closer trade ties with the United States. This led to the Canada-United States Free Trade Agreement in January 1989. Mexican presidents Miguel de la Madrid, in the early 1980s and Carlos Salinas de Gortari in the late 1980s, started implementing liberal economic strategies that were seen as a good move. However, Mexico experienced a strong economic recession in 1982 and the Mexican peso suffered a devaluation. In the United States president Ronald Reagan attempted to move the United States back towards a hard anti-communist line in foreign affairs, in what his supporters saw as an attempt to assert moral leadership (compared to the Soviet Union) in the world community. Domestically, Reagan attempted to bring in a package of privatization and regulation to stimulate the economy.

The end of the Cold War and the beginning of the era of sustained economic expansion coincided during the 1990s. On January 1, 1994, Canada, Mexico and the United States signed the North American Free Trade Agreement, creating the world's largest free trade area. In 2000, Vicente Fox became the first non-PRI candidate to win the Mexican presidency in over 70 years. The optimism of the 1990s was shattered by the 9/11 attacks of 2001 on the United States, which prompted military intervention in Afghanistan, which also involved Canada. Canada did not support the United States' later move to invade Iraq, however.

In the U.S. the Reagan Era of conservative national policies, deregulation and tax cuts took control with the election of Ronald Reagan in 1980. By 2010, political scientists were debating whether the election of Barack Obama in 2008 represented an end of the Reagan Era, or was only a reaction against the bubble economy of the 2000s (decade), which burst in 2008 and became the Late-2000s recession with prolonged unemployment.

Central America

Despite the failure of a lasting political union, the concept of Central American reunification, though lacking enthusiasm from the leaders of the individual countries, rises from time to time. In 1856–1857 the region successfully established a military coalition to repel an invasion by United States adventurer William Walker. Today, all five nations fly flags that retain the old federal motif of two outer blue bands bounding an inner white stripe. (Costa Rica, traditionally the least committed of the five to regional integration, modified its flag significantly in 1848 by darkening the blue and adding a double-wide inner red band, in honor of the French tricolor).

In 1907, a Central American Court of Justice was created. Between November 14 and December 20, 1907, after a proposal by Mexico and the United States, five Central American nations (Costa Rica, El Salvador, Guatemala, Honduras and Nicaragua) took part in the Central American Peace Conference in Washington, D.C. sponsored by United States Secretary of State Elihu Root. The five nations, all former Spanish colonies, had previously tried to form a political alliance. Their first attempt was the Federal Republic of Central America, and the most recent effort was the founding of the Republic of Central America 11 years earlier.

The participants concluded the conference with an agreement creating the Central American Court of Justice *(Corte de Justicia Centroamericana)*. The court would remain in effect for ten years from the final ratification, and communication would be through the government of Costa Rica. It was composed of five judges, one from each member state. The court heard ten cases, five of which were brought by private individuals (and declared inadmissible) and three begun by the court. The court operated until April 1918 from its headquarters in Costa Rica; despite efforts beginning in March 1917 (when Nicaragua submitted a notice of termination of the agreement), it then dissolved.

Reasons for the agreement's failure include:

- No effective system of judicial procedure

- Judges were not independent of their respective governments.

- Jurisdiction was too broad to satisfy its member states

1900–1920

By the start of the century, the United States continued its interventionist attitude, which aimed to directly defend its interests in the region. This was officially articulated in Theodore Roosevelt's Big Stick Doctrine, which modified the old Monroe Doctrine, which had simply aimed to deter European intervention in the hemisphere.

The Great Depression posed a challenge to the region. The collapse of the world economy meant that the demand for raw materials drastically declined, undermining many of the economies of South America. Intellectuals and government leaders in South America turned their backs on the older economic policies and turned toward import substitution industrialization. The goal was to create self-sufficient economies, which would have their own industrial sectors and large middle classes and which would be immune to the ups and downs of the global economy. Despite the potential threats to United States commercial interests, the Roosevelt administration (1933–1945) understood that the United States could not wholly oppose import substitution. Roosevelt implemented a good neighbor policy and allowed the nationalization of some American companies in South America. The Second World War also brought the United States and most Latin American nations together.

On December 13, 1960, Guatemala, El Salvador, Honduras, and Nicaragua established the Central American Common Market ("CACM"). Costa Rica, because of its relative economic prosperity and political stability, chose not to participate in the CACM. The goals for the CACM were to create greater political unification and success of import substitution industrialization policies. The project was an immediate economic success, but was abandoned after the 1969 "Football War" between El Salvador and Honduras. A Central American Parliament has operated, as a purely advisory body, since 1991. Costa Rica has repeatedly declined invitations to join the regional parliament, which seats deputies from the four other former members of the Union, as well as from Panama and the Dominican Republic.

South America

In the 1960s and 1970s, the governments of Argentina, Brazil, Chile, and Uruguay were overthrown or displaced by U.S.-aligned military dictatorships. These dictatorships detained tens of thousands of political prisoners, many of whom were tortured and/or killed (on inter-state collaboration, see Operation Condor). Economically, they began a transition to neoliberal economic policies. They placed their own actions within the United States Cold War doctrine of "National Security" against internal subversion. Throughout the 1980s and 1990s, Peru suffered from an internal conflict (see Túpac Amaru Revolutionary Movement and Shining Path). Revolutionary movements and right-wing military dictatorships have been common, but starting in the 1980s a wave of democratization came through the continent, and democratic rule is widespread now. Allegations of corruption remain common, and several nations have seen crises which have forced the resignation of their presidents, although normal civilian succession has continued.

International indebtedness became a notable problem, as most recently illustrated by Argentina's default in the early 21st century. In recent years, South American governments have drifted to the left, with socialist leaders being elected in Chile, Bolivia, Brazil, Venezuela, and a leftist president in Argentina and Uruguay. Despite the move to the left, South America is still largely capitalist. With the founding of the Union of South American Nations, South America has started down the road of economic integration, with plans for political integration in the European Union style.

1930–1960

The history of South America during World War II is of importance because of the significant economic, political, and military changes that occurred throughout much of the region as a result of the war.

The war caused a considerable degree of panic in Latin America over economics, because South Americans depended on the European investment capital which was shut down. Latin America tried to stay neutral but the warring countries were endangering their neutrality. Most countries used propaganda to turn the neutral countries to their side, while Berlin wanted Latin America neutral.

In order to better protect the Panama Canal (which provided a link between the Atlantic and Pacific Oceans that was vital to both commerce and defense), combat Axis influence, and optimize the production of goods for the war effort, the United States through Lend-Lease and similar programs greatly expanded its interests in Latin America, resulting in large-scale modernization and a major economic boost for the countries that participated.

Strategically, Brazil was of great importance because of its having the closest point in the Americas to Africa where the Allies were actively engaged in fighting the the Germans and Italians in Africa.

For the Axis, the Southern Cone nations of Argentina and Chile were where they found most of their South American support, and they utilised it to the fullest by interfering with internal affairs, conducting espionage, and distributing propaganda.

Brazil was the only country to send an Expeditionary force to the European theatre. The Brazilian Expeditionary Force or FEB (Portuguese: *Força Expedicionária Brasileira*; FEB) consisted of about 25,700 men arranged by the army and air force to fight alongside the Allied forces in the Mediterranean Theatre of World War II. This air–land force consisted of (replacements included) a complete infantry division, a liaison flight, and a fighter squadron. It fought in Italy from September 1944 to May 1945, while the Brazilian Navy as well as the Air Force also acted in the Battle of the Atlantic from the middle of 1942 until the end of the war. The FEB took 20,573 Axis prisoners, including two generals.

The Cuban Navy worked closely with the United States in patrolling the waters of the Caribbean. On 7 January 1944, the *CS-13*, commanded by Mario Ramirez Delgado sank a German U-boat during World War II. Several countries had skirmishes with German U-Boats and cruisers in the Caribbean and South Atlantic. Mexico sent a fighter squadron of 300 volunteers to the Pacific, the *Escuadrón 201* were known as the Aztec Eagles (*Aguilas Aztecas - Escuadrón Aéreo de Pelea 201*). The Brazilian active participation on the battle field in Europe was divined after the Casablanca Conference. The President of the U.S., Franklin D. Roosevelt on his way back from Morocco met the President of Brazil, Getulio Vargas, in Natal, Rio Grande do Norte, this meeting is known as the Potenji River Conference, and defined the creation of the Brazilian Expeditionary Force.

United States Role

In 1940, after he expressed his concern to President Franklin D. Roosevelt over Nazi influence in Latin America, Nelson Rockefeller of the famous family was appointed to the new position of Coordinator of Inter-American Affairs (CIAA) in the Office of the Coordinator of Inter-American Affairs (OCIAA). Rockefeller was charged with overseeing a program of U.S. cooperation with the nations of Latin America to help raise the standard of living, to achieve better relations among the nations of the western hemisphere, and to counter rising Nazi influence in the region. He facilitated this form of cultural diplomacy by collaborating with the Director of Latin American Relations at the CBS radio network Edmund A. Chester.

Anti-fascist propaganda was a major U.S. project across Latin America, and was run by Rockefeller's office. It spent millions on radio broadcasts and motion pictures, hoping to reach a large audience. Madison Avenue techniques generated a push back in Mexico, especially, where well-informed locals resisted heavy-handed American influence. Nevertheless, Mexico was a valuable ally in the war. A deal was reached whereby 250,000 Mexican citizens living in the United States served in the American forces; over 1000 were killed in combat. In addition to propaganda, large sums were allocated for economic support and development. On the whole the Roosevelt policy was a political success, except in Argentina, which tolerated German influence, and refused to follow Washington's lead until the war was practically over.

Economics

According to author Thomas M. Leonard, World War II had a major impact on Latin American economies. Many countries raised prices on their exports so that they could support themselves economically. Following the December 7, 1941 Japanese attack on Pearl Harbor, most of Latin America either severed relations with the Axis powers or declared war on them. As a result, many nations (including all of Central America, the Dominican Republic, Mexico, Chile, Peru, Argentina, and Venezuela) suddenly found that they were now a major trading partner of the United States and highly valued for their trade.

The United States' high demand for particular products and commodities during the war further distorted trade. For example, the United States wanted all of the platinum produced in Colombia, all of Chile's copper, and all of Peru's cotton. The parties agreed upon set prices, often with a high premium favoring Latin Americans, but the various nations lost their ability to bargain and trade in the open market.

Shortages of consumer goods and other products were also a problem during the war years. The demands of the American war industry and a scarcity of shipping caused many goods to be unavailable in Latin America, and so the prices for what was available increased. Gasoline and other oil products were expensive and difficult to obtain. Food shortages were a problem in the cities. Ultimately, all of these factors resulted in inflation.

Most of Latin America used the war to their advantage by siding with the United States and receiving aid. Peru, however, was an exception. In Peru, the government placed price controls on various products; hence, its foreign reserves did not increase as much as some of the other Latin American states and it lost badly-needed capital. Argentina, despite its pro-German leanings and its hostility towards the United States, did very well as trade increased rapidly. Panama also benefited economically, mainly because of increased ship traffic and goods passing through the canal.

In Puerto Rico, the alcohol industry boomed because access to European markets ceased. Petroleum-rich Mexico and Venezuela benefitted from the elevated price of oil. Mexico used this commodity to force a deal on its terms with American and European oil companies for the nationalization of its oil industry in 1938. Furthermore, during the war President Manuel Ávila Camacho capitalized on the situation to improve Mexico's bargaining position with the United States.

Lend-Lease

On March 22, 1942, the United States government enacted Lend-Lease, which was a program which gave war materials and other assistance from the United States in exchange for military bases and participation in the defense of the Western Hemisphere. The United Kingdom and other European nations, including their colonies, logically received the majority of the aid, because the chaos of war was much closer to them. Latin America, however, received approximately $400 million in war materials, which was a small fraction compared of what was distributed to the European nations.

Because of Cuba's geographical position at the entrance of the Gulf of Mexico, Havana's role as the principal trading port in the West Indies, and the country's natural resources, Cuba was an important participant in the American Theater of World War II, and subsequently one of the greatest beneficiaries of the United States' Lend-Lease program. Cuba declared war on the Axis powers in December 1941, making it one of the first Latin American countries to enter the conflict, and by the war's end in 1945 its military had developed a reputation as being the most efficient and cooperative of all the Caribbean nations.

Federico Laredo Brú was the President of Cuba when the war began in 1939. His one significant World War II-related crisis before leaving office in 1940 was the MS *St. Louis* affair. The MS *St. Louis* was a German ocean liner carrying over 900 Jewish refugees from Germany to Cuba. Upon arriving in Havana, the Cuban government refused to allow the refugees to land because they did not have proper permits and visas. After sailing north, the United States and Canadian governments also refused to accept the refugees, and so the *St. Louis* sailed back across the Atlantic, and dropped her passengers off in Europe. Some thenceforth went to Britain, but most went to Belgium and France, which were soon overrun by German forces. Ultimately, because of the refusal to take in the Jewish refugees, many were taken prisoner by the Germans and subsequently killed in concentration camps.

Following the 1940 Cuban elections, Brú was succeeded by the "strongman and chief" of the Cuban Army, Fulgencio Batista. Any possible Nazi leanings by Batista was dispelled when he sent the British a large quantity of sugar as a gift. Later, fear of Batista's possible sympathy for Franco was also dispelled when the president suggested to the United States that it launch a joint US-Latin American invasion of Spain, in order to overthrow Franco and his régime. This plan, however, did not materialize.

Batista's support for the Allied cause was confirmed in February 1941, when he ordered all German and Italian consular officials to leave his country. Cuba entered the war on December 9, 1941, by declaring war on Japan, which a few days before had launched a devastating attack on the United States Navy base at Pearl Harbor, Hawaii. Cuba then declared war on Germany and Italy on December 11, 1941, and - following the Americans' example - broke relations with Vichy France on November 10, 1942.

Contribution to the Battle of the Caribbean

According to Rear Admiral Samuel Eliot Morison, Cuba's military was the "most cooperative and helpful of all the Caribbean states" during the war, and that its navy was "small but efficient" in its fight against German U-boats. Upon Cuba's declaration of war on the Axis powers, Batista signed an agreement with the United States that gave the latter permission to build airfields in Cuba for the protection of the Caribbean sealanes, and he also signed a mutual defense pact with Mexico for the defense against enemy submarines in the Gulf of Mexico. Among the new American bases was the San Antonio Air Base near San Antonio de los Baños, and the San Julián Air Base in Pinar del Rio, both of which were built in 1942 and turned over to the Cuban military after the war. The United States also supplied Cuba with modern military aircraft, which were vital for coastal defense and anti-submarine operations, and refitted the Cuban Navy with modern weapons and other equipment. During World War II, the Cuban Navy escorted hundreds of Allied ships through hostile waters, sailed nearly 400,000 miles on convoy and patrol duty, flew over 83,000 hours on convoy and patrol duty, and rescued over 200 U-boat victims from the sea, all without losing a single warship or aircraft to enemy action.

Out of all of the Latin American nations, Brazil benefited the most from Lend-Lease during the war, mainly because of its geographical position at the northeastern corner of South America, which allowed for patrolling between South America and West Africa, as well as providing a ferry point for the transfer of American-made war materials to the Allies fighting in North Africa, but also because it was seen as a possible German invasion route that had to be defended. New and favorable trade treaties were signed with the United States, which offered loans and military aid, but of more importance was the drop in competition in Brazil's manufacturing industry. Brazil received three-quarters of the Lend-Lease assistance distributed in Latin America. Ecuador received some, mainly for the building of an airbase in the Galapagos, and both Colombia and the Dominican Republic used Lend-Lease to modernize their militaries in exchange for their participation in the defense of the Panama Canal and the Caribbean sea lanes.

In contrast, Argentina and Chile received very little military aid, because for most of the war neither would heed American demands that they sever all relations with the Axis powers. Peru received some aid, but by 1943 the western coast of South America had lost all strategic significance, because it was so far away from the main theaters of war, and thus Peru lost its immediate justification for Lend-Lease weaponry. The Central American nations suffered a similar fate as Peru. By 1943, the Pan-American Highway, which the United States was building for defense purposes, ceased to be a priority, and so work on the road, as well as military aid, was halted.

According to Leonard, Lend-Lease changed the balance of power in Latin America and "rekindled old rivalries." The Chilean government, for example, was very concerned about its lack of military assistance, not out of fear of an attack by Axis forces, but because it was concerned that Bolivia and Peru might attempt to use their newly acquired weapons to take back territory lost to Chile sixty years before during the War of the Pacific. Ecuador also was unhappy because, at the end of the 1941 Ecuadorian-Peruvian War, it had lost to Peru. Finally, Argentina was threatened by its old rival, Brazil, because of the latter's access to modern American weaponry. Leonard says that the Argentine dictator Juan Perón came to power partially by claiming that he would "redress this change in military status."

Axis Activity

At the beginning of World War II, fascism was seen as a positive alternative by some Latin American leaders and groups that were impressed by Germany's Adolf Hitler, Italy's Benito Mussolini, Japan's

Emperor Hirohito, Spain's Francisco Franco (although Spain remained neutral throughout the war) and the fascist dictators of the minor Axis Powers (Romania and Hungary). President Rafael Trujillo of the Dominican Republic, for example, admired Hitler for his style and his militaristic rallies. Similar views were held by Jorge Ubico and Maximiliano Hernández Martínez, the dictators of Guatemala and El Salvador, respectively. According to Leonard, in Brazil, Argentina, and Chile, the strong sense of unity and purpose created by fascism was quite attractive. Brazil's Integralists dressed in jackboots and green military-style shirts, and were open admirers of Mussolini.

The politics of fascism were not all that was attractive, as in the pre-war years the Germans also enjoyed growing economic penetration using strict binational trade agreements to ensure that the economic relationship with various Latin American nations would be equal. With the start of the war in September 1939, Axis ships could no longer cross the Atlantic for commerce, and so trade between Latin America and Germany and Italy ceased.

Almost all of the Latin American states had to respond to Axis espionage activity. Mexico, and to a lesser extent Brazil, cooperated with the United States in shutting down Axis cells. Chile and Argentina, on the other hand, allowed enemy agents to operate in their countries for most of the war, which was a source of considerable discord between the two nations and the United States. Many of the Latin American states also had to deal with large numbers of immigrants from Axis countries. Colombia, for example, had a population of about 4,000 German immigrants in 1941, as well as a small village of Japanese farmers in Cauca. Many of the Germans in Colombia were involved in the air transportation industry as employees of SCADTA, so the United States was concerned that they might be engaged in espionage or even plot to convert civilian aircraft into bombers for an attack against the Panama Canal. As a result, the United States government pressured Colombia into monitoring and interning the immigrants or, in some cases, deporting them to the United States. The same occurred in other Latin American countries as well.

The threat of German and Spanish espionage was much more real. Throughout much of the war, the Germans operated spy networks in all of the most prominent countries of the region, including Argentina, Chile, Paraguay, Brazil, Cuba, Mexico, and others. Operation *Bolivar*, as it was called, was centered on clandestine radio communications from their base in Argentina to Berlin in Germany, but it also utilized Spanish merchant vessels for the shipment of paper-form intelligence back to Europe. The latter was possible because of Spanish cooperation with German intelligence agencies during the war. Although Argentina and

Chile eventually "cracked down" on the Axis agents operating in their countries in early 1944, some *Bolivar* activity continued up until the end of the European war in May 1945.

In addition to German espionage and sabotage in Latin America, the United States was also concerned about Nazi propaganda. For example, Germany's embassy in Guatemala City served as the distribution center for Nazi propaganda in Central America. Prior to the beginning of the war in 1939, the propaganda focused on the superiority of German manufactured goods, and claimed that Germany was the center for scientific research, because it had the "world's most advanced educational system." Between September 1939 and late 1943, the propaganda focused on German victories and the superiority of its military equipment. From Guatemala the propaganda made its way to the German embassies in other countries, often as packages aboard the Salvadoran airline TACA.

Soviet–Latin American Relations

Hitler's invasion of June 1941 provoked support and aid for the Soviet Union in many countries in Latin America, generally organized through voluntary organizations or trade unions. Cuba dispatched 40,000 cigars to the Red Army and in October 1942 became the first Latin American country to extend diplomatic recognition to the USSR. The war led to a diplomatic thaw more generally: by 1945, 11 Latin American states, including Colombia, Chile, Argentina and the Central American republics, had normalized relations with Moscow.

At the end of World War II in Europe, Mexican president Manuel Ávila Camacho declared: *"Al enterarme del retroceso definitivo del Ejército alemán recuerdo junto con mi país los esfuerzos admirables del heroico pueblo soviético durante los años de la lucha contra las tropas fascistas."* (Upon hearing of the definitive retreat of the German army, I, along with my country, remembered the admirable efforts of the heroic Soviet people during the years of struggle against fascist troops.)

Jewish Passports-El Salvador

While Jews were trying to escape the Axis powers, Colonel José Castellanos Contreras, the Salvadoran Consul General in Geneva, Switzerland, saved 25,000 Jews by providing them with Salvadoran passports which could be used as a form of political asylum. This was however a very quiet and unrecognized part of El Salvador contribution in World War 2.

Cold War Era

Wars became less frequent in the later 20th century, with Bolivia-Paraguay and Peru-Ecuador fighting the last inter-state wars. Early in the 20th century, the three wealthiest South American countries engaged in a vastly expensive naval arms race which was catalyzed by the introduction of a new warship type, the "dreadnought". At one point, the Argentine government was spending a fifth of its entire yearly budget for just two dreadnoughts, a price that did not include later in-service costs, which for the Brazilian dreadnoughts was sixty percent of the initial purchase.

The continent became a battlefield of the Cold War in the late 20th century. Some democratically elected governments of Argentina, Brazil, Chile, Uruguay, and Paraguay were overthrown or displaced by military dictatorships in the 1960s and 1970s. To curtail opposition, their governments detained tens of thousands of political prisoners, many of whom were tortured and/or killed on inter-state collaboration. Economically, they began a transition to neoliberal economic policies. They placed their own actions within the US Cold War doctrine of "National Security" against internal subversion. Throughout the 1980s and 1990s, Peru suffered from an internal conflict. South America, like many other continents, became a battlefield for the superpowers during the Cold War in the late 20th century. In the postwar period, the expansion of communism became the greatest political issue for both the United States and governments in the region. The start of the Cold War forced governments to choose between the United States and the Soviet Union.

Late 20th Century Military Régimes and Revolutions

By the 1970s, leftists had acquired a significant political influence which prompted the right-wing, ecclesiastical authorities and a large portion of each individual country's upper class to support coups d'état to avoid what they perceived as a communist threat. This was further fueled by Cuban and United States intervention which led to a political polarization. Most South American countries were in some periods ruled by military dictatorships that were supported by the United States of America.

Also around the 1970s, the régimes of the Southern Cone (Argentina, Chile and Uruguay) collaborated in Operation Condor killing many leftist dissidents, including some urban guerrillas. However, by the early 90's all countries had restored their democracies.

Colombia has had an ongoing, though diminished internal conflict, which started in 1964 with the creation of Marxist guerrillas (FARC-EP) and then involved several illegal armed groups of leftist-leaning ideology as well as the private armies of powerful drug lords. Many of these are now defunct, and only a small portion of the ELN remains, along with the stronger, though also greatly reduced FARC. These leftist groups smuggle narcotics out of Colombia to fund their operations, while also using kidnapping, bombings, land mines and assassinations as weapons against both elected and non-elected citizens.

Revolutionary movements and right-wing military dictatorships became common after World War II, but since the 1980s, a wave of democratisation came through the continent, and democratic rule is widespread now. Nonetheless, allegations of corruption are still very common, and several countries have developed crises which have forced the resignation of their governments, although, in most occasions, regular civilian succession has continued.

In the 1960s and 1970s, the governments of Argentina, Brazil, Chile, and Uruguay were overthrown or displaced by U.S.-aligned military dictatorships. These detained tens of thousands of political prisoners, many of whom were tortured and/or killed (on inter-state collaboration, i.e., Operation Condor). Economically, they began a transition to neoliberal economic policies. They placed their own actions within the U.S. Cold War doctrine of "National Security" against internal subversion. Throughout the 1980s and 1990s, Peru suffered from a prolonged internal conflict with the Túpac Amaru Revolutionary Movement and Shining Path gueurilla groups. Revolutionary movements and right-wing military dictatorships have been common, but starting in the 1980s a wave of democratization came through the continent, and democratic rule is now widespread. Allegations of corruption remain common, and several nations have seen crises which have forced the resignation of their presidents, although normal civilian succession has continued. International indebtedness became a recurrent problem, with examples like the 1980s debt crisis, the mid 1990s Mexican peso crisis and Argentina's 2001 default.

Washington Consensus

The set of specific economic policy prescriptions that were considered the "standard" reform package were promoted for crisis-wracked developing countries by Washington, DC-based institutions such as the International Monetary Fund (IMF), World Bank, and the US Treasury Department during the 1980s and '90s. The prescriptions encompassed policies for economic openings with respect to both trade and investment, and the expansion of market forces within the domestic economy in order to achieve macroeconomic stabilization.

The Cold War: A Synopsis of the Southern Hemisphere

- CUBA

  - 26th of July Movement topples Fulgencio Batista (denied arms by the Eisenhower administration for its excesses) in January 1959.

  - Castro denies that he is a communist. US intelligence/Eisenhower at first unsure if Castro is a communist.

  - Eisenhower administration plans invasion to land at City of Trinidad to topple Castro with help of CIA.

  - January 1961: Expropriation of land by Cuban government accelerated. Censorship implemented. Opponents and suspects are sent to firing squads in a reign of terror.

  - Eisenhower severs relations with the Cuban government.

  - April 1961, JFK mounted an unsuccessful invasion of the island. Changes invasion site to Playa Girón in the Bay of Pigs. JFK makes other substantial changes to invasion plans, including air cover, which guarantees failure. Changes made in the name of "plausible deniability".

  - Castro openly embracing Marxism-Leninism, and the Soviet Union pledged to provide support.

  - Kennedy continues covert ops: Cuban Project/Operation Mongoose (Operation Mongoose was a secret program of propaganda, psychological warfare, and sabotage against Cuba to remove the communists from power).

  - The USSR placed multiple nuclear missiles in Cuba, sparking heated tension with the Americans and leading to the Cuban Missile Crisis of 1962, where full-scale nuclear war is threatened. Outcome of negotiations kept secret to prevent public outrage in US. Cuba instrumental in subversive movements in the Americas and Africa.

- DOMINICAN REPUBLIC

- April 1965 Operation Power Pack: LBJ lands 22,000 troops in the DR for a one-year occupation citing the threat of the emergence of a Cuban-style revolution in Latin America via Juan Bosch.

- In 1966 DR elections, conservative Joaquín Balaguer wins. The PRD's activists were violently harassed by the Dominican police and armed forces.

- CHILE

  - 1970: Socialist Party candidate Salvador Allende (Popular Unity) narrowly wins election becoming the first democratically elected Marxist president in the Americas.

  - Allende heads coalition of leftists in 3 way race.

  - Ties w/Cuba, nationalization of industries and collectivization cause severe recession. Anti-Allende protest groups grow which are also funded by Nixon/CIA.

  - Chilean Supreme Court opposes Allende and the Chamber of Deputies; formally asks the military to restore rule of law on August 22, 1973.

  - On September 11, General Augusto Pinochet carries out coup and becomes dictator. Leftist opponents were killed or detained in internment camps under the Dirección de Inteligencia Nacional (DINA).

- OPERATION CONDOR

  - Implemented officially 1975: Employed by authoritarian governments in Argentina, Brazil, Bolivia, Chile, Uruguay, and Paraguay to terminate socialist/communist influence by leftist opposition movements through assassination and intelligence operations. Ecuador and Peru joining later in more peripheral roles

  - Many opposition groups, but not all, Soviet/Cuban supported

  - The US/CIA served in a supervisory capacity.

  - Manuel Contreras, chief of DINA (the Chilean secret police), in Santiago de Chile, officially created the Plan Condor

- Cooperation between hemispheric security services existed previously: Xth Conference of American Armies (Caracas, September 3, 1973), Brazilian General Breno Borges Fortes, proposed to "extend the exchange of information" between various services.

- Additionally in March 1974, representatives of the police forces of Chile, Uruguay and Bolivia met with Alberto Villar, deputy chief of the Argentine Federal Police and co-founder of the Triple A death squad, to implement cooperation guidelines in order to destroy the "subversive" threat represented by the presence of thousands of political exiles in Argentina.

- ARGENTINA

  - 1976-1983: the Dirty War (Guerra Sucia) a period of state-sponsored violence against left-wing activists, trade unionists, students, journalists, Marxists and Peronist guerrillas or sympathizers. Esp. the Montoneros (leftist Peronist group) and People's Revolutionary Army (ERP) guerillas.

  - Estimates of killed or "disappeared" 9,000 to 30,000. Carried out primarily by military dictatorship of Jorge Rafael Videla's (part of Operation Condor) until the return to civilian rule in 1983.

  - Origins of the Dirty War can be traced back to either the Bombing of Plaza de Mayo (1955), the Trelew massacre of 1972 (leftist prisoners executed in a faked prison escape), the Argentine Anticommunist Alliance (1973) and Isabel Martínez de Perón's "annihilation decrees" against leftist guerrillas during Operativo Independencia (1975).

- NICARAGUA

  - 1979: The Sandinista National Liberation Front (Frente Sandinista de Liberación Nacional, FSLN) ousts the dictatorship of Anastasio Somoza Debayle with help provided by Cuba clandestinely.

  - The FSLN governed from 1979 until 1990, and tried to remake Nicaragua along socialist lines.

  - The Sandinistas are opposed by the Contras, an umbrella of various anti-communist groups. g the July 1979 overthrow of dictatorship. The Nicaraguan Democratic Force (FDN) emerged as by far the largest of Contra groups

- All Contra groups are separate & possess different political aims US worked to maintain unity among the Contra groups.

- In June 1985 most of the groups reorganized as the United Nicaraguan Opposition (UNO), under the leadership of Adolfo Calero, Arturo Cruz and Alfonso Robelo, all originally supporters of the anti-Somoza revolution.

- 1987: Virtually all Contra organizations are united as the Nicaraguan Resistance. The Contras received both overt and covert financial and military support from the US/Reagan/CIA.

- US Congress wished to distance itself from the Contras and withdrew all overt support. Some rebels disliked the term "Contras", feeling that it implied a desire to restore the old order, and referred to themselves as commandos. Peasant sympathizers called the rebels "los primos" ("the cousins"). The revolution played a substantial role in foreign policy for Nicaragua, Central America and the Americas.

- The revolutionary conflict also marked one of the most important proxy wars in the Cold War.

- Mediation by other Central American governments under Costa Rican leadership led to the Sapoa Accord ceasefire of March 23, 1988, which, along with additional agreements in February and August 1989, provided for the Contras' disarmament and reintegration into Nicaraguan society and politics.

- February 25, 1990: internationally-monitored election. Violeta Chamorro, a former Sandinista ally who turned into a vocal opponent, and widow of murdered anti-Somoza journalist Pedro Joaquín Chamorro Cardenal, defeated Sandinista leader Daniel Ortega by a huge margin and became President with the backing of the center-right UNO.

- Some Contra elements and disgruntled Sandinistas would return briefly to armed opposition in the 1990s, but these groups were subsequently persuaded to disarm.

- JAMAICA

  - 1972: Jamaica began pursuing closer relations with the Cuban government as a result of Michael Manley's election (in a speech he said, "All anti-imperialists know that the balance of forces in the world shifted irrevocably in 1917 when there was a movement and a man in the October Revolution, and Lenin was the man."

- Manley saw Cuba and the Cuban model as having much to offer both Jamaica and the world.

- The United States' covert response included financing Manley's political opponents, the instigation of mutiny in the Jamaican army, and the fitting out of a private mercenary army against the Manley government.

- Violence ensued and grew in January 1976 in anticipation of elections.

- A State of Emergency was declared by Manley's party the PNP in June and 500 people, including some prominent members of the JLP, were detained, without charges, in a specially created prison at the Up-Park Camp military headquarters.

- Violence continued to blight political life in the 1970s. Gangs armed by both parties fought for control of urban constituencies.

- In the 1980 elections, Seaga's JLP won and he became Prime Minister.

- GUATEMALA

  - 1954: CIA-backed military coup ousted the left-wing President Jacobo Arbenz Guzmán. The new government, a military junta headed by Carlos Castillo Armas, returned nationalized American property, set up a National Committee of Defense Against Communism, and decreed a Preventive Penal Law Against Communism at the request of the United States.

- GUIANA

  - 1953: In British Guiana, the leftist People's Progressive Party (PPP) candidate Cheddi Jagan won the position of chief minister in a colonially-administered election, but was quickly forced to resign from power after Britain's suspension of the still-dependent nation's constitution.

- EL SALVADOR

- 1980-1992: A civil war fought primarily between the government and a coalition of four leftist groups and one communist group known as the Farabundo Martí National Liberation Front (FMLN).

- Subversive activity started when the guerrilla forces were small and did not have military training. This changed over time.

- Approximately 75,000 people were killed in the war.

- The Salvadoran Civil war was fought in the context of the global Cold War, with the United States backing the right wing military Salvadoran government. The United States is reputed to have poured some 5 billion dollars into the war.

- January 16, 1992: President Alfredo Cristiani and the guerrillas represented by the commanders of the five guerrilla groups such as Shafick Handal, Joaquin Villalobos, Salvador Sanchez Ceren, Francisco Jovel and Eduardo Sancho signed the Peace Agreements ending a 12-years civil war in the Chapultepec Castle in Mexico.

- PERU

  - 1980-1997: The Túpac Amaru Revolutionary Movement, a Marxist revolutionary group led by Víctor Polay Campos (comrade "Rolando") until his incarceration and by Néstor Cerpa Cartolini (comrade "Evaristo") until his death in 1997.

  - The MRTA took its name from the last indigenous leader of the Inca people.

  - The first action by the MRTA occurred on 31 May 1982, when its members robbed a bank in La Victoria, Lima.

  - Peru's counterterrorist program diminished the group's ability to carry out terrorist attacks, and the MRTA suffered from infighting as well as violent clashes with Maoist rival Shining Path.

  - In December 1996, fourteen MRTA members occupied the Japanese Ambassador's residence in Lima, holding 72 hostages for more than four months. Under orders from then-President Alberto Fujimori, armed forces stormed the residence in April 1997, rescuing all but one of the remaining hostages and killing all fourteen MRTA militants.

- Fujimori was publicly acclaimed for the decisive action, but the affair was later tainted by subsequent revelations that at least three, and perhaps as many as eight, of the MRTistas were summarily executed after surrendering.

- Shining Path (Sendero Luminoso in Spanish) is a Maoist insurgent guerrilla organization also in Peru. The Shining Path believed in imposing a dictatorship of the proletariat, inducing cultural revolution, and eventually sparking world revolution. It was widely condemned for its brutality against peasants, trade union organizers, popularly elected officials and the general civilian population.

- Since the capture of its leader Abimael Guzmán in 1992, the Shining Path has only been sporadically active. Some factions of Shining Path have reinvented themselves as cocaine-smugglers.

- COLOMBIA

  - The Revolutionary Armed Forces of Colombia-People's Army (Spanish: Fuerzas Armadas Revolucionarias de Colombia-Ejército del Pueblo), also known by the acronym of FARC or FARC-EP, is a Marxist-Leninist revolutionary guerrilla organization based in Colombia.

  - FARC-EP has proclaimed itself to be a revolutionary agrarian, anti-imperialist Marxist-Leninist organization represent the rural poor.

  - It funds itself principally through ransom kidnappings, taxation, and the illegal drug trade. FARC-EP remains the largest and oldest insurgent group in the Americas.

  - According to Colombian Armed Forces Commander Admiral Édgar Cely, FARC-EP had a total of 18,000 members in 2010, with an estimated 9,000 of those being armed combatants and the remaining 9,000 made up of plainclothes militia who provide intelligence or logistical support.

  - They have been weakened and retreated to mountainous regions since President Álvaro Uribe took office in 2002.

  - In 2011, Colombian President Juan Manuel Santos claimed FARC-EP may have less than 8,000 members.

- In 2007 FARC-EP Commander Raúl Reyes claimed that their force consisted of 18,000 guerrillas.

- The largest concentrations of FARC-EP guerrillas are believed to be located throughout the southeastern parts of Colombia's 193,000 square miles of jungle and in the plains at the base of the Andean mountains.

- Venezuelan President Hugo Chávez publicly rejected their classification as "terrorists" in January 2008, considering them to be "real armies", and called on the Colombian and other governments to recognize the guerrillas as a "belligerent force", arguing that this would then oblige them to renounce kidnappings and terror acts, and respect the Geneva Conventions.

THE GREAT DEPRESSION

In this March 6, 1930 file photo, demonstrators organized by the
Unemployed Council gather in front of the White House in Washington
before a major protest.

The Great Depression was the longest, deepest, and most pervasive depression in American history, lasted from 1929 to 1939. Its effects were felt in virtually all corners of the world, and it is one of the great economic calamities in history.

In previous depressions, such as those of the 1870s and 1890s, real per capita gross domestic product (GDP)—the sum of all goods and services produced, weighted by market prices and adjusted for inflation—had returned to its original level within five years. In the Great Depression, real per capita GDP was still below its 1929 level a decade later.

Economic activity began to decline in the summer of 1929, and by 1933 real GDP fell more than 25 percent, erasing all of the economic growth of the previous quarter century. Industrial production was especially hard hit, falling some 50 percent. By comparison, industrial production had fallen 7 percent in the 1870s and 13 percent in the 1890s.

From the depths of depression in 1933, the economy recovered until 1937. This expansion was followed by a brief but severe recession, and then another period of economic growth. It was not until the 1940s that previous levels of output were surpassed. This led some to wonder how long the depression would have continued without the advent of World War II.

In the absence of government statistics, scholars have had to estimate unemployment rates for the 1930s. The sharp drop in GDP and the anecdotal evidence of millions of people standing in soup lines or wandering the land as hoboes suggest that these rates were unusually high. It is widely accepted that the unemployment rate peaked above 25 percent in 1933 and remained above 14 percent into the 1940s. Yet these figures may underestimate the true hardship of the times: those who became too discouraged to seek work would not have been counted as unemployed. Likewise, those who moved from the cities to the countryside in order to feed their families would not have been counted. Even those who had jobs tended to see their hours of work fall: the average work week, 47 to 49 hours in the 1920s, fell to 41.7 hours in 1934 and stayed between 42 and 45 until 1942.

The banking system witnessed a number of "panics" during which depositors rushed to take their money out of banks rumored to be in trouble. Many banks failed under this pressure, while others were forced to merge: the number of banks in the United States fell 35 percent between 1929 and 1933.

While the Great Depression affected some sectors of the economy more than others, and thus some regions of the country more than others, all sectors and regions experienced a serious decline in output and a sharp rise in unemployment. The hardship of unemployment, though concentrated in the working class, affected millions in the middle class as well. Farmers suffered too, as the average price of their output fell by half (whereas the aggregate price level fell by only a third).

The Great Depression followed almost a decade of spectacular economic growth. Between 1921 and 1929, output per worker grew about 5.9 percent per year, roughly double the average in the twentieth century. Unemployment and inflation were both very low throughout this period as well. One troublesome characteristic of the 1920s, however, was that income distribution became significantly less equal. Also, a boom in housing construction, associated in part with an automobile-induced rush to the suburbs, collapsed in the late 1920s. And automakers themselves worried throughout the late 1920s that they had saturated their market fighting for market share; auto sales began to slide in the spring of 1929.

Technological advances in production processes (notably electrification, the assembly line, and continuous processing of homogenous goods such as chemicals) were largely responsible for the advances in productivity in the 1920s. These advances induced the vast bulk of firms to invest in new plants and equipment In the early 1920s, there were also innovative new products, such as radio, but the decade after 1925 was the worst in the twentieth century for new product innovation.

Causes of the Great Depression

In 1929 the standard economic theory suggested that a calamity such as the Great Depression could not happen: the economy possessed equilibrating mechanisms that would quickly move it toward full employment. For example, high levels of unemployment should put downward pressure on wages, thereby encouraging firms to increase employment. Before the Great Depression, most economists urged governments to concentrate on maintaining a balanced budget. Since tax receipts inevitably fell during a downturn, governments often increased tax rates and reduced spending. By taking money out of the economy, such policies tended to accelerate the downturn, though the effect was likely small.

As the depression continued, many economists [led by John Maynard Keyes] advised the federal government to increase spending, in order to provide employment. Economists also searched for theoretical justifications for such policies. Some thought the depression was caused by overproduction: consumers did not wish to consume all that was produced. These analysts often attributed overproduction to the increased disparity in income that developed in the 1920s, for the poor spend a greater percentage of their income than do the rich. Others worried about a drop in the number of profitable investment opportunities. Often, these arguments were couched in apocalyptic terms: the Great Depression was thought to be the final crisis of capitalism, a crisis that required major institutional restructuring. Others, notably Joseph Schumpeter, pointed the finger at technology and suggested that the Great Depression reflected the failure of entrepreneurs to bring forth new products. He felt the depression was only temporary and a recovery would eventually occur.

The stock market crash of 1929 and the bank panics of the early 1930s were dramatic events. Many commentators emphasized the effect these had in decreasing the spending power of those who lost money. Some went further and blamed the Federal Reserve System for allowing the money supply, and thus average prices, to decline.

John Maynard Keynes in 1936 put forward a theory arguing that the amount individuals desired to save might exceed the amount they wanted to invest. In such an event, they would necessarily consume less than was produced (since, if we ignore foreign trade, total income must be either consumed or saved, while total output is the sum of consumption goods and investment goods). Keynes was skeptical of the strength of equilibrating mechanisms and shocked many economists who clung to a faith in the ability of the market system to govern itself. Yet within a decade the profession had largely embraced his approach, in large part because it allowed them to analyze deficient consumption and investment demand without reference to a crisis of capitalism. Moreover, Keynes argued that, because a portion of income was used for taxes and output included government services, governments might be able to correct a situation of deficient demand by spending more than they tax.

In the early postwar period, Keynesian theory dominated economic thinking. Economists advised governments to spend more than they taxed during recessions and tax more than spend during expansions. Although governments were not always diligent in following this prescription, the limited severity of early postwar business cycles was seen as a vindication of Keynesian theory. Yet little attention was paid to the question of how well it could explain the Great Depression.

In 1963, Milton Friedman and Anna Schwartz proposed a different view of the depression. They argued that, contrary to Keynesian theory, the deflationary actions of the Federal Reserve were primarily at fault. In the ensuing decades, Keynesians and "monetarists" argued for the supremacy of their favored theory. The result was a recognition that both explanations had limitations. Keynesians struggled to comprehend why either consumption or investment demand would have fallen so precipitously as to trigger the depression (though saturation in the housing and automobile markets, among others, may have been important). Monetarists struggled to explain how smallish decreases in the money supply could trigger such a massive downturn, especially since the price level fell as fast as the supply of money, and thus real (inflation-adjusted) aggregate demand need not have fallen.

In the 1980s and 1990s, some economists argued that the actions of the Federal Reserve had caused banks to decrease their willingness to loan money, leading to a severe decrease in consumption and, especially, investment. Others argued that the Federal Reserve and central banks in other countries were constrained by the gold standard, under which the value of a particular currency is fixed to the price of gold.

Effects of the Great Depression

The psychological, cultural, and political repercussions of the Great Depression were felt around the world, but it had a significantly different impact in different countries. In particular, it is widely agreed that the rise of the Nazi Party in Germany and was associated with the economic turmoil of the 1930s. No similar threat emerged in the United States. While President Franklin Roosevelt did introduce a variety of new programs, he was initially elected on a traditional platform that pledged to balance the budget. Why did the depression cause less political change in the U.S. than elsewhere? A much longer experience with democracy may have been important. In addition, a faith in the "American dream," whereby anyone who worked hard could succeed, was apparently retained and limited the agitation for political change.

Effects on Individuals

Much of the unemployment experience of the depression can be accounted for by workers who moved in and out of periods of employment and unemployment that lasted for weeks or months. These individuals suffered financially, to be sure, but they were generally able to save, borrow, or beg enough to avoid the severest hardships. Their intermittent periods of employment helped to stave off a psychological sense of failure. Yet there were also numerous workers who were unemployed for years at a time. Among this group were those with the least skills or the poorest attitudes. Others found that having been unemployed for a long period of time made them less attractive to employers. Long-term unemployment appears to have been concentrated among people in their late teens and early twenties and those older than fifty-five. For many that came of age during the depression, World War II would provide their first experience of full-time employment.

With unemployment rates exceeding 25 percent, it was obvious that most of the unemployed were not responsible for their plight. Yet the ideal that success came to those who worked hard remained in place, and thus those who were unemployed generally felt a severe sense of failure. The incidence of mental health problems rose, as did problems of family violence. For both psychological and economic reasons, decisions to marry and to have children were delayed. Although the United States provided more relief to the unemployed than many other countries (including Canada), coverage was still spotty. In particular, recent immigrants to the United States were often denied relief. Severe malnutrition afflicted many, and the palpable fear of it, many more.

Effects by Gender and Race

Federal, state, and local governments, as well as many private firms, introduced explicit policies in the 1930s to favor men over women for jobs. Married women were often the first to be laid off. At a time of widespread unemployment, it was felt that jobs should be allocated only to male "breadwinners." Nevertheless, unemployment rates among women were lower than for men during the 1930s, in large part because the labor market was highly segmented by gender, and the service sector jobs in which women predominated were less affected by the depression. The female labor force participation rate—the proportion of women seeking or possessing paid work—had been rising for decades; the 1930s saw only a slight increase; thus, the depression acted to slow this societal change (which would greatly accelerate during World War II, and then again in the postwar period).

Many surveys found unemployment rates among blacks to be 30 to 50 percent higher than among whites. Discrimination was undoubtedly one factor: examples abound of black workers being laid off to make room for white workers. Yet another important factor was the preponderance of black workers in industries (such as automobiles) that experienced the greatest reductions in employment. And the migration of blacks to northern industrial centers during the 1920s may have left them especially prone to seniority-based layoffs.

Cultural Effects

One might expect the Great Depression to have induced great skepticism about the economic system and the cultural attitudes favoring hard work and consumption associated with it. As noted, the ideal of hard work was reinforced during the depression, and those who lived through it would place great value in work after the war. Those who experienced the depression were disposed to thrift, but they were also driven to value their consumption opportunities. Recall that through the 1930s it was commonly thought that one cause of the depression was that people did not wish to consume enough: an obvious response was to value consumption more.

The New Deal

The [New Deal's] nonmilitary spending of the federal government accounted for 1.5 percent of GDP in 1929 but 7.5 percent in 1939. Not only did the government take on new responsibilities, providing temporary relief and temporary public works employment, but it established an ongoing federal presence in social security (both pensions and unemployment insurance), welfare, financial regulation and deposit insurance, and a host of other areas. The size of the federal government would grow even more in the postwar period. Whether the size of government today is larger than it would have been without the depression is an open question. Some scholars argue for a "ratchet effect," whereby government expenditures increase during crises, but do not return to the original level thereafter. Others argue that the increase in government brought on by the depression would have eventually happened anyhow.

Some economists have suggested that public works programs exacerbated the unemployment experience of the depression. They argue that many of those on relief would have otherwise worked elsewhere. However, there were more workers seeking employment than there were job openings; thus, even if those on relief did find work elsewhere, they would likely be taking the jobs of other people.

The introduction of securities regulation in the 1930s has arguably done much to improve the efficiency, fairness, and thus stability of American stock markets. Enhanced bank supervision, and especially the introduction of deposit insurance from 1934, ended the scourge of bank panics: most depositors no longer had an incentive to rush to their bank at the first rumor of trouble. But deposit insurance was not an unmixed blessing; in the wake of the failure of hundreds of small savings and loan institutions decades later, many noted that deposit insurance allowed banks to engage in overly risky activities without being penalized by depositors. The Roosevelt administration also attempted to stem the decline in wages and prices by establishing "industry codes," whereby firms and unions in an industry agreed to maintain set prices and wages. Firms seized the opportunity to collude and agreed in many cases to restrict output in order to inflate prices; this particular element of the New Deal likely served to slow the recovery. Similar attempts to enhance agricultural prices were more successful, at least in the goal of raising farm incomes (but thus increased the cost of food to others).

International Effects

It was long argued that the Great Depression began in the United States and spread to the rest of the world. Many countries, including Canada and Germany, experienced similar levels of economic hardship. In the case of Europe, it was recognized that World War I and the treaties ending it (which required large reparation payments from those countries that started and lost the war) had created weaknesses in the European economy, especially in its financial system. Thus, despite the fact that trade and capital flows were much smaller than today, the American downturn could trigger downturns throughout Europe.

Many Third World countries were heavily dependent on exports and suffered economic contractions as these markets dried up. At the same time, they were hit by a decrease in foreign investment flows, especially from the United States, which was a reflection of the monetary contraction in the United States. Many Third World countries, especially in Latin America, responded by introducing high tariffs and striving to become self-sufficient. This may have helped them recover from the depression, but probably served to seriously slow economic growth in the postwar period.

Developed countries also introduced high tariffs during the 1930s. In the United States, the major one was the Smoot-Hawley Tariff of 1930, which arguably encouraged other countries to retaliate with tariffs of their own. Governments hoped that the money previously spent on imports would be spent locally and enhance employment. In return, however, countries lost access to foreign markets, and therefore employment in export-oriented sectors. The likely effect of the increase in tariffs was to decrease incomes around the world by reducing the efficiency of the global economy; the effect the tariffs had on employment is less clear.

BAY OF PIGS

The Bay of Pigs (Bahía de Cochinos) is a small bay on the southern coast of Cuba that was invaded on April 17, 1961 by approximately 1,500 Cuban [anti-communist] exiles organized and armed by the U.S. Central Intelligence Agency. The invasion was [initially] meant to appear to be an attempt by independent Cuban rebels to overthrow communist Cuban leader Fidel Castro, but became obviously known as an American project, and confirmed when President John F. Kennedy immediately admitted responsibility when the invasion failed. The Bay of Pigs, as the whole episode came to be known, was a major embarrassment for the U.S., which was caught deceiving the United Nations. One hundred and fourteen invaders and 157 Cuban soldiers were killed and 1,189 invaders were taken prisoner.

Fidel Castro became the leader of Cuba's government when his revolutionary forces overthrew the Batista régime in January, 1959. At first, Washington was not hostile to Castro. President Dwight D. Eisenhower recognized his government a few days after Batista's downfall, and Castro even traveled to Washington to meet with Vice President Richard Nixon (later President Nixon). Nixon decided that Castro could not be relied upon to pursue U.S. interests and began to agitate privately for his removal.

In October, 1959, Eisenhower approved a secret program to depose Castro proposed by the CIA and the State Department. Eisenhower told his advisors that "our hand should not show in anything that is done"—in other words, that the operation should be carried out in such a way that U.S. responsibility could be plausibly denied. To this end, the CIA gathered, funded, armed, and trained an anti-Castro rebel organization in Florida, the Panama Canal Zone, and Guatemala. The CIA began military training of 300 Cuban expatriates in March of 1960, and in May began broadcasting anti-Castro propaganda over the whole Caribbean from a station on a small, disputed territory named Swan Island. The programs were taped in Miami under CIA control, but claimed to be the voice of an authentic Cuban rebel movement without U.S. ties. In September, addressing the General Assembly of the United Nations, Castro accurately accused the U.S. of operating Radio Swan; the U.S. denied the charge.

In July, 1960, the Cuban fighters of "Brigade 2506"—named for the number of a brigade member killed in an accident—were transferred to a training camp in Guatemala built and run by the CIA.

On November 4, 1960, John Kennedy was elected president. Once in office, Kennedy gave his approval for the training of Brigade 2506 to continue. Like Eisenhower before him, however, Kennedy was adamant that U.S. armed forces should not take part in any effort to overthrow Castro. U.S. planners hoped that when news of the invasion reached the Cuban populace, an anti-Castro rebellion would arise and cast him out. At the very least, planners believed, the invaders could fight their way overland to the Escambray Mountains, about 100 miles west of the landing zone, and join rebel forces already fighting there. However, the Kennedy administration made important changes in the invasion plan which guaranteed it's failure, a landing in the remote Bay of Pigs area (surrounded by the Zapata Swamps) instead of the City of Trinidad, and especially in the cancellation of the 2nd and 3rd airstrikes by the invaders to eliminate Castro's air force.

On April 15, 1961, the first part of the invasion plan was carried out. Eight B-26 bombers supplied by the CIA bombed Cuban military aircraft on the ground at several locations. Later, a B-26 bearing Cuban markings and marked with bullet-holes landed at Miami International Airport. The pilots claimed to be defecting Cuban pilots, the goal being to make the raids on Cuba earlier that morning look like an internal action by defecting Cuban pilots. However, reporters on the scene noted that the plane's machine guns had not been fired and that the plane was not of the type actually used by Cuba. Castro, hearing the reports, commented that even Hollywood would not have tried to film such a feeble story. The goal of the bombings themselves was to destroy the Cuban government's small air force.

Two days later, on April 17, a landing was made at Playa Girón (Girón Beach) in the Bay of Pigs. A small beachhead was quickly achieved by Brigade 2506, but one of their freighter vessels, containing food, fuel, medical equipment, and a ten days' supply of ammunition, was quickly sunk. Combat was heavy around the beachhead as Cuban government forces responded to the attack. The remnants of the Cuban Air Force bombed and strafed the invading forces, as Brigade 2506 had not been supplied with fighter aircraft and President Kennedy categorically refused to allow U.S. fighters to go into combat.

The military situation deteriorated steadily (from the invaders' point of view) over the next 48 hours. On April 18, while the fighting was at its peak, Adlai Stevenson denied to the United Nations, in response to Cuban accusations, that the U.S. was attacking Cuba. Eventually, Kennedy was persuaded to authorize unmarked U.S. fighter jets from the aircraft carrier *Essex* to provide escort cover for the invasion's B-26 bombers, some of which were now being flown by CIA agents in support of the ground invasion. The jets from the *Essex* missed their rendezvous with the B-26s by an hour due to a misunderstanding about time zones; in the subsequent, unescorted bombing raid over Cuba, two B-26s were shot down and four Americans were killed. The fighting ended on April 20, 1961, with the defeat of Brigade 2506.

The project, some critics would later conclude, had been made hopeless from the beginning. Fidel Castro enacted mass arrests of anyone suspected of disloyalty to the régime prior to the invasion (even filling sports stadiums with thousands of the detained), preventing an uprising. Castro had just consolidated a military victory against the Batista régime; without air support, a few thousand invaders could not possibly have taken the island. Furthermore, the idea that the U.S. could keep its role secret had become ridiculous long before the invasion was attempted. The *New York Times* had run a story on March 17, 1961, predicting a U.S. invasion of Cuba in the coming weeks, and another story on April 7, entitled "Anti-Castro Units Trained to Fight at Florida Bases," which noted that invasion plans were in their final stages. Although the *Times* had watered down the latter story considerably at President Kennedy's personal request, when Kennedy saw the paper he exclaimed that Castro didn't need spies; all he had to do was read the news. But Castro, and others, did have spies, and the Soviet Union was fairly well-informed of U.S. invasion plans ahead of time.

The costs of the Bay of Pigs were high, and not only in lives lost. In the wake of the invasion, Castro totally consolidated his régime, eliminated all pretenses of not being a communist, and concluded a mutual-defense agreement with the Soviet Union. The Russians exploited this relationship to get Cuban permission to place ballistic-missile launch sites on Cuban soil. These launch sites, detected by U.S. aerial photography, were the immediate cause of the Cuban Missile Crisis of 1962, generally agreed to have been the closest approach to all-out nuclear war that the world has yet encountered. Furthermore, it allowed a communist foothold in the Americas, from which the Castro/Soviet alliance could foster guerrilla movements.

CUBAN MISSILE CRISIS

Perhaps no single event in the history of the Cold War presented as great a challenge to world peace and the continued existence of humankind as the thirteen days of the Cuban Missile Crisis in October 1962. The outcome of the crisis was been linked to the development of a direct Teletype "hotline" between Moscow and Washington, D.C., the initial stages of superpower détente, and the ratification of a bilateral atmospheric testing ban on nuclear weapons.

LEADING UP TO OCTOBER 1962

Despite the failed U.S. effort to overthrow Cuban communist dictator Fidel Castro during the Bay of Pigs invasion in April 1961, President John F. Kennedy continued to make Castro's removal a primary goal. In November 1961, Kennedy initiated Operation Mongoose, a covert operations plan designed to infiltrate anti-communist guerrilla groups into Cuba and incite dissident Cubans against Castro. Perhaps as a result, Castro, who enjoyed the Soviet Union's economic, political, and military backing, began receiving regular covert shipments of Soviet arms, ostensibly for "defensive" purposes only.

SOVIET NUCLEAR MISSILES IN CUBA

On October 14, 1962, a U2 spy plane, flying a routine Strategic Air Command mission over Cuba, snapped a series of photographs that became the first direct evidence of Soviet medium-range ballistic nuclear missiles in Cuba. These missiles clearly constituted an offensive weapons buildup on the island.

On the morning of October 16, National Security Adviser McGeorge Bundy presented a detailed analysis of the photographic evidence to Kennedy at an Oval Office briefing. Just before noon, Kennedy convened the first meeting of fourteen administration officials and advisers. The group became known as the Executive Committee of the National Security Council, or ExComm.

Time was of the essence. ExComm members received estimates that the Soviet missiles could be at full operation within fourteen days, with individual missiles readied within eighteen hours under a crash program. Most missiles were determined to be SS-4s, with a range of approximately 1,100 nautical miles (1,266 statute miles). This placed major American cities, including Dallas and Washington, D.C., within range of a strike. Later, photographic evidence concluded that several SS-5s, with a range of 2,200 nautical miles, were also included in the Soviet arms shipments.

For the next seven days, ExComm debated the merits of three general approaches to the developing crisis, all while keeping a tight public lid on the Cuban discovery. The first was a surgical airstrike targeting as many missile sites as possible. The second was an air strike followed by a U.S. military invasion of Cuba. The third was a blockade of Soviet ships thought to be carrying additional materials in support of the offensive weapons program.

In an attempt to allow diplomatic approaches an opportunity to work, Kennedy opted for the blockade, which was termed a "quarantine" so as to avoid warlike denotations. The term quarantine was appealing to the Kennedy administration because it implied the isolation and neutralizing of a problem from a public relations standpoint. Obviously, *there was no quarantine, since the missiles were already on the island.*

THE QUARANTINE

On October 22, in anticipation of a Cuban and/or Soviet reaction to the quarantine, the joint chiefs of staff placed U.S. military forces worldwide on DEFCON 3 alert. At five that afternoon, Kennedy met with seventeen congressional leaders from both major parties to discuss the situation. The president received some support for the quarantine, but notable exceptions included Senators J. William Fulbright and Richard B. Russell, both of whom believed that the strategy would not compel the Soviets to abandon their missiles.

By six that evening, Secretary of State Dean Rusk met with the Soviet ambassador to the United States, Anatoly Dobrynin, and presented the ambassador with an advanced copy of Kennedy's address. At seven, Kennedy addressed the American public in a seventeen-minute speech. His major objective, in addition to calling public attention to the Soviet missiles in Cuba, was to outline the U.S. response—the quarantine of all offensive military equipment under shipment to Cuba.

Soviet premier Nikita Khrushchev's reply to Kennedy's speech arrived on the morning of October 23. Premier Khrushchev's letter insisted that the Soviet missiles in Cuba were defensive in nature, and that the proposed U.S. response constituted a grave threat to world peace.

Kennedy was concerned that the German capital of Berlin, which was divided into segments of East and West at the end of World War II, would become a focal point for Soviet retaliation. As such, he directed the Central Intelligence Agency (CIA) to develop plans for protecting Berlin in the event the Soviets mounted a quarantine around the city.

By the evening of October 23, Kennedy and ExComm had new worries much closer to home. Earlier in the day, the CIA began tracking several Soviet submarines unexpectedly moving toward Cuba. This made the Navy's job of conducting the quarantine more complicated, as it now had to track the changing position of the Soviet subs in order to ensure the safety of its own vessels.

The quarantine, which received the unanimous backing of the Organization of American States (OAS) went into effect at 10:00 a.m. on October 24.

Early morning intelligence on that day suggested that sixteen of the nineteen Soviet cargo ships identified as Cuban bound were reversing course. The remaining three, however, were nearing the quarantine line, including the *Gagarin* and *Komiles*. Naval intelligence reported that one of the Soviet subs had taken a position between the two ships. Kennedy, though wishing to avoid conflict with the sub, authorized the aircraft carrier USS *Essex* to take whatever defensive measures were necessary against the submarine. This was perhaps the most dangerous moment of the cold war, as both superpowers were armed and mere moments from turning the war hot. Just prior to any armed hostilities, however, both Soviet ships stopped dead in the water, and eventually reversed course.

Realizing that a diplomatic resolution to the crisis was imperative, Kennedy and senior ExComm advisers began to consider offering the Soviets a missile trade. Specifically, if Khrushchev pulled his missiles out of Cuba, the United States would dismantle and remove its Jupiter missiles in Turkey and northern Italy (to prevent an electoral backlash, this action was kept secret for the next 10 years). *Kennedy also promised never to invade Cuba.*

RAISING THE STAKES

October 25 found the U.S. ambassador to the United Nations, Stevenson, publicly confronting the Soviet ambassador, Valerian Zorin, in front of the United Nations Security Council. The Soviet Union had, until this date, denied that offensive Soviet missiles were in Cuba. At this point, Stevenson showed the council, and the world, several reconnaissance photographs of the Cuban missiles.

This triumph was short-lived. By five that evening, CIA director John McCone reported to ExComm that some of the Cuban missiles were now operational.

By the morning of October 26, Kennedy was convinced that only an invasion of Cuba could succeed in removing the missiles. ExComm initiated preliminary civil defense measures for the American Southeast, while the State Department began to devise plans for establishing a new civil government in the wake of Castro's deposing. By that afternoon, the U.S. military was poised to conduct a land invasion. Secretary of Defense Robert McNamara advised Kennedy to expect heavy American casualties in the campaign.

At six that evening, the State Department received a letter from Khruschev proposing that the U.S. declare it would not invade Cuba in exchange for the Soviets dismantling the missiles. Later that evening, Attorney General Robert F. Kennedy, the president's closest adviser and brother, held another in a series of private meetings with Dobrynin. It was at this meeting that Kennedy, with the president's approval, began to specifically discuss the option of a Turkey-for-Cuba missile trade.

Any positive momentum from this meeting stalled on the morning of October 27. A second letter from Khrushchev arrived at the State Department around eleven. This letter replaced the non-invasion pledge with the requirement of a complete removal of U.S. missiles in Turkey. This raised the stakes for the Kennedy administration, as any public agreement on the Jupiter missiles would appear as a quid pro quo, with the U.S. forced to develop its security and foreign policies under severe threat.

The situation deteriorated even further when a U2, piloted by Major Rudolf Anderson, was shot down over Cuba around noon. Sensing that he was losing control of the crisis, Kennedy decided not to retaliate against the anti-aircraft site that fired on Anderson, much to the consternation of his military leaders.

At an ExComm meeting later that evening, the idea of responding only to the offer in Khrushchev's first letter—the non-invasion pledge—while ignoring the terms of the second letter, was debated. President Kennedy eventually came to adopt the proposal. Robert Kennedy was sent to discuss the terms with Dobrynin, which included an agreement not to publicly disclose the Turkey-for-Cuba missile trade, so as to avoid the appearance of a quid pro quo.

MAXIMUM DANGER AVERTED

President Kennedy, while hopeful that a deal would be reached, activated twenty-four Air Force units in preparation for a Cuban invasion to occur no later than October 29.

A CIA update in the early morning of October 28 claimed that all MRBM sites in Cuba were now operational. At nine that morning, Radio Moscow broadcast Khrushchev's reply to the terms outlined to Dobrynin the night before. In it, Khrushchev stated that all Soviet missiles in Cuba would be dismantled and crated. No public mention of the missile trade deal was made. The Cuban Missile Crisis was over, and a world war with nuclear weapons had most likely been averted.

Many historians generally view President Kennedy's performance in the crisis as exemplary. However, some scholars have criticized Kennedy's interpretation of the threat posed by the Cuban missiles as an under-reaction not warranted by a sober assessment of Soviet intentions and strategic goals. In promising to never invade Cuba, Kennedy accepted a Soviet outpost in the Americas that would promote communist insurgencies. Others argue that the Soviets politically outmaneuvered the Americans by reducing the number of U.S. missiles confronting them in Turkey and Europe. Still others point out that had Kennedy assured the success of the Bay of Pigs invasion, the Castro-communists would have been overthrown and no missile crisis would have occurred.

THE CIVIL RIGHTS MOVEMENT

The civil rights movement is essentially a movement of social reform. Such movements begin when a large group of people, feeling frustrated and unhappy with some aspects of society, join together to create change. A number of social reform movements greatly altered American society during the twentieth century. In particular, the civl rights movement achieved dramatic and significant gains. It not only changed the way African Americans live, but also affected the thoughts and beliefs of mainstream white America. It prompted many citizens to demand that the government live up to its principles, uphold standards of fairness, and provide equal protection to all.

The main civil rights movement in America took place throughout the 1950s and 1960s. It involved displays of extraordinary courage and determination on the part of the movement's leaders and millions of activists. For opponents of equal rights for African Americans, the civil rights movement brought on intense feelings of fear, resentment, and rage. This often led to acts of hostility and outright violence. On many occasions, civil rights activists placed themselves in the midst of heated confrontations. They risked their jobs, their homes, and their personal safety to fight for justice. The conflicts of that era were played out on the streets and in the schools, in courthouses, and in the halls of government, both state and federal. Victories were achieved with great difficulty, and the setbacks and obstacles were numerous.

However, progress was made slowly and a nation was changed. The civil rights movement helped improve African Americans' access to education and jobs. It also safeguarded voting rights and provided equal protection under the law. The struggle against racism (the belief that race determines traits and abilities, and the discrimination based on race) continues today. Yet the victories of the civil rights movement provided the framework for ongoing progress.

Civil rights are basic rights guaranteed by the U.S. Constitution (the laws and principles of the nation) to all citizens. These freedoms include the right to have a fair trial, to vote, and to choose where to live and where to go to school. When historians discuss the civil rights movement, they note its origins in the Thirteenth, Fourteenth, and Fifteenth Amendments to the U.S. Constitution. The Thirteenth Amendment, which was ratified, or formally approved, in 1865, abolished slavery. The Fourteenth Amendment, ratified in 1868, states that any person born in the United States—or any person naturalized, or admitted to citizenship—is a citizen. All citizens, as written in the Fourteenth Amendment, are guaranteed "the equal protection of the laws."

Essential Terms

- Civil disobedience: The purposeful and usually peaceful violation of laws or rules that are considered unfair or morally wrong.

- Civil rights: Personal rights guaranteed by law to all citizens.

- Desegregation: To eliminate laws or conditions that create or force segregation.

- Integration: The mixing together of racial, cultural, or religious groups that had been formerly separated.

- Jim Crow: A set of laws, customs, and regulations in the American South that separated blacks from whites to ensure that blacks were kept on a lower social footing. "Jim Crow" also describes the time period during which such laws were common, from the Reconstruction Era (1865–77) until the mid-1960s.

- Nonviolence: The deliberate avoidance of violence during demonstrations or protests designed to change a law or custom.

- Racist: A person who discriminates or is prejudiced against a group due to the group's race. Racism is based on the notion that one race is naturally superior to another based on genetic makeup.

- Reconstruction Era: A period from 1865 to 1877 of rebuilding after the American Civil War (1861–65) when the southern states were re-admitted to the Union and former slaves were briefly granted basic civil rights.

- Segregation: The separation of groups based on racial or cultural differences.

- Sit-in: A nonviolent form of protest popular during the civil rights movement that involved activists occupying seats in a segregated establishment, like a restaurant, and refusing to leave until they were served.

- In addition, no one can be deprived of "life, liberty, or property" without due process, which means a strict upholding of the rules of a legal proceeding, like a trial. Ratified in 1870, the Fifteenth Amendment states that all U.S. citizens have the right to vote, regardless of race. The Fifteenth Amendment granted voting rights to African Americans, but it applied only to men.

Many historians mark the beginning of the civil rights movement with the landmark 1954 Supreme Court case *Brown v. Board of Education of Topeka, Kansas*. This ruling outlawed segregation in schools. The end of the movement, although difficult to pinpoint exactly, is thought by many to be during the summer of 1965. During that summer, the last significant civil rights law of that era, the Voting Rights Act of 1965, was passed. Also, several of the major organizations behind the civil rights movement began to splinter, weakening the movement. The battle for equality and freedom did not suddenly end during the summer of 1965, and in fact it continues today. Similarly, the American civil rights movement did not suddenly begin with a single court case in 1954. It had been building momentum for decades.

Slavery and Reconstruction

In the early history of America, most Africans came to the country not by choice but rather in chains. They arrived on slave ships beginning in the 1600s. Slavery thrived in the United States for more than two hundred years. The practice of owning and selling slaves was gradually outlawed in northern states. However, it remained legal in the South until the Thirteenth Amendment banned the practice in 1865. Slavery, an explosive issue between the northern and southern states, was one of the major causes of the American Civil War (1861–65). At the end of the Civil War, President Abraham Lincoln (1809–1865; served 1861–65) began a program known as Reconstruction. This program was a plan to reunite a divided nation and help the South cope with its postwar status. But Lincoln never saw this plan take shape as he was assassinated just days after the war ended. His successor, Andrew Johnson (1808–1875; served 1865–69), continued with the Reconstruction.

During the post-Civil War period, the U.S. Congress was controlled by Republican Party lawmakers. These politicians helped pass constitutional amendments and civil rights laws that outlined and protected the rights of the newly freed slaves. The Fourteenth Amendment, which gave blacks the rights of citizenship and legal protection, and the Fifteenth Amendment, which gave all citizens the right to vote, became the basis for Civil Rights Acts in 1866, 1871, and 1875. These laws attempted to protect African Americans from racially motivated discrimination and violence. Many black men voted for the first time during this period. However, women of all races were prevented from voting nationally until 1920. As a result of the new voting power, a number of black politicians were elected to local, state, and even some national offices.

Despite the legal protections offered to blacks, their daily lives continued to be marked by brutality and restrictions. After the slaves were freed, many southerners were afraid the free blacks would rise up in a violent rebellion against their former masters. In addition, southern landowners were concerned that they would no longer have laborers to work their fields. In response to these fears, many southern states, controlled by the Democrat Party, passed Black Codes. These rules placed severe limitations on the liberty of black citizens and imposed harsh penalties for criminal acts committed by blacks. The Black Codes were designed to keep blacks fearful of whites and constantly aware of their status as second-class citizens.

Blacks' fears were further heightened by random and brutal attacks by gangs of white southern men. These groups, including the Ku Klux Klan (KKK) and several others, terrorized black citizens. African Americans were subjected to kidnappings, beatings, fires being set to destroy their homes, and in some cases murder. Such murders, also known as lynchings, often involved hanging the victim from a tree and leaving his/her body in a public place to serve as a warning to other blacks.

The few freedoms granted to blacks following the Civil War faded away with the end of Reconstruction. The conclusion of the Reconstruction Era occurred after an 1877 political compromise between northern and southern lawmakers. Following Reconstruction, the federal government's role as protector of African American civil rights ended for many decades.

Supreme Court Reversals and Jim Crow laws

The legal protections offered by the civil rights laws and constitutional amendments crafted after the Civil War were weakened in the South. Widespread opposition had formed on the part of ordinary citizens, state and local lawmakers, and even the U.S. Supreme Court. Although the Civil Rights Act of 1875 was supposed to guarantee black citizens equal access to public places like hotels, theaters, and trains, many whites simply refused to comply. Blacks were routinely turned away from inns or forced to sit in black-only train compartments. In 1883 the U.S. Supreme Court allowed such refusals to be legal when it overturned part of the 1875 law, ruling that it was unconstitutional.

The Civil Rights Act of 1875 had been based on the rights guaranteed by the recently drafted Fourteenth Amendment. This amendment offered citizenship and equal protection under the law to all citizens, regardless of race. The U.S. Supreme Court argued that the Fourteenth Amendment prohibited discrimination by the government and its officials. The court decided, however, that private companies or citizens who owned businesses used by the public could do as they wished.

A few years later, with the landmark *Plessy v. Ferguson* case, the U.S. Supreme Court issued another ruling supporting racial discrimination. This 1896 decision supported a Louisiana law that mandated separate railway cars for black and white passengers. The court ruled that the law was not discriminatory. The judges stated that the law allowed all passengers access to the railway cars, but in separate facilities. The *Plessy v. Ferguson* case gave rise to the expression "separate but equal." It became the basis for widespread legal discrimination throughout the South for many decades to come. The separate but equal ruling offered a way out for governments wishing to adhere to the Constitution but wanting to continue segregation, or separation of the races. In reality, facilities for blacks, whether in railway cars, schools, or hospitals, were far from equal to those for whites.

Decisions like that of *Plessy v. Ferguson* allowed state and local governments in the South to make numerous laws that restricted or denied blacks access to places like beaches and parks. Known as Jim Crow laws, these regulations provided for strict separation of the races. Blacks had to use separate bathrooms and water fountains. They were sent to separate schools. Many restaurants and hotels barred African Americans completely, while hospitals treated black patients in segregated areas. Even in death, the races could not mix. Blacks could only be buried in all-black cemeteries. Everywhere they turned, African Americans received the message that they were not just separate, but somehow lower class. The Jim Crow laws remained in place for decades, until they were overturned by civil rights laws in the 1960s.

Voting Restrictions

One of the most significant ways southern states prevented black citizens from achieving equality was to reduce their political power. Technically, the Fifteenth Amendment guaranteed all citizens the right to vote.

However, the governments of southern states, predominantly run by the Democrat Party, became skilled at drafting laws that lessened that right for African Americans. One such law, the poll tax, effectively denied many black voters the ability to cast their ballots. The poll tax required voters to pay a fee to vote. Most black southerners, barred from finding quality jobs, were extremely poor and could not afford to pay a poll tax. Some states started residency requirements, demanding that voters live in one place for two years prior to an election in order to vote. African Americans generally did not own homes and moved around frequently, preventing them from meeting residency requirements.

The Origins of "Jim Crow"

The phrase "Jim Crow" was commonly used to describe the system of racial discrimination and segregation in the American South during the nineteenth and twentieth centuries. It had its origins in an 1820s minstrel show. Minstrel shows were popular song-and-dance routines featuring white performers dressed up as exaggerated stereotypes of black people. The shows, considered extremely racist and insulting today, serve as an indication of just how widespread racial prejudice was toward African Americans during that era. Minstrel performers blackened their faces, a practice known as blackface. They also dressed in sloppy, clownish clothes. They performed silly dances, told jokes, and sang songs designed to comically illustrate the unfair stereotype of blacks as lazy, ignorant, and foolish.

In the 1820s, a white actor named Thomas Dartmouth Rice wrote a minstrel routine featuring a song called "Jump Jim Crow." The popularity of the song led to the common usage of the term "Jim Crow" to refer to a black person in a negative way. Over time, the phrase evolved to refer specifically to the separation of the white and black races, or segregation. By the early 1900s, Jim Crow systems, in the form of laws and social customs, were established throughout the South. Blacks were separated from whites in their housing, jobs, schools, and hospitals. The Jim Crow laws were designed to keep black citizens "in their place," humiliated and defeated.

Most southern blacks were illiterate, or unable to read. Some states in the South required voters to pass a literacy test, an impossibility for many blacks. Literacy tests often required voters to read and explain the meaning of a complicated document, such as the state constitution. Many southern whites would have had difficulty with the literacy test as well, but most were able to get around that requirement through a 'grandfather clause. ' This clause stated that a voter did not have to pass the literacy test if he was the descendant of someone who had been able to vote prior to the passage of the Fifteenth Amendment. All such descendants were white, since blacks could not vote prior to that amendment's passage.

In some southern states, black votes were made meaningless by a policy known as the white primary. A primary is an election that determines the candidate of a political party who will later run in the general election. The Democrats had overwhelming power in the South. This meant that the winner of the Democratic primary was virtually guaranteed to win the general election. By 1915 every southern state had instituted the white primary, excluding blacks from voting in the primary elections. Once the white voters had chosen their Democratic candidate in the primary, it wouldn't matter which person black citizens voted for in the general election because whites outnumbered blacks. The Democrat was sure to win.

In addition to poll taxes, literacy tests, and white primaries, many southern whites relied on violence and intimidation to prevent black voters from having a voice in politics. Black citizens who tried to register to vote faced the threat of being fired from their jobs, being beaten by angry mobs, or having their homes set on fire. Some were even threatened with the prospect of being lynched.

In his book *The Civil Rights Movement*, John M. Dunn points out that the combined impact of these tactics effectively erased black political power. In Louisiana alone, the number of black voters went from 130,334 to just 1,342 between 1896 and 1904. With most blacks prevented from voting, it didn't take long for the few African Americans who had been elected to local or national office to be voted out. The modest gains of the Reconstruction Era had been completely reversed.

The Beginnings of a Movement

The decades following the end of Reconstruction in the South were marked by poverty, humiliation, and violence for African Americans. Many former slaves continued working as farm laborers in a system known as sharecropping. White landowners allowed black laborers to farm a portion of their land and share in the profits made from selling the crop. The sharecroppers borrowed money from the landowners for seed and living expenses. This system, often corrupt, kept many black workers in constant debt to the landowners. The sharecroppers could never repay their debts after receiving their portion of the crop's profits. Thus, they began each new planting season in debt to the landowners and were continually unable to pay off that debt. The law said that they had been freed from slavery, but their daily lives had changed little since the Civil War ended.

Southern blacks also lived with constant reminders that the larger society considered them inferior and even unclean. Blacks could not drink from the same water fountains as whites, nor could they sit near whites on trains or boats. In addition to these daily assaults on their self-esteem, African Americans in the South also faced the threat of physical violence. Black people, particularly men, were expected to behave in a certain way around white people. They were to address whites as "sir" or "ma'am," keep their eyes lowered, and generally act in a submissive, or obedient, way. Any violations of this unwritten code of conduct could result in a scolding at best, a beating, or even murder at worst.

Angry white mobs terrorized black communities. They usually attacked at night, under the cover of darkness. They took victims from their homes and then beat and tortured them. Many such victims were hung from tree branches, a crime known as lynching. A common excuse given for a lynching was that the black man had raped or otherwise assaulted a white woman. However, few of these supposed offenses were ever officially reported to the police. Other excuses for lynchings included lesser "crimes," such as speaking to a white woman or showing disrespect to a white person. Regardless of the imagined or real offenses committed by the victims of lynchings, the white gangs that conducted these murders were acting outside of the law. They were rarely, however, brought to trial. Lynchings usually went completely unpunished. Between 1889 and 1918, more than three thousand people, most of them black, were killed by lynching.

The Emancipation Proclamation, President Abraham Lincoln's declaration on January 1, 1863, that all slaves shall be free, had held great promise for African Americans. But the reality of post-Civil War life in America was very disappointing. The hope of someday achieving equality among the races still burned brightly for many, however. Significant civil rights organizations took shape in the late nineteenth and early twentieth centuries. The Afro-American Council (AAC) is considered the first civil rights organization in the United States. Founded by black journalist T. Thomas Fortune (1856–1928) in 1898 in New York City, the AAC focused primarily on the issue of racially motivated violence. The organization lasted only a few years, but it gained attention and historical importance, in part, for its Anti-Lynching Bureau. The head of this bureau, a black journalist named Ida B. Wells-Barnett (1862–1931), investigated and reported on the problem of lynchings at great personal risk.

Booker T. Washington

Early civil rights activists differed in their goals and in their means of accomplishing them. One of the most influential and controversial civil rights leaders of that era was Booker T. Washington (1856–1915). Washington suggested that acceptance and cooperation on the part of blacks would be the most effective path to improving their condition. Washington was a former slave and the founder of the Tuskegee Normal and Industrial Institute (also known simply as the Tuskegee Institute) in Alabama. The institute trained black students to be teachers and schooled them in farming methods or in a trade such as carpentry or plumbing. Washington believed that the first goal for African Americans should be receiving a moral and practical education that would help them become part of the American economy. Only then, he felt, would they have any hope of achieving social equality.

In 1895 Washington gave a famous speech, known as the Atlanta Compromise. Speaking at the white-organized Cotton States and International Exposition in Atlanta, Georgia, Washington urged white people to offer blacks economic opportunities. He suggested they donate money to black schools and make jobs available to trained black workers. He also suggested that black people give up their hopes for social and political equality, for the time being. Washington's recommendations met with approval by most whites. They agreed with the suggestion that black people accept their second-class status. Some blacks agreed with Washington's views, believing that any progress, even if it just meant better education and job training, would improve their lives. Washington did earn the financial support of a number of wealthy northerners, enabling many poor students to attend the institute. And he quietly worked behind the scenes to make changes to the laws that so restricted African Americans' lives.

W. E. B. Du Bois and the Niagara Movement

Many prominent black citizens felt strongly that Washington did great harm to the cause of black equality by publicly urging blacks to give in to the wishes of the white majority and to passively accept their situation. John Hope (1868–1936), an African American and later the president of Atlanta University, responded angrily. As quoted in Sanford Wexler's *The Civil Rights Movement:* "If we are not striving for equality, in heaven's name for what are we living?"

One of the best-known critics of Washington's policies was William Edward Burghardt Du Bois (pronounced due-BOYZ; 1868–1963), better known as W. E. B. Du Bois. A professor and writer, Du Bois was the first black person to earn a Ph.D. from Harvard University in Cambridge, Massachusetts. He objected to Washington's suggestion that black people accept their fate.

In his landmark 1903 collection of essays, *The Souls of Black Folk*, Du Bois argued that "Negroes must insist continually, in season and out of season, that voting is necessary to modern manhood, that color discrimination is barbarism [backwards and primitive], and that black boys need education as well as white boys." (Du Bois left it to later activists to defend the importance of girls having the right to vote and be educated.) He also pointed out a flaw in Washington's reasoning. He contended that even the smallest goals of Washington's compromise, simply economic progress, could not be met without political equality and access to higher education.

During the summer of 1905, Du Bois arranged a meeting with twenty-eight other black leaders at Niagara Falls, in Ontario, Canada. The purpose of this secret meeting was to forge a plan for working toward complete civil rights and the end of racial discrimination. Known as the Niagara Movement, this organization marked the beginning of the modern civil rights movement. The Niagara Movement soon began recruiting members, setting up chapters throughout the United States. The organization struggled financially, however, and only lasted about five years.

However, several key members of the Niagara Movement, including Du Bois and Wells-Barnett, joined together with black ministers and a group of whites sympathetic to the African American cause to form the National Negro Committee in 1909. The following year, that organization changed its name to the National Association for the Advancement of Colored People, or NAACP. This institution continues to have a prominent role in the ongoing struggle for civil rights today.

The Civil Rights Movement Grows

In the early decades of the twentieth century, the NAACP and other civilrights organizations worked to achieve gains for African Americans primarily through legal challenges. One of the first goals of the NAACP was to lobby Congress for the passage of federal antilynching laws. This legislation to make lynching a federal crime was supported by many in Congress. However, a number of southern lawmakers prevented the bills from passing.

A number of court cases from that period met with greater success. In 1915 the U.S. Supreme Court struck down the grandfather clause that allowed many southern states to limit the voting rights of African Americans. The grandfather clause forced black citizens to pass a difficult literacy test in order to vote, while white voters could register as their grandfathers had done—without passing any such test. Two years later, in 1917, the U.S. Supreme Court declared unconstitutional any city ordinances that dictated where blacks could live. In 1923 the court overturned a murder conviction against a black man, saying his trial had been unfair because none of the jurors were black. One aspect of a fair trial involves being tried by a jury of one's peers, meaning people of similar social standing. The U.S. Supreme Court decided that a black man facing an all-white jury would be less likely to meet with justice than if some of the jurors had been black.

World War I and its Aftermath

When the United States entered World War I (1914–18) in 1917, many African Americans enlisted in the military. Despite the fact that they were placed in segregated units and assigned menial, or low-skill tasks that no one else wanted, more than 360,000 black American soldiers served during the war. They risked their lives fighting to ensure freedom and democracy abroad, only to return home to a nation that continued to deny them opportunities.

Returning black soldiers expected fellow citizens to be grateful to them for their service. Instead, these veterans were treated the same way they had been before the war: as inferior, and even dangerous, citizens. Some whites feared that black soldiers, having experienced the importance and power associated with being a soldier during wartime, would rebel against their low social status at home. White citizens' fear, along with the raised expectations of the black soldiers, increased tensions between the two races.

One source of conflict between blacks and whites involved job opportunities. During the pre-World War I military buildup, jobs in northern defense industries had been plentiful, and many southern blacks moved north in search of work. After the war, when American soldiers returned home and the defense industries were no longer flourishing, competition for jobs increased. Many blacks were forced out of their jobs, a situation that only worsened the problems of poverty and overcrowding in northern cities. In many U.S. cities, north and south, hostility between the races continued to grow in the years following World War I. Lynchings and other violent crimes against African Americans rose. In 1919, in some twenty-five cities all across the country, blacks responded to violence with violence. Riots erupted in cities like Chicago, Illinois; Washington, D.C.; and Tulsa, Oklahoma.

During the 1920s, black citizens, particularly in the North, did find some reasons to celebrate. Blacks in the North were free to vote. They exercised that right, resulting in increasing political power. In 1928 Oscar De Priest became the first black U.S. congressman of the twentieth century. He represented a district in Chicago and served three terms. The 1920s also brought a period of extraordinary accomplishment among African American artists and writers. It was a time known as the Harlem Renaissance. African Americans were encouraged to celebrate their heritage, a welcome change from past pressures to accept second-class status in white society.

The Great Depression and the New Deal

The end of the 1920s marked the beginning of a period of terrible hardship for many Americans as well as much of the industrialized world. With the stock market crash of October 29, 1929, the Great Depression began. Many Americans were plunged into poverty, losing their jobs and sometimes their homes. Unemployment rates were high, with as many as 25 percent of Americans out of work. For blacks, the consequences of the Depression were even more severe. As many as 50 percent of black laborers could not find work.

With the election of President Franklin Delano Roosevelt (1882–1945; served 1933–45) in 1932 came some promise of aid. Roosevelt spearheaded an aggressive plan of economic recovery and relief for the poor. He called his program the New Deal. The Roosevelt administration launched dozens of programs in an attempt to stabilize the U.S. economy, get as many people as possible back to work, and provide some government support for those hit hardest by the Depression. With his New Deal programs and strong leadership at a time of crisis, Roosevelt earned widespread admiration.

Roosevelt was popular with African Americans in part because he organized an unofficial advisory committee known as the Black Cabinet. Unlike his official Cabinet, a group of presidential advisers including the Secretary of State and Secretary of Defense, the members of the Black Cabinet were not actually part of the executive branch of the government. Many were community leaders and some held important roles in various New Deal agencies. Roosevelt consulted with the Black Cabinet periodically on issues significant to the African American community.

Eleanor Roosevelt (1884–1962), the president's wife, also earned the respect of African Americans for her dedication to civil rights. In 1939 opera singer Marian Anderson was invited by the Daughters of the American Revolution (DAR), a patriotic women's organization, to perform at Constitution Hall in Washington, D.C. When the DAR realized that Anderson was black, they canceled the performance. Furious with this act of racial discrimination, Eleanor Roosevelt ended her membership in the DAR. She later staged a free outdoor concert on the steps of the Lincoln Memorial at which Anderson performed for an audience of seventy-five thousand people. Their admiration for the Roosevelts prompted many black voters to change their political loyalty from the Republican Party, the party of Abraham Lincoln, the president who had freed the slaves, to the Democratic Party.

Court Victories Chip Away at School Segregation

In the mid-1930s, just as it had done twenty years earlier, the NAACP achieved some measure of racial justice through the nation's court system. Led by the organization's chief legal counsel, Charles Houston (1895–1950), the NAACP launched a campaign to end school segregation. Houston's ultimate goal was to end segregation for black students of all ages. He chose to begin this effort by addressing inequalities at the graduate-school level. He felt that the integration of graduate schools would be less threatening to whites than the integration of elementary schools. In addition, he believed that the inequality was far more obvious at the graduate-school level.

For school-age black children in the South, all-black schools, though inferior to the all-white schools, were always provided. Many black students wishing to pursue graduate studies, however, had no options. They were not admitted to the all-white programs, and in many states there were no black graduate schools. Houston felt this circumstance obviously violated the "separate but equal" principle established by *Plessy v. Ferguson*.

Houston enlisted the help of a talented young lawyer named Thurgood Marshall (1908–1993), a man who later became the first African American U.S. Supreme Court justice. In 1935 Houston and Marshall took on the case of Donald Gaines Murray, a black man who had been denied admission to the all-white law school at the University of Maryland. The lawyers argued that the university must admit Murray to the white law school because the state offered no black law school as an alternative. The Baltimore city court agreed, ordering the University of Maryland to admit Murray to its law school.

Charles Houston Leads the Charge

Other civil rights activists may be better known than Charles Houston. Yet his years of behind-the-scenes work to end school desegregation laid the groundwork for the landmark U.S. Supreme Court ruling *Brown v. Board of Education*, which declared school segregation unconstitutional.

Charles Hamilton Houston was born on September 3, 1895, the only child of William and Mary Houston. He grew up in Washington, D.C. William Houston earned a law degree from Howard University, a black school, by attending night classes. He established a successful law practice and later became an instructor at Howard. Mary Houston, trained as a schoolteacher, opted to work as a hairdresser because she could earn more money that way and help provide for her child.

Unlike many black schoolchildren, Charles Houston attended a high-quality all-black school that focused on preparing students for college, rather than training them for a trade. He excelled in school, graduating as class valedictorian, an honor usually reserved for the student with the highest grades. Graduating early from high school, Houston moved to Massachusetts to attend Amherst College at age sixteen. The sole black student in his class, Houston performed well academically, graduating with honors in 1915.

As the United States began planning to enter World War I (1914–18; U.S. involvement, 1917–18), Houston knew that he would probably be drafted. If so, he would likely end up performing unpleasant duties that white soldiers never wanted to do. He and several Howard faculty members persuaded the government that black troops should have black officers. Thus, he served during the war as an officer. While in the army, Houston became involved in legal cases and was dismayed at the unfair treatment black soldiers received as compared to whites. He decided at that time to become a lawyer and work to help those who were powerless in the legal system.

Houston attended Harvard University Law School, where he became the first black student to join the editorial board of the Harvard Law Review. After graduating, Houston worked at his father's law firm and taught part-time at Howard University's School of Law. In 1929 Houston became vice dean of the law school and set about making dramatic changes. He ended the program's popular part-time night school, hired established black scholars as professors, and quickly raised the school's reputation to that of an institution that turned out high-quality black lawyers. With all of his students, Houston emphasized the importance of using legal knowledge to improve society and to help those who needed it most.

In 1935 Houston began work as the chief legal counsel for the NAACP and began his mission of using the courts to attack school segregation.

After winning high-profile cases to integrate graduate schools, Houston left the NAACP work to Thurgood Marshall and other young lawyers he had helped train. He then returned to Washington, D.C. Over the next several years, he took on numerous cases that challenged segregation and discrimination. In 1948 he began work on another school segregation case. He devoted more than two years to the case, but in early 1950 had to hand it off to a colleague following a severe heart attack. He died on April 20, 1950.

The school segregation case that Houston had worked on was *Bolling v. Sharpe*, one of the five cases that were argued together in front of the U.S. Supreme Court as *Brown v. Board of Education of Topeka, Kansas*. The *Brown* case, decided in 1954, marked the end of legal segregation in U.S. public schools.

A few years later, in 1938, Houston and Marshall took a similar case all the way to the U.S. Supreme Court. A black student named Lloyd Lionel Gaines had been denied admission to the all-white law school at the University of Missouri. After more than two years of court battles, the case was heard by the U.S. Supreme Court, which ordered the University of Missouri law school to admit Gaines. These legal victories weakened the *Plessy v. Ferguson* decision, the basis for all segregationist laws. The next step for the NAACP was to address segregation in public elementary and secondary schools and to try to bring down *Plessy v. Ferguson* completely.

World War II

As the lawyers of the NAACP fought for school desegregation, other civil rights activists tackled inequalities elsewhere. When it became clear that the United States might be drawn into another largescale war, jobs in defense-related industries became abundant. Still, such jobs were primarily reserved for white workers. African American labor leader A. Philip Randolph (1889–1979) approached the U.S. government with a demand. He called for an end to discrimination against black workers in the defense plants. In 1925, Randolph had founded the first black union in the United States. He had organized railroad porters into the Brotherhood of Sleeping Car Porters.

In 1941, on the eve of U.S. entry into World War II (1939–45), Randolph announced that if his demand for defense jobs for blacks was not met, he would organize a massive march on Washington, D.C. He promised that tens of thousands of protesters would gather in the nation's capital to demand equality in the workplace. President Roosevelt was concerned that such a protest would be too disruptive at a time when the nation was preparing for war. So, he agreed to Randolph's demand. The march was canceled, and Roosevelt issued Executive Order 8802 on June 25, 1941. The order desegregated defense-related industries with government contracts.

During World War II, about one million African Americans served in the military. Randolph had tried to achieve desegregation of the military, but he had not succeeded. As they had done during World War I, black soldiers served in segregated units and were often stuck with the jobs no white soldiers wanted. They were prevented from combat positions, except in cases where the need for additional soldiers was particularly high. Black soldiers risked their lives and performed heroic acts, but they received few medals for their service.

As with World War I, African Americans played a significant role in the fight for democracy overseas, but they returned home to the dreary realities of racial discrimination. It wasn't until three years after the end of World War II that the military was desegregated. In 1948 President Harry S Truman (1884–1972; served 1945–53) issued Executive Order 9981, calling for the desegregation of armed forces and government agencies.

Asian American Civil Rights

Asian Americans have experienced racially motivated discrimination and violence for many years. For example, during the 1800s, many Asian immigrants could only find work in low wage jobs. Some worked as cooks and servants; others built railroads. Many Chinese immigrants worked on the Transcontinental Railroad. Paid lower wages than whites, they were often given the most dangerous tasks, such as setting dynamite to clear rocky cliffs. Lowered on ropes, the men placed and lighted explosives. Some died in the blasts or fell to their deaths. Many were treated as if they were expendable.

Anti-Asian sentiment surged during World War II, particularly toward Japanese Americans. This occurred after the Japanese military bombed the U.S. naval base at Pearl Harbor, Hawaii, bringing the United States into the war in December 1941. Many citizens became fearful of all Japanese Americans, regardless of how long such families had lived and worked in the country. Some worried that Japanese Americans would help Japan's war effort by spying on or sabotaging U.S. military facilities. This culture of fear made life difficult for Japanese Americans, who were surprised by such accusations.

In February of 1942, President Roosevelt issued Executive Order 9066 requiring Japanese Americans and Japanese immigrants living on the West Coast to be relocated to internment camps. Allowed to bring only what they could carry, they were forced to sell their remaining property quickly, often receiving far less than fair market value. The camps were set up in remote, desert areas where farming was difficult. The men, women, and children interned were surrounded by fences and guards. Some 120,000 people lived in the camps in long, wooden barracks. The camps were often overcrowded and offered poor living conditions. In 1945 the executive order was repealed.

Many Americans came to view the internment as a major civil rights violation. In 1976 President Gerald R. Ford issued a presidential proclamation noting that the internment was a national mistake. In 1989 a federal law awarded $20,000 to each surviving victim. Four years later, the courts ruled that the internment of Japanese Americans had violated their constitutional rights.

In the late 1960s Asian Americans joined together to fight for civil rights. For the first time, Asians from various countries—Japan, China, Korea, the Philippines, and others—joined forces to make their voices heard. The Asian American movement did not receive the same level of attention as the other civil rights movement of the era, but it did make significant gains. Asian American organizations set up community centers in urban areas to provide food for the poor as well as legal aid and other types of assistance.

During 1968 and 1969 Asian American students joined with other students of color, including Hispanic Americans, Native Americans, and African Americans, to demonstrate at two California universities for equal rights. The students conducted these "third world strikes" to persuade universities to admit more students of color and to establish special departments devoted to the study of various ethnic groups. Not every demand was met to their satisfaction, but their protests led to the creation of ethnic studies departments at the universities. Since then, universities across the nation have created similar departments.

In 1982 the murder of Vincent Chin, a Chinese American, brought renewed interest to the Asian American civil rights movement. The incident shows how during troubled economic times, many white Americans have blamed high unemployment rates on competition from Japan and other Asian countries. Chin was beaten to death by two autoworkers in Detroit with a baseball bat. The two men had assumed Chin was Japanese and vented their anger at Japanese carmakers on Chin. They were convicted of manslaughter, sentenced to probation, and fined a few thousand dollars. Asian Americans throughout the United States were angered that Chin's killers received no prison time. The two men were later tried for violating Chin's civil rights. One was acquitted and the other's guilty verdict was overturned.

Brown Case Marks Beginning of Eew era

The NAACP's modest victories in the 1930s that led to the integration of some all-white graduate schools had little impact on the lives of black schoolchildren in the South. Many southern states had increased spending on black schools to head off any lawsuits stating that their school systems were separate and unequal. But the segregation of elementary and secondary schools was still the law in many states. The situation seemed nearly impossible to change. The NAACP, however, became determined to prove that school segregation was unconstitutional.

In the early 1950s the NAACP filed lawsuits in several states attacking segregation. Unsuccessful in the lower courts, five such cases earned the right in 1952 to be heard by the nation's highest court, the U.S. Supreme Court. The court combined these cases under the name of one case that had originated in Kansas, one of four western states that permitted school segregation. *Brown v. Board of Education of Topeka, Kansas* had originated from the frustration of an African American named Oliver Brown. He was unhappy that his seven-year-old daughter Linda had to take a bus across town to attend a black school when they lived just a few blocks from a white school. So, Brown filed a lawsuit against the Topeka Board of Education.

Arguments in the *Brown* case, as well as the four other related cases, were presented to the Supreme Court in December 1952. The attorneys in each case argued that the separate school facilities for black and white children were grossly unequal. They contended that the situation violated the Fourteenth Amendment, which guaranteed equal protection under the law for all citizens. In addition, the lawyers said racial segregation of schools was psychologically damaging to the black children. They noted that black students clearly understood society's message that they were considered inferior to white children.

More than a year later, on May 17, 1954, the court issued its decision. It declared that school segregation was unconstitutional. As quoted in *Eyes on the Prize*, Chief Justice Earl Warren wrote: "We conclude, unanimously, that in the field of public education the doctrine of 'separate but equal' has no place. Separate educational facilities are inherently unequal." The Brown decision came to be considered one of the most important U.S. Supreme Court cases of the twentieth century. Although it took many years before southern schools were truly integrated, the *Brown* case set in motion a movement that altered nearly every aspect of life for African Americans in the South.

Fear and Fury in the South

It soon became clear that the *Brown* decision would not bring a swift end to school segregation. The southern states that bordered northern states generally held moderate views. However, many in the so-called Deep South (states like Mississippi, Alabama, and Georgia) clung to Civil War-era beliefs. They felt that individual states should make their own rules, and the federal government should have little power over their lives.

The growing civil rights movement and court rulings like the *Brown* decision struck fear into the hearts of many southerners. Supporters of segregation became increasingly nervous that their way of life was being threatened. They feared any change to the balance of power between whites and blacks. They worried that the black population would rise up in revolt and try to dominate southern society. Large numbers of southern citizens and lawmakers reacted to the *Brown* decision with a furious determination to ignore the ruling.

Many white southerners responded to the potential changes in their lifestyle with a sense of angry rebellion and determination to preserve the old ways. Citizens' Councils, made up of middle class and professional whites, arose throughout the South with the purpose of economically intimidating any black citizens who supported desegregation. The councils threatened to take away the jobs and homes of African Americans who defied their will. And if such tactics failed to intimidate, then the KKK would be called into service to terrorize blacks through physical violence. The number of lynchings and other violent acts toward blacks rose during the mid-1950s. One case in particular represented the powerlessness of blacks in the Jim Crow South, and the lengths some people would go to prevent change.

Emmett Till was a fourteen-year-old African American visiting relatives in a small Mississippi town in August of 1955. He came from Chicago, where he lived in a black neighborhood and attended an all-black public school. But while Till understood the realities of a segregated community, he was unfamiliar with the social customs in the South. Visiting a country market with his cousin and some friends one evening, Till whistled at the white woman behind the counter. He said "Bye, baby" on his way out the door. That small act of teenage rebellion in a region where blacks were expected to keep their distance from whites, especially white women, would cost Emmett Till his life.

Three days after the incident, the woman's husband, Roy Bryant, and another man, J. W. Milam, showed up at the house where Till was staying and abducted the boy. They beat him severely, shot him in the head, and dumped his body in the Tallahatchie River. The two men were arrested and tried for murder, but an all-white jury acquitted them after deliberating for just about one hour. The men later admitted their guilt to a journalist who paid them $4,000 for their story. They claimed that the boy needed to be taught a lesson for his bold behavior.

Millions of people, particularly in the North, reacted with outrage and disgust that such a crime had occurred and that the perpetrators had gone unpunished. Emmett Till's mother, Mamie Bradley, insisted on an open casket at her son's funeral. She wanted all to see the horrifying evidence of her son's brutal murder. Thousands lined up to view the body over a four-day period. The tragedy of the Emmett Till case awakened many in the North, both black and white, of the need for change.

In *Eyes on the Prize*, Juan Williams reflected on the incident's impact. "It is difficult to measure just how profound an effect the public viewing of Till's body created. But without question it moved black America in a way the Supreme Court ruling on school desegregation could not match." Bradley, as quoted in *Eyes on the Prize*, explained how her son's murder changed her own perspective: "When something happened to the Negroes in the South [before the murder] I said, 'That's their business, not mine.' Now I know how wrong I was. The murder of my son has shown me that what happens to any of us, anywhere in the world, had better be the business of us all.'

The Montgomery Bus Boycott

After the *Brown* case delivered its blow to school segregation, more and more African Americans began to feel it was possible to get rid of segregation in other aspects of their lives. In Montgomery, Alabama, a highly segregated city, the treatment blacks received on the city bus lines became a focus of their frustration. African American passengers were forced to sit in "colored" sections at the back of the bus. If a bus became too crowded, black passengers were required to give up seats in the colored section for white riders. In addition, black passengers had to pay at the front of the bus, then exit and re-enter through the rear door. Those who dared break these rules faced arrest and, in some cases, severe beatings from angry white passengers.

Black citizens of Montgomery became increasingly fed up with the system. Some began to speak of a boycott. Three-quarters of the city's bus riders were black. Thus, if they banded together and refused to ride the buses, the bus company would suffer a significant loss of income. Jo Ann Robinson, the president of a black women's organization called the Women's Political Council, began to plan for a citywide boycott. She and other black community leaders waited for an incident to take place that would inspire enough anger and frustration on the part of black citizens to unite them behind the boycott. On December 1, 1955, that incident occurred.

On that day, a forty-three-year-old black seamstress named Rosa Parks (1913–2005) boarded a bus after work. Parks had been active in the NAACP for many years, working at one time as secretary of the Montgomery chapter. She had run into trouble on a city bus twelve years earlier, in 1943, getting kicked off for refusing to enter through the rear door. On this Thursday in December 1955, Parks took a seat in the colored section. Later, as the bus became more crowded, the driver ordered Parks and three others to give up their seats for white riders. The others complied, but Parks refused to get up. The bus driver called the police, and Parks was arrested. Immediately, black community activists like Robinson began to spread the word that a one-day bus boycott would be held the following Monday to protest bus segregation in general and Parks's arrest in particular.

The one-day boycott was a huge success, with most black bus riders finding other ways to reach their destinations that day. Many walked, some carpooled, others took taxis or rode bicycles. The Montgomery Improvement Association (MIA), a group of religious and community leaders, formed to plan the next steps. They elected as their leader a young, educated, charismatic minister who had recently moved to Montgomery and who would become the civil rights movement's most visible leader: Martin Luther King Jr. (1929–1968). Ralph Abernathy (1926–1990), another major force in the movement, was also an instrumental figure in the MIA. With the support of the black community, the MIA voted to extend the boycott.

The bus company, as well as many downtown businesses, quickly began to lose money. The city's white leaders tried various measures to force the boycott to end, including arresting King and dozens of others. Montgomery's black citizens faced tremendous pressure, including harassment, beatings, and the threat of losing their jobs. Yet they continued to stay off the city's buses. King's home and that of another black leader, E. D. Nixon (1899–1987), were bombed by mobs of angry white citizens. But in spite of the risks, the boycott continued. What had begun as a one-day demonstration stretched into a year-long movement.

In addition to the boycott, the MIA and NAACP attempted to end segregation of the city bus lines through the court system. After months of legal battles, the Montgomery City Lines bus company was forced to end its policy of racial segregation on December 20, 1956. Black passengers could enter through whichever door they wished and sit wherever they wanted. The Montgomery bus boycott ended the next day.

Martin Luther King Jr. and the SCLC

Through his role in the Montgomery bus boycott, Martin Luther King Jr. became known as a gifted and inspiring civil rights leader. He had the ability to persuade reluctant citizens to become dedicated activists, passing along his considerable passion for justice to all who heard him speak. Soon after the bus boycott ended, Ella Jo Baker (1903–1986), a dedicated civil rights activist, approached King about forming a new organization that would coordinate civil rights activities throughout the South. In early January 1957, King and a group of more than sixty black ministers gathered at Ebenezer Baptist Church in Atlanta, Georgia, the church led by King's father. The ministers created the Southern Christian Leadership Conference (SCLC) and elected King as its president. Ella Jo Baker spent more than two years as the SCLC's master organizer and strategist, lending her years of experience as an activist to the new organization and its young leader.

The SCLC played a significant role in the early years of the civil rights movement. Its basic mission involved ending segregation and pursuing social justice through nonviolent means. King and other SCLC leaders preached repeatedly about the importance of fighting hate with love. The SCLC worked with local organizations all over the South, staging demonstrations, marches, and voter registration drives. By coordinating the activities of numerous other groups, the SCLC helped to build a massive grassroots, or locally based, movement throughout the southern states.

Conflict in Little Rock

The 1954 *Brown v. Board of Education* Supreme Court ruling declared that school segregation had to end. But the Supreme Court and other branches of the federal government gave no guidance as to how, or how quickly, to achieve integration.

In addition, the Supreme Court issued a 1955 ruling known as *Brown v. Board of Education II* that further confused the situation. Stating that schools should desegregate with "all deliberate speed," the decision allowed for school boards to come up with plans for gradual integration. While "speed" suggests quickness, "deliberate" means to come to a decision carefully and even slowly. In states where integration was strongly opposed, *Brown II* was interpreted as a victory. The Supreme Court seemed to approve of long delays for school desegregation.

The school board of Little Rock, Arkansas, became one of the first in the nation to come up with a plan to gradually integrate the public schools. The plan initially called for the voluntary integration of one all-white high school, meaning that any black student brave enough to attend the white school could choose to do so. Only nine black students agreed to step forward. The integration of Little Rock's Central High School was supposed to begin in early September 1957, but in the weeks leading up to the first day of school, politicians and citizens scrambled to block the black students from entering the school.

Arkansas Governor Orval Faubus had not expressed strong views about segregation. However, in 1957 he became a staunch supporter of separate facilities for blacks and whites. His political opponents were gaining followers with their segregationist views, and Faubus worried that he would lose the re-election if he didn't express the same views. Two days before the first day of school, Governor Faubus announced on television that he had called in 250 National Guard troops to keep the black students out of Central High. Claiming to be concerned about violence and rioting, Faubus declared that if the troops were not there to block the black students, blood would "run in the streets" of Little Rock.

The first day of school was September 4. The school board had cautioned the parents of the nine black students not to take their children to school that day out of concern that their presence might spark a riot. The parents complied. Daisy Bates, the president of the Arkansas NAACP chapter, agreed to accompany the students in place of their parents. Unable to reach one of the students, Elizabeth Eckford, the night before, Bates met the other eight at an intersection in Little Rock, where two police cars waited to drive the children to school.

Eckford approached the school alone, enduring threats and racist jeers shouted at her from the white crowd. She made her way toward the line of guards, thinking they would protect her. Instead, the guards raised their weapons and closed ranks, preventing her from entering the school. She made her way back through the crowd, away from the school. With the help of some sympathetic whites, she boarded a city bus and rode away. The other black students met with similar resistance from the crowd and the guards, and they, too, were turned away from the school.

A federal judge and the U.S. Justice Department intervened and forced Governor Faubus to call off the National Guard troops. On September 23, the Little Rock Nine, as the students came to be called, entered Central High with a police escort. The victory was short-lived, however. The threat of violence from students inside the school and angry white mobs outside convinced the authorities that the students were not safe and should be taken home. The following day, after President Eisenhower, a Republican (1890–1969; served 1953–61), got involved, the students returned to the school accompanied by one thousand U.S. Army paratroopers. Eisenhower had also put the Arkansas National Guard under federal control, enlisting them to keep the peace in Little Rock. For the remainder of the school year, armed National Guardsmen patrolled the hallways of Central High.

Much of the conflict in Little Rock was captured by television news cameras. Many people around the world were shocked by the level of racial hatred shown there. But even some who supported integration in theory wondered if the results were worth all the trouble.

The Rise of the Student Movement

In the years following the Little Rock crisis, school integration continued to proceed very slowly. Even in Little Rock, the gains made in 1957 were reversed in 1958, when Governor Faubus closed down the public schools altogether. A number of southern states took similar actions to avoid complying with the *Brown* decision. By 1960, six years after *Brown*, very few schools had desegregated. African Americans who had been schoolchildren in 1954, the year of *Brown*, were now young adults. As each year passed and they realized they would not personally reap the benefits of the momentous Supreme Court decision, many of these young people decided to become activists and attempt to bring about change on their own. Although victories in courts and legislatures were significant, this growing group of activists realized there were other ways to achieve social justice.

Sit-ins

Civil rights organizations like the Congress of Racial Equality (CORE), founded in 1942, and the SCLC and NAACP held training sessions to teach young activists about the principles of nonviolence. They explained the application of those principles to civil disobedience or the peaceful violation of a law that many consider unjust or immoral. In early 1960, a new organization formed that embodied the restless, activist spirit of many young African Americans. The Student Nonviolent Coordinating Committee, or SNCC (pronounced "snick"), adhered to the principles of nonviolence supported by the more established civil rights groups. But SNCC took a more aggressive approach to civil rights than the older groups had, expressing the energy and idealism of the student members.

SNCC was formed in the midst of a successful series of demonstrations held throughout the South. Activists were attempting to make lunch counters in department stores and drugstores open to people of all races. Many such businesses would sell clothing or other items to black customers but denied them service at the lunch counters within the stores. During the late 1950s, a few incidents were staged to challenge lunch-counter segregation. Activists undertook sit-ins at white-only counters. A sit-in involved black customers sitting at a lunch counter, asking to be served, and remaining in their seats after being denied service. On occasion, sympathetic whites joined the sit-in.

In February 1960, a group of four black students from North Carolina A & T (Agricultural and Technical) College, an all-black school in Greensboro, took action. They decided to stage a sit-in at the lunch counter of Woolworth's drugstore. They were refused service but stayed in their seats until the store closed. The following day, the Greensboro Four, as they came to be known, returned with nineteen black students to stage another sit-in. By the end of the week, several hundred students, including many white supporters, were taking turns occupying the seats of Woolworth's lunch counter.

Word spread quickly of the actions of the Greensboro Four, thanks in part to television coverage of the sit-ins. In the following weeks, student demonstrators staged sit-ins in cities throughout the South. Over the next year and a half, tens of thousands of black and white students participated in sit-ins at lunch counters, movie theaters, public swimming pools, hotels, and other places that served the public. Often conducted in conjunction with a boycott of those businesses and large demonstrations in the streets, the sit-ins proved extremely effective. They forced the integration of businesses in more than one hundred communities throughout the South.

Freedom Rides

In the wake of the *Brown* decision and many other court rulings that banned segregation, civil rights activists learned that legal victories did not always bring real change. The U.S. Supreme Court could declare that a certain kind of segregation was illegal, but without the support of law enforcement officials, such rulings were ineffective. In much of the South, particularly the states known as the Deep South, there was strong opposition to integration. Most state officials refused to honor the authority of the nation's courts. Many black southerners kept quiet about instances of illegal segregation, fearing physical assault and other forms of intimidation.

A 1947 U.S. Supreme Court ruling had banned segregation on interstate buses and trains. At that time, the civil rights group CORE had sent black and white volunteers on bus rides in the South to determine if that ruling was being enforced. The riders found that segregation remained the custom, if not the law, and they were harassed and ultimately arrested. In 1961 the U.S. Supreme Court expanded on the 1947 ruling. The court specified that the waiting areas for interstate buses and trains could not be segregated either. Once again, CORE, under the leadership of James Farmer (1920–1999), set out to test the South's compliance with this ruling.

In May 1961, white and black CORE volunteers began a journey from Washington, D.C., to New Orleans, Louisiana. The plan involved black riders sitting in the front of the bus and refusing to move if ordered to do so. At rest stops, the black volunteers would enter the all-white waiting rooms. These volunteers, who came to be known as Freedom Riders, knew that their actions would provoke outcry and possibly violence from white southerners. In fact, the activists intended to spark a reaction. They figured that assaults on the Freedom Riders would force the U.S. government to acknowledge that federal laws were being ignored in the South. In turn, the government would have to step in to remedy the situation.

The Freedom Riders met with minor resistance in Virginia and North Carolina. They suffered a beating from a group of white men in Rock Hill, South Carolina. Dedicated to the principles of nonviolence, they refused to fight back. On May 14 the Freedom Riders split into two groups in Atlanta, Georgia, with some riding on a Trailways bus and others on a Greyhound bus. They then began the most dangerous leg of their journey as they approached Alabama and Mississippi, two of the states most hostile to civil rights efforts.

When the Greyhound bus pulled into the station in Anniston, Mississippi, an angry crowd threw stones at the bus and slashed its tires. The driver hastily pulled away, driving a few miles outside town until the flat tires forced him to stop. Many of those in the mob at the bus station followed in cars. When the bus stopped, one of them threw a firebomb through a window of the bus. As smoke filled the vehicle, the passengers were forced to leave through an emergency exit. The bus became consumed with flames, and the fleeing passengers were beaten by the waiting mobs. The beatings stopped due to the actions of an undercover Alabama patrolman, who had boarded the bus in Atlanta. Feeling duty-bound to prevent murder, he fired his gun into the air and threatened to shoot anyone who continued.

The Trailways bus also encountered attacks in Anniston and met with similar violence in Birmingham, Alabama. There, the riders were assaulted by a large crowd of people, many of whom beat the riders with metal pipes. In both Anniston and Birmingham, in spite of advance warnings that violence might take place, the local police departments were absent. Although they endured beatings, the Freedom Riders were determined to continue, prepared to give their lives to the cause. After the incidents in Anniston and Birmingham, however, no bus driver would agree to transport them.

Inspired by the bravery of the Freedom Riders, hundreds of volunteers traveled to the South to try to continue the journey. When Alabama Governor John Patterson promised to protect the riders, the Freedom Rides resumed. On May 20, in Montgomery, Alabama, it became clear that the governor had not kept his promise. Hundreds of angry whites surrounded the buses of the Freedom Riders, rioting in the streets and brutally attacking the civil rights workers. The state of Alabama seemed to have come unhinged. The situation improved when President John F. Kennedy (1917–1963; served 1961–63) ordered hundreds of federal marshals to the state to restore order.

Volunteers continued to show up for duty as the Freedom Riders prepared to enter Mississippi. Fearful for the riders' safety and concerned about alienating southern Democrats, the Kennedy administration chose the president's brother, Robert F. Kennedy (1925–1968), to negotiate an agreement with Mississippi officials. The state would guarantee that the Freedom Riders would not be attacked in Mississippi. And the U.S. government would allow Mississippi to enforce its segregation laws and arrest the black passengers who attempted to integrate waiting areas. Although the federal government controlled interstate travel, individual states retained control of bus stations within their state lines. The state laws permitting segregation conflicted with federal anti-segregation laws. Kennedy allowed Mississippi's state laws to prevail in the case of the Freedom Riders. Hundreds of Freedom Riders were subsequently arrested.

James Meredith and Ole Miss

Many of the conflicts during the civil rights era came down to tension between the southern states' desire to preserve their rights, including their longstanding tradition of racial discrimination, and the federal government's assertion of its power. One of several explosive civil rights battles took place in Mississippi, which was considered by many to be the South's most strongly segregated state. Governor Ross Barnett, Democrat (1898–1987) pledged to prevent the integration of any Mississippi school as long as he was in office. His pledge came in the fall of 1962, when federal courts ordered the University of Mississippi to admit James Meredith. A black Air Force veteran, Meredith was a sophomore at the all-black Jackson State University. The University of Mississippi, nicknamed "Ole Miss," was a symbol of traditional white southern values. It had never admitted a black student, and Meredith set out to change that.

With the backing of the U.S. court system, Meredith attempted to register for classes in September, but he was blocked from doing so. In one instance, Governor Barnett personally prevented Meredith from registering. Barnett had appointed himself as the university registrar on the day the young student was to sign up for classes. The following day, Meredith was stopped by state troopers as he tried to register at the campus in Oxford, Mississippi. On Sunday, September 30, President Kennedy ordered federal marshals and state troopers to accompany Meredith to the university. The appearance of federal troops in Mississippi angered the governor and many white citizens in the state. Thousands of whites gathered on campus to engage in battle with the marshals. The outraged white mobs attacked the marshals with bats, bricks, bombs, and guns. Outnumbered, the marshals fought back. More than 150 people were wounded, many by gunshot. By early morning, Kennedy sent army troops to Oxford, and the rioting ended.

Later that morning, Meredith registered without incident and began attending classes. He graduated from the University of Mississippi in the summer of 1963. He had been accompanied by armed guards during his entire time at the school. Although Meredith's victory came at a great price, his battle against segregation at Ole Miss gave hope to blacks throughout the state that change was indeed possible.

The Freedom Rides did not achieve the dramatic changes to the enforcement of desegregation laws like the riders had hoped would occur. However, by autumn of 1961 the Interstate Commerce Commission (ICC) had issued new rules forcing bus and train companies to integrate waiting rooms. In communities throughout the South, Freedom Rides and other methods of confronting segregation laws continued. The original Freedom Riders, revered for their courage in the face of certain danger, were viewed as heroes by blacks throughout the South for many years to come.

The Albany Movement

In late November 1961, civil rights workers from SNCC, the SCLC, and the NAACP, among others, converged on Albany, Georgia. They were attempting to reverse segregation laws in that city. They faced an uphill battle, in part because the various civil rights groups working in Albany could not always agree about what goals or methods to use. In spite of their differences, numerous organizations banded together to form the Albany Movement, an umbrella organization to oversee civil rights activities in that city.

For the next several months, the Albany Movement coordinated a flurry of protest actions. These included sit-ins at transportation terminals, libraries, and restaurants, as well as protest marches and prayer vigils. The hope in Albany, as with civil rights actions in other cities, was to provoke a violent and angry reaction from the white community and Albany police, drawing the attention of the press and the sympathy of supporters from around the country. The Albany police, however, under the guidance of police chief Laurie Pritchett, undermined that effort. They treated the protesters courteously and protected them from angry white crowds.

Many demonstrators were arrested by the Albany police, but the clashes remained largely nonviolent. Albany officials stated publicly that the arrests were for such violations as parading without a permit, trespassing, or loitering. They carefully avoided using inflammatory language about the racial issues behind the protests. The Albany police kept tabs on the Albany Movement through informers. Once they learned of the tension within the movement, they exploited that weakness.

In July 1962 the Albany Movement was dealt a blow when a federal judge issued a restraining order prohibiting further demonstrations in Albany. A few days later, an appeals court judge reversed the order. Protesters responded by staging a huge march through the streets of Albany. The march eventually broke into violence on the part of protesters, some of whom threw rocks and bricks at police. That event was a great disappointment to the civil rights leaders who had long argued for nonviolent resistance.

Although the Albany Movement continued until 1965, it became clear by the end of the summer of 1962 that the movement had lost much of its steam. Civil rights organizations turned their efforts elsewhere. Some observers suggested that the Albany Movement had been a failure, but many of those involved disagreed. The demonstrations in Albany had involved numerous African Americans who had never stood up for their rights before, and the experience profoundly changed them. In addition, the civil rights groups in Albany learned many valuable lessons about waging a successful campaign, lessons they applied to future efforts.

Conflict Erupts in Birmingham

Like many other cities in the Deep South, Birmingham, Alabama, was thoroughly segregated and extremely hostile to African Americans working for change. The city's public safety commissioner, Theophilus Eugene "Bull" Connor (1897–1973), had repeatedly expressed his contempt for civil rights activists and made no secret of his racist views. Between 1957 and 1963, eighteen bombs had exploded in Birmingham's black neighborhoods. None of the bombing cases had been solved, primarily because the Birmingham police had no interest in investigating the incidents. The city had thus earned the nickname "Bombingham."

Many of the city's leaders were involved in the KKK, which attracted broad support from Birmingham's white citizens. Segregation in Birmingham was the law and the custom. When a federal desegregation order came through in 1962, the city closed down its parks, playgrounds, public pools, and golf courses rather than comply with the order. Alabama Governor George Wallace (1919–1998) was one of segregation's most vocal supporters. He brought cheers from the crowds at his inauguration speech. As quoted in *The Washington Post*, Wallace said: "I draw the line in the dust and toss the gauntlet before the feet of tyranny, and I say, segregation now, segregation tomorrow, segregation forever."

In early 1963, the SCLC, along with the Alabama Christian Movement for Human Rights, began planning its strategy for desegregating Birmingham. Their plan was dubbed "Project C," with the "C" standing for "confrontation." It involved a variety of protest tactics, including sit-ins, boycotts, marches, and other types of demonstrations. The civil rights groups focused on downtown department stores. Such businesses allowed black customers to enter but refused to serve them at lunch counters and discouraged them from trying on clothes before buying. Black customers had to use separate bathrooms and fitting rooms. And, black employees served in menial positions, never allowed to advance to higher jobs.

On April 3 the protests began. The police responded by arresting hundreds of demonstrators at a time. On Palm Sunday (the Sunday before Easter), April 6, Martin Luther King Jr.'s brother, A. D. King, led a march through the streets. The protesters were attacked by the police with batons and dogs. A few days later, a circuit court judge issued an order banning King and more than one hundred other leaders from participating in any demonstrations. Martin Luther King Jr. chose to violate the order, knowing it would result in his arrest. He led a march on April 12, which was Good Friday, the Friday before Easter. King and others were immediately arrested, and King was put in solitary confinement.

A number of moderate white religious leaders criticized King's actions in a full-page advertisement in one of Birmingham's newspapers. Disappointed by their lack of support, King quickly wrote a lengthy response, scribbling on toilet paper scraps and in the margins of the newspaper. His essay, titled "Letter from Birmingham Jail," was soon published as a pamphlet and distributed widely. King's "Letter" became one of the best-known writings of the civil rights movement. In it, he wrote, "We know from painful experience that freedom is never voluntarily given by the oppressor; it must be demanded by the oppressed."

After weeks of demonstrations and mass arrests, the campaign in Birmingham had lost many supporters, some of whom feared getting arrested and losing their jobs. In a controversial move, the leaders of the campaign decided to stage a children's march, noting that an aggressive police response to young protesters would be unacceptable to the American public. On May 2, hundreds of young people age six to eighteen marched through the streets. The Birmingham police arrested more than 950 of them, carting them off in school buses. The following day, more than one thousand children showed up to march. Bull Connor, desperate to halt the march, ordered firefighters to turn their hoses on the marchers. Children crouched in the street and were sent tumbling into curbs and parked cars by streams of water powerful enough to take bark off trees.

The nation was outraged by footage of the young marchers being attacked by the police. African Americans in Birmingham turned out in full force to continue the demonstrations, many of which then turned violent. As the protests threatened to become out of control, the civil rights leaders and white business owners, who had suffered economic setbacks during the weeks of protests, forged a secret deal. On May 10, the deal was announced. The protests would end, and the downtown stores would desegregate, with black store employees promised better positions.

The fragile truce began to unravel when angry members of the KKK bombed the hotel where King was staying as well as the home of his brother, A. D. King. Riots erupted, and the chaos was only brought under control when President Kennedy threatened to send in federal troops. The events in Birmingham brought civil rights to the forefront of the Kennedy administration's agenda. In June 1963 Kennedy announced that he would send a bill to Congress ending segregation in places that served the public. This included restaurants, hotels, libraries, and stores, as well as buses and trains.

The March on Washington

Leaders of the civil rights movement rejoiced at the possibility of a sweeping law to protect the rights of African Americans. They had been planning a large-scale, peaceful march in Washington, D.C., the seat of the federal government, to demand their rights. When President Kennedy sent the civil rights bill to Congress, the goals of the march expanded to include a show of support for the legislation. A number of organizations came together to plan the March on Washington for Jobs and Freedom, scheduled for August 28, 1963. Black civil rights groups, as well as white activists and representatives of the Catholic, Protestant, and Jewish faiths, joined forces to coordinate the massive demonstration. The principal planners were A. Philip Randolph and Bayard Rustin (c. 1910–1987), both of whom had been involved in many significant civil rights actions.

Initially, President Kennedy opposed the march. He was concerned that it might turn violent and would be seen as threatening to the white lawmakers. Faced with the insistence of civil rights leaders that the march take place, Kennedy agreed to offer his support.

The planners expected, and hoped for, about 100,000 attendees. On the morning of August 28, more than 250,000 people showed up in the nation's capital, including some 60,000 white people. The marchers had come from all over the country, traveling to Washington by train, bus, car, and even on foot. They marched from the Washington Monument to the Lincoln Memorial, where they gathered for an afternoon of stirring music and rousing speeches. Folksingers and gospel singers including Joan Baez, Bob Dylan, Odetta, and Mahalia Jackson performed.

The leaders of the movement, including Randolph, John Lewis (1940–) of SNCC, and Martin Luther King Jr., spoke of their views of the future

—a future that held unparalleled opportunities for African Americans. King delivered his "I Have a Dream" speech, one of his most moving and famous orations. The audience at the Lincoln Memorial and those watching the events on television listened intently as King spoke of his dream of a day "when little black boys and black girls will be able to join hands with little white boys and white girls as sisters and brothers." In his passionate and emotional delivery, King asked the entire nation to "let freedom ring."

The largest demonstration in American history to that point, the March on Washington showed the world that African Americans would not accept second-class citizenship any longer. It also demonstrated that harmony between the races was possible, with whites and blacks marching, singing, and praying side by side.

Victories mingled with tragedies

While the March on Washington stood out as a high point of the civil rights era, the movement also endured many dark days at that time. Two months before the march, Medgar Evers (1925–1963), the field secretary of the NAACP in Mississippi, had been murdered in his own driveway. Evers's murder, in addition to the troubles in Birmingham, sparked hundreds of protests and riots in towns throughout the South during the summer of 1963. Less than three weeks after the March on Washington, on September 15, a bomb exploded inside Birmingham's Sixteenth Street Baptist Church, a black church. Four black girls, at the church for Sunday school, were killed. Later that day, a black teenage boy was shot and killed by the police, and another teenage boy was murdered by white teenagers who had earlier attended a segregationist rally.

On November 22, 1963, President Kennedy was shot and killed by an assassin. The nation mourned the loss of the young president, and civil rights activists worried about the future. Kennedy had been the first president of the modern era to actively promote civil rights. His successor, Lyndon Baines Johnson (1908–1973; served 1963–69), was a southerner. Black leaders feared that he would be less likely to support the civil rights bill. However, Johnson quieted their fears a few days later when he announced his support for the bill during an address to a joint session of Congress.

Several months later, after intense lobbying from supporters and detractors of the bill and a lively debate in Congress, the bill became law. The Civil Rights Act of 1964 was passed on July 2. It marked the end of Jim Crow segregationist laws, prohibiting racial discrimination in places serving the public, in schools, and in the workplace. The law also banned discrimination based on gender. It established the Equal Employment Opportunity Commission (EEOC), which enforces the law as it relates to employment. The Civil Rights Act of 1964 was the most significant civil rights legislation since the Reconstruction Era after the Civil War.

Freedom Summer

Although the passage of the Civil Rights Act was celebrated by activists, the law failed to guarantee African Americans the right to vote, a freedom that had become the primary focus of the civil rights movement. SNCC and other organizations zeroed in on Mississippi, a state that had rigidly resisted any attempts at desegregation. They sought to raise the number of black voters there. Blacks made up 45 percent of the population in that state, but only 5 percent of the black population was registered to vote in 1960. The state officials were hard-line segregationists, and the state had the highest number of lynchings, beatings, and unexplained disappearances of blacks in the South. Mississippi was the poorest state in the nation, and black residents were the poorest of the poor.

Black and white SNCC workers, many of whom dropped out of college to devote themselves full-time to the movement, had been risking their lives to increase voter registration in Mississippi since 1960. In 1962 SNCC, CORE, SCLC, the NAACP, and several local civil rights groups joined forces to create the Council of Federated Organizations, or COFO. The civil rights activists working to register black voters in Mississippi were threatened, beaten, and arrested. At that time, they had very little to show for their efforts. Black voter registration increased by less than 2 percent between 1960 and the summer of 1963.

The Life and Death of Medgar Evers

Medgar Evers was born in 1925 in Decatur, Mississippi. As a young child, he quickly became acquainted with the racism and violence that marked the daily lives of blacks in Mississippi. He was taunted by whites on his way to school. He witnessed blacks being harassed by whites on a regular basis. On occasion, Evers even faced the horror of a black person in his community being lynched by white gangs.

After fighting for democracy and freedom abroad as a soldier during World War II, Evers became determined to improve the lives of blacks in the South, particularly in Mississippi. He attended Alcorn A & M (Agricultural and Mechanical) College from 1948 to 1952, becoming increasingly involved at that time with the NAACP. During his senior year, he married Myrlie Beasley.

After graduating from college, Evers began selling insurance. His work took him through many small towns in Mississippi. He became more and more disturbed by the desperate poverty of his fellow black citizens. He quit the insurance business and began working full-time for the NAACP. He was soon promoted to field secretary, coordinating voter registration efforts and following up on reports of anti-black intimidation and violence. Evers was regarded as a dangerous man by many white Mississippians. The activist and his family received death threats regularly.

Even after his home was bombed, Evers remained dedicated to the cause of civil rights. He was determined to make a better life for his children and all future generations. On June 11, 1963, he returned home late at night from NAACP functions. Evers was shot in the back after getting out of his car. The thirty-seven-year-old civil rights leader died less than an hour later.

Much of the evidence, including fingerprints on the murder weapon, pointed to a white supremacist, someone who believes in the absolute superiority of the white race. The suspect, Byron De La Beckwith (1920–2001), was tried for Evers's murder twice in the months following the crime. Each time, an all-white jury failed to deliver a guilty verdict. At the time, Beckwith was treated with respect and admiration by many white Mississippians, who regarded him as a hero for his actions. Many years later, in 1994, Beckwith was tried a third time for the murder. He was convicted by a racially mixed jury in Mississippi. He went to prison for the remainder of his life, dying in 2001 at the age of eighty.

Although the number of registered voters did not change dramatically, the civil rights workers felt they achieved a great deal in terms of education. Many poor blacks had been denied an education and did not even know they had the right to vote. The civil rights activists spoke to workers in the fields and in the factories, informing them of their rights. They spread the notion that black voters could potentially elect black officials, who could then effect real change in Mississippi.

Activists planned to renew their efforts during the summer of 1964, which came to be known as Freedom Summer. They called for volunteers to travel to Mississippi that summer. Hundreds responded. They knew that their activism came with great personal risk. Many of the volunteers were white, and many came from northeastern upper-middle-class families. Their average age was twenty-one. A primary goal for the summer was to register black voters and prepare them for the upcoming presidential election.

On June 20, the first group of volunteers traveled to Mississippi. The following day, one of the volunteers, a white man named Andrew Goodman, disappeared, along with two CORE workers: Michael Schwerner, a white man, and James Chaney, a black Mississippi native. After driving to the town of Lawndale to investigate the burning of a black church, the three men had been arrested and then later released. Soon after they were let go, they disappeared. When they failed to check in at Freedom Summer headquarters, fellow activists became greatly concerned.

The bodies of Goodman, Schwerner, and Chaney were found later that summer. All three men had been shot, and Chaney had also been brutally beaten. The families wanted the three men to be buried together, but Mississippi officials denied the request. They would only allow Chaney's body to be buried in an all-black cemetery.

The nation was outraged over the murder of the three young men, a detail that many southern blacks attributed to the fact that two of the victims were white. Time and again black people had disappeared and were later found murdered. However, those crimes failed to attract attention or sympathy from the rest of the country. Twenty-one men were eventually arrested in connection with the murder of the three civil rights workers, though the murder charges were later dropped. Twelve of the suspects later faced federal charges of civil rights violation, and seven were convicted.

But the quest to bring the killers to justice did not end. In June 2005 a jury convicted Edgar Ray Killen of manslaughter in the slayings. An ordained minister and a member of the KKK, Killen was in his late thirties when the murders occurred. He had been tried in 1967, but the jury became deadlocked because one juror could not bring herself to convict a minister. At his retrial in 2005, Killen was eighty and suffering from ill health. His conviction occurred forty-one years after the murders of Chaney, Goodman, and Schwerner.

The Mississippi Freedom Democratic Party

In addition to educating African Americans about voter registration, the Freedom Summer volunteers also set up "freedom schools" to educate black children, health clinics to provide free medical advice and care, and legal clinics to help protect the rights of blacks. Volunteers also worked to sign people up as

Native American Civil Rights

Native Americans, a group also known as American Indians, have endured racial prejudice from white Americans for hundreds of years, since the first white settlers arrived in the New World from Europe. Many of these settlers viewed Native American tribes as savage and violent because the Indian way of life was so different from their lifestyle. Settlers used such characterizations to justify waging war with the Indians and taking their land. Native Americans lost many people to wars as well as diseases that were brought to America by the Europeans. They lost their land to settlers who overpowered them with military might.

In many cases, Native American also lost land and power after agreeing to treaties with the U.S. government that were subsequently broken. By the twentieth century, Native Americans were primarily living on reservations, land that had been set aside for them by the government. Poverty, segregation, and discrimination in jobs and housing have been major problems for the various Native American nations throughout the twentieth and into the twenty-first century.

Throughout the 1960s and 1970s, spurred on by the gains of the African American civil rights movement, Native American activists began filing lawsuits. They attempted to retrieve Indian lands that had been taken as a result of treaty violations in previous decades. The American Indian Movement (AIM) formed in 1968 to help protect the rights of Native Americans. That same year, the U.S. Congress passed the American Indian Civil Rights Act, guaranteeing for Native Americans the same rights that all other Americans were entitled to under the Constitution. This law also, however, limited the authority of tribal governments, each of which is considered a sovereign, or self-governing, nation. Native American civil rights groups, with AIM being the best known and most visible, led a number of militant protest actions throughout the 1970s. These groups often clashed with police just as African American activists had done. A number of AIM members were killed during confrontations with police, and many allege that others were killed under mysterious circumstances.

One of the most notorious actions took place in early 1973. Members of the Oglala Sioux nation (also known as the Lakota) occupied the area known as Wounded Knee with the help of AIM activists. Located on the Pine Ridge Reservation in South Dakota, Wounded Knee was the site of a tragic massacre of Indians by U.S. troops in 1890. In 1973 the Native American occupiers demanded that the government investigate broken treaties and ill treatment of the Oglala Sioux. The government responded by surrounding the area with massive military firepower.

The standoff ended after seventy-one days with the government making promises but ultimately failing to meet the Oglala Sioux's demands. The years following the standoff proved highly volatile, with the U.S. government and Indian tribes intensely distrustful of each other. A firefight between Federal Bureau of Investigation (FBI) agents and residents of the Pine Ridge Reservation led to the controversial arrest of AIM activist Leonard Peltier (1944–) and others for the murder of two agents. The case was hotly debated. Claims were made that those prosecuting Peltier had committed improprieties. The American Indian activist was convicted of the agents' murders and sent to prison for two life sentences. Supporters from around the world have continued to protest his imprisonment.

Although individual protest actions of the Native American civil rights movement were not always successful, taken together these protests raised awareness among Native Americans, Americans of other races and ethnicities, and the U.S. government. Crime, alcoholism, and poverty continue to be significant problems for many Native American nations. However, a number of gains have been made through civil rights laws, victories in court, and the schooling of many Americans on the value and richness of Native American history and culture.

members of the Mississippi Freedom Democratic Party (MFDP). An official, legal political party, it was set up as an alternative to the all-white Democratic party in Mississippi. By the end of the summer, 80,000 African Americans had signed up for the MFDP.

One of MFDP's most visible and inspiring activists was a black woman named Fannie Lou Hamer (1917–1977). The youngest of twenty children, Hamer had worked in the fields alongside her parents from the age of six. She had endured terrible poverty and never received much education. At the age of forty-four, Hamer attended a voter registration meeting held by the SNCC and soon became a full-time activist. She worked tirelessly to register African Americans to vote.

Activists had been campaigning to have delegates from the MFDP replace the white delegates from the Democratic party at the Democratic National Convention in Atlantic City, New Jersey, in August of 1964. Each state would be sending delegates to the party's national convention to determine the Democrats' nominee for president. MFDP members argued that they more accurately represented the people of Mississippi and that their political views were more in line with the national party than the white Mississippi Democrats.

Although the MFDP gained considerable support from Democrats in many states, President Johnson and many other Democrats opposed the idea of MFDP delegates replacing the traditional Democrats at the convention. Eventually the MFDP was offered a compromise: the white Democratic delegates from Mississippi would be seated and have a vote at the convention, while just two MFDP delegates would be allowed to attend but would not be associated with Mississippi. The compromise also stated that in the future, the Mississippi delegation would have to be integrated.

Some in the MFDP urged acceptance of the compromise, but others felt it was an all-or-nothing situation. The differences among members of the party pointed to a growing rift between the civil rights movement's "old guard," represented by Martin Luther King Jr. and the SCLC, and the more aggressive members of SNCC. SCLC members preached patience, insisting that change could only happen slowly. However, SNCC members were tired of waiting and felt ready to demand their rights rather than politely requesting them.

The MFDP lost its bid to gain political strength at the convention, but it did lay the groundwork for the integration of Mississippi's Democratic party. In addition, the many other projects of Freedom Summer continued on. President Johnson provided federal funding for health clinics, schools, nutrition programs, and legal clinics in rural Mississippi. And Johnson's Head Start, the national preschool program for low-income families, evolved from activities begun during Freedom Summer. Perhaps most important, numerous poor blacks developed a sense of empowerment and dignity through their participation in the political process.

A Power Struggle in Selma

In early 1965 King and the SCLC joined SNCC for a campaign for voting rights in Selma, Alabama. The two groups set out to increase pressure on the federal government to pass a law protecting voting rights for all. They hoped to stage demonstrations, provoke a hostile response from law enforcement, and compel the federal government to step in and make changes. Like many other cities in the Deep South, Selma had a large black population, about 15,000, which was half of the city's total population. Nevertheless, it had very few registered voters. Only 156 blacks were registered to vote in Selma as of 1963. Also like many other southern cities, the law enforcement and political officials were deeply opposed to integration in any form and readily used violence to crush signs of activism.

The Johnson administration had already begun writing legislation that would eliminate obstacles to voting imposed by southern states. However, civil rights activists felt that Johnson was acting too slowly and that voting rights needed to be a higher priority for the president. On January 18, King and the SCLC began conducting marches to the courthouse in an attempt to register voters. The marchers were prevented from registering. A series of marches followed over the next several days, with hundreds of protesters being arrested. King himself was arrested on February 1, an act that guaranteed the national spotlight would remain on Selma. A few days later, the controversial civil rights leader Malcolm X (1925–1965) traveled to Selma to make a speech in support of King. He suggested that white people should be grateful to King for preaching peaceful protest, suggesting that not all civil rights leaders urged their followers to refrain from violence.

In early March, civil rights leaders announced an upcoming march from Selma to Montgomery, the capital of Alabama, to present a list of complaints to the governor. Alabama Governor George Wallace (Democrat) had no intention of receiving this list and tried to prevent the march from taking place. Determined, hundreds of marchers set out for Montgomery on March 7. They marched without being harassed at first. But when they reached the Edmund Pettus Bridge leading out of Selma, they saw the Selma police as well as one hundred state troopers, all decked out in riot gear. The marchers were ordered to disperse. But before they could react, the police were upon them. The activists were attacked with batons, chains, electric cattle prods, and tear gas. Dozens of marchers were injured, some seriously. The entire incident was captured on film by television news reporters. Once again, the nation reacted with shock to the scenes of police brutality directed toward civil rights activists. That day became known as "Bloody Sunday."

On March 9, fifteen hundred marchers again attempted to reach Montgomery. When they arrived at the bridge, a crowd of state troopers awaited them and ordered them to turn around. The marchers sang "We Shall Overcome," the song that had become the anthem of the civil rights movement. King and other leaders knelt in prayer. Then, to the surprise of many, King turned the crowd around and headed back. He wished to avoid further beatings. He felt they had made their point, revealing again that peaceful demonstration was being met with the threat of violence. Many of his followers felt betrayed, however, wondering why King had refused to confront the police. That night, a group of three white ministers who supported the civil rights movement were attacked by white thugs in Selma. One of them, James Reeb, was beaten with a club and later died of his injuries.

A few days later, President Johnson (Democrat) announced at a press conference that he would send a voting rights bill to Congress that would prevent states from restricting a person's right to vote. The following day, a federal judge ruled that the march from Selma to Montgomery could legally take place. Governor Wallace refused to provide the marchers with police protection from angry white mobs. President Johnson stepped in and placed the Alabama National Guard under federal control, ordering the troops to protect the marchers. Johnson also called in two thousand soldiers from the U.S. Army as well as hundreds of other federal agents. Some four thousand marchers left Selma on March 25, 1965. Five days and fifty-four miles later, twenty-five thousand people reached Montgomery. A few months later, on August 6, President Johnson signed into law the Voting Rights Act of 1965, passed with Republican support, outlawing such voting restrictions as poll taxes and literacy tests.

Hispanic American Civil Rights

Hispanic Americans are a large and fast-growing population with roots in one of a number of Spanish-speaking countries, including Spain, Mexico, and many nations in Central and South America and in the Caribbean. The term "Latino," which refers to people from Latin America, is often used instead of "Hispanic." Hispanic America immigrants to the United States, as well as later generations, have at times endured a great deal of discrimination.

Like African Americans, Hispanics have often been segregated in schools, housing, and other aspects of their lives. They have been denied employment or offered nothing but the most menial, unpleasant jobs. They have suffered higher rates of poverty, joblessness, and imprisonment than the white population.

The Hispanic American civil rights movement was most active during the 1960s and 1970s. An important action in the movement involved the formation of a union of farm laborers in 1962 known as the National Farm Workers Association. The organization later became the United Farm Workers (UFW) in 1966. Led by a charismatic community organizer named Ceésar Chávez (1927–1993), the group consisted primarily of Hispanics. In September 1965, the organization began a strike against grape growers. They fought for years for the right to organize as a union and to bargain with growers. The growers fought back, using the court system and violence to limit the strikers' effectiveness.

As the strike continued for months on end with little sign of success, Chávez initiated a boycott of grapes. He persuaded many consumers around the country to boycott grapes grown by targeted companies. Activist groups in many states pressured supermarket chains not to carry grapes that weren't approved by the UFW. The boycott was eventually expanded to cover all table grapes (the type usually bought by consumers) grown in California. After five years of striking and close to three years of the boycott, the grape growers finally gave in. They agreed to the demands of the farm workers. Soon, other growers followed suit, giving farm laborers the same types of workplace rights that other laborers have.

Hispanic American civil rights gained attention during spring 2006, as the U.S. Congress debated a controversial immigration bill. Activists for immigrants' rights, represented in large numbers by Hispanic immigrants from Central and South America, organized national protests. During April, students staged walk-outs while thousands attended marches throughout the country. On May 1, a day to celebrate the achievements of working people, thousands of immigrants, including a significant number of illegal, or undocumented, immigrants in the United States, participated in a one-day boycott to emphasize their importance to the national economy. In many cities, students stayed out of school and others refrained from going to work or spending any money in stores or restaurants. Although the economic impact of the one-day boycott was minimal, the events received tremendous media notice, focusing the nation's attention on the difficulties encountered by immigrants living and working in the country illegally.

A Divided Movement

The passage of the Voting Rights Act was a meaningful victory for the civil rights movement. Within months, black voter registration had increased significantly throughout the South. Black voters soon began electing black officials, primarily for local offices. And more and more blacks occupied positions of importance in the federal government. Thurgood Marshall, for example, was appointed the first black justice of the U.S. Supreme Court in 1967.

Legislative victories, however, were not enough to satisfy restless, frustrated urban blacks. While many of the legal methods of discrimination had been prohibited, overwhelming numbers of blacks still suffered from crushing poverty and faced considerable obstacles to jobs, housing, and education. A massive race riot in the Los Angeles neighborhood of Watts in August 1965 left dozens dead and hundreds injured. Over the next three years, 150 race riots tore apart cities all over the nation.

The leaders of the civil rights movement seemed unsure of how to address the needs of a diverse population of African Americans. The movement became weakened by strong differences of opinion among its leaders. Some continued to advocate nonviolent resistance, while others, like Stokely Carmichael (1941–1998), leader of SNCC from 1966 to 1967, took a more militant stance. He roused crowds with chants of "Black Power." Leaders like King had always worked toward integration. However, a number of younger black community leaders, including Malcolm X and Carmichael, supported separatism, a rejection of white culture and the embrace of African American heritage.

Another development that weakened the civil rights movement was the assassination of some of its most powerful leaders. Malcolm X was gunned down on February 21, 1965, and Martin Luther King Jr. was murdered on April 4, 1968. Without the leadership of these charismatic men, many of their followers drifted away from the cause. In addition, growing opposition to the Vietnam War (1954–75), especially among the nation's youth, drew attention and energy away from African American issues.

A Mixed Legacy

The civil rights movement unquestionably brought about vast and important changes, particularly in the American South. Over time, the Jim Crow laws were overturned and racially discriminating voting restrictions were prohibited. The lives of many southern blacks changed significantly in the span of a few decades. A major blow was dealt to institutional racism—racism that is woven into the fabric of a government or organization.

Legislation cannot overcome personal racism, however, and outlawing discrimination does not make it disappear. Millions of blacks, particularly in urban areas, remain in ghettoes, poor neighborhoods where residents struggle with inadequate housing and dead-end jobs. Black inmates far outnumber white inmates in the nation's prisons. The United States has yet to achieve the equality and justice envisioned by participants in the civil rights movement. However, the gains of the movement continue to demonstrate the power ordinary people possess in achieving social reform.

A SUMMARY OF THE 20TH CENTURY

The 20th century was dominated by a chain of events that heralded significant changes in world history as to redefine the era: flu pandemic, World War I and World War II, nuclear power and space exploration, nationalism and decolonization, the Cold War and post-Cold War conflicts; intergovernmental organizations and cultural homogenization through developments in emerging transportation and communications technology; poverty reduction and world population growth, awareness of environmental degradation, ecological extinction; and the birth of the Digital Revolution. It saw great advances in communication and medical technology that by the late 1980s allowed for near-instantaneous worldwide computer communication and genetic modification of life.

The 20th century was saw the largest transformation of the world order since the Fall of Rome: a rise in global total fertility rates, ecological collapses; the resulting competition for land and dwindling resources, accelerated deforestation, water depletion, and the mass extinction of some of the world's species and decline in the population of others; consequences which are now being dealt with. It took over two-hundred thousand years of human history up to 1804 for the world's population to reach 1 billion; world population reached an estimated 2 billion in 1927; by late 1999, the global population reached 6 billion. Global literacy averaged 80%; global lifespan-averages exceeded 40+ years for the first time in history, with over half achieving 70+ years (three decades *longer* than it was a century ago).

The century had the first global-scale total wars between world powers across continents and oceans in World War I and World War II. Nationalism became a major political issue in the world in the 20th century, acknowledged in international law along with the right of nations to self-determination, official decolonization in the mid-century, and related regional conflicts.

The century saw a major shift in the way that many people lived, with changes in politics, ideology, economics, society, culture, science, technology, and medicine. The 20th century may have seen more technological and scientific progress than all the other centuries combined since the dawn of civilization. Terms like *ideology, world war, genocide,* and *nuclear war* entered common usage. Scientific discoveries, such as the theory of relativity and quantum physics, profoundly changed the foundational models of physical science, forcing scientists to realize that the universe was more complex than previously believed, and dashing the hopes (or fears) at the end of the 19th century that the last few details of scientific knowledge were about to be filled in. It was a century that started with horses, simple automobiles, and freighters but ended with high-speed rail, cruise ships, global commercial air travel and the Space Shuttle. Horses, Western society's basic form of personal transportation for thousands of years, were replaced by automobiles and buses within a few decades. These developments were made possible by the exploitation of fossil fuel resources, which offered energy in an easily portable form, but also caused concern about pollution and long-term impact on the environment. Humans explored space for the first time, taking their first footsteps on the Moon.

Mass media, telecommunications, and information technology (especially computers, paperback books, public education, and the Internet) made the world's knowledge more widely available. Advancements in medical technology also improved the health of many people: the global life expectancy increased from 35 years to 65 years. Rapid technological advancements, however, also allowed warfare to reach unprecedented levels of destruction. World War II alone killed over 60 million people, while nuclear weapons gave humankind the means to annihilate itself in a short time. However, these same wars resulted in the destruction of the imperial system. For the first time in human history, empires and their wars of expansion and colonization ceased to be a factor in international affairs, resulting in a far more globalized and cooperative world. The last time major powers clashed openly was in 1945, and since then, violence has seen an unprecedented decline.

The world also became more culturally homogenized than ever with developments in transportation and communications technology, popular music and other influences of Western culture, international corporations, and what was arguably a truly global economy by the end of the 20th century.

Technological advancements during World War I changed the way war was fought, as new inventions such as tanks, chemical weapons, and aircraft modified tactics and strategy. After more than four years of trench warfare in Western Europe, and 20 million dead, the powers that had formed the Triple Entente (France, Britain, and Russia, later replaced by the United States and joined by Italy and Romania) emerged victorious over the Central Powers (Germany, Austria-Hungary, the Ottoman Empire and Bulgaria). In addition to annexing many of the colonial possessions of the vanquished states, the Triple Entente exacted punitive restitution payments from them, plunging Germany in particular into economic depression. The Austro-Hungarian and Ottoman empires were dismantled at the war's conclusion. The Russian Revolution resulted in the overthrow of the Tsarist régime of Nicholas II and the onset of the

Russian Civil War. The victorious Bolsheviks then established the Soviet Union, the world's first communist state.

At the beginning of the period, the British Empire was the world's most powerful nation, having acted as the world's policeman for the past century. Fascism, a movement which grew out of post-war angst and which accelerated during the Great Depression of the 1930s, gained momentum in Italy, Germany, and Spain in the 1920s and 1930s, culminating in World War II, sparked by Nazi Germany's aggressive expansion at the expense of its neighbors. Meanwhile, Japan had rapidly transformed itself into a technologically advanced industrial power and, along with Germany and Italy, formed the Axis powers. Japan's military expansionism in East Asia and the Pacific Ocean brought it into conflict with the United States, culminating in a surprise attack which drew the US into World War II. After some years of dramatic military success, Germany was defeated in 1945, having been invaded by the Soviet Union and Poland from the East and by the United States, the United Kingdom, Canada, and France from the West. After the victory of the Allies in Europe, the war in Asia ended with the dropping of two atomic bombs on Japan by the US, the first nation to develop and use nuclear weapons. In total, World War II left some 60 million people dead. After the war, Germany was occupied and divided between the Western powers and the Soviet Union. East Germany and the rest of Eastern Europe became Soviet puppet states under communist rule. Western Europe was rebuilt with the aid of the American Marshall Plan, resulting in a major post-war economic boom, and many of the affected nations became close allies of the United States.

With the Axis defeated and Britain and France rebuilding, the United States and the Soviet Union were left standing as the world's only superpowers. Allies during the war, they soon became hostile to one another as their competing ideologies of communism and democratic capitalism proliferated in Europe, which became divided by the Iron Curtain and the Berlin Wall. They formed competing military alliances (NATO and the Warsaw Pact) which engaged in a decades-long standoff known as the Cold War. The period was marked by a new arms race as the USSR became the second nation to develop nuclear weapons, which were produced by both sides in sufficient numbers to end most human life on the planet had a large-scale nuclear exchange ever occurred. Mutually assured destruction is credited by many historians as having prevented such an exchange, each side being unable to strike first at the other without ensuring an equally devastating retaliatory strike. Unable to engage one another directly, the conflict played out in a series of proxy wars around the world–particularly in China, Korea, Vietnam, and Afghanistan–as the USSR sought to export communism while the US attempted to contain it. The technological competition between the two sides led to substantial investment in research and development which produced innovations that reached far beyond the battlefield, such as space exploration and the Internet.

In the latter half of the century, most of the European-colonized world in Africa and Asia gained independence in a process of decolonization. Meanwhile, globalization opened the door for several nations to exert a strong influence over many world affairs. The US's global military presence spread American culture around the world with the advent of the Hollywood motion picture industry, Broadway, rock and roll, pop music, fast food, big-box stores, and the hip-hop lifestyle. Britain also continued to influence world culture, including the "British Invasion" into American music, leading many rock bands from other countries (such as Swedish ABBA) to sing in English. After the Soviet Union collapsed under internal pressure in 1991, most of the communist governments it had supported around the world were dismantled—with the notable exceptions of China, North Korea, Cuba, Vietnam, and Laos —followed by awkward transitions into market economies.

Following World War II, the United Nations, successor to the League of Nations, was established as an international forum in which the world's nations could discuss issues diplomatically. It enacted resolutions on such topics as the conduct of warfare, environmental protection, international sovereignty, and human rights. Peacekeeping forces consisting of troops provided by various countries, with various United Nations and other aid agencies, helped to relieve famine, disease, and poverty, and to suppress some local armed conflicts. Europe slowly united, economically and, in some ways, politically, to form the European Union, which consisted of 15 European countries by the end of the 20th century.

In the last third of the century, concern about humankind's impact on the Earth's environment made environmentalism popular. In many countries, especially in Europe, the movement was channeled into politics through Green parties. Increasing awareness of global warming began in the 1980s, commencing decades of social and political debate.

The Nature of Innovation and Change

Due to continuing industrialization and expanding trade, many significant changes of the century were, directly or indirectly, economic and technological in nature. Inventions such as the light bulb, the automobile, and the telephone in the late 19th century, followed by supertankers, airliners, motorways, radio, television, antibiotics, nuclear power, frozen food, computers and microcomputers, the Internet, and mobile telephones affected people's quality of life across the developed world. Scientific research, engineering professionalization and technological development —much of it motivated by the Cold War arms race—drove changes in everyday life.

Social Change

At the beginning of the century, strong discrimination based on race and sex was significant in general society. The fight for equality for non-white people in the white-dominated societies of North America, Europe, and South Africa continued. During the century, the social taboo of sexism fell. By the end of the 20th century, women had the same legal rights as men in many parts of the world, and racism had come to be seen as abhorrent. Attitudes towards homosexuality also began to change in the later part of the century.

The World at the End of the 20th century

Communications and information technology, transportation technology, and medical advances had radically altered daily lives. Europe appeared to be at a sustainable peace for the first time in recorded history. The people of the Indian subcontinent, a sixth of the world population at the end of the 20th century, had attained an indigenous independence for the first time in centuries. China, an ancient nation comprising a fifth of the world population, was finally open to the world, creating a new state after the near-complete destruction of the old cultural order. With the end of colonialism and the Cold War, nearly a billion people in Africa were left in new nation states after centuries of foreign domination.

The world was undergoing its second major period of globalization; the first, which started in the 18th century, having been terminated by World War I. Since the US was in a dominant position, a major part of the process was Americanization. The influence of China and India was also rising, as the world's largest populations were rapidly integrating with the world economy.

Terrorism, dictatorship, and the spread of nuclear weapons were pressing global issues. The world was still blighted by small-scale wars and other violent conflicts, fueled by competition over resources and by ethnic conflicts. Despots such as Kim Jong-il of North Korea continued to lead their nations toward the development of nuclear weapons.

Disease threatened to destabilize many regions of the world. New viruses such as SARS and West Nile continued to spread. Malaria and other diseases affected large populations. Millions were infected with HIV, the virus which causes AIDS. The virus was becoming an epidemic in southern Africa.

Based on research done by climate scientists, the majority of the scientific community consider that in the long term environmental problems may threaten the planet's habitability. One argument is that of global warming occurring due to human-caused emission of greenhouse gases, particularly carbon dioxide produced by the burning of fossil fuels. This prompted many nations to negotiate and sign the Kyoto treaty, which set mandatory limits on carbon dioxide emissions.

World population increased from about 1.6 billion people in 1901 to 6.1 billion at the century's end.

Wars and Politics

The number of people killed during the century by government actions was in the hundreds of millions. This includes deaths caused by wars, genocide, politicide and mass murders. The deaths from acts of war during the two world wars alone have been estimated at between 50 and 80 million. Political scientist Rudolph Rummel estimated 262,000,000 deaths caused by democide, which excludes those killed in war battles, civilians unintentionally killed in war and killings of rioting mobs. According to Charles Tilly, "Altogether, about 100 million people died as a direct result of action by organized military units backed by one government or another over the course of the century. Most likely a comparable number of civilians died of war-induced disease and other indirect effects." It is estimated that approximately 70 million Europeans died through war, violence and famine between 1914 and 1945.

- After gaining political rights in the United States and much of Europe in the first part of the century, and with the advent of new birth control techniques, women became more independent throughout the century.

- Rising nationalism and increasing national awareness were among the many causes of World War I (1914–1918), the first of two wars to involve many major world powers including Germany, France, Italy, Japan, Russia/USSR, the British Empire and the United States. World War I led to the creation of many new countries, especially in Eastern Europe. At the time, it was said by many to be the "war to end all wars".

- Industrial warfare greatly increased in its scale and complexity during the first half of the 20th century. Notable developments included chemical warfare, the introduction of military aviation and the widespread use of submarines. The introduction of nuclear warfare in the mid-20th century marked the definite transition to modern warfare.

- Civil wars occurred in many nations. A violent civil war broke out in Spain in 1936 when General Francisco Franco rebelled against the Second Spanish Republic. Many consider this war as a testing battleground for World War II, as the fascist armies bombed some Spanish territories.

- The Great Depression in the 1930s led to the rise of Fascism and Nazism in Europe.

- World War II (1939–1945) involved Eastern Asia and the Pacific, in the form of Japanese aggression against China and the United States. Civilians also suffered greatly in World War II, due to the aerial bombing of cities on both sides, and the German genocide of the Jews and others, known as the Holocaust.

- During World War I, in the Russian Revolution of 1917, 300 years of Romanov reign were ended and the Bolsheviks, under the leadership of Vladimir Lenin, established the world's first Communist state. After the Soviet Union's involvement in World War II, communism became a major force in global politics, notably in Eastern Europe, China, Indochina and Cuba, where communist parties gained near-absolute power. This led to the Cold War and proxy wars with the Western bloc, including wars in Korea (1950–1953) and Vietnam (1957–1975).

- The Cold War had caused an arms race and increasing competition between the two major players in the world: the Soviet Union and the United States. This competition included the development and improvement of nuclear weapons and the Space Race.

- The Soviet authorities caused the deaths of millions of their own citizens in order to eliminate domestic opposition. More than 18 million people passed through the Gulag, with a further 6 million being exiled to remote areas of the Soviet Union.

- The civil rights movement in the United States and the movement against apartheid in South Africa challenged racial segregation in those countries.

- The two world wars led to efforts to increase international cooperation, notably through the founding of the League of Nations after World War I, and its successor, the United Nations, after World War II.

- Nationalist movements in the subcontinent led to the independence and partition of India and Pakistan.

- Gandhi's nonviolence and Indian independence movement against the British Empire influenced many political movements around the world, including the civil rights movement in the U.S., and freedom movements in South Africa and Burma.

- The creation in 1948 of Israel, a Jewish state in the Middle East, by the British Mandate of Palestine fueled many regional conflicts. These were also influenced by the vast oil fields in many of the other countries of the mostly Arab region.

- The end of colonialism led to the independence of many African and Asian countries. During the Cold War, many of these aligned with the United States, the USSR, or China for defense.

- After a long period of civil wars and conflicts with western powers, China's last imperial dynasty ended in 1912. The resulting republic was replaced, after another civil war, by a communist People's Republic in 1949. At the end of the 20th century, though still ruled by a communist party, China's economic system had largely transformed to capitalism.

- The Great Chinese Famine was a direct cause of the death of tens of millions of Chinese peasants between 1959 and 1962. It is thought to be the largest famine in human history.

- The Vietnam War caused two million deaths, changed the dynamics between the Eastern and Western Blocs, and altered North-South relations.

- The Soviet War in Afghanistan caused one million deaths and contributed to the downfall of the Soviet Union.

- The revolutions of 1989 released Eastern and Central Europe from Soviet supremacy. Soon thereafter, the Soviet Union, Czechoslovakia, and Yugoslavia dissolved, the latter violently over several years, into successor states, many rife with ethnic nationalism. Meanwhile, East Germany and West Germany were reunified in 1990.

- The Tiananmen Square protests of 1989, culminating in the deaths of hundreds of civilian protesters, were a series of demonstrations in and near Tiananmen Square in Beijing, China. Led mainly by students and intellectuals, the protests occurred in a year that saw the collapse of a number of communist governments around the world.

- European integration began in earnest in the 1950s, and eventually led to the European Union, a political and economic union that comprised 15 countries at the end of the 20th century.

Culture and Entertainment

- As the century began, Paris was the artistic capital of the world, where both French and foreign writers, composers and visual artists gathered. By the end of the century New York City had become the artistic capital of the world.

- Theater, films, music and the media had a major influence on fashion and trends in all aspects of life. As many films and much music originate from the United States, American culture spread rapidly over the world.

- 1953 saw the coronation of Queen Elizabeth II, an iconic figure of the century.

- Visual culture became more dominant not only in films but in comics and television as well. During the century a new skilled understanding of narrativist imagery was developed.

- Computer games and internet surfing became new and popular form of entertainment during the last 25 years of the century.

- In Literature, science fiction, fantasy (with well-developed fictional worlds, rich in detail), and alternative history fiction gained unprecedented popularity. Detective fiction gained unprecedented popularity in the interwar period. In the United States in 1961 Grove Press published *Tropic of Cancer* a novel by Henry Miller redefining pornography and censorship in publishing in America.

Music

The invention of music recording technologies such as the phonograph record, and dissemination technologies such as radio broadcasting, massively expanded the audience for music. Prior to the 20th century, music was generally only experienced in live performances. Many new genres of music were established during the 20th century.

Film, television and theatre

Film as an artistic medium was created in the 20th century. The first modern movie theatre was established in Pittsburgh in 1905. Hollywood developed as the center of American film production. While the first films were in black and white, technicolor was developed in the 1920s to allow for color films. Sound films were developed, with the first full-length feature film, *The Jazz Singer*, released in 1927. The Academy Awards were established in 1929.

Video Games

Video games—due to the great technological steps forward in computing since the second post-war period—are the new form of entertainment emerged in the 20th century alongside films.

- Video games emerged as an industry during the 1970s, and then exploded into social and cultural phenomenon such as the golden age of arcade video games, the worldwide success of Nintendo's *Super Mario Bros.* and the release in the 1990s of Sony PlayStation console, the first one to break the record of 100 million units sold.

Art and Architecture

- The art world experienced the development of new styles and explorations such as fauvism, expressionism, Dadaism, cubism, de stijl, surrealism, abstract expressionism, color field, pop art, minimal art, lyrical abstraction, and conceptual art.

- The modern art movement revolutionized art and culture and set the stage for both Modernism and its counterpart postmodern art as well as other contemporary art practices.

- Art Nouveau began as advanced architecture and design but fell out of fashion after World War I. The style was dynamic and inventive but unsuited to the depression of the Great War.

- In Europe, modern architecture departed from the decorated styles of the Victorian era. Streamlined forms inspired by machines became commonplace, enabled by developments in building materials and technologies. Before World War II, many European architects moved to the United States, where modern architecture continued to develop.

- The automobile increased the mobility of people in the Western countries in the early-to-mid-century, and in many other places by the end of the 20th century. City design throughout most of the West became focused on transport via car.

Sport

- The popularity of sport increased considerably—both as an activity for all, and as entertainment, particularly on television.

- The modern Olympic Games, first held in 1896, grew to include tens of thousands of athletes in dozens of sports.

Physics

- New areas of physics, like special relativity, general relativity, and quantum mechanics, were developed during the first half of the century. In the process, the internal structure of atoms came to be clearly understood, followed by the discovery of elementary particles.

- Discovery of nuclear reactions, in particular nuclear fusion, finally revealed the source of solar energy.

- Radiocarbon dating was invented, and became a powerful technique for determining the age of prehistoric animals and plants as well as historical objects.

Astronomy

- A much better understanding of the evolution of the universe was achieved, its age (about 13.8 billion years) was determined, and the Big Bang theory on its origin was proposed and generally accepted.

- The planets of the solar system and their moons were closely observed via numerous space probes. Pluto was discovered in 1930 on the edge of the solar system, although in the early 21st century, it was reclassified as a plutoid instead of a planet proper, leaving eight planets.

- No trace of life was discovered on any of the other planets in our solar system (or elsewhere in the universe), although it remained undetermined whether some forms of primitive life might exist, or might have existed, somewhere. Extrasolar planets were observed for the first time.

Biology

- Genetics was unanimously accepted and significantly developed. The structure of DNA was determined in 1953 by James Watson, Francis Crick,Rosalind Franklin and Maurice Wilkins, following by developing techniques which allow to read DNA sequences and culminating in starting the Human Genome Project (not finished in the 20th century) and cloning the first mammal in 1996.

- The convergence of various sciences for the formulation of the modern evolutionary synthesis (produced between 1936 and 1947), providing a widely accepted account of evolution.

Medicine

- Placebo-controlled, randomized, blinded clinical trials became a powerful tool for testing new medicines.

- Antibiotics drastically reduced mortality from bacterial diseases and their prevalence.

- A vaccine was developed for polio, ending a worldwide epidemic. Effective vaccines were also developed for a number of other serious infectious diseases, including influenza, diphtheria, pertussis (whooping cough), tetanus, measles, mumps, rubella (German measles), chickenpox, hepatitis A, and hepatitis B.

- Epidemiology and vaccination led to the eradication of the smallpox virus in humans.

- X-rays became powerful diagnostic tool for wide spectrum of diseases, from bone fractures to cancer. In the 1960s, computerized tomography was invented. Other important diagnostic tools developed were sonography and magnetic resonance imaging.

- Development of vitamins virtually eliminated scurvy and other vitamin-deficiency diseases from industrialized societies.

- The role of tobacco smoking in the causation of cancer and other diseases was proven during the 1950s (see British Doctors Study).

- New methods for cancer treatment, including chemotherapy, radiation therapy, and immunotherapy, were developed. As a result, cancer could often be cured or placed in remission.

- The development of blood typing and blood banking made blood transfusion safe and widely available.

- The invention and development of immunosuppressive drugs and tissue typing made organ and tissue transplantation a clinical reality.

- New methods for heart surgery were developed, including pacemakers and artificial hearts.

- Contraceptive drugs were developed, which reduced population growth rates in industrialized countries, as well as decreased the taboo of premarital sex throughout many western countries.

- Vaccines, hygiene and clean water improved health and decreased mortality rates, especially among infants and the young.

Notable diseases

- An influenza pandemic, Spanish Flu, killed anywhere from 20 to 100 million people between 1918 and 1919.

- A new viral disease, called the Human Immunodeficiency Virus, or HIV, arose in Africa and subsequently killed millions of people throughout the world. HIV leads to a syndrome called Acquired Immunodeficiency Syndrome, or AIDS. Treatments for HIV remained inaccessible to many people living with AIDS and HIV in developing countries, and a cure has yet to be discovered.

- Because of increased life spans, the prevalence of cancer, Alzheimer's disease, Parkinson's disease, and other diseases of old age increased slightly.

- Sedentary lifestyles, due to labor-saving devices and technology, along with the increase in home entertainment and technology such as television, video games, and the internet contributed to an "epidemic" of obesity, at first in the rich countries, but by the end of the 20th century spreading to the developing world.

Energy and the environment

- The dominant use of fossil sources and nuclear power, considered the conventional energy sources.

- Widespread use of petroleum in industry—both as a chemical precursor to plastics and as a fuel for the automobile and airplane —led to the geopolitical importance of petroleum resources. The Middle East, home to many of the world's oil deposits, became a center of geopolitical and military tension throughout the latter half of the century. (For example, oil was a factor in Japan's decision to go to war against the United States in 1941, and the oil cartel, OPEC, used an oil embargo of sorts in the wake of the Yom Kippur War in the 1970s).

- The increase in fossil fuel consumption also fueled a major scientific controversy over its effect on the environment.

- Pesticides, herbicides and other toxic chemicals accumulated in the environment, including in the bodies of humans and other animals.

- Overpopulation and worldwide deforestation diminished the quality of the environment.

Engineering and technology

One of the prominent traits of the 20th century was the dramatic growth of technology. Organized research and practice of science led to advancement in the fields of communication, engineering, travel, medicine, and war.

- The number and types of home appliances increased dramatically due to advancements in technology, electricity availability, and increases in wealth and leisure time. Such basic appliances as washing machines, clothes dryers, furnaces, exercise machines, refrigerators, freezers, electric stoves, and vacuum cleaners all became popular from the 1920s through the 1950s. The microwave oven became popular during the 1980s and have become a standard in all homes by the 1990s. Radios were popularized as a form of entertainment during the 1920s, which extended to television during the 1950s. Cable and satellite television spread rapidly during the 1980s and 1990s. Personal computers began to enter the home during the 1970s–1980s as well. The age of the portable music player grew during the 1960s with the development of the transistor radio, 8-track and cassette tapes, which slowly began to replace record players. These were in turn replaced by the CD during the late 1980s and 1990s. The proliferation of the Internet in the mid-to-late 1990s made digital distribution of music (mp3s) possible. VCRs were popularized in the 1970s, but by the end of the 20th century, DVD players were beginning to replace them, making the VHS obsolete by the end of the first decade of the 21st century.

- The first airplane was flown in 1903. With the engineering of the faster jet engine in the 1940s, mass air travel became commercially viable.

- The assembly line made mass production of the automobile viable. By the end of the 20th century, billions of people had automobiles for personal transportation. The combination of the automobile, motor boats and air travel allowed for unprecedented personal mobility. In western nations, motor vehicle accidents became the greatest cause of death for young people. However, expansion of divided highways reduced the death rate.

- Aluminum became an inexpensive metal and became second only to iron in use.

Space exploration

- The Space Race between the United States and the Soviet Union gave a peaceful outlet to the political and military tensions of the Cold War, leading to the first human spaceflight with the Soviet Union's *Vostok 1* mission in 1961, and man's first landing on another world—the Moon—with America's *Apollo 11* mission in 1969. Later, the first space station was launched by the Soviet space program. The United States developed the first reusable spacecraft system with the Space Shuttle program, first launched in 1981. As the century ended, a permanent manned presence in space was being founded with the ongoing construction of the International Space Station.

- In addition to human spaceflight, unmanned space probes became a practical and relatively inexpensive form of exploration. The first orbiting space probe, *Sputnik 1*, was launched by the Soviet Union in 1957. Over time, a massive system of artificial satellites was placed into orbit around Earth. These satellites greatly advanced navigation, communications, military intelligence, geology, climate, and numerous other fields. Also, by the end of the 20th century, unmanned probes had visited the Moon, Mercury, Venus, Mars, Jupiter, Saturn, Uranus, Neptune, and various asteroids and comets. The Hubble Space Telescope, launched in 1990, greatly expanded our understanding of the Universe and brought brilliant images to TV and computer screens around the world.

- The Global Positioning System, a series of satellites that allow land-based receivers to determine their exact location, was developed and deployed.

Religion

- The Vatican II council was held from 1962 to 1965, and resulted in significant changes in the Catholic Church.

- The Wahhabi sect of Sunni Islam gained in influence with the growth of Saudi Arabia.

- Atheism became considerably more common, both in secular Western countries, and Communist countries with a policy of state atheism.

Economics

- The Great Depression was a worldwide economic slowdown that lasted throughout the early 1930s.

- The Soviet Union implemented a series of five-year plans for industrialization and economic development.

- Most countries abandoned the gold standard for their currency. The Bretton Woods system involved currencies being pegged to the United States dollar; after the system collapsed in 1971 most major currencies had a floating exchange rate.

SOURCES

AUTHORITARIAN STATES

NAZI GERMANY

Céspedes, Juan R. (2013). *The Myopic Vision: The Causes of Totalitarianism, Authoritarianism, and Statism.* Mundus Novus Publishers. https://www.amazon.com/Myopic-Vision-Totalitarianism-Authoritarianism-Statism-ebook/dp/B00E65NSFE.

"Nazi Germany." Gale Encyclopedia of World History: Governments. . *Encyclopedia.com.* 17 Jun. 2019 <https://www.encyclopedia.com>.

Shirer, William L. (1960). *The Rise and Fall of the Third Reich* . New York: Simon & Schuster.

Vashem, Yad (2000). Encyclopedia of the Holocaust . London: Routledge.

Wilt, Alan F. (1994). *Nazi Germany* . Arlington Heights, IL: Harlan Davison.

Authoritarian Dictators

The Rise of Adolf Hitler

Céspedes, Juan R. (2013). *The Myopic Vision: The Causes of Totalitarianism, Authoritarianism, and Statism.* Mundus Novus Publishers. https://www.amazon.com/Myopic-Vision-Totalitarianism-Authoritarianism-Statism-ebook/dp/B00E65NSFE.

"Adolf Hitler." Encyclopedia of World Biography. . Retrieved June 18, 2019 from Encyclopedia.com: https://www.encyclopedia.com/history/encyclopedias-almanacs-transcripts-and-maps/adolf-hitler

Monteshire, Henry Charles (1950). *Hitler: A Study of Despotism.* Cranstaff & Robinson Books, LTD.

FASCIST ITALY

Céspedes, Juan R. (2013). *The Myopic Vision: The Causes of Totalitarianism, Authoritarianism, and Statism.* Mundus Novus Publishers. https://www.amazon.com/Myopic-Vision-Totalitarianism-Authoritarianism-Statism-ebook/dp/B00E65NSFE.

Gentile, Emilio (2003). *The Struggle For Modernity Nationalism Futurism and Fascism* (Westport, CT: Praeger, 2003), p. 87.

Harrison, Mark (2000). *The Economics of World War II: Six Great Powers in International Comparison. Cambridge University Press. p. 3. ISBN 9780521785037. Retrieved 2 October 2017.*

Italy (2019). https://www.britannica.com/place/Italy/Italy-since-1945

Mussolini, Benito (1935). Fascism: Doctrine and Institutions. Rome: Ardita Publishers. p. 14.

Pauley, Bruce F (2003). *Hitler, Stalin, and Mussolini: Totalitarianism in the Twentieth Century Italy*, Wheeling: Harlan Davidson, Inc., p. 107.

Payne, Stanley G. (1996). *A History of Fascism, 1914–1945.* p. 212

The Rise of Benito Mussolini

"Benito Mussolini." Encyclopedia of World Biography. . *Encyclopedia.com.* 17 Jun. 2019 <https://www.encyclopedia.com>.

Bosworth, R. J. B. 2002. *Mussolini.* New York: Oxford University Press.

Cardoza, Anthony L. 2006. *Benito Mussolini: The First Fascist.* New York: Pearson Longman.

Céspedes, Juan R. (2013). *The Myopic Vision: The Causes of Totalitarianism, Authoritarianism, and Statism.* Mundus Novus Publishers. https://www.amazon.com/Myopic-Vision-Totalitarianism-Authoritarianism-Statism-ebook/dp/B00E65NSFE.

Mack Smith, Denis. 1983. *Mussolini.* New York: Vintage.

Mussolini, Benito. 1998. *My Rise and Fall.* Ed. Max Ascoli. New York: Da Capo.

"Mussolini, Benito." International Encyclopedia of the Social Sciences. . *Encyclopedia.com.* 17 Jun. 2019 <https://www.encyclopedia.com>.

IMPERIAL JAPAN

First Sino-Japanese War

Céspedes, Juan R. (2013). *The Myopic Vision: The Causes of Totalitarianism, Authoritarianism, and Statism.* Mundus Novus Publishers. https://www.amazon.com/Myopic-Vision-Totalitarianism-Authoritarianism-Statism-ebook/dp/B00E65NSFE.

Chang, Jung (2013). *The Concubine Who Launched Modern China: Empress Dowager Cixi.* New York: Anchor Books. *ISBN 9780307456700.*

Duus, Peter (1998). *The Abacus and the Sword: The Japanese Penetration of Korea. University of California Press. ISBN 978-0-520-92090-3.*

Elleman, Bruce A. (2001). *Modern Chinese Warfare, 1795–1989. Routledge. ISBN 978-0-415-21474-2.*

Evans, David C; Peattie, Mark R (1997). *Kaigun: strategy, tactics, and technology in the Imperial Japanese Navy, 1887–1941. Annapolis, Maryland: Naval Institute Press. ISBN 978-0-87021-192-8.*

Jansen, Marius B. (1995). *The Emergence of Meiji Japan. Cambridge University Press. ISBN 978-0-521-48405-3.*

Jansen, Marius B. (2002). *The Making of Modern Japan. Harvard University Press. ISBN 978-0-674-00334-7.*

Jowett, Philip (2013). *China's Wars: Rousing the Dragon 1894-1949. Bloomsbury Publishing. ISBN 978-1-47280-673-4.*

Keene, Donald (2002). *Emperor of Japan: Meiji and His World, 1852–1912. New York: Columbia University Press. ISBN 978-0-231-12341-9.*

Kim, Jinwung (2012). *A History of Korea: From "Land of the Morning Calm" to States in Conflict. New York: Indiana University Press. ISBN 978-0-253-00024-8.*

Kwang-Ching, Liu (1978). *John King Fairbank (ed.). The Cambridge History of China. Volume 11, Late Ch'ing, 1800–1911 Part 2 (illustrated ed.). Cambridge University Press. ISBN 978-0-521-22029-3.*

Lone, Stewart (1994). *Japan's First Modern War: Army and Society in the Conflict with China, 1894–1895. New York: St. Martin's Press.*

Olender, Piotr (2014). *Sino-Japanese Naval War 1894–1895. MMPBooks. ISBN 978-83-63678-30-2.*

Paine, S.C.M (2003). *The Sino-Japanese War of 1894–1895: Perceptions, Power, and Primacy. Cambridge University Press. ISBN 978-0-521-81714-1.*

Palais, James B. (1975). *Politics and Policy in Traditional Korea. Harvard University Asia Center. ISBN 978-0-674-68770-7.*

Seth, Michael J. (2011). *A History of Korea: From Antiquity to the Present. Rowman & Littlefield. ISBN 978-0-742-56715-3.*

Sondhaus, Lawrence (2001). *Naval Warfare, 1815–1914. Routledge. ISBN 978-0-415-21477-3.*

Schencking, J. Charles (2005). *Making Waves: Politics, Propaganda, And The Emergence Of The Imperial Japanese Navy, 1868–1922. Stanford University Press. ISBN 978-0-8047-4977-0.*

Willmott, H. P. (2009). *The Last Century of Sea Power: From Port Arthur to Chanak, 1894–1922, Volume 1. Indiana University Press. ISBN 978-0-25300-356-0.*

Zachmann, Urs Matthias (2009). *China and Japan in the Late Meiji Period: China Policy and the Japanese Discourse on National Identity, 1895-1904. Routledge. ISBN 978-0415481915.*

Second Sino-Japanese War (and the following sections)

Bix, Herbert P. (1992), *"The Showa Emperor's 'Monologue' and the Problem of War Responsibility", Journal of Japanese Studies, **18** (2): 295–363, doi:10.2307/132824*

Black, Jeremy (2012). *Avoiding Armageddon: From the Great Wall to the Fall of France, 1918–40. p. 171. ISBN 978-1-4411-2387-9.*

Brinkley, Douglas. *The New York Times Living History: World War II, 1942–1945: The Allied Counteroffensive. Retrieved September 1, 2018.*

Céspedes, Juan R. (2011). *War Interminable:The Origins, Causes, Practices and Effects of International Conflict. https://www.amazon.com/dp/1463767293/ref=rdr_ext_tmb*

Chevrier, Marie Isabelle; Chomiczewski, Krzysztof; Garrigue, Henri, eds. (2004). *The Implementation of Legally Binding Measures to Strengthen the Biological and Toxin Weapons Convention: Proceedings of the NATO Advanced Study Institute, Held in Budapest, Hungary, 2001. Volume 150 of NATO science series: Mathematics, physics, and chemistry (illustrated ed.). Springer. p. 19. ISBN 1-4020-2097-X. Retrieved March 10, 2019.*

"China Offensive". Center of Military History. United states Army. October 3, 2003. Retrieved November 14, 2018.

Clodfelter, Michael "Warfare and Armed Conflicts: A Statistical Reference", Vol. 2, pp. 956.

Combs, Jerald A. (2002). Embargoes and Sanctions. *Encyclopedia of American Foreign Policy.*

Crawford, Keith A.; Foster, Stuart J. (2007). *War, nation, memory : international perspectives on World War II in school history textbooks. Charlotte, NC: Information Age. p. 90. ISBN 9781607526599. OCLC 294758908.*

Fenby, Jonathan (2003). *Generalissimo: Chiang Kai-shek and the China He Lost (illustrated ed.). Simon and Schuster. p. 319. ISBN 0-7432-3144-9. Retrieved April 24, 2018.*

Feng, Liu (2007). "血祭太阳旗: 百万侵华日军亡命实录". Central Compilation and Translation Press. ISBN 978-7-80109-030-0. *Note*: This Chinese publication analyses statistics provided by Japanese publications.

Ferris, John; Mawdsley, Evan (2015). *The Cambridge History of the Second World War, Volume I: Fighting the War. Cambridge: Cambridge University Press.*

Fu Jing-hui (2003). An Introduction of Chinese and Foreign History of War, pp. 109–111

Goodman, David S. G. (2004). *"Qinghai and the Emergence of the West: Nationalities, Communal Interaction and National Integration" (PDF). The China Quarterly. Cambridge University Press for the School of Oriental and African Studies. University of London, UK.: 385. ISSN 0305-7410. Retrieved July 13, 2018.*

Gordon, David M. "The China–Japan War, 1931–1945" *Journal of Military History* (January 2006). v. 70#1, pp, 137–82. Historiographical overview of major books from the 1970s through 2006

Guoxiang, Meng & Zhang Qinyuan (1995). "关于抗日战争中我国军民伤亡数字问题".

Horner, David Murray (July 24, 2003). *The Second World War: The Pacific. Taylor & Francis. pp. 14–15. ISBN 978-0-415-96845-4. Retrieved March 6, 2019.*

Hotta, E. (December 25, 2007). *Pan-Asianism and Japan's War 1931-1945. Palgrave Macmillan US. p. 40. ISBN 978-0-230-60992-1.*

Hsiung, James C. *(1992). China's Bitter Victory: The War With Japan, 1937–1945. New York: M.E. Sharpe publishing. ISBN 1-56324-246-X.*

Hsiung, James C., and Steven I. Levine, eds. (1992). *China's Bitter Victory: The War with Japan, 1937–1945.* Armonk, NY: M.E. Sharpe. xxv, 333p. ISBN 0-87332-708-X. Chapters on military, economic, diplomatic aspects of the war.

Hsu, Long-hsuen; Chang Ming-kai (1972). History of the Sino-Japanese war (1937–1945). Chung Wu Publishers. ASIN B00005W210.

Huang, Zheping; Huang, Zheping. *"China is rewriting textbooks so its "eight-year war of resistance" against Japan is now six years longer". Quartz. Retrieved April 8, 2019.*

Januszewski, Tadeusz (2013). *Mitsubishi A5M Claude (Yellow Series). P.O. Box 123 27–600 Sandomierz 1, Poland: STRATUS. ISBN 978-83-61421-99-3.*

Linebarger, Paul M. A. (May 1941). *"The Status of the China Incident". American Academy of Political and Social Science. Sage Publications, Inc.* **215**: *8. JSTOR 1022596.*

Kao, Yao-Han (2011). Kao Chih-Hang Biography: Air Force Ares. Taiwan: Dawn Cultural Undertaking Corp. ISBN 978-957-16-0819-8.

Kirby, Major General Woodburn, S (1958). *The War against Japan, Vol 2: India's Most Dangerous Hour. London: Her Majesty's Stationery Office.*

Long-hsuen, Hsu (1972) "History of the Sino-Japanese war (1937–1945)". Taipei.

"Memorandum by Mr J. McEwen, Minister for External Affairs 10 May 1940". Info.dfat.gov.au. Archived from the original on February 21, 2011. Retrieved December 2, 2018.

Mitter, Rana (2014). Forgotten Ally: China's World War II, 1937–1945. Mariner Books. ISBN 978-0-544-33450-2.

O'Connell, John F. (2007). The Effectiveness of Airpower in the 20th Century. 2021 Pine Lake Rd. Suite 100 Lincoln, NE 68512: iUniverse. ISBN 978-0-595-43082-6.

Oi, Mariko (March 14, 2013). "What Japanese history lessons leave out". BBC.

Paine, S. C. M. (August 20, 2012). The Wars for Asia, 1911–1949. Cambridge University Press. p. 123. ISBN 978-1-139-56087-0.

Rea, George Bronson (1935). The Case for Manchoukuo. New York: D. Appleton-Century Company, Pp 164.

Rummel, R. J. (1991). China's Bloody Century. Transaction. ISBN 0-88738-417-X.

Schaller, Michael (1979). The U. S. Crusade in China, 1938.

Schoppa, R. Keith (2011). In a Sea of Bitterness, Refugees during the Sino-Japanese War. Harvard University Press. p. 28. ISBN 978-0-674-05988-7.

Slim, William (1956). Defeat into Victory. London: Cassell. ISBN 0-304-29114-5.

Stevens, Keith (2005). "A Token Operation: 204 Military Mission to China, 1941–1945". Asian Affairs. Risk Management Reference Center, EBSCOhost. 36 (1): 66, 74. doi:10.1080/03068370500039151.

"The Senkaku or Diaoyu Islands: Narrative of an empty space". The Economist. London: Economist Group (Christmas Specials 2012). December 22, 2012. ISSN 0013-0613. Archived from the original on February 26, 2014. Retrieved February 26, 2018.

US Congress. Investigation of Concentration of Economic Power. Hearings before the Temporary National Economic Committee. 76th Congress, 2nd Session, Pt. 21. Washington, 1940, p. 11241

Wang, Zheng (April 23, 2014). *"History Education: The Source of Conflict Between China and Japan"*. The Diplomat.

"War, Leadership and Ethnopolitics: Chiang Kai-shek and China's frontiers, 1941–1945". *Informaworld.com. Retrieved December 2, 2018.*

Zarrow, Peter (2005). "The War of Resistance, 1937–45". China in war and revolution 1895–1949. London: Routledge.

Наджафов, Д. Г. (1990). Нейтралитет США. 1935—1941. М., "Наука", стр.157

"马家军悲壮的抗战: 百名骑兵集体投河殉国(1)". 军事- 中华网. *September 19, 2008. Archived from the original on April 11, 2011.* (Eng.: "Ma Jiajun's tragic anti-Japanese war: 100 cavalry collectively voted for the country (1)"

Analysis: Japan During World War II (and the following sections)

Barenblatt, Daniel (2004). *A Plague upon Humanity*, pp. xii, 173.

Céspedes, Juan R. (2011). *War Interminable:The Origins, Causes, Practices and Effects of International Conflict. https://www.amazon.com/dp/1463767293/ref=rdr_ext_tmb.*

Céspedes, Juan R. (2015). *Japanese Asian Expansionism in the 20th Century.* Class notes, Florida International University (unpublished document).

"Chronological table 5 1 December 1946 - 23 June 1947". *National Diet Library. Retrieved September 30, 2017.*

Dave Flitton (1994). *Battlefield: Pearl Harbor (Documentary). Event occurs at 8 minutes, 40 seconds – via distributor: PBS.*

Dower, J. W. (1993). *Japan in War & Peace*, New press, p. 11

Gill, G. Hermon (1957). *Royal Australian Navy 1939–1942. Australia in the War of 1939–1945. Series 2 – Navy. 1. Canberra: Australian War*

Memorial. p. 485. LCCN 58037940. Archived from the original on May 25, 2009. Retrieved June 16, 2019.

Grajdanzev, A. J. (1 January 1942). *"Formosa (Taiwan) Under Japanese Rule". Pacific Affairs.* **15** *(3): 311–324. doi:10.2307/2752241. JSTOR 2752241.*

Hotta, Eri (2013). *Japan 1941 : Countdown to Infamy. New York: Knpf. ISBN 978-0307739742.*

Klemen, L. (1999–2000). *"Forgotten Campaign: The Dutch East Indies Campaign 1941–1942". Archived from the original on July 26, 2011.*

Lankov, Andrei (March 23, 2006). *"The Dawn of Modern Korea (360): Settling Down". The Korea Times. Retrieved December 18, 2018.*

Morton, Louis. *"Japan's Decision for War". U.S. Army Center Of Military History. Retrieved 5 May 2018.*

Newman, T. (2018, February 28). Biological weapons and bioterrorism: Past, present, and future. Retrieved from https://www.medicalnewstoday.com/articles/321030.php.

Racing the Enemy: Stalin, Truman, and the Surrender of Japan Tsuyoshi Hasegawa Belknap Press (Oct. 30 2006) ISBN 978-0674022416

"Russia Acknowledges Sending Japanese Prisoners of War to North Korea". Mosnews.com. April 1, 2005. Archived from the original on November 13, 2006. Retrieved February 23, 2018. http://web.archive.org/web/20061113081334/http://www.mosnews.com/news/2005/04/01/japanesedied.shtml

Tanaka, Yuki (1998). *Poison Gas, the Story Japan Would Like to Forget,* Bulletin of the Atomic Scientists, October, p. 16-17.

Totani, Yuma (April 1, 2009). *The Tokyo War Crimes Trial: The Pursuit of Justice in the Wake of World War II. Harvard University Asia Center. p. 57.*

Yoshiaki Yoshimi and Seiya Matsuno, *Dokugasusen Kankei Shiryō II* (Materials on poison gas Warfare II), Kaisetsu, Hōkan 2, Jūgonen sensô gokuhi shiryōshū, Funi Shuppankan, 1997, pp. 25–29.

Hideki Tojo (and the following sections)

Baudot, Marcel (1980). *The Historical encyclopedia of World War II. Infobase Publishing. ISBN 978-0-87196-401-4.*

Browne, Courtney (1998). *Tojo The Last Banzai. Boston: Da Capo Press. ISBN 0306808447.*

Butow, Robert Joseph Charles (1961). *Tojo and the coming of the war. Stanford University Press. ISBN 978-0-8047-0690-2.*

Céspedes, Juan R. (2015). *Japanese Asian Expansionism in the 20th Century.* Class notes, Florida International University (unpublished document).

Crowe, David M. (2014). *War Crimes, Genocide, and Justice: A Global History. New York City, New York: St. Martin's Press, LLC. ISBN 978-0-230-62224-1. Retrieved February 24, 2019.*

Dower, John (1986). *War Without Mercy: Race and Power in the Pacific War. New York: Pantheon. ISBN 0075416522.*

Falk, Stanley (December 1961). *"Organization and Military Power: The Japanese High Command in World War II". Political Science Quarterly. 76. pp. 503–518.*

Fredrikson, John C. (2001). *America's military adversaries: from colonial times to the present. ABC-CLIO. ISBN 978-1-57607-603-3.*

Gorman, Jacqueline Laks (2009). *Pearl Harbor: A Primary Source History. Gareth Stevens. ISBN 978-1-4339-0047-1.*

"Hideki Tojo." Encyclopedia of World Biography. *Encyclopedia.com.* 27 Jun. 2019 <https://www.encyclopedia.com>.

Karnow, Stanley (1989). *"Hideki Tojo/Hideko Tojo". In Our Image: America's Empire in the Philippines. Random House. ISBN 978-0-394-54975-0.*

Kristof, Nicholas (November – December 1998). *"The Problem of Memory". Foreign Affairs. 77. pp. 37–49.*

Lamont-Brown, Raymond (1988). *Kempeitai: Japan's dreaded military police. The History Press. ISBN 978-0-7509-1566-3.*

Toland, John (1970). *The Rising Sun: The Decline and Fall of the Japanese Empire, 1936–1945. New York: Random House. LCCN 77117669.*

CULT OF PERSONALITY

Bown, Matthew C. 1991. The Cult of Personality: The Apotheosis of Stalin, 1945–56. In *Art under Stalin*. New York: Holmes and Meier.

Céspedes, Juan R. *(2013). Collapse of the Soviet Empire. https://www.amazon.com/Collapse-Soviet-Empire-C%C3%A9spedes-Ph-D-ebook/dp/B00DFLFOMU.*

Chandler, David P. 1999. *Brother Number One: A Political Biography of Pol Pot.* Boulder, CO: Westview.

Hollander, Paul. 2002. The Cult of Personality in Communist States. In *Discontents: Postmodern and Postcommunist.* New Brunswick, NJ: Transaction.

Khrushchev, Nikita S. 1989. О КуЛьТе ЛИЧНОСТИ Иего ПОСЛеДСТВИЯХ [On the Cult of Personality and Its Consequences]. ИЗВеСТИЯ Ц ПСС [The News of the Central Committee of the Communist Party of the Soviet Union] 3 (March).

Overy, Richard J. 1997. The Cult of Personality: Stalin and the Legacy of War. In *Russia's War: Blood upon the Snow.* New York: TV Books.

"Personality, Cult of." International Encyclopedia of the Social Sciences. *Rossen Vassilev. Encyclopedia.com. 27 Jun. 2019 <https://www.encyclopedia.com>.*

Ryan, Louise. 2001. The Cult of Personality: Reassessing Leadership and Suffrage Movements in Britain and Ireland. In *Leadership and Social Movements,* ed. Colin Barker, Alan Johnson, and Michael Lavalette, 196–212. Manchester, U.K.: Manchester University Press.

Secondary Sources

International Encyclopedia of the Social Sciences

Encyclopedia of Russian History

The Soviet/Communist Phenomena

Brooks, Jeffrey. (2000). *Thank You, Comrade Stalin!* Princeton, NJ: Princeton University Press.

Céspedes, Juan R. *(2013). Collapse of the Soviet Empire. https:// www.amazon.com/Collapse-Soviet-Empire-C%C3%A9spedes-Ph-D-ebook/dp/B00DFLFOMU.*

Gill, Graeme. (1980). "The Soviet Leader Cult: Reflections on the Structure of Leadership in the Soviet Union." *British Journal of Political Science* 10(2):167–186.

"Cult of Personality." Encyclopedia of Russian History. . *Encyclopedia.com.* 27 Jun. 2019 <https://www.encyclopedia.com>. Karen Petrone.

"How Likely is a Putin Cult of Personality?" (2001). [Panel Discussion] *Current Digest of the Post-Soviet Press* 53(21):4–6.

Khrushchev, Nikita. (1956). "On the Cult of Personality and Its Harmful Consequences" *Congressional Proceedings and Debates of the 84th Congress, 2nd Session* (May 22–June 11), C11, Part 7 (June 4), pp. 9,389–9,403.

Tucker, Robert C. (1973). *Stalin as Revolutionary, 1879–1929.* New York: Norton.

Tucker, Robert C. (1992). *Stalin in Power: The Revolution from Above, 1928–1941.* New York: Norton.

Tumarkin, Nina. (1983). *Lenin Lives! The Lenin Cult in Russia.* Cambridge, MA: Harvard University Press.

THE MOVE TO GLOBAL WAR (and the following sections)

Bassford, Christopher. 2002. *Clausewitz in English: The Reception of Clausewitz in Britain and America, 1815-1945.* Oxford University Press. ISBN 978-0195083835

Bell, David (2007). *The First Total War: Napoleon's Europe and the Birth of Warfare as We Know It.* Houghton Mifflin. ISBN 978-0618349654

Boemeke, Manfred, Robert Chickering, and Stig Forster (1999). *Total War: The German and American Experiences, 1871-1914.* ISBN 978-0521622943

Céspedes, Juan R. (2011). *War Interminable:The Origins, Causes, Practices and Effects of International Conflict. https://www.amazon.com/dp/1463767293/ref=rdr_ext_tmb.*

Kopf, David and Eric Markusen (1995). *The Holocaust and Strategic Bombing: Genocide and Total War in the Twentieth Century.* Westview Press. ISBN 0813375320

McWhiney, Grady and Daniel Sutherland (1998). *The Emergence of Total War.* McWhiney Foundation Press. Retrieved September 20, 2018.

Neely, Mark (2004). *Was the Civil War a Total War?* Civil War History. Retrieved September 20, 2017.

Trueman, Chris (2007). Military Developments in the Thirty Years War, *History Learning Site.* Retrieved August 6, 2017.

Death from the Air (and the following sections)

Bell, David A (12 January 2007). *The First Total War: Napoleon's Europe and the Birth of Warfare as We Know It (First ed.). Houghton Mifflin Harcourt. ISBN 0618349650. Retrieved 19 January 2019.*

Broers, Michael (2008). "The Concept of 'Total War' in the Revolutionary —Napoleonic Period" *War in History* v.15 n.3 pp.247-268.

Céspedes, Juan R. (2011). *War Interminable:The Origins, Causes, Practices and Effects of International Conflict. https://www.amazon.com/dp/1463767293/ref=rdr_ext_tmb.*

"The Impact of Total War." World War II Reference Library. *Encyclopedia.com.* 17 Jun. 2019 <https://www.encyclopedia.com>.

WORLD WAR II (and the following sections)

Adamthwaite, Anthony P. (1992). *The Making of the Second World War. New York: Routledge. ISBN 978-0-415-90716-3.*

Breuer, William B. *Undercover Tales of World War II.* New York: J. Wiley, 1999.

Farago, Ladislas. *The Game of the Foxes: The Untold Story of German Espionage in the United States and Great Britain during World War II.* City: Publisher, 1971.

Persico, Joseph E. *Roosevelt's Secret War: FDR and World War II Espionage.* New York: Random House, 2001.

Shirer, William. *The Rise and Fall of the Third Reich.* New York: Simon and Schuster, 1960.

West, Nigel. *A Thread of Deceit: Espionage Myths of World War II.* New York: Random House, 1985.

"World War II." Encyclopedia of Espionage, Intelligence, and Security. *Encyclopedia.com.* 16 Jun. 2019 <https://www.encyclopedia.com>

CONSEQUENCES OF WORLD WAR II (and the following sections)

Barber, John, and Harrison, Mark. (1991). *The Soviet Home Front: A Social and Economic History of the USSR in World War II.* London: Longman.

Erickson, John. (1975). *Stalin's War with Germany,* vol. 1: *The Road to Stalingrad.* London: Weidenfeld & Nicolson.

Erickson, John. (1983). *Stalin's War with Germany,* vol. 2: *The Road to Berlin.* London: Weidenfeld & Nicolson.

Erickson, John. (1997). "Red Army Battlefield Performance, 1941–1945: The System and the Soldier." In *Time to Kill: The Soldier's Experience of War in the West, 1939–1945,* eds. Paul Addison and Angus Calder. London: Pimlico.

Glantz, David M., and House, Jonathan. (1995). *When Titans Clashed: How the Red Army Stopped Hitler.* Lawrence: University Press of Kansas.

Gorodetsky, Gabriel. (1999). *Grand Delusion: Stalin and the German Invasion of Russia.* New Haven, CT: Yale University Press.

Haslam, Jonathan. (1992). *The Soviet Union and the Threat from the East, 1933–41: Moscow, Tokyo, and the Prelude to the Pacific War.* London: Macmillan.

Kershaw, Ian, and Lewin, Moshe, eds. (1997). *Stalinism and Nazism: Dictatorships in Comparison.* Cambridge, UK: Cambridge University Press.

Overy, Richard. (1997). *Russia's War.* London: Allen Lane.

Reese, Roger R. (2000). *The Soviet Military Experience*. London: Routledge.

Roberts, Geoffrey. (1995). *The Soviet Union and the Origins of the Second World War: Russo-German Relations and the Road to War, 1933–1941*. Basingstoke, UK: Macmillan.

Roberts, Geoffrey. (2000). *Victory at Stalingrad: The Battle That Changed History*. London: Longman.

Salisbury, Harrison. (1969). *The 900 Days: The Siege of Leningrad*. London: Pan.

Volkogonov, Dmitri. (1991). *Stalin: Triumph and Tragedy*. London: Weidenfeld & Nicholson.

Wegner, Bernd, ed. (1997). *From Peace to War: Germany, Soviet Russia, and the World, 1939–1941*. Providence, RI: Berghahn.

Weinberg, Gerhard L. (1995). *A World at Arms: A Global History of World War II*. Cambridge, UK: Cambridge University Press.

Werth, Alexander. (1964). *Russia at War, 1941–1945*. London: Barrie & Rockliff.

"World War II." Encyclopedia of Russian History. *Encyclopedia.com.* 16 Jun. 2019 <https://www.encyclopedia.com>.

Secondary Sources

Boyer, Paul S. *The Oxford Companion to United States History* (2001) excerpt and text search; online at many libraries

Carnes, Mark C., and John A. Garraty. *The American Nation: A History of the United States: AP Edition* (2008)

Dear, Ian C. B. and Michael Foot, eds. *The Oxford Companion to World War II* (2005), comprehensive encyclopedia for all countries

Lee, Loyd, ed. *World War II in Europe, Africa, and the Americas, with General Sources: A Handbook of Literature and Research* (1997) excerpt and text search

THE COLD WAR

Acheson, Dean. *Present at the Creation: My Years in the State Department.* New York, 1969.

Brands, H. W., Jr. *Cold Warriors: Eisenhower's Generation and the American Foreign Policy.* New York, 1988.

Brinkley, Douglas. *Dean Acheson: The Cold War Years, 1953–1971.* New Haven, Conn., 1992.

Cannon, Lou. *President Reagan: The Role of a Lifetime.* New York, 1991.

Chace, James. *Acheson: The Secretary of State Who Created the American World.* New York, 1998.

Clark, Suzanne. *Cold Warriors: Manliness on Trial in the Rhetoric of the West.* Carbondale, Ill., 2000. The subtitle suggests how much the field of Cold War studies has changed since the early 1990s.

"Cold Warriors." Encyclopedia of American Foreign Policy. . *Encyclopedia.com.* 17 Jun. 2019 <https://www.encyclopedia.com>.

Conquest, Robert. *Stalin: Breaker of Nations.* New York, 1991.

Fitz Gerald, Frances. *Way Out There in the Blue: Reagan, Star Wars, and the End of the Cold War.* New York, 2000.

Goncharov, Sergei N., John W. Lewis, and Xue Litai. *Uncertain Partners: Stalin, Mao, and the Korean War.* Stanford, Calif., 1993.

Hunt, Michael H. *The Genesis of Chinese Communist Foreign Policy.* New York, 1996.

Isaacson, Walter, and Evan Thomas. *The Wise Men: Six Friends and the World They Made: Acheson, Bohlen, Harriman, Kennan, Lovett, McCloy.* New York, 1986.

Khrushchev, Nikita. *Khrushchev Remembers: The Last Testament.* Translated and edited by Strobe Talbott. Boston, 1974.

Mastny, Vojtech. *Russia's Road to the Cold War.* New York, 1979.

McLellan, David S. *Dean Acheson: The State Department Years.* New York, 1976.

Raack, R. C. *Stalin's Drive to the West, 1938–1945: The Origins of the Cold War.* Stanford, Calif., 1995.

Radzinsky, Edvard. *Stalin.* New York, 1996.

Reagan, Ronald. *An American Life.* New York, 1990.

Schmertz, Eric J., Natalie Datlof, and Alexej Ugrinsky, eds. *President Reagan and the World.* Westport, Conn., 1997.

Schram, Stuart. *Mao Tse-tung.* New York, 1966.

Spence, Jonathan. *Mao Zedong.* New York, 1999.

Tucker, Robert C. *Stalin in Power: The Revolution from Above, 1928–1941.* New York, 1990.

Wills, Garry. *Reagan's America: Innocents at Home.* Garden City, N.Y., 1987.

Zubok, Vladislav, and Constantine Pleshakov. *Inside the Kremlin's Cold War: From Stalin to Khrushchev.* Cambridge, Mass., 1996.

Secondary Sources

Encyclopedia of American Foreign Policy

The Oxford Companion to American Military History

Encyclopedia of Russian History

Encyclopedia of Espionage, Intelligence, and Security

Dictionary of American History

A Military & Ideological Struggle (1945–91)

Cardona, Luis (2007). *Cold War KFA. Routledge.*

Céspedes, Juan R. *(2013). Collapse of the Soviet Empire. https:// www.amazon.com/Collapse-Soviet-Empire-C%C3%A9spedes-Ph-D-ebook/dp/B00DFLFOMU.*

Hanhimäki, Jussi and Odd Arne Westad, eds. *The Cold War: A History in Documents and Eyewitness Accounts* (Oxford University Press, 2003). ISBN 0-19-927280-8.

Kirkendall, Andrew J. (November 2014). "Cold War Latin America: The State of the Field", *H-Diplo Essay No. 119: An H-Diplo State of the Field Essay.*

LaFeber, Walter (1993). *America, Russia, and the Cold War, 1945–1992. McGraw-Hill. ISBN 978-0-07-035853-9.*

Leffler, Melvyn (1992). *A Preponderance of Power: National Security, the Truman Administration, and the Cold War. Stanford University Press. ISBN 978-0-8047-2218-6.*

Leffler, Melvyn P. and Odd Arne Westad, eds. *The Cambridge History of the Cold War* (3 vol, 2010) 2000 pp; new essays by leading scholars

Leffler, Melvyn P. (September 2008). *For The Soul of Mankind: The United States, the Soviet Union, and the Cold War. New York: Farrar, Strauss, and Giroux. ISBN 9780374531423.*

Lüthi, Lorenz M (2008). *The Sino-Soviet Split: Cold War in the Communist World. Princeton University Press. ISBN 978-0-691-13590-8.*

Mastny, Vojtech. *The Cold War and Soviet Insecurity: The Stalin Years* (1996) online edition

Miller, Roger Gene (2000). *To Save a City: The Berlin Airlift, 1948–1949. Texas A&M University Press. ISBN 978-0-89096-967-0.*

Njølstad, Olav (2004). *The Last Decade of the Cold War. Routledge. ISBN 978-0-7146-8371-3.*

Pearson, Raymond (1998). *The Rise and Fall of the Soviet Empire. Macmillan. ISBN 978-0-312-17407-1.*

Porter, Bruce; Karsh, Efraim (1984). *The USSR in Third World Conflicts: Soviet Arms and Diplomacy in Local Wars. Cambridge University Press. ISBN 978-0-521-31064-2.*

Service, Robert (2015). *The End of the Cold War: 1985–1991. Macmillan. ISBN 978-1-61039-499-4.*

Tucker, Spencer, ed. *Encyclopedia of the Cold War: A Political, Social, and Military History* (5 vol. 2008), world coverage

Westad, Odd Arne (2017). *The Cold War: A World History. Basic Books. ISBN 978-0-465-05493-0.* online review

Zubok, Vladislav M. (2008). *A Failed Empire: The Soviet Union in the Cold War from Stalin to Gorbachev*

The Role of Nuclear Weapons (and the following sections)

Boughton, G. J. (1974). Journal of Interamerican Studies and World Affairs (16th ed.). Miami, United States of America: Center for Latin American Studies at the University of Miami.

Brown, A. Reform, Coup and Collapse: The End of the Soviet State. BBC History. Retrieved November 22, 2012

Cold War: A Brief History. (n.d.). Atomic Archive. Retrieved November 16, 2012

Doty, P., Carnesale, A., & Nacht, M. (1976, October). The Race to Control Nuclear Arms.   •

Joyce, A., Bates Graber, R., Hoffman, T. J., Paul Shaw, R., & Wong, Y. (1989, February). The Nuclear Arms Race: An Evolutionary Perspective.

Maloney, S. M. (2007). Learning to love the bomb: Canada's nuclear weapons during the Cold War. Washington, D.C: Potomac Books.

May, E. R. (n.d.). John F Kennedy and the Cuban Missile Crisis. BBC History. Retrieved November 22, 2012

Van, C. M. (1993). Nuclear proliferation and the future of conflict. New York, United States: Free Press.

The Endgame

Andrew, Christopher M., and Mitrokhin, Vasili (1999). *The Sword and the Shield: The Mitrokhin Archive and the Secret History of the KGB.* New York: Basic Books.

Cohen Warren I., and Tucker, Nancy Bernkopf, eds. (1994). *Lyndon Johnson Confronts the World: American Foreign Policy, 1963–1968.* New York: Cambridge University Press.

"Cold War." Encyclopedia of Russian History. . *Encyclopedia.com.* 17 Jun. 2019 <https://www.encyclopedia.com>.

Cold War International History Project Bulletin (1992–). Washington, DC: Woodrow Wilson International Center for Scholars.

Fursenko, Aleksandr, and Naftali, Timothy (1997). *"One Hell of a Gamble": Khrushchev, Castro, and Kennedy, 1958–1964.* New York: Norton.

Gaddis, John Lewis (1972). *The United States and the Origins of the Cold War, 1941–1947.* New York: Columbia University Press.

Gaddis, John Lewis (1982). *Strategies of Containment: A Critical Appraisal of Postwar American National Security Policy.* New York: Oxford University Press.

Haynes, John Earl Haynes, and Klehr, Harvey (1999). *Venona: Decoding Soviet Espionage in America.* New Haven, CT: Yale University Press.

Hogan, Michael J. (1998). *A Cross of Iron: Harry S. Truman and the Origins of the National Security State.* New York: Cambridge University Press.

Holloway, David (1994). *Stalin and the Bomb: The Soviet Union and Atomic Energy, 1939–1956.* New Haven, CT: Yale University Press.

Journal of Cold War Studies (quarterly, 1999–). Cambridge, MA: MIT Press.

Leffler, Melvyn P. (1992). *A Preponderance of Power: National Security, the Truman Administration, and the Cold War.* Stanford, CA: Stanford University Press.

Naimark, Norman, and Gibianskii, Leonid, eds. (1997). *The Establishment of Communist Regimes in Eastern Europe.* Boulder, CO: Westview Press.

Schmidt, Gustáv, ed. (2001). *A History of NATO: The First Fifty Years,* 3 vols. New York: Palgrave.

Stokes, Gale (1993). *The Walls Came Tumbling Down: The Collapse of Communism in Eastern Europe.* New York: Oxford University Press.

Taubman, William C. (2003). *Khrushchev: The Man and His Era.* New York: Norton.

Thornton, Richard C. (2001). *The Nixon-Kissinger Years: Reshaping America's Foreign Policy,* rev. ed. St. Paul: Paragon House.

The Unforeseen Collapse of the Soviet Empire (and the following sections)

Baucom, Donald. *The Origins of SDI.* Lawrence, KS: University Press of Kansas, 1992.

Brown, Archie. *The Gorbachev Factor.* Oxford: Oxford University Press, 1997.

Céspedes, Juan R. (2013). *Collapse of the Soviet Empire.* https://www.amazon.com/Collapse-Soviet-Empire-C%C3%A9spedes-Ph-D-ebook/dp/B00DFLFOMU.

"Cold War (1972–1989): the Collapse of the Soviet Union." Encyclopedia of Espionage, Intelligence, and Security. . *Encyclopedia.com.* 17 Jun. 2019 <https://www.encyclopedia.com>.

Colton, Timothy, and Robert Legvold. *After the Soviet Union.* New York: W. W. Norton, 1992.

McGuire, Michael. *Perestroika and Soviet National Security.* Washington, D.C.: Brookings Institute, 1991.

McMahon, Robert. *The Cold War on the Periphery.* New York: Columbia University Press, 1994.

Secondary Sources

Cold War (1945–1950), The Start of the Atomic Age

Cold War (1950–1972)

Ford Administration (1974–1977), United States National Security Policy

Nixon Administration (1969–1974), United States National Security Policy

Reagan Administration (1981–1989), United States National Security Policy

Civil Rights and the Cold War

Borstelmann, Thomas. 2001. *The Cold War and the Color Line: American Race Relations in the Global Arena*. Cambridge, MA: Harvard University Press.

"Civil Rights, Cold War." International Encyclopedia of the Social Sciences. . *Encyclopedia.com*. 17 Jun. 2019 <https://www.encyclopedia.com>.

Dudziak, Mary L. 2000. *Cold War Civil Rights: Race and the Image of American Democracy*. Princeton, NJ: Princeton University Press.

Giddins, Gary. 2001. *Satchmo: The Genius of Louis Armstrong*. 2nd ed. Cambridge, MA: Da Capo Press.

Plummer, Brenda Gayle. 1996. *Rising Wind: Black Americans and U.S. Foreign Affairs, 1935–1960*. Chapel Hill: University of North Carolina Press.

THE BLACKLIST (and the following sections)

Cook, Bruce (1977). *Dalton Trumbo*. New York: Scribners.

Cook, Fred J. (1971). *The Nightmare Decade: The Life and Times of Senator Joe McCarthy*. New York: Random House. ISBN 0-394-46270-X

Denning, Michael (1998). *The Cultural Front: The Laboring of American Culture in the Twentieth Century*. London and New York: Verso. ISBN 1-85984-170-8

Dmytryk, Edward. *It's a Hell of a Life but Not a Bad Living*. New York: Time Books, 1978.

Hanson, Peter (2001). *Dalton Trumbo, Hollywood Rebel: A Critical Survey and Filmography*. Jefferson, NC: McFarland.

Tender Comrade (1943), *Murder, My Sweet* (1944), *Crossfire* (1947), *The Caine Mutiny* (1954), *Broken Lance* (1954), *Warlock* (1959)

Trumbo, Dalton (1939). *Johnny Got His Gun*. Lippincott.

THE "HIP" COLD WAR

Belfrage, Cedric. *The American Inquisition, 1945–1960: A Profile of the "McCarthy Era."* New York: Thunder's Mouth, 1989.

Bernstein, Walter. *Inside Out: A Memoir of the Blacklist.* New York: Knopf, 1996.

Biskind, Peter. *Seeing Is Believing: How Hollywood Taught Us to Stop Worrying and Love the Fifties.* New York: Pantheon, 1983.

Boyer, Paul. *By the Bomb's Early Light: American Thought and Culture at the Dawn of the Atomic Age.* New York: Pantheon, 1985.

Ceplair, Larry, and Steven Englund. *The Inquisition in Hollywood: Politics in the Film Community, 1930–1960.* Berkeley: University of California Press, 1979.

"Cold War." Schirmer Encyclopedia of Film. *Kim Newman. Encyclopedia.com.* 17 Jun. 2019 <https://www.encyclopedia.com>.

Cole, Lester. *Hollywood Red.* Palo Alto, CA: Ramparts Press, 1981.

Henriksen, Margot A. *Dr. Strangelove's America: Society and Culture in the Atomic Age.* Berkeley: University of California Press, 1997.

Kahn, Gordon. *Hollywood on Trial: The Story of the Ten Who Were Indicted.* New York: Boni and Gaer, 1948.

Kazan, Elia. *Elia Kazan: A Life.* New York: Knopf, 1988.

McGilligan, Patrick, and Paul Buhle, eds. *Tender Comrades: A Backstory of the Hollywood Blacklist.* New York: St. Martin's Press, 1997.

Miller, Arthur. *Timebends: A Life.* New York: Grove Press, 1987.

Navasky, Victor S. *Naming Names.* New York: Viking Press, 1980.

Smith, Julian. *Looking Away: Hollywood and Vietnam.* New York: Scribners, 1975.

Warren, Bill. *Keep Watching the Skies!: American Science Fiction Movies of the Fifties, Vol. 1, 1950–1957.* Jefferson, NC, and London: McFarland, 1982.

———. *Keep Watching the Skies!: American Science Fiction Movies of the Fifties, Vol. 2, 1958–1962.* Jefferson, NC, and London: McFarland, 1986.

The Berlin Airlift (and the following sections)

Céspedes, Juan R. (2013). *Collapse of the Soviet Empire.* https://www.amazon.com/Collapse-Soviet-Empire-C%C3%A9spedes-Ph-D-ebook/dp/B00DFLFOMU.

Céspedes, Juan R. (2011). *War Interminable: The Origins, Causes, Practices and Effects of International Conflict.* https://www.amazon.com/War-Interminable-Practices-International-Conflict/dp/1463767293.

"Cold War." Encyclopedia of Modern Europe: Europe Since 1914: Encyclopedia of the Age of War and Reconstruction. . *Encyclopedia.com.* 17 Jun. 2019 <https://www.encyclopedia.com>.

Hanhimäki, Jussi M., and Odd Arne Westad, eds. (2003). *The Cold War: A History in Documents and Eyewitness Accounts.* Oxford, U.K.,

Orwell, George. The Collected Essays, Journalism, and Letters of George Orwell, edited by Sonia Orwell and Ian Angus . Vol. 4. London, 1968.

Secondary Sources

Crockatt, Richard (1995). *The Fifty Years War: The United States and the Soviet Union in World Politics, 1941–1991.* London, 1995.

Fox, William T. R. (1944). *The Super-Powers: The United States, Britain, and the Soviet Union.* New York.

Gaddis, John (1997). *We Now Know: Rethinking Cold War History.* Oxford, U.K.,.

Halliday, Fred (1986). *The Making of the Second World War.* 2nd ed. London.

Reynolds, David (2000). *One World Divisible: A Global History since 1945.* New York. Sets the Cold War within larger global patterns.

Westad, Odd Arne, ed. (2000). *Reviewing the Cold War: Approaches, Interpretations, and Theory.* London. A stimulating set of essays.

TOTALITARIANISM IN THE 20TH CENTURY (and the following sections)

Applebaum, Anne (2003). *Gulag: A History.* New York: Doubleday.

Arendt, Hannah (1968). *The Origins of Totalitarianism.* 1951. Reprint, New York: Harcourt Brace.

Baehr, Peter, and Melvin Richter, eds. (2004). *Dictatorship in History and Theory: Bonapartism, Caesarism, and Totalitarianism.* Cambridge, U.K.: Cambridge University Press.

Berman, Paul (2003). *Terror and Liberalism.* New York: Norton.

Burleigh, Michael (2001). *The Third Reich: A New History.* New York: Hill and Wang.

Canovan, Margaret (1992). *Hannah Arendt: A Reinterpretation of Her Political Thought.* Cambridge, U.K.: Cambridge University Press.

Céspedes, Juan R. (2013). *Collapse of the Soviet Empire.* https://www.amazon.com/Collapse-Soviet-Empire-C%C3%A9spedes-Ph-D-ebook/dp/B00DFLFOMU.

Céspedes, Juan R. (2013). *The Myopic Vision: The Causes of Totalitarianism, Authoritarianism, and Statism.* Mundus Novus Publishers. https://www.amazon.com/Myopic-Vision-Totalitarianism-Authoritarianism-Statism-ebook/dp/B00E65NSFE.

Chandler, David (1999). *Voices from S-21: Terror and History in Pol Pot's Secret Prison.* Berkeley: University of California Press.

Courtois, Stéphane, et al. (1999). *The Black Book of Communism: Crimes, Terror, Repression.* 1997. Reprint, Cambridge, Mass.: Harvard University Press.

Friedrich, Carl J., ed. (1954). *Totalitarianism: Proceedings of a Conference Held at the American Academy of Arts and Sciences, March 1953.* Cambridge, Mass.: Harvard University Press.

Friedrich, Carl J., and Zbigniew K. Brzezinski (1965). *Totalitarian Dictatorship and Autocracy.* 2nd rev. ed. Cambridge, Mass.: Harvard University Press.

Furet, François, and Ernst Nolte (1998). *Fascism and Communism.* Translated by Katherine Golsan. Reprint, Lincoln: University of Nebraska Press, 2001.

Gentile, Emilio (2000). "The Sacralization of Politics: Definitions, Interpretations, and Reflections on the Question of Secular Religion and

Totalitarianism." Translated by Robert Mallett. *Totalitarian Movements and Political Religions* 1, no. 1: 18–55.

Gleason, Abbott (1995). *Totalitarianism: The Inner History of the Cold War.* New York: Oxford University Press.

Griffin, Roger, ed. (1995). *Fascism.* Oxford: Oxford University Press.

Hobsbawm, Eric (1994). *Age of Extremes.* New York: Pantheon.

Kershaw, Ian, and Moshe Lewin, eds. (1997). *Stalinism and Nazism: Dictatorships in Comparison.* Cambridge, U.K.: Cambridge University Press.

Kirkpatrick, Jeane (1992). *Dictatorships and Double Standards: Rationalism and Reason in Politics.* New York: Simon and Schuster.

Lifka, Thomas E. (1988). *The Concept "Totalitarianism" and American Foreign Policy, 1933–1949.* New York: Garland.

Lifton, Robert Jay (1961). *Thought Reform and the Psychology of Totalism.* New York: Norton.

Linz, Juan J. (2000). *Totalitarian and Authoritarian Regimes.* Boulder, Colo.: Rienner.

Menze, Ernest A., ed. (1981). *Totalitarianism Reconsidered.* Port Washington, N.Y.: Kennikat.

Nathan, Andrew (1997). *China's Transition.* New York: Columbia University Press.

Schapiro, Leonard (1972). *Totalitarianism.* New York: Praeger.

Schoenhals, Michael, ed. (1996). *China's Cultural Revolution, 1966–1969: Not a Dinner Party.* Armonk, N.Y.: Sharpe.

Talmon, Jacob L. (1985). *The Origins of Totalitarian Democracy.* 1952. Reprint, Boulder, Colo.: Westview.

Todorov, Tsvetan (1997). *Facing the Extreme: Moral Life in the Concentration Camps.* Translated by Arthur Denner and Abigail Pollak. New York: Owl.

Zaslavsky, Victor (1999). "The Katyn Massacre: 'Class Cleansing' as Totalitarian Praxis." Translated by Joseph Cardinale. *Telos* 114: 67–107.

Totalitarian Systems (and the following sections)

American Academy of Arts and Sciences (1954). *Totalitarianism.* Edited with an introduction by Carl J. Friedrich. Cambridge, Mass.: Harvard Univ. Press. -" Proceedings of a conference held at the American Academy of Arts and Sciences, March 1953.

Arendt, Hannah (1951). 1958 *The Origins of Totalitarianism.* 2d enl. ed. New York: Meridian.

Arendt, Hannah 1963 *Eichmann in Jerusalem: A Report on the Banality of Evil.* New York: Viking.

Brzezinski, Zbigniew K. (1962). Deviation Control: A Study in the Dynamics of Doctrinal Conflict. *American Political Science Review* 56:5-22.

Céspedes, Juan R. (2013). *Collapse of the Soviet Empire.* https:// www.amazon.com/Collapse-Soviet-Empire-C%C3%A9spedes-Ph-D-ebook/dp/B00DFLFOMU.

Céspedes, Juan R. (2013). *The Myopic Vision: The Causes of Totalitarianism, Authoritarianism, and Statism.* Mundus Novus Publishers. https://www.amazon.com/Myopic-Vision-Totalitarianism-Authoritarianism-Statism-ebook/dp/B00E65NSFE.

Cobban, Alfred (1939). *Dictatorship: Its History and Theory.* New York: Scribner.

Friedrich, Carl J.; and Brzezinski, Zbigniew K. (1956). *Totalitarian Dictatorship and Autocracy.* Cambridge, Mass.: Harvard Univ. Press.

Kautsky, John H. (1962). *Political Change in Underdeveloped Countries: Nationalism and Communism.* New York: Wiley.

Moore, Barrington, Jr. (1954). *Terror and Progress— USSR: Some Sources of Change and Stability in the Soviet Dictatorship.* Harvard University, Russian Research Center Studies, No. 12. Cambridge, Mass.: Harvard Univ. Press.

Moore, Barrington, Jr. (1958). *Political Power and Social Theory: Six Studies.* Cambridge, Mass.: Harvard Univ. Press.

Neumann, Franz L. (1942). 1963 *Behemoth: The Structure and Practice of National Socialism, 1933-1944.* 2d ed. New York: Octagon Books.

Neumann, Fkanz L. (1957). Notes on the Theory of Dictatorship. Pages 233-256 in Franz L. Neumann, *The Democratic and the Authoritarian State: Essays in Political and Legal Theory.* Glencoe, 111.: Free Press.

Neumann, Sigmund (1942). *Permanent Revolution: The Total State in a World at War.* New York: Harper.

Nolte, Ernst (1965, 1966). *Three Faces of Fascism: Action Frangaise, Italian Fascism, National Socialism.* New York: Holt. -" First published in German.

Rossiter, Clinton L. (1948). *Constitutional Dictatorship: Crisis Government in the Modern Democracies.* Princeton Univ. Press.

Spiro, Herbert J. (1962). Comparative Politics: A Comprehensive Approach. *American Political Science Review* 56:577-595.

Talmon, J. L. (1952). *The Rise of Totalitarian Democracy.* Boston: Beacon.

"Totalitarianism." International Encyclopedia of the Social Sciences. *Encyclopedia.com.* 18 Jun. 2019 <https://www.encyclopedia.com>.

Utis, O. (1952). Generalissimo Stalin and the Art of Government. *Foreign Affairs* 30:197-214.

George Orwell (and the following sections)

Arendt, Hannah. *The Origins of Totalitarianism,* San Diego, New York, and London: Harcourt Brace Jonvanovich, 1951.

Aristotle, *Politics*, in Ebenstein, William and Alan Ebenstein. *Great Political Thinkers, Plato to the Present,* New York: Harcourt College Publishers, 2000.

Céspedes, Juan R. (2013). *The Myopic Vision: The Causes of Totalitarianism, Authoritarianism, and Statism.* Mundus Novus Publishers. https://www.amazon.com/Myopic-Vision-Totalitarianism-Authoritarianism-Statism-ebook/dp/B00E65NSFE.

Ebenstein, William and Alan Ebenstein (2000). *Great Political Thinkers, Plato to the Present,* New York: Harcourt College Publishers.

Friedrich, Carl J., and Zbigniew K. Brzezinski (1956). Totalitarian Dictatorship and Autocracy, *New York: Frederick A. Praeger.*

Magstadt, Thomas M. (1998). *Nations and Governments, Comparative Politics in Regional Perspective,* New York: St. Martin's Press.

Nietzsche, Friedrich (2000). *Thus Spake Zarathustra,* in Ebenstein, William and Alan Ebenstein. *Great Political Thinkers, Plato to the Present,* New York: Harcourt College Publishers.

Orwell, George (1949). *1984,* New York: Harcourt, Brace and Company.

Plato (2000). *The Republic,* in Ebenstein, William and Alan Ebenstein. *Great Political Thinkers, Plato to the Present,* New York: Harcourt College Publishers.

"Totalitarianism." Political Theories for Students. *Encyclopedia.com.* 18 Jun. 2019 <https://www.encyclopedia.com>.

Secondary Sources

Aburish, Said K. (1995). *The Rise, Corruption and Coming Fall of the House of Saud,* New York: Saint Martin's.

Bakhash, Shaul (1991). *The Reign of the Ayatollahs: Iran and the Islamic Revolution,* San Bernardino, California: Borgo Press.

De Klerk, F.W. (1999). *The Last Trek — A New Beginning,* New York: St. Martin's Press.

Deutscher, Isaac (1960). *Stalin: A Political Biography,* New York: Vintage Books.

Hunter, Wendy (1996). *Eroding Military Influence in Brazil: Politicians against Solider,* Chapel Hill, North Carolina: University of North Carolina Press.

Springborg, Robert (1989). *Mubarak's Egypt: Fragmentation of the Political Order,* Boulder, Colorado: Westview Press.

CUBAN IMPACT ON HEMISPHERIC AND WORLD AFFAIRS

Background

Britannica, Encyclopedia (2014, July 31). Fulgencio Batista: Cuban Dictator. Retrieved from http://www.britannica.com/biography/Fulgencio-Batista

Corrales, Javier (2014, January 6). The Cuban Paradox: Why is Havana so cautious about reform? Perhaps because its reformer-in-chief is also a stalwart of the revolution. FP (Foreign Policy). Retrieved from http://foreignpolicy.com/2014/01/06/the-cuban-paradox/

Farber, Samuel (2015). CUBA'S CHALLENGE: WHAT DID THE CUBAN REVOLUTION ACCOMPLISH AND WHERE CAN IT GO FROM HERE? The Cuban Economy. Tag Archives: *Special Period.* Retrieved from http://thecubaneconomy.com/articles/tag/special-period/

UC Sandiego (n.p.d.) Elections and Events 1933-1959. The Library. Retrieved from http://act.ucsd.edu/cwp/tools/search?site=cascade-lib&q=elections+and+events%20more:cascade-lib

Schoonover, Thomas (2008). *Hitler's Man in Havana: Heinz Luning and Nazi Espionage in Latin America.* University Press of Kentucky.

International Involvement Pre-1959

World War II

Chicago Daily Tribune (1942, June 12). U.S. Ship Shells, Rams, and Sinks U-Boat off Cuba. Retrieved from http://archives.chicagotribune.com/1942/06/12/page/7/article/u-s-ship-shells-rams-and-sinks-u-boat-off-cuba.

Kelshall, Gaylord T. M. (1994). The U-Boat War in the Caribbean United States. Naval Institute Annapolis Maryland.

Morison, Samuel Eliot (2002). History of United States Naval Operations in World War II: The Atlantic. University of Illinois Press.

Polmar, Norman; Thomas B. Allen. *World War II: The Encyclopedia of the War Years 1941-1945.*

Schoonover, Thomas (2008). Hitler's Man in Havana: Heinz Luning and Nazi Espionage in Latin America. University Press of Kentucky.

Post 1959 International Relations

Amnesty International Publications (1989). *When the State Kills: The Death Penalty v. Human Rights.*

Anti-Cuba Bandits: terrorism in past tense (2007, February 22). Escambray Digital Newspaper in central Sancti Spíritus province, Cuba. Retrieved from https://web.archive.org/web/20070222204658/http://www.escambray.cu/Eng/Bandits/FpasadoE.htm

Encinosa, Enrique G. (n.p.d.). "Escambray: La Guerra Olvidada": Un Libro Historico De Los Combatientes Anticastristas En Cuba (1960-1966). Latin American Studies. p. 18. Retrieved from http://www.latinamericanstudies.org/book/escambray-18.htm

Faria Jr., Miguel A. (2002, November 18). Cuban War Criminal Touring U.S. Hacienda Publishing. Excerpts from original by Faria: *Cuba in Revolution: Escape From a Lost Paradise.* Macon, GA, Hacienda Publishing, Inc., 2002, pp. 88-104. Retrieved from http://www.haciendapub.com/articles/cuban-war-criminal-touring-us

Thomas, Hugh (1998). Cuba or the Pursuit of Freedom. Longitude. Retrieved from http://www.longitudebooks.com/find/p/7230/mcms.html

U.S. Department of State (2015, July 21). U.S. Relations With Cuba. BUREAU OF WESTERN HEMISPHERE AFFAIRS, Fact Sheet. Retrieved from http://www.state.gov/r/pa/ei/bgn/2886.htm

Vargas Llosa, Alvaro (2005, July 11). The Killing Machine Che Guevara, from Communist Firebrand to Capitalist Brand. Independent Institute. Also published in *The New Republic.* Retrieved from http://www.independent.org/newsroom/article.asp?id=1535

A Dependable Soviet Proxy

BBC News (2008, February 19). Castro: Profile of the great survivor. Retrieved from http://news.bbc.co.uk/2/hi/americas/244974.stm

Bourne, Peter G. (1986). Fidel: A Biography of Fidel Castro. New York City: Dodd, Mead & Company. pp. 68–69.

Clark, Jonas (2008, February). Fidel Castro: A collection of Atlantic writings assesses Castro and his legacy. Retrieved from http://www.theatlantic.com/magazine/archive/2008/02/fidel-castro/306692/

Haggerty, Richard A.; Hudson, Rex A., Merrill, Tim (1990, June). "CUBAN PRESENCE AND ACTIVITIES IN THE THIRD WORLD : A

Report Prepared under an Interagency Agreement by the Federal Research Division, Library of Congress". Dtic.mil. Retrieved from http:// www.dtic.mil/cgi-bin/GetTRDoc?AD=ADA305100

lanic (Latin American Network Information Center) (n.p.d.). Castro Speech Date Base. Retrieved from http://lanic.utexas.edu/project/castro/db/1963/19630605.html

Nuri, Maqsud Ul Hasan (1987, Second Quarter). THE SOVIET-CUBAN MILITARY INTERVENTION IN SUBSAHARAN AFRICA: PROXY OR PARTNER RELATIONSHIP? Pakistan Horizon, Vol. 40, No. 2, pp. 58-83. Published by: Pakistan Institute of International Affairs. Retrieved from http://www.jstor.org/stable/41394245?seq=1#page_scan_tab_contents

O'Grady, Mary Anastasia (2005, October 30). "Counting Castro's Victims". Wallstreet Journal, Center for a Free Cuba. Archived from the original on 2006-04-18. Retrieved from http://web.archive.org/web/20060418094333/http://www.cubacenter.org/media/news_articles/countingcastrosvictims.php

Quirk, Robert (1995, August). Fidel Castro. W. W. Norton & Company.

Sofinski, Nikolai (2016, May 4). Russia Highlights Cuba's Role As Most Loyal Ally in Western Hemisphere. Cuba Confidential: The source for news on Cuban espionage worldwide. Retrieved from https://cubaconfidential.wordpress.com/2016/05/04/russia-highlights-cubas-role-as-most-loyal-ally-in-western-hemisphere/

The Gazette, Montreal (1979, September 4). Castro opens Third World talks by denying Cuba isa Soviet 'tool'. Retrieved from https://news.google.com/newspapers?nid=1946&dat=19790904&id=yYw1AAAAIBAJ&sjid=aKQFAAAAIBAJ&pg=1106,853808&hl=en

U.S. DEPARTMENT OF STATE BACKGROUND NOTES (1994, November). CUBA. PUBLISHED BY THE BUREAU OF PUBLIC AFFAIRS. Retrieved from http://dosfan.lib.uic.edu/ERC/bgnotes/wha/cuba9411.html

Première Expérience - Santo Domingo

Cuba Confidential: The source for news on Cuban espionage worldwide (2012, June 14). This Date in History: Cuba Attacked the Dominican

Republic. Retrieved from https://cubaconfidential.wordpress.com/
2012/06/14/this-date-in-history-cuba-attacked-the-dominican-republic/

Cuban Information Archives (n.p.d.. Invasion of Cuba from Dominican
Republic. Document 0155. [Reference: RIF 124-10294-10051, FBI
record 2-1423-9TH NR 36] DATE: 05/05/59. Retrieved from http://
cuban-exile.com/doc_151-175/doc0155.html

The Congo

Mail & Guardian Arica (2015, August 17). As Cuba returns to the fold,
15 things about Havana in Africa, plus how Congo broke Che Guevara's
heart. Retrieved from http://mgafrica.com/article/2015-08-15-as-cuba-
returns-to-the-fold-15-things-you-didnt-know-about-cuba-in-africa-plus-
how-congo-broke-che-guevaras-heart

McClintock, Michael (2002). Waging Unconventional Warfare:
Guatemala, the Congo, and the Cubans: Eisenhower and Unconventional
Warfare. StateCraft.org. Retrieved from http://www.statecraft.org/
chapter5.html

Falk, Pamela S. (1987, Summer). Cuba in Africa. Foreign Affairs.
Retrieved from https://www.foreignaffairs.com/articles/africa/
1987-06-01/cuba-africa

The Guardian (2000, August 11). From Cuba to Congo, dream to disaster
for Che Guevara. Retrieved from http://www.theguardian.com/books/
2000/aug/12/cuba.artsandhumanities

Failure in the Bolivian Ñancahuazú

Billups, Andrea and Kathleen Walter (2013, October 10), On Anniversary
of Che Killing, CIA's Felix Rodriguez Remembers Archived. Newsmax.
Retrieved from http://www.newsmax.com/Newsfront/che-guevara-cia-
cuba-killing/2013/10/08/id/529906/

Brooks, Douglas J. (1989, August). THE PHOENIX PROGRAM: A
RETROSPECTIVE ASSESSMENT. MA thesis, Baylor University, pp.
iv, 38-40, 50, 57, 60, 114-18, 127, 140-144, and 148-56. Retrieved from
http://www.hoosier84.com/phx.pdf

Cupull, Adys; González, Froilán (1993). *La CIA contra el Che* (Spanish:
The CIA against el Che). Bolivia: Editora Política. Retrieved from
https://books.google.ca/books?
id=IcJ1AAAAMAAJ&q=Félix+Ismael+Rodr%C3%ADguez+Mendigutia

+1941&dq=Félix+Ismael+Rodr%C3%ADguez+Mendigutia+1941&sourc
e=bl&ots=t-
8XGw5d&sig=I_VNyhXF1EZo1td_zUC_KvxV5Co&hl=en&sa=X&ei
=i8waUMrAF-3piQLX74DoBQ&redir_esc=y

Fox News Latino (2015, April 28). Fidel Castro 'betrayed' Che Guevara,
'abandoned' him in Bolivia, Cuban journalist says. Retrieved from http://
latino.foxnews.com/latino/news/2015/04/28/fidel-betrayed-che-
abandoned-him-in-bolivia-cuban-journalist-says/

Nordlinger, Jay (2013, August 5). "The Anti-Che; Felix Rodriguez,
freedom fighter and patriot". *National Review*. Retrieved from https://
www.nationalreview.com/nrd/articles/353799/anti-che

Rodriguez, Felix (1989, November). Memoirs of the Man the White
House Said Didn't Exist. Book review by Robert Parry, *Washington
Monthly*, pp. 50-54. Retrieved from https://www.unz.org/Pub/
WashingtonMonthly-1989nov-00050

Rodriguez, Felix I. and John Weisman (1989). *Shadow Warrior/the CIA
Hero of a Hundred Unknown Battles*. New York: Simon & Schuster.

Woodward, Bob (2002). Bush At War, Simon and Schuester, p. 317

1961: The Revolution Imperiled

Bethell, Leslie (1993). *Cuba*. Cambridge University Press

Bohning, Don (1997, January 5). Site change called fatal to invasion;
Bay of Pigs bad choice, planner says. The Miami Herald. Retrieved from
http://www.latinamericanstudies.org/bay-of-pigs/site.htm

Bohning, Don (2005). *The Castro Obsession: U.S. Covert Operations
Against Cuba, 1959–1965*. Washington, D.C.: Potomac Books, Inc.

Colhoun, Jack (2014, February 24). How JFK Slammed the Door on Che
Guevara's Offer to Improve U.S.-Cuban Relations. History News
Network (HNN). Retrieved from http://historynewsnetwork.org/article/
154814

Cooper, Tom (2003). Clandestine US Operations: Cuba, 1962, Bay of
Pigs. Retrieved from http://www.acig.info/CMS/index.php?
option=com_content&task=view&id=83&Itemid=47

de Quesada, Alejandro; Walsh, Stephen. 2009. *The Bay of Pigs: Cuba 1961*. Osprey Elite series #166

Fernandez, Jose Ramon (2001). *Playa Giron/Bay of Pigs: Washington's First Military Defeat in the Americas*. Pathfinder.

Ferrer, Edward B. 1975 (Spanish), 1982 (English). *Operation Puma: The Air Battle of the Bay of Pigs*. International Aviation Consultants.

Gleijeses, Piero (1995, February). "Ships in the Night: The CIA, the White House and the Bay of Pigs". *Journal of Latin American Studies*, vol. 27, no. 1, pp. 1–42 (via JSTOR)

John F. Kennedy Presidential Library and Museum (n.p.d.). The Bay of Pigs. Retrieved from http://www.jfklibrary.org/JFK/JFK-in-History/The-Bay-of-Pigs.aspx

Johnson, Haynes (1964, 1974). *The Bay of Pigs: The Leaders' Story of Brigade 2506*. W. W. Norton & Co.

Jones, Howard (2008). *Bay of Pigs (Pivotal Moments in American History)*. OUP USA

Lazo, Mario (1968, 1970). *Dagger in the heart: American policy failures in Cuba*. Twin Circle. New York. 1968 edition Library of Congress number 6831632, 1970 edition

MacPhall, Doug & Acree, Chuck (2003). "Bay of Pigs: The Men and Aircraft of the Cuban Revolutionary Air Force". LAAHS (Latin American Aviation Historical Society). Retrieved from http://www.laahs.com/content/19-Bay-of-Pigs-The-Men-and-Aircraft-of-the-Cuban-Revolutionary-Air-Force

Reeves, Richard (1993). *President Kennedy: Profile of Power*. Simon & Schuster

Rodriguez, Juan Carlos (1999). *Bay of Pigs and the CIA*. Ocean Press.

Ros, Enrique. 1994 (1998). *Girón la verdadera historia*. Ediciones Universales (Colección Cuba y sus jueces) third edition.

Szulc, Tad, and Karl E. Meyer (1962). *The Cuban Invasion. The chronicle of a disaster*. Praegar

The National Security Archives (n.p.d.) Bay of Pigs: 40 years after, Chronology. Retrieved from http://nsarchive.gwu.edu/bayofpigs/chron.html

Triay, Victor Andres (2001). *Bay of Pigs: An Oral History of Brigade 2506*. University Press of Florida

Wyden, Peter (1979). *Bay of Pigs - The Untold Story*. Simon and Schuster

Operation Mongoose

Alleged Plots Involving Foreign Leaders, U.S. Senate, Select Committee to Study Governmental Operations with Respect to Intelligence Activities, S. Rep. No. 755, 94th Cong., 2d sess. Retrieved from http://www.intelligence.senate.gov/sites/default/files/94465.pdf

Anderson, Jack (1971-01-18). "6 Attempts to Kill Castro Laid to CIA". The Washington Post.

Domínguez, Jorge I. (2000, Spring). "The @#$%& Missile Crisis (Or, What was 'Cuban' about US Decisions during the Cuban Missile Crisis.Diplomatic History: The Journal of the Society for Historians of Foreign Relations, Vol. 24, No. 2: pp. 305–315.)

Escalante Font, Fabián (1996). CIA Targets Fidel: Secret 1967 CIA Inspector General's Report on Plots to Assassinate Fidel Castro. Melbourne, Vic., Australia: Ocean Press.

Grow, Michael (2008). "Cuba, 1961". U.S. Presidents and Latin American Interventions: Pursuing Regime Change in the Cold War. Lawrence: University of Kansas Press, p. 42.

Husain, Aiyaz (2005, February). "Covert Action and US Cold War Strategy in Cuba, 1961-62". *Cold War History*.

Lia, Kari (Producer) (Oliver Huddleston, Editor; Dollan Cannell, Director) (2006, November 28). 638 Ways to Kill Castro. Documentary film, broadcast in the United Kingdom, Channel 4. Retrieved from the Internet Movie Database http://www.imdb.com/title/tt0918485/

Office of the Historian (1962, January 18). FOREIGN RELATIONS OF THE UNITED STATES, 1961–1963, VOLUME X, CUBA, JANUARY 1961–SEPTEMBER 1962: 291. Program Review by the Chief of

Operations, Operation Mongoose (Lansdale). Retrieved from https://history.state.gov/historicaldocuments/frus1961-63v10/d291

US Department of State, Foreign Relations of the United States 1961–1963, Volume X Cuba, 1961–1962 Washington, DC

Cuban Missile Crisis

Faria, Miguel A. (2002). *Cuba in Revolution: Escape from a Lost Paradise*. Macon, GA: Hacienda Pub.

Gibson, David R. (2012) T*alk at the Brink: Deliberation and Decision during the Cuban Missile Crisis*. Princeton, New Jersey: Princeton University Press. pp. 135–56.

Gibson, David R. (2012). Talk at the Brink: Deliberation and Decision during the Cuban Missile Crisis. Princeton University Press.

Gott, Richard (2012, October 12). How Cuba won the missile crisis. The Guardian. Retrieved from http://www.theguardian.com/commentisfree/2012/oct/12/what-cuban-missile-crisis

Cuba Nature Travel (n.p.d.). History. Retrieved from http://www.cubanaturetravel.com/history

Office of the Historian (1962, October 27). FOREIGN RELATIONS OF THE UNITED STATES, 1961–1963, VOLUME VI, KENNEDY-KHRUSHCHEV EXCHANGES. 67. Telegram From the Department of State to the Embassy in the Soviet Union. Retrieved from https://history.state.gov/historicaldocuments/frus1961-63v06/d67

The National Security Archive (n.p.d.). George Washington University. Audio Clips from the Kennedy White House. Tuesday October 16, 11:50 A.M., Cabinet Room, The White House. Retrieved from http://nsarchive.gwu.edu/nsa/cuba_mis_cri/audio.htm

Early Diplomatic Coup: Schism in the OAS

Filip, Brysen (2015, April 10). The Organization of American States (OAS) and the Re-establishment of Ties between the U.S. and Cuba. Global Research. Retrieved from http://www.globalresearch.ca/the-organization-of-american-states-oas-and-the-re-establishment-of-ties-between-the-u-s-and-cuba/5442045

New York Times (1962, January 24). "U.S. is Advancing Plan to Suspend Cuba from O.A.S." Retrieved from http://query.nytimes.com/gst/abstract.html?res=9901E2DE1531EF3BBC4C51DFB7668389679EDE

Organization of American States (1979, December 14). SIX REPORT ON THE SITUATION OF POLITICAL PRISONERS IN CUBA. Inter_American Commission on Human Rights. OEA/Ser.L/V/II.48 doc. 24. Original: Spanish. Retrieved from http://www.cidh.oas.org/countryrep/Cuba79eng/intro.htm

Organization of American States (1998, February 4). MEXICO CALLS FOR CUBA'S REINSTATEMENT INTO THE OAS. Organization of American States News Release. Retrieved from http://www.oas.org/OASpage/press2002/en/Press98/020498ce.htm

Schlesinger Jr., Arthur (1965). *A Thousand Days: John F. Kennedy in the White House.* Houghton Mifflin, Boston. pp 669-673.

Time Magazine (1960, August 22). THE AMERICAS: The Testing of the OAS. Retrieved from http://content.time.com/time/magazine/article/0,9171,869814,00.html

Chile

Ampuero, Roberto (1999). Nuestros años verde olivo (Spanish Language Edition). Editorial Planeta.

"Bultos Cubanos". *Special edition* (in Spanish) ("Que Pasa" magazine). 1982. p. 21.

Collier, Simon; Sater, William F. (2004). *A History of Chile, 1808-1994.* (Cambridge Latin American Studies) 2nd Edition.

Conservapedia (2016, May 29). Salvador Allende. Retrieved from http://www.conservapedia.com/Salvador_Allende

Friedman, Norman (2007, March 7). *The Fifty-Year War: Conflict and Strategy in the Cold War.* Naval Institute Press.

Ortega, Javier (n.p.d.). La historia inédita de los años verde olivo. Encuentro en la Red: Dario Independiente de Asuntos Cubanos. Dossier/Historia de una intervención Cubana en Chile. pp. 208-242. Retrieved from http://arch1.cubaencuentro.com/pdfs/21-22/21jo208.pdf

Vial-Correa, Gonzalo (Patricio Carvajal Prado, Editor) (1973). Libro Blanco del Cambio de Gobierno en Chile: 11 de Septiembre de 1973. 2a Edición. Editado por Lord Cochrane S.A., Santiago, Chile. Retrieved from Libro_Blanco_del_cambio_de_Gobierno_en_Chile.pdf

Wright, Thomas C. (2001). Latin America in the era of the Cuban Revolution. Praeger Publishers. p. 140.

Nicaragua

Andrew, Christopher (September 2000). *The Sword and the Shield: The Mitrokhin Archive and the Secret History of the KGB*. Basic Books. p. 385.

Fauriol, Georges, & Eva Loser, editors (1990). Cuba: The International Dimension. p. 21. Transaction Publishers. Retyrieved from https://books.google.ie/books?id=VyqOhCUb66AC&pg=PA21&lpg=PA21&dq=cuba+assistance+fsln&source=bl&ots=p-09UO4MB4&sig=BOTkmO7QFTQBR0ljjXX01NZ_Nac&hl=en&ei=jzkdSv7zKYPR-AavjMTDCw&sa=X&oi=book_result&ct=result#v=onepage&q=cuba%20assistance%20fsln&f=false

Glazov, Jaime (2002, June 5). Remembering Sandinista Genocide. FrontPageMag. Retrieved from http://archive.frontpagemag.com/readArticle.aspx?ARTID=25257

Shulltz, Jr., Richard H. (1988). The Soviet Union and Revolutionary Warfare: Principles, Practices, and Regional Comparisons. Hoover Institution, Stanford University. pp. 179-185. Retrieved from http://books.google.ie/books?id=wtebWixsIdYC&pg=PA184&lpg=PA184&dq=cuba+assistance+fsln&source=bl&ots=PoWGOlfqka&sig=h4boRqnTv-ixnNL9c4zTAX0tilU&hl=en&ei=jzkdSv7zKYPR-AavjMTDCw&sa=X&oi=book_result&ct=result&resnum=4

The Spokesman Review (1987, June 15). U.S. Touts Contra Victories. Retrieved from https://news.google.com/newspapers?nid=1314&dat=19870615&id=SlpWAAAAIBAJ&sjid=gu8DAAAAIBAJ&pg=5587,8293358&hl=en

El Salvador

Chase, Michelle (2014). The End of an Era: The Cold War in El Salvador and Cuba. North American Congress on Latin America (NACLA).

Retrieved from https://nacla.org/news/end-era-cold-war-el-salvador-and-cuba

Elton, Catherine (2004, March 19). El Salvador vote recalls cold-war power play: Salvadorans choose a new president on Sunday. The Christian Science Monitor. Retrieved from http://www.csmonitor.com/2004/0319/p07s02-woam.html

McClintock, Michael (2002). Instruments of Statecraft: U.S. Guerilla Warfare, Counterinsurgency, and Counterterrorism, 1940-1990. Counterterror and Counterorganization: Terror Option. Retrieved from http://www.statecraft.org/chapter10.html

Grenada

Haggerty, Richard A.; Hudson, Rex A., Merrill, Tim (1990, June). "CUBAN PRESENCE AND ACTIVITIES IN THE THIRD WORLD : A Report Prepared under an Interagency Agreement by the Federal Research Division, Library of Congress". Dtic.mil. Retrieved from http://www.dtic.mil/cgi-bin/GetTRDoc?AD=ADA305100

James, Vonnie (2009-01-01). TIMELINE: GRENADA –CUBA RELATION. Retrieved from http://archive.is/4bnV

Military.com (n.p.d.). Invasion of Grenada: Operation Urgent Fury. Retrieved from http://www.military.com/Resources/HistorySubmittedFileView?file=history_grenada.htm

Russell, Lee; Mendez, Albert (1985). *Grenada 1983*. 12-14 Long Acre, London WC2E 9LP: Osprey Publishing Ltd. pp. 3-16, 24-34, 40.

Sylvia, Stephen; O'Donnell, Michael (1984). *Guns of Grenada*. Orange, VA, 22960: Moss Publications. pp. 24–28.

Varona, Arnoldo (editor) (2011, December 17). CUBAN AND US INVASION OF GRENADA. CubanHistory.com. Retrieved from http://www.thecubanhistory.com/2011/12/cuban-and-us-invasion-of-grenada-2/

Zunes, Stephen (2003, October). The U.S. Invasion of Grenada. Global Policy Forum. Retrieved from https://www.globalpolicy.org/component/content/article/155/25966.html

Yom Kippur War

Bourne, Peter G. (1986), *Fidel: A Biography of Fidel Castro*. New York: Dodd, Mead & Company.

Perez, Cuba, *Between Reform and Revolution*, pp. 377–379. Gott, Cuba, *A New History*, p. 280, 377-379.

Williams, John Hoyt (1988, August). Cuba: Havana's Military Machine: On Castro's island, most of the population is under arms. The Atlantic. Retrieved from http://www.theatlantic.com/magazine/archive/1988/08/cuba-havanas-military-machine/305932/

Ethio-Somali War

BBC News (1999, December 22). "US admits helping Mengistu escape", Retrieved from http://news.bbc.co.uk/2/hi/africa/575405.stm

Coutsoukis, Photius (2004). Somalia Irredentism and the Changing Balance of Power. Geographic.org. Retrieved from http://www.photius.com/countries/somalia/national_security/somalia_national_security_irredentism_and_the_~1624.html

Cuban American Military Council (n.p.d.). Cuban Expeditionary Forces In Ethiopia. CubaHeritage.com. Article ID 258. Retrieved from http://www.cubaheritage.org/articles.asp?lID=1&artID=258

Dagne, Haile Gabriel (2006). The commitment of the German Democratic Republic in Ethiopia: a study based on Ethiopian sources. Münster, London: Lit; Global.

Federal Research Division (2004). *Somalia: A Country Study*. Kessinger Publishing, LLC, p. 38

Zolberg, Aristide R., et al. (1992). *Escape from Violence: Conflict and the Refugee Crisis in the Developing World*. Oxford University Press, p. 106

Angolan Civil War

Centro de Informacion de la Defensa de las Fuerzas Armadas Revolucionarias (1975). Document: CIDFAR, [Center of Information of the Armed Forces]. Ministry of the Interior. Retrieved from http://nsarchive.gwu.edu/NSAEBB/NSAEBB67/gleijeses3.pdf

Foss, Clive (2010, March). Cuba's African Adventure. History Today, Vol 60, Issue 3. Retrieved from http://www.historytoday.com/clive-foss/cubas-african-adventure

Mallin, Jay (1987). *Cuba in Angola*. Coral Gables, Fla.: Research Institute for Cuban Studies, Graduate School of International Studies, University of Miami.

Marcum, John (1976, April). Lessons of Angola, Foreign Affairs 54, No. 3

Wood, Emma (2016, April 29). The Angola Handbook - Everything You Need To Know About Angola. Emereo Publishing.

Wright, George (1997). *The Destruction of a Nation: United States' Policy toward Angola since 1945*, Pluto Press, London, Chicago, pp. 58, 131.

Cuba's Role in the Non-Aligned Movement

Council on Hemispheric Affairs (2006, October 16). Cuba's Leadership of the Non-Aligned Movement: Challenge to U.S. Hegemony? Retrieved from http://www.coha.org/cuba's-leadership-of-the-non-aligned-movement-challenge-to-us-hegemony/

EXECUTIVE INTELLIGENCE REVIEW (1979, August 21-August 27). "The Nonaligned meet in Havana: The challenge of guaranteeing Third World development. Retrieved from http://www.larouchepub.com/eiw/public/1979/eirv06n33-19790821/eirv06n33-19790821_027-the_nonaligned_meet_in_havana.pdf

Government of India, Ministry of External Affairs (2012, August 22). History and Evolution of Non-Aligned Movement. Retrieved from http://mea.gov.in/in-focus-article.htm?20349/History+and+Evolution+of+NonAligned+Movement

Levi, Rozita (edited by Cole Blasier and Carmelo Mesa-Lago) (1979). Cuba in the World. University of Pittsburg Press, p. 147. Retrieved from https://books.google.com/books?id=9neZWKRI49oC&pg=PA147&lpg=PA147&dq=Cuba's+Role+in+the+Non-Aligned+Movement&source=bl&ots=eLE_n7y4Xn&sig=0EP_AQgGSBcLuWu3A141yv52sko&hl=en&sa=X&ved=0ahUKEwj5hLjjkZfNAhWBFh4KHelqDncQ6AEIZDAJ#v=onepage&q=Cuba's%20Role%20in%20the%20Non-Aligned%20Movement&f=false

Narayanan, R. (1981). Cuba and the Nonaligned Movement. International Studies, vol. 20 no. 1-2 411-413. Sage Publications. Retrieved from http://isq.sagepub.com/content/20/1-2/411.extract

Riechers, C. Russell (2012, April 29). Cuba and the Non-Aligned Movement: Interactions of Pragmatic Idealism. Retrieved from http://aladinrc.wrlc.org/bitstream/handle/1961/10667/Riechers,%20C.%20Russell%20-%20Spring%202012.pdf?sequence=1

Medical Internationalism

Brouwer, Steve (2009, January 8). The Cuban Revolutionary Doctor: The Ultimate Weapon of Solidarity. Monthly Review, Vol. 60. Retrieved from http://monthlyreview.org/2009/01/01/the-cuban-revolutionary-doctor-the-ultimate-weapon-of-solidarity/

Milne, Seumas (2014, December 3). Cuba's extraordinary global medical record shames the US blockade. The Guardian. Retrieved from http://www.theguardian.com/commentisfree/2014/dec/03/cuba-global-medical-record-shames-us-blockade-ebola

Ceasar, Mike (2007, August 1). "Cuban Doctors Abroad Helped to Defect by New U.S. Visa Policy", *World Politics Review*. Retrieved from http://www.worldpoliticsreview.com/articles/981/cuban-doctors-abroad-helped-to-defect-by-new-u-s-visa-policy

Drug Trafficking & the Ochoa Trial

Adams, Nathan M. (1982, July). Havana's Drug-Smuggling Connection. Reader's Digest. pp 98-102. Retrieved from http://www.latinamericanstudies.org/cuba/drugs.htm

George, Edward (2005). The Cuban Intervention in Angola, 1965-1991: From Che Guevara to Cuito Cuanavale. Frank Cass Publishers, pp. 262, 266. Retrieved from https://books.google.com/books?id=gcR_AgAAQBAJ&pg=PA266&lpg=PA266&dq=ochoa+scapegoat&source=bl&ots=SlZUWVnL6S&sig=JvpKS8HK6NMm_PRMCQ9L-Ted6Zo&hl=en&sa=X&ved=0ahUKEwiLzNmprMjMAhVFkx4KHcqZCLMQ6AEIKTAD#v=onepage&q=ochoa%20scapegoat&f=false

GlobalSecurity.org (2016). The Ochoa Affair. Military. Retrieved from http://www.globalsecurity.org/military/world/cuba/ochoa.htm

Hudson, Rex A. (2002). Cuba: A Country Study. Government Printing Office, p. 296. Retrieved from https://books.google.com/books? id=OjFA2QFqnioC&pg=PA296&lpg=PA296&dq=Ochoa+ %22serious+acts+of+corruption+and+illegal+use+of+economic+resourc es&source=bl&ots=dFDSy47qnR&sig=Ed3Gy7j0fbWXq2t7k3cXEo9xg zM&hl=en&sa=X&ved=0ahUKEwiV_q2rnqHNAhXC9R4KHTMNCtA Q6AEIIzAB#v=onepage&q=Ochoa%20%22serious%20acts%20of%20c orruption%20and%20illegal%20use%20of%20economic%20resources&f =false

Moses, Harry (Producer) (with CBS News Correspondents Mike Wallace, Morley Safer and Dan Rather) (1978, February 26). "THE CASTRO CONNECTION?" 60 MINUTES, Volume X, Number 26 as broadcast over the CBS TELEVISION NETWORK. Retrieved from http:// www.latinamericanstudies.org/drugs/60-minutes.htm

Pear, Robert (1989, July 14). Cuban General and Three Others Executed for Sending Drugs to U.S. The New York Times. Retrieved from http://www.nytimes.com/1989/07/14/world/ cuban-general-and-three-others-executed-for-sending-drugs-to-us.html

Tamayo, Juan O. (2014, June 22). Arnaldo Ochoa — a problem for Castro brothers 25 years ago. The Miami Herald. Retrieved from http://www.miamiherald.com/news/nation-world/world/ americas/article1967653.html

Tepper, Stephanie and Cran, William (1991, February 5). Cuba and Cocaine, #910. Retrieved from http://www.pbs.org/wgbh/ pages/frontline/shows/drugs/archive/cubaandcocaine.html

The Washington Post (1982, November 6). Four Cuban Officials Indicted in Drug Smuggling: Havana Said Haven For Colombia Goods. Retrieved from http://www.latinamericanstudies.org/drugs/smugglers.htm

Guinea-Bissau

Blasier, Cole; Carmelo Mesa-Lago (1979). Cuba in the World, University of Pittsburgh Press, pp. 95-96.

Cabral, Amilcar (2002). Revolutionary Leadership and People's War, Cambridge University Press, p. 86.

George, Edward (2005). The Cuban Intervention in Angola, 1965-1991: From Che Guevara to Cuito Cuanavale, Routledge. p. 354.

Gleijeses, Piero (1997). "The First Ambassadors: Cuba's Contribution to Guinea-Bissau's War of Independence". *Journal of Latin American Studies* **29** (1): pp. 45–88.

Gleijeses, Piero (2002). Conflicting Missions: Havana, Washington, and Africa, 1959-1976. University of North Carolina Press. p. 197

Gleijeses, Piero (2003, November 17). Cubans in Guinea-Bissau's independence struggle. The Militant, Vol. 67/No. 40. Retrieved from http://www.themilitant.com/2003/6740/674061.html

Laqueur, Walter (1976). Guerrilla Warfare: A Historical and Critical Study, Transaction Publishers. p. 362.

van Ness, Peter (1971). Revolution and Chinese Foreign Policy: Peking's Support for Wars of National Liberation, University of California Press. pp. 143.

Mozambique

Cuba Entry 1975 Exit 1987 Combat Forces 150.000 Population 8.700.000 Losses 3.000

CubaHeritage.org (n.p.d.) Renamo Insurgency: The Mozambique War. Article ID 253. Retrieved from http://www.cubaheritage.org/articles.asp?lID=1&artID=253

Hoile, David (1994). Mozambique, Resistance and Freedom: A Case for Reassessment. Mozambique Institute, pp. 64.

Mittleman, James H. (2013). Underdevelopment and the Transition to Socialism: Mozambique and Tanzania. Academic Press. pp 38.

Stockholm International Peace Research Institute (1976). Southern Africa The Escalation of a Conflict : a Politico-military Study. Harcourt School, pp. 99.

Suchlicki, Jaime (1989). The Cuban Military Under Castro, University of Miami North-South Center, pp. 45

Yemen and Oman

Allen, Calvin H.; Rigsbee, W. Lynn (2000). Oman under Qaboos: From Coup to Constitution, 1970-1996. Routledge. Retrieved from Google Books https://books.google.com/books?

id=f3pV457NIE4C&printsec=frontcover&source=gbs_navlinks_s#v=one page&q&f=false

Beckett, Ian; Pimlott, John (1985). Armed Forces & Modern Counter-insurgency. New York: St. Martin's

Burrowes, Robert D. (1999). Middle East dilemma: the politics and economics of Arab integration Columbia University Press, pp. 187-210

Burrowes, Robert D. (2010). Historical Dictionary of Yemen. Rowman & Littlefield. p. 190

Captain N. G.R. Hepworth (1970). 'The Unknown War'in The White Horseand FleurdeLys, journal of the King's Regiment, Vol.VI, No. 6, Winter.

Fiennes, Ranulph (1976). Where soldiers fear to tread. New English Library.

Gardiner, Ian (2006). In the Service of the Sultan. Pen and Sword Military.

Gimenez, David (2016). Cuba Intervention in Yemen. CubaHeritage.org, Article ID 256. Retrieved from http://www.cubaheritage.org/articles.asp?lID=1&artID=256

Halliday, Fred. Arabia Without Sultans. London: Penguin, 1974.

Hermann, Richard, Perceptions and behavior in Soviet foreign policy, University of Pittsburgh Pre, 1985, page 152. Retrieved from Google Books https://books.google.com/books?id=fvx_mozejjgC&pg=PA241&dq=yemen+1979&hl=en&ei=DeOMTYijCcaw0QHzg7C8Cw&sa=X&oi=book_result&ct=result#v=onepage&q=yemen%201979&f=false

Hoyt Williams, John (1988, August). Cuba: Havana's Military Machine. The Atlantic, Retrieved from http://www.theatlantic.com/magazine/archive/1988/08/cuba-havanas-military-machine/305932/

Kohn, George C. (2006). "Dictionary of Wars". Infobase Publishing. p. 615.

University of Central Arkansas (2016). Middle East/North Africa/Persian Gulf Region. Political Science. Retrieved 2011. http://uca.edu/politicalscience/dadm-project/middle-eastnorth-africapersian-gulf-region/

Trinidad and Tobago Meeting

CARICOM: Caribbean Community (2016, June 8). Caribbean integration is possible, St Vincent PM tells ACS summit. Retrieved from http://caricom.org/media-center/communications/news-from-the-community/caribbean-integration-is-possible-st-vincent-pm-tells-acs-summit

CARICOM: Caribbean Community (2016, June 8). Havana Declaration. Retrieved from http://caricom.org/media-center/communications/news-from-the-community/havana-declaration

CARICOM: Caribbean Community (2016, June 8). Association of Caribbean States' 7th Summit to Be Held in Cuba on June 4. Retrieved from http://caricom.org/media-center/communications/news-from-the-community/association-of-caribbean-states-7th-summit-to-be-held-in-cuba-on-june-4

CARICOM: Caribbean Community (2016, June 6). Raúl Castro Meets Presidents of Haiti, Guyana, Jamaica and Suriname. Retrieved from http://caricom.org/media-center/communications/news-from-the-community/caribbean-integration-is-possible-st-vincent-pm-tells-acs-summit

Cuba Min Rex (editor) (2016, June 6). Trinidad and Tobago: Prime Minister of Trinidad and Tobago present for 7th ACS Summit. Retrieved from http://www.minrex.gob.cu/en/bilaterales/america-latina-y-el-caribe/trinidad-y-tobago

NBC News (2009). Obama: U.S. seeks 'new beginning' with Cuba. Retrieved from http://www.nbcnews.com/id/30261514/ns/world_news-americas/t/obama-us-seeks-new-beginning-cuba/#.V1y6R0vknwI

Newsday (2015, April 12). PM Kamla: Cuba/US meeting a great day. Retrieved from http://www.newsday.co.tt/news/0,209558.html

Whitefield, Mimi (2015, November 30). Emerging Cuba worries Caribbean. The Miami Herald. Retrieved from http://www.miamiherald.com/news/nation-world/world/americas/cuba/article47182355.html

Intelligence Directorate

Andrew, Christopher; Mitrokhin, Vasili (1999). *The sword and the Shield: The Mitrokhin Archive and the Secret History of the KGB*. Basic Books. p. 386.

Carroll, Rory (2013). Comandante : myth and reality in Hugo Chávez's Venezuela. Penguin Press: New York. pp. 98–100.

CI Centre (2011). 159: An Introduction to Cuban Intelligence and Counterintelligence Methodologies. The Centre for Counterintelligence and Securities Studies. Retrieved from http://www.cicentre.com/?page=159

Cuba Confidential (2016, May 30): The source for news on Cuban espionage worldwide. U.S. Academics Honor Expelled Spy With Award. Retrieved from https://cubaconfidential.wordpress.com

Demaris, Ovid (1977, November 7). "Carlos: The Most Dangerous Man In The World", *New York Magazine*, p. 35. Retrieved from https://books.google.com/books?id=EegCAAAAMBAJ&pg=PA35#v=onepage&q=cuba&f=false

Edward González and Kevin McCarthy, "Cuba After Castro: Legacies, Challenges, and Impediments," RAND (Santa Monica, CA: RAND, 2004), 44, PDF retrieved from https://www.rand.org/pubs/technical_reports/2005/RAND_TR131.pdf.

Foro Militar General (Cuban Military and Intelligence Forum) (2016, May 19). Las Fuerzas Armadas Revolucionarias (FAR) y la historia militar cubana. Retrieved from http://www.militar.org.ua/foro/

Global Security (2016). Directorate General of Intelligence (DGI). Retrieved from http://www.globalsecurity.org/intell/world/cuba/dgi.htm

Golinger, Eva (2016, May 2). Leftist Attorney and "Journalist" Eva Golinger Interviews Cuban Spies. Cuba Confidential: The source for news on Cuban espionage worldwide. Retrieved from https://cubaconfidential.wordpress.com/2016/05/02/leftist-attorney-and-journalist-eva-golinger-interviews-cuban-spies/

Harris, Shan (2016, March 6) The Stupidly Simple Spy Messages No Computer Could Decode. Cuba Confidential: The source for news on Cuban espionage worldwide. Retrieved from https://cubaconfidential.wordpress.com/2016/03/06/the-stupidly-simple-spy-messages-no-computer-could-decode/

Harris, Shan (2016, March 6). The Unauthorized Biography of Cuban Spy-Diplomat Rodrigo Malmierca Diaz. Cuba Confidential: The source for news on Cuban espionage worldwide. Retrieved from https://

cubaconfidential.wordpress.com/2016/03/13/the-unauthorized-biography-of-cuban-spy-diplomat-rodrigo-malmierca-diaz/

Protestas en Venezuela (2014, February 19). "Herido con golpes y perdigones el Padre José Palmar en el Zulia". *El Nacional*. Retrieved from http://www.eluniversal.com/nacional-y-politica/protestas-en-venezuela/140219/herido-con-golpes-y-perdigones-el-padre-jose-palmar-en-el-zulia

Urribarres, Ruben (2013). Cuban Aviation. Retrieved from http://www.urrib2000.narod.ru/index-e.html

Fontaine, Roger (1988, June 4). Cuba's Terrorist Connection. The Heritage Foundation archives. Backgrounder #655 on Latin America. Retrieved from http://www.heritage.org/research/reports/1988/06/cubas-terrorist-connection

Cuba's Military Machine

Defense Intelligence Agency (1997, November 18). The Cuban Threat to U.S. National Security. Retrieved from https://fas.org/irp/dia/product/980507-dia-cubarpt.htm

Global Firepower (2016). Cuba Military Strength: Current military capabilities and available firepower for 2016 detailed. Retrieved from http://www.globalfirepower.com/country-military-strength-detail.asp?country_id=cuba

MilitaryBudget.org (n.p.d.). Cuban Military Budget. Military Expenditures 2001-2012. Retrieved from http://militarybudget.org/cuba/

NationMaster (n.p.d.). Cuba Military Stats. Retrieved from http://www.nationmaster.com/country-info/profiles/Cuba/Military

Thomas, Hugh (1998). Cuba or the Pursuit of Freedom (Paperback). Da Capo Press.

Williams, John Hoyt (1988, August). Cuba: Havana's Military Machine. On Castro's island, most of the population is under arms. The Atlantic. Retrieved from http://www.theatlantic.com/magazine/archive/1988/08/cuba-havanas-military-machine/305932/.

The "Special Period"

Acosta, Dalia (2004, August 11). August 5, 1994: The Day the 'Hottest Summer' Exploded in Cuba. Cuba Culture News. Retrieved from http://havanajournal.com/culture/entry/august_5_1994_the_day_the_hottest_summer_exploded_in_cuba/

Benjamin, Medea (2015, March 10). Dividing the Pie: Cuba's Ration System After 50 Years. Common Dreams. Retrieved from http://www.commondreams.org/views/2015/03/10/dividing-pie-cubas-ration-system-after-50-years

Deere, Carmen Diana (1991, July–August). Cuba's struggle for self-sufficiency - aftermath of the collapse of Cuba's special economic relations with Eastern Europe. Retrieved from https://www.questia.com/magazine/1G1-11063036/cuba-s-struggle-for-self-sufficiency

Donovan, Sandy; Rao, Sujay; Sandmann, Alexa L. (2008). *Teens in Cuba*. Capstone. p. 26. Retrieved from https://books.google.com/books?id=8YzDOtRjNlcC&lpg=PT14&dq=cuban+lost+kilograms&pg=PT14&hl=en#v=onepage&q=cuban%20lost%20kilograms&f=false

Fifty years of the Castro regime: Time for a (long overdue) change (2008, December 30). The Economist. From the print edition. Retrieved from http://www.economist.com/node/12853934

Henken, Ted (2008). *Cuba: A Global Studies Handbook*. ABC-CLIO. Google Books. p. 438. Retrieved from https://books.google.com/books?id=Mv7anQoCbzgC&lpg=PT467&ots=v_i5kpr7cw&dq=%22Per%C3%ADDodo+especial%22+%221990%22+-wikipedia&pg=PT467&hl=en#v=onepage&q=%22Per%C3%ADDodo%20especial%22%20%221990%22%20-wikipedia&f=false

Hillyard, Mick; Miller, Vaughne (1998, December 14). "Cuba and the Helms-Burton Act" (PDF). *House of Commons Library Research Papers* (Great Britain. Parliament. House of Commons.) 98 (114): 3. Archived from the original (PDF) on August 19, 2000. Retrieved from https://web.archive.org/web/20000819014257/http://www.parliament.uk/commons/lib/research/rp98/rp98-114.pdf

Notes from the Cuban Exile Quarter (2012, August 5). Cuba's Day of National Rebellion: August 5, 1994. Retrieved from http://cubanexilequarter.blogspot.com/2012/08/cubas-day-of-national-rebellion-august.html

Oxfam America (2001, June 1). Cuba: Going Against the Grain - The Food Crisis in Cuba. Retrieved from http://www.oxfamamerica.org/static/oa4/OA-CubaGoingAgainstGrain_FoodCrisis.pdf

Parrot diplomacy: Venezuela and Cuba (2008, July 24). Having rescued Cuba with cheap oil, Venezuela is to be paid back in zebras. The Economist. Retrieved from http://www.economist.com/node/11792274

Pérez, Jr., Louis A. (n.p.d.). Cuba's Special Period
an excerpt from: "Cuba: Between Reform & Revolution". Chapter 12 - Socialist Cuba Section XII - Pages 381-387. Retrieved from http://www.historyofcuba.com/history/havana/lperez2.htm

Reyes, Hector (2000, Spring). Cuba: The Crisis of State Capitalism. International Socialist Review (ISR), Issue 11. Retrieved from http://www.isreview.org/issues/11/cuba_crisis.shtml

A Look Toward the Future

Amnesty International (2016). Cuba Human Rights: Civil and political rights continue to be severely restricted by Cuban authorities. Retrieved from http://www.amnestyusa.org/our-work/countries/americas/cuba

Berrien, Hank (2016, April 3). IN CASE YOU MISSED IT: President Obama Posed In Front of The Ministry of the Interior, From Where All Repression in Cuba is Orchestrated. Cuba Confidential: The source for news on Cuban espionage worldwide. Retrieved from https://cubaconfidential.wordpress.com/2016/04/03/in-case-you-missed-it-president-obama-posed-in-front-of-the-ministry-of-the-interior-from-where-all-repression-in-cuba-is-orchestrated/

Carbonell, Brenden M. (2007). FAR from Perfect: The Military and Corporatism (Chapter 10). City University of New York, Graduate Center Publications. Retrieved from http://www.gc.cuny.edu/CUNY_GC/media/CUNY-Graduate-Center/PDF/Centers/Bildner%20Center%20for%20Western%20Hemisphere%20Studies/Publications/Carbonell10_000.pdf

Flagblackened.net (n.p.d.). Cuba, socialist paradise or Castro's fiefdom? Originally from Worker's Solidarity - Irish anarchist paper, No40, 1993. Retrieved from http://flag.blackened.net/liberty/cuba-ws40.html

Human Rights Watch (2015). World Report 2015: Cuba. Retrieved from https://www.hrw.org/world-report/2015/country-chapters/cuba

Martí (2004, April 15). HUMAN RIGHTS COMMISSION CONDEMNS CUBA. Retrieved from http://www.martinoticias.com/a/human-rights-co/3303.html

United States Department of State, Bureau of Public Affairs, Washington, D.C. (1981, December 14). Cuba's Renewed Support of Violence in Latin America. Special Report No. 90. Retrieved from Cuban Information Archives, Document 0224, http://cuban-exile.com/doc_201-225/doc0224.html

Images/illustration for the above section found in *Cuban Communism and Its Impact on World Affairs: 1959 - 2015* by Dr. Juan R. Céspedes (https://www.amazon.com/Cuban-Communism-Impact-World-Affairs/dp/1534703888).

1: José Martí: https://commons.wikimedia.org/wiki/Category:José_Mart%C3%AD#/media/File:Jose-Marti.jpg

2: Havana 1956: http://1.bp.blogspot.com/_L3Sr52SjMHw/RdkP6SN8zXI/AAAAAAAAAB4/xbix10d3kCU/s1600-h/Tarjeta+postal+-+Focsa+-+Hotel+Nacional+-+monumento+Maine+-+1956.jpg

3: Battleship USS Texas: https://upload.wikimedia.org/wikipedia/commons/1/13/USS_Texas_Havana_1940.jpg

4: Castro in Washington: https://upload.wikimedia.org/wikipedia/commons/c/c5/Fidel_Castro_-_MATS_Terminal_Washington_1959.jpg

5: Castro and Krushchev: https://upload.wikimedia.org/wikipedia/commons/2/25/Castro-kruschev.jpg

6: Dominican Rebels: http://www.latinamericanstudies.org/dominican-republic/mil-cumbres-1.jpg

7: Guevara in the Congo: https://upload.wikimedia.org/wikipedia/commons/f/f8/CheInCongo1965.jpg

8: Guevara in Bolivia: https://en.wikipedia.org/wiki/Che_Guevara#/media/File:CheinBolivia1.jpg

9: Czech anti-aircraft: http://www.latinamericanstudies.org/bay-of-pigs/4-boca.jpg

10: Mongoose: https://en.wikipedia.org/wiki/Cuban_Project#/media/File:Mangoose.jpg

11: Soviet Missile: https://en.wikipedia.org/wiki/Cuban_Missile_Crisis#/media/File:Soviet-R-12-nuclear-ballistic_missile.jpg

12: Castro at UN: https://en.wikipedia.org/wiki/Fidel_Castro#/media/File:Fidel_Castro_-_UN_General_Assembly_1960.jpg

13: Castro and Allende: http://www.periodismosinfronteras.org/wp-content/uploads/2014/08/castro-y-salvador-allende.jpg

14: Castro and Ortega https://diplomatdc.files.wordpress.com/2009/02/castro.jpg?w=500&h=330

15: Salvadoran guerrillas: http://eltorogoz.net/COLUMNA_GUAZAPA_1981.JPG

16: Ortega, Bishop, and Castro: https://renegadeslave.files.wordpress.com/2013/05/tumblr_mnkq7og7k71qap9gno1_5001.jpg

17: Cuban tanks in 1973 Yom Kippur War: http://militaryhistorynow.com/2016/01/29/the-cuban-army-abroad-fidel-castros-forgotten-foreign-wars/

18: Cuban-manned Ethiopian tanks: http://www.acig.info/UserFiles/File/SubSaharanAfr/Ogaden_War_1977_1978/ethiopian_002.jpg

19: A Cuban tank crew in Angola: http://i0.wp.com/ militaryhistorynow.com/wp-content/uploads/2014/10/Cuba-in-Angola.jpg?resize=560%2C343

20: Castro is met by Indira Gandhi: http://forbesindia.com/media/images/ 2014/Aug/img_76985_indira_gandhi.jpg

21: Cuban doctors and medical personnel before being shipped on "a mission": http://translatingcuba.com/wp-content/uploads/2014/11/ MACdicos-cubanos-salir-misiAn-EFE_CYMIMA20141110_0002_13.jpg

22: General Arnaldo T. Ochoa Sánchez: http://www.executedtoday.com/ images/Arnaldo_Ochoa.jpg

23: Amílcar Cabral with Nicolae Ceaușescu: https:// upload.wikimedia.org/wikipedia/commons/e/ed/ Amilcar_Cabral_FOCR.jpg

24: Fidel Castro and Samora Machel: https:// thegatvolblogger.files.wordpress.com/2014/10/image20.jpg

25: South Yemeni leadership: http://fuldagap.tumblr.com/post/ 48396287624/president-salim-rubai-ali-secretary-general-of

26: President Obama in front Che Guevara mural: http://nypost.com/ 2016/03/22/in-cuba-to-make-history-obama-stands-in-the-shadow-of-tyranny/

27: Fidel Castro in North Vietnam: http://english.hcma.gov.vn/Uploads/ 2015/10/3/media-thumb1379645321.jpg

28: Cuban military on parade: https://s-media-cache-ak0.pinimg.com/ 736x/45/a3/ff/45a3ffc06d433b0468d481c33c48866c.jpg

29: Police arrest and brutalize a demonstrator during *El Maleconazo*: http://babalublog.com/wpr/wp-content/uploads/2010/08/ maleconazo2005.jpg

30: The new leftist alliances in the Americas: https://c1.staticflickr.com/ 5/4144/5091920037_d7fc854286.jpg

31: Front cover: http://www.history.com/topics/cold-war/fidel-castro LARGE

32: Back cover: http://assets.nydailynews.com/polopoly_fs/
1.1187563.1418836646!/img/httpImage/image.jpg_gen/derivatives/
gallery_1200/fidel-castro-nikita-khrushchev-united-nations-1960.jpg

Appendices

Appendix A: CIA, *The Fall of Che Guevara and the Changing Face of the Cuban Revolution*, October 18, 1965

This intelligence memorandum, written by a young CIA analyst, Brian
Latell, presents an assessment that Guevara's preeminence as a leader of
the Cuban revolution has waned, and his internal and international
policies have been abandoned. In domestic policy, his economic strategy
of rapid industrialization has "brought the economy to its lowest point
since Castro came to power," the paper argues. In foreign policy, he
"never wavered from his firm revolutionary stand, even as other Cuban
leaders began to devote most of their attention to the internal problems of
the revolution." With Guevara no longer in Cuba, the CIA's assessment
concludes, "there is no doubt that Castro's more cautious position on
exporting revolution, as well as his different economic approach, led to
Che's downfall."

Declassified document referenced at http://nsarchive.gwu.edu/NSAEBB/
NSAEBB5/docs/doc01.pdf

Appendix B: The Shipment of Comrades to Angola and Mozambique. November 22, 1972, Memorandum, from Major Manuel Piñeiro Lozada to Major Raúl Castro Ruz. (Document from the Centro de Informacion de la Defensa de las Fuerzas Armadas Revolucionarias, CIDFAR, [Center of Information of the Armed Forces]).

This document, written by Cuba's famous intelligence operative, Manuel
Piñeiro, shows the early Cuban Government contacts with the MPLA
(Popular Movement for the Liberation of Angola) and original MPLA
requests for low-level training and logistical assistance in Angola. The
memo describes Cuban plans to send a delegation to Angola and
Mozambique to ascertain what kind of support Cuba could give to
independence struggles in those two nations.

Declassified document referenced at http://nsarchive.gwu.edu/NSAEBB/
NSAEBB67/gleijeses7.pdf

SPOTLIGHT ON MAO ZEDONG (and the following sections)

Li, Zhisui (1994). *The Private Life of Chairman Mao: The Memoirs of Mao's Personal Physician*. Trans. Tai Hung-chao. New York: Random House.

"Mao Zedong." International Encyclopedia of the Social Sciences. *Encyclopedia.com*. 18 Jun. 2019 <https://www.encyclopedia.com>.

Schram, Stuart R. (1969). *The Political Thought of Mao Tse-tung*. Harmondsworth, U.K.: Penguin.

Short, Phillip (2001). *Mao: A Life*. New York: Holt.

Snow, Edgar P. (1968). *Red Star over China*. Rev. ed. New York: Grove. (Orig. pub. 1937.)

Spence, Jonathan D. (1999). *Mao Zedong*. New York: Viking.

Wylie, Raymond F. (1980). *The Emergence of Maoism: Mao Tsetung, Ch'en Po-ta, and the Search for Chinese Theory, 1935–1945*. Stanford, CA: Stanford University Press.

Secondary Sources

International Encyclopedia of the Social Sciences

Encyclopedia of World Biography

UXL Encyclopedia of World Biography

The Columbia Encyclopedia, 6th ed.

World Encyclopedia

Cold War Reference Library

Encyclopedia of Genocide and Crimes Against Humanity

SPOTLIGHT ON JOSEPH STALIN

Applebaum, Anne (2003). *Gulag: A History. Doubleday. ISBN 978-0-7679-0056-0.*

Bideleux, Robert; Jeffries, Ian (1998). *A History of Eastern Europe: Crisis and Change. Routledge. ISBN 978-0-203-05024-8.*

Boobbyer, Phillip (2000). *The Stalin Era. Routledge. ISBN 978-0-7679-0056-0.*

Conquest, Robert (1997). *"Victims of Stalinism: A Comment" (PDF). Europe-Asia Studies. 49 (7): 1317–1319. doi: 10.1080/09668139708412501.*

Harris, James (2017). *The Great Fear: Stalin's Terror of the 1930s. Oxford University Press. ISBN 978-0-19-879786-9.*

Hasegawa, Tsuyoshi. (2005) *Racing the enemy: Stalin, Truman, and the surrender of Japan.* https://archive.org/details/racingenemystali00hase.

"Joseph Stalin." Encyclopedia of World Biography. *Encyclopedia.com.* 18 Jun. 2019 <https://www.encyclopedia.com>.

Khlevniuk, Oleg V. (2008). *Master of the House: Stalin and His Inner Circle. New Haven and London.*

Kun, Miklos (2003). *Stalin: An Unknown Portrait. Budapest and New York.*

Kuromiya, Hiroaki (2005). *Stalin: Profiles in Power. New York.*

Nekrich, Aleksandr Moiseevich; Ulam, Adam Bruno; Freeze, Gregory L. (1997). *Pariahs, Partners, Predators: German-Soviet Relations, 1922–1941. Columbia University Press. ISBN 978-0-231-10676-4.*

Plamper, Jan (2012). *The Stalin Cult: A Study in the Alchemy of Power. New Haven.*

Radzinsky, Edvard (1997). *Stalin: The First In-Depth Biography Based on Explosive New Documents from Russia's Secret Archive. New York.*

Rayfield, Donald (2005). *Stalin and His Hangmen: The Tyrant and Those Who Killed For Him. New York: Penguin. ISBN 978-0-14-191419-0.*

Roberts, Geoffrey (2007). "Stalin at the Tehran, Yalta, and Potsdam conferences." *Journal of Cold War Studies* 9.4: 6–40.

Thurston, Robert W. (1998). *Life and Terror in Stalin's Russia, 1934–1941. Yale University Press. ISBN 978-0-300-07442-0.*

Tucker, Robert C. (1973). *Stalin as Revolutionary: 1879–1929: A Study in History and Personality.*

Tucker, Robert C. (1990). *Stalin in Power: The Revolution from Above, 1928–1941. New York.*

Ulam, Adam B. (1973). *Stalin: The Man and His Era. New York.*

van Ree, Erik (2002). *The Political Thought of Joseph Stalin: A Study in Twentieth-Century Revolutionary Patriotism. London and New York.*

Wheatcroft, Stephen G. (1999). *"Victims of Stalinism and the Soviet Secret Police: The Comparability and Reliability of the Archival Data. Not the Last Word" (PDF). Europe-Asia Studies. 51 (2): 340–342. doi: 10.1080/09668139999056.*

Secondary Sources

Encyclopedia of World Biography

Encyclopedia of World Biography

UXL Encyclopedia of World Biography

World Encyclopedia

Korean War Reference Library

SPOTLIGHT ON POL POT (and the following sections)

Céspedes, Juan R. (n.p.d.) WAR IN CAMBODIA: A SOMBER PARALLEL TO THE VIETNAM CONFLICT. Class notes. https://www.academia.edu/6698530/WAR_IN_CAMBODIA_A_SOMBER_PARALLEL_TO_THE_VIETNAM_CONFLICT.

Heder, Stephen (1991). *Pol Pot and Khieu Samphan.* Clayton, Victoria: Centre of Southeast Asian Studies, 1991.

Kiernan, Ben (1997). *The Pol Pot regime: Race, power and genocide in Cambodia under the Khmer Rouge*, 1975–79. New Haven, Conn: Yale University Press.

Kiernan, Ben (2004). *How Pol Pot came to power: A history of Cambodian communism, 1930–1975.* New Haven, Conn.: Yale University Press.

Locard, Henri (March 2005). "State Violence in Democratic Kampuchea (1975–1979) and Retribution (1979–2004)", *European Review of History —Revue européenne d'Histoire*, vol. 12, no. 1, pp. 121–143.

"Pol Pot." Encyclopedia of World Biography. . *Encyclopedia.com*. 18 Jun. 2019 <https://www.encyclopedia.com>.

Ponchaud, François (1978). *Cambodia: Year Zero*. New York: Holt, Rinehart and Winston, 1978

Pescali, Piergiorgio (2015). *S-21 Nella prigione di Pol Pot*. Milan: La Ponga Edizioni.

Short, Philip (2004). *Pol Pot: The History of a Nightmare. London: John Murray. ISBN 978-0719565694.*

Secondary Sources

Encyclopedia of World Biography

International Encyclopedia of the Social Sciences

The Columbia Encyclopedia, 6th ed.

World Encyclopedia

Vietnam War Reference Library

Encyclopedia of Genocide and Crimes Against Humanity

The Cult of Personality

Bown, Matthew C. 1991. The Cult of Personality: The Apotheosis of Stalin, 1945–56. In *Art under Stalin*. New York: Holmes and Meier.

Chandler, David P. 1999. *Brother Number One: A Political Biography of Pol Pot*. Boulder, CO: Westview.

Hollander, Paul. 2002. The Cult of Personality in Communist States. In *Discontents: Postmodern and Postcommunist*. New Brunswick, NJ: Transaction.

Khrushchev, Nikita S. 1989. О КуЛьТе ЛИЧНОСТИ Иего ПОСЛеДСТВИЯХ [On the Cult of Personality and Its Consequences].

ИЗВеСТИЯ Ц ПСС [The News of the Central Committee of the Communist Party of the Soviet Union] 3 (March).

Overy, Richard J. 1997. The Cult of Personality: Stalin and the Legacy of War. In *Russia's War: Blood upon the Snow*. New York: TV Books.

Ryan, Louise. 2001. The Cult of Personality: Reassessing Leadership and Suffrage Movements in Britain and Ireland. In *Leadership and Social Movements*, ed. Colin Barker, Alan Johnson, and Michael Lavalette, 196–212. Manchester, U.K.: Manchester University Press.

"Personality, Cult of." International Encyclopedia of the Social Sciences. Rossen Vassilev. *Encyclopedia.com*. 27 Jun. 2019 <https://www.encyclopedia.com>.

Secondary Sources

Home History Modern Europe Russian, Soviet, and CIS History Cult of Personality

International Encyclopedia of the Social Sciences

International Encyclopedia of the Social Sciences

Encyclopedia of Russian History

DEATH BY COMMUNISM (and the following sections)

Alexopoulos, Golfo (January 7, 2013). *The Gulag's Veiled Mortality, Hoover Institution, retrieved September 21, 2018*

Alexopolus, Golfo (April 25, 2017). *Illness and Inhumanity in Stalin's Gulag, Yale University, ISBN 978-0-300-17941-5, retrieved September 3, 2018*

Amstutz, Mark R. (January 28, 2005). *International ethics: concepts, theories, and cases in global politics (2nd ed.). Rowman & Littlefield, ISBN 978-0-7425-3583-1*

Andrew, Christopher; Mitrokhin, Vasili (2006). *The World Was Going Our Way: The KGB and the Battle for the Third World, Basic Books, ISBN 978-0-465-00313-6*

Barry, Ellen (November 26, 2010). *"Russia: Stalin Called Responsible for Katyn Killings", The New York Times*

Baron, Udo (2011). *Hertle, Hans-Hermann; Nooke, Maria (eds.). The Victims at the Berlin Wall 1961-1989: A Biographical Handbook, Ch. Links Verlag, ISBN 978-3-861-53632-1*

Bilinsky, Yaroslav (1999). *"Was the Ukrainian Famine of 1932–1933 Genocide?", Journal of Genocide Research, 1 (2): 147–156, doi: 10.1080/14623529908413948*

Boobbyer, Phillip (2000). *The Stalin Era, Routledge, ISBN 978-0-7679-0056-0*

Brady, Brendan (July 27, 2010). *"Sentence reduced for former Khmer Rouge prison chief", The Los Angeles Times*

Brent, Jonathan (2008). *Inside the Stalin Archives: Discovering the New Russia (PDF), Atlas & Co., ISBN 978-0-9777433-3-9*

Céspedes, Juan R. (2013). *The Myopic Vision: The Causes of Totalitarianism, Authoritarianism, & Statism. https://www.amazon.com/ Myopic-Vision-Totalitarianism-Authoritarianism-Statism-ebook/dp/ B00E65NSFE.*

Céspedes, Juan R. (2016). *Cuban Communism and its Impact on World Affairs: 1959 - 2015. https://www.amazon.com/Cuban-Communism-Impact-World-Affairs/dp/1534703888.*

Chang, Jung; Halliday, Jon (2005). *Mao: The Unknown Story, London, ISBN 978-0-224-07126-0*

Charny, Israel (1999). *Encyclopedia of Genocide, Santa Barbara: ABC-Clio, ISBN 9780874369281*

Clayton, Jonathan (December 13, 2006). *"Guilty of genocide: the leader who unleashed a 'Red Terror' on Africa", The Times Online*

Conquest, Robert (1970). *The Nation Killers, New York: Macmillan, ISBN 978-0-333-10575-7*

Conquest, Robert (2007) [1990]. *The Great Terror: A Reassessment, 40th Anniversary Edition, Oxford: Oxford University Press, ISBN 978-0-195-31699-5*

Courtois, Stéphane, ed. (1999). *The Black Book of Communism: Crimes, Terror, Repression, translated by Jonathan Murphy and Mark Kramer;*

Mark Kramer (consulting ed.), Cambridge, MA: Harvard University Press, ISBN 978-0-674-07608-2

Dallin, Alexander (2000). "Reviewed Work(s): The Black Book of Communism: Crimes, Terror, Repression by Stéphane Courtois, Nicolas Werth, Jean-Louis Panné, Andrzej Paczkowski, Karel Bartošek, Jean-Louis Margolin, Jonathan Murphy and Mark Kramer", Slavic Review, 59 (4): 882–883, doi:10.2307/2697429, JSTOR 2697429

Dangerfield, Katie (December 13, 2017). North Korea defector says prisoners fled to dogs, women forced to have abortions, Global News, retrieved August 8, 2018

Davies, R. W.; Wheatcroft, S. G. (2004). The Years of Hunger: Soviet Agriculture, 1931-1933, The Industrialisation of Soviet Russia, 5, Basingstoke: Palgrave Macmillan

Dikötter, Frank (2010). Mao's Great Famine: The History of China's Most Devastating Catastrophe, 1958-1962, Walker & Company, ISBN 978-0-8027-7768-3

Dissident (July 28, 2016). Victims by the Numbers, Victims of Communism Memorial Foundation, archived from the original on March 14, 2018, retrieved August 19, 2018

Doyle, Kevin (July 26, 2007). "Putting the Khmer Rouge on Trial", Time

Dulić, Tomislav (2004). "Tito's Slaughterhouse: A Critical Analysis of Rummel's Work on Democide", Journal of Peace Research, 41 (1): 85–102, doi:10.1177/0022343304040051, JSTOR 4149657

Ellman, Michael (2002). "Soviet Repression Statistics: Some Comments" (PDF), Europe-Asia Studies, 54 (7): 1151–1172, doi: 10.1080/0966813022000017177

Ellman, Michael (September 2005). "The Role of Leadership Perceptions and of Intent in the Soviet Famine of 1931–1934" (PDF), Europe-Asia Studies, 57 (6): 823–841, doi:10.1080/09668130500199392, retrieved July 4, 2018.

Ellman, Michael (2007). "Stalin and the Soviet Famine of 1932–33 Revisited", Europe-Asia Studies, 59 (4), archived from the original (PDF) on October 14, 2007

Fein, Helen (1993). *"Soviet and Communist genocides and 'Democide'"*, *Genocide: a sociological perspective; Contextual and Comparative Studies I: Ideological Genocides*, Sage Publications, ISBN 978-0-8039-8829-3

Fenby, Jonathan (2008). *Modern China: The Fall and Rise of a Great Power, 1850 to the Present*, Ecco, ISBN 978-0-06-166116-7

Figes, Orlando (1997). *A People's Tragedy: The Russian Revolution 1891–1924*, Viking, ISBN 978-0-19-822862-2

Figes, Orlando (2007). *The Whisperers: Private Life in Stalin's Russia*, Metropolitan Books, ISBN 978-0-8050-7461-1

Finn, Peter (April 27, 2008). *"Aftermath of a Soviet Famine"*, The Washington Post

Fischer, Ruth; Leggett, John C. (2006). *"Stalin and German Communism: A Study in the Origins of the State Party"*, *Studies in Intelligence*, Edison, New Jersey: Transaction Publishers, ISBN 978-0-87855-822-3

Fitzpatrick, Sheila (2008). *The Russian Revolution*, Oxford University Press, ISBN 978-0-19-923767-8

Gellately, Robert (2007). *Lenin, Stalin, and Hitler: The Age of Social Catastrophe*, Knopf, ISBN 978-1-4000-4005-6

Getty, Arch; Rittersporn, Gábor; Zemskov, Viktor (1993). *"Victims of the Soviet penal system in the pre-war years: a first approach on the basis of archival evidence" (PDF)*, *American Historical Review*, 98 (4): 1017–1049, doi:10.2307/2166597, JSTOR 2166597

Gregory, Stephen (June 14, 2017). *"Remembering the Victims of Communism—for Them, and for Us"*, The Epoch TimesGoldhagen, Daniel (2009), *Worse Than War: Genocide, Eliminationism, and the Ongoing Assault on Humanity*, PublicAffairs, ISBN 978-1-58648-769-0

Haggard, Stephan; Noland, Marcus; Sen, Amartya (2009). *Famine in North Korea*, Columbia University Press

Hardy, Jeffrey S. (Spring 2018). *"Illness and Inhumanity in Stalin's Gulag. By Golfo Alexopoulos. New Haven: Yale University Press, 2007. xi, 308 pp. Notes. Index. Maps. $65.00, hard bound"*, *Slavic Review*, 77 (1): 269–270, doi:10.1017/slr.2018.57

Harff, Barbara; Gurr, Ted R. (1988). *Toward Empirical Theory of Genocides and Politicides: Identification and Measurement of Cases since 1945, 32*

Harff, Barbara (1996). *"Death by Government by R. J. Rummel", The Journal of Interdisciplinary History, 27 (1): 117–119, doi: 10.2307/206491, JSTOR 206491*

Harff, Barbara (2017). *"12. The Comparative Analysis of Mass Atrocities and Genocide", in Gleditsch, N. P. (ed.), R.J. Rummel: An Assessment of His Many Contributions, SpringerBriefs on Pioneers in Science and Practice, 37, SpringerBriefs on Pioneers in Science and Practice, pp. 116–125, doi:10.1007/978-3-319-54463-2_12, ISBN 978-3-319-54463-2*

Haynes, John Earl; Klehr, Harvey (2003). *In Denial: Historians, Communism, and Espionage, San Francisco, California: Encounter Books, ISBN 978-1-893554-72-6*

Hollander, Paul, ed. (2006). *From the Gulag to the Killing Fields: Personal Accounts of Political Violence and Repression in Communist States, Applebaum, Anne (foreword) and Hollander, Paul (introduction), Intercollegiate Studies Institute, ISBN 978-1-932-23678-1*

Holocaust by communist governments. https://en.wikipedia.org/wiki/ Mass_killings_under_communist_regimes.

Holquist, Peter (January – June 1997). *""Conduct Merciless Mass Terror": Decossackization on the Don, 1919" (PDF), Cahiers du Monde Russe : Russie, Empire Russe, Union Soviétique, États Indépendants, Guerre, guerres civiles et conflits nationaux dans l'Empire russe et en Russie soviétique, 1914 - 1922, 38 (1–2): 127–162, doi:10.3406/cmr. 1997.2486*

Jambrek, Peter, ed. (2008). *Crimes Committed by Totalitarian Regimes (PDF) (DRAFT BEFORE FINAL EDITING ed.), Slovenian Presidency of the Council of the European Union, p. 156, ISBN 978-961-238-977-2*

Jones, Adam (2010). *Genocide: A Comprehensive Introduction (2nd ed.), New York: Routledge, ISBN 978-0-415-48619-4*

Kakar, M. Hassan (1995). *Afghanistan: The Soviet Invasion and the Afghan Response, 1979–1982, University of California Press*

Kaplonski, Christopher (2002). *"Thirty thousand bullets" (PDF), Historical Injustice and Democratic Transition in Eastern Asia and Northern Europe, London*

Karlsson, Klas-Göran; Schoenhals, Michael (2008). *Crimes against humanity under communist regimes – Research review (PDF), Forum for Living History, ISBN 978-91-977487-2-8*

Keep, John (1997). *"Recent Writing on Stalin's Gulag: An Overview", Crime, Histoire & Sociétés / Crime, History & Societies, 1 (2): 91–112, doi:10.4000/chs.1014*

Kiernan, Ben (2003). *"The Demography of Genocide in Southeast Asia: The Death Tolls in Cambodia, 1975-79, and East Timor, 1975-80" (PDF), Critical Asian Studies, 35 (4): 585–597, doi: 10.1080/1467271032000147041*

Kort, Michael (2001). *The Soviet Colossus: History and Aftermath, Armonk, New York: M.E. Sharpe, ISBN 978-0-7656-0396-8*

Kotkin, Stephen (November 3, 2017). *"Communism's Bloody Century", The Wall Street Journal, archived from the original on November 3, 2017*

Krain, Matthew (June 1997). *"State-Sponsored Mass Murder: The Onset and Severity of Genocides and Politicides", The Journal of Conflict Resolution, 41 (3): 331–360, doi:10.1177/0022002797041003001, JSTOR 174282*

Kuisong, Yang (March 2008). *"Reconsidering the Campaign to Suppress Counterrevolutionaries", The China Quarterly, 193*

Kuromiya, Hiroaki (2001). *"Review Article: Communism and Terror. Reviewed Work(s): The Black Book of Communism: Crimes, Terror, and Repression by Stephane Courtois; Reflections on a Ravaged Century by Robert Conquest", Journal of Contemporary History, 36 (1): 191–201, doi:10.1177/002200940103600110, JSTOR 261138*

Leggett, George (1987). *The Cheka: Lenin's Political Police, Oxford University Press, ISBN 978-0-19-822862-2*

Locard, Henri (March 2005). *"State Violence in Democratic Kampuchea (1975–1979) and Retribution (1979–2004)", European Review of History, 12 (1): 121–143, CiteSeerX 10.1.1.692.8388, doi: 10.1080/13507480500047811*

Lorenz, Andreas (May 15, 2007). *"The Chinese Cultural Revolution: Remembering Mao's Victims"*, Der Spiegel Online

MacFarquhar, Roderick; Schoenhals, Michael (2006). *Mao's Last Revolution*, Harvard University Press

Maksymiuk, Jan (November 29, 2006). *Ukraine: Parliament Recognizes Soviet-Era Famine As Genocide*, RFE/RL

Malia, Martin (1999). *"Foreword: The Uses of Atrocity"*, in Courtois, Stéphane; Kramer, Mark (eds.), The Black Book of Communism: Crimes, Terror, Repression, Harvard University Press, pp. ix–xx, ISBN 978-0-674-07608-2, retrieved August 24, 2017.

Mann, Michael (2005). *The Dark Side of Democracy: Explaining Ethnic Cleansing*, New York: Cambridge University Press, ISBN 978-0-521-53854-1

Materski, Wojciech; Szarota, Tomasz (2009). *Polska 1939–1945. Straty osobowe i ofiary represji pod dwiema okupacjami*, Warszawa: Institute of National Remembrance (IPN), ISBN 978-83-7629-067-6

Mawdsley, Evan (2003). *The Stalin Years: The Soviet Union 1929–1953*, Manchester, England: Manchester University Press, ISBN 978-0-7190-6377-0

McKirdy, Euan (August 7, 2014). *"Top Khmer Rouge leaders found guilty of crimes against humanity, sentenced to life in prison"*, CNN

McLoughlin, Barry (2002). *"Mass Operations of the NKVD, 1937–1938: a survey"*, in McLoughlin, Barry; McDermott, Kevin (eds.), Stalin's Terror: High Politics and Mass Repression in the Soviet Union, Palgrave Macmillan, ISBN 978-1-4039-0119-4

Midlarsky, Manus (2005). *The Killing Trap: Genocide in the Twentieth Century*, New York: Cambridge University Press, ISBN 978-0-521-81545-1

Möller, Horst (1999). *Der rote Holocaust und die Deutschen. Die Debatte um das 'Schwarzbuch des Kommunismus' [The red Holocaust and the Germans. The debates on the 'Black Book of Communism']*, Piper Verlag, ISBN 978-3-492-04119-5

Montefiore, Simon Sebag (2005). *Stalin: The Court of the Red Tsar*, New York: Vintage Books, ISBN 978-1-4000-7678-9

Morré, Jörg (1997). *"Einleitung. – Sowjetische Internierungslager in der SBZ", in Morré, Jörg (ed.), Speziallager des NKWD. Sowjetische Internierungslager in Brandenburg 1945–1950 (PDF), Potsdam: Brandenburgische Landeszentrale für politische Bildung*

Mosher, Steven W. (1992). *China Misperceived: American Illusions and Chinese Reality, Basic Books, ISBN 978-0-465-09813-2*

Perry, Mark J. (2016). *Counting victims of the Castro regime: Nearly 11,000 to date.* [From a 2005 *Wall Street Journal* article by Mary Anastasia O'Grady "Counting Castro's Victims"]. http://www.aei.org/publication/counting-victims-of-the-castro-regime-nearly-11000-to-date/.

WAR: ITS CAUSES AND EFFECTS (and the following sections)

Allison, Graham (1971). *Essence of Decision.* Boston: Little, Brown.

Bueno de Mesquita, Bruce (1980). "Theories of International Conflict: An Analysis and Appraisal." In Ted Robert Gurr, ed., *Handbook of Political Conflict.* New York: Free Press.

Céspedes, Juan R. (2011). War Interminable: The Origins, Causes, Practices and Effects of International Conflict. https://www.amazon.com/War-Interminable-Practices-International-Conflict/dp/1463767293.

Gilpin, Robert (1981). *War and Change in World Politics.* Cambridge, UK: Cambridge University Press.

Golstein, Joshua (1988). *Long Cycles.* New Haven, Conn.: Yale University Press.

Hobson, J. A. (1902). 1954 *Imperialism.* London: Allen and Unwin.

Janis, Irving (1972). *Victims of Groupthink.* Boston: Houghton Mifflin.

Kant, Immanuel (1795). 1949 "Eternal Peace." In C. J. Friedrich, ed., *The Philosophy of Kant.* New York: Modern Library.

Lenin, V. I. (1917). 1939 *Imperialism.* New York: International.

Levy, Jack S. (1989). "The Causes of War: A Review of Theories and Evidence." In Philip E. Tetlock, Robert Jarvis, Paul Stern, and Charles Tilly, eds., *Behavior, Society and Nuclear War.* Oxford, UK: Oxford University Press.

Morgenthau, Hans (1967). *Politics among Nations*. New York: Knopf.

Organski, J. F. K. (1968). *World Politics*. New York: Knopf.

Waltz, Kenneth (1959). *Man, the State, and War*. New York: Columbia University Press.

"War." Encyclopedia of Sociology. *Encyclopedia.com.* 18 Jun. 2019 <https://www.encyclopedia.com>.

"war." The Oxford Dictionary of Phrase and Fable. *Encyclopedia.com.* 18 Jun. 2019 <https://www.encyclopedia.com>.

"war." World Encyclopedia. *Encyclopedia.com.* 18 Jun. 2019 <https://www.encyclopedia.com>.

—— 1981 *The War Trap*. New Haven, Conn.: Yale University Press.

War: Legal Questions (and the following sections)

Céspedes, Juan R. (2011). *War Interminable: The Origins, Causes, Practices and Effects of International Conflict*. https://www.amazon.com/War-Interminable-Practices-International-Conflict/dp/1463767293.

Céspedes, Juan R. (2013). *Collapse of the Soviet Empire*. https://www.amazon.com/Collapse-Soviet-Empire-C%C3%A9spedes-Ph-D-ebook/dp/B00DFLFOMU.

Céspedes, Juan R. (2013). *The Myopic Vision: The Causes of Totalitarianism, Authoritarianism, and Statism*. Mundus Novus Publishers. https://www.amazon.com/Myopic-Vision-Totalitarianism-Authoritarianism-Statism-ebook/dp/B00E65NSFE.

Chesterman, Simon, ed. (2001). *Civilians in War.* Boulder, Colo.: Lynne Rienner.

Claude, Inis, Jr. (1956). *Swords into Plowshares*. New York: Random House.

Commission of Inquiry into the Events at the Refugee Camps in Beirut (1983). *Final Report of the Commission of Inquiry into the Events at the Refugee Camps in Beirut The Jerusalem Post*. February 9, 1983.

Goodrich, Leyland M. (1960). *The United Nations*. London: Stevens.

Goodrich, Leyland M., Edward Hambro, and Ann P. Simons (1969). *Charter of the United Nations,* 3rd edition. New York: Columbia University Press.

Gutman, Roy, and David Rieff (1999). *Crimes of War.* New York: Norton.

Holzgrefe, J. L., and Robert O. Keohane, eds. (2003). *Humanitarian Intervention: Ethical, Legal, and Political Dilemmas.* Cambridge, Mass.: Cambridge University Press.

International Commission on Intervention and State Sovereignty (2001). *Report of the International Commission on Intervention and State Sovereignty: The Responsibility to Protect.* Ottawa: International Development Research Center.

International Committee of the Red Cross (ICRC). Available from: http://www.icrc.org.

Report of the Independent Inquiry into the Actions of the United Nations During the 1994 Genocide in Rwanda. UN Doc. S/99/1257. Published 1999.

Simma, Bruno (2002). *The Charter of the United Nations: A Commentary,* 2nd edition. New York: Oxford University Press.

Schabas, William A. (2000). *Genocide in International Law.* Cambridge, Mass.: Cambridge University Press.

Schabas, William A. (2004). *An Introduction to the International Criminal Court,* 2nd Edition. Cambridge, Mass.: Cambridge University Press.

United Nations (1999). *Report of the Secretary General Pursuant to General Assembly Resolution 53/35: The Fall of Srebrenica.* UN Doc. A/54/549.

White, Nigel D. (1997). *Keeping the Peace,* 2nd edition. New York: Manchester University Press.

"War." Encyclopedia of Genocide and Crimes Against Humanity. *Encyclopedia.com.* 18 Jun. 2019 <https://www.encyclopedia.com>.

THE NATURE OF WAR (and the following sections)

Céspedes, Juan R. (2011). *War Interminable:The Origins, Causes, Practices and Effects of International Conflict.* https://www.amazon.com/dp/1463767293/ref=rdr_ext_tmb

Frehling, John E. (1993). *Struggle for a Continent: The Wars of Early America.*

Gardner, Lloyd C. (1984). *A Covenant with Power: America and World Order from Wilson to Reagan.*

Perret, Geoffrey (1989). *A Country Made by War: From the Revolution to Vietnam—The Story of America's Rise to Power.*

Russell F. Weigley (1973). *The American Way of War: A History of United States Military Strategy and Policy.*

Sherry, Michael (1995). *In the Shadow of War: The United States since the 1930s.*

Watts, Stephen (1987). *The Republic Reborn: War and the Making of Liberal America, 1790–1820.*

Whiteclay Chambers II, John and G. Kurt Piehler, eds., (1999). *Major Problems in American Military History.*

Peace and Anti-War Movements (and the following sections)

Blainey, Geoffrey (1988). *The Causes of War, 3rd ed.*

Cashman, Greg (, 1993). *What Causes War? An Introduction to Theories of International Conflict.*

Céspedes, Juan R. (2011). *War Interminable:The Origins, Causes, Practices and Effects of International Conflict.* https://www.amazon.com/dp/1463767293/ref=rdr_ext_tmb

George, Alexander L. (1989). *Domestic Constraints on Regime Change in U.S. Foreign Policy, in G. John Ikenberry, ed., American Foreign Policy, pp. 583–608.*

Gleditsch, Nils Petter (1992). *Democracy and Peace, Journal of Peace Research, 29, pp. 369–76.*

Jervis, Robert (1976). *Perception and Misperception in International Politics, 1976.*

Levy, Jack (1989). *The Causes of War: A Review of Theories, in Philip E. Tetlock, et al., eds., Behavior, Society, and Nuclear War, 1, pp. 209–333.*

The Effects of War on the Economy

Clayton, James L., ed., (1970). *The Economic Impact of the Cold War.*

Hacker, Louis (1940). *The Triumph of American Capitalism.*

Kennedy, Paul (1987). *The Rise and Fall of the Great Powers.*

Kennedy, Paul (1993). *Preparing for the Twenty–First Century, esp. chaps. 13 and 14.*

"War." The Oxford Companion to American Military History. *Encyclopedia.com.* 18 Jun. 2019 <https://www.encyclopedia.com>.

Wright, Chester W. (1943). *The More Enduring Economic Consequences of America's Wars, in the Journal of Economic History.*

MORAL JUSTIFICATIONS FOR WAR (and the following sections)

Céspedes, Juan R. (2011). *War Interminable:The Origins, Causes, Practices and Effects of International Conflict. https://www.amazon.com/dp/1463767293/ref=rdr_ext_tmb*

Denton Jr., Robert E., ed., (1993). *The Media and the Persian Gulf War.*

Fornari, Franco (1974). *The Psychoanalysis of War. Translated by Pfeifer, Alenka. NY: Doubleday Anchor Press.*

Fry, Douglas (2004). *"Conclusion: Learning from Peaceful Societies". In Kemp, Graham (ed.). Keeping the Peace. Routledge. pp. 185–204.*

Fry, Douglas (2005). *The Human Potential for Peace: An Anthropological Challenge to Assumptions about War and Violence.* Oxford University Press.

Fry, Douglas (2009). *Beyond War.* Oxford University Press.

Gat, Azar (2006). *War in Human Civilization.* Oxford University Press.

Graber, Doris A. (1968). *Public Opinion, the President, and Foreign Policy: Four Case Studies from the Formative Years.*

Knightly, Philip (, 1975). *The First Casualty: From the Crimea to Vietnam: The War Correspondent as Hero, Propagandist, and Myth Maker.*

"News Media, War, and the Military." The Oxford Companion to American Military History. *Encyclopedia.com.* 18 Jun. 2019 <https://www.encyclopedia.com>.

Vaughn, Stephen (1980). *Holding Fast the Inner Lines: Democracy, Nationalism, and the Committee on Public Information.*

Winkler, Allan M. (1975). *The Politics of Propaganda: The Office of War Information, 1942–1945.*

DIRECT IMPACT ON HUMANS AND THE ENVIRONMENT (and the following sections)

Amnesty International (1991). *Health Personnel: Victims of Human Rights Violations.* London: Author.

Arms Project of Human Rights Watch and Physicians for Human Rights (1993). *Landmines: A Deadly Legacy.* New York: Human Rights Watch.

British Medical Association (1992). *Medicine Betrayed: The Participation of Doctors in Human Rights Abuses.* London: Zed Books.

Carnegie Commission on Preventing Deadly Conflict (1997). *Preventing Deadly Conflict: Final Report.* Washington, DC: Author.

Forrow, L. F.; Blair, B. G.; Helfand, I.; Lewis, G.; Postol, T.; Sidel, V. W.; Levy, B. S.; Abrams, H.; and Cassel, C. (1998). "Accidental Nuclear War: A Post-Cold War Assessment." *New England Journal of Medicine* 338:1326–1331.

Forrow, L. F., and Sidel, V. W. (1998). "Medicine and Nuclear War: From Hiroshima to Mutual Assured Destruction to Abolition 2000." *Journal of the American Medical Association* 280:456–461.

Geiger, H. J., and Cook-Deegan, R. M. (1993). "The Role of Physicians in Conflicts and Humanitarian Crises." *Journal of the American Medical Association* 270:616–620.

Institute of Medicine (1988). *The Future of Public Health.* Washington, DC: National Academy Press.

International Physicians for the Prevention of Nuclear War (1997). *Landmines: A Global Health Crisis.* Cambridge, MA: Author.

Levy, B. S., and Sidel, V. W., eds. (1997). *War and Public Health.* New York: Oxford University Press.

Sidel, V. W. (1989). "Weapons of Mass Destruction: The Greatest Threat to Public Health." *Journal of the American Medical Association* 262:680–682.

Sidel, V. W., and Goldwyn, R. M. (1966). "Chemical and Biological Weapons—A Primer." *New England Journal of Medicine* 242:21–27.

Sidel, V. W., and Shahi, G. (1997). "The Impact of Military Activities on Development, Environment and Health." In *International Perspectives in Environment, Development and Health: Toward A Sustainable World,* eds. G. Shahi, B. S. Levy, A. Binger, T. Kjellstrom and R. Lawrence. New York: Springer.

"War." Encyclopedia of Public Health. . *Encyclopedia.com.* 18 Jun. 2019 <https://www.encyclopedia.com>.

Wright S., ed. (1990). *Preventing a Biological Arms Race.* Cambridge, MA: MIT Press.

—— (1995) "The International Arms Trade and Its Impact on Health." British Medical Journal 311:1677–1680.

—— (1996). *Prescription for Change: Health Professionals and the Exposure of Human Rights Violations.* London: Author.

—— (1996). "The Role of Physicians in the Prevention of Nuclear War." In *Genocide, War, and Human Survival,* eds. B. C. Strozier and M. Flynn. Lanham, MD: Rowman and Littlefield Publishers.

WORLD WAR I

Berghahn, Volker R. (1973). Germany and the Approach of War in 1914.

Céspedes, Juan R. (2011). *War Interminable:The Origins, Causes, Practices and Effects of International Conflict.* *https://www.amazon.com/dp/1463767293/ref=rdr_ext_tmb*

Fischer, Fritz (1967). Germany: War Aims in the First World War, 1967.
Jarausch, Konrad (1972). The Enigmatic Chancellor.

The Oxford Companion to American Military History 2000, originally
published by Oxford University Press 2000.

THE SPANISH CIVIL WAR

Bolloten, Burnett (1991). *The Spanish Civil War: Revolution and
Counterrevolution*. Durham: University of North Carolina Press.

Coverdale, John F. (1975). *Italian Intervention in the Spanish Civil War*.
Princeton, NJ: Princeton University Press.

Payne, Stanley G. (1987). *The Franco Regime 1936–1975*. Madison:
University of Wisconsin Press.

Payne, Stanley G. (2003). *The Spanish Civil War, the Soviet Union, and
Communism*. New Haven, CT: Yale University Press.

Payne, Stanley G. (2006). *The Collapse of the Spanish Republic, 1933–
1936. Origins of the Civil War*. New Haven, CT: Yale University Press.

Preston, Paul. (1993). *Franco. A Biography*. London: HarperCollins.

"Spanish Civil War." International Encyclopedia of the Social Sciences.
Encyclopedia.com. 18 Jun. 2019 <https://www.encyclopedia.com>.

Thomas, Hugh. (1986). *The Spanish Civil War*. New York: Harper &
Row.

Whealey, Robert H. (1989). *Hitler and Spain. The Nazi Role in the
Spanish Civil War*. Lexington: University of Kentucky Press.

Secondary Sources

International Encyclopedia of the Social Sciences

International Encyclopedia of the Social Sciences

The Columbia Encyclopedia, 6th ed.

Encyclopedia of Russian History

World Encyclopedia

Encyclopedia of Modern Europe: Europe Since 1914: Encyclopedia of the Age of War and Reconstruction

THE CHINESE CIVIL WAR

"Chinese Civil War, U.S. Involvement in the." The Oxford Companion to American Military History. *Encyclopedia.com.* 16 Jun. 2019 <https://www.encyclopedia.com>.

Dreyer, Edward L. (1995). China at War: 1901–1949.

THE KOREAN WAR

Appleman, Roy E. (1961). South to the Naktong, North to the Yalu, June–November 1950.

Foot, Rosemary (1990). A Substitute for Victory: The Policy of Peacemaking at the Korean Armistice Talks.

Goulden, Joseph C. (1982). Korea: the Untold Story of the War.

Kaufman, Burton I. (1986). The Korean War: Challenges in Crisis, Credibility and Command.

"Korean War." The Oxford Companion to American Military History. *Encyclopedia.com.* 15 Jun. 2019 <https://www.encyclopedia.com>.

Zhang, Shu Guang (1992). Deterrence and Strategic Culture: Chinese American Confrontations, 1949–1958.

THE VIETNAM WAR

Beckett, I. F. W. (15 September 2009). Encyclopedia of Guerrilla Warfare (Hardcover). Santa Barbara, California: Abc-Clio Inc. ISBN 978-0874369298. ISBN 9780874369298

Hinckle, Warren (with Steven Chain and David Goldstein) (1971): Guerrilla-Krieg in USA (Guerrilla war in the USA), Stuttgart (Deutsche Verlagsanstalt). ISBN 3-421-01592-9

Keats, John (1990). They Fought Alone. Time Life. ISBN 0-8094-8555-9

Oller, John (2016). The Swamp Fox: How Francis Marion Saved the American Revolution. Boston: Da Capo Press. ISBN 978-0-306-82457-9.

Peers, William R.; Brelis, Dean (1963). Behind the Burma Road: The Story of America's Most Successful Guerrilla Force. Boston: Little, Brown & Co..

Powers, Thomas (2018). "The War without End" (review of Steve Coll, Directorate S: The CIA and America's Secret Wars in Afghanistan and Pakistan, Penguin, 757 pp.), The New York Review of Books, vol. LXV, no. 7 (19 April 2018), pp. 42–43.

Schmidt, L.S. (1982). "American Involvement in the Filipino Resistance on Mindanao During the Japanese Occupation, 1942-1945". M.S. Thesis. U.S. Army Command and General Staff College. 274 pp.

Sutherland, Daniel E. (2000). "Sideshow No Longer: A Historiographical Review of the Guerrilla War." Civil War History 46.1: 5-23; American Civil War, 1861–65

Secondary Sources

The Oxford Companion to American Military History

International Encyclopedia of the Social Sciences

Encyclopedia of the American Constitution

GUERRILLA WARS

Anderson, David L. (2004). Columbia Guide to the Vietnam War. New York: Columbia University Press. ISBN 978-0231114929.

Appy, Christian G. (2006). Vietnam: The Definitive Oral History, Told from All Sides. London: Ebury Press. ISBN 978-0091910112.

Céspedes, Juan R. (2011). *War Interminable:The Origins, Causes, Practices and Effects of International Conflict. https://www.amazon.com/dp/1463767293/ref=rdr_ext_tmb*

Cooper, Chester L. (1970). The Lost Crusade: America in Vietnam. ISBN 978-0396062417. a Washington insider's memoir of events.

Duiker, William J. (1981). The Communist Road to Power in Vietnam. Westview Press. ISBN 978-0891587941.

Herring, George C. (2001). America's Longest War: The United States and Vietnam, 1950–1975 (4th ed.). New York: McGraw-Hill. ISBN 978-0072536188.

Kolko, Gabriel (1985). Anatomy of a War: Vietnam, the United States, and the Modern Historical Experience. New York: Pantheon Books. ISBN 978-0394747613.

Kutler, Stanley I., ed. (1996). Encyclopedia of the Vietnam War. New York: Charles Scribner's Sons. ISBN 978-0132769327.

——— (2010). "The Indochina wars and the Cold War, 1945–1975". In Melvyn P. Leffler and Odd Arne Westad, eds., The Cambridge History of the Cold War, Volume II: Crises and Détente (pp. 281–304). Cambridge: Cambridge University Press. ISBN 978-0521837200.

NUCLEAR WAR (and the following sections)

Associated Press. "16,000 Now Believed Used in Radiation Experiments." San Antonio Express-News, 18 August 1995, 6A.

Boyer, Paul (1985). By the Bomb's Early Light: American Thought and Culture at the Dawn of the Atomic Age. New York: Pantheon.

Broad, William J. (1996, February 16). "U.S., in First Atomic Accounting, Says It Shipped a Ton of Plutonium to 39 Countries." New York Times, 10.

Ford, Daniel (1982). The Cult of the Atom: The Secret Papers of the Atomic Energy Commission. New York: Simon and Schuster.

Institute for Energy and Environmental Research and the International Physicians for the Prevention of Nuclear War. Radioactive Heaven and Earth: The Health and Environmental Effects of Nuclear Weapons Testing In, On and Above the Earth. New York: Apex Press, 1991.

Subak, Susan (1984). "The Soviet Union's Nuclear Realism." The New Republic, 17 December 1984.

Tikhonov, Valentin (2001). Russia's Nuclear and Missile Complex: The Human Factor in Proliferation. Washington, DC: Carnegie Endowment for International Peace.

Toynbee, Arnold (1950). War and Civilization. New York: Oxford University Press.

HISTORY OF THE AMERICAS (and the following sections)

Boyer, Paul S. (2001). *The Oxford Companion to United States History*, excerpt and text search; online at many libraries

Carnes, Mark C., and John A. Garraty (2008). *The American Nation: A History of the United States: AP Edition.*

Egerton, Douglas R. et al. (2007). *The Atlantic World: A History, 1400–1888*, college textbook; 530 pp

Jacobs, Heidi Hayes, and Michal L. LeVasseur (2007). *World Studies: Latin America: Geography - History - Culture.*

Keen, Benjamin, and Keith Haynes (2008). *A History of Latin America.*

Marsh, James C., ed. (1985). *The Canadian Encyclopedia* (4 vol) online edition

Cold War Era (and the following sections)

Brands, H. W. (1988). *Cold Warriors. Eisenhower's Generation and American Foreign Policy.*

Céspedes, Juan R. (n.p.d.). The Cold War: A Focus on the Southern Hemisphere. https://www.academia.edu/6987909/The_Cold_War_A_Focus_on_the_Southern_Hemisphere.

Chang, Laurence and Peter Kornbluh, eds., (1992). *The Cuban Missile Crisis, 1962.*

Divine, Robert A. (1981). *Eisenhower and the Cold War.*

Freedman, Lawrence *(2000). Kennedy's Wars: Berlin, Cuba, Laos, and Vietnam.*

Gaddis, John Lewis (1990). *Russia, the Soviet Union and the United States. An Interpretative History* 2nd ed.

Heiss, Mary Ann (2003). "The Economic Cold War: America, Britain, and East-West Trade, 1948–63" *The Historian*, Vol. 65.

Kolko, Gabriel (1971). *The Limits of Power* New York.

LaFeber, Walter (1993). *America, Russia, and the Cold War, 1945–1992* 7th ed.

THE GREAT DEPRESSION (and the following sections)

Barnard, Rita (1995). *The Great Depression and the Culture of Abundance: Kenneth Fearing, Nathanael West, and Mass Culture in the 1930s.* New York: Cambridge University Press.

Bernstein, Michael A. (1987). *The Great Depression: Delayed Recovery and Economic Change in America, 1929–1939.* New York: Cambridge University Press.

Bordo, Michael D., Claudia Goldin, and Eugene N. White, eds. (1998). *The Defining Moment: The Great Depression and the American Economy in the Twentieth Century.* Chicago: University of Chicago Press.

Friedman, Milton, and Anna J. Schwartz (1963). *A Monetary History of the United States, 1867–1960.* Princeton, N.J.: Princeton University Press.

Hall, Thomas E., and J. David Ferguson (1998). *The Great Depression: An International Disaster of Perverse Economic Policies.* Ann Arbor: University of Michigan Press.

Keynes, John M. (1964, Original edition published in 1936). *The General Theory Of Employment, Interest, and Money.* New York: St. Martin's Press, 1964.

Margo, Robert A. (spring 1993). "Employment and Unemployment in the 1930s." *Journal of Economic Perspectives* 7, no. 2: 41–59.

Rosenof, Theodore. (1997). *Economics in the Long Run: New Deal Theorists and Their Legacies, 1933–1993.* Chapel Hill: University of North Carolina Press.

Rothermund, Dietmar (1996). *The Global Impact of the Great Depression, 1929–1939.* London: Routledge.

Szostak, Rick. https://www.encyclopedia.com/history/united-states-and-canada/us-history/great-depression.

Temin, Peter (1976). *Did Monetary Forces Cause the Great Depression?* New York: Norton.

————. *Lessons from the Great Depression* (1989). Cambridge, Mass.: MIT Press.

Secondary Sources

International Encyclopedia of the Social Sciences

Gale Encyclopedia of U.S. Economic History

The Columbia Encyclopedia, 6th ed.

World Encyclopedia

Everyday Finance: Economics, Personal Money Management, and Entrepreneurship

BAY OF PIGS

Blight, James and Peter Kornbluh. *Politics of Illusion: The Bay of Pigs Invasion Reexamined.* Boulder, CO: Lynne Rienner Publishers, 1998.

Céspedes, Juan R. (2016). *Cuban Communism and its Impact on World Affairs. 1959 - 2015. For IB the Americas Paper 3 Exam.* Kindle Edition. https://www.amazon.com/Cuban-Communism-Impact-World-Affairs-ebook/dp/B01HWSMPGO/ref=sr_1_1? keywords=dr+juan+cespedes+cuba&qid=1561563535&s=gateway&sr=8-1

Gilman, Larry. https://www.encyclopedia.com/history/latin-america-and-caribbean/cuban-history/bay-pigs.

Kornbluh, Peter. *Bay of Pigs Declassified: The Secret CIA Report on the Invasion of Cuba.* New York: The New Press, 1998.

CUBAN MISSILE CRISIS (ing sections)

Allison, Graham, and Philip Zelikow. (1999). *Essence of Decision: Explaining the Cuban Missile Crisis.* 2nd ed. New York: Longman.

Brune, Lester H. 1985. *The Missile Crisis of October 1962: A Review of Issues and References.* Claremont, CA: Regina Books.

Céspedes, Juan R. (2016). *Cuban Communism and its Impact on World Affairs. 1959 - 2015. For IB the Americas Paper 3 Exam.* Kindle Edition. https://www.amazon.com/Cuban-Communism-Impact-World-Affairs-

ebook/dp/B01HWSMPGO/ref=sr_1_1?
keywords=dr+juan+cespedes+cuba&qid=1561563535&s=gateway&sr=8
-1

"Cuban Missile Crisis." International Encyclopedia of the Social
Sciences. *Brian Robert Calfano. Encyclopedia.com.* 26 Jun. 2019
<https://www.encyclopedia.com>

Hilsman, Roger. (1967). *To Move a Nation: The Politics of Foreign
Policy in the Administration of John F. Kennedy.* Garden City, NY:
Doubleday.

Medland, William J. (1990). The Cuban Missile Crisis: Evolving
Historical Perspectives. *The History Teacher* 23: 433–447.

Rostow, Walt W. (1972). *The Diffusion of Power: An Essay in Recent
History.* New York: Macmillan.

Sorensen, Theodore C. (1965). *Kennedy.* New York: Harper and Row.

THE CIVIL RIGHTS MOVEMENT (ing sections)

Andryszewski, Tricia (1996). *The March on Washington 1963: Gathering
to Be Heard.* Brookfield, CT: Millbrook Press.

Dunn, John M. (1998). *The Civil Rights Movement.* San Diego, CA:
Lucent Books.

McKissack, Patricia and Fredrick (1987). *The Civil Rights Movement in
America from 1865 to the Present.* Chicago: Children's Press.

Meltzer, Milton (2001). *There Comes a Time: The Struggle for Civil
Rights.* New York: Landmark Books.

"The Civil Rights Movement." American Social Reform Movements
Reference Library. *Encyclopedia.com.* 3 Jul. 2019 <https://
www.encyclopedia.com>.

Wexler, Sanford (1999). *The Civil Rights Movement.* New York: Facts on
File.

Williams, Juan (1987). *Eyes on the Prize: America's Civil Rights Years,
1954–1965.* New York: Viking.

Winters, Paul A., ed. (2000). *The Civil Rights Movement*. San Diego, CA: Greenhaven Press.

A SUMMARY OF THE 20TH CENTURY (and the following sections)

Brower, Daniel R. and Thomas Sanders (7th Ed, 2013). *The World in the Twentieth Century*.

Ferguson, Niall (2004). *Empire: The rise and demise of the British world order and the lessons for global power. New York: Basic Books. ISBN 978-0-465-02328-8.*

Grenville, J. A. S. (1994). *A History of the World in the Twentieth Century*.

Hallock, Stephanie A. (2012). *The World in the 20th Century: A Thematic Approach.*

Harrison, Mark (2002). *Accounting for War: Soviet Production, Employment, and the Defence Burden, 1940–1945*. Cambridge University Press. p. 167. ISBN 0-521-89424-7

Pinker, Stephen (2011). *The Better Angels of Our Nature. Viking. ISBN 978-0-670-02295-3.*

Thee, Marek (1976). *"The Indochina Wars: Great Power Involvement - Escalation and Disengagement". Journal of Peace Research. Sage Publications. **13** (2): 117–129. doi:10.1177/002234337601300204. ISSN 1460-3578. JSTOR 423343.*

*UNESCO (February 28, 2008). "The Twentieth Century". History of Humanity. **VII**. Routledge. p. 600. ISBN 978-0-415-09311-8.*

Weaver, Gary Rodger (1998). *Culture, Communication, and Conflict*. Simon & Schuster. p. 474. ISBN 0-536-00373-4

Whittaker, Jason (2004), The cyberspace handbook, Routledge, p. 122, ISBN 978-0-415-16835-9.

Illustrations

The images and illustrations in this book are unburdened with copyright and available and authorized for use under (a) the Creative Commons Attribution 2.0 Generic license through Wikimedia Commons, other public domain, or open content sources, (b) works of an employee of the United States government, the United States armed forces, or a member of the United Nations, (c) in the public domain because they have exceeded the copyright term, (d) freely available throughout the Internet and other media, unidentifiable, or uncopyrightable. The author of this book does not claim ownership of the images or illustrations. Thus, the images and illustrations are free and may be used by anyone for any purpose following the requirement of attribution, which is referenced below. The attribution herein does not in any way suggest that the originator of the images or illustrations endorses the author of this book, the contents of this book, or the author's use of the work.

History under magnifying glass. Source: https://www.the-rampage.org/2896/features/history-department-looks-to-the-future/

Authoritarian States. Benito Mussolini (left), dictator of Italy from 1922 to 1943 and, Adolf Hitler (right), dictator of Germany from 1933 to 1945. Source: https://en.wikipedia.org/wiki/Dictator#/media/File:Hitlermusso2_edit_cropped.JPG

The Move to Global War. German King Tiger tanks. Source: https://www.historyonthenet.com/world-war-2-timeline-2.

Totalitarianism in the 20th Century. Left to right: Marx, Engels, Lenin, Stalin, Mao. Source: https://www.quora.com/Can-we-mix-Marxism-with-Leninism-Trotskyism-Maoism-and-socialism.

Death by Communism. Skulls of Khmer Rouge victims. Source: https://www.aboutasiatravel.com/cambodia/history/the-khmer-rouge.htm

War: Its Causes and Effects. Soviet troops charging German positions near Leningrad, World War II. Source: https://ww2db.com/image.php?image_id=15263

History of the Americas. Mexican fighter pilot and air crew, World War II. Source: https://www.thoughtco.com/mexican-involvement-in-world-war-two-2136644

The Great Depression. In this March 6, 1930 file photo, demonstrators organized by the Unemployed Council gather in front of the White House in Washington before a major protest. Source: https://www.peoplesworld.org/article/the-communist-party-in-the-30s-the-depression-and-the-great-upsurge/

Mennonite clock machinery. Source: https://www.mysteinbach.ca/blogs/9078/a-mennonite-wall-clock-as-steampunk/

Clocks scattered. Source: https://solutionsreview.com/business-process-management/the-history-of-bpm-software/

Books Available at Amazon and Other Fine Book Emporiums

IB Exam Prep Textbooks. High-powered, user-friendly and reasonably priced books to help you pass your IB Examinations, and get the full benefits of your diploma! Available at Amazon and other fine book emporiums world-wide!

IB History Exam https://www.amazon.com/History-Exam-Study-Guide-International/dp/1475055633/ref=asap_bc?ie=UTF8

IB History Exam Study Guide: International Contemporary History 1848-2008 by Dr. Juan R. Céspedes, Ph.D. A comprehensive study guide for students preparing for the IB examination, extensively covering material on papers 1, 2, & 3. Also an excellent review source for any student of contemporary history (years 1848-2008). Examines the root causes of events leading to the history of the 20th century, as well as thought provoking material necessary for the critical thinking aspects found in IB examinations. Dr. Juan R. Céspedes' scholarly perspective is concise and covers the following topics: "Communism in Crisis: 1976-1991", "Causes, Practices and Effects of Wars", "Origins and Development of Authoritarian and Single Party States", "The Cold War", and "History of the Americas".

THE IB SPANISH EXAM: https://www.amazon.com/s/ref=nb_sb_noss?url=search-alias%3Dstripbooks&field-keywords=dr+cespedes+ib+spanish

THE IB SPANISH EXAM: SL, HL and AB INITIO: ¡Mira, Que Fácil!

The IB Spanish Exam is extremely challenging, and thorough test preparation is essential for success. This is the ideal prep solution for anyone who wants to pass the IB Spanish Exam. When it comes to value for money and overall effectiveness, it's hard to do better than this study guide. A huge amount of learning material is packed into each level for a very reasonable price. The lessons go into greater depth and enables you to develop your retention, pronunciation, writing and listening skills. The study guide reviews the most important components of the exam. You get: ***A breakdown of linguistic-cultural knowledge***An examination of spelling, pronunciation, punctuation, and grammar.***Comprehensive practice questions***Critical information you'll need in order to do well on the test ***Concepts, procedures, principles, and vocabulary that the examiners expect you to have mastered before sitting for the exam.***Knowledge beforehand of the structure of the testComprehension questionsThe guide is laid out in a logical and organized fashion so that one section naturally flows from the one preceding it. Because it's written with an eye for both technical accuracy and accessibility, you will not have to worry about getting lost in dense academic language.

IB History Paper 2: War Interminable: The Origins, Causes, Practices and Effects of International Conflict: https://www.amazon.com/War-Interminable-Practices-International-Conflict/dp/1463767293

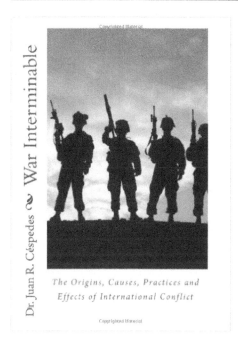

IB Paper 2: War Interminable: The Origins, Causes, Practices and Effects of International Conflict!

A definitive and comprehensive examination on the origins, causes, practices and effects of warfare. An excellent review source for the IB history examination or for those interested in historical research. A sampling of the subject matter covered is "The Origins of War"; the "Anthropological Roots of War"; "The Nation-State and War"; the "School of Realism in International Relations"; "Zero-sum" gamesmanship; "National Interest and the Rule of Law"; "Waging War"; "Military Strategy & Planning"; war from the perspective of Clausewitz, Sun Tzu, Napoleon, Machiavelli, and other great thinkers; "The Causes of War"; "The Nature of War"; the role of women; "The Practice of War"; "Different types of 20th century warfare"; "The Effects and Results of War"; "Post-war economic problems"..."Possible IB Exam-Related Questions" and much more. Each chapter ends with a synopsis of the material covered for easy review.

IB HISTORY INTERNAL ASSESSMENT https://www.amazon.com/IB-History-Internal-Assessment-Steps/dp/149100598X/ref=asap_bc?ie=UTF8

<u>The IB History Internal Assessment: An "A+" in 6 Easy Steps!</u>

The Internal Assessment is one of the core requirements of the IB Diploma Programme. Written on a topic chosen by the student, it culminates in a 2,000 word essay with specific requirements. These requirements often makes the Internal Assessment a difficult task for many students, but Dr. Céspedes breaks this into 6 simple steps. Dr. Céspedes has helped thousands of students with their writing, including doctoral candidates at the university level! Inside are tips for selecting a top-scoring topic, researching quickly and effectively, structuring your essay for maximum impact, and concluding impressively. Follow the step-by-step instructions in this guide and you will maximize your final score.

IB EXTENDED ESSAY https://www.amazon.com/IB-Extended-Essay-Easy-Steps/ dp/1467989169/ref=asap_bc?ie=UTF8IB

The IB Extended Essay: An "A+" in 6 Easy Steps!

The Extended Essay is one of the core requirements of the IB Diploma Programme. Written on a topic chosen by the student, it culminates in a 4,000 word essay. This seems to be a daunting task for many students, but Dr. Céspedes breaks this seemingly difficult task into 6 simple steps. Dr. Céspedes has helped thousands of students with their writing, including doctoral candidates! Inside are tips for selecting a top-scoring topic, researching quickly and effectively, structuring your essay for maximum impact, and concluding impressively. Follow the step-by-step instructions in this guide and you will maximize your final score!

IB HISTORY QUESTIONS https://www.amazon.com/101-IB-History-Exam-related-Questions/dp/1482344823/ref=asap_bc?ie=UTF8

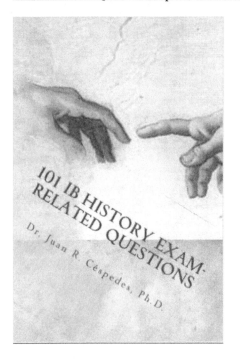

101 IB History Exam-related Questions... and their answers!

101 IB History Exam-related Questions! This book is a terrific resource for helping both students and teachers prepare for the demanding IB history examinations SL and HL. With this book you will learn from an experienced IB instructor and college professor, with 30 years in the educational field. You will improve your understanding of how questions should be answered in order to receive the highest possible scores. This book will help you build confidence by answering the questions provided, then checking your answers with those in the book. The book is great at covering the historical material for each question. Finally, it will help you understand the IB history syllabus and learn the proper way to approach your exams!

IB Paper 1-2: Collapse of the Soviet Empire - A Preparation for the International Baccalaureate History Examination!

An in-depth examination of the causes of the collapse of communism in the Soviet Union and Eastern Europe. An excellent review source for the IB history examination or for the historical researcher. Comprehensive and packed with IB-related thought provoking questions and material. Dr. Juan R. Céspedes' scholarly perspective engages the reader with details of the cultural, economic, social, and political life under communism. A sampling of the subject matter covered is "The Decline and Disintegration of the Soviet Union", "Achievements at Home and Abroad", "Outlook for Brezhnev", "Incursion into Afghanistan", "Enter Gorbachev", "Glasnost", "Perestroika", "Attempts at Democratization", "A Chronology of Key Events", "Possible Exam-Related Questions and Outline of Answers" and much more. Each chapter ends with a synopsis of the material covered for easy review.!

AMERICAS PAPER 3 - CUBA https://www.amazon.com/Cuban-Communism-Impact-World-Affairs-ebook/dp/B01HWSMPGO/ref=asap_bc?ie=UTF8

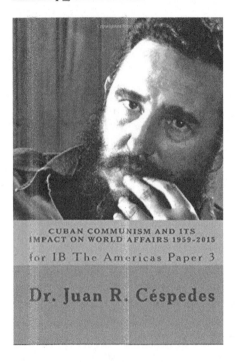

Cuban Communism and its Impact on World Affairs: 1959 - 2015 (for IB the Americas - Paper 3)

Cuba is a relatively small country, but with the foreign policy of a major league international player. It has carried out such a policy since the start of Castro's 1959 revolution. Because of its close alliance with the Soviet Union, by the early to mid 1960's it had the external resources, internal conditions, and lack of significant US opposition to begin to visibly impact conditions throughout the world; from Latin America, to Africa and Asia. In this book, Dr. Céspedes sees a Cuban foreign policy that has been both aggressive ideologically, militaristic, yet highly pragmatic. The Castro brothers saturated the media with altruistic images of themselves in a campaign to justify and encourage, or directly spread, radical change. Using previously unexplored sources, Dr. Céspedes constructs a compelling and detailed exposé which focuses on Cuban political subversion throughout the world, either through direct military intervention, or disguised as development aid for health, economic, and civic programs. This is a must read for history students written by a prominent historian.

IB ECONOMICS EXAM https://www.amazon.com/IB-Economics-Complete-Essential-Preparation/dp/1981954961

IB Economics: The Complete and Essential Exam Preparation for SL and HL

The IB Economics exam can be a challenge. However, it is your to conquer with this outstanding preparation guide. No pressure—this exam prep contains to-the-point clear analysis, summaries, and explicit charts and diagrams galore. The authors have gone through the curriculum very carefully to ensure a depth of coverage that is perfect for what is covered by the IB. This guide is prepared by Drs. Juan R. Céspedes and Charles E. W. Wadesworth, credentialed instructors with decades of experience helping students successfully pass the IB examination. Each chapter contains an introductory paragraph, illustrations further clarifying the points being made, and an outline and explanation of important terms. The guide concludes with an amazing 264 IB economics related questions.

IB MATH EXAM https://www.amazon.com/IB-MATH-EXAM-PREP-SL/dp/ 1522993657/ref=sr_1_9? s=books&ie=UTF8&qid=1522286201&sr=1-9&keywords=ib+math

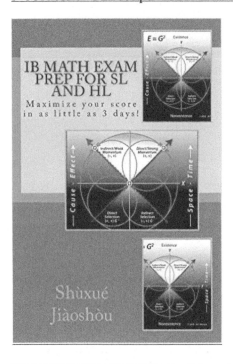

IB MATH EXAM PREP for SL and HL

How you prepare for the IB math exam is more important than how many hours you spend preparing! This study guide provides everything you need to master the challenging concepts from basic Algebra to Calculus, and will help you focus your studies on the most important math topics to maximize your score!

This comprehensive study guide contains many essential and unique features to help improve exam scores, including: * Detailed explanations for solving each formula presented * Methods and strategies to improve your math score * Review of important Math Concepts

This study guide provides you with everything you need to improve your Math score—unquestionably. These test-taking techniques, methods, and strategies work. This study guide is the must-have preparation tool for every student looking to score higher on the IB Math Exams and get into their top-choice college!

IB TOK EXAM https://www.amazon.com/TOK-Essential-Compendium-John-Garden-ebook/dp/B00LY7HXOY/ref=sr_1_1?ie=UTF8&qid=1522286411&sr=8-1&keywords=tok+john+garden

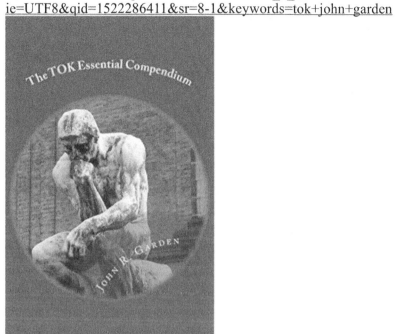

The TOK Essential Compendium!

An indispensable guide that provides an inside understanding of the TOK program from John R. Garden, an instructor with over 30 years of teaching experience! Centered around the "How We Know" and "Ways of Knowing" of 33 essential philosophers from Laozi to Albert Camus. Provides 350 TOK-oriented thinking questions, a blueprint for a top scoring essay, and blueprint for a top scoring presentation. A practical, easy to understand, and thorough examination of the Theory of Knowledge program.

B BIOLOGY EXAM https://www.amazon.com/Complete-IB-Biology-Exam-Preparation/dp/1539598152

THE COMPLETE IB BIOLOGY EXAM PREPARATION FOR SL & HL

IB Biology is challenging, college-level course, so there will be times when you will need more help than your class notes give you in preparing for the final exam. In this comprehensive and easy to understand exam preparation, Dr. Goulds compiles both SL and HL information into one user-friendly resource, and provides you with many IB Biology related practice questions. Written by, Dr. Goulds, an American professor, biologist, and one of the most widely read writers of her generation, this exam preparation is a must for students wishing to maximize their score. If you are looking for material that closely parallels the questions in the whole IB Biology Exam, you can skip to the end of the book to the reviews/questions section for great overall study resources. We highly recommend that you use this guide throughout the year as a refresher before tests and quizzes, as well as for additional support if you did not entirely understand a specific lesson in your IB Biology class.

IB PSYCHOLOGY EXAM https://www.amazon.com/Essential-Psychology-Guide-Empowering-Examination/dp/1976271312/ref=sr_1_1?s=books&ie=UTF8&qid=1522287153&sr=1-1&keywords=Felix+Dr.+Felix+Albrecht-Erikson

The Essential IB Psychology Guide SL & HL

The IB Psychology Exam Guide (SL & HL) is UNIQUE. Beat the "test taking game" with the most important exam preparation book you will find. This comprehensive study guide is written by a psychology and test-taking expert, Dr. Felix Albrecht-Erikson, who has painstakingly researched every topic and concept you need to know to pass your IB psychology exam. He has utilized his many years of expertise to guarantee your success in the SL or HL IB psychology exam.

The standards set by Dr. Albrecht-Erikson are very strict. Along with his staff, he has years of combined research experience in mastering the content and skills necessary to succeed on the toughest exams.

Some academic studies have revealed that test takers do not really benefit from most traditional test preparation process. Dr. Albrecht-Erikson has developed a set of secret keys to the exam that will open the door of success for you.

This is a thorough, concise study guide that we believe allows any test taker, at any skill level, to improve his or her results dramatically with a minimum of effort.

Dr. Albrecht-Erikson has made the critical connection between the material to be learned and how to use the material to succeed on the IB test. You're going to save time, money, and aggravation with this guide.

IB CHEMISTRY EXAM https://www.amazon.com/IB-Chemistry-SL-Ivan-Reshtenkov-ebook/dp/B06XSNHBYC/ref=sr_1_1?s=books&ie=UTF8&qid=1522287247&sr=1-1&keywords=Ivan+Reshtenkov

IB Chemistry SL & HL: A Complete Exam Review Course

This IB Chemistry book may be your best bet for a comprehensive and effective review of the SL or HL course material.

The book has friendly and understandable explanations of complex concepts, with 250 practice questions for the test, as well as a complete listing of all related terms and their explanation.

Important equations are listed throughout each content chapter, covering what you need to know in order to excel in the SL or HL test. Questions with answers include an overview section, and an additional in-depth section if you need further clarification. The user-friendly format makes it one of the best IB Chemistry review book available. It provides a means for developing study plans that you can customize to fit your needs. It isn't too skimpy or too overwhelming with information. It also provides a great way for structuring your studying, which is helpful if you consider yourself somewhat less than a totally organized student.

IB Philosophy: Conversations with a Centurion: about Life, Death, and God https://www.amazon.com/Conversations-Centurion-about-Life-Death/dp/1535004134

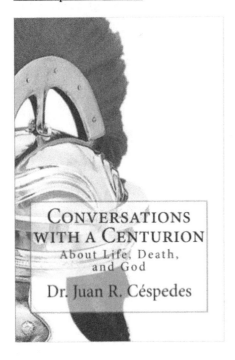

Conversations with a Centurion: about Life, Death, and God

We struggle with work and overcoming the challenges of daily life, only to experience the same end...death. Rich or poor, educated or not, death is the great equalizer for all of humanity. One measure of adulthood is the realization that "bad" things happen to "good" people. Why am I here? Is there a God, what is the meaning of life, is there an afterlife? If there is a God...why does God let these things happen? These questions are answered in a meeting with a Roman Centurion that appears magically, mystically, inexplicably, in a museum in modern Rome. The Centurion turns out to be a Roman army officer who was assigned to Capernaum, a fishing village in Judea, where he met Jesus. Most people in our time, devout Christians and Jews included, understand little about the world of first-century Palestine, and think that the Jews were an undifferentiated and united people in their disgruntlement and opposition to the rule of Rome. This is a gross oversimplification of the historical, political, and cultural reality of the time. The Centurion helps the reader understand the life of Romans, Jews, their leaders, and others; as well as the geographical, cultural, and political divisions which existed at the time.

The book examines many aspects of Jesus' world that are unknown to many. Dr. Céspedes also delves into mathematical and scientific explanations for the existence of God, near death experiences, the crucifixion, the resurrection of Jesus, the early Christian church, and the great personal sacrifices made by the apostles. This fascinating and carefully researched book concludes with suggestions for living a more meaningful life, and how to battle sadness and loneliness.

IB History Papers 1 & 2: The Myopic Vision - The Causes of
Totalitarianism, Authoritarianism, & Statism https://www.amazon.com/
Myopic-Vision-Totalitarianism-Authoritarianism-Statism/dp/1468091255

IIB Paper 1 & 2 - The Myopic Vision: The Causes of Totalitarianism, Authoritarianism, and Statism!

In this benchmark of political and historical analysis, Dr. Juan R. Céspedes provides a fascinating and comprehensive look at the "Myopic Vision" which has resulted in totalitarianism, authoritarianism, and statism. The Myopic Vision has inspired many governments and is responsible for the deaths of approximately 250 million human beings in the 20th century. What are the reasons behind this slaughter? The advocates of the Myopic Vision believe they are the holders of scientifically demonstrable truths concerning man, history, and social evolution. Thus, Dr. Céspedes coins a new phrase, as well as issues a warning for the future. Can the Myopic Vision be corrected or reversed? What does the future hold? This is a "must read" for all those which cherish and wish to preserve democracy and human dignity.

More books for the IB/AP student and the advanced thinker. Available at Amazon and other fine book emporiums!

Footsteps to World War III https://www.amazon.com/Footsteps-World-Juan-C%C3%A9spedes-Ph-D/dp/1495336476/ref=sr_1_1_twi_pap_2?s=books&ie=UTF8&qid=1527523297&sr=1-1&keywords=footsteps+to+world+war+IIi+Dr+cespedes

Footsteps to World War III

A riveting, enlightening and often frightening look at the next major war involving the United States and the world. In his thought-provoking book, Dr. Céspedes draws from a multitude of sources to carefully analyze the likelihood, and the outcomes, of a major military encounter between the United States and its major potential adversaries. Asserting that we are at the doorstep of a new epoch, he constructs a lucid and highly comprehensible forecast of the challenges that the United States can expect from around the world. As a Europe continues to weaken militarily and chose neutralist policies, or policies contrary to those of the United States, what new alliances can the United States formulate? With this panorama, will the United States remain the dominant global superpower, as other nations challenge American preeminence? Will such a war ultimately end with a victory by the United States and its allies? Captivating and compelling from the first to the last page, "Footsteps to World War III" is a fascinating exploration of what the future may hold for the world at large.

The New Global Threat: Transnational Crime

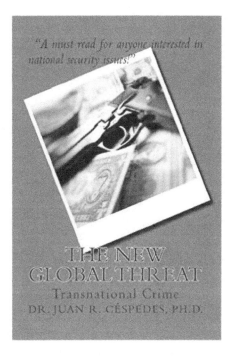

The New Global Threat: Transnational Crime

Transnational organized crime is a growing cancer, and a threat to the security of North America . . . as well as to the entire world! What was once the dominion of countries and regions separated by geography is increasingly a concern to the Department of State and for the U.S. military. Transgressing the laws of multiple nations, these criminal activities have a negative impact on society, the global economy, and greatly impede the progress of developing nations and governments. Unfortunately, many of the nations affected lack the resources or the political will to provide an adequate level of security and countermeasures that matches the threat to its security and its borders. This work reveals the dangers and horrors of modern transnational crime; a menace which challenges the modern hierarchies and methods of response, and helps to piece together the construction of pragmatic and workable policies to counter such a menace. This is a must read for anyone interested in national security issues!

Victory Over Terrorism: The Unthinkable Solution

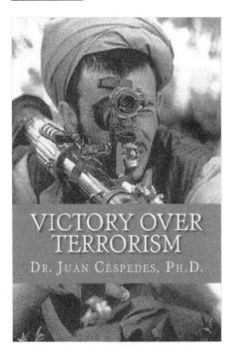

Victory Over Terrorism: The Unthinkable Solution!

Extremists have made, and will continue into the future, varied attempts to attack the US and its allies with varying levels of organization and skill. We shake our heads with a certain degree of disbelief and say, "When will it end?" After the destruction of the World Trade Center and the accompanying damages to the Pentagon and the national psyche, government has enacted laws and strategies to prevent terrorist activities. However, as democratic societies which value individual rights, we are challenged to not provoke a response which undermines our Constitutional system of government. In a thorough investigative fashion, "Victory Over Terrorism" takes readers through the strange and often sordid methods that are routinely utilized by terrorists organizations, the prevailing thoughts and beliefs of Muslim communities throughout the world, and the anti-terrorist practices that intensified in recent years.

Cancer Free by Dr. John Hunter https://www.amazon.co.uk/Cancer-Free-Dr-John-Hunter/dp/1508584672

Cancer Free!

Your physician tells you the bad news: "You have cancer." The shock leaves you speechless, but you must go on. This book will give you hope. It is "must" reading for those that have cancer, or those with family members who have the disease. Motivated by a family history of cancer that caused the deaths of his grandfather, father, uncle, and eventually his wife, Dr. John Hunter engages in a personal quest to fully research and provide answers to dealing with this dreaded disease. Dr. Hunter explains which are the most advantageous options from the thousands of case-control studies, comprehensive reviews, and biologic parameters published on the topic, while informing the reader of the reasons for those selections. Dr. John Hunter sorts through the morass of disinformation that often accompanies the topic and sheds light on a complex disease, providing the public with interconnected facts and whole truths. Dr. Hunter accurately describes the current status of scientific and holistic thinking on many topics included in his book. He describes a multitude of strategies from quitting smoking to learning the warning signs of cancer.

Coup d'État USA: The coming overthrow of the U.S. Constitution https://www.amazon.com/Coup-d%C3%89tat-USA-Overthrow-Constitution/dp/1544919557

Coup d'État USA: The coming overthrow of the U.S. Constitution

Our vigilance is imperative—democracy and our way of life in America is threatened with collapse. There is a coup d'etat brewing in America, and the warning signals are both abundant and frightening. Dr. Céspedes, a notable contemporary historian, author, researcher, and geopolitical analyst has spent over three decades studying the rise and fall of democratic governments throughout history. His exacting research reveals the many and factual reasons to be alarmed.

The clearest warnings include a failure by the coup plotters to refuse the use of violence unequivocally, their rejection of the democratic process, and their eagerness to strangle the civil rights of their political opponents. Political extremism such as this, once considered to be confined to the periphery of American politics and inconsequential, has now become established and expected behavior. Worse yet is the fact that the existence of a coup is unknown to most Americans. Dr. Céspedes points out that when this has happened in other countries during the 19th and 20th centuries, the invariable result was social and political chaos, the disappearance of democratic rights, and the reversal of individual opportunity and economic prosperity. With this research Dr. Céspedes coins two new terms that enter the lexicon of political analysis: the *coup d'état typique,* and the *coup d'état graduel.*

Dr. Céspedes argues that our democratic traditions must be reinforced by strengthening the rules that have guided American democratic values—fair play, political moderation, and bipartisan consensus. These are deep-rooted traditions that have existed in the United States since its founding, and disrupted only momentarily by the Civil War. Prepare to be transfixed by this book, and its factual, useful, and mind-opening details.

APUSH Cruncher https://www.amazon.co.uk/APUSH-Cruncher-Passing-American-History-ebook/dp/B00HOH5CO6

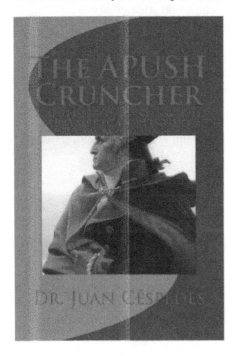

The APUSH Cruncher: A Guide for Passing the AP American History Exam with Ease!

As its name implies, The APUSH CRUNCHER is specifically designed for crunching the information you need to master the AP US History exam. From Pre-Columbian societies to 20th Century politics, this AP US History prep is designed for either short-term intense review or lengthier study. You have a choice! Develop your AP history skills in every test area. The CRUNCHER coaches you on the most important parts of the test, the weight given to each section, and proven strategies on how to effectively answer the questions for top scores. The author's goal is for you become a star-spangled winner in AP US history. This book is written by Dr. Juan R. Céspedes, a Ph.D. in education with over 30 years of experience!

Cambridge History Exam Prep

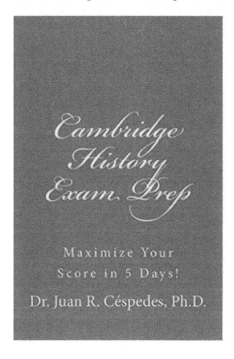

Cambridge History Exam Prep: Maximize your score in 5 days!

Scientifically, the very best way to prepare for the Cambridge History exam! Studying for the Cambridge history exam can be a stressful time for all students–there is so much information to cover! So, knowing HOW to properly prepare for the exam is the key to avoiding stress and maximizing your score. This guide provides a clear and uniform way to focus and make the best use of your study time, while assessing your performance. Say "no" to cramming blindly. Focus specifically on questions that are likely to come up in the exam! Maximize your retention; this guide makes clear the sometimes missed associations between the curriculum covered in Cambridge and the areas of examination. Avoid the "all-nighter" which wastes time, impairs reasoning and memory. The summations provided in this guide are the most effective way to study.

Peace, Conflict, and Security: The Widening Gap

Peace, Conflict, and Security: The Widening Gap

This influential book is destined to be a classic in the discipline of peace studies. Finding the balance between peace, conflict, and security, the author says, requires a pivotal and decisive paradigm shift in our understanding of the nation-state and its historical role. Today an assortment of regional or international organizations are involved in peacekeeping and peacemaking activities in addition to the United Nations. The research of Dr. Juan R. Céspedes is a core contribution in the development of peace and security as it relates to international studies and security analysis. A widely published and internationally recognized expert on history and geopolitics, Dr. Céspedes' thoughts provide important keys to understanding the avenues leading to effective mediation, negotiation, and settlement of international disputes. This book brings together and analyzes a multitude of diverse theories concerning peace, conflict, and security in one volume. Dr. Céspedes defines, creates valid measures, and finds ways of dealing with current and future conflicts. Thus, attention is also paid here to conflict prevention, peace agreements, sanctions and third-party activity for preventing and ending armed conflict, and building a lasting world peace. This book will be of great interest to all students of peace studies, conflict resolution, war and conflict studies.

IB Coordinator Guide for a Top-Notch Program: A tried and true comprehensive blueprint for coordinators, principals, & teachers.

IB Coordinator Guide

https://www.amazon.com/COORDINATOR-GUIDE-TOP-NOTCH-PROGRAM-Comprehensive/dp/109539360X

This book is what happens when a group of highly successful and credentialed IB professionals collaborate, sharing their experiences and ideas on implementing a top-notch IB program. When IB Coordinators, teachers, and administrators like these band together, they form important symbiotic professional relationships, find ways of streaming tasks, increase effectiveness, share information, and contribute to IB program improvement and student success!

The ultimate goal of that collaboration is increased student performance.

This book enables you to profit from the expertise of others, and create an environment of accomplishment from demonstrably good ideas and perspectives.

As an IB Coordinator, administrator, or teacher, you may have felt isolated, left-out, or wondering how others have reached a higher level of success than you. This book dares to share the expertise and knowledge of successful professionals in the IB program. This book unlocks and opens the "idea and experience vault" of seasoned IB professionals. It is a professional learning showcase in IB education.

The objective of this book is to make your brain "explode" with an amazing, motivating, useful, and captivating information overload that you didn't know was possible. You won't find this in other IB-related books. This volcanic compilation may result in a sudden and alarmingly Zen-like realization that your IB program can be incredibly better in every conceivable way.